Fundamentals of
Literature

for Christian Schools®

Donna L. Hess

June Cates

Bob Jones University Press, Greenville, South Carolina 29614

Advisory Committee

Ronald A. Horton, B.A., M.A., Ph.D.
Chairman of the Division of English Language and Literature, Bob Jones University.

Janie Caves McCauley, B.A., M.A., Ph.D.
English professor, Bob Jones University. Literary advisor.

William L. Yost, B.S., M.A., Ph.D.
Chairman of the Division of Secondary Education, Bob Jones University. Educational advisor.

NOTE:
The fact that materials produced by other publishers are referred to in this volume does not constitute an endorsement by Bob Jones University Press of the content or theological position of materials produced by such publishers. The position of Bob Jones University Press, and the University itself, is well known. Any references and ancillary materials are listed as an aid to the student or the teacher and in an attempt to maintain the accepted academic standards of the publishing industry.

FUNDAMENTALS OF LITERATURE for Christian Schools®

Donna L. Hess, B.S., M.A.
June Cates

Produced in cooperation with the Bob Jones University Division of English Language and Literature of the College of Arts and Science, the School of Religion, and Bob Jones Academy.

©1988 Bob Jones University Press
Greenville, South Carolina 29614

Printed in the United States of America

ISBN 0-89084-423-2

20   19   18   17   16   15   14   13   12   11   10   9   8

Acknowledgments

Alfred A. Knopf, Inc.: "In the Ring with Jack Dempsey," an excerpt from "The Feel." From *Farewell to Sport* by Paul Gallico. Copyright 1938 and renewed 1966 by Paul Gallico. Reprinted by permission of Alfred A. Knopf, Inc.

"Neighbour Rosicky." Copyright 1932 by Willa Cather and renewed 1960 by the Executors of the Estate of Willa Cather. Reprinted from *Obscure Destinies* by Willa Cather, by permission of Alfred A. Knopf, Inc.

Doubleday & Company, Inc.: "A Lightning Gleam" by Matsuo Bashō from *An Introduction to Haiku* by Harold G. Henderson. Copyright © 1958 by Harold G. Henderson. Reprinted by permission of Doubleday, a division of Bantam, Doubleday, Dell Publishing Group, Inc.

Harcourt Brace Jovanovich, Inc.: "Splinter." From *Good Morning, America,* copyright 1928, 1956 by Carl Sandburg. Reprinted by permission of Harcourt Brace Jovanovich, Inc.

Harold Matson Company, Inc.: "Top Man." Copyright 1940. © renewed 1968 by James Ramsey Ullman. Reprinted by permission of Harold Matson Company, Inc.

Harper & Row, Publisher, Inc.: "Through the Tunnel," originally published in the *New Yorker,* from *The Habit of Loving* by Doris Lessing. Copyright © 1955 by Doris Lessing. Reprinted by permission of Harper & Row, Publishers, Inc.

Henry Holt and Company: From *Cyrano de Bergerac* by Edmond Rostand, translated by Brian Hooker. Copyright 1923 by Henry Holt and Company, Inc. and renewed 1951 by Doris C. Hooker. Reprinted by permission of Henry Holt and Company, Inc.

Macmillan Publishing Co.: John Galsworthy, "Quality" from *The Inn of Tranquility.* Copyright 1912 Charles Scribner's Sons; copyright renewed 1940 Ada Galsworthy. Reprinted with the permission of Charles Scribner's Sons, an imprint of Macmillan Publishing Co.

"When You Are Old." From *The Poems of W. B. Yeats: A New Edition,* edited by Richard J. Finneran (New York: Macmillan, 1983).

Princeton University Press: "Lightning Flashes" by Matsuo Bashō, Alex Preminger et al, ed. *Encyclopedia of Poetry and Poetics.* Copyright © 1965 by Princeton University Press. Excerpt reprinted with permission of Princeton University Press.

Viking Penguin Inc.: "400-Meter Freestyle," *Our Ground Time Here Will Be Brief* by Maxine Kumin. Copyright © 1975 by Maxine Kumin. All rights reserved. Reprinted by permission of Viking Penguin Inc.

"The Open Window," *The Complete Short Stories of Saki* by H. H. Munro. Copyright 1930 by The Viking Press, Inc. Copyright renewed 1958 by The Viking Press, Inc. All rights reserved. Reprinted by permission of Viking Penguin Inc.

Contents

CONFLICT

CHARACTER

THEME

STRUCTURE

POINT OF VIEW

MORAL TONE

UNIT ONE

Conflict

Conflict

A story is war, a struggle for victory or supremacy. The battlefield may be a small town or a stormy sea; the foe may be an evil ruler or a guilty conscience; and the fight may be over a parcel of land or a man's soul. Regardless of the setting, the characters, or the situation, in a good story there is always war, always **conflict.** Have you ever wondered why this is true? It is true because good literature reflects life, and life involves conflict.

Conflict began in the Garden of Eden when Adam and Eve rebelled and placed themselves and their descendants at war with the Creator. As a direct result of this rebellion, God cursed the ground, and man also found himself at odds with nature. These incidents in Genesis 3 are our first record of **man in conflict with a power or powers greater than himself.**

Out of this initial struggle a second type of conflict emerged, **man at war with himself.** After the fall when Adam and Eve "heard the voice of the Lord God," they hid themselves. And when the Lord asked them why they had fled, Adam replied, "I heard thy voice in the garden, and *I was afraid*" (Gen. 3:8, 10). Adam's sin not only severed his fellowship with God but also destroyed his inner peace.

This second conflict produced yet another, **man against man.** When confronted with his disobedience, Adam's loving attitude toward his wife vanished. Fear drove him to protect himself first, and he laid the blame for his sin on Eve saying, "The woman whom thou gavest to be with me, she gave me of the tree, and I did eat" (3:12). What a contrast this accusation was to Adam's initial tender, poetic utterance about his wife: "This is now bone of my bones, and flesh of my flesh: she shall be called Woman, because she was taken out of Man" (2:23). Eve, quick to follow Adam's example, sought to protect herself as well by laying the blame for her sin on the serpent.

These conflicts were "reborn" in Adam and Eve's son Cain, the first murderer, and the agony that resulted was expressed in his lament: "My punishment is greater than I can bear. Behold, thou hast driven [me] out this day from the face of the earth; and from thy face shall I be hid; and I shall be a fugitive and a vagabond in the earth" (4:13-14).

All the struggles observed in life and reflected in literature can be traced to one or more of these three original conflicts recorded in Scripture: man against a power greater than himself, man against himself, man against man. Scripture, however, does more than simply record man's struggles; it also provides a **resolution** for these conflicts. Good literature should do the same. When an author fails to provide a satisfying resolution to the conflict he creates—as many modern authors do—the story may end with the same feeling of despair echoed in Cain's lament. The more familiar you become with good writing, the more you will see the beauty inherent in the pattern set for us in Scripture. You will see that conflict and resolution are not only an integral part of life but also the essence of good literature.

Escape literature, whose primary purpose is to entertain (like *Treasure Island*) or to teach an obvious moral point (like *Cinderella*), tends to emphasize the most concrete conflict, man against man. Interpretive or sophisticated literature is more subtle or complex. This literature tends to emphasize either man in conflict with a larger force or man in conflict with himself. Edgar Allan Poe's "The Masque of the Red Death" is an example of man in conflict with a larger force. In this story, a rich prince named Prospero clashes with Death (personified). Despite Prospero's efforts to fortify his castle and protect himself and his friends, Death gains entrance into the fortress during a masquerade and succeeds in overcoming all the revelers.

A literary example of a central character's struggling to overcome something within himself is found in Margaret Deland's "Many Waters" (pp. 201-19). In this story, the most important battle is fought and resolved inside the central character.

In interpretive literature you may also find a character ensnared in more than one type of conflict at once, though one conflict will eventually emerge as dominant. For example, in the opening of Baroness Orczy's *The Scarlet Pimpernel,* Percy Blakeney is combating the evil forces set in motion by the French Revolution. As the story progresses, however, a cruel foe named Chauvelin emerges. This conflict between Blakeney and Chauvelin eventually dominates the story. The author chose to emphasize the personal conflict because it generated greater sympathy for her hero and helped crystallize her story's theme.

Like Baroness Orczy, the authors in this unit's stories recognized that the first step in discerning a story's meaning is identifying the central conflict and its resolution, and they provided several clues to help make this identification possible. To draw out this information, ask yourself the following questions as you read: Who is the central character, or **protagonist,** in the story? Who or what is the central character fighting against? Is there more than one opposing force, or **antagonist?** If there is more than one antagonist, which one becomes the dominant enemy? How is the fight between the protagonist and antagonist resolved?

Miss Hinch

Henry Syndor Harrison

It seems unlikely that an aging clergyman and a decent-looking old woman would be pitted against each other in a life-and-death struggle. But as the story of "Miss Hinch" unfolds, you will discover that things are not always as they seem; nor is it always easy to discern who is the hero and who is the villain. If you follow the details of the action carefully, however, you can unravel the mystery before reaching the story's end.

In going from a given point on 126th Street to a subway station at 125th, it is not usual to begin by circling the block to 127th Street, especially in sleet, darkness, and deadly cold. When two people pursue such a course at the same time, moving unobtrusively on opposite sides of the street, in the nature of things the coincidence is likely to attract the attention of one or the other of them.

In the bright light of the entrance of the tube* they came almost face to face, and the clergyman took a good look at her. Certainly she was a decent-looking old body, if any woman was: white-haired, wrinkled, spec-

tacled, and stooped. A poor but thoroughly respectable domestic servant of the better class she looked, in her old black hat, neat veil, and grey shawl; and her brief glance at the reverend gentleman was precisely what it should have been from her to him—deference* itself. Nevertheless, he, going more slowly down the draughty* steps, continued to study her from behind with a singular intentness.

---

tube: British: subway
deference: a humble yielding to the wishes or judgment of another
draughty: British: drafty

An express was just thundering in, which the clergyman, handicapped as he was by his clubfoot and stout cane, was barely in time to catch. He entered the same car with the woman and chanced to take a seat directly across from her. It must have been then after twelve o'clock, and the wildness of the weather was discouraging to travel. The car was almost deserted. Even in this underground retreat the bitter breath of the night blew and bit, and the old woman shivered under her shawl. At last, her teeth chattering, she got up in an apologetic sort of way, and moved toward the better protected rear of the car, feeling the empty seats as she went, plainly in search of hot pipes. The clergyman's eyes followed her candidly, and watched her sink down, presently, into a seat on his own side of the car. A young couple sat between them now; he could no longer see the woman, beyond occasional glimpses of her black knees and her faded bonnet, fastened on with a long steel hatpin.

Nothing could have seemed more natural or more trivial than this change of seats on the part of a thin-blooded and half-frozen passenger. But it happened to be at a time of mutual doubt and misgivings, of alert suspicions and hair-trigger watchfulness, when men looked askance into every strange face and the smallest incidents were likely to take on a hysterical importance. Through days of fruitless searching for a fugitive outlaw of extraordinary gifts, the nerve of the city had been slowly strained to the breaking-point. All jumped, now, when anybody cried "Boo!" and the hue and cry went up falsely twenty times a day.

The clergyman pondered; mechanically he turned up his coat collar and fell to stamping his icy feet. He was an Episcopal clergyman, by his garb—rather short, very full-bodied, not to say fat, bearded and somewhat puffy-faced, with heavy cheeks cut by deep creases. Well-lined against the cold though he was, however, he, too, began to suffer visibly, and presently was forced to retreat in his turn, seeking out a new place where the heating apparatus gave a better account of itself. He found one, two seats beyond the old serving-woman, limped into it, and soon relapsed into his own thoughts.

The young couple, now half a dozen seats away, were thoroughly absorbed in each other's society. The fifth traveler, a withered old gentleman sitting next the middle door across the aisle, napped fitfully upon his cane. The woman in the hat and shawl sat in a sad kind of silence; and the train hurled itself roaringly through the tube. After a time, she glanced timidly at the meditating clergyman, and her look fell swiftly from his face to the discarded "ten o'clock extra" lying by his side. She removed her dim gaze and let it travel casually about the car; but before long it returned, pointedly, to the newspaper. Then, with some hesitation, she bent forward and said, above the noises of the train:

"Excuse me, Father, but would you let me look at your paper a minute, sir?"

The clergyman came out of his reverie instantly, and looked up with a quick smile.

"Certainly. Keep it if you like: I am quite through with it. But," he added, in a pleasant deep voice, "I am an Episcopal minister, not a priest."

"Oh, sir—I beg your pardon! I thought—"

He dismissed the apology with a nod and a good-natured hand.

The woman opened the paper with decent cotton-gloved fingers. The garish headlines told the story at a glance: "Earth Opened and Swallowed Miss Hinch—Headquarters Virtually Abandons Case—Even Jessie Dark," so the bold capitals ran on—"Seems Stumped." Below the spread was a luridly written but flimsy narrative "By Jessie Dark," which at once confirmed the odd implication of the caption. "Jessie Dark," it appeared, was one of those most extraordinary of the products of yellow journalism,* a woman "crime expert," now in action. More than this, she was a "crime expert" to be taken seriously it seemed—no mere office-desk sleuth, but an actual performer with, unexpectedly enough, a somewhat formidable list of notches on her gun. So much, at least, was to be gathered from her paper's display of "Jessie Dark's Triumphs:"

---

yellow journalism: sensational and melodramatic journalism; also called "muckraking."

March 2, 1901. Caught Julia Victorian, alias Gregory, the brains of the "Heally Ring" kidnappers.

October 7-29, 1903. Found Mrs. Trotwood and secured the letter that convicted her of the murder of her lover, Ellis E. Swan.

December 17, 1903. Ran down Charles Bartsch in a Newark laundry and trapped a confession from him.

July 4, 1904. Caught Mary Calloran and recovered the Stratford jewels.

And so on—nine "triumphs" in all; and nearly every one of them, as the least observant reader could hardly fail to notice, involved the capture of a woman.

Nevertheless, it could not be pretended that the "snappy" paragraphs in this evening's extra seemed to foreshadow a new or tenth triumph for Jessie Dark at an early date; and the old serving-woman in the car presently laid down the sheet with a look of marked depression.

The clergyman looked at her again. Her expression was so speaking that it seemed to be almost an invitation; besides, public interest in the great case made conversation between total strangers the rule wherever two or three were gathered together.

"You were reading about this strange mystery, perhaps."

The woman with a sharp intake of breath, answered. "Yes, sir. Oh, sir, it seems as if I couldn't think of anything else."

"Ah?" he said, without surprise. "It certainly appears to be a remarkable affair."

Remarkable, indeed, the affair seemed. In a tiny little room within ten steps of Broadway at half-past nine o'clock on a fine evening, Miss Hinch had killed John Catherwood with the light sword she used in her famous representation of the Father of his Country. Catherwood, it was known, had come to tell her of his coming marriage, and ten thousand amateur detectives, fired by unusual rewards, had required no further motive of a creature already notorious for fierce jealousy. So far the tragedy was commonplace enough, and even vulgar. What had redeemed it to romance from this point on was the extraordinary faculty of the woman, which had made her celebrated while she was still in her teens. Coarse, violent, utterly unmoral she might be, but she happened also to be the most astonishing impersonator of her time. Her brilliant "act" consisted of a series of character changes, many of them done in full view of the audience with the assistance only of a small table of properties half concealed under a net. Some of these transformations were so amazing as to be beyond belief, even after one had sat and watched them. Not her appearance only, but voice, speech, manner, carriage, all shifted incredibly to fit the new part; so that the woman appeared to have no permanent form or fashion of her own, but to be only so much plastic human material out of which her cunning could mold at will man, woman, or child, great lady of the Louisan Court* or Tammany statesman* with the modernest of

East Side modernisms upon his lip.

Louisan Court: the court of any of a line of extravagant
  French monarchs
Tammany statesman: a member of a Democratic party
  organization in New York City that was very powerful in
  the nineteenth and early twentieth centuries

With this strange skill, hitherto used only to enthrall large audiences and wring extortionate contracts from managers, the woman known as Miss Hinch—she appeared to be without a first name—was now fighting for her life somewhere against the police of the world. Without artifice, she was a tall, thin-chested young woman with strongly marked features and considerable beauty of a bold sort. What she would look like at the present moment nobody could venture a guess. Having stabbed John Catherwood in her dressing-room at the Amphitheater, she had put on her hat and coat, dropped two wigs and her make-up kit into a handbag, and walked out into Broadway. Within ten minutes the dead body of Catherwood was found and the chase had begun. At the stage door, as she passed out, Miss Hinch had met an acquaintance, a young comedian named Dargis, and exchanged a word of greeting with him. That had been ten days ago. After Dargis, no one

had seen her. The earth, indeed, seemed to have opened and swallowed her. Yet her natural features were almost as well known as the President's, and the newspapers of a continent were daily reprinting them in a thousand variations.

"A very remarkable case," repeated the clergyman, rather absently; and his neighbor, the old woman, respectfully agreed that it was. Then, as the train slowed up for the stop at 86th Street, she added with sudden bitterness:

"Oh, they'll never catch her, sir—never! She's too smart for 'em all, Miss Hinch is."

Attracted by her tone, the stout divine inquired if she were particularly interested in the case.

"Yes, sir—I got reason to be. Jack Catherwood's mother and me was at school together, and great friends all our life long. Oh, sir," she went on, as if in answer to his look of faint surprise, "Jack was a fine gentleman, with manners and looks and all beyond his people. But he never grew away from his old mother—no, sir, never! And I don't believe ever a Sunday passed that he didn't go up and set the afternoon away with her, talking and laughing just like he was a little boy again. Maybe he done things he

hadn't ought, as high-spirited lads will, but oh, sir, he was a good boy in his heart—a good boy. And it does seem too hard for him to die like that—and that hussy free to go her way, ruinin' and killin'—"

"My good woman," said the clergyman presently, "compose yourself. No matter how diabolical this woman's skill is, her sin will assuredly find her out."

The woman dutifully lowered her handkerchief and tried to compose herself, as bidden.

"But, oh, she's that clever—diabolical, just as ye say, sir. Through poor Jack we of course heard much gossip about her, and they do say that her best tricks was not done on the stage at all. They say, sir, that, sittin' around a table with her friends, she could begin and twist her face so strange and terrible that they would beg her stop, and jump up and run from the table—frightened out of their lives, sir, grown-up people, by the terrible faces she could make. And let her only step behind her screen for a minute—for she kept her secrets well, Miss Hinch did—and she'd come walking out to you, and you could go right up to her in the full light and take her hand, and still you couldn't make yourself believe it was her."

"Yes," said the clergyman, "I have heard that she is remarkably clever—though, as a stranger in this part of the world, I never saw her act. I must say, it is all very interesting and strange."

He turned his head and stared through the rear of the car at the dark flying walls. At the same moment the woman turned her head and stared full at the clergyman. When the train halted again, at Grand Central Station, he turned back to her.

"I'm a visitor in the city, from Denver, Colorado," he said pleasantly, "and knew little or nothing about the case until an evening or two ago, when I attended a meeting of gentlemen here. The men's club of St. Matthias' Church—perhaps you know the place? Upon my word, they talked of nothing else. I confess they got me quite interested in their gossip. So tonight I bought this paper to see what this extraordinary woman detective it employs had to say about it. We don't have such things in the West, you know. But I must say I was disappointed after all the talk about her."

"Yes, sir, indeed, and no wonder, for she's told Mrs. Catherwood herself that she never made such a failure as this so far. It seemed like she could always catch women, up to this. It seemed like she knew in her own mind just what a woman would do, where she'd try to hide and all, and so she could find them time and time when the men detectives didn't know where to look. But, oh, sir, she's never had to hunt for such a woman as Miss Hinch before!"

"No! I suppose not," said the clergyman. "Her story here in the paper certainly seems to me very poor."

"Story, sir! Bless my soul!" suddenly exploded the old gentleman across the aisle, to the surprise of both. "You don't suppose the clever little woman is going to show her hand in those stories, with Miss Hinch in the city and reading every line of them! In the city, sir—such is my positive belief!"

The approach to his station, it seemed, had roused him from his nap just in time to overhear the episcopate criticism. Now he answered the looks of the old woman and the clergyman with an elderly cackle.

"Excuse my intrusion, I'm sure! But I can't sit silent and hear anybody run down Jessie Dark—Miss Mathewson in private life, as perhaps you don't know. No, sir! Why, there's a man at my boarding-place—astonishing young fellow named Hardy, Tom Hardy—who's known her for years! As to those stories, sir, I can assure you that she puts in there exactly the opposite of what she really thinks!"

"You don't tell me!" said the clergyman encouragingly.

"Yes, sir! Oh, she plays the game—yes, yes! She has her private ideas, her clues, her schemes. The woman doesn't live who is clever enough to hoodwink Jessie Dark. I look for developments any day—any day, sir!"

A new voice joined in. The young couple down the car, their attention caught by the old man's pervasive tones, had been frankly listening; and it was illustrative of the public mind at the moment that, as they now rose for the station and drew nearer, the young man felt perfectly free to offer his contribution.

"Dramatic situation, isn't it, when you stop to think. Those two clever women pitted against each other in a life-and-death struggle, fighting it out silently in the underground somewhere—keen professional pride on one side and the fear of the electric chair on the other. Good heavens, there's—"

"Oh, yes! Oh, yes!" exclaimed the old gentleman rather testily. "But my dear sir, it's not professional pride that makes Jessie Dark so resolute to win. It's sex jealousy, if you follow me—no offense, madam! Yes, sir! Women never have the slightest respect for each other, either! I tell you, Jessie Dark'd be ashamed to be beaten by another woman. Read her stories between the lines, sir—as I do. Invincible determination—no weakening—no mercy! You catch my point, sir?"

"It sounds reasonable," answered the Colorado clergyman, with his courteous smile. "All women, we are told, are natural rivals at heart—"

"Oh, I'm for Jessie Dark every time!" the young fellow broke in eagerly—"especially since the police have practically laid down. But—"

"Why, she's told my young friend Hardy," the old gentleman rode him down, "that she'll find Hinch if it takes her lifetime! Knows a thing or two about actresses, she says. Says the world isn't big enough for the creature to hide from her. Well! What do you think of that?"

"Tell what we were just talking about, George," said the young wife, looking at her husband with admiring eyes.

"But oh, sir," began the old woman timidly, "Jack Catherwood's been dead ten days now, and—and—"

"Ten days, madam! And what is that, pray?" exploded the old gentleman, rising triumphantly. "A lifetime, if necessary! Oh, never fear! Mrs. Victorian was considered pretty clever, eh? Wasn't she? Remember what Jessie Dark did for her? Nan Parmalee, too—though the police did their best to steal her credit. She'll do just as much for Miss Hinch—you may take it from me!"

"But how's she going to make the capture, gentlemen?" cried the young fellow, getting his chance at last. "That's the point my wife and I've been discussing. Assuming that she succeeds in spotting this woman-devil, what will she do? Now—"

"Do! Yell for the police!" burst from the old gentleman at the door.

"And have Miss Hinch shoot her—and then herself, too? Wouldn't she have to—"

"Grand Central!" cried the guard for the second time; and the young fellow broke off reluctantly to find his bride towing him strongly toward the door.

"Hope she nabs her soon, anyway," he called back to the clergyman over his shoulder. "The thing's getting on my nerves. One of these kindergarten reward-chasers followed my wife for five blocks the other day, just because she's got a pointed chin, and I don't know what might have happened if I hadn't came along and—"

Doors rolled shut behind him, and the train flung itself on its way. Within the car a lengthy silence ensued. The clergyman stared thoughtfully at the floor, and the old woman fell back upon her borrowed paper. She appeared to be re-reading the observations of Jessie Dark with considerable care. Presently she lowered the paper and began a quiet search for something under the folds of her shawl; and at length, her hands emerging empty, she broke the silence in a lifted voice.

"Oh, sir—have you a pencil you could lend me, please? I'd like to mark something in the piece to send to Mrs. Catherwood. It's what she says here about the disguises, sir."

The kindly divine felt in his pockets, and after some hunting produced a pencil—a white one with blue lead. She thanked him gratefully.

"How is Mrs. Catherwood bearing all this strain and anxiety?" he asked suddenly. "Have you seen her today?"

"Oh, yes, sir! I've been spending the evening with her since nine o'clock, and am just back from there now. Oh, she's very much broke up, sir."

She looked at him uncertainly. He stared straight in front of him, saying nothing, though conceivably he knew, in common with the rest of the reading world, that Jack Catherwood's mother lived, not on 126th Street, but on East Houston Street. Possibly he might have wondered if his silence had not been an error of judgment. Perhaps that misstatement had not been a slip, but something cleverer?

The woman went on with a certain eagerness: "Oh, sir, I only hope and pray those gentlemen may be right, but it does look to Mrs. Catherwood, and me too, that if Jessie Dark was going to catch her at all, she'd have done it before now. Look at those big blue eyes she had, sir, with the lashes an inch long, they say, and that terrible long chin of hers. They do say she can change the color of her

eyes, not forever of course, but put a few of her drops into them and make them look entirely different for a time. But that chin, ye'd say—"

She broke off; for the clergyman, without preliminaries of any sort, had picked up his heavy stick and suddenly risen.

"Here we are at Fourteenth Street," he said nodding pleasantly. "I must change here. Good night. Success to Jessie Dark, I say!"

He was watching the woman's faded face and he saw just that look of respectful surprise break into it that he had expected.

"Fourteenth Street! I'd no notion at all we'd come so far. It's where I get out, too, sir, the express not stopping at my station."

"Ah?" said the clergyman, smiling a little.

He led the way, limping and leaning on his stick. They emerged upon the chill and cheerless platform, not exactly together, yet still with some reference to their acquaintance-ship on the car. But the clergyman, after stumping along a few steps, all at once realized

that he was walking alone, and turned. The woman had halted. Over the intervening space their eyes met.

"Come," said the man gently. "Come, let us walk about a little to keep warm."

"Oh, sir—it's too kind of you, sir," said the woman, coming forward.

From other cars two or three blue-nosed people had got off to make the change; one or two more came straggling in from the street; but scattered over the bleak concrete expanse, they detracted little from the isolation that seemed to surround the woman and the clergyman. Step for step, the odd pair made their way to the extreme northern end of the platform.

"By the way," said the clergyman, halting abruptly, "May I see that paper again for a moment?"

"Oh, yes, sir—of course," said the woman, producing it from beneath her shawl. "I thought you had finished with it, and I—"

He said that he wanted only to glance at it for a moment; but he fell to looking through it page by page, with considerable care. The woman glanced at him several times. At last she said hesitatingly:

"I thought, sir, I'd ask the ticket-chopper could he say how long before the next train. I'm very late as it is, sir, and I still must stop to get something to eat before I go to bed."

"An excellent idea," said the clergyman.

He explained that he, too, was already behind time, and was spending the night with cousins in Jersey, to boot. Side by side, they retraced their steps down the platform, questioned the chopper with scant results, and then, as by tacit* consent, started back again. However, before they had gone far, the woman stopped short and, with a white face, leaned against a pillar.

tacit: unspoken

"Oh, sir, I'm afraid I'll have to stop and get a bite somewhere before I go on. You'll think me foolish, sir, but I missed my supper entirely tonight, and there is quite a faint feeling coming over me."

The clergyman looked at her with apparent concern. "Do you know, my friend, you seem to anticipate all my own wants. Your mentioning something to eat just now reminded me that I myself was all but famishing." He glanced at his watch, appearing to deliberate. "Yes—it will not take long. Come, we'll find a modest eating-house together."

"Oh, sir," she stammered, "but—you wouldn't want to eat with a poor old woman like me, sir."

"And why not? Are we not all equal in the sight of God?"

They ascended the stairs together, like any prosperous parson and his poor parishioner, and coming out into Fourteenth Street, started west. On the first block they came to a restaurant, a brilliantly lighted, tiled and polished place of a quick-lunch variety. But the woman timidly preferred not to stop here, saying that the glare of such places was very bad for her old eyes. The divine accepted the objection as valid, without an argument. Two blocks farther on they found on a corner a quieter resort, an unpretentious little haven which yet boasted a "Ladies' Entrance" down the side street.

They entered by the front door, and sat down at a table, facing each other. The woman read the menu through, and finally, after some embarrassed uncertainty, ordered poached eggs on toast. The clergyman ordered the same. The simple meal was soon dispatched. Just as they were finishing it, the woman said apologetically:

"If you'll excuse me, sir—could I see the bill of fare a minute? I think I'd best take a little pot of tea to warm me up, if they do not charge too high."

"I haven't the bill of fare," said the clergyman.

They looked diligently for the cardboard strip, but it was nowhere to be seen. The waiter drew near.

"Yes, sir! I left it there on the table when I took the order."

"I'm sure I can't imagine what's become of it," repeated the clergyman, rather insistently.

He looked hard at the woman, and found that she was looking hard at him. Both pairs of eyes fell instantly.

The waiter brought another bill of fare; the woman ordered tea; the waiter came back with it. The clergyman paid for both orders with a bill that looked hard-earned.

The tea proved to be very hot; it could not be drunk down at a gulp. The clergyman, watching the woman sidewise as she sipped, seemed to grow more restless. His fingers drummed the tablecloth: he could hardly sit still. All at once he said: "What is that calling in the street? It sounds like newsboys."

The woman put her old head on one side and listened. "Yes, sir. There seems to be an extra out."

"Upon my word," he said after a pause. "I believe I'll go get one. Good gracious! Crime is a very interesting thing, to be sure!"

He rose slowly, took down his shovel-hat from the hanger near him, grasped his heavy stick, limped to the door. Leaving it open behind him, much to the annoyance of the proprietor in the cashier's cage, he stood a moment in the little vestibule, looking up and down the street. Then he took a few slow steps eastward, beckoning with his hand as he went, and so passed out of sight of the woman at the table.

The eating-place was on the corner, and outside the clergyman paused for half a breath.

North, east, south and west he looked and nowhere he found what his flying glance sought. He turned the corner into the darker cross-street, and began to walk, at first slowly, continually looking about him. Presently his pace quickened, quickened, so that he no longer even stayed to use his stout cane. In another moment he was all but running, his clubfoot pounding the icy sidewalk heavily as he went. A newsboy thrust an extra under his very nose, but he did not even see it.

Far down the street, nearly two blocks away, a tall figure in a blue coat stood and stamped in the freezing sleet; and the hurrying divine sped straight toward him. But he did not get very near. For, as he passed the side entrance at the extreme rear of the restaurant, a departing guest dashed out so recklessly as to run full into him, stopping him dead.

Without looking at her, he knew who it was. In fact, he did not look at her at all, but turned his head hurriedly north and south, sweeping the dark street with a swift eye. But the old woman, having drawn back with a sharp exclamation as they collided, rushed breathlessly into apologies:

"Oh, sir—excuse me! A newsboy popped his head into the side door just after you went out, and I ran to get you the paper. But he got away too quick for me, sir, and so I—"

"Exactly," said the clergyman in his quiet deep voice. "That must have been the very boy I myself was after."

On the other side, two men had just turned into the street, well muffled against the night, talking cheerfully as they trudged along. Now the clergyman looked full at the woman, and she saw that there was a smile on his face.

"As he seems to have eluded us both, suppose we return to the subway?"

"Yes, sir; it's full time I—"

"The sidewalk is so slippery," he went on gently, "perhaps you had better take my arm."

Behind the pair in the dingy restaurant, the waiter came forward to shut the door, and lingered to discuss with the proprietor the sudden departure of his two patrons. However, the score had been paid with a liberal tip for service, so there was no especial complaint to make. After listening to some unfavorable comments on the ways of the clergy, the waiter returned to his table to set it in order.

On the floor in the carpeted aisle between tables lay a white piece of cardboard, which his familiar eye recognized as part of one of his own bills of fare, face downward. He stooped and picked it up. On the back of it was some scribbling, made with a blue lead pencil.

The handwriting was very loose and irregular, as if the writer had had his eyes elsewhere while he wrote, and it was with some difficulty that the waiter deciphered this message:

"Miss Hinch 14th St. subway Get police quick."

The waiter carried this curious document to the proprietor, who read it over a number of times. He was a dull man, and had a dull man's suspiciousness of a practical joke. However, after a good deal of irresolute discussion, he put on his overcoat and went out for a policeman. He turned west, and halfway up the block met an elderly bluecoat trudging east. The policeman looked at the scribbling, and dismissed it profanely as a wag's foolishness of the sort that was bothering the life out of him a dozen times a day. He walked along with the proprietor, and as they drew near to the latter's place of business both become aware of footsteps thudding nearer up the cross-street from the south. As they looked up, two young policemen, accompanied by a man in uniform like a street-car conductor's, swept around the corner and dashed straight into the restaurant.

The first policeman and the proprietor ran in after them, and found them staring about rather vacantly. One of the arms of the law demanded if any suspicious characters had been seen about the place, and the dull proprietor said no. The officers, looking rather flat, explained their errand. It seemed that a few moments before, the third man, who was a ticket-chopper at the subway station, had found a mysterious message lying on the floor by his box. Whence it had come, how long it had lain there, he had not the slightest idea. However, there it was. The policeman exhibited a crumpled scrap torn from a newspaper, on which was scrawled in blue pencil:

"Miss Hinch Miller's Restaurant Get police quick."

The first policeman, who was both the oldest and the fattest of the three, produced the message on the bill of fare, so utterly at odds with this. The dull proprietor, now bethinking himself, mentioned the clergyman and the old woman who had taken poached eggs and tea together, called for a second bill of fare, and departed so unexpectedly by different doors. The ticket-chopper recalled that he had seen the same pair at his station; they had come up, he remembered, and questioned him about trains. The three policemen were momentarily puzzled by this testimony. But it was soon plain to them if either the woman or the clergyman really had any information about Miss Hinch—a highly improbable supposition in itself—they would never have stopped with peppering the neighborhood with silly little contradictory messages.

"They're a pair of old fools tryin' to have sport with the police, and I'd like to run them in for it," growled the fattest of the officers; and it was the general verdict.

The little conference broke up. The dull proprietor returned to his cage, the waiter to his table; the subway man departed for his chopping box; the three policemen passed out into the bitter night. They walked together, grumbling, and their feet, perhaps by some subconscious impulse, turned toward the subway. And in the next block a man came running up to them.

"Officer, look what I found on the sidewalk a minute ago. Read that scribble!"

"Police! Miss Hinch 14th St subw"

The hand trailed off on the *w* as though the writer had been suddenly interrupted. The fat policeman blasphemed and threatened arrests. But the second policeman, who was dark and wiry, raised his head from the bill of fare and said suddenly: "Tim, I believe there's something in this."

"There'd ought to be ten days on the Island in it for them," growled fat Tim.

"Suppose, now," said the other policeman, staring intently at nothing, "the old woman was Miss Hinch, herself, f'r instance, and the parson was shadowing her, and Miss Hinch not darin' to cut and run for it till she was sure she had a clean getaway. Well, now, Tim, what better could he do—"

"That's right!" exclaimed the third policeman. "'Specially when ye think that Hinch carries a gun, an'll use it, too! Why not have a look in at the subway station?"

The proposal carried the day. The three officers started for the subway, the citizen following. They walked at a good pace and without more talk; and both their speed and their silence had a psychological reaction. As the minds of the policemen turned inward upon the odd behavior of the pair in Miller's Restaurant, the conviction that, after all, something important might be afoot grew and strengthened within each one of them. Unconsciously their pace quickened. It was the wiry policeman who first broke into a run, but the two others had been for twenty paces

on the verge of it.

However, these consultations had taken time. The stout clergyman and the poor old woman had five minutes' start on the officers of the law, and that, as it happened, was all that the occasion required. On Fourteenth Street, as they made their way arm in arm to the station, they were seen and remembered by a number of belated pedestrians. It was observed by more than one that the woman lagged as if she were tired, while the club-footed divine, supporting her on his arm, steadily kept her up to his own brisk gait.

So walking, the pair descended the subway steps, came out upon the bare platform again, and presently stood once more at the extreme uptown end of it, just where they had waited half an hour before. Nearby a careless porter had overturned a bucket of water, and a splotch of thin ice ran out and over the edge of the concrete. Two young men who were taking lively turns up and down distinctly heard the clergyman warn the woman to look out for this ice. Far away to the north was to be heard the faint roar of the approaching train.

The woman stood nearer the track, and the clergyman stood in front of her. In the vague light their looks met, and each was struck by the pallor of the other's face. In addition, the woman was breathing hard, and her hands and feet betrayed some nervousness. It was difficult now to ignore the fact that for an hour they had been clinging desperately to each other, at all costs; but the clergyman made a creditable effort to do so. He talked ramblingly, in a voice sounding only a little unnatural, for the most part of the deplorable weather and his train to Jersey, for which he was now so late. And all the time both of them were incessantly turning their heads toward the station entrances, as if expecting some arrival.

As he talked, the clergyman kept his hands

unobtrusively busy. From the bottom edge of his black sack-cloth he drew a pin, and stuck it deep into the ball of the middle finger. He took out a handkerchief to dust the hard sleet from his hat; and under his overcoat he pressed the handkerchief against his bleeding finger. While making these small arrangements, he held the woman's eyes with his own, talking on; and, still holding them, he suddenly broke off his random talk and peered at her cheek with concern.

"My good woman, you've scratched your cheek somehow! Why, bless me, it's bleeding quite badly."

"Never mind—never mind," said the woman and swept her eyes hurriedly toward the entrance.

"But good gracious, I must mind! The blood will fall on your shawl. If you will permit me—ah!"

Too quick for her, he leaned forward, and, through the thin veil, swept her cheek hard with the handkerchief; removing it, he held it up so that she might see the blood for herself. But she did not glance at the handkerchief; and neither did he. His gaze was riveted upon her cheek, which looked smooth and clear where he had smudged the clever wrinkles away.

Down the steps and upon the platform pounded the feet of three flying policemen. But it was evident now that the train would thunder in just ahead of them. The clergyman, standing close in front of the woman, took a firmer grip on his heavy stick, and a look of stern triumph came into his face.

"You're not so terribly clever, after all!"

The woman had sprung back from him with an irrepressible exclamation, and in that instant she was aware of the police.

However, her foot slipped upon the treacherous ice—or it may have tripped on the stout cane, when the clergyman suddenly shifted its position. And in the next breath the train came roaring past.

By one of those curious chances which sometimes refute all experience, the body of the woman was not mangled or mutilated in the least. There was a deep blue bruise on the left temple, and apparently that was all; even the ancient hat remained on her head, skewered fast by the long pin. It was the clergyman who found the body huddled at the side of the dark track where the train had flung it—he who covered the still face and superintended the removal to the platform. Two eyewitnesses of the tragedy pointed out the ice on which the unfortunate woman had slipped, and described their horror as they saw her companion spring forward just too late to save her.

Not wishing to bring on a delirium of excitement among the bystanders, two policemen drew the clergyman quietly aside and showed him the mysterious messages. Much affected by the shocking end of his sleuthery* as he was, he readily admitted having written them. He briefly recounted how the woman's strange movements on 126th Street had arrested his attention and how, watching her closely on the car, he had finally detected that she wore a wig. Unfortunately, however, her suspicions had been aroused by his interest in her, and thereafter a long battle of wits had ensued between them—he trying to summon the police without her knowledge, she dogging him close to prevent that, and at the same time watching her chance to give him the slip. He rehearsed how, in the restaurant, when he had invented an excuse to leave her for an instant, she had made a bolt and narrowly missed getting away; and finally how, having brought her back to the subway and seeing the police at last near, he had decided to risk exposing her make-up with this unexpectedly shocking result.

---

sleuthery: acting as a detective

"And now," he concluded in a shaken voice, "I am naturally most anxious to know whether I am right—or have made some terrible mistake. Will you look at her, officer, and tell me if it is indeed—she?"

But the fat policeman shook his head over the well-known ability of Miss Hinch to look like everybody but herself.

"It'll take God Almighty to tell ye that, sir, saving your presence. I'll leave it f'r headquarters," he continued, as if that were the same thing. "But, if it is her, she's gone to her reward, sir."

"God pity her!" said the clergyman.

"Amen! Give me your name, sir. They'll likely want you in the morning."

The clergyman gave it: Rev. Theodore Shaler, of Denver; city address, a number on East 11th Street. Having thus discharged his duty in the affair, he started sadly to go away; but, passing by the silent figure stretched on a bench under the ticket-seller's overcoat, he bared his head and stopped for one last look at it.

The parson's gentleness and efficiency had already won favorable comments from the bystanders, and of the first quality he now gave a final proof. The dead woman's balled-up handkerchief, which somebody had recovered from the track and laid upon her breast, had slipped to the floor; and the clergyman, observing it, stooped silently to restore it again. This last small service chanced to bring his head close to the head of the dead woman; and, as he straightened up again, her projecting hatpin struck his cheek and ripped a straight line down it. This in itself would have been a trifle, since scratches soon heal. But it happened that the point of the hatpin caught the lining of the clergyman's perfect beard and ripped it clean from him; so that, as he rose with a suddenly shrilled cry, he turned upon the astonished onlookers the bare, smooth chin of a woman, curiously long and pointed.

There were not many such chins in the world, and the urchins in the street would have recognized this one. Amid a sudden uproar which ill became the presence of the dead, the police closed in on Miss Hinch and handcuffed her with violence, fearing suicide, if not some new witchery; and at the station-house an unemotional matron divested the famous impersonator of the last and best of her disguises.

This much the police did. But it was everywhere understood that it was Jessie Dark who had really made the capture, and the papers next morning printed pictures of the unconquerable little woman and of the hatpin with which she had reached back from another world to bring her greatest adversary to justice.

About the Story

1. What is the setting of the story?
2. Who is the central character? The antagonist?
3. What type of conflict does the story reveal?
4. What is the first clue to the true identity of the old woman?
5. How is the conflict resolved?

About the Author

Henry Syndor Harrison (1880-1930) was born in Sewanee, Tennessee, the son of a professor of classical languages at the University of the South. Harrison attended Columbia University and then went into newspaper work as a staffer at the Richmond *Times-Dispatch* from 1900 to 1930. His experiences in journalism helped him in creating the main character of his first novel, *Queed*. Instantly popular, this novel was later made into a play. Six more novels followed in addition to short stories such as "Miss Hinch," an excellent example of using a story's structure to create conflict and sustain a high level of suspense.

Like Charles Dickens, Harrison used his pen to promote social reform, though he never enjoyed Dickens's critical acclaim. Yet even when dealing with problems such as factory working conditions and child-labor disputes, Harrison maintained a lively, entertaining, and optimistic style. It is this light-hearted quality in his writing that still makes Henry Syndor Harrison a pleasure to read.

Robin Hood
and Little John

The actual existence of Robin Hood is as doubtful as that of King Arthur. But the outlaw of Sherwood Forest has as firm a place in the world of imagination as does the legendary ruler of Camelot.

The Robin Hood legend comes down to us mostly through ballads. Many of them follow the pattern of "Robin Hood and Little John." Robin meets a stranger in the woods and challenges him. They fight. Robin gets the worst of the match. The stranger, oddly, submits and asks to be accepted into Robin's band of foresters.

It is interesting that in literature as in life the leader is not always the strongest or most gifted of the group. Something else about him inspires the loyalty and confidence of others. Notice the resolution of Robin and Little John's conflict. Can you find some clue as to why others readily followed Robin Hood?

Though he was called Little, his limbs they were large
    And his stature was seven foot high.
Wherever he came, they quaked at his name
    For soon he would make them to fly.

They happened to meet on a long narrow bridge,   5
    And neither of them would give way;
Quoth bold Robin Hood, and sturdily stood,
    "I'll show you right Nottingham play!"

With that from his quiver an arrow he drew,
    A broad arrow with a goose wing.   10
The stranger replied, "I'll tear off thy hide
    If thou offer to touch the string!

"With my whole heart," the stranger went on,
    "I scorn in the least to give out!"*   *give out:* give way
This said, they fell to it without more dispute,   15
    And their staffs they did flourish about.

At first Robin gave the stranger a bang,
    So hard that he made his bones ring;
The stranger he said, "This must be repaid,
    I'll give you as good as you bring."   20

The stranger gave Robin a crack on the crown,
    Which caused the blood to appear;
Then Robin, enraged, more fiercely engaged,
    And followed his blows more severe.

O then in a fury the stranger he grew,   25
    And gave him a furious look,
And with a blow laid Robin full low
    And tumbled him into the brook.

Then unto the bank he did presently wade
    And pulled him* out by a thorn;*   30   *him:* himself
                                                  thorn: branch of a
Which done at the last he blew a loud blast   hawthorn tree
    Straightway on his fine bugle horn.

"O what is the matter?" quoth Will Stutely,
   "Good master, you are wet to the skin!"
"No matter," quoth he, "the lad that you see   35
   In fighting hath tumbled me in."

"He shall not go scot free!" the others replied,
   So straight they were seizing him there
To duck him likewise, but Robin Hood cries,
   "He is a stout fellow, forbear!"   40

"O here is my hand," the stranger replied,
   "I'll serve you with all my whole heart;
My name is John Little, a man of good mettle*   *mettle:* quality
   Ne'er doubt me, for I'll play my part."

"His name shall be altered," quoth Will Stutely,   45
   "And I will his godfather be;
Prepare then a feast, and none of the least,
   For we will be merry," quoth he.

"This infant was called John Little," quoth he,
   "Which name shall be changed anon;*   50   *anon:* immediately
The words we'll transpose so wherever he goes,
   His name shall be called Little John!"

Then music and dancing did finish the day.
   At length, when the sun waxed low,
Then all the whole train* the grove did refrain   55   *train:* group
   And unto their caves they did go.

And so ever after, as long as he lived,
   Although he was proper* and tall,   *proper:* handsome
Yet nevertheless, the truth to express,
   Still Little John they did him call.   60

About the Poem

1. Was Little John aptly named? Why or why not?
2. How did Robin summon his men?
3. How was Robin kind to John Little?
4. Paraphrase the action of this ballad.
5. Is this folk ballad simple or complex? Support your answer.

Through the Tunnel

Doris Lessing

In this suspenseful story, eleven-year-old Jerry attempts to test his courage and endurance by "mastering" the blue sea and its great rocks that "lay like discolored monsters under the surface."

Though nature could be viewed as a type of antagonist in this story, it is better viewed as the agent which measures the central character's maturity. There is another, more dominant antagonist Jerry must deal with. Doris Lessing makes the identification of this central conflict easier through her emphasis of certain descriptive details. What does this artful control of sound and syntax tell you about Jerry's attitude toward the beach, the bay, and his mother? Does this understanding of Jerry's thoughts and attitudes help you discern the central conflict?

Going to the shore on the first morning of the vacation, the young English boy stopped at a turning of the path and looked down at a wild and rocky bay, and then over to the crowded beach he knew so well from other years. His mother walked on in front of him, carrying a bright striped bag in one hand. Her other arm, swinging loose, was very white in the sun. The boy watched that white, naked arm, and turned his eyes, which had a frown behind them, toward the bay and back again to his mother. When she felt he was not with her, she swung around. "Oh, there you are, Jerry!" she said. She looked impatient, then smiled. "Why, darling, would you rather not come with me? Would you rather—" She frowned, conscientiously worrying over what amusements he might secretly be longing for, which she had been too busy or too careless to imagine. He was very familiar with that anxious apologetic smile. Contrition* sent him running after her. And yet, as he ran, he looked back over his shoulder at the wild bay; and all morning, as he played on the safe beach, he was thinking of it.

---

contrition: heartfelt remorse for doing wrong

Next morning, when it was time for the routine of swimming and sunbathing, his mother said, "Are you tired of the usual beach, Jerry? Would you like to go somewhere else?"

"Oh, no!" he said quickly, smiling at her out of that unfailing impulse of contrition— a sort of chivalry. Yet, walking down the path with her, he blurted out, "I'd like to go and have a look at those rocks down there."

She gave the idea her attention. It was a wild-looking place, and there was no one there; but she said, "Of course, Jerry. When you've had enough, come to the big beach. Or just go straight back to the villa, if you like." She walked away, that bare arm, now slightly reddened from yesterday's sun, swinging. And he almost ran after her again, feeling it unbearable that she should go by herself, but he did not.

She was thinking, Of course he's old enough to be safe without me. Have I been keeping him too close? He mustn't feel he ought to be with me. I must be careful.

He was an only child, eleven years old. She was a widow. She was determined to be neither possessive nor lacking in devotion. She went worrying off to her beach.

As for Jerry, once he saw that his mother had gained her beach, he began the steep descent to the bay. From where he was, high up among red-brown rocks, it was a scoop of moving bluish green fringed with white. As he went lower, he saw that it spread among small promontories* and inlets of rough, sharp rock, and the crisping, lapping surface showed stains of purple and darker blue. Finally, as he ran sliding and scraping down the last few yards, he saw an edge of white surf and the shallow, luminous movement of water over white sand, and, beyond that, a solid, heavy blue.

---

promontories: projecting coastal cliffs

He ran straight into the water and began swimming. He was a good swimmer. He went out fast over the gleaming sand, over a middle region where rocks lay like discolored monsters under the surface, and then he was in the real sea—a warm sea where irregular cold currents from the deep water shocked his limbs.

When he was so far out that he could look back not only on the little bay but past the promontory that was between it and the big beach, he floated on the buoyant surface and looked for his mother. There she was, a speck of yellow under an umbrella that looked like a slice of orange peel. He swam back to shore, relieved at being sure she was there, but all at once very lonely.

On the edge of a small cape that marked the side of the bay away from the promontory was a loose scatter of rocks. Above them, some boys were stripping off their clothes. They came running down to the rocks. The English boy swam toward them, but kept his distance at a stone's throw. They were of that coast; all of them were burned smooth dark brown and speaking a language he did not understand. To be with them, of them, was a craving that filled his whole body. He swam a little closer; they turned and watched him with narrowed, alert dark eyes. Then one smiled and waved. It was enough. In a minute, he had swum in and was on the rocks beside them, smiling with a desperate, nervous supplication. They shouted cheerful greetings at him; and then, as he preserved his nervous, uncomprehending smile, they understood that he was a foreigner strayed from his own beach, and they proceeded to forget him. But he was happy. He was with them.

They began diving again and again from a high point into a well of blue sea between rough, pointed rocks. After they had dived and come up, they swam around, hauled themselves up, and waited their turn to dive again. They were big boys—men, to Jerry. He dived, and they watched him; and when he swam around to take his place, they made way for him. He felt he was accepted and he dived again, carefully, proud of himself.

Soon the biggest of the boys poised himself, shot down into the water, and did not come up. The others stood about, watching. Jerry, after waiting for the sleek brown head to appear, let out a yell of warning; they looked at him idly and turned their eyes back toward the water. After a long time, the boy came up on the other side of a big dark rock, letting the air out of his lungs in a spluttering gasp and a shout of triumph. Immediately the rest of them dived in. One moment, the morning seemed full of clattering boys; the next, the air and the surface of the water were empty. But through the heavy blue, dark shapes could be seen moving and groping.

Jerry dived, shot past the school of underwater swimmers, saw a black wall of rock looming at him, touched it, and bobbed up at once to the surface, where the wall was a low barrier he could see across. There was no one visible; under him, in the water, the dim shapes of the swimmers had disappeared. Then one, and then another of the boys came up on the far side of the barrier of rock, and he understood that they had swum through some gap or hole in it. He plunged down again.

He could see nothing through the stinging salt water but the blank rock. When he came up the boys were all on the diving rock, preparing to attempt the feat again. And now, in a panic of failure, he yelled up, in English, "Look at me! Look!" and he began splashing and kicking in the water like a foolish dog.

They looked down gravely, frowning. He knew the frown. At moments of failure, when he clowned to claim his mother's attention, it was with just this grave, embarrassed inspection that she rewarded him. Through his hot shame, feeling the pleading grin on his face like a scar that he could never remove, he looked up at the group of big brown boys on the rock and shouted, "*Bonjour! Merci! Au revoir! Monsieur, monsieur!*" while he hooked his fingers round his ears and waggled them.

Water surged into his mouth; he choked, sank, came up. The rock, lately weighted with boys, seemed to rear up out of the water as their weight was removed. They were flying down past him, now, into the water; the air was full of falling bodies. Then the rock was empty in the hot sunlight. He counted one, two, three. . . .

At fifty, he was terrified. They must all be drowning beneath him, in the watery caves of the rock! At a hundred, he stared around him at the empty hillside, wondering if he should yell for help. He counted faster, faster, to hurry them up, to bring them to the surface quickly, to drown them quickly—anything rather than the terror of counting on and on into the blue emptiness of the morning. And then, at a hundred and sixty, the water beyond the rock was full of boys blowing like brown whales. They swam back to the shore without a look at him.

He climbed back to the diving rock and sat down, feeling the hot roughness of it under his thighs. The boys were gathering up their bits of clothing and running off along the shore to another promontory. They were leaving to get away from him. He cried openly, fists in his eyes. There was no one to see him, and he cried himself out.

It seemed to him that a long time had passed, and he swam out to where he could see his mother. Yes, she was still there, a yellow spot under an orange umbrella. He swam back to the big rock, climbed up, and dived into the blue pool among the fanged and angry boulders. Down he went, until he touched the wall of rock again. But the salt was so painful in his eyes that he could not see.

He came to the surface, swam to shore and went back to the villa to wait for his mother. Soon she walked slowly up the path, swinging her striped bag, the flushed, naked arm dangling beside her. "I want some swimming goggles," he panted, defiant and beseeching.

She gave him a patient, inquisitive look as she said casually, "Well, of course, darling."

But now, now, now! He must have them this minute, and no other time. He nagged and pestered until she went with him to a shop. As soon as she had bought the goggles, he grabbed them from her hand as if she were going to claim them for herself, and was off, running down the steep path to the bay.

Jerry swam out to the big barrier rock, adjusted the goggles, and dived. The impact of the water broke the rubber-enclosed vacuum, and the goggles came loose. He understood that he must swim down to the base of the rock from the surface of the water. He fixed the goggles tight and firm, filled his lungs, and floated, face down, on the water. Now, he could see. It was as if he had eyes of a different kind—fish eyes that showed everything clear and delicate and wavering in the bright water.

Under him, six or seven feet down, was a floor of perfectly clean, shining white sand, rippled firm and hard by the tides. Two grayish shapes steered there, like long, rounded pieces of wood or slate. They were fish. He saw them nose toward each other, poise motionless, make a dart forward, swerve off, and come around again. It was like a water dance. A few inches above them the water sparkled as if sequins were dropping through it. Fish again—myriads of minute fish, the length of his fingernail, were drifting through the water, and in a moment he could feel the innumerable tiny touches of them against his limbs. It was like swimming in flaked silver. The great rock the big boys had swum through rose sheer out of the white sand—black, tufted lightly with greenish weed. He could see no gap in it. He swam down to its base.

Again and again he rose, took a big chestful of air, and went down. Again and again he groped over the surface of the rock, feeling it, almost hugging it in the desperate need to find the entrance. And then, once, while he was clinging to the black wall, his knees came up and he shot his feet out forward and they met no obstacle. He had found the hole.

He gained the surface, clambered about the stones that littered the barrier rock until he found a big one, and, with this in his arms, let himself down over the side of the rock. He dropped, with the weight, straight to the sandy floor. Clinging tight to the anchor of stone, he lay on his side and looked in under the dark shelf at the place where his feet had gone. He let go of his anchor, clung with his hands to the edges of the hole, and tried to push himself in.

He got his head in, found his shoulders jammed, moved them in sidewise, and was inside as far as his waist. He could see nothing ahead. Something soft and clammy touched his mouth; he saw a dark frond moving against the grayish rock, and panic filled him. He thought of octopuses, of clinging weed. He pushed himself out backward and caught a glimpse, as he retreated, of a harmless tentacle of seaweed drifting in the mouth of the tunnel. But it was enough. He reached the sunlight, swam to shore, and lay on the diving rock. He knew he must find his way through that cave, or hole, or tunnel, and out the other side.

First, he thought, he must learn to control his breathing. He let himself down into the water with another big stone in his arms, so that he could lie effortlessly on the bottom of the sea. He counted. One, two, three. He counted steadily. He could hear the movement of blood in his chest. Fifty-one, fifty-two . . . . His chest was hurting. He let go of the rock and went up into the air. He saw that the sun was low. He rushed to the villa and found his mother at her supper. She said only "Did you enjoy yourself?" and he said "Yes."

All night the boy dreamed of the water-filled cave in the rock, and as soon as breakfast was over he went to the bay.

That night, his nose bled badly. For hours he had been underwater, learning to hold his breath, and now he felt weak and dizzy. His mother said, "I shouldn't overdo things, darling, if I were you."

That day and the next, Jerry exercised his lungs as if everything, the whole of his life, all that he could become, depended upon it. Again his nose bled at night, and his mother insisted on his coming with her the next day. It was a torment to him to waste a day of his careful self-training, but he stayed with her on that other beach, which now seemed a place for small children, a place where his mother might lie safe in the sun. It was not his beach.

He did not ask for permission, on the following day, to go to his beach. He went, before his mother could consider the complicated rights and wrongs of the matter.

A day's rest, he discovered, had improved his count by ten. The big boys had made the passage while he counted a hundred and sixty. He had been counting fast, in his fright. Probably now, if he tried, he could get through that long tunnel, but he was not going to try yet. A curious, most unchildlike persistence, a controlled impatience, made him wait. In the meantime, he lay underwater on the white sand, littered now by stones he had brought down from the upper air, and studied the entrance to the tunnel. He knew every jut and corner of it, as far as it was possible to see. It was as if he already felt its sharpness about his shoulders.

He sat by the clock in the villa when his mother was not near, and checked his time. He was incredulous and then proud to find he could hold his breath without strain for two minutes. The words "two minutes," authorized by the clock, brought close the adventure that was so necessary to him.

In another four days, his mother said casually one morning, they must go home. On the day before they left, he would do it. He would do it if it killed him, he said defiantly to himself. But two days before they were to leave—a day of triumph when he increased his count by fifteen—his nose bled so badly that he turned dizzy and had to lie limply over the big rock like a bit of seaweed, watching the thick red blood flow on to the rock and trickle slowly down to the sea. He was frightened. Supposing he died there, trapped? Supposing—his head went around, in the hot sun, and he almost gave up. He thought he would return to the house and lie down, and next summer, perhaps, when he had another year's growth in him—*then* he would go through the hole.

But even after he had made the decision, or thought he had, he found himself sitting up on the rock and looking down into the

water; and he knew that now, this moment, when his nose had only just stopped bleeding, when his head was still sore and throbbing— this was the moment when he would try. If he did not do it now, he never would. He was trembling with fear that he would not go; and he was trembling with horror at that long, long tunnel under the rock, under the sea. Even in the open sunlight, the barrier rock seemed very wide and very heavy; tons of rock pressed down on where he would go. If he died there, he would lie until one day—perhaps not before next year—those big boys would swim into it and find it blocked.

He put on his goggles, fitted them tight, tested the vacuum. His hands were shaking. Then he chose the biggest stone he could carry and slipped over the edge of the rock until half of him was in the cool, enclosing water and half in the hot sun. He looked up once at the empty sky, filled his lungs once, twice, and then sank fast to the bottom with the stone. He let it go and began to count. He took the edges of the hole in his hands and drew himself into it, wriggling his shoulders in sidewise as he remembered he must, kicking himself along with his feet.

Soon he was clear inside. He was in a small rockbound hole filled with yellowish-gray water. The water was pushing him up against the roof. The roof was sharp and pained his back. He pulled himself along with his hands— fast, fast—and used his legs as levers. His head knocked against something; a sharp pain dizzied him. Fifty, fifty-one, fifty-two . . . . He was without light, and the water seemed to press upon him with the weight of rock. Seventy-one, seventy-two . . . . There was no strain on his lungs. He felt like an inflated balloon, his lungs were so light and easy, but his head was pulsing.

He was being continually pressed against the sharp roof, which felt slimy as well as sharp.

Again he thought of octopuses, and wondered if the tunnel might be filled with weed that could tangle him. He gave himself a panicky, convulsive kick forward, ducked his head, and swam. His feet and hands moved freely, as if in open water. The hole must have widened out. He thought he must be swimming fast, and he was frightened of banging his head if the tunnel narrowed.

A hundred, a hundred and one . . . . The water paled. Victory filled him. His lungs were beginning to hurt. A few more strokes and he would be out. He was counting wildly; he said a hundred and fifteen, and then, a long time later, a hundred and fifteen again. The water was a clear jewel-green all around him. Then he saw above his head, a crack running up through the rock. Sunlight was falling through it, showing the clean, dark rock of the tunnel, a single mussel shell, and darkness ahead.

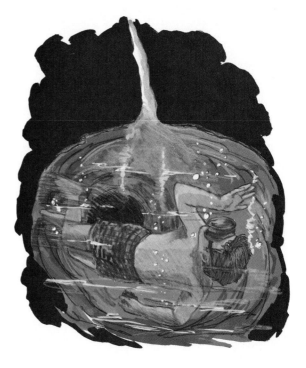

He was at the end of what he could do. He looked up at the crack as if it were filled with air and not water, as if he could put his mouth to it to draw in air. A hundred and fifteen, he heard himself say inside his head— but he had said that long ago. He must go on into the blackness ahead, or he would drown. His head was swelling, his lungs cracking. A hundred and fifteen, a hundred and fifteen pounded through his head, and he feebly clutched at rocks in the dark, pulling himself forward, leaving the brief space of sunlit water behind. He felt he was dying. He was no longer quite conscious. He struggled on in the darkness between lapses into unconsciousness. An immense, swelling pain filled his head, and then the darkness cracked with an explosion of green light. His hands, groping forward, met nothing; and his feet, kicking back, propelled him out into the open sea.

He drifted to the surface, his face turned up to the air. He was gasping like a fish. He felt he would sink now and drown; he could not swim the few feet back to the rock. Then he was clutching it and pulling himself up on to it. He lay face down, gasping. He could see nothing but a red-veined, clotted dark. His eyes must have burst, he thought; they were full of blood. He tore off his goggles and a gout of blood went into the sea. His nose was bleeding, and the blood had filled the goggles.

He scooped up handfuls of water from the cool, salty sea, to splash on his face, and did not know whether it was blood or salt water he tasted. After a time, his heart quieted, his eyes cleared, and he sat up. He could see the local boys diving and playing half a mile away. He did not want them. He wanted nothing but to get back home and lie down.

In a short while, Jerry swam to shore and climbed slowly up the path to the villa. He flung himself on his bed and slept, waking at the sound of feet on the path outside. His mother was coming back. He rushed to the bathroom, thinking she must not see his face with bloodstains, or tearstains, on it. He came out of the bathroom and met her as she walked into the villa, smiling, her eyes lighting up.

"Have a nice morning?" she asked, laying her hand on his warm brown shoulder a moment.

"Oh, yes, thank you," he said.

"You look a bit pale." And then, sharp and anxious, "How did you bang your head?"

"Oh, just banged it," he told her.

She looked at him closely. He was strained; his eyes were glazed-looking. She was worried. And then she said to herself, Oh, don't fuss! Nothing can happen. He can swim like a fish.

They sat down to lunch together.

"Mummy," he said, "I can stay under water for two minutes—three minutes, at least." It came bursting out of him.

"Can you, darling?" she said. "Well, I shouldn't overdo it. I don't think you ought to swim any more today."

She was ready for a battle of wills, but he gave in at once. It was no longer of the least importance to go to the bay.

About the Story

1. Does the setting of the story help portray the conflict? Why or why not?
2. What colors does the author use to describe the mother and the beach?
3. What colors are used to describe the boys swimming in the bay and the bay itself?
4. What do you think this contrast in colors implies?
5. How would you describe Jerry's and his mother's relationship at the opening of the story (note paragraphs 5 and 6)? How does this relationship change when the conflict is resolved?

About the Author

Doris Lessing (1919-   ) was reared in Southern Rhodesia, where her English parents ran a farm. The people, animals, and scenery of that land deeply impressed her, not only forming a rich reservoir of descriptive imagery for her writings but also shaping a social and political conscience that would surface in her work.

While growing up, Doris Lessing was exposed to the conflicts that raged between native Africans and English colonizers. This experience, coupled with her reading of nineteenth-century Russian authors like Tolstoy and Dostoevsky, caused her to draw a comparison between pre-revolutionary Russia and the English colonies in Africa. As a result, she began to look to communism as an engine of social justice. In 1949 when she returned to England, she began to support the Communist party of Great Britain. Like so many other British intellectuals of the postwar period, Lessing became disillusioned with the party during the Hungarian Revolt in 1956. Her later works continue to emphasize the need for social change, but they also reflect a disillusionment with communism as a viable agent of such change.

In her novels and short stories, Doris Lessing's underlying theme is commitment—to political causes, to love, to family, to friends, and to oneself. Personal integrity and independence rise above all other goals in the lives of many of Lessing's later characters. Although the inner conflicts of her characters are often well drawn and realistically portrayed, they are usually resolved in ways unacceptable to a Christian reader. An exception is "Through the Tunnel," in which Jerry successfully fulfills his commitment to himself without shirking his responsibility to his mother. This proving of oneself is another important theme in Lessing's writings.

The Duel

Nikolai Dmitrievitch Teleshov

Like the hero in "Through the Tunnel," the central character in this story faces a test of courage. Unlike Jerry, however, Ivan Golubenko does not take up his challenge willingly. How does Ivan's attitude toward conflict affect the resolution of the story?

It was early morning—

Vladimir Kladunov, a tall, graceful young man, twenty-two years of age, almost boyish in appearance, with a handsome face and thick, fair curls, dressed in the uniform of an officer and in long riding boots, minus overcoat and cap, stood upon a meadow covered with new-fallen snow, and gazed at another officer, a tall, red-faced, mustached man, who faced him at a distance of thirty paces, and was slowly lifting his hand in which he held a revolver, and aimed it straight at Vladimir.

With his arms crossed over his breast and also holding in one hand a revolver, Kladunov, almost with indifference, awaited the shot of his opponent. His handsome, young face, though a little paler than usual, was alight with courage, and wore a scornful smile. His dangerous position, and the merciless determination of his adversary, the strenuous attention of the seconds* who silently stood at one side, and the imminence of death, made the moment one of terrible intensity—mysterious, almost solemn. A question of honor was to be decided. Every one felt the importance of the question; the less they understood what they were doing, the deeper seemed the solemnity of the moment.

seconds: official attendants of the contestants in a duel

A shot was fired; a shiver ran through all. Vladimir threw his hands about, bent his knees, and fell. He lay upon the snow, shot through the head, his hands apart, his hair, face, and even the snow around his head covered with blood. The seconds ran toward him and lifted him; the doctor certified his death, and the question of honor was solved. It only remained to announce the news to the regiment and to inform, as tenderly and carefully as possible, the mother, who was now left alone in the world, for the boy that had been killed was her only son. Before the duel no one had given her even a thought; but now they all became very thoughtful. All knew and loved her, and recognized the fact that she must be prepared by degrees for the terrible news. At last Ivan Golubenko was chosen as most fit to tell the mother, and smooth out matters as much as possible.

. . . .

Pelageia Petrovna had just risen and was preparing her morning tea when Ivan Golubenko, gloomy and confused, entered the room.

"Just in time for tea, Ivan Ivanovich!" amiably exclaimed the old lady, rising to meet her guest. "You have surely called to see Vladimir!"

"No, I—in passing by—" Golubenko stammered, abashed.

"You will have to excuse him; he is still asleep. He walked up and down his room the whole of last night, and I told the servant not to wake him, as it is a—holy day. But probably you came on urgent business?"

"No, I only stepped in for a moment in passing—"

"If you wish to see him, I will give the order to wake him up."

"No, no, do not trouble yourself!"

But Pelageia Petrovna, believing that he had called to see her son on some business or other, left the room, murmuring to herself.

Golubenko walked excitedly to and fro, wringing his hands, not knowing how to tell her the terrible news. The decisive moment was quickly approaching, but he lost control of himself, was frightened, and cursed fate that had so mixed him up with the whole business.

"Now! How can a body trust you young people!" Pelageia exclaimed good-naturedly to her guest, reentering the room. "Here I have been taking care not to make the least noise with the cups and saucers, and asking you not to wake my boy, and he has long ago departed without leaving a trace! But why do you not take a seat, Ivan Ivanovich, and have a cup of tea? You have been neglecting us terribly lately!"

She smiled as with a secret joy, and added in a low voice:

"And we have had so much news during that time!—Vladimir surely could not keep it. He must have told you all about it by this time; for he is very straightforward and open-hearted, my Vladimir. I was thinking last night, in my sinful thoughts: 'Well, when my Vladimir paces the room the whole night—that means that he is dreaming of Lenochka!' That is always the case with him: if he paces the room the whole night he will surely leave to-morrow. —Ah, Ivan Ivanovich, I only ask the Lord to send me this joy in my old age. What more does an old woman need? I have but one desire, one joy—and it seems to me I shall have nothing more to pray for after Vladimir and Lenochka are married. So joyful and happy it would make me! —I do not need anything besides Vladimir; there is nothing dearer to me than his happiness."

The old lady became so affected that she had to wipe away the tears which came to her eyes.

"Do you remember," she continued, "things did not go well in the beginning—either between the two or on account of the money— you young officers are not even allowed to marry without bonds—well, now everything has been arranged; I have obtained the necessary five thousand rubles for Vladimir, and they could go to the altar even to-morrow! Yes, and Lenochka has written such a lovely letter to me—my heart is rejoicing!"

Continuing to speak, Pelageia Petrovna took a letter out of her pocket, which she showed to Golubenko, and then put it back again.

"She is such a dear girl! And so good!"

Ivan Golubenko, listening to her talk, sat as if on red-hot coals. He wanted to interrupt her flow of words, to tell her that everything was at an end, that her Vladimir was dead, and that in one short hour nothing would remain to her of all her bright hopes; but he listened to her and kept silent. Looking upon her good, gentle face, he felt a convulsive gripping in his throat.

"But why are you looking so gloomy to-day?" the old lady at last asked. "Why, your face looks as black as night!"

Ivan wanted to say, "Yes! And yours will be the same when I tell you!" But instead of telling her anything, he turned his head away, and began to twirl his mustaches.

Pelageia Petrovna did not notice it, and, wholly absorbed in her own thoughts, continued:

"I have a greeting for you. Lenochka writes that I should give Ivan Ivanovich her regards, and should compel him to come with Vladimir and pay her a visit—you know yourself how she likes you, Ivan Ivanovich! —No, it seems I am not able to keep it to myself. I must show you the letter. Just see for yourself how loving and sweet it is."

And Pelageia Petrovna again took out the package of letters from her pocket, took from it a thin letter-sheet, closely written, and unfolded it before Ivan Golubenko, whose face had become still gloomier, and he tried to push away with his hand the extended note, but Pelageia Petrovna had already started to read:

"Dear Pelageia Petrovna: When will the time arrive when I will be able to address you, not as above, but as my dear, sweet mother! I am anxiously awaiting the time, and hope so much that it will soon come that even now I do not want to call you otherwise than mama—"

Pelageia Petrovna lifted her head, and, ceasing to read, looked at Golubenko with eyes suffused with tears.

"You see, Ivan Ivanovich," she added; but seeing that Golubenko was biting his mustaches, and that his eyes too were moist, she rose, placed a trembling hand upon his hair, and quietly kissed him on the forehead. "Thank you, Ivan Ivanovich," she whispered, greatly moved. "I always thought that you and Vladimir were more like brothers than like simple friends—forgive me—I am so very happy, God be thanked!"

Tears streamed down her cheeks, and Ivan Golubenko was so disturbed and confused that he could only catch in his own her cold, bony hand and cover it with kisses; tears were suffocating him, and he could not utter a word, but in this outburst of motherly love he felt such a terrible reproach to himself that he would have preferred to be lying himself upon the field, shot through the head, than to hear himself praised for his friendship by this woman who would in half an hour find out the whole truth; what would she then think of him? Did not he, the friend, the almost brother, stand quietly by when a revolver was pointed at Vladimir? Did not this brother himself measure the space between the two antagonists and load the revolvers? All this he did himself, did consciously; and now this friend and brother silently sat there without having even the courage to fulfil his duty.

He was afraid; at this moment he despised himself, but could not prevail upon himself to say even one word. His soul was oppressed by a strange lack of harmony; he felt sick at heart and stifling. And in the meanwhile time flew—he knew it, and the more he knew it the less had he the courage to deprive Pelageia Petrovna of her few last happy moments. What should he say to her? How should he prepare her? Ivan Golubenko lost his head entirely.

He had had already time enough to curse in his thoughts all duels, all quarrels, every kind of heroism, and all kinds of so-called questions of honor, and he at last rose from his seat ready to confess or to run away. Silently and quickly he caught the hand of Pelageia Petrovna, and stooping over it to touch it with his lips, thus hid his face, over which a torrent of tears suddenly streamed down; impetuously, without another thought, he ran out into the corridor, snatching his great coat, and then out of the house without having said a word.

Pelageia Petrovna looked after him with astonishment, and thought:

"He also must be in love, poor fellow—well, that is their young sorrow—before happiness!" . . .

And she soon forgot him, absorbed in her dreams of the happiness which seemed to her so inviolable and entire.

About the Story

1. Who is the central character of the story?
2. Whom or what is the central character fighting against? Support your answer with specific quotations from the story.
3. How is the dominant conflict resolved?
4. What is the secondary conflict in this story?
5. How is this secondary conflict resolved?

About the Author

Little is known about Nikolai Dmitrievitch Teleshov (1867-1945), a Russian writer during the latter part of the nineteenth and the early twentieth century. We do know that Teleshov was influenced by and wrote for the famous author Maxim Gorky, the "father of Soviet literature" and the initiator of Socialist Realism. Like Gorky, Teleshov was perceived as a radical writer. His sketches and stories often depict the plight of the Russian peasant or the Siberian exile. Like many of his stories, "The Duel" is a vivid portrayal of psychological conflict. It is free, however, from the political and social propaganda that characterizes much of his work. Though a supporter of the Bolshevik cause, Teleshov (like Gorky and other intellectuals of the era) was not an avid supporter of Lenin. Following Lenin's rise to power in 1917, Teleshov devoted his energies to writing reminiscences of such famous authors as Gorky, Chekhov, and Andreyev, thus contributing to several of his contemporaries the literary fame he himself was denied.

Top Man

James Ramsey Ullman

As you have already discovered, the descriptive details in a story are invaluable in helping you pinpoint the central conflict, especially if there is more than one type of conflict presented.

After reading only the first few paragraphs of "Top Man," you can see that one conflict in the story will be man against nature. But as you continue reading about the men and their ascent, you will notice that Ullman brings two other conflicts to our attention: man struggling with himself, and man struggling with man. Which of these conflicts becomes the dominant conflict? Does the title of the story give you a clue?

The gorge bent. The walls fell suddenly away, and we came out on the edge of a bleak, boulder-strewn valley. . . . *And there it was.*

Osborn saw it first. He had been leading the column, threading his way slowly among the huge rock masses of the gorge's mouth. Then he came to the first flat bare place and stopped. He neither pointed nor cried out, but every man behind him knew instantly what it was. The long file sprang taut, like a jerked rope. As swiftly as we could, but in complete silence, we came out one by one into the open space where Osborn stood, and we raised our eyes with his.

In the records of the Indian Topographical Survey it says: "Kalpurtha: altitude 27,930 feet. The highest peak in the Garhwal Himalayas and probably fourth highest in the world. Also known as K3. A tertiary formation of sedimentary limestone. . . ."

There were men among us who had spent months of their lives—in some cases years—reading, thinking, planning about what now lay before us; but at that moment statistics and geology, knowledge, thought, and plans, were as remote and forgotten as the faraway western cities from which we had come. We were men bereft of everything but eyes, everything but the single electric perception: *there it was!*

Before us the valley stretched into miles of rocky desolation. To right and left it was bounded by low ridges; which, as the eye followed them, slowly mounted and drew closer together, until the valley was no longer a valley at all, but a narrowing, rising corridor between the cliffs. What happened then I can describe only as a stupendous crash of music. At the end of the corridor and above it—so far above it that it shut out half the sky—hung the blinding white mass of K3.

It was like the many pictures I had seen, and at the same time utterly unlike them. The shape was there, and the familiar distinguishing features: the sweeping skirt of glaciers; the monstrous vertical precipices of the face and the jagged ice-line of the east ridge; finally, the symmetrical summit pyramid that transfixed the sky. But whereas in the pictures the mountain had always seemed unreal—a dream-image of cloud, snow, and crystal—it was now no longer an image at all. It was a mass: solid, immanent, appalling. We were still too far away to see the windy whipping of its snow plumes or to hear the cannonading of its avalanches, but in that sudden silent moment every man of us was for the first time aware of it not as a picture in his mind, but as a thing, an antagonist. For all its twenty-eight thousand feet of lofty grandeur it seemed, somehow, less to tower than to crouch—a white-hooded giant, secret and remote, but living. Living and on guard.

I turned my eyes from the dazzling glare and looked at my companions. Osborn still stood a little in front of the others. He was absolutely motionless, his young face tense and shining. One could feel in the very set of his body the overwhelming desire that swelled in him to act, to come to grips, to conquer. A little behind him were ranged the other white men of the expedition: Randolph, our leader, Wittmer and Johns, Dr. Schlapp and Bixler. All were still, their eyes cast upward. Off to one side a little stood Nace, the Englishman, the only one among us who was not staring at K3 for the first time. He had been the last

to come up out of the gorge and stood now with arms folded on his chest, squinting at the great peak he had known so long and fought so tirelessly and fiercely. His lean British face, under its mask of stubble and windburn, was expressionless. His lips were a thin line, and his eyes seemed almost shut. Behind the sahibs* ranged the porters, bent forward over their brown seamed faces straining upward from beneath their loads.

sahibs: Europeans

For a long while no one spoke or moved. The only sounds between earth and sky were the soft hiss of our breathing and the pounding of our hearts.

Through the long afternoon we wound slowly between the great boulders of the valley and at sundown pitched camp in the bed of a dried-up stream. The porters ate their rations in silence, wrapped themselves in their blankets, and fell asleep under the stars. The rest of us, as was our custom, sat close about the fire that blazed in the circle of tents, discussing the events of the day and the plans for the

next. It was a flawlessly clear Himalayan night, and K3 tiered up* into the blackness like a monstrous beacon lighted from within. There was no wind, but a great tide of cold air crept down the valley from the ice fields above, penetrating our clothing, pressing gently against the canvas of the tents.

tiered up: ascended in layers

"Another night or two and we'll be needing the sleeping bags," commented Randolph.

Osborn nodded. "We could use them tonight would be my guess."

Randolph turned to Nace. "What do you say, Martin?"

The Englishman puffed at his pipe a moment. "Rather think it might be better to wait," he said at last.

"Wait? Why?" Osborn jerked his head up.

"Well, it gets pretty nippy high up, you know. I've seen it thirty below at twenty-five thousand on the east ridge. Longer we wait for the bags, better acclimated we'll get."

Osborn snorted. "A lot of good being acclimated will do, if we have frozen feet."

"Easy, Paul, easy," cautioned Randolph. "It seems to me Martin's right."

Osborn bit his lip, but said nothing. The other men entered the conversation, and soon it had veered to other matters: the weather, the porters and pack animals, routes, camps, and strategy, the inevitable, inexhaustible topics of the climber's world.

There were all kinds of men among the eight of us, men with a great diversity of background and interest. Sayre Randolph, whom the Alpine Club had named leader of our expedition, had for years been a well-known explorer and lecturer. Now in his middle fifties, he was no longer equal to the grueling physical demands of high climbing, but served as planner and organizer of the enterprise. Wittmer was a Seattle lawyer who

had recently made a name for himself by a series of difficult ascents in the Coast Range of British Columbia. Johns was an Alaskan, a fantastically strong, able sourdough* who had been a ranger in the U.S. Forestry Service and had accompanied many famous Alaskan expeditions. Schlapp was a practicing physician from Milwaukee, Bixler a government meteorologist with a talent for photography. I, at the time, was an assistant professor of geology at an eastern university.

sourdough: northern prospector, pioneer

Finally, and preeminently, there were Osborn and Nace. I say "preeminently" because, even at this time, when we had been together as a party for little more than a month, I believe all of us realized that these were the two key men of our venture. None, to my knowledge, ever expressed it in words, but the conviction was nonetheless there that if any of us were eventually to stand on the summit of K3, it would be one of them, or both. They were utterly dissimilar men. Osborn was twenty-three and a year out of college, a compact, buoyant mass of energy and high spirits. He seemed to be wholly unaffected by either the physical or mental hazards of mountaineering and had already, by virtue of many spectacular ascents in the Alps and Rockies, won a reputation as the most skilled and audacious of younger American climbers. Nace was in his forties—lean, taciturn,* introspective. An official in the Indian Civil Service, he had explored and climbed in the Himalayas for twenty years. He had been a member of all five of the unsuccessful British expeditions to K3, and in his last attempt had attained to within five hundred feet of the summit, the highest point which any man had reached on the unconquered giant. This had been the famous, tragic attempt in which his fellow climber and lifelong friend, Captain

Furness, had slipped and fallen ten thousand feet to his death. Nace rarely mentioned his name, but on the steel head of his ice ax were engraved the words: TO MARTIN FROM JOHN. If fate were to grant that the ax of any one of us should be planted upon the summit of K3, I hoped it would be this one.

taciturn: untalkative

Such were the men who huddled about the fire in the deep, still cold of a Himalayan night. There were many differences among us, in temperament as well as in background. In one or two cases, notably that of Osborn and Nace, there had already been a certain amount of friction, and as the venture continued and the struggles and hardships of the actual ascent began, it would, I knew, increase. But differences were unimportant. What mattered—all that mattered—was that our purpose was one: to conquer the monster of rock and ice that now loomed above us in the night; to stand for a moment where no man, no living thing, had ever stood before. To that end we had come from half a world away, across oceans and continents to the fastnesses* of inner Asia. To that end we were prepared to endure cold, exhaustion, and danger, even to the very last extremity of human endurance. . . . Why? There is no answer, and at the same time every man among us knew the answer; every man who has ever looked upon a great mountain and felt the fever in his blood to climb and conquer knows the answer. George Leigh Mallory, greatest of mountaineers, expressed it once and for all when he was asked why he wanted to climb unconquered Everest.

fastnesses: fortifications, mountain heights

"I want to climb it," said Mallory, "because it is there."

Day after day we crept on and upward.

Sometimes the mountain was brilliant above us, as it had been when we first saw it; sometimes it was partially or wholly obscured by tiers of clouds. The naked desolation of the valley was unrelieved by any motion, color, or sound; and as we progressed, the great rock walls that enclosed it grew so high and steep that its floor received the sun for less than two hours each day. The rest of the time it lay in ashen half-light, its gloom intensified by the dazzling brilliance of the ice slopes above. As long as we remained there we had the sensation of imprisonment; it was like being trapped at the bottom of a deep well or in a sealed court between great skyscrapers. Soon we were thinking of the ascent of the shining mountain not only as an end in itself, but as an escape.

In our nightly discussions around the fire our conversation narrowed more and more to the immediate problems confronting us, and during them I began to realize that the tension between Osborn and Nace went deeper than I had at first surmised. There was rarely any outright argument between them—they were both far too able mountain men to disagree on fundamentals—but I saw that at almost every turn they were rubbing each other the wrong way. It was a matter of personalities, chiefly. Osborn was talkative, enthusiastic, optimistic, always chafing* to be up and at it, always wanting to take the short straight line to the given point. Nace, on the other hand, was matter-of-fact, cautious, slow. He was the apostle of trial-and-error and watchful waiting. Because of his far greater experience and intimate knowledge of K3, Randolph almost invariably followed his advice, rather than Osborn's, when a difference of opinion arose. The younger man usually capitulated with good grace, but I could tell that he was irked.

chafing: straining against a prohibition, delay, or limitation

During the days in the valley I had few occasions to talk privately with either of them, and only once did either mention the other in any but the most casual manner. Even then, the remarks they made seemed unimportant and I remember them only in view of what happened later.

My conversation with Osborn occurred first. It was while we were on the march, and Osborn, who was directly behind me, came up suddenly to my side. "You're a geologist, Frank," he began without preamble. "What do you think of Nace's theory about the ridge?"

"What theory?" I asked.

"He believes we should traverse* under it from the glacier up. Says the ridge itself is too exposed."

---

traverse: pass across

"It looks pretty mean through the telescope."

"But it's been done before. He's done it himself. All right, it's tough—I'll admit that. But a decent climber could make it in half the time the traverse will take."

"Nace knows the traverse is longer," I said. "But he seems certain it will be much easier for us."

"Easier for *him* is what he means." Osborn paused, looking moodily at the ground. "He was a great climber in his day. It's a shame a man can't be honest enough with himself to know when he's through." He fell silent and a moment later dropped back into his place in line.

It was that same night, I think, that I awoke to find Nace sitting up in his blanket and staring at the mountain.

"How clear it is!" I whispered.

The Englishman pointed. "See the ridge?"

I nodded, my eyes fixed on the great, twisting spine of ice that climbed into the sky.

I could see now, more clearly than in the blinding sunlight, its huge indentations and jagged, wind-swept pitches. "It looks impossible," I said.

"No, it can be done. Trouble is, when you've made it you're too done in for the summit."

"Osborn seems to think its shortness would make up for its difficulty."

Nace was silent a long moment before answering. Then for the first and only time I heard him speak the name of his dead companion. "That's what Furness thought," he said quietly. Then he lay down and wrapped himself in his blanket.

For the next two weeks the uppermost point of the valley was our home and workshop. We established our base camp as close to the mountain as we could, less than half a mile from the tongue of its lowest glacier, and plunged into the arduous tasks of preparation for the ascent. Our food and equipment were unpacked, inspected and sorted, and finally repacked in lighter loads for transportation to more advanced camps. Hours were spent poring over maps and charts and studying the monstrous heights above us through telescope and binoculars. Under Nace's supervision, a thorough reconnaissance of the glacier was made and the route across it laid out; then began the backbreaking labor of moving up supplies and establishing the chain of camps.

Camps I and II were set up on the glacier itself, in the most sheltered sites we could find. Camp III we built at its upper end, as near as possible to the point where the great rock spine of K3 thrust itself free of ice and began its precipitous ascent. According to our plans, this would be the advance base of operations during the climb. The camps to be established higher up, on the mountain proper, would be too small and too exposed to serve as anything more than one or two nights' shelter. The total distance between the base camp and Camp III was only fifteen miles, but the utmost daily progress of our porters was five miles, and it was essential that we should never be more than twelve hours' march from food and shelter. Hour after hour, day after day, the long file of men wound up and down among the hummocks* and crevasses of the glacier, and finally the time arrived when we were ready to advance.

---

hummocks: mounds or ridges

Leaving Dr. Schlapp in charge of eight porters at the base camp, we proceeded easily and on schedule, reaching Camp I the first night, Camp II the second, and the advance base the third. No men were left at Camps I and II, inasmuch as they were designed simply as caches for food and equipment; and furthermore we knew we would need all the manpower available for the establishment of the higher camps on the mountain proper.

For more than three weeks now the weather had held perfectly, but on our first night at the advance base, as if by malignant prearrangement of nature, we had our first taste of the fury of a high Himalayan storm. It began with great streamers of lightning that flashed about the mountain like a halo; then heavily through the weird glare, snow began to fall. The wind rose. At first it was only sound— a remote, desolate moaning in the night high above us—but soon it descended, sucked down the deep valley as if into a gigantic funnel. Hour after hour it howled about the tents with hurricane frenzy, and the wild flapping of the canvas dinned in our ears like machine-gun fire.

There was no sleep for us that night or the next. For thirty-six hours the storm raged without lull, while we huddled in the icy gloom of the tents, exerting our last ounce of strength to keep from being buried alive or blown into eternity. At last, on the third morning, it was over, and we came out into a world transformed by a twelve-foot cloak of snow. No single landmark remained as it had been before, and our supplies and equipment were in the wildest confusion. Fortunately there had not been a single serious injury, but it was another three days before we had regained our strength and put the camp in order.

Then we waited. The storm did not return, and the sky beyond the ridges gleamed flawlessly clear; but night and day we could hear the roaring thunder of avalanches on the mountain above us. To have ventured so much as one step into that savage vertical wilderness before the new-fallen snow froze tight would have been suicidal. We chafed or waited patiently, according to our individual temperaments, while the days dragged by.

It was late one afternoon that Osborn returned from a short reconnaissance up the ridge. His eyes were shining and his voice jubilant.

"It's tight!" he cried. "Tight as a drum. We can go!" All of us stopped whatever we were doing. His excitement leaped like an electric spark from one to another. "I went about a thousand feet, and it's sound all the way. What do you say, Sayre? Tomorrow?"

Randolph hesitated, then looked at Nace.

"Better give it another day or two," said the Englishman.

Osborn glared at him. "Why?" he challenged.

"It's usually safer to wait till—"

"Wait! Wait!" Osborn exploded. "Don't you ever think of anything but waiting? The snow's firm, I tell you!"

"It's firm down here," Nace replied quietly, "because the sun hits it only two hours a day. Up above it gets the sun twelve hours. It may not have frozen yet."

"The avalanches have stopped."

"That doesn't necessarily mean it will hold a man's weight."

"It seems to me Martin's point—" Randolph began.

Osborn wheeled on him. "Sure," he snapped. "I know. Martin's right. The cautious English are always right. Let him have his way, and we'll be sitting here chewing our nails until the mountain falls down on us." His eyes flashed to Nace. "Maybe with a little less of that cautiousness you English wouldn't have made such a mess of Everest. Maybe your pals Mallory and Furness wouldn't be dead."

"Osborn!" commanded Randolph sharply.

The youngster stared at Nace for another moment, breathing heavily. Then abruptly he turned away.

The next two days were clear and windless, but we still waited, following Nace's advice. There were no further brushes between him and Osborn, but an unpleasant air of restlessness and tension hung over the camp. I found myself chafing almost as impatiently as Osborn himself for the moment when we would break out of that maddening inactivity and begin the assault.

At last the day came. With the first paling of the sky a roped file of men, bent almost double beneath heavy loads, began slowly to climb the ice slope, just beneath the jagged line of the great east ridge. In accordance with the prearranged plan, we proceeded in relays, this first group consisting of Nace, Johns, myself, and eight porters. It was our job to ascend approximately two thousand feet in a day's climbing and establish Camp IV at the most level and sheltered site we could find. We would spend the night there and return to the advance base next day, while the second relay, consisting of Osborn, Wittmer, and eight more porters, went up with their loads. This process was to continue until all necessary supplies were at Camp IV, and then the whole thing would be repeated between Camps IV and V and V and VI. From VI, at an altitude of about twenty-six thousand feet, the ablest and fittest men—presumably Nace and Osborn—would make the direct assault on the summit. Randolph and Bixler were to remain at the advance base throughout the operations, acting as directors and co-ordinators. We were under the strictest orders that any man—sahib or porter—who suffered illness or injury should be brought down immediately.

How shall I describe those next two weeks beneath the great ice ridge of K3? In a sense there was no occurrence of importance, and at the same time everything happened that could possibly happen, short of actual disaster. We established Camp IV, came down again, went up again, came down again. Then we crept laboriously higher. With our axes we hacked uncountable thousands of steps in the gleaming walls of ice. Among the rocky outcroppings of the cliffs we clung to holds and strained at ropes until we thought our arms would spring from their sockets. Storms swooped down on us, battered us, and passed. The wind increased, and the air grew steadily colder and more difficult to breathe. One morning two of the porters awoke with their feet frozen black; they had to be sent down. A short while later Johns developed an uncontrollable nosebleed and was forced to descend to a lower camp. Wittmer was suffering from racking headaches and I from a continually dry throat. But providentially, the one enemy we feared the most in that icy gale-lashed hell did not again attack us. No snow fell. And day by day, foot by foot, we ascended.

It is during ordeals like this that the surface trappings of a man are shed and his secret mettle* laid bare. There were no shirkers or quitters among us—I had known that from the beginning—but now, with each passing day, it became more manifest which were the

strongest and ablest among us. Beyond all argument, these were Osborn and Nace.

mettle: courage

Osborn was magnificent. All the boyish impatience and moodiness which he had exhibited earlier were gone, and, now that he was at last at work in his natural element, he emerged as the peerless mountaineer he was. His energy was inexhaustible, his speed, both on rock and ice, almost twice that of any other man in the party. He was always discovering new routes and short cuts. Often he ascended by the ridge itself, instead of using the traverse beneath it, as had been officially prescribed; but his craftsmanship was so sure and his performance so brilliant that no one ever thought of taking him to task. Indeed, there was such vigor, buoyancy, and youth in everything he did that it gave heart to all the rest of us.

In contrast, Nace was slow, methodical, unspectacular. Since he and I worked in the same relay, I was with him almost constantly, and to this day I carry in my mind the clear image of the man: his tall body bent almost double against endless shimmering slopes of ice; his lean brown face bent in utter concentration on the problem in hand, then raised searchingly to the next; the bright prong of his ax rising, falling, rising, falling, with tireless rhythm, until the steps in the glassy incline were so wide and deep that the most clumsy of the porters could not have slipped from them had he tried. Osborn attacked the mountain head-on. Nace studied it, sparred with it, wore it down. His spirit did not flap from his sleeve like a pennon;* it was deep inside him—patient, indomitable.

pennon: flag

The day soon came when I learned from him what it is to be a great mountaineer. We were making the ascent from Camp IV to V, and an almost perpendicular ice wall had made it necessary for us to come out for a few yards on the exposed crest of the ridge. There were six of us in the party, roped together, with Nace leading, myself second, and four porters bringing up the rear. The ridge at this particular point was free of snow, but razor-thin, and the rocks were covered with a smooth glaze of ice. On either side the mountain dropped away in sheer precipices of five thousand feet.

Suddenly the last porter slipped. I heard the ominous scraping of boot nails behind me and, turning, saw a gesticulating figure plunge sideways into the abyss. There was a scream as the next porter was jerked off too. I remember trying frantically to dig into the ridge with my ax, realizing at the same time it would no more hold against the weight of the falling men than a pin stuck in a wall. Then I heard Nace shout, "Jump!" As he said it, the rope went tight about my waist, and I went hurtling after him into space on the opposite side of the ridge. After me came the nearest porter . . . .

What happened then must have happened in five yards and a fifth of a second. I heard myself cry out, and the glacier a mile below rushed up at me spinning. Then both were blotted out in a violent spasm, as the rope jerked taut. I hung for a moment, an inert mass, feeling that my body had been cut in two; then I swung in slowly to the side of the mountain. Above me the rope lay tight and motionless across the crest of the ridge, our weight exactly counterbalancing that of the men who had fallen on the far slope.

Nace's voice came up from below. "You chaps on the other side!" he shouted. "Start climbing slowly. We're climbing too."

In five minutes we had all regained the ridge. The porters and I crouched panting on the jagged rocks, our eyes closed, the sweat beading our faces in frozen drops. Nace carefully examined the rope that again hung loosely between us.

"All right, men," he said presently. "Let's get on to camp for a cup of tea."

Above Camp V the whole aspect of the ascent changed. The angle of the ridge eased off, and the ice, which lower down had covered the mountain like a sheath, lay only in scattered patches between the rocks. Fresh enemies, however, instantly appeared to take the place of the old. We were now laboring at an altitude of more than twenty-five thousand feet—well above the summits of the highest surrounding peaks—and day and night, without protection or respite, we were buffeted by the fury of the wind. Worse than this was that the atmosphere had become so rarefied it could scarcely support life. Breathing itself was a major physical effort, and our progress upward consisted of two or three painful steps followed by a long period of rest in which our hearts pounded wildly and our burning lungs gasped for air. Each of us carried a small cylinder of oxygen in his pack, but we used it only in emergencies and found that, while its immediate effect was salutary,* it left us later even worse off than before. My throat dried and contracted until it felt as if it were lined with brass. The faces of all of us, under our beards and windburn, grew haggard* and strained.

---

salutary: beneficial to health
haggard: appearing worn and tired

But the great struggle was now mental as much as physical. The lack of air induced a lethargy of mind and spirit; confidence and the powers of thought and decision waned, and dark foreboding crept out from the secret recesses of the subconscious. The wind seemed to carry strange sounds, and we kept imagining we saw things which we knew were not there. The mountain, to all of us, was no longer a mere giant of rock and ice; it had become a living thing, an enemy, watching us, waiting for us, hostile, relentless, and aware. Inch by inch we crept upward through that empty forgotten world above the world, and only one last thing remained to us of human consciousness and human will: to go on. To go on.

On the fifteenth day after we had first left the advance base we pitched Camp VI at an altitude of almost twenty-six thousand feet. It was located near the uppermost extremity of the great east ridge, directly beneath the so-called shoulder of the mountain. On the far side of the shoulder the monstrous north face of K3 fell sheer to the glaciers, two miles below. And above it and to the left rose the symmetrical bulk of the summit pyramid. The topmost rocks of its highest pinnacle were clearly visible from the shoulder, and the intervening two thousand feet seemed to offer no insuperable* obstacles.

---

insuperable: not able to be overcome

Camp VI, which was in reality no camp at all, but a single tent, was large enough to accommodate only three men. Osborn established it with the aid of Wittmer and one porter; then, the following morning, Wittmer and the porter descended to Camp V, and Nace and I went up. It was our plan that Osborn and Nace should launch the final assault—the next day, if the weather held—with myself in support, following their progress through binoculars and going to their aid or summoning help from below if anything went wrong. As the three of us lay in the tent that night, the summit seemed already within arm's reach, victory securely in our grasp.

And then the blow fell. With malignant timing, which no power on earth could have made us believe was a simple accident of nature, the mountain hurled at us its last line of defense. It snowed.

For a day and a night the great flakes drove down on us, swirling and swooping in the wind, blotting out the summit, the shoulder, everything beyond the tiny white-walled radius of our tents. Hour after hour we lay in our sleeping bags, stirring only to eat or to secure the straining rope and canvas. Our feet froze under their thick layers of wool and rawhide. Our heads and bodies throbbed with a dull nameless aching, and time crept over our numbed minds like a glacier. At last, during the morning of the following day, it cleared.

The sun came out in a thin blue sky, and the summit pyramid again appeared above us, now whitely robed in fresh snow. But still we waited. Until the snow either froze or was blown away by the wind it would have been the rashest courting of destruction for us to have ascended a foot beyond the camp. Another day passed. And another.

By the third nightfall our nerves were at the breaking point. For hours on end we had scarcely moved or spoken, and the only sounds in all the world were the endless moaning of the wind outside and the harsh sucking noise of our breathing. I knew that, one way or another, the end had come. Our meager food supply was running out; even with careful rationing there was enough left for only two more days.

Presently Nace stirred in his sleeping bag and sat up. "We'll have to go down tomorrow," he said quietly.

For a moment there was silence in the tent. Then Osborn struggled to a sitting position and faced him.

"No," he said.

"There's still too much loose snow above. We can't make it."

"But it's clear. As long as we can see—"

Nace shook his head. "Too dangerous. We'll go down tomorrow and lay in a fresh supply. Then we'll try again."

"Once we go down we're licked. You know it."

Nace shrugged. "Better to be licked than . . ." The strain of speech was suddenly too much for him and he fell into a violent paroxysm of coughing. When it had passed there was a long silence.

Then suddenly Osborn spoke again. "Look, Nace," he said, "I'm going up tomorrow."

The Englishman shook his head.

"I'm going—understand?"

For the first time since I had known him

I saw Nace's eyes flash in anger. "I'm the senior member of this group," he said. "I forbid you to go!"

Osborn jerked himself to his knees, almost upsetting the tiny tent. "You forbid me? This may be your sixth time on this mountain, and all that, but you don't *own* it! I know what you're up to. You haven't got it in you to make the top yourself, so you don't want anyone else to make it. That's it, isn't it? Isn't it?" He sat down again suddenly, gasping for breath.

Nace looked at him with level eyes. "This mountain has beaten me five times," he said softly. "It killed my best friend. It means more to me to climb it than anything else in the world. Maybe I'll make it and maybe I won't. But if I do, it will be as a rational intelligent human being—not as a fool throwing my life away. . . ."

He collapsed into another fit of coughing and fell back in his sleeping bag. Osborn, too, was still. They lay there inert, panting, too exhausted for speech.

It was hours later that I awoke from dull, uneasy sleep. In the faint light I saw Nace fumbling with the flap of the tent.

"What is it?" I asked.

"Osborn. He's gone."

The words cut like a blade through my lethargy. I struggled to my feet and followed Nace from the tent.

Outside, the dawn was seeping up the eastern sky. It was very cold, but the wind had fallen and the mountain seemed to hang suspended in a vast stillness. Above us the summit pyramid climbed bleakly into space, like the last outpost of a spent and lifeless planet. Raising my binoculars, I swept them over the gray waste. At first I saw nothing but rock and ice; then, suddenly, something moved.

"I've got him," I whispered.

As I spoke, the figure of Osborn sprang into clear focus against a patch of ice. He took three or four slow upward steps, stopped, went on again. I handed the glasses to Nace.

The Englishman squinted through them, returned them to me, and reentered the tent. When I followed, he had already laced his boots and was pulling on his outer gloves.

"He's not far," he said. "Can't have been gone more than half an hour." He seized his ice ax and started out again.

"Wait," I said. "I'm going with you."

Nace shook his head. "Better stay here."

"I'm going with you," I said.

He said nothing further, but waited while I made ready. In a few moments we left the tent, roped up, and started off.

Almost immediately we were on the shoulder and confronted with the paralyzing two-mile drop of the north face; but we negotiated the short exposed stretch without mishap, and in ten minutes were working up the base of the summit pyramid. The going here was easier, in a purely climbing sense: the angle of ascent was not steep, and there was firm rock for hand- and foot-holds between the patches of snow and ice. Our progress, however, was creepingly slow. There seemed to be literally no air at all to breathe, and after almost every step we were forced to rest, panting and gasping as we leaned forward against our axes. My heart swelled and throbbed with every movement until I thought it would explode.

The minutes crawled into hours and still we climbed. Presently the sun came up. Its level rays streamed across the clouds, far below, and glinted from the summits of distant peaks. But, although the pinnacle of K3 soared a full three thousand feet above anything in the surrounding world, we had scarcely any sense of height. The wilderness of mountain valley and glacier that spread beneath us to the horizon was flattened and remote, an unreal, insubstantial landscape seen in a dream. We had no connection with it, or it with us. All living, all awareness, purpose, and will, was concentrated in the last step and the next: to put one foot before the other; to breathe; to ascend. We struggled on in silence.

I do not know how long it was since we had left the camp—it might have been two hours, it might have been six—when we suddenly sighted Osborn. We had not been able to find him again since our first glimpse through the binoculars; but now, unexpectedly and abruptly, as we came up over a jogged outcropping rock, there he was. He was at a point, only a few yards above us, where the mountain steepened into an almost vertical wall. The smooth surface directly in front of him was obviously unclimbable, but two alternate routes were presented. To the left, a chimney* cut obliquely across the wall, forbiddingly steep, but seeming to offer adequate holds. To the right was a gentle slope of snow that curved upward and out of sight behind the rocks. As we watched, Osborn ascended to the edge of the snow, stopped, and probed it with his ax. Then, apparently satisfied that it would bear his weight he stepped out on the slope.

---

chimney: vertical groove

I felt Nace's body tense. "Paul!" he cried out.

His voice was too weak and hoarse to carry. Osborn continued his ascent.

Nace cupped his hands and called his name again, and this time Osborn turned. "Wait!" cried the Englishman.

Osborn stood still, watching us, as we struggled up the few yards to the edge of the snow slope. Nace's breath came in shuddering gasps, but he climbed faster than I had ever seen him climb before.

"Come back!" he called. "Come off the snow!"

"It's all right. The crust is firm," Osborn called back.

"But it's melting. There's . . ." Nace paused, fighting for air. "There's nothing underneath!"

In a sudden sickening flash I saw what he meant. Looked at from directly below, at the point where Osborn had come to it, the slope on which he stood appeared as a harmless covering of snow over the rocks. From where we were now, however, a little to one side, it could be seen that it was in reality no covering at all, but merely a cornice or unsupported platform clinging to the side of the mountain. Below it was not rock, but ten thousand feet of blue air.

"Come back!" I cried. "Come back!"

Osborn hesitated, then took a downward step. But he never took the next. For in that same instant the snow directly in front of him disappeared. It did not seem to fall or to break away. It was just soundlessly and magically no longer there. In the spot where Osborn had been about to set his foot there was now revealed the abysmal drop of the north face of K3.

I shut my eyes, but only for a second, and when I reopened them Osborn was still, miraculously, there. Nace was shouting, "Don't move! Don't move an inch!"

"The rope—" I heard myself saying.

The Englishman shook his head. "We'd have to throw it, and the impact would be too much. Brace yourself and play it out." As he spoke, his eyes were traveling over the rocks that bordered the snow bridge. Then he moved forward.

I wedged myself into a cleft in the wall and let out the rope which extended between us. A few yards away Osborn stood in the snow, transfixed, one foot a little in front of the other. But my eyes now were on Nace. Cautiously, but with astonishing rapidity, he edged along the rocks beside the cornice. There was a moment when his only support was an inch-wide ledge beneath his feet, another where

there was nothing under his feet at all, and he supported himself wholly by his elbows and hands. But he advanced steadily and at last reached a shelf wide enough for him to turn around on. At this point he was perhaps six feet away from Osborn.

"It's wide enough here to hold both of us," he said in a quiet voice. "I'm going to reach out my ax. Don't move until you're sure you have a grip on it. When I pull, jump."

He searched the wall behind him and found a hold for his left hand. Then he slowly extended his ice ax, head foremost, until it was within two feet of Osborn's shoulder. "Grip it!" he cried suddenly. Osborn's hands shot out and seized the ax. "Jump!"

There was a flash of steel in the sunlight and a hunched figure hurtled inward from the snow to the ledge. Simultaneously another figure hurtled out. The haft* of the ax jerked suddenly from Nace's hand, and he lurched forward and downward. A violent spasm convulsed his body as the rope went taut. Then it was gone. Nace did not seem to hit the snow; he simply disappeared through it, soundlessly. In the same instant the snow itself was gone. The frayed, yellow end of broken rope spun lazily in space. . . .

---

haft: handle

Somehow my eyes went to Osborn. He was crouched on the ledge where Nace had been a moment before, staring dully at the ax he held in his hands. Beyond his head, not two hundred feet above, the white untrodden pinnacle of K3 stabbed the sky.

Perhaps ten minutes passed, perhaps a half hour. I closed my eyes and leaned forward motionless against the rock, my face against my arm. I neither thought nor felt; my body and mind alike were enveloped in a suffocating numbness. Through it at last came the sound

of Osborn moving. Looking up, I saw he was standing beside me.

"I'm going to try for the top," he said tonelessly.

I merely stared at him.

"Will you come?"

"No," I said.

Osborn hesitated, then turned and began slowly climbing the steep chimney above us. Halfway up he paused, struggling for breath. Then he resumed his laborious upward progress and presently disappeared beyond the crest.

I stayed where I was, and the hours passed. The sun reached its zenith above the peak and sloped away behind it. And at last I heard above me the sound of Osborn returning. As I looked up, his figure appeared at the top of the chimney and began the descent. His clothing was in tatters, and I could tell from his movements that only the thin flame of his will stood between him and collapse. In another few minutes he was standing beside me.

"Did you get there?" I asked dully.

He shook his head. "I couldn't make it," he answered. "I didn't have what it takes."

We roped together silently and began the descent to the camp.

There is nothing more to be told of the sixth assault on K3—at least not from the experiences of the men who made it. Osborn and I reached Camp V in safety, and three days later the entire expedition gathered at the advance base. It was decided, in view of the tragedy that had occurred, to make no further attempt on the summit, and by the end of the week we had begun the evacuation of the mountain.

It remained for another year and other men to reveal the epilogue.

The summer following our attempt a combined English-Swiss expedition stormed the peak successfully. After weeks of hardship and struggle they attained the topmost pinnacle of the giant, only to find that what should have been their great moment of triumph was, instead, a moment of the bitterest disappointment. For when they came out at last upon the summit they saw that they were *not* the first. An ax stood there. Its haft was embedded in rock and ice and on its steel head were the engraved words: TO MARTIN FROM JOHN.

They were sporting men. On their return to civilization they told their story, and the name of the conqueror of K3 was made known to the world.

About the Story

1. Who is the central character of the story?
2. Who opposes the central character?
3. Describe the three conflicts in the story.

4. Explain how each conflict is resolved.
5. Which of these conflicts would you say is the dominant conflict? Why?

About the Author

James Ramsey Ullman (1907-1971), author and expert mountaineer, was one of the first Americans to climb Mount Everest. The life-long pursuit of his three favorite activities—writing, mountain-climbing, and traveling—yielded many short stories and seven adventure novels rich with realistic detail. When Ullman was an undergraduate at Princeton University, he took a vacation to Switzerland and scaled the Matterhorn. He continued to climb, devoting his time between ascents to his writing career. After four years spent in journalism, Ullman turned to writing and producing plays. Of all ten of the plays he produced, the most successful was a Pulitzer-prize winner by Sidney Kingsley, *Men in White*. When his success in dramatic production waned, Ullman decided to make a journey to South America. The trip gave him the material he needed for *The Other Side of the Mountain* and *River of the Sun*.

Ullman interrupted his writing career only to serve honorably as an ambulance driver during World War II. *The White Tower,* his first and best-known novel, reflects the attitudes not only of one who has scaled mountains but also of one who has known life's valleys. Regarding the book he says, "The climbing of the White Tower, as I conceived it, was primarily an act of faith—an affirmation of the will-to-hope and the will-to-do in a tired, despairing, and shattered world. Today the fighting [of World War II] is over. . . . But it would be a rash optimist indeed who would say that the need for that faith and that will has passed, or that humanity has advanced perceptibly farther up the slopes of its mountain."

Under the Lion's Paw

Hamlin Garland

Garland's story, like Ullman's, presents all three types of conflict. It would be difficult, however, to discern the dominant conflict of "Under the Lion's Paw" without understanding the historical context in which the story was written. The story is set during a time when the Midwest was plagued by greedy land speculators. Through unethical practices these speculators swindled the tenant farmers hired to work the land. Initially the law sided with the speculators. But with the emergence of the Populist Movement, midwestern farmers were eventually granted protection from wily, opportunistic men.

Keep this background information in mind as you read; it will help you decide if the dominant conflict is simply man against man, or if Garland is using the conflict between Butler and Haskins to expose a larger struggle.

I

It was the last of autumn and first day of winter coming together. All day long the plowmen on their prairie farms had moved to and fro in their wide level fields through the falling snow, which melted as it fell, wetting them to the skin—all day, notwithstanding the frequent squalls of snow, the dripping, desolate clouds, and the muck of the furrows, black and tenacious* as tar.

---

tenacious: holding firmly together

Under their dripping harness the horses swung to and fro silently, with that marvelous uncomplaining patience which marks the horse. All day the wild geese, honking wildly as they sprawled sidewise down the wind, seemed to be fleeing from an enemy behind, and with neck outthrust and wings extended, sailed down the wind, soon lost to sight.

Yet the plowman behind his plow, though the snow lay on his ragged great-coat, and the cold, clinging mud rose on his heavy boots, fettering him like gyves,* whistled in the very beard of the gale. As day passed, the snow, ceasing to melt, lay along the plowed land, and lodged in the depth of the stubble, till on each slow round the last furrow stood out black and shining as jet* between the plowed land and the gray stubble.

---

gyves: shackles for legs
jet: dense black coal

When night began to fall, and the geese, flying low, began to alight invisibly in the near corn-field, Stephen Council was still at work "finishing a land." He rode on his sulky* plow when going with the wind, but walked when facing it. Sitting bent and cold but cheery under his slouch hat, he talked encouragingly to his four-in-hand.*

---

sulky: lightweight two-wheel vehicle which holds one person
four-in-hand: team of four horses

"Come round there, boys!—Round agin! We got t' finish this land. Come in there, Dan! *Stiddy,* Kate,—stiddy! None o' y'r tantrums, Kittie. It's purty tuff, but got a be did. *Tchk! Tchk!* Step along, Pete! Don't let Kate git y'r single-tree on the wheel. *Once* more!"

They seemed to know what he meant, and that this was the last round, for they worked so with greater vigor than before.

"Once more, boys, an' than, sez I, oats an' a nice warm stall, an' sleep f'r all."

By the time the last furrow was turned on the land it was too dark to see the house, and the snow was changing to rain again. The tired and hungry man could see the light from the kitchen shining through the leafless hedge, and he lifted a great shout, "Supper f'r a half a dozen!"

It was nearly eight o'clock by the time he had finished his chores and started for supper. He was picking his way carefully through the mud, when the tall form of a man loomed up before him with a premonitory cough.

"Waddy ye want?" was the rather startled question of the farmer.

"Well, ye see," began the stranger, in a deprecating* tone, "we'd like t' git in f'r the night. We've tried every house f'r the last two miles, but they hadn't any room f'r us. My wife's jest about sick, 'n' the children are cold and hungry—"

---

deprecating: belittling

"Oh, y' want 'o stay all night, eh?"

"Yes, sir; it 'ud be a great accom—"

"Waal, I don't make it a practice t' turn anybuddy way hungry, not on sech nights as this. Drive right in. We ain't got much, but sech as it is—"

But the stranger had disappeared. And soon his steaming, weary team, with drooping heads and swinging single-trees, moved past the well to the block beside the path. Council stood at the side of the "schooner" and helped the children out—two little half-sleeping children—and then a small woman with a babe in her arms.

"There ye go!" he shouted jovially, to the children. "*Now* we're all right! Run right along to the house there, an' tell Mam' Council you wants sumpthin' t' eat. Right this way, Mis'—keep right off t' the right there. I'll go an' git a lantern. Come," he said to the dazed and silent group at his side.

"Mother," he shouted, as he neared the fragrant and warmly lighted kitchen, "here are some wayfarers an' folks who need sumpthin' t' eat an' a place t' snooze." He ended by pushing them all in.

Mrs. Council, a large, jolly, rather coarse-looking woman, took the children in her arms. "Come right in, you little rabbits. 'Most asleep, hey? Now here's a drink o' milk f'r each o' ye. I'll have s'm tea in a minute. Take off y'r things and set up t' the fire."

While she set the children to drinking milk, Council got out his lantern and went out to the barn to help the stranger about his team, where his loud, hearty voice could be heard as it came and went between the haymow and the stalls.

The woman came to light as a small, timid and discouraged-looking woman, but still pretty, in a thin and sorrowful way.

"Land sakes! An' you've traveled all the way from Clear Lake t'-day in this mud! Waal! waal! No wonder you're all tired out. Don't wait f'r the men, Mis'—" She hesitated, waiting for the name.

"Haskins."

"Mis' Haskins, set right up to the table an' take a good swig o' tea whilst I make y' s'm toast. It's green tea, an' it's good. I tell Council as I git older I don't seem to enjoy Young Hyson n'r Gunpowder. I want the reel green tea, jest as it comes off'n the vines. Seems t'have more heart in it, some way. Don't s'pose it has. Council says it's all in m' eye."

Going on in this easy way, she soon had the children filled with bread and milk and the woman thoroughly at home, eating some toast and sweet-melon pickles, and sipping the tea.

"See the little rats!" she laughed at the children. "They're full as they can stick now, and they want to go to bed. Now, don't git up, Mis' Haskins; set right where you are an' let me look after 'em. I know all about young ones, though I'm all alone now. Jane went an' married last fall. But, as I tell Council, it's lucky we keep our health. Set right there, Mis' Haskins; I won't have you stir a finger."

It was an unmeasured pleasure to sit there in the warm, homely kitchen, the jovial chatter of the housewife driving out and holding at bay the growl of the impotent, cheated wind.

The little woman's eyes filled with tears which fell down upon the sleeping baby in her arms. The world was not so desolate and cold and hopeless, after all.

"Now I hope Council won't stop out there and talk politics all night. He's the greatest man to talk politics an' read the *Tribune*— How old is it?"

She broke off and peered down at the face of the babe.

"Two months 'n' five days." said the mother, with a mother's exactness.

"Ye don't say! I want 'o know! The dear little pudzy-wudzy!" she went on, stirring it up in the neighborhood of the ribs with her fat forefinger.

"Pooty tough on 'oo go gallivant'n' 'cross lots this way—"

"Yes, that's so; a man can't lift a mountain," said Council, entering the door. "Mother, this is Mr. Haskins, from Kansas. He's been eat up 'n' drove out by grasshoppers."

"Glad t' see yeh!—Pa, empty that washbasin 'n' give him a chance t' wash."

Haskins was a tall man, with a thin, gloomy face. His hair was a reddish brown, like his coat, and seemed equally faded by the wind and sun, and his sallow face, though hard and set, was pathetic somehow. You would have felt that he had suffered much by the line of his mouth showing under his thin, yellow mustache.

"Hain't Ike got home yet, Sairy?"

"Hain't seen 'im."

"W-a-a-l, set right up, Mr. Haskins; wade right into what we've got; 'tain't much, but we manage to live on it—she gits fat on it," laughed Council, pointing his thumb at his wife.

After supper, while the women put the children to bed, Haskins and Council talked on, seated near the huge cooking-stove, the steam rising from their wet clothing. In the Western fashion Council told as much of his own life as he drew from his guest. He asked but few questions, but by and by the story of Haskins' struggles and defeat came out. The story was a terrible one, but he told it quietly, seated with his elbows on his knees, gazing most of the time at the hearth.

"I didn't like the looks of the country, anyhow," Haskins said, partly rising and glancing at his wife. "I was ust t' northern Ingyannie, where we have lots o' timber 'n' lots o' rain, 'n' I didn't like the looks o' that dry prairie. What galled me the worst was goin' s' far away acrosst so much fine land layin' all through here vacant."

"And the 'hoppers eat ye four years, hand runnin', did they?"

"Eat! They wiped us out. They chawed everything that was green. They jest set around waitin' f'r us to die t' eat us, too. I ust t' dream of 'em sittin' 'round on the bedpost, six feet long, workin' their jaws. They eet the fork-handles. They got worse 'n' worse till they jest rolled on one another, piled up like snow in winter. Well, it ain't no use. If I was t' talk all winter I couldn't help thinkin' of all that land back here that nobuddy was usin' that I ought 'o had 'stead o' bein' out there in that cussed country."

"Waal, why didn't ye stop an' settle here?" asked Ike, who had come in and was eating his supper.

"Fer the simple reason that you fellers wantid ten 'r fifteen dollars an acre fer the bare land, and I hadn't no money fer that kind o' thing."

"Yes, I do my own work," Mrs. Council was heard to say in the pause which followed. "I'm a gettin' purty heavy t' be on m' laigs all day, but we can't afford t' hire, so I keep rackin' around somehow, like a foundered horse. S'lame—I tell Council he can't tell how lame I am, f'r I'm jest as lame in one laig as t' other." And the good soul laughed at the joke on herself as she took a handful of flour and dusted the biscuit-board to keep the dough from sticking.

"Well, I hain't *never* been very strong," said Mrs. Haskins. "Our folks was Canadians an' small-boned, and then since my last child I hain't got up again fairly. I don't like t' complain. Tim has about all he can bear now—but they was days this week when I jes wanted to lay right down an' die."

"Waal, now, I'll tell ye," said Council, from his side of the stove, silencing everybody with his good-natured roar, "I'd go down and *see* Butler, *anyway,* if I was you. I guess he'd let you have his place purty cheap; the farm's all run down. He's ben anxious t' let t' somebuddy next year. It 'ud be a good chance fer you. Anyhow, you go to bed and sleep like a babe. I've got some plowin' t' do, anyhow, an' we'll see if somethin' can't be done about your case. Ike, you go out an' see if the horses is all right, an' I'll show the folks t' bed."

When the tired husband and wife were lying under the generous quilts of the spare bed, Haskins listened a moment to the wind in the eaves, and then said, with a slow and solemn tone,

"There are people in this world who are good enough t' be angels, an' only haff t' die to *be* angels."

II

Jim Butler was one of those men called in the West "land poor." Early in the history of Rock River he had come into the town and started in the grocery business in a small way, occupying a small building in a mean part of the town. At this period of his life he earned all he got, and was up early and late sorting beans, working over butter, and carting his goods to and from the station. But a change came over him at the end of the second year, when he sold a lot of land for four times what he paid for it. From that time forward he believed in land speculation as the surest way of getting rich. Every cent he could save or spare from his trade he put into land at forced sale, or mortgages on land, which were "just as good as the wheat," he was accustomed to say.

Farm after farm fell into his hands, until he was recognized as one of the leading landowners of the county. His mortgages were scattered all over Cedar County, and as they slowly but surely fell in he sought usually to retain the former owner as tenant.

He was not ready to foreclose; indeed, he had the name of being one of the "easiest" men in the town. He let the debtor off again and again, extending the time whenever possible.

"I don't want y'r land," he said. "All I'm after is the int'rest on my money—that's all. Now, if y' want 'o stay on the farm, why, I'll give y' a good chance. I can't have the land layin' vacant." And in many cases the owner remained as tenant.

In the meantime he had sold his store; he couldn't spend time in it; he was mainly occupied now with sitting around town on rainy days smoking and "gassin' with the boys," or in riding to and from his farms. In fishing-time he fished a good deal. Doc Grimes, Ben Ashley, and Cal Cheatham were his cronies on these fishing excursions or hunting trips in the time of chickens or partridges. In winter they went to Northern Wisconsin to shoot deer.

In spite of all these signs of easy life Butler persisted in saying he "hadn't enough money to pay taxes on his land," and was careful to convey the impression that he was poor in spite of his twenty farms. At one time he was said to be worth fifty thousand dollars, but land had been a little slow of sale of late, so that he was not worth so much.

A fine farm, known as the Higley place, had fallen into his hands in the usual way the previous year, and he had not been able to find a tenant for it. Poor Higley, after working himself nearly to death on it in the attempt to lift the mortgage, had gone off to Dakota, leaving the farm and his curse to Butler.

This was the farm which Council advised Haskins to apply for; and the next day Council hitched up his team and drove down town to see Butler.

"You jest let *me* do the talkin'," he said. "We'll find him wearin' out his pants on some salt barrel somew'ers; and if he thought you *wanted* a place he'd sock it to you hot and heavy. You jest keep quiet; I'll fix 'im."

Butler was seated in Ben Ashley's store telling fish yarns when Council sauntered in casually.

"Hello, Butler; lyin' agin, hey!"

"Hellow, Steve! how goes it?"

"Oh, so-so. Too much rain these days. I thought it was going' t' freeze up f'r good last night. Tight squeak if I get m' plowin' done. How's farmin' with *you* these days?"

"Bad. Plowin' ain't half done."

"It 'ud be a religious idee f'r you t' go out an' take a hand y'rself."

"I don't haff to," said Butler, with a wink.

"Got anybody on the Higley place?"

"No. Know of anybody?"

"Waal, no; not eggsackly. I've got a relation

back t' Michigan who's ben hot an' cold on the idee o' comin' West f'r sometime. *Might* come if he could get a good layout. What do you talk on the farm?"

"Well, I d'know. I'll rent it on shares or I'll rent it money rent."

"Waal, how much money, say?"

"Well, say ten per cent, on the price—two fifty."

"Waal, that ain't bad. Wait on 'im till 'e thrashes?"

Haskins listened eagerly to his important question, but Council was coolly eating a dried apple which he had speared out of a barrel with his knife. Butler studied him carefully.

"Well, knocks me out of twenty-five dollars interest."

"My relation'll need all he's got t' git his crops in," said Council, in the safe, indifferent way.

"Well, all right; *say* wait," concluded Butler.

"All right; this is the man. Haskins, this is Mr. Butler—no relation to Ben—the hardest-working man in Cedar County."

On the way home Haskins said: "I ain't much better off. I'd like that farm; it's a good farm, but it's all run down, an' so 'm I. I could make a good farm of it if I had half a show. But I can't stock it n'r seed it."

"Waal, now, don't you worry," roared Council in his ear. "We'll pull y' through somehow till next harvest. He's agreed t' hire it plowed, an' you can earn a hundred dollars plowin' an' y' e'n git the seed o' me, an' pay me back when y' can."

Haskins was silent with emotion, but at last he said, "I ain't got nothin' t' live on."

"Now, don't you worry 'bout that. You jest make your headquarters at ol' Steve Council's. Mother'll take a pile o' comfort in havin' y'r wife an' children 'round. Y' see, Jane's married off lately, an' Ike's away a good 'eal, so we'll be glad t' have y' stop with us this winter.

Nex' spring we'll see if y' can't git a start agin." And he chirruped to the team, which sprang forward with the rumbling, clattering wagon.

"Say, looky here, Council, you can't do this. I never saw—" shouted Haskins in his neighbor's ear.

Council moved about uneasily in his seat and stopped his stammering gratitude by saying: "Hold on, now: don't make such a fuss over a little thing. When I see a man down, an' things all on top of 'm, I jest like t' kick 'em off an' help 'm up."

They rode the rest of the way home in silence. And when the red light of the lamp shone out into the darkness of the cold and windy night, and he thought of this refuge for his children and wife. Haskins could have put his arm around the neck of his burly companion and squeezed him. But he contented himself with saying, "Steve Council, you'll git y'r pay f'r this some day."

"Don't want any pay. My religion ain't run on such business principles."

The wind was growing colder, and the ground was covered with a white frost, as they turned into the gate of the Council farm, and the children came rushing out, shouting, "Papa's come!" They hardly looked like the

same children who had sat at the table the night before. Their torpidity,* under the influence of sunshine and Mother Council, had given way to a sort of spasmodic cheerfulness, as insects in winter revive when laid on the hearth.

---

torpidity: motionlessness; numbness

III

Haskins worked like a fiend, and his wife, like the heroic woman that she was, bore also uncomplainingly the most horrible burdens. They rose early and toiled without intermission till the darkness fell on the plain, then tumbled into bed, every bone and muscle aching with fatigue, to rise with the sun next morning to the same round of the same ferocity of labor.

The eldest boy drove a team all through the spring, plowing and seeding, milked the cows, and did chores innumerable, in most ways taking the place of a man.

An infinitely pathetic but common figure, this boy on the American farm, where there is no law against child labor. To see him in his coarse clothing, his huge boots, and his ragged cap, as he staggered with a pail of water from the well, or trudged in the cold and cheerless dawn out into the frosty field behind his team, gave the city-bred visitor a sharp pang of sympathetic pain. Yet Haskins loved his boy, and would have saved him from this if he could, but he could not.

By June the first year the result of such Herculean toil began to show on the farm. The yard was cleaned up and sown to grass, the garden plowed and planted, and the house mended.

Council had given them four of his cows.

"Take 'em an' run 'em on shares. I don't want 'o milk s' many. Ike's away s' much now, Sat'd'ys an' Sund'ys, I can't stand the bother anyhow."

Other men, seeing the confidence of Council in the newcomer, had sold him tools on time; and as he was really an able farmer, he soon had round him many evidences of his care and thrift. At the advice of Council he had taken the farm for three years, with the privilege of re-renting or buying at the end of the term.

"It's a good bargain, an' y' want 'o nail it." said Council. "If you have any kind of a crop, you c'n pay y'r debts, an' keep seed an' bread."

The new hope which now sprang up in the heart of Haskins and his wife grew great almost as a pain by the time the wide field of wheat began to wave and swirl in the wind of July. Day after day he would snatch a few moments after supper to go and look at it.

"Have ye seen the wheat t'-day, Nettie?" he asked one night as he rose from supper.

"No, Tim, I ain't had time."

"Well, take time now. Le's go look at it."

She threw an old hat on her head—Tommy's hat—and looking almost pretty in her thin, sad way, went out with her husband to the hedge.

"Ain't it grand, Nettie? Just look at it."

It was grand. Level, russet here and there, heavy-headed, wide as a lake, and full of multitudinous whispers and gleams of wealth, it stretched away before the gazers like the fabled field of the cloth of gold.

"Oh, I think—I *hope* we'll have a good crop, Tim; and, oh, how good the people have been to us!"

"Yes; I don't know where we'd be t'-day if it hadn't ben f'r Council and his wife."

"They're the best people in the world," said the little woman, with a great sob of gratitude.

"We'll be in the field on Monday, sure," said Haskins, gripping the rail on the fence as if already at the work of the harvest.

The harvest came, bounteous glorious, but the winds came and blew it into tangles, and the rain matted it here and there close to the ground, increasing the work of gathering it threefold.

Oh, how they toiled in those glorious days! Clothing dripping with sweat, arms aching, filled with briers, fingers raw and bleeding, backs broken with the weight of heavy bundles, Haskins and his man toiled on. Tommy drove the harvester, while his father and a hired man bound on the machine. In this way they cut ten acres every day, and almost every night after supper, when the hand went to bed, Haskins returned to the field shocking the bound grain in the light of the moon. Many a night he worked till his anxious wife came out at ten o'clock to call him in to rest and lunch.

At the same time she cooked for the men, took care of the children, washed and ironed, milked the cows at night, made the butter, and sometimes fed the horses and watered them while her husband kept at the shocking.

No slave in the Roman galleys could have toiled so frightfully and lived, for this man thought himself a free man, and that he was working for his wife and babes.

When he sank into his bed with a deep groan of relief, too tired to change his grimy, dripping clothing, he felt that he was getting nearer and nearer to a home of his own, and pushing the wolf of want a little farther from his door.

There is no despair so deep as the despair of a homeless man or woman. To roam the roads of the country or the streets of the city, to feel there is no rood of ground on which the feet can rest, to halt weary and hungry outside lighted windows and hear laughter and song within—these are the hungers and rebellions that drive men to crime and women to shame.

It was the memory of this homelessness, and the fear of its coming again, that spurred Timothy Haskins and Nettie his wife, to such ferocious labor during that first year.

IV

"'M, yes; 'm, yes; first-rate," said Butler, as his eye took in the neat garden, the pigpen, and the well-filled barnyard. "You're gitt'n' quite a stock around yeh. Done well, eh?"

Haskins was showing Butler around the place. He had not seen it for a year, having spent the year in Washington and Boston with Ashley, his brother-in-law, who had been elected to Congress.

"Yes, I've laid out a good deal of money durin' the last three years. I've paid out three hundred dollars f'r fencin'."

"Um—h'm! I see, I see," said Butler while Haskins went on:

"The kitchen there cost two hundred: the barn ain't cost much in money, but I've put a lot o' time on it. I've dug a new well, and I—"

"Yes, yes, I see. You've done well. Stock worth a thousand dollars," said Butler, picking his teeth with a straw.

"About that," said Haskins, modestly. "We begin to feel's if we was gitt'n a home f'r ourselves; but we've worked hard. I tell you we began to feel it, Mr. Butler, and we're goin' t' begin to ease up purty soon. We've been kind o' plannin' a trip back t' *her* folks after the fall plowin's done."

"*Eggs*-actly!" said Butler, who was evidently thinking of something else. "I suppose you've kind o' calc'lated on stayin' here three years more?"

"Well, yes. Fact is, I think I c'n buy the farm this fall, if you'll give me a reasonable show."

"Um—m! What do you call a reasonable show?"

"Well, say a quarter down and three years time."

Butler looked at the huge stacks of wheat, which filled the yard, over which the chickens were fluttering and crawling, catching grasshoppers, and out of which the crickets were singing innumerable. He smiled in a peculiar way as he said, "Oh, I won't be hard on yeh. But what did you expect to pay f'r the place?"

"Why, about what you offered it for before, two thousand five hundred, or *possibly* three thousand dollars," he added quickly as he saw the owner shake his head.

"This farm is worth five thousand and five hundred dollars," said Butler, in a careless and decided voice.

"*What!*" almost shrieked the astounded Haskins. "What's that? Five thousand? Why, that's double what you offered it for three years ago."

"Of course, and it's worth it. It was all run down then; now it's in good shape. You've laid out fifteen hundred dollars in improvements, according to your own story."

"But *you* had nothin' t' do about that. It's my work an' my money."

"You bet it was; but it's my land."

"But what's to pay me for all my—"

"Ain't you had the use of 'em?" replied Butler, smiling calmly into his face.

Haskins was like a man struck on the head with a sandbag; he couldn't think; he stammered as he tried to say: "But—I never'd git the use—You'd rob me! More'n that: you agreed—you promised that I could buy or rent at the end of three years at—"

"That's all right. But I didn't say I'd let you carry off the improvements, nor that I'd go on renting the farm at two-fifty. The land is doubled in value, it don't matter how; it don't enter into the question; an' now you can pay me five hundred dollars a year rent, or take it on your own terms at fifty-five hundred, or—git out."

He was turning away when Haskins, the sweat pouring from his face, fronted him, saying again:

"But *you've* done nothing to make it so. You hain't added a cent. I put it all there myself, expectin' to buy. I worked an' sweat to improve it. I was workin' for myself an' babes—"

"Well, why didn't you buy when I offered to sell? What y' kickin' about?"

"I'm kickin' about payin' you twice f'r my own things,—my own fences, my own kitchen, my own garden."

Butler laughed. "You're too green t'eat, young feller. *Your* improvements! The law will sing another tune."

"But I trusted your word."

"Never trust anybody, my friend. Besides, I didn't promise not to do this thing. Why, man, don't look at me like that. Don't take me for a thief. It's the law. The reg'lar thing. Everybody does it."

"I don't care if they do. It's stealin' jest the same. You take three thousand dollars of my money—the work o' my hands and my wife's." He broke down at this point. He was not a strong man mentally. He could face hardship, ceaseless toil, but he could not face the cold and sneering face of Butler.

"But I don't take it," said Butler, coolly. "All you've got to do is to go on jest as you've been a-doin', or give me a thousand dollars down, and a mortgage at ten per cent on the rest."

Haskins sat down blindly on a bundle of oats near by, and with staring eyes and drooping head went over the situation. He was under the lion's paw. He felt a horrible numbness in his heart and limbs. He was hid in a mist, and there was no path out.

Butler walked about, looking at the huge stacks of grain, and pulling now and again a few handfuls out, shelling the heads in his hands and blowing the chaff away. He hummed a little tune as he did so. He had an accommodating air of waiting.

Haskins was in the midst of the terrible toil of the last year. He was walking again in the rain and the mud behind his plow; he felt the dust and dirt of the threshing. The ferocious husking-time, with its cutting wind and biting, clinging snows, lay hard upon him. Then he thought of his wife, how she had cheerfully cooked and baked, without holiday and without rest.

"Well, what do you think of it?" inquired the cool, mocking, insinuating voice of Butler.

"I think you're a thief and a liar!" shouted Haskins, leaping up. "A black-hearted houn'!" Butler's smile maddened him; with a sudden leap he caught a fork in his hands, and whirled it in the air. "You'll never rob another man!" he grated through his teeth, a look of pitiless ferocity in his accusing eyes.

Butler shrank and quivered, expecting the blow; stood, held hypnotized by the eyes of the man he had a moment before despised— a man transformed into an avenging demon. But in the deadly hush between the lift of the weapon and its fall there came a gush of faint, childish laughter and then across the range of his vision, far away and dim, he saw the sun-bright head of his baby girl, as, with the pretty, tottering run of a two-year-old, she moved across the grass of the dooryard. His hands relaxed; the fork fell to the ground; his head lowered.

"Make out y'r deed an' mor'gage, an' git off'n my land, an' don't ye never cross my line agin; if y' do, I'll kill ye."

Butler backed away from the man in wild haste, and climbing into his buggy with trembling limbs drove off down the road, leaving Haskins seated dumbly on the sunny piles of sheaves, his head sunk into his hands.

About the Story

1. What are the different types of conflicts?
2. How are the different conflicts resolved?
3. Which is the dominant conflict in the story?
4. Speculate on what Haskins thinks as he faces Butler with the pitchfork.
5. What does Council mean when he says, "Don't want any pay. My religion ain't run on such business principles"?
6. Explain the significance of the title of the story.

About the Author

Hamlin Garland's (1860-1940) goal as an author was to present realistically the lives of the pioneers who settled the Midwest after the Civil War. He sought to convey a sense of not only the pleasure but also the toil and heartache of pioneering, without sentimentalizing these aspects.

Garland's background well qualified him for this work. A childhood spent on family farms instilled in him a deep appreciation for the courage and self-discipline of settlers. His youth was as full of joy as it was hard work, however. His father's family had much natural musical ability, and his mother's family enjoyed reading and prized education. Garland himself claimed to have been "born with a hunger for print." This hunger drove him to work his way through school. Then upon graduating he traveled east, where his grammar-school background in oratory and his innate love of learning helped gain him lecturing opportunities and teaching positions. Garland later returned to his parents' farm in the Midwest to regain a flavor of the countryside and gather material for stories through recording his mother's vivid recollections of fellow-settlers.

Although raised in a loving, moral home, Garland had no religious background. He did attend lectures by advocates of modernism and evolution, and while a young man he read much of the writings of Charles Darwin, Aldous Huxley, and Herbert Spencer. These writings convinced Garland that evolutionary principles were reliable and applicable to social behavior. Like many other writers of the time, Garland's works encouraged social reform and often promoted the idea that a person's environment determines his destiny. Unlike many of his contemporaries, however, Garland endeavored to keep his writing free of blatant objectionable elements, stating, "[Though] I am an evolutionist, I do not enjoy seeing men and women returning to the morality of monkeys."

During the last forty years of his life, Garland researched psychic phenomena, a curious pursuit for a man who claimed to have lost his belief in the supernatural as a youth and who, even after years of study, did not hold firmly to a belief in the afterlife.

Although his later works were of such an agnostic nature as to be unsuitable for the Christian reader, Garland's autobiographical works, especially *A Son of the Middle Border,* and many of his short stories dealing with pioneers are rich and readable sources of information on the inspiring lives of our American homesteaders.

UNIT TWO

Character

Character

Though conflict is the essence of a story's action, characters bring it to life. The better you know the characters, the more the story "comes alive." But how do you get to know characters? You get to know them the same way you would people: you listen to what they say; you listen to what others say about them; and you observe what they do. From this information you draw conclusions about what they are like. An author provides such information for you either directly (through exposition, description, and dialogue) or indirectly (through action).

To understand the process of character revelation, let us draw an example from Scripture. As you will see, it supernaturally excels in artistry of form as well as in truth of content. Notice, for example, how the Lord reveals the historical character of Job to us. In the opening **exposition** the narrator tells us that "There was a man in the land of Uz, whose name was Job: and that man was perfect and upright, and one that feared God, and eschewed evil" (Job 1:1).

This picture of Job is enhanced through the **description** given during the confrontation between God and Satan. In verse 8, for example, the Lord reinforces the opening exposition and adds that there was "none like [Job] in the earth." God describes Job not just as upright, but as more upright than any other man. Satan, however, contradicts the Lord by giving a description of Job which implies that Job is self-seeking rather than godly. Attempting to prove the validity of his assessment, Satan challenges God, saying, "put forth thine hand now, and touch all that he hath, and he will curse thee to thy face." The Lord responds, "Behold, all that he hath is in thy power; only upon himself put not forth thine hand" (1:9-12). Thus, Satan departs and launches his first attack on Job, killing all his children and destroying all his earthly possessions.

What was Job's response? He "arose, and rent his mantle, and shaved his head, and fell down upon the ground, and *worshipped*" (1:20). Job's **action** is the most powerful statement of his character we have yet had, for it blots out Satan's accusation and affirms the narrator's exposition and the Lord's description. And though Satan is permitted to torment God's servant further by afflicting him with "sore boils from the crown of his head to the sole of his foot," Job continues to maintain his integrity.

As the story progresses, we come to know Job even better through the **dialogue** between him and his three friends. We learn that he has been a godly father and a compassionate master, that he has often given shelter to orphans and protection to widows, and that he has upheld the cause of the poor and given counsel to both young and old. We also see that in his pain, this wise, strong man craves support and sympathetic understanding, both of which his wife and his friends deny him. We learn too that his limited knowledge of God and of Satan's devices causes him to misinterpret the source of his suffering. As a result he is tormented not only physically but also intellectually and emotionally. His speeches are filled with contradictory thoughts and feelings. In despair he laments, "What is my strength, that I should hope? and what is mine end, that I should prolong my life?" (6:11). Yet he also proclaims, "I know that my redeemer liveth, and that he shall stand at the latter day upon the earth: And though after my skin worms destroy this body, yet in my flesh shall I see God" (19:25-26). He also repeatedly cries out for death (3:2-23). But then he prays, "Remember, I beseech thee, that thou hast made me as the clay; and wilt thou bring me into dust again?" (10:9). He also acknowledges that God "is not a man, as I am, that I should answer him. . ." (9:32). Then shortly thereafter he demands of God, "Call thou, and I will answer: or let me speak and answer thou me" (13:22). These poetic utterances not only reveal Job's character to us but also illustrate the type of character he is. Job is a multifaceted or **round character,** a man as complex as the problem of pain he faces. Unlike Job, however, his three friends are one-dimensional or **flat characters.** We learn nothing of their past, nor are we given any details about their circumstances nor any proof of their personal integrity. We know only that they believe suffering to be a result of sin. Though Eliphaz seems to base his argument on a vision, Bildad on tradition, and Zophar on personal experience, all three reach the the same conclusion.

Job's friends are also unchanging or **static characters.** Their conversations with Job show no change in their attitudes or development in their thinking. They are simple men who hammer the same point in every speech. Job, on the other hand, is a changing or **dynamic character.** His speeches reveal a man working his way through a desperate struggle, a man rushing down every avenue of reasoning, seeking either an answer to his dilemma or a way of escape. Only when the Lord speaks to him out of the whirlwind does his questioning cease and his despair vanish; both are consumed by the majesty of God.

Job never learns the specific reason for his suffering. He does, however, gain a clearer view of himself and his Creator. As a result he is no longer tormented by what he does not or cannot understand. It is enough for Job that God knows and understands all things. His response to the Lord evidences the extent of his growth: "Then Job answered the LORD, and said, I know that thou canst do every thing, and that no thought can be withholden from thee. . . . Therefore have I uttered that I understood not; things too wonderful for me, which I knew not. . . . I have heard of thee by the hearing of the ear: but now mine eye seeth thee. Wherefore I abhor myself, and repent in dust and ashes" (42:1-3, 5-6).

This growth in Job is believable because it is consistent with what has been revealed as the essence of his character; throughout the book he is a man who fears God and hates evil. Though limited knowledge causes Job to question the Lord, he never blasphemes. And though his pain makes him loathe his own life, we never see any indication that he loathes his Maker. Thus, it is not surprising that when God *does* speak, Job readily listens.

In the final scene not only does the Lord reiterate His opening assessment of Job's integrity (with no contradiction from Satan), but He also gives us a clearer view of Job's friends. Then "the Lord said to Eliphaz the Temanite, My wrath is kindled against thee, and against thy two friends: *for ye have not spoken of me the thing that is right, as my servant Job hath.* Therefore take unto you now seven bullocks and seven rams, and go to my servant Job. . . . and my servant Job shall pray for you: for *him will I accept:* lest I deal with you after your folly, in that ye have not spoken of me the thing which is right, like my servant Job. And the Lord turned the captivity of Job, when he prayed for his friends: also the LORD gave Job twice as much as he had before" (42: 7-8, 10).

It is interesting to note that thirty-five of the forty-two chapters of Job challenge rather than affirm his nobility. But despite the incessant attacks of Satan and the three friends, the words and actions of Job and His God in the few remaining chapters leave no doubt as to what this godly man is really like.

As you read this unit's stories, you can apply the same principles of character analysis that you apply when studying a historical character like Job. Notice what each character says or thinks, what others say about him, and what he does. Then ask yourself: How well do I know each character? Which character do I know best? Does this character change? If so, is the change positive or negative? Also, what does the author reveal about the character that makes me accept the change as believable and consistent with the characterization?

Laborers in the Vineyard, Frederick Lamb. Bob Jones University Collection of Sacred Art. (A portion of this stained-glass window also appears on pp. 64-65.)

Treasure Island

Robert Louis Stevenson

Though Robert Louis Stevenson's Treasure Island *can be called simple escape literature, its exciting action and intriguing characters have made it a classic.*

The hero and narrator of the story is a boy, Jim Hawkins. In this excerpt from the novel, the "Admiral Benbow" inn is threatened by a pirate raid the day after Jim's father's funeral. The raid is only the beginning of a series of dangerous adventures for Jim. How much can you learn about Jim through his actions, reactions and observations? Based on that knowledge, would you say that he is a flat or a round character?

The Old Sea Dog at the "Admiral Benbow"

Squire Trelawney, Dr. Livesey, and the rest of these gentlemen having asked me to write down the whole particulars about Treasure Island, from the beginning to the end, keeping nothing back but the bearings of the island, and that only because there is still treasure not yet lifted, I take up my pen in the year of grace 17—, and go back to the time when my father kept the "Admiral Benbow" inn, and

the brown old seaman with the saber cut first took up his lodging under our roof.

I remember him as if it were yesterday, as he came plodding to the inn door, his sea chest following behind him in a handbarrow; a tall, strong, heavy, nutbrown man; his tarry* pigtail falling over the shoulders of his soiled blue coat; his hands ragged and scarred, with black, broken nails; and the saber cut across one cheek, a dirty, livid white. I remember him looking round the cove and whistling to himself as he did so, and then breaking out in that old sea song that he sang so often afterward:

"Fifteen men on the dead man's chest—
　　Yo-ho-ho, and a bottle of rum!"

in the high, old, tottering voice that seemed to have been tuned and broken at the capstan* bars. Then he rapped on the door with a bit of stick like a handspike that he carried, and when my father appeared, called roughly for a glass of rum. This, when it was brought to him, he drank slowly, like a connoisseur, lingering on the taste, and still looking about him at the cliffs and up at our signboard.

---

tarry: black as if smeared with tar
capstan: a mechanism made of a vertical cylinder rotated
　　manually or by motor, used for lifting weights by winding
　　in the cable

　　"This is a handy cove," says he at length, "and a pleasant sittyated grogshop.* Much company, mate?"

---

grogshop: tavern; place where diluted rum was offered

　　My father told him no, very little company, the more was the pity.

　　"Well, then," said he, "this is the berth for me. Here you, matey," he cried to the man who trundled the barrow, "bring up alongside and help up my chest. I'll stay here a bit," he continued. "I'm a plain man; rum and bacon and eggs is what I want, and that head up there for to watch ships off. What you mought call me? You mought call me captain. Oh, I see what you're at—there," and he threw down three or four gold pieces on the threshold. "You can tell me when I've worked through that," says he, looking as fierce as a commander.

　　And, indeed, bad as his clothes were and coarsely as he spoke, he had none of the appearance of a man who sailed before the mast; but seemed like a mate or skipper, accustomed to be obeyed or to strike. The man who came with the barrow told us the mail* had set him down the morning before at the "Royal George"; that he had inquired what inns there were along the coast, and hearing ours well spoken of, I suppose, and described as lonely, had chosen it from the others for his place of residence. And that was all we could learn of our guest.

---

mail: mail coach

　　He was a very silent man by custom. All day he hung round the cove or upon the cliffs, with a brass telescope; all evening he sat in a corner of the parlor next to the fire, and drank rum and water very strong. Mostly he would not speak when spoken to; only look up sudden and fierce, and blow through his nose like a foghorn; and we and the people who came about our house soon learned to let him be. Every day, when he came back from his stroll, he would ask if any seafaring men had gone by along the road. At first we thought it was the want of company of his own kind that made him ask this question, but at last we began to see he was desirous to avoid them. When a seaman put up at the "Admiral Benbow" (as now and then some did, making by the coast road from Bristol), he would look in at him through the curtained door before he entered the parlor; and he was always sure to be as silent as a mouse when any such was present. For me, at least, there was no secret about the matter, for I was, in a way, a sharer in his alarms. He had taken me aside one day and promised me a silver fourpenny* on the first of every month if I would only keep my "weather eye open for a seafaring man with one leg," and let him know the moment he appeared. Often enough, when the first of the month came round, and I applied to him for my wage, he would only blow through his nose at me and stare me down; but before the week was out he was sure to think better of it, bring me my fourpenny* piece, and then repeat his former orders to look out for "the seafaring man with one leg."

---

fourpenny: valued at four pence (British pennies); a token sum

---

How that personage haunted my dreams I need scarcely tell you. On stormy nights, when the wind shook the four corners of the house and the surf roared along the cove and up the cliffs, I would see him in a thousand forms and with a thousand diabolical expressions. Now the leg would be cut off at the knee, now at the hip; now he as a monstrous kind of creature who had never had but the one leg, and that in the middle of his body. To see him leap and run and pursue me over hedge and ditch was the worst of nightmares. And altogether I paid pretty dear for my monthly fourpenny piece, in the shape of these abominable fancies.

But though I was so terrified by the idea of the seafaring man with one leg, I was far less afraid of the captain himself than anybody else who knew him. There were nights when he took a deal more rum and water than his head would carry; and then he would sometimes sit and sing his wicked, old, wild sea songs, minding nobody; but sometimes he would call for glasses round and force all the trembling company to listen to his stories or bear a chorus to his singing. Often I have heard the house shaking with "Yo-ho-ho, and a bottle of rum," all the neighbors joining in for dear life, with the fear of death upon them, and each singing louder than the other to avoid remark. For in these fits he was the most overriding companion ever known; he would slap his hand on the table for silence all round;

he would fly up in a passion of anger at a question, or sometimes because none was put, and so he judged the company was not following his story. Nor would he allow anyone to leave the inn till he had drunk himself sleepy and reeled off to bed.

His stories were what frightened people worst of all. Dreadful stories they were: about hanging, and walking the plank, and storms at sea, and the Dry Tortugas,* and wild deeds and places on the Spanish Main. By his own account he must have lived his life among some of the wickedest men that God ever allowed upon the sea; and the language in which he told these stories shocked our plain country people almost as much as the crimes that he described. My father was always saying the inn would be ruined, for people would soon cease coming there to be tyrannized over and put down, and sent shivering to their beds; but I really believe his presence did us good. People were frightened at the time, but on looking back they rather liked it; it was a fine excitement in a quiet country life; and there was even a party of the younger men who pretended to admire him, calling him a "true sea dog," and a "real old salt," and suchlike names, and saying there was the sort of man that made England terrible at sea.

---

the Dry Tortugas: an island group off the coast of south Florida, about sixty miles west of Key West

---

In one way, indeed, he bade fair to ruin us, for he kept on staying week after week, and at last month after month, so that all the money had been long exhausted, and still my father never plucked up the heart to insist on having more. If ever he mentioned it, the captain blew through his nose so loudly that you might say he roared, and stared my poor father out of the room. I have seen him wringing his hands after such a rebuff, and I am sure the annoyance and the terror he lived in must have greatly hastened his early and unhappy death.

All the time he lived with us the captain made no change whatever in his dress but to buy some stockings from a hawker.* One of the cocks* of his hat having fallen down, he let it hang from that day forth, though it was a great annoyance when it blew. I remember the appearance of his coat, which he patched himself upstairs in his room, and which, before the end, was nothing but patches. He never wrote or received a letter, and he never spoke with any but the neighbors, and with these, for the most part, only when drunk on rum. The great sea chest none of us had ever seen open.

hawker: peddler
cocks: points

He was only once crossed, and that was toward the end, when my poor father was far gone in a decline that took him off. Dr. Livesey came late one afternoon to see the patient, took a bit of dinner from my mother, and went into the parlor to smoke a pipe until his horse should come down from the hamlet, for we had no stabling at the old "Benbow." I followed him in, and I remember observing the contrast the neat, bright doctor, with his powder* as white as snow, and his bright, black eyes and pleasant manners, made with the coltish countryfolk, and above all, with that filthy, heavy, bleared scarecrow of a pirate of ours, sitting far gone in rum with his arms on the table. Suddenly he—the captain, that is—began to pipe up his eternal song:

powder: wig

"Fifteen men on the dead man's chest—
   Yo-ho-ho, and a bottle of rum!
Drink and the devil had done for the rest—
   Yo-ho-ho, and a bottle of rum!"

At first I had supposed "the dead man's chest" to be that identical big box of his upstairs in the front room, and the thought had been mingled in my nightmares with that of the one-legged seafaring man. But by this time we had all long ceased to pay any particular notice to the song; it was new, that night, to nobody but Dr. Livesey, and on him I observed it did not produce an agreeable effect, for he looked up for a moment quite angrily before he went on with his talk to old Taylor, the gardener, on a new cure for the rheumatics. In the meantime, the captain gradually brightened up at his own music and at last flapped his hand upon the table before him in a way we all knew to mean—silence. The voices stopped at once, all but Dr. Livesey's; he went on as before, speaking clear and kind and drawing briskly at his pipe between every word or two. The captain glared at him for awhile, flapped his hand again, glared still harder, and at last broke out with a villainous, low oath: "Silence, there, between decks!"

"Were you addressing me, sir?" says the doctor; and when the ruffian had told him, with another oath, that this was so, "I have only one thing to say to you, sir," replied the doctor, "that if you keep on drinking rum, the world will soon be quit of a very dirty scoundrel!"

The old fellow's fury was awful. He sprang to his feet, drew and opened a sailor's clasp knife, and, balancing it open on the palm of his hand, threatened to pin the doctor to the wall.

The doctor never so much as moved. He spoke to him, as before, over his shoulder, and in the same tone of voice; rather high, so that all the room might hear, but perfectly calm and steady:

"If you do not put that knife this instant in your pocket, I promise, upon my honor, you shall hang at the next assizes."*

---

assizes: court sessions

Then followed a battle of looks between them; but the captain soon knuckled under, put up his weapon, and resumed his seat, grumbling like a beaten dog.

"And now, sir," continued the doctor, "since I now know there's such a fellow in my district, you may count I'll have an eye upon you day and night. I'm not a doctor only, I'm a magistrate; and if I catch a breath of complaint against you, if it's only for a piece of incivility like tonight's, I'll take effectual means to have you hunted down and routed* out of this. Let that suffice."

---

routed: driven out

Soon after, Dr. Livesey's horse came to the door and he rode away; but the captain held his peace that evening and for many evenings to come.

About the Story

1. Why does the old seaman choose this particular inn?
2. For whom is Jim instructed to keep his "weather-eye" open?
3. What makes most people fear the old seaman?
4. What is the basic description of the old seaman?
5. Why is Jim less afraid of the old seaman than others?
6. About what is the doctor condemning the old seaman?

Black Dog Appears and Disappears

It was not very long after this that there occurred the first of the mysterious events that rid us at last of the captain, though not, as you will see, of his affairs. It was a bitter cold winter, with long, hard frosts and heavy gales; and it was plain from the first that my poor father was little likely to see the spring. He sank daily, and my mother and I had all the inn upon our hands; and were kept busy enough, without paying much regard to our unpleasant guest.

It was one January morning, very early— a pinching, frosty morning—the cove all gray with hoarfrost, the ripple lapping softly on the stones, the sun still low and only touching the hilltops and shining far to seaward. The captain had risen earlier than usual, and set out down the beach, his cutlass swinging under the broad skirts of the old blue coat, his brass telescope under his arm, his hat tilted back upon his head. I remember his breath hanging like smoke in his wake as he strode off, and the last sound I heard of him, as he turned the big rock, was a loud snort of indignation, as though his mind was still running upon Dr. Livesey.

Well, mother was upstairs with father; and I was laying the breakfast table against the captain's return, when the parlor door opened and a man stepped in on whom I had never set my eyes before. He was a pale, tallowy* creature, wanting two fingers of the left hand; and, though he wore a cutlass, he did not look much like a fighter. I had always my eye open for seafaring men, with one leg or two, and I remember this one puzzled me. He was not sailorly, and yet he had a smack of the sea about him too.

---

tallowy: appearing as if covered with tallow, a whitish solid fat obtained from the bodies of cattle, sheep, or horses, and used in some food products or to make candles

---

I asked him what was for his service, and he said he would take rum; but as I was going out of the room to fetch it, he sat down upon a table and motioned me to draw near. I paused where I was with my napkin in my hand.

"Come here, sonny," says he. "Come nearer here."

I took a step nearer.

"Is this here table for my mate Bill?" he asked, with a kind of leer.*

---

leer: sideways evil look

I told him I did not know his mate Bill, and this was for a person who stayed in our house, whom we called the captain.

"Well," said he, "my mate Bill would be called the captain, as like as not. He has a cut on one cheek, and a mighty pleasant way with him, particularly in drink, has my mate Bill. We'll put it, for argument like, that your captain has a cut on one cheek—and we'll put it, if you like, that that cheek's the right one. Ah, well! I told you. Now, is my mate Bill in this here house?"

I told him he was out walking.

"Which way, sonny? Which way is he gone?"

And when I had pointed out the rock and told him how the captain was likely to return, and how soon, and answered a few other questions, "Ah," said he, "this'll be as good as drink to my mate Bill."

The expression of his face as he said these words was not at all pleasant, and I had my own reasons for thinking that the stranger was mistaken, even supposing he meant what he said. But it was no affair of mine, I thought; and, besides, it was difficult to know what to do. The stranger kept hanging about just inside the inn door, peering round the corner like a cat waiting for a mouse. Once I stepped out myself into the road, but he immediately called me back, and, as I did not obey quick enough for his fancy, a most horrible change came over his tallowy face, and he ordered me in, with an oath that made me jump. As soon as I was back again he returned to his former manner, half fawning,* half sneering, patted me on the shoulder, told me I was a good boy, and he had taken quite a fancy to me. "I have a son of my own," said he, "as like you as two blocks, and he's all the pride of my 'art. But the great thing for boys is discipline, sonny—discipline. Now, if you had sailed along of Bill, you wouldn't have stood there to be spoke to twice—not you. That was never Bill's way, nor the way of sich as sailed with him. And here, sure enough, is my mate Bill, with a spyglass under his arm, bless his 'art, to be sure. You and me'll just go back into the parlor, sonny, and get behind the door, and we'll give Bill a little surprise—bless his 'art, I say again."

fawning: seeking attention through flattery

So saying, the stranger backed along with me into the parlor, and put me behind him in the corner, so that we were both hidden by the open door. I was very uneasy and alarmed, as you may fancy, and it rather added to my fears to observe that the stranger was certainly frightened himself. He cleared the hilt of his cutlass and loosened the blade in the sheath; and all the time we were waiting there he kept swallowing as if he felt what we used to call a lump in the throat.

At last in strode the captain, slammed the door behind him, without looking to the right or left, and marched straight across the room to where his breakfast awaited him.

"Bill," said the stranger, in a voice that I thought he had tried to make bold and big.

The captain spun round on his heel and fronted us; all the brown had gone out of his face, and even his nose was blue; he had the look of a man who sees a ghost, or the evil one, or something worse, if anything can be; and, upon my word, I felt sorry to see him, all in a moment, turn so old and sick.

"Come, Bill, you know me; you know an old shipmate, Bill, surely," said the stranger.

The captain made a sort of gasp.

"Black Dog!" said he.

"And who else?" returned the other, getting more at his ease. "Black Dog as ever was, come

for to see his old shipmate Billy, at the 'Admiral Benbow' inn. Ah, Bill, Bill, we have seen a sight of times, us two, since I lost them two talons,"* holding up his mutilated hand.

---

talons: claws (of animals) or fingers (of human beings)

"Now, look here," said the captain, "you've run me down; here I am; well, then, speak up: what is it?"

"That's you, Bill," returned Black Dog, "you're in the right of it, Billy. I'll have a glass of rum from this dear child here, as I've took such a liking to, and we'll sit down, if you please, and talk square, like old shipmates."

When I returned with the rum they were already seated on either side of the captain's breakfast table—Black Dog next to the door, and sitting sideways, so as to have one eye on his old shipmate and one, as I thought, on his retreat.

He bade me go, and leave the door wide open. "None of your keyholes for me, sonny," he said; and I left them together, and retired into the bar.

For a long time, though I certainly did my best to listen, I could hear nothing but a low gabbling;* but at last the voices began to grow higher, and I could pick up a word or two, mostly oaths, from the captain.

---

gabbling: rapid or senseless speech

"No, no, no, no; and an end of it!" he cried once. And again, "If it comes to swinging, swing all, say I."

Then all of a sudden there was a tremendous explosion of oaths and other noises—the chair and table went over in a lump, a clash of steel followed, and then a cry of pain, and the next instant I saw Black Dog in full flight, and the captain hotly pursuing, both with drawn cutlasses, and the former streaming blood from the left shoulder. Just at the door,

the captain aimed at the fugitive one last tremendous cut, which would certainly have split him to the chin had it not been intercepted by our signboard of Admiral Benbow. You may see the notch on the lower side of the frame to this day.

That blow was the last of the battle. Once out upon the road, Black Dog, in spite of his wound, showed a wonderful clean pair of heels, and disappeared over the edge of the hill in half a minute. The captain, for his part, stood staring at the signboard like a bewildered man. Then he passed his hand over his eyes several times, and at last turned back into the house.

"Jim," says he, "rum"; and as he spoke, he reeled a little, and caught himself with one hand against the wall.

"Are you hurt?" cried I.

"Rum," he repeated. "I must get away from here. Rum! Rum!"

I ran to fetch it; but I was quite unsteadied by all that had fallen out, and I broke one glass and fouled the tap, and while I was still getting in my own way I heard a loud fall in the parlor and, running in, beheld the captain lying full length upon the floor. At the same instant my mother, alarmed by the cries and fighting, came running downstairs to help me. Between us we raised his head. He was breathing very loud, and hard; but his eyes were closed, and his face a horrible color.

"Dear, deary me," cried my mother, "what a disgrace upon the house! And your poor father sick!"

In the meantime, we had no idea what to do to help the captain, nor any other thought but that he had got his death-hurt in the scuffle with the stranger. I got the rum, to be sure, and tried to put it down his throat, but his teeth were tightly shut and his jaws as strong as iron. It was a happy relief for us when the door opened and Dr. Livesey came in, on his visit to my father.

"Oh, doctor," we cried, "what shall we do? Where is he wounded?"

"Wounded? A fiddlestick's end!" said the doctor. "No more wounded than you or I. The man has had a stroke, as I warned him. Now, Mrs. Hawkins, just you run upstairs to your husband, and tell him, if possible, nothing about it. For my part, I must do my best to save this fellow's trebly worthless life; and, Jim, you get me a basin."

When I got back with the basin, the doctor had already ripped up the captain's sleeve, and exposed his great sinewy arm. It was tattooed in several places. "Here's luck," "A fair wind," and "Billy Bones his fancy" were very neatly and clearly executed on the forearm; and up near the shoulder there was a sketch of a gallows and a man hanging from it—done, as I thought, with great spirit.

"Prophetic," said the doctor, touching this picture with his finger. "And now, Master Billy Bones, if that be your name, we'll have a look at the color of your blood. Jim," he said, "are you afraid of blood?"

"No, sir," said I.

"Well, then," said he, "you hold the basin," and with that he took his lancet from his case and opened a vein.

A great deal of blood was taken before the captain opened his eyes and looked mistily about him. First he recognized the doctor with an unmistakable frown; then his glance fell upon me, and he looked relieved. But suddenly his color changed, and he tried to raise himself, crying:

"Where's Black Dog?"

"There is no Black Dog here," said the doctor, "except what you have on your own back. You have been drinking rum; you have had a stroke, precisely as I told you; and I have just, very much against my own will, dragged you head foremost out of the grave. Now, Mr. Bones—"

"That's not my name," he interrupted.

"Much I care," returned the doctor. "It's the name of a buccaneer of my acquaintance, and I call you by it for the sake of shortness; and what I have to say to you is this: one glass of rum won't kill you, but if you take one you'll take another and another, and I stake my wig if you don't break off short you'll die—do you understand that?—die, and go to your own place, like the man in the Bible.* Come, now, make an effort. I'll help you to your bed for once."

---

the man in the Bible: Judas Iscariot, as described in Acts 1:25

Between us, with much trouble, we managed to hoist him upstairs, and laid him on his bed, where his head fell back on the pillow as if he were almost fainting.

"Now, mind you," said the doctor, "I clear my conscience—the name of rum for you is death."

And with that he went off to see my father, taking me with him by the arm.

"This is nothing," he said, as soon as he had closed the door. "I have drawn blood enough to keep him quiet awhile; he should lie for a week where he is—that is the best thing for him and you; but another stroke would settle him."

About the Story

1. Who is the old seaman's unexpected visitor?
2. Describe this visitor, using quotations from the story.
3. What happens to the old seaman after the visitor leaves?
4. What is the old seaman's complete name?
5. What is the treatment that the doctor gives Billy?

The Black Spot

About noon I stopped at the captain's door with some cooling drinks and medicines. He was lying very much as we had left him, only a little higher, and he seemed both weak and excited.

"Jim," he said, "you're the only one here that's worth anything; and you know I've been always good to you. Never a month but I've given you a silver fourpenny for yourself. And now you see, mate, I'm pretty low, and deserted by all; and, Jim, you'll bring me one noggin of rum, now, won't you, matey?"

"The doctor—" I began.

But he broke in cursing the doctor, in a feeble voice but heartily. "Doctors is all swabs,"* he said; "and that doctor there, why, what do he know about seafaring men? I been in places hot as pitch, and mates dropping round with yellow jack,* and the blessed land a-heaving like the sea with earthquakes—what do the doctor know of lands like that?—and I lived on rum, I tell you. It's been meat and drink, and man and wife, to me; and if I'm not to have my rum now I'm a poor old hulk on a lee shore,* my blood'll be on you, Jim, and that doctor swab," and he ran on again for a while with curses. "Look, Jim, how my fingers fidges," he continued in the pleading tone. "I can't keep 'em still, not I. I haven't had a drop this blessed day. That doctor's a fool, I tell you. If I don't have a drain o' rum, Jim, I'll have the horrors; I seen some on 'em already. I seen old Flint in the corner there, behind you; as plain as print, I seen him; and if I get the horrors, I'm a man that has lived rough, and I'll raise Cain. Your doctor hisself said one glass wouldn't hurt me. I'll give you a golden guinea for a noggin, Jim."

---

swabs: awkward, stupid persons
yellow jack: yellow fever
lee shore: shore away from the wind

He was growing more and more excited, and this alarmed me for my father, who was very low that day and needed quiet; besides, I was reassured by the doctor's words, now quoted to me, and rather offended by the offer of a bribe.

"I want none of your money," said I, "but what you owe my father. I'll get you one glass, and not more."

When I brought it to him, he seized it greedily and drank it out.

"Aye, aye," said he, "that's some better, sure enough. And now, matey, did that doctor say how long I was to lie here in this old berth?"

"A week at least," said I.

"Thunder!" he cried. "A week! I can't do that; they'd have the black spot on me by then. The lubbers is going about to get the wind of me this blessed moment; lubbers* as couldn't keep what they got, and want to nail what is another's. Is that seamanly behavior, now, I want to know? But I'm a saving soul. I never wasted good money of mine, nor lost it neither; and I'll trick 'em again. I'm not afraid on 'em. I'll shake out another reef,* matey, and daddle* 'em again."

---

lubbers: clumsy sailors
shake out another reef: unfurl a sail with a good shake
daddle: dawdle; trifle with

As he was thus speaking he had risen from bed with great difficulty, holding to my shoulder with a grip that almost made me cry out, and moving his legs like so much dead weight. His words, spirited as they were in meaning, contrasted sadly with the weakness of the voice in which they were uttered. He paused when he had got into a sitting position on the edge.

"That doctor's done me," he murmured. "My ears is singing. Lay me back."

Before I could do much to help him he had fallen back again to his former place, where he lay for a while silent.

"Jim," he said, at length, "you saw that seafaring man today!"

"Black Dog?" I asked.

"Ah! Black Dog," says he. "He's a bad 'un; but there's worse that put him on. Now, if I can't get away nohow, and they tip me the black spot, mind you, it's my old sea chest they're after; you get on a horse—you can, can't you? Well, then, you get on a horse, and go to—well, yes, I will!—to that eternal doctor swab, and tell him to pipe all hands—magistrates and sich—and he'll lay 'em aboard at the 'Admiral Benbow'—all old Flint's crew, man and boy, all on 'em that's left. I was first mate, I was, old Flint's first mate, and I'm the on'y one as knows the place. He gave it me at Savannah, when he lay a-dying, like as if I was to now, you see. But you won't peach* unless they get the black spot on me, or unless you see that Black Dog again, or a seafaring man with one leg, Jim—him above all."

peach: turn informer

"But what is the black spot, captain?" I asked.

"That's a summons, mate. I'll tell you if they get that. But you keep your weather eye open, Jim, and I'll share with you equals, upon my honor."

He wandered a little longer, his voice growing weaker; but soon after I had given him his medicine, which he took like a child, with the remark, "If ever a seaman wanted drugs, it's me," he fell at last into a heavy, swoonlike sleep, in which I left him. What I should have done had all gone well I do not know. Probably I should have told the whole story to the doctor; for I was in mortal fear lest the captain should repent of his confessions and make an end of me. But as things fell out, my poor father died quite suddenly that evening, which put all other matters on one side. Our natural distress, the visits of the neighbors, the arranging of the funeral, and all the work of the inn to be carried on in the meanwhile, kept me so busy that I had scarcely time to think of the captain, far less to be afraid of him.

He got downstairs next morning, to be sure, and had his meals as usual, though he ate little, and had more, I am afraid, than his usual supply of rum, for he helped himself out of the bar, scowling and blowing through his nose, and no one dared to cross him. On the night before the funeral he was as drunk as ever; and it was shocking, in that house of mourning, to hear him singing away at his ugly old sea song; but, weak as he was, we were all in the fear of death for him, and the doctor was suddenly taken up with a case many miles away and was never near the house after my father's death. I have said the captain was weak; and indeed, he seemed rather to grow weaker than regain his strength. He clambered up and down stairs, and went from the parlor to the bar and back again, and sometimes put his nose out of doors to smell the sea, holding onto the walls as he went for support, and breathing hard and fast like a man on a steep mountain. He never particularly addressed me, and it is my belief he had as good as forgotten his confidences; but his temper was more flighty and, allowing for his bodily weakness, more violent than ever. He had an alarming way now, when he was drunk, of drawing his cutlass and laying it bare before him on the table. But, with all that, he minded people less, and seemed shut up in his own thoughts and rather wandering. Once, for instance, to our extreme wonder, he piped up to a different air, a kind of country love song, that he must have learned in his youth before he had begun to follow the sea.

So things passed until, the day after the funeral, and about three o'clock of a bitter,

foggy, frosty afternoon, I was standing at the door for a moment, full of sad thoughts about my father, when I saw someone drawing slowly near along the road. He was plainly blind, for he tapped before him with a stick, and wore a great green shade over his eyes and nose; and he was hunched, as if with age or weakness, and wore a huge old tattered sea cloak with a hood, that made him appear positively deformed. I never saw in my life a more dreadful-looking figure.

He stopped a little distance from the inn, and, raising his voice in an odd singsong, addressed the air in front of him:

"Will any kind friend inform a poor blind man, who has lost the precious sight of his eyes in the gracious defense of his native country, England, and God bless King George!—where or in what part of this country he may now be?"

"You are at the 'Admiral Benbow,' Black Hill Cove, my good man," said I.

"I hear a voice," said he, "a young voice. Will you give me your hand, my kind, young friend, and lead me in?"

I held out my hand, and the horrible, soft-spoken, eyeless creature gripped it in a moment like a vise. I was so much startled that I struggled to withdraw; but the blind man pulled me close up to him with a single action of his arm.

"Now, boy," he said, "take me in to the captain."

"Sir," said I, "upon my word I dare not."

"Oh," he sneered, "that's it! Take me in straight, or I'll break your arm."

And he gave it, as he spoke, a wrench that made me cry out.

"Sir," said I, "it is for yourself I mean. The captain is not what he used to be. He sits with a drawn cutlass. Another gentleman—"

"Come, now, march," interrupted he; and I never heard a voice so cruel, and cold, and ugly as that blind man's. It cowed me more than the pain; and I began to obey him at once, walking straight in at the door and toward the parlor, where our sick old buccaneer was sitting, dazed with rum. The blind man clung close to me, holding me in one iron fist, and leaning almost more of his weight on me than I could carry. "Lead me straight up to him, and when I'm in view, cry out, 'Here's a friend for you, Bill.' If you don't, I'll do this"; and with that he gave me a twitch that I thought would have made me faint. Between this and that, I was so utterly terrified of the blind beggar that I forgot my terror of the captain, and as I opened the parlor door, cried out the words he had ordered in a trembling voice.

The poor captain raised his eyes, and at one look the rum went out of him, and left him staring sober. The expression of his face was not so much of terror as of mortal sickness. He made a movement to rise, but I do not believe he had enough force left in his body.

"Now, Bill, sit where you are," said the beggar. "If I can't see, I can hear a finger stirring. Business is business. Hold out your left hand. Boy, take his left hand by the wrist, and bring it near to my right."

We both obeyed him to the letter, and I saw him pass something from the hollow of the hand that held his stick into the palm of the captain's, which closed upon it instantly.

"And now that's done," said the blind man; and at the words he suddenly left hold of me, and, with incredible accuracy and nimbleness, skipped out of the parlor and into the road, where, as I still stood motionless, I could hear his stick go tap-tap-tapping into the distance.

It was some time before either I or the captain seemed to gather our senses; but at length, and about at the same moment, I released his wrist, which I was still holding, and he drew in his hand and looked sharply into the palm.

"Ten o'clock!" he cried. "Six hours. We'll do them yet." And he sprang to his feet.

Even as he did so, he reeled, put his hand to his throat, stood swaying for a moment, and then, with a peculiar sound, fell from his whole height face foremost to the floor.

I ran to him at once, calling to my mother. But haste was all in vain. The captain had been struck dead by thundering apoplexy.* It is a curious thing to understand, for I had certainly never liked the man, though of late I had begun to pity him, but as soon as I saw that he was dead I burst into a flood of tears. It was the second death I had known, and the sorrow of the first was still fresh in my heart.

---

apoplexy: stroke

About the Story

1. What three things must happen before Jim is to tell the authorities about the contents of the chest?
2. Describe the blind man that Jim sees coming up the road on the day after the funeral.
3. What action of the blind man contradicts his initial friendly greeting to Jim?
4. What is the blind man's business at the inn?
5. How many hours does the summons give Billy Bones?

The Sea Chest

I lost no time, of course, in telling my mother all that I knew, and perhaps should have told her long before, and we saw ourselves at once in a difficult and dangerous position. Some of the man's money—if he had any—was certainly due to us; but it was not likely that our captain's shipmates, above all the two specimens seen by me, Black Dog and the blind beggar, would be inclined to give up their booty in payment of the dead man's debts. The captain's order to mount at once and ride for Dr. Livesey would have left my mother alone and unprotected, which was not to be thought of. Indeed, it seemed impossible for either of us to remain much longer in the house: the fall of coals in the kitchen grate, the very ticking of the clock, filled us with alarms. The neighborhood, to our ears, seemed haunted by approaching footsteps; and what between the dead body of the captain on the parlor floor and the thought of that detestable blind beggar hovering near at hand, and ready to return, there were moments when, as the saying goes, I jumped in my skin for terror. Something must speedily be resolved upon; and it occurred to us at last to go forth together and seek help in the neighboring hamlet. No sooner said than done. Bareheaded as we were, we ran out at once in the gathering evening and the frosty fog.

The hamlet lay not many hundred yards away though out of view, on the other side of the next cove; and what greatly encouraged me, it was in an opposite direction from that whence the blind man had made his appearance, and whither he had presumably returned. We were not many minutes on the road, though we sometimes stopped to lay hold of each other and hearken. But there was no unusual sound—nothing but the low wash of the ripple and the croaking of the inmates of the wood.

It was already candlelight when we reached the hamlet, and I shall never forget how much I was cheered to see the yellow shine in doors and windows; but that, as it proved, was the best of the help we were likely to get in that quarter. For—you would have thought men would have been ashamed of themselves—no soul would consent to return with us to the "Admiral Benbow." The more we told of our troubles, the more—man, woman, and child—they clung to the shelter of their houses. The name of Captain Flint, though it was strange to me, was well enough known to some there and carried a great weight of terror. Some of the men who had been to field work on the far side of the "Admiral Benbow" remembered, besides, to have seen several strangers on the road, and, taking them to be smugglers, to have bolted away; and one at least had seen a little lugger* in what we called Kitt's Hole. For that matter, anyone who was a comrade of the captain's was enough to frighten them to death. And the short and the long of the matter was that, while we could get several who were willing enough to ride to Dr. Livesey's, which lay in another direction, not one would help us to defend the inn.

---

lugger: small boat with two or three masts, each with a lugsail, and two or three jibs set on the bowsprit

---

They say cowardice is infectious, but then argument is, on the other hand, a great emboldener;* and so when each had said his say, my mother made them a speech. She would not, she declared, lose money that belonged to her fatherless boy; "if none of the rest of you dare," she said, "Jim and I dare. Back we will go, the way we came, and small thanks to you big, hulking, chickenhearted men. We'll have that chest open, if we die for it. And I'll thank you for that bag, Mrs. Crossley, to bring back our lawful money in."

---

emboldener: object that fosters boldness

Of course I said I would go with my mother, and of course they all cried out at our foolhardiness; but even then not a man would go along with us. All they would do was to give me a loaded pistol, lest we were attacked; and to promise to have horses ready saddled, in case we were pursued on our return; while one lad was to ride forward to the doctor's in search of armed assistance.

My heart was beating finely when we two set forth in the cold night upon this dangerous venture. A full moon was beginning to rise and peered redly through the upper edges of the fog, and this increased our haste, for it was plain that, before we came forth again, all would be as bright as day, and our departure exposed to the eyes of any watchers. We slipped along the hedges, noiseless and swift, nor did we see or hear anything to increase our terrors, till, to our relief, the door of the "Admiral Benbow" had closed behind us.

I slipped the bolt at once, and we stood and panted for a moment in the dark, alone in the house with the dead captain's body. Then my mother got a candle in the bar, and, holding each other's hands, we advanced into the parlor. He lay as we had left him, on his back, with his eyes open, and one arm stretched out.

"Draw down the blind, Jim," whispered my mother; "they might come and watch outside. And now," said she, when I had done so, "we have to get the key off that; and who's to touch it, I should like to know!" and she gave a kind of sob as she said the words.

I went down on my knees at once. On the floor close to his hand there was a little round of paper, blackened on the one side. I could not doubt that *this* was the *black spot;* and taking it up, I found written on the other side, in a very good clear hand, this short message: "You have till ten tonight."

"He had till ten, mother," said I; and just as I said it, our old clock began striking. This sudden noise startled us shockingly; but the news was good, for it was only six.

"Now, Jim," she said, "that key."

I felt in his pockets, one after another. A few small coins, a thimble, and some thread and big needles, a piece of pigtail tobacco bitten away at the end, his gully* with the cracked handle, a pocket compass, and a tinderbox,* were all that they contained, and I began to despair.

---

gully: large knife
tinderbox: metal box holding combustible material used to start a fire

---

"Perhaps it's round his neck," suggested my mother.

Overcoming a strong repugnance, I tore open his shirt at the neck, and there, sure enough, hanging to a bit of tarry string, which I cut with his own gully, we found the key. At this triumph we were filled with hope and hurried upstairs, without delay, to the little room where he had slept so long and where his box had stood since the day of his arrival.

It was like any other seaman's chest on the outside, the initial "B" burned on the top of it with a hot iron, and the corners somewhat smashed and broken as by long, rough usage.

"Give me the key," said my mother; and though the lock was very stiff, she had turned it and thrown back the lid in a twinkling.

A strong smell of tobacco and tar rose from the interior, but nothing was to be seen on the top except a suit of very good clothes, carelessly brushed and folded. They had never been worn, my mother said. Under that, the miscellany began—a quadrant,* a tin canni-kin,* several sticks of tobacco, two brace* of very handsome pistols, a piece of bar silver, an old Spanish watch and some other trinkets of little value and mostly of foreign make, a pair of compasses mounted with brass, and five or six curious West Indian shells. I have often wondered since why he should have carried about these shells with him in his wandering, guilty, and hunted life.

---

quadrant: navigational instrument for measuring the altitude of stars (distance from the horizon)
cannikin: mug
brace: pair

In the meantime, we had found nothing of any value but the silver and the trinkets, and neither of these were in our way. Underneath there was an old boat cloak, whitened with sea salt on many a harbor bar. My mother pulled it up with impatience, and there lay before us, the last things in the chest, a bundle tied up in oilcloth, and looking like papers, and a canvas bag, that gave forth, at a touch, the jingle of gold.

"I'll show these rogues that I'm an honest woman," said my mother. "I'll have my dues, and not a farthing over. Hold Mrs. Crossley's bag." And she began to count over the amount of the captain's score from the sailor's bag into the one that I was holding.

It was a long, difficult business, for the coins were of all countries and sizes—doubloons, and louis d'ors, and guineas, and pieces of eight, and I know not what besides, all shaken together at random. The guineas, too, were about the scarcest, and it was with these only that my mother knew how to make her count.

When we were about halfway through, I suddenly put my hand upon her arm; for I had heard in the silent, frosty air a sound that brought my heart into my mouth—the tap-tapping of the blind man's stick upon the frozen road. It drew nearer and nearer, while we sat holding our breath. Then it struck sharp on the inn door, and then we could hear the handle being turned, and the bolt rattling as the wretched being tried to enter; and then there was a long time of silence both within and without. At last the tapping recommenced and, to our indescribable joy and gratitude, died slowly away again until it ceased to be heard.

"Mother," said I, "take the whole and let's be going." For I was sure the bolted door must have seemed suspicious and would bring the whole hornet's nest about our ears; though how thankful I was that I had bolted it, none could tell who had never met that terrible blind man.

But my mother, frightened as she was, would not consent to take a fraction more than was due to her, and was obstinately unwilling to be content with less. It was not yet seven, she said, by a long way; she knew her rights and she would have them; and she was still arguing with me when a little low whistle sounded a good way off upon the hill. That

was enough, and more than enough, for both of us.

"I'll take what I have," she said, jumping to her feet.

"And I'll take this to square the count," said I, picking up the oilskin packet.

Next moment we were both groping downstairs, leaving the candle by the empty chest; and the next we had opened the door and were in full retreat. We had not started a moment too soon. The fog was rapidly dispersing; already the moon shone quite clear on the high ground on either side; and it was only in the exact bottom of the dell and round the tavern door that a thin veil still hung unbroken to conceal the first steps of our escape. Far less than halfway to the hamlet,

very little beyond the bottom of the hill, we had to come forth into the moonlight. Nor was this all; for the sound of several footsteps running came already to our ears, and as we looked back in their direction, a light tossing to and fro and still rapidly advancing showed that one of the newcomers carried a lantern.

"My dear," said my mother suddenly, "take the money and run on. I am going to faint."

This was certainly the end for both of us, I thought. How I cursed the cowardice of the neighbors; how I blamed my poor mother for her honesty and her greed, for her past foolhardiness and present weakness! We were just at the little bridge, by good fortune; and I helped her, tottering as she was, to the edge of the bank, where, sure enough, she gave a sigh and fell on my shoulder. I do not know how I found the strength to do it at all, and I am afraid it was roughly done; but I managed to drag her down the bank and a little way under the arch. Farther I could not move her, for the bridge was too low to let me do more than crawl below it. So there we had to stay— my mother almost entirely exposed and both of us within earshot of the inn.

About the Story

1. Why will no one return to the inn with Jim and his mother?
2. What is found inside the chest?
3. What does Jim hear while looking through the chest?
4. What does Jim take from the chest? What does his mother take?
5. At the end of the chapter, where are Jim and his mother? Why are they there?

The Last of the Blind Man

My curiosity, in a sense, was stronger than my fear; for I could not remain where I was, but crept back to the bank again, whence, sheltering my head behind a bush of broom, I might command the road before our door. I was scarcely in position ere my enemies began to arrive, seven or eight of them, running hard, their feet beating out of time along the road, and the man with the lantern some paces in front. Three men ran together, hand in hand; and I made out, even through the mist, that the middle man of this trio was the blind beggar. The next moment his voice showed me that I was right.

"Down with the door!" he cried.

"Aye, aye, sir!" answered two or three; and a rush was made upon the "Admiral Benbow," the lantern bearer following. And then I could see them pause, and hear speeches passed in a lower key, as if they were surprised to find the door open. But the pause was brief, for the blind man again issued his commands. His voice sounded louder and higher, as if he were afire with eagerness and rage.

"In, in, in!" he shouted, and cursed them for their delay.

Four or five of them obeyed at once, two remaining on the road with the formidable* beggar. There was a pause, then a cry of surprise, and then a voice shouting from the house:

formidable: fearsome

"Bill's dead!"

But the blind man swore at them again for their delay.

"Search him, some of you shirking lubbers, and the rest of you aloft and get the chest," he cried.

I could hear their feet rattling up our old stairs, so that the house must have shook with it. Promptly afterwards fresh sounds of astonishment arose; the window of the captain's room was thrown open with a slam and a jingle of broken glass; and a man leaned out into the moonlight, head and shoulders, and addressed the blind beggar on the road below him.

"Pew," he cried, "they've been before us. Someone's turned the chest out alow and aloft."*

---

alow and aloft: from the hold to the crow's nest (of a ship); below and above; thoroughly

---

"Is it there?" roared Pew.

"The money's there."

The blind man cursed the money.

"Flint's fist, I mean," he cried.

"We don't see it here nohow," returned the man.

"Here, you below there, is it on Bill?" cried the blind man again.

At that, another fellow, probably the one who had remained below to search the captain's body, came to the door of the inn. "Bill's been overhauled a'ready," said he, "nothin' left."

"It's these people of the inn—it's that boy. I wish I had put his eyes out!" cried the blind man, Pew. "They were here no time ago—they had the door bolted when I tried it. Scatter, lads, and find 'em."

"Sure enough, they left their glim* here," said the fellow from the window.

---

glim: source of light, such as a candle

"Scatter and find 'em! Rout the house out!" reiterated Pew, striking with his stick upon the road.

Then there followed a great to-do through all our old inn, heavy feet pounding to and fro, furniture thrown over, doors kicked in, until the very rocks re-echoed, and the men came out again, one after another, on the road, and declared that we were nowhere to be found.

And just then the same whistle that had alarmed my mother and myself over the dead captain's money was once more clearly audible through the night, but this time twice repeated. I had thought it to be the blind man's trumpet, so to speak, summoning his crew to the assault; but I now found that it was a signal from the hillside toward the hamlet, and, from its effect upon the buccaneers, a signal to warn them of approaching danger.

"There's Dirk again," said one. "Twice! We'll have to budge, mates."

"Budge, you skulk!" cried Pew. "Dirk was a fool and a coward from the first—you wouldn't mind him. They must be close by; they can't be far; you have your hands on it. Scatter and look for them, dogs! Oh, shiver my soul," he cried, "if I had eyes!"

This appeal seemed to produce some effect, for two of the fellows began to look here and there among the lumber, but halfheartedly, I thought, and with half an eye to their own danger all the time, while the rest stood irresolute* on the road.

---

irresolute: undecided

"You have your hands on thousands, you fools, and you hang a leg! You'd be as rich as kings if you could find it, and you know it's here, and you stand there skulking. There wasn't one of you dared face Bill, and I did it—a blind man! And I'm to lose my chance for you! I'm to be a poor, crawling beggar, sponging for rum, when I might be rolling in a coach! If you had the pluck of a weevil in a biscuit you would catch them still."

"Hang it, Pew, we've got the doubloons!" grumbled one.

"They might have hid the blessed thing," said another. "Take the Georges,* Pew, and don't stand here squalling."

Georges: coins

Squalling was the word for it, Pew's anger rose so high at these objections; till at last, his passion completely taking the upper hand, he struck at them right and left in his blindness, and his stick sounded heavily on more than one.

These, in their turn, cursed back at the blind miscreant,* threatened him in horrid terms, and tried in vain to catch the stick and wrest it from his grasp.

---

miscreant: villain

This quarrel was the saving of us, for while it was still raging, another sound came from the top of the hill on the side of the hamlet— the tramp of horses galloping. Almost at the same time a pistol shot, flash and report, came from the hedge side. And that was plainly the last signal of danger, for the buccaneers turned at once and ran, separating in every direction, one seaward along the cove, one slant across the hill, and so on, so that in half a minute not a sign of them remained but Pew. Him they had deserted, whether in sheer panic or out of revenge for his ill words and blows, I know not; but there he remained behind, tapping up and down the road in a frenzy, and groping and calling for his comrades. Finally he took the wrong turn, and ran a few steps past me, toward the hamlet, crying:

"Johnny, Black Dog, Dirk," and other names, "you won't leave old Pew, mates—not old Pew!"

Just then the noise of horses topped the rise and four or five riders came in sight in the moonlight and swept at full gallop down the slope.

At this Pew saw his error, turned with a scream, and ran straight for the ditch, into which he rolled. But he was on his feet again in a second and made another dash, now utterly bewildered, right under the nearest of the coming horses.

The rider tried to save him, but in vain. Down went Pew with a cry that rang high into the night; and the four hoofs trampled and spurned him and passed by. He fell on his side, then gently collapsed upon his face, and moved no more.

I leaped to my feet and hailed the riders. They were pulling up, at any rate, horrified at the accident; and I soon saw what they were. One, tailing out behind the rest, was a lad that had gone from the hamlet to Dr. Livesey's; the rest were revenue officers, whom he had met by the way and with whom he had had the intelligence to return at once. Some news of the lugger in Kitt's Hole had found its way to Supervisor Dance and set him forth that night in our direction, and to that circumstance my mother and I owed our preservation from death.

Pew was dead, stone dead. As for my mother, when we had carried her up to the hamlet, a little cold water and salts very soon brought her back again, and she was none the worse for her terror, though she still continued to deplore the balance of the money. In the meantime the supervisor rode on, as fast as he could, to Kitt's Hole; but his men had to dismount and grope down the dingle,* leading, and sometimes supporting, their horses, and in continual fear of ambushes; so it was no great matter for surprise that when they got down to the Hole the lugger was already under way, though still close in. He hailed her. A voice replied, telling him to keep out of the moonlight or he would get some lead in him, and at the same time a bullet whistled close by his arm. Soon after, the lugger doubled* the point and disappeared. Mr. Dance stood there, as he said, "like a fish out of water," and all he could do was to dispatch a man to B— to warn the cutter. "And that," said he, "is just about as good as nothing. They've got off clean, and there's an end. Only," he added, "I'm glad I trod on Master Pew's corns," for by this time he had heard my story.

---

dingle: wooded hollow
doubled: rounded

I went back with him to the "Admiral Benbow," and you cannot imagine a house in such a state of smash; the very clock had been thrown down by these fellows in their furious hunt after my mother and myself; and though nothing had actually been taken away except the captain's moneybag and a little silver from the till, I could see at once that we were ruined. Mr. Dance could make nothing of the scene.

"They got the money, you say? Well, then, Hawkins, what in fortune were they after? More money, I suppose?"

"No, sir; not money, I think," replied I. "In fact, sir, I believe I have the thing in my breast pocket; and, to tell you the truth, I should like to get it put in safety."

"To be sure, boy; quite right," said he. "I'll take it, if you like."

"I thought, perhaps, Dr. Livesey—" I began.

"Perfectly right," he interrupted very cheerily, "perfectly right—a gentleman and a magistrate. And, now I come to think of it, I might as well ride round there myself and report to him or squire. Master Pew's dead, when all's done; not that I regret it, but he's dead, you see, and people will make it out against an officer of his majesty's revenue, if make it out they can. Now, I'll tell you, Hawkins: if you like, I'll take you along."

I thanked him heartily for the offer, and we walked back to the hamlet where the horses were. By the time I had told mother of my purpose they were all in the saddle.

"Dogger," said Mr. Dance, "you have a good horse; take up this lad behind you."

As soon as I was mounted, holding onto Dogger's belt, the supervisor gave the word and the party struck out at a bouncing trot on the road to Dr. Livesey's house.

About the Story

1. Describe Pew.
2. What is Pew looking for in the chest?
3. What happens to Pew?
4. Based on your reading, decide which of the following characters are round characters.
   a. Jim
   b. Billy Bones
   c. Jim's mother
   d. Dr. Livesey
   e. Pew
   f. Dirk, Johnny, Black Dog (buccaneers)
5. Take *one* of the round characters from above and find three quotations from the story to support your belief that the character is round. Choose quotations that illustrate the following three categories: something the character actually said; something another character said about him; some action he performed.

About the Author

Robert Louis Stevenson (1850-1894) is an author whose life is as rich and interesting as his writing. Often held up to children as a figure to emulate, Stevenson expounded some ideas that a Christian young person might safely adopt. This author's personal philosophy, however, is harmful when taken as a whole. In his youth an atheist and in later life an agnostic at best, Stevenson taught a religion of sturdy effort, a "gospel of work." He did not hold to any kind of religious dogma, except that "the meaning of religion is a rule of life; it is an obligation to do well. . . ." Speaking of religion, he said, "I cannot transfer my interests, not even my religious interests, to any different sphere" from that of human life. Although he attended church sporadically, was a supporter of missions, and for a short time even taught Sunday school, Stevenson claimed no personal relationship with Christ; in fact, he held that sudden changes such as conversions were unnatural. He equated good works from a sincere heart with salvation.

Although he had only a sentiment of God and a form of godliness, Stevenson put much of true moral values into his works. Specifically, they reflect his upbringing, in that evil is recognized and presented as very unappealing, while doing good is portrayed as the best course of action. Undoubtedly, this is a result of his having been reared by strong Protestant parents and a pious, loving nurse who instilled in him a strong sense of right and wrong and a thorough knowledge of the Scriptures, though no evidence exists of any emphasis on personal conversion in his or his parents' lives. According to John Kelman, Stevenson's biographer, the young boy's "earliest memories were of nursery rhymes, the Bible, and Mr. [Robert Murray] M'Cheyne," the latter being a special favorite of Alison Cunningham, the nurse that cared for Stevenson during his sickly childhood.

Though he later studied law, he never practiced it, choosing rather to follow his literary ambitions. To improve his fragile health, Stevenson took walking tours in France. He also toured throughout Scotland, his beloved homeland. On this and other trips worldwide, Stevenson gathered vivid details with which he flavored his dramatic stories. The author of such classics as *Kidnapped* and *Dr. Jekyll and Mr. Hyde,* Stevenson spent his last days in a setting as exotic as any found in his works. Stevenson and his American wife, Fanny Osbourne, journeyed to the South Sea island of Samoa, in a final attempt to alleviate the discomfort of his lung disease. There he died at forty-four, and he was buried by the natives, who looked upon this man not merely as a great storyteller from a faraway country but as a noble and good friend.

Phaëthon

translated by Edith Hamilton

Classical myths like Phaëthon (pronounced FAY uh THON) descended primarily from the Greeks and Romans. These old tales about gods and mortals were written to explain the world and man's place in it. Of course, as Christians we look to Scripture, not mythology, for understanding life and its purpose. We can, however, appreciate the literary beauty and the universal themes presented in mythology. In a limited sense, myths are profitable as moral fables, for they teach such virtues as courage, wisdom, hospitality, and constancy in love. They also warn against such vices as pride, rashness, and reckless ambition.

The story of Phaëthon was told—or retold—by the master Roman storyteller named Ovid. Its vivid description makes it one of his best. The protagonist, Phaëthon, is a flat character, but his one-dimensional characterization clearly thrusts home the moral point of the story. What is the negative quality characterized by Phaëthon's actions and dialogue?

The palace of the Sun was a radiant place. It shone with gold and gleamed with ivory and sparkled with jewels. Everything without and within flashed and glowed and glittered. It was always high noon there. Shadowy twilight never dimmed the brightness. Darkness and night were unchanging brilliancy of light, but few had ever found their way thither.

Nevertheless, one day a youth, mortal on his mother's side, dared to approach. Often he had to pause and clear his dazzled eyes, but the errand which had brought him was so urgent that his purpose held fast and he pressed on, up to the palace, through the burnished doors, and into the throne-room where, surrounded by a blinding, blazing splendor, the Sun-god sat. There the lad was forced to halt. He could bear no more.

Nothing escapes the eyes of the Sun. He saw the boy instantly and he looked at him very kindly. "What brought you here?" he asked.

"I have come," the other answered boldly, "to find out if you are my father or not. My mother said you were, but the boys at school laugh when I tell them I am your son. They will not believe me. I told my mother and she said I had better go and ask you."

Smiling, the Sun took off his crown of burning light so that the lad could look at him without distress. "Come here, Phaëthon," he said. "You are my son. Clymenë told you the truth. I expect you will not doubt my word too? But I will give you a proof. Ask anything you want of me, and you shall have it. I call the Styx to be witness to my promise, the river of the oath of the gods."

No doubt Phaëthon had often watched the Sun riding through the heavens and had told himself with a feeling, half awe, half excitement, "It is my father up there." And then he would wonder what it would be like to be in that chariot, guiding the steeds along that dizzy course, giving light to the world. Now at his

father's words this wild dream had become possible. Instantly he cried, "I choose to take your place, Father. That is the only thing I want. Just for a day, a single day, let me have your car to drive."

The Sun realized his own folly. Why had he taken that fatal oath and bound himself to give in to anything that happened to enter a boy's rash young head? "Dear lad," he said, "this is the only thing I would have refused you. I know I cannot refuse. I have sworn by the Styx. I must yield if you persist. But I do not believe you will. Listen while I tell you what this is you want. You are Clymenë's son as well as mine. You are mortal, and no mortal could drive my chariot. Indeed, no god except myself can do that. The ruler of the gods cannot. Consider the road. It rises up from the sea so steeply that the horses can hardly climb it, fresh though they are in the early morning. In midheaven it is so high that even I do not like to look down. Worst of all is the descent, so precipitous that the sea-gods waiting to receive me wonder how I can

avoid falling headlong. To guide the horses, too, is a perpetual struggle. Their fiery spirits grow hotter as they climb and they scarcely suffer my control. What would they do with you?

"Are you fancying that there are all sorts of wonders up there, cities of the gods full of beautiful things? Nothing of the kind. You will have to pass beasts, fierce beasts of prey, and they are all that you will see. The Bull, the Lion, the Scorpion, the great Crab, each will try to harm you. Be persuaded. Look around you. See all the goods the rich world holds. Choose from them your heart's desire and it shall be yours. If what you want is to be proved my son, my fears for you are proof enough that I am your father."

But none of all this wise talk meant anything to the boy. A glorious prospect opened before him. He saw himself proudly standing in that wondrous car, his hands triumphantly guiding those steeds which Jove himself could not master. He did not give a thought to the dangers his father detailed. He felt not a quiver of fear, not a doubt of his own powers. At last the Sun gave up trying to dissuade him. It was hopeless, as he saw. Besides, there was no time. The moment for starting was at hand. Already the gates of the east glowed purple, and Dawn had opened her courts full of rosy light. The stars were leaving the sky; even the lingering morning star was dim.

There was need for haste, but all was ready. The seasons, the gatekeepers of Olympus, stood waiting to fling the doors wide. The horses had been bridled and yoked to the car. Proudly and joyously Phaëthon mounted it, and they were off. He had made his choice. Whatever came of it he could not change now. Not that he wanted to in that first exhilarating rush through the air, so swift that the East Wind was outstripped and left far behind. The horses' flying feet went through the low-banked clouds near the ocean as through a thin sea mist and then up and up in the clear air, climbing the height of heaven. For a few ecstatic moments Phaëthon felt himself the Lord of the Sky. But suddenly there was a change. The chariot was swinging wildly to and fro; the pace was faster; he had lost control. Not he but the horses were directing the course. That light weight in the car, those feeble hands clutching the reins, had told them their own driver was not there. They were the masters then. No one else could command them. They left the road and rushed where they chose, up, down, to the right, to the left. They nearly wrecked the chariot against the Scorpion; they brought up short and almost ran into the Crab. By this time the poor charioteer was half fainting with terror, and he let the reins fall.

That was the signal for still more mad and reckless running. The horses soared up to the very top of the sky and then, plunging headlong down, they set the world on fire. The highest mountains were the first to burn, Ida and Helicon, where the Muses dwell, Parnassus, and the heaven-piercing Olympus. Down their slopes the flame ran to the low-lying valleys and the dark forest lands, until all things everywhere were ablaze. The springs turned into steam; the rivers shrank. It is said that it was then the Nile fled and hid his head, which still is hidden.

In the car Phaëthon, hardly keeping his place there, was wrapped in thick smoke and heat as if from a fiery furnace. He wanted nothing except to have this torment and terror ended. He would have welcomed death. Mother Earth, too, could bear no more. She uttered a great cry which reached up to the gods. Looking down from Olympus they saw that they must act quickly if the world was to be saved. Jove seized his thunderbolt and hurled it at the rash, repentant driver. It struck him dead, shattered the chariot, and made the maddened horses rush down into the sea.

Phaëthon all on fire fell from the car through the air to the earth. The mysterious river Eridanus, which no mortal eyes have ever seen, received him and put out the flames and cooled the body. The naiads,* in pity for him, so bold and so young to die, buried him and carved upon the tomb:

Here Phaëthon lies
who drove the Sun-god's car.
Greatly he failed,
but he had greatly dared.

---

naiads: nymphs that live in and preside over streams and brooks

---

His sisters, the Heliades, the daughters of Helios, the Sun, came to his grave to mourn for him. There they were turned into poplar trees, on the bank of the Eridanus,

Where sorrowing they weep
into the stream forever.
And each tear as it falls shines in the
water a glistening drop of amber.

About the Story

1. Describe Phaëthon.
2. What incident motivates Phaëthon to visit the Sun-god?
3. Who are Phaëthon's parents?
4. Why does the Sun call his oath "folly"?
5. What tragic flaw causes Phaëthon's downfall?

About the Translator

Edith Hamilton (1867-1963) gained her interest in learning at a young age from her father, who challenged her to read about and master any subject that interested her. Taking up this challenge, Hamilton taught herself myriad subjects ranging from math to classical literature. She also became proficient in Latin, Greek, French, and German. Always, however, her first love was the study of classical literature, especially Greek.

Also important in the Hamilton household was a thorough knowledge of the Scriptures. Hamilton later wrote that "the Bible was more familiar to us than any other book." This intimate knowledge of the Bible, however, was limited to a recognition of its worth as literature. To Hamilton, a love of the Scripture was essential for a proper appreciation of culture. She especially loved the thirteenth chapter of I Corinthians, which she studied in the original Greek. Unfortunately, she did not view the Bible as the infallible Word of God, the rule for faith and practice. As a result, the Christ she reverenced was not the Christ of Scripture. To her, Christ was a great example, a wonderful teacher, even the incarnate essence of everything divine, but He was not the Saviour of men. According to Hamilton, there was no truth or dogma revealed in the Bible that required a heart response. Truth was simply a pleasurable goal to be sought and found by anyone willing to look for it.

Though Hamilton was deficient in her understanding of Scripture, she did have an abundant supply of human insight and a gift for rendering the universal truths in classical literature accessible to the modern English reader. She felt that more than histories or social studies, "a people's literature is the great textbook for real knowledge of them." In books such as *The Greek Way,* she interpreted the thoughts and values of cultures different from our own and conveyed an appreciation for the effects of Greek thought on modern man. Certainly she brought out much that is noble and of literary merit in Greek literature.

Marjorie Daw

Thomas Bailey Aldrich

"Marjorie Daw" is a story with a delightful ironic twist. The conclusion, though quite unexpected, is entirely consistent with the characterizations Aldrich has developed. Notice, for example, Dr. Dillon's opening letter. What do we learn about John Flemming from the doctor? What do we learn about Edward Delaney? How are the doctor's descriptions and implications reinforced by John and Edward's letters to each other? How do these revelations help prepare us for the ending of the story?

I

Dr. Dillon to Edward Delaney, Esq.,
at the Pines, near Rye, N.H.

August 8, 1872

My dear Sir:

I am happy to assure you that your anxiety is without reason. Flemming will be confined to the sofa for three or four weeks, and will have to be careful at first how he uses his leg. A fracture of this kind is always a tedious affair. Fortunately the bone was very skillfully set by the surgeon who chanced to be in the drugstore where Flemming was brought after his fall, and I apprehend no permanent inconvenience from the accident. *Flemming is doing perfectly well physically;* but I must confess that the irritable and morbid state of mind into which he has fallen causes me a great deal of uneasiness. You know how impetuous our friend is ordinarily, what a soul of restlessness and energy, never content unless he is rushing at some object, like a sportive bull at a red shawl, but amiable withal. He is no longer amiable. His temper has become something frightful. He has a complete set of Balzac's works, twenty-seven volumes, piled up near his sofa, to throw at Watkins whenever that exemplary serving-man appears with his meals. Yesterday I very innocently brought Flemming a small basket of lemons. You know it was a strip of lemon-peel on the curbstone that caused our friend's mischance. Well, he no sooner set his eyes upon those lemons than he fell into such a rage as I cannot adequately describe. This is only one of his moods, and the least distressing. At other times he sits with bowed head regarding his splintered limb, silent, sullen, despairing. When this fit is on him—and it sometimes lasts all day—nothing can distract his melancholy. He refuses to eat, does not even read the newspaper; books, except as projectiles for Watkins, have no charms for him. His state is truly pitiable.

Now, if he were a poor man, with a family depending on his daily labor, this irritability and despondency would be natural enough. But in a young fellow of twenty-four, with plenty of money and seemingly not a care in the world, the thing is monstrous. If he continues to give way to his vagaries* in this manner, he will end by bringing on an inflammation of the fibula. It was the fibula he broke. I am at my wits' end to know what to prescribe for him. I have anaesthetics and lotions to make people sleep and to soothe pain; but I've no medicine that will make a man have a little common sense. That is beyond my skill, but maybe it is not beyond yours. You are Flemming's intimate friend, his *fidus Achates*.* Write to him, write to him frequently, distract his mind, cheer him up, and prevent him from becoming a confirmed case of melancholia. Perhaps he has some important plans disarranged by his present confinement. If he has, you will know, and will know how to advise him judiciously. I trust your father finds the change beneficial? I am, my dear sir, with great respect, etc.

---

vagaries: erratic actions
fidus Achates: Latin: faithful Achates; Aeneas's companion in Virgil's epic poem *The Aenied*

II

Edward Delaney to John Flemming, West 38th Street, New York

August 9, 1872

My dear Jack:

I had a line from Dillon this morning, and was rejoiced to learn that your hurt is not so bad as reported. Like a certain personage, you are not so black and blue as you are painted. Dillon will put you on your pins again in two or three weeks, if you will only have patience and follow his counsels. Did you get my note of last Wednesday? I was greatly troubled when I heard of the accident.

I can imagine how tranquil and saintly you are with your leg in a trough! It is awkward, to be sure, just as we had promised ourselves a glorious month together at the sea-side; but we must make the best of it. It is unfortunate, too, that my father's health renders it impossible for me to leave him. I think he has much improved; the sea air is his native element; but he still needs my arm to lean upon in his walks, and requires some one more careful than a servant to look after him. I cannot come to you, dear Jack, but I have hours of unemployed time on hand, and I will write you a whole post office full of letters, if that will divert you. Heaven knows, I haven't anything to write about. It isn't as if we were living at one of the beach houses; then I could do you some character studies, and fill your imagination with groups of sea-goddesses, with their (or somebody else's) raven and blond manes hanging down their shoulders. You should have Aphrodite* in morning wrapper, in evening costume. But we are far from all that here. We have rooms in a farmhouse, on a crossroad, two miles from the hotels, and lead the quietest of lives.

Aphrodite: Greek goddess of love and beauty

I wish I were a novelist. This old house, with its sanded floors and high wainscots,* and its narrow windows looking out upon a cluster of pines that turn themselves into aeolian harps every time the wind blows, would be the place in which to write a summer romance. It should be a story with the odors of the forest and the breath of the sea in it. It should be a novel like one of that Russian fellow's—what's his name?—Tourguenieff, Turguenef, Turgenif, Toorguniff, Turgenjew—nobody knows how to spell him. Yet I wonder if even a Liza or an Alexandra Paulovna could stir the heart of a man who has constant twinges in his leg. I wonder if one of our own Yankee girls of the best type, haughty and *spirituelle,** would be of any comfort to you in your present deplorable condition. If I thought so, I would hasten down to the Surf House and catch one for you; or, better still, I would find you one over the way.

---

wainscots: wood paneling on interior walls
spirituelle: French: extremely refined character

Picture to yourself a large white house just across the road, nearly opposite our cottage. It is not a house, but a mansion, built, perhaps, in the colonial period, with rambling extensions, and gambrel roof, and a wide piazza on three sides—a self-possessed, high-bred piece of architecture, with its nose in the air. It stands back from the road, and has an obsequious* retinue* of fringed elms and oaks and weeping willows. Sometimes in the morning, and oftener in the afternoon, when the sun has withdrawn from that part of the mansion, a young woman appears on the piazza with some mysterious Penelope* web of embroidery in her hand, or a book. There is a hammock over there—of pineapple fiber, it looks from here. A hammock is very becoming when one is eighteen, and has golden hair, and dark eyes and an emerald-colored illusion dress looped up after the fashion of a Dresden china shepherdess, and is *chaussée** like a belle of the time of Louis Quatorze.* All this splendor goes into that hammock, and sways there like a pond-lily in the golden afternoon. The window of my bedroom looks down on that piazza—and so do I.

---

obsequious: totally compliant
retinue: group of attendants accompanying person of high rank
Penelope: faithful wife of Odysseus in Homer's *Odyssey*
chaussée: French: booted
Louis Quatorze: Louis XIV, the "sun king"

But enough of this nonsense, which ill becomes a sedate young attorney taking his vacation with an invalid father. Drop me a line, dear Jack, and tell me how you really are. State your case. Write me a long, quiet letter. If you are violent or abusive, I'll take the law to you.

III

John Flemming to Edward Delaney
August 11, 1872

Your letter, dear Ned, was a god-send. Fancy what a fix I am in—I, who never had a day's sickness since I was born. My left leg weighs three tons. It is embalmed in spices and smothered in layers of fine linen, like a mummy. I can't move. I haven't moved for five thousand years. I'm of the time of Pharaoh.

I lie from morning till night on a lounge, staring into the hot street. Everybody is out of town enjoying himself. The brown-stone-front houses across the street resemble a row of particularly ugly coffins set up on end. A green mold is settling on the names of the deceased, carved on the silver doorplates. Sardonic* spiders have sewed up the keyholes. All is silence and dust and desolation.—I interrupt this a moment, to take a shot at Watkins with the second volume of *César Birotteau.* Missed him! I think I could bring

him down with a copy of Sainte-Beuve or the *Dictionnaire Universel,* if I had it. These small Balzac books somehow do not quite fit my hand; but I shall fetch him yet. You should see him: he glides into my chamber, with that colorless, hypocritical face of his drawn out long like an accordion; but I know he grins all the way downstairs, and is glad I have broken my leg. Was not my evil star in the very zenith when I ran up to town to attend that dinner at Delmonico's? I didn't come up altogether for that. It was partly to buy Frank Livingstone's roan mare Margot. And now I shall not be able to sit in the saddle these two months. I'll send the mare down to you at The Pines—is that the name of the place?

---

sardonic: contemptibly mocking

Old Dillon fancies that I have something on my mind. He drives me wild with lemons. Lemons for a mind diseased! Nonsense. I am only restless under this confinement—a thing I'm not used to. Take a man who has never had so much as a headache or a toothache in his life, strap one of his legs in a section of water-spout, keep him in a room in the city for weeks, with the hot weather turned on, and then expect him to smile and purr and be happy! It is preposterous. I can't be cheerful or calm.

Your letter is the first consoling thing I have had since my disaster, ten days ago. It really cheered me up for half an hour. Send me a screed,* Ned, as often as you can, if you love me. Anything will do. Write me more

about that little girl in the hammock. That was very pretty, all that about the Dresden china shepherdess and the pond-lily; the imagery a little mixed, perhaps, but very pretty. I didn't suppose you had so much sentimental furniture in your upper story. It shows how one may be familiar for years with the reception-room of his neighbor, and never suspect what is directly under his mansard.* I supposed your loft stuffed with dry legal parchments, mortgages, and affidavits; you take down a package of manuscript, and lo! there are lyrics and sonnets and canzonettas. You really have a graphic descriptive touch, Edward Delaney, and I suspect you of anonymous love-tales in the magazines.

---

screed: long letter
mansard: roof with two slopes on all four sides

I shall be a bear until I hear from you again. Tell me all about your pretty *inconnue** across the road. What is her name? Who is she? Who's her father? Where's her mother? Who's her lover? You cannot imagine how this will occupy me. The more trifling, the better. My imprisonment has weakened me intellectually to such a degree that I find your epistolary* gifts quite considerable. I am passing into my second childhood. In a week or two I shall take to India-rubber rings and prongs of coral. A silver cup, with an appropriate inscription, would be a delicate attention on your part. In the meantime, write!

---

inconnue: French: unknown lady
epistolary: related to letters or letter writing

IV

Edward Delaney to John Flemming
                                    August 12, 1872

The sick pasha* shall be amused—he wills it so. But truly, Jack, I have a hard task. There is literally nothing here—except the little girl over the way. She is swinging in the hammock at this moment. It is to me compensation for many of the ills of life to see her now and then put out a small kid boot, which fits like a glove, and set herself going. Who is she, and what is her name? Her name is Daw. Only daughter of Mr. Richard W. Daw, ex-colonel and banker. Mother dead. One brother at Harvard, elder brother killed at the battle of Fair Oaks, ten years ago. Old, rich family, the Daws. This is the homestead, where father and daughter pass eight months of the twelve; the rest of the year in Baltimore and Washington. The New England winter too much for the old gentleman. The daughter is called Marjorie—Marjorie Daw. Sounds odd at first, doesn't it? But after you say it over to yourself half a dozen times, you like it. There's a pleasing quaintness to it, something prim and violet-like. Must be a nice sort of girl to be called Marjorie Daw.

---

pasha: title formerly used after the name of a Turkish military leader

---

I had my host of The Pines in the witness-box last night, and drew the foregoing testimony from him. He has charge of Mr. Daw's vegetable garden, and has known the family these thirty years. Of course I shall make the acquaintance of my neighbors before many days. It will be next to impossible for me not to meet Mr. Daw or Miss Daw in some of my walks. The young lady has a favorite path to the sea-beach. I shall intercept her some morning and touch my hat to her. Then the princess will bend her fair head to me with courteous surprise not unmixed with haughtiness. Will snub me, in fact. All this for thy sake. O Pasha of the Snapt Axle-tree! . . . How oddly things fall out! Ten minutes ago I was called down to the parlor—you know the kind of parlors in farmhouses on the coast, a sort of amphibious parlor, with sea-shells on the mantelpiece and spruce branches in the chimney place—where I found my father and Mr. Daw doing the antique polite to each other. He had come to pay his respects to his new neighbors. Mr. Daw is a tall, slim gentleman of about fifty-five, with a florid face and snow-white mustache and side-whiskers. Looks like Mr. Dombey, or as Mr. Dombey would have looked if he had served a few years in the British Army. Mr. Daw was a colonel in the late war, commanding the regiment in which his son was a lieutenant. Plucky old boy, backbone of New Hampshire granite. Before taking his leave, the colonel delivered himself of an invitation as if he were issuing a general order. Miss Daw had a few friends coming, at 4 P.M., to play croquet on the lawn (parade-ground) and have tea (cold rations) on the piazza. Will we honor them with our company? (or be sent to the guard-house.) My father declines on the plea of ill-health. My father's son bows with as much suavity as he knows, and accepts.

In my next I shall have something to tell you. I shall have seen the little beauty face to face. I have a presentiment, Jack, that this Daw is a *rara avis!** Keep up your spirits, my boy, until I write you another letter—and send me along word how's your leg.

---

rara avis: Latin: rare bird

V

Edward Delaney to John Flemming

August 13, 1872

The party, my dear Jack, was as dreary as possible. A lieutenant of the navy, the rector of the Episcopal Church at Stillwater, and a society swell from Nahant. The lieutenant looked as if he had swallowed a couple of his buttons, and found the bullion rather indigestible; the rector was a pensive youth, of the daffydowndilly sort; and the swell from Nahant was a very weak tidal wave indeed. The women were much better, as they always are; the two Miss Kingsburys of Philadelphia, staying at the Seashell House, two bright and engaging girls. But Marjorie Daw!

The company broke up soon after tea, and I remained with the colonel on the piazza. It was like seeing a picture, to see Miss Marjorie hovering around the old soldier, and doing a hundred gracious little things for him. As we sat there, she came and went in the summer twilight, and seemed, with her white dress and pale gold hair, like some lovely phantom that had sprung into existence. If she had melted into air, like the statue of Galatea* in the play, I should have been more sorry than surprised.

Galatea: in Greek mythology, an ivory statue of a young girl, brought to life by Aphrodite

---

It was easy to perceive that the old colonel worshiped her, and she him. I think the relation between an elderly father and a daughter just blooming into womanhood the most beautiful possible. There is in it a subtile sentiment that cannot exist in the case of mother and daughter, or that of son and mother. But this is getting into deep water.

I sat with the Daws until half past ten, and saw the moon rise on the sea. The ocean, that had stretched motionless and black against the horizon, was changed by magic into a broken field of glittering ice, interspersed with marvelous silvery fjords.* In the far distance the Isles of Shoals loomed up like a group of huge bergs drifting down on us. The Polar Regions in a June thaw! It was exceedingly fine. What did we talk about? We talked about the weather—and you. The weather has been disagreeable for several days past—and so have you. I glided from one topic to the other very naturally. I told my friends of your accident; how it had frustrated all our summer plans, and what our plans were. I played quite a spirited solo on the fibula. Then I described you; or, rather, I didn't. I spoke of your amiability, of your patience under this severe affliction; of your touching gratitude when Dillon brings you little presents of fruit; of your tenderness to your sister Fanny, whom you would not allow to stay in town to nurse you, and how you heroically sent her back to Newport, preferring to remain alone with Mary, the cook, and your man Watkins, to whom, by the way, you were devotedly attached. If you had been there, Jack, you wouldn't have known yourself. I should have excelled as a criminal lawyer, if I had not turned my attention to a different branch of jurisprudence.

---

fjords: lengthy, often deep inlets from the sea between high cliffs

---

Miss Marjorie asked all manner of leading questions concerning you. It did not occur to me then, but it struck me forcibly afterwards, that she evinced a singular interest in the conversation. When I got back to my room, I recalled how eagerly she leaned forward, with her full, snowy throat in strong moonlight, listening to what I said. Positively, I think I made her like you!

Miss Daw is a girl whom you would like immensely, I can tell you that. A beauty without affectation, a high and tender nature—

if one can read the soul in the face. And the old colonel is a noble character, too.

I am glad that the Daws are such pleasant people. The Pines is an isolated spot, and my resources are few. I fear I should have found life here somewhat monotonous before long, with no other society than that of my excellent sire. It is true, I might have made a target of the defenseless invalid; but I haven't a taste for artillery, *moi.**

moi: French: me; I

VI

John Flemming to Edward Delaney
August 17, 1872

For a man who hasn't a taste for artillery, it occurs to me, my friend, you are keeping up a pretty lively fire on my inner works. But go on. Cynicism is a small brass field-piece that eventually bursts and kills the artilleryman.

You may abuse me as much as you like, and I'll not complain; for I don't know what I should do without your letters. They are curing me. I haven't hurled anything at Watkins since last Sunday, partly because I have grown more amiable under your teaching, and partly because Watkins captured my ammunition one night, and carried it off to the library. He is rapidly losing the habit he had acquired of dodging whenever I rub my ear, or make any slight motion with my right arm.

Ned, that Miss Daw must be a charming person. I should certainly like her. I like her already. When you spoke in your first letter of seeing a young girl swinging in a hammock under your chamber window, I was somehow strangely drawn to her. I cannot account for it in the least. What you have subsequently written of Miss Daw has strengthened the impression. You seem to be describing a woman I have known in some previous state

of existence, or dreamed of in this. Upon my word, if you were to send me her photograph, I believe I should recognize her at a glance. Her manner, that listening attitude, her traits of character, as you indicate them, the light hair and the dark eyes—they are all familiar things to me. Asked a lot of questions, did she? Curious about me? That is strange.

You would laugh in your sleeve, you wretched old cynic, if you knew how I lie awake nights, thinking of The Pines and the house across the road. How cool it must be down there! I long for the salt smell in the air. I picture the colonel on the piazza. I send you and Miss Daw off on afternoon rambles along the beach. Sometimes I let you stroll with her under the elms in the moonlight, for you are great friends by this time, I take it, and see each other every day. I know your ways and your manners! Then I fall into a truculent mood, and would like to destroy somebody. Have you noticed anything in the shape of a lover hanging around the colonial Lares and Penates?* Does that lieutenant of the horse-marines or that young Stillwater parson visit the house much? Not that I am pining for news of them, but any gossip of the kind would be in order. I wonder, Ned, that you don't fall in love with Miss Daw. I am ripe to do it myself. Speaking of photographs, couldn't you manage to slip one of her *cartes-de-visite** from her album—she must have an album, you know—and send it to me? I will return it before it could be missed. That's a good fellow! Did the mare arrive safe and sound? It will be a capital animal this autumn for Central Park.

Lares and Penates: guardian household gods in early Roman times
cartes-de-visite: small photographs sometimes used as calling cards

Oh—my leg? I forgot about my leg. It's better.

VII

Edward Delaney to John Flemming

August 20, 1872

You are correct in your surmises. I am on the most friendly terms with our neighbors. I pass an hour or two of the day or the evening with the daughter. I am more and more struck by the beauty, modesty, and intelligence of Miss Daw.

You ask me why I do not fall in love with her. I will be frank, Jack: I have thought of that. She is young, rich, accomplished, uniting in herself more attractions, mental and personal, than I can recall in any girl of my acquaintance; but she lacks the something that would be necessary to inspire in me that kind of interest. Possessing this unknown quantity, a woman neither beautiful nor wealthy nor very young could bring me to her feet. But not Miss Daw. I would like to have her for a sister, that I might shield her and counsel her, and spend half my income on old threadlace and camel's-hair shawls. If such were not my feeling, there would still be an obstacle to my loving Miss Daw. A greater misfortune could scarcely befall me than to love her. Flemming, I am about to make a revelation that will astonish you. I may be all wrong in my premises and consequently in my conclusions; but you shall judge.

That night when I returned to my room after the croquet party at the Daws', and was thinking over the trivial events of the evening, I was suddenly impressed by the air of eager attention with which Miss Daw had followed my account of your accident. I think I mentioned this to you. Well, the next morning, as I went to mail my letter, I overtook Miss Daw on the road to Rye, where the post-office is, and accompanied her thither and back, an hour's walk. The conversation again turned on you, and again I remarked that inexplicable look of interest which had lighted up her face the previous evening. Since then, I have seen Miss Daw perhaps ten times, perhaps oftener, and on each occasion I found that when I was not speaking of you, or your sister, or some person or place associated with you, I was not holding her attention. She would be absent-minded, her eyes would wander away from me to the sea, or to some distant object in the landscape; her fingers would play with the leaves of a book in a way that convinced me she was not listening. At these moments if I abruptly changed the theme—I did it several times as an experiment—and dropped some remark about my friend Flemming, then the somber blue eyes would come back to me instantly.

Now, is not this the oddest thing in the world? No, not the oddest. The effect which you tell me was produced on you by my casual mention of an unknown girl swinging in a hammock is certainly as strange. You can conjecture how that passage in your letter of Friday startled me. Is it possible, then, that two people who have never met, and who are hundreds of miles apart, can exert a magnetic influence on each other? I have read of such psychological phenomena, but never credited them. I leave the solution of the problem to you. As for myself, all other things being favorable, it would be impossible for me to fall in love with a woman who listens to me only when I am talking of my friend!

I am not aware that anyone is paying marked attention to my fair neighbor. The lieutenant of the navy—he is stationed at Rivermouth—sometimes drops in of an evening, and sometimes the rector from Stillwater; the lieutenant the oftener. He was there last night. I should not be surprised if he had an eye to the heiress; but he is not formidable. Mistress Daw carries a neat little spear of irony, and the honest lieutenant seems to have a particular facility for impaling himself on the point of it. He is not dangerous, I should say; though I have known a woman to satirize a man for years, and marry him after all. Decidedly, the lowly rector is not dangerous; yet, again, who has not seen Cloth of Frieze* victorious in the lists* where Cloth of Gold* went down?

Cloth of Frieze: coarse wool cloth, symbolic of the clergy
lists: scenes of combat
Cloth of Gold: cloth in which gold threads are interwoven with silk or wool, symbolic of royalty

---

As to the photograph. There is an exquisite ivory-type of Marjorie on the drawing-room mantelpiece. It would be missed at once if taken. I would do anything reasonable for you, Jack; but I've no burning desire to be hauled up before the local justice of the peace on a charge of petty larceny.

P.S.—Enclosed is a spray of mignonette,* which I advise you to treat tenderly. Yes, we talked of you again last night, as usual. It is becoming a little dreary for me.

---

mignonette: a plant usually grown for its clusters of fragrant greenish flowers

---

VIII

Edward Delaney to John Flemming
August 22, 1872

Your letter in reply to my last has occupied my thoughts all the morning. I do not know what to think. Do you mean to say that you are seriously half in love with a woman whom you have never seen—with a shadow, a chimera?* for what else can Miss Daw be to you? I do not understand it at all. I understand neither you nor her. You are a couple of ethereal beings moving in finer air than I can breathe with my commonplace lungs. Such delicacy of sentiment is something that I admire without comprehending. I am bewildered. I am of the earth earthy,* and I find myself in the incongruous position of having to do with mere souls, with natures so finely tempered that I run some risk of shattering them in my awkwardness. I am as Caliban* among the spirits!

---

chimera: something created in the imagination
of the earth earthy: Biblical allusion to I Corinthians 15:47
Caliban: an outlandish slave in Shakespeare's *The Tempest*

Reflecting on your letter, I am not sure that it is wise in me to continue this correspondence. But no, Jack; I do wrong to doubt the good sense that forms the basis of your character. You are deeply interested in Miss Daw; you feel that she is a person whom you may perhaps greatly admire when you know her: at the same time you bear in mind that the chances are ten to five that, when you do come to know her, she will fall far short of your ideal, and you will not care for her in the least. Look at it in this sensible light, and I will hold back nothing from you.

Yesterday afternoon my father and myself rode over to Rivermouth with the Daws. A heavy rain in the morning had cooled the atmosphere and laid the dust. To Rivermouth is a drive of eight miles, along a winding road lined all the way with wild barberry-bushes. I never saw anything more brilliant than these bushes, the green of the foliage and the faint blush of the berries intensified by the rain. The colonel drove, with my father in front, Miss Daw and I on the back seat. I resolved that for the first five miles your name should not pass my lips. I was amused by the artful attempt she made, at the start, to break through my reticence.* Then a silence fell upon her; and then she became suddenly gay. That keenness which I enjoyed so much when it was exercised on the lieutenant was not so satisfactory directed against myself. Miss Daw has great sweetness of disposition, but she can be disagreeable. She is like the young lady in the rhyme, with the curl on her forehead,

---

reticence: keeping one's feelings and thoughts to oneself

"When she is good,
She is very, very good,
And when she is bad, she is horrid!"

I kept to my resolution, however; but on the return home I relented, and talked of your mare! Miss Daw is going to try a side-saddle on Margot some morning. The animal is a trifle too light for my weight. By the bye, I nearly forgot to say that Miss Daw sat for a picture yesterday to a Rivermouth artist. If the negative turns out well, I am to have a copy. So our ends will be accomplished without crime. I wish, though, I could send you the ivory-type in the drawing-room; it is cleverly colored, and would give you an idea of her hair and eyes, which of course the other will not.

No, Jack, the spray of mignonette did not come from me. A man of twenty-eight doesn't enclose flowers in his letters—to another man. But don't attach too much significance to the circumstance. She gives sprays of mignonette to the rector, sprays to the lieutenant. She had even given a rose from her bosom to your slave. It is her jocund nature to scatter flowers, like Spring.

If my letters sometimes read disjointedly, you must understand that I never finish one at a sitting, but write at intervals, when the mood is on me.

The mood is not on me now.

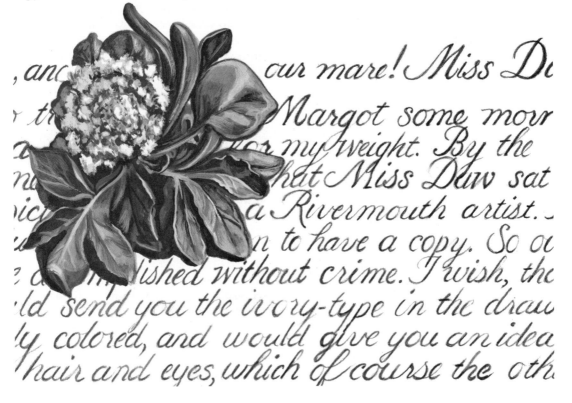

IX

Edward Delaney to John Flemming

August 23, 1872

I have just returned from the strangest interview with Marjorie. She has all but confessed to me her interest in you. But with what modesty and dignity! Her words elude my pen as I attempt to put them on paper; and, indeed, it was not so much what she said as her manner; and that I cannot reproduce. Perhaps it was of a piece with the strangeness of this whole business, that she should tacitly acknowledge to a third party the love she feels for a man she had never beheld! But I have lost, through your aid, the faculty of being surprised. I accept things as people do in dreams. Now that I am again in my room, it all appears like an illusion—the black masses of Rembrandtish shadow under the trees, the fireflies whirling in Pyrrhic dances* among the shrubbery, the sea over there, Marjorie sitting on the hammock!

Pyrrhic dances: ancient Greek war-dances in which motions of actual war were depicted

---

It is past midnight, and I am too sleepy to write more.

Thursday Morning

My father has suddenly taken it into his head to spend a few days at the Shoals. In the meanwhile you will not hear from me. I see Marjorie walking in the garden with the colonel. I wish I could speak to her alone, but shall probably not have an opportunity before we leave.

X

Edward Delaney to John Flemming

August 28, 1872

You were passing into your second childhood, were you? Your intellect was so reduced that my epistolary gifts seemed quite considerable to you, did they? I rise superior to the sarcasm in your favor of the 11th instant, when I notice that five days' silence on my part is sufficient to throw you into the depths of despondency.

We returned only this morning from Appledore, that enchanted island—at four dollars per day. I find on my desk three letters from you! Evidently there is no lingering doubt in your mind as to the pleasure I derive from your correspondence. These letters are undated, but in what I take to be the latest are two passages that require my consideration. You ask my advice on a certain point. I will give it. In my opinion you could do nothing more unwise than to address a note to Miss Daw, thanking her for the flower. It would, I am sure, offend her delicacy beyond pardon. She knows you only through me; you are to her an abstraction, a figure in a dream—a dream from which the faintest shock would awaken her. Of course, if you enclose a note to me and insist on its delivery, I shall deliver it; but I advise you not to do so.

You say you are able, with the aid of a cane, to walk about your chamber, and that you purpose to come to The Pines the instant Dillon thinks you strong enough to stand the journey. Again I advise you not to. Do you not see that, every hour you remain away, Marjorie's glamor deepens, and your influence over her increases? You will ruin everything by precipitancy. Wait until you are entirely recovered; in any case, do not come without giving me warning. I fear the effect of your abrupt advent here—under the circumstances.

Miss Daw was evidently glad to see us back again, and gave me both hands in the frankest way. She stopped at the door a moment this afternoon in the carriage; she had been over to Rivermouth for her pictures. Unluckily the photographer had spilt some acid on the plate, and she was obliged to give him another sitting. I have an intuition that something is troubling Marjorie. She had an abstracted air not usual with her. However, it may be only my fancy. . . . I end this, leaving several things unsaid, to accompany my father on one of those long walks which are now his chief medicine—and mine!

XI

Edward Delaney to John Flemming

August 29, 1872

I write in great haste to tell you what has taken place here since my letter of last night. I am in the utmost perplexity. Only one thing is plain—you must not dream of coming to The Pines. Marjorie has told her father everything! I saw her for a few minutes, an hour ago, in the garden; and, as near as I could gather from her confused statement, the facts are these: Lieutenant Bradly—that's the naval officer stationed at Rivermouth—has been paying court to Miss Daw for some time past, but not so much to her liking as to that of the colonel, who it seems is an old friend of the young gentleman's father. Yesterday (I knew she was in some trouble when she drove up to our gate) the colonel spoke to Marjorie of Bradly—urged his suit, I infer. Marjorie expressed her dislike for the lieutenant with characteristic frankness, and finally confessed to her father—well, I really do not know what she confessed. It must have been the vaguest of confessions, and must have sufficiently puzzled the colonel. At any rate, it exasperated him. I suppose I am implicated in the matter, and that the colonel feels bitterly towards me. I do not see why: I have carried no messages between you and Miss Daw; I have behaved with the greatest discretion. I can find no flaw anywhere in my proceeding. I do not see that anybody has done anything—except the colonel himself.

It is probable, nevertheless, that the friendly relations between the two houses will be broken off. "A plague o' both your houses,"* say you. I will keep you informed, as well as I can, of what occurs over the way. We shall remain here until the second week in September. Stay where you are, or, at all events, do not dream of joining me. . . . Colonel Daw is sitting on the piazza, looking rather wicked. I have not seen Marjorie since I parted with her in the garden.

"A plague . . . houses": from *Romeo and Juliet*, Act III, Scene i, line 96

XII

Edward Delaney to Thomas Dillon, M.D., Madison Square, New York

August 30, 1872

My dear Doctor:

If you have any influence over Flemming, I beg of you to exert it to prevent his coming to this place at present. There are circumstances, which I will explain to you before long, that make it of the first importance that he should not come into this neighborhood. His appearance here, I speak advisedly, would be disastrous to him. In urging him to remain in New York, or to go to some inland resort, you will be doing him and me a real service. Of course you will not mention my name in this connection. You know me well enough, my dear doctor, to be assured that, in begging your secret co-operation, I have reasons that will meet your entire approval when they are made plain to you. We shall return to town on the 15th of next month, and my first duty will be to present myself at your hospitable door and satisfy your curiosity, if I have excited it. My father, I am glad to state, has so greatly improved that he can no longer be regarded as an invalid. With great esteem, I am, etc., etc.

XIII

Edward Delaney to John Flemming

August 31, 1872

Your letter, announcing your mad determination to come here, has just reached me. I beseech you to reflect a moment. The step would be fatal to your interests and hers. You would furnish just cause for irritation to R.W.D.; and, though he loves Marjorie devotedly, he is capable of going to any lengths if opposed. You would not like, I am convinced, to be the means of causing him to treat her with severity. That would be the result of your presence at The Pines at this juncture. I am annoyed to be obliged to point out these things to you. We are on very delicate ground, Jack; the situation is critical, and the slightest mistake in a move would cost us the game. If you consider it worth winning, be patient. Trust a little to my sagacity.* Wait and see what happens. Moreover, I understand from Dillon that you are in no condition to take so long a journey. He thinks the air of the coast would be the worst thing possible for you; that you ought to go inland, if anywhere. Be advised by me. Be advised by Dillon.

---

sagacity: quality of wisdom

XIV

Telegrams

September 1, 1872

To Edward Delaney

Letter received. Dillon be hanged. I think I ought to be on the ground.

J.F.

To John Flemming

Stay where you are. You would only complicate matters. Do not move until you hear from me.

E.D.

To Edward Delaney

My being at The Pines could be kept secret. I must see her.

J.F.

To John Flemming

Do not think of it. It would be useless. R.W.D. has locked M. in her room. You would not be able to effect an interview.

E.D.

To Edward Delaney

Locked in her room! That settles the question. I shall leave by the twelve-fifteen express.

J.F.

XV

The Arrival

On the second day of September, 1872, as the down express, due at 3:40, left the station at Hampton, a young man, leaning on the shoulder of a servant, whom he addressed as Watkins, stepped from the platform into a hack, and requested to be driven to "The

Pines." On arriving at the gate of a modest farmhouse, a few miles from the station, the young man descended with difficulty from the carriage, and, casting a hasty glance across the road, seemed much impressed by some peculiarity in the landscape. Again leaning on the shoulder of the person Watkins, he walked to the door of the farmhouse and inquired for Mr. Edward Delaney. He was informed by the aged man who answered his knock, that Mr. Edward Delaney had gone to Boston the day before, but that Mr. Jonas Delaney was within. This information did not appear satisfactory to the stranger who inquired if Mr. Edward Delaney had left any message for Mr. John Flemming. There was a letter for Mr. Flemming, if he were that person. After a brief absence the aged man reappeared with a letter.

XVI

Edward Delaney to John Flemming
September 1, 1872

I am horror-stricken at what I have done! When I began this correspondence I had no other purpose than to relieve the tedium of your sick-chamber. Dillon told me to cheer you up. I tried to. I thought that you entered into the spirit of the thing. I had no idea, until within a few days, that you were taking matters *au grand sérieux.**

---

au grand sérieux: French: of great seriousness

What can I say? I am in sackcloth and ashes.* I am a pariah,* a dog of an outcast. I tried to make a little romance to interest you, something soothing and idyllic, and, I have done it only too well! My father doesn't know a word of this, so don't jar the old gentleman any more than you can help. I fly from the wrath to come*—when you arrive! For, oh, dear Jack, there isn't any colonial mansion on the other side of the road, there isn't any piazza, there isn't any hammock—there isn't any Marjorie Daw!

---

in sackcloth and ashes: thoroughly repentant; from Matthew 11:21
pariah: outcast
fly from the wrath to come: from Bunyan's *Pilgrim's Progress;* the warning Evangelist gives Christian when admonishing him to flee the City of Destruction

About the Story

1. Who are the primary characters? Secondary characters?
2. Explain why the primary characters are considered round, static characters.
3. Notice the methods Aldrich uses to reveal the character to the reader. Give a specific example of each method listed.

> Description: the person's appearance and/or environment
> Dialogue: what the character says; what others say about him
> Action: what the character does; how other characters react to him

About the Author

Thomas Bailey Aldrich (1836-1907) was born in Portsmouth, New Hampshire, the son of an old New England family who had moved to New Orleans when Aldrich was ten. Three years later they returned to Portsmouth to allow their son to begin preparing for college. There he lived with his grandfather, a man greatly respected and loved by the young Aldrich. He later recalled the older man's "unquestioning faith" and tender thoughtfulness. Although Aldrich himself did not share his grandfather's faith, he never lost respect for the traditional moral values his grandfather upheld. Nor did he ever forget his grandfather's old trunk full of classic adventure novels such as *Robinson Crusoe* and the *Arabian Nights,* stories which sparked his imagination and love of reading.

Aldrich's hope of a college education vanished when his father died. Finances made it imperative that he and his mother move to New York City to stay with an uncle who gave Aldrich a job as a clerk. Though his opportunity for formal training had been thwarted, Aldrich used every spare moment to write and to read, and at nineteen he published his first volume of poetry, which brought him immediate acclaim and helped him obtain an editorial position on the staff of a popular periodical. Over the next several years he published myriad poems, short stories, and novels, and eventually he became the editor of the prestigious periodical *The Atlantic Monthly.*

Aldrich's most famous and enduring novel, *The Story of a Bad Boy,* was published in 1869. Like his other works, this story is witty and entertaining; it is also a significant work in literary history for its contribution to Realism and the local-color movement. Unlike many other Realistic writers, however, Aldrich chose to emphasize the "pleasurable aspects of life to the neglect of the sordid." He was a charming man, full of life and seemingly always young.

The Revolt of Mother

Mary E. Wilkins Freeman

In the three previous stories, you have observed both flat and round characters. All of these characters, however, have been static. In "The Revolt of Mother" the two central characters are dynamic. Both the father and the mother evidence change throughout the course of the story. Although these changes may be considered positive, the method used to evoke the change is not necessarily the best. As you read, list some specific ways in which the two central characters change. What is the husband's response? What is the wife's response? Do you think these responses indicate a positive change in these two central characters? What different methods might have been used to encourage the same results?

"Father!"

"What is it?"

"What are them men diggin' over there in the field for?"

There was a sudden dropping and enlarging of the lower part of the old man's face, as if some heavy weight had settled therein; he shut his mouth tight and went on harnessing the great bay mare. He hustled the collar on to her neck with a jerk.

"Father!"

The old man slapped the saddle upon the mare's back.

"Look here, Father, I want to know what them men are diggin' over in the field for, an' I'm goin' to know."

"I wish you'd go into the house, Mother, an' 'tend to your own affairs," the old man said then. He ran his words together, and his speech was almost as inarticulate as a growl.

But the woman understood; it was her native tongue. "I ain't goin' into the house till you tell me what them men are doin' over there in the field," said she.

Then she stood waiting. She was a small woman, short and straight-waisted like a child in her brown cotton gown. Her forehead was mild and benevolent between the smooth curves of gray hair; there were meek downward lines about her nose and mouth; but her eyes, fixed upon the old man, looked as if the meekness had been the result of her own will, never of the will of another.

They were in the barn, standing before the wide open doors. The spring air, full of the smell of growing grass and unseen blossoms, came in their faces. The deep yard in front was littered with farm wagons and piles of wood; on the edges, close to the fence and the house, the grass was a vivid green, and there were some dandelions.

The old man glanced doggedly at his wife as he tightened the last buckles on the harness. She looked as immovable to him as one of the rocks in his pasture land, bound to the earth with generations of blackberry vines. He slapped the reins over the horse, and started forth from the barn.

"Father!" said she.

The old man pulled up. "What is it?"

"I want to know what them men are diggin' over there in that field for."

"They're diggin' a cellar, I s'pose, if you've got to know."

"A cellar for what?"

"A barn."

"A barn? You ain't goin' to build a barn over there where we was goin' to have a house, Father?"

The old man said not another word. He hurried the horse into the farm wagon and clattered out of the yard, jouncing as sturdily on his seat as a boy.

The woman stood a moment looking after him, then she went out of the barn across a corner of the yard to the house. The house, standing at right angles with the great barn and a long reach of sheds and outbuildings, was infinitesimal compared with them. It was scarcely as commodious* for people as the little boxes under the barn eaves were for doves.

---

commodious: roomy

A pretty girl's face, pink and delicate as a flower, was looking out of one of the house windows. She was watching three men who were digging over in the field which bounded the yard near the road line. She turned quietly when the woman entered.

"What are they digging for, Mother?" said she. "Did he tell you?"

"They're diggin' for—a cellar for a new barn."

"Oh, Mother, he ain't going to build another barn?"

"That's what he says."

A boy stood before the kitchen glass combing his hair. He combed slowly and painstakingly, arranging his brown hair in a smooth hillock over his forehead. He did not seem to pay any attention to the conversation.

"Sammy, did you know Father was going to build a new barn?" asked the girl.

The boy combed assiduously.*

---

assiduously: diligently

"Sammy!"

He turned and showed a face like his father's under his smooth crest of hair. "Yes, I s'pose I did," he said reluctantly.

"How long have you known it?" asked his mother.

" 'Bout three months, I guess."

"Why didn't you tell of it?"

"Didn't think 'twould do no good."

"I don't see what Father wants another barn for," said the girl, in her sweet, slow voice. She turned again to the window and stared out at the digging men in the field. Her tender, sweet face was full of gentle distress. Her forehead was as bald and innocent as a baby's, with the light hair strained back from it in a row of curl papers. She was quite large, but her soft curves did not look as if they covered muscles.

Her mother looked sternly at the boy. "Is

he goin' to buy more cows?" said she.

The boy did not reply; he was tying his shoes.

"Sammy, I want you to tell me if he's goin' to buy more cows."

"I s'pose he is."

"How many?"

"Four, I guess."

His mother said nothing more. She went into the pantry, and there was a clatter of dishes. The boy got his cap from a nail behind the door, took an old arithmetic from the shelf, and started for school. He was lightly built, but clumsy. He went out of the yard with a curious spring in the hips, that made his loose homemade jacket tilt up in the rear.

The girl went to the sink and began to wash the dishes that were piled up there. Her mother came promptly out of the pantry and shoved her aside. "You wipe 'em," said she; "I'll wash. There's a good many this mornin'."

The mother plunged her hands vigorously into the water; the girl wiped the plates slowly and dreamily. "Mother," said she, "don't you think it's too bad Father's going to build that new barn, much as we need a decent house to live in?"

Her mother scrubbed a dish fiercely. "You ain't found out yet we're womenfolks, Nanny Penn," said she. "You ain't seen enough of menfolks yet to. One of these days you'll find it out, an' then you'll know that we know only what menfolks think we do, so far as any use of it goes, an' how we'd ought to reckon menfolks in with Providence an' not complain of what they do any more than we do of the weather."

"I don't care; I don't believe George is anything like that, anyhow," said Nanny. Her delicate face flushed pink, her lips pouted softly, as if she were going to cry.

"You wait an' see. I guess George Eastman ain't no better than other men. You hadn't ought to judge Father, though. He can't help it, 'cause he don't look at things jest the way we do. An' we've been pretty comfortable here, after all. The roof don't leak—ain't never but once—that's one thing. Father's kept it shingled right up."

"I do wish we had a parlor."

"I guess it won't hurt George Eastman any to come to see you in a nice clean kitchen. I guess a good many girls don't have as good a place as this. Nobody's ever heard me complain."

"I ain't complained either, Mother."

"Well, I don't think you'd better, a good father an' a good home as you've got. S'pose your father made you go out an' work for your livin'? Lots of girls have to that ain't no stronger an' better able to than you be."

Sarah Penn washed the frying pan with a conclusive air. She scrubbed the outside of it as faithfully as the inside. She was a masterly keeper of her box of a house. Her one living room never seemed to have in it any of the dust which the friction of life with inanimate matter produces. She swept, and there seemed to be no dirt to go before the broom; she cleaned, and one could see no difference. She was like an artist so perfect that he has apparently no art. Today she got out a mixing bowl and a board and rolled some pies, and there was no more flour upon her than upon her daughter who was doing finer work. Nanny was to be married in the fall, and she was sewing on some white cambric* and embroidery. She sewed industriously while her mother cooked; her soft milk-white hands and wrists showed whiter than her delicate work.

---

cambric: white linen or cotton fabric

"We must have the stove moved out in the shed before long," said Mrs. Penn. "Talk about not havin' things, it's been a real blessin' to be able to put a stove up in that shed in hot weather. Father did one good thing when he fixed that stovepipe out there."

Sarah Penn's face as she rolled her pies had that expression of meek vigor which might have characterized one of the New Testament saints. She was making mince pies. Her husband, Adoniram Penn, liked them better than any other kind. She baked twice a week. Adoniram often liked a piece of pie between meals. She hurried this morning. It had been later than usual when she began, and she wanted to have a pie baked for dinner. However deep a resentment she might be forced to hold against her husband, she would never fail in sedulous* attention to his wants.

---

sedulous: diligent

Nobility of character manifests itself at loopholes when it is not provided with large doors. Sarah Penn's showed itself today in flaky dishes of pastry. So she made the pies faithfully, while across the table she could see, when she glanced up from her work, the sight that rankled in her patient and steadfast soul—the digging of the cellar of the new barn in the place where Adoniram forty years ago had promised her their new house should stand.

The pies were done for dinner. Adoniram and Sammy were home a few minutes after twelve o'clock. The dinner was eaten with serious haste. There was never much conversation at the table in the Penn family. Adoniram asked a blessing, and they ate promptly, then rose up and went about their work.

Sammy went back to school, taking soft sly lopes out of the yard like a rabbit. He wanted a game of marbles before school and feared his father would give him some chores to do. Adoniram hastened to the door and called after him, but he was out of sight.

"I don't see what you let him go for, Mother," said he. "I wanted him to help me unload that wood."

Adoniram went to work out in the yard unloading wood from the wagon. Sarah put away the dinner dishes, while Nanny took down her curl papers and changed her dress. She was going down to the store to buy some more embroidery and thread.

When Nanny was gone, Mrs. Penn went to the door. "Father!" she called.

"Well, what is it!"

"I want to see you jest a minute, Father."

"I can't leave this wood nohow. I've got to git it unloaded an' go for a load of gravel afore two o'clock. Sammy had ought to helped me. You hadn't ought to let him go to school so early."

"I want to see you jest a minute."

"I tell ye I can't, nohow, Mother."

"Father, you come here." Sarah Penn stood in the door like a queen; she held her head as if it bore a crown; there was that patience which makes authority royal in her voice. Adoniram went.

Mrs. Penn led the way into the kitchen and pointed to a chair. "Sit down, Father," said she; "I've got somethin' I want to say to you."

He sat down heavily; his face was quite stolid, but he looked at her with restive* eyes. "Well ,what is it, Mother?"

---

restive: nervous or restless

"I want to know what you're buildin' that new barn for, Father?"

"I ain't got nothin' to say about it."

"It can't be you think you need another barn?"

"I tell ye I ain't got nothin' to say about it, Mother; an' I ain't goin' to say nothin'."

"Be you goin' to buy more cows?"

Adoniram did not reply; he shut his mouth tight.

"I know you be, as well as I want to. Now,

Father, look here"—Sarah Penn had not sat down; she stood before her husband in the humble fashion of a Scripture woman—"I'm goin' to talk real plain to you; I never have sence I married you, but I'm goin' to now. I ain't never complained, an' I ain't goin' to complain now, but I'm goin' to talk plain. You see this room here, Father; you look at it well. You see there ain't no carpet on the floor, an' you see the paper is all dirty an' droppin' off the walls. We ain't had no new paper on it for ten year, an' then I put it on myself, an' it didn't cost but ninepence a roll. You see this room, Father; it's all the one I've had to work in an' eat in an' sit in sence we was married. There ain't another woman in the whole town whose husband ain't got half the means you have but what's got better. It's all the room Nanny's got to have her company in; an' there ain't one of her mates but what's got better, an' their fathers not so able as hers is. It's all the room she'll have to be married in. What would you have thought, Father, if we had had our weddin' in a room no better than this? I was married in my mother's parlor, with a carpet on the floor, an' stuffed furniture,

an' a mahogany card table. An' this is all the room my daughter will have to be married in. Look here, Father!"

Sarah Penn went across the room as though it were a tragic stage. She flung open a door and disclosed a tiny bedroom, only large enough for a bed and bureau, with a path between. "There, Father," said she— "there's all the room I've had to sleep in forty year. All my children were born there—the two that died, an' the two that's livin'. I was sick with a fever there."

She stepped to another door and opened it. It led into the small, ill-lighted pantry. "Here," said she, "is all the buttery I've got—every place I've got for my dishes, to set away my victuals in, an' to keep my milk pans in. Father, I've been takin' care of the milk of six cows in this place, an' now you're going to build a new barn, an' keep more cows, an' give me more to do in it."

She threw open another door. A narrow crooked flight of stairs wound upward from it. "There, Father," said she, "I want you to look at the stairs that go up to them two unfinished chambers that are all the places our son an' daughter have had to sleep in all their lives. There ain't a prettier girl in town nor a more ladylike one than Nanny, an' that's the place she has to sleep in. It ain't so good as your horse's stall; it ain't so warm an' tight."

Sarah Penn went back and stood before her husband. "Now, Father," said she, "I want to know if you think you're doin' right an' accordin' to what you profess. Here, when we was married, forty year ago, you promised me faithful that we should have a new house built in that lot over in the field before the year was out. You said you had money enough, an' you wouldn't ask me to live in no such place as this. It is forty year now, an' you've been makin' more money, an' I've been savin' of it for you ever sence, an' you ain't built no house yet. You've built sheds an' cow houses an' one new barn an' now you're goin' to build another. Father, I want to know if you think it's right. You're lodgin' your dumb beasts better than you are your own flesh an' blood. I want to know if you think it's right."

"I ain't got nothin' to say."

"You can't say nothin' without ownin' it ain't right, Father. An' there's another thing—I ain't complained; I've got along forty year, an' I s'pose I should forty more, if it wa'n't for that—if we don't have another house. Nanny she can't live with us after she's married. She'll have to go somewheres else to live away from us, an' it don't seem as if I could have it so, noways, Father. She wa'n't ever strong. She's got considerable color, but there wa'n't never any backbone to her. I've always took the heft of everything off her, an' she ain't fit to keep house an' do everything herself. She'll be all worn out inside of a year. Think of her doin' all the washin' an' ironin' an' bakin' with them soft white hands an' arms, an' sweepin'! I can't have it so noways, Father."

Mrs. Penn's face was burning; her mild eyes gleamed. She had pleaded her little cause like a Webster;* she had ranged from severity to pathos;* but her opponent employed that obstinate silence which makes eloquence futile with mocking echoes. Adoniram arose clumsily.

[Daniel] Webster: famous American speaker (1782-1852)
pathos: a quality which arouses feelings of sympathy, pity, or sorrow

---

"Father, ain't you got nothin' to say?" said Mrs. Penn.

"I've got to go off after that load of gravel. I can't stan' here talkin' all day."

"Father, won't you think it over an' have a house built there instead of a barn?"

"I ain't got nothin to say."

Adoniram shuffled out. Mrs. Penn went into her bedroom. When she came out, her eyes were red. She had a roll of unbleached cotton cloth. She spread it out on the kitchen table and began cutting out some shirts for her husband. The men over in the field had a team to help them this afternoon; she could hear their halloos. She had a scanty pattern for the shirts; she had to plan and piece the sleeves.

Nanny came home with her embroidery and sat down with her needlework. She had taken down her curl papers and there was a soft roll of fair hair like an aureole* over her forehead; her face was as delicately fine and clear as porcelain. Suddenly she looked up, and the tender red flamed all over her face and neck. "Mother," said she.

---

aureole: halo

"What say?"

"I've been thinking—I don't see how we're goin' to have any—wedding in this room. I'd be ashamed to have his folks come if we didn't have anybody else."

"Mebbe we can have some new paper before then; I can put it on. I guess you won't have no call to be ashamed of your belongin's."

"We might have the wedding in the new barn," said Nanny, with gentle pettishness. "Why, Mother, what makes you look so?"

Mrs. Penn had started, and was staring at her with a curious expression. She turned again to her work and spread out a pattern carefully on the cloth. "Nothin,' " said she.

Presently Adoniram clattered out of the yard in his two-wheeled dump cart, standing as proudly upright as a Roman charioteer. Mrs. Penn opened the door and stood there a minute looking out; the halloos of the men sounded louder.

It seemed to her all through the spring months that she heard nothing but the halloos and the noises of saws and hammers. The new barn grew fast. It was a fine edifice for this little village. Men came on pleasant Sundays, in their meeting suits and clean shirt bosoms, and stood around it admiringly. Mrs. Penn did not speak of it, and Adoniram did not mention it to her, although sometimes, upon a return from inspecting it, he bore himself with injured dignity.

"It's a strange thing how your mother feels about the new barn," he said, confidentially, to Sammy one day.

Sammy only grunted after an odd fashion for a boy; he had learned it from his father.

The barn was all completed ready for use by the third week in July. Adoniram had planned to move his stock in on Wednesday; on Tuesday he received a letter which changed his plans. He came in with it early in the morning. "Sammy's been to the post office," said he, "an' I've got a letter from Hiram." Hiram was Mrs. Penn's brother, who lived in Vermont.

"Well," said Mrs. Penn, "what does he say about the folks?"

"I guess they're all right. He says he thinks if I come up country right off there's a chance to buy jest the kind of a horse I want." He stared reflectively out of the window at the new barn.

Mrs. Penn was making pies. She went on clapping the rolling pin into the crust, although she was very pale, and her heart beat loudly.

"I dun' know but what I'd better go," said Adoniram. "I hate to go off jest now, right in the midst of hayin', but the ten-acre lot's cut, an' I guess Rufus an' the others can git along without me three or four days. I can't get a horse round here to suit me, nohow, an' I've got to have another for all that wood haulin' in the fall. I told Hiram to watch out, an' if he got wind of a good horse to let me know. I guess I'd better go."

"I'll get out your clean shirt an' collar," said Mrs. Penn calmly.

She laid out Adoniram's Sunday suit and his clean clothes on the bed in the little bedroom. She got his shaving water and razor ready. At last she buttoned on his collar and fastened his black cravat.*

---

cravat: fabric scarf worn as a tie

Adoniram never wore his collar and cravat except on extra occasions. He held his head high, with a rasped dignity. When he was all ready, with his coat and hat brushed, and a lunch of pie and cheese in a paper bag, he hesitated on the threshold of the door. He looked at his wife, and his manner was defiantly apologetic, "If them cows come today, Sammy can drive 'em into the new barn," said he; "an when they bring the hay up, they can pitch it in there."

"Well," replied Mrs. Penn.

Adoniram set his shaven face ahead and started. When he had cleared the doorstep, he turned and looked back with a kind of nervous solemnity. "I shall be back by Saturday if nothin' happens," said he.

"Do be careful, Father," replied his wife.

She stood in the door with Nanny at her elbow and watched him out of sight. Her eyes had a strange, doubtful expression in them; her peaceful forehead was contracted. She went in and about her baking again. Nanny sat sewing. Her wedding day was drawing nearer, and she was getting pale and thin with her steady sewing. Her mother kept glancing at her.

"Have you got that pain in your side this mornin'?" she asked.

"A little."

Mrs. Penn's face, as she worked, changed, her perplexed forehead smoothed, her eyes were steady, her lips firmly set. She formed a maxim for herself, although incoherently with her unlettered thoughts. "Unsolicited opportunities are the guideposts of the Lord to the new roads of life," she repeated in effect, and she made up her mind to her course of action.

"S'posin' I *had* wrote to Hiram," she muttered once, when she was in the pantry— "s'posin' I had wrote an' asked him if he knew of any horse? But I didn't an' Father's goin' wa'n't none of my doin'. It looks like a providence."* Her voice rang out quite loud at the last.

---

providence: foreordained circumstance

"What you talkin' about, Mother?" called Nanny.

"Nothin'."

Mrs. Penn hurried her baking; at eleven o'clock it was all done. The load of hay from the west field came slowly down the cart track and drew up at the new barn. Mrs. Penn ran out. "Stop!" she screamed—"stop!"

The men stopped and looked; Sammy upreared from the top of the load and stared at his mother.

"Stop!" she cried out again. "Don't you put the hay in that barn; put it in the old one."

"Why, he said to put it in here," returned one of the haymakers, wonderingly. He was a young man, a neighbor's son, whom Adoniram hired by the year to help on the farm.

"Don't you put the hay in the new barn; there's room enough in the old one, ain't there?" said Mrs. Penn.

"Room enough," returned the hired man, in his thick, rustic tones. "Didn't need the new barn, nohow, far as room's concerned. Well, I s'pose he changed his mind." He took hold of the horses' bridles.

Mrs. Penn went back to the house. Soon the kitchen windows were darkened, and a fragrance like warm honey came into the room.

Nanny laid down her work. "I thought father wanted them to put the hay into the new barn?" she said wonderingly.

"It's all right," replied her mother.

Sammy slid down from the load of hay and came in to see if dinner was ready.

"I ain't goin' to get a regular dinner today, as long as Father's gone," said his mother. "I've let the fire go out. You can have some bread an' milk an 'pie. I thought we could get along." She set out some bowls of milk, some bread, and a pie on the kitchen table. "You better eat your dinner now," said she. "You might jest as well get through with it. I want you to help me afterward."

Nanny and Sammy stared at each other. There was something strange in their mother's manner. Mrs. Penn did not eat anything herself. She went into the pantry, and they heard her moving dishes while they ate. Presently she came out with a pile of plates. She got the clothes basket out of the shed and packed them in it. Nanny and Sammy watched. She brought out cups and saucers and put them in with the plates.

"What you goin' to do, Mother?" inquired Nanny, in a timid voice. A sense of something unusual made her tremble, as if it were a ghost. Sammy rolled his eyes over his pie.

"You'll see what I'm goin' to do," replied Mrs. Penn. "If you're through, Nanny, I want you to go upstairs an' pack up your things; an' I want you, Sammy, to help me take down the bed in the bedroom."

"Oh, Mother, what for?" gasped Nanny.

"You'll see."

During the next few hours a feat was performed by the simple, pious New England mother which was equal in its way to Wolfe's storming of the Heights of Abraham.* It took no more genius and audacity of bravery for Wolfe to cheer his wondering soldiers up those steep precipices, under the sleeping eyes of the enemy, than for Sarah Penn, at the head of her children, to move all their little household goods into the new barn while her husband was away.

Heights of Abraham: plain situated on top of some steep cliffs near the city of Quebec; the site where the English general Wolfe defeated the French general Montcalm in 1759

Nanny and Sammy followed their mother's instructions without a murmur; indeed, they were overawed. There is a certain uncanny and superhuman quality about all such purely original undertakings as their mother's was to them. Nanny went back and forth with her light loads, and Sammy tugged with sober energy.

At five o'clock in the afternoon the little house in which the Penns had lived for forty years had emptied itself into the new barn.

Every builder builds somewhat for unknown purposes and is in a measure a prophet. The architect of Adoniram Penn's barn, while he designed it for the comfort of four-footed animals, had planned better than he knew for the comfort of humans. Sarah Penn saw at a glance its possibilities. Those great box stalls, with quilts hung before them, would make better bedrooms than the one she had occupied for forty years, and there was a tight carriage room. The harness room, with its chimney and shelves, would make a kitchen of her dreams. The great middle space would make a parlor, by and by, fit for a palace. Upstairs there was as much room as down. With partitions and windows, what a house would there be! Sarah looked at the row of stanchions* before the allotted space for the cows and reflected that she would have her front entry there.

---

stanchions: vertical posts

At six o'clock the stove was up in the harness room, the kettle was boiling, and the table was set for tea. It looked almost as homelike as the abandoned house across the yard had ever done. The young hired man milked, and Sarah directed him calmly to bring the milk to the new barn. He came gaping, dropping little blots of foam from the brimming pails on the grass. Before the next morning he had spread the story of Adoniram Penn's wife moving into the new barn all over the little village. Men assembled in the store and talked it over, women with shawls over their heads scuttled into each other's houses before their work was done. Any deviation from the ordinary course of life in this quiet town was enough to stop all progress in it. Everybody paused to look at the staid, independent figure on the side track. There was a difference of opinion with regard to her. Some held her to be insane; some, of a lawless and rebellious spirit.

Friday the minister went to see her. It was in the forenoon, and she was at the barn door shelling peas for dinner. She looked up and returned his salutation with dignity, then she went on with her work. She did not invite him in. The saintly expression of her face remained fixed, but there was an angry flush over it.

The minister stood awkwardly before her and talked. She handled the peas as if they were bullets. At last she looked up, and her eyes showed the spirit that her meek front had covered for a lifetime.

"There ain't no use talkin', Mr. Hersey," said she. "I've thought it all over, an' I believe I'm doin' what's right. I've made it the subject of prayer, an' it's betwixt me an' the Lord an' Adoniram. There ain't no call for nobody else to worry about it."

"Well, of course, if you have brought it to the Lord in prayer and feel satisfied that you are doing right, Mrs. Penn," said the minister, helplessly.

"I think it's right jest as much as I think it was right for our forefathers to come over from the old country 'cause they didn't have what belonged to 'em," said Mrs. Penn. She arose. The barn threshold might have been Plymouth Rock from her bearing. "I don't doubt you mean well, Mr. Hersey," said she. "but there are things people hadn't ought to interfere with. I've been a member of the church for over forty years. I've got my own mind an' my own feet, an' I'm goin' to think my own thoughts an' go my own ways, an' nobody but the Lord is goin' to dictate to me unless I've a mind to have him. Won't you come in an' set down? How is Mis' Hersey?"

"She is well, I thank you," replied the minister. He added some more perplexed apologetic remarks; then he retreated.

He could expound the intricacies of every character study in the Scriptures, he was competent to grasp the Pilgrim Fathers and all historical innovators, but Sarah Penn was beyond him. He could deal with primal cases, but parallel ones worsted him. But, after all, although it was aside from his province, he wondered more how Adoniram Penn would deal with his wife than how the Lord would. Everybody shared the wonder. When Adoniram's four new cows arrived, Sarah ordered three to be put in the old barn, the other in the house shed where the cooking stove had stood. That added to the excitement. It was whispered that all four cows were domiciled in the house.

Toward sunset on Saturday, when Adoniram was expected home, there was a knot of men in the road near the new barn. The hired man had milked, but he still hung around the premises. Sarah Penn had supper all ready. There were brown bread and baked beans and a custard pie; it was the supper that Adoniram loved on a Saturday night. She had on a clean calico, and she bore herself imperturbably.* Nanny and Sammy kept close at her heels. Their eyes were large, and Nanny was full of nervous tremors. Still there was to them more pleasant excitement than anything else. An inborn confidence in their mother over their father asserted itself.

imperturbably: unshakably calmly

Sammy looked out of the harness-room window. "There he is," he announced, in an awed whisper. He and Nanny peeped around the casing. Mrs. Penn kept on about her work. The children watched Adoniram leave the new horse standing in the drive while he went to the house door. It was fastened. Then he went around to the shed. That door was seldom locked, even when the family was away. The thought how her father would be confronted by the cow flashed upon Nanny. There was a hysterical sob in her throat. Adoniram emerged from the shed and stood looking about in a dazed fashion. His lips moved. He was saying something, but they could not hear what it was. The hired man was peeping around a corner of the old barn, but nobody saw him.

Adoniram took the new horse by the bridle and led him across the yard to the new barn. Nanny and Sammy slunk close to their mother.

The barn doors rolled back, and there stood Adoniram, with the long mild face of the great Canadian farm horse looking over his shoulder.

Nanny kept behind her mother, but Sammy stepped suddenly forward and stood in front of her.

Adoniram stared at the group. "What on airth you all down here for?" said he. "What's the matter over to the house?"

"We've come here to live, Father," said Sammy. His shrill voice quavered out bravely.

"What"—Adoniram sniffed—"what is it smells like cookin'?" said he. He stepped forward and looked in the open door of the harness room. Then he turned to his wife. His old bristling face was pale and frightened. "What on airth does this mean, Mother?" he gasped.

"You come in here, Father," said Sarah. She led the way into the harness room and shut the door. "Now, Father," said she, "you needn't be scared. I ain't crazy. There ain't

nothin' to be upset over. But we've come here to live, an' we're goin' to live here. We've got jest as good a right here as new horses an' cows. The house wa'n't fit for us to live in any longer, an' I made up my mind I wa'n't goin' to stay there. I've done my duty by you forty year, an' I'm goin' to do it now; but I'm goin' to live here. You've got to put in some windows and partitions; an' you'll have to buy some furniture."

"Why, Mother!" the old man gasped.

"You'd better take your coat off an' get washed—there's the washbasin—and then we'll have supper."

"Why, Mother!"

Sammy went past the window, leading the new horse to the old barn. The old man saw him and shook his head speechlessly. He tried to take off his coat, but his arms seemed to lack the power. His wife helped him. She poured some water into the tin basin and put in a piece of soap. She got the comb and brush

and smoothed his thin gray hair after he had washed. Then she put the beans, hot bread, and tea on the table. Sammy came in, and the family drew up. Adoniram sat looking dazedly at his plate, and they waited.

"Ain't you goin' to ask a blessin', Father?" said Sarah. And the old man bent his head and mumbled.

All through the meal he stopped eating at intervals and stared furtively at his wife, but he ate well. The home food tasted good to him, and his old frame was too sturdily healthy to be affected by his mind. But after supper he went out and sat down on the step of the smaller door at the right of the barn, through which he had meant his Jerseys to pass in stately file, but which Sarah designed for her front house door, and he leaned his head on his hands.

After the supper dishes were cleared away and the milk pans washed, Sarah went out to him. The twilight was deepening. There was a clear green glow in the sky. Before them stretched the smooth level of field; in the distance was a cluster of haystacks like the huts of a village; the air was very cool and calm and sweet. The landscape might have been an ideal one of peace.

Sarah bent over and touched her husband on one of his thin, sinewy shoulders. "Father!"

The old man's shoulder heaved; he was weeping.

"Why, don't do so, Father," said Sarah.

"I'll—put up the—partitions, an'—everything you—want, Mother."

Sarah put her apron up to her face; she was overcome by her own triumph.

Adoniram was like a fortress whose walls had no active resistance and went down the instant the right besieging tools were used. "Why, Mother," he said, hoarsely, "I hadn't no idee you was so set on't as all this comes to."

About the Story

1. Who are the primary characters?
2. Who are the secondary characters?
3. Explain why the main characters are considered round, dynamic characters.
4. What does the author mean when she says, "Nobility of character manifests itself at loopholes when it is not provided with large doors"?
5. How does Sarah Penn get the idea of moving into the barn?
6. How does the community react to Mrs. Penn's revolt?
7. How do Mr. and Mrs. Penn change in the story?
8. Mr. and Mrs. Penn have various character traits: some the same and some different. Put the trait under the proper character. Be prepared to give an example of the trait from the story.

Hard working
Thrifty
Patient   Mr. Penn
Stubborn
Respectful
Strong-willed
Unfaithful in   Mrs. Penn
    promises
Selfish

9. Peter tells us, "Yea, all of you be subject one to another, and be clothed with humility" (I Peter 5:5). In what ways do Mr. and Mrs. Penn fail to apply this principle in the story. In what ways do they succeed?
10. What different method(s) might have been used to evoke the same resolution to the story?

About the Author

Mary E. Wilkins Freeman (1852-1930) was born in Massachusetts and lived her whole life in New England. Her work reflects her intimate knowledge of the countryside and the people of that region. Her greatest talent was not in constructing plots but in creating characters. In her smooth prose style, Freeman often presented eccentric and stubborn folk. She could portray with gentle humor the peculiarities of her New England characters while offering tempered insights into their hearts and minds.

Many of Freeman's characters resemble her, in that they bear quietly a great deal of heartache. By the time she was thirty-one, Freeman's immediate family had all died. After these losses, she lived with a childhood friend for many years, writing stories to help support herself and her aunt. Although she had been too sickly as a child to attend school regularly, she had read and learned to appreciate good literature. Surprisingly, she was unfamiliar with much well-known literature, even the work of writers such as Sara Orne Jewett, another New England-genre writer whose style resembles Freeman's.

Although she was eventually married at fifty, the marriage was an unhappy one, for her husband drank heavily, and she struggled with a serious hearing loss. She wrote little after her marriage, but among her life's accomplishments are her long employment as secretary to Oliver Wendell Holmes, and her acquisition of several literary awards, one of which placed her among the first four women in the National Institute of Arts and Letters. Despite her hardships, Freeman remained pleasant and good-natured.

Though many of Freeman's characters are as stubborn as Mrs. Penn in "The Revolt of Mother," they do not usually resolve their conflicts as concretely as Mrs. Penn does. Instead, they either do not recognize or choose to ignore possible solutions to their problems. Sarah Penn, however, has the capacity to feel deeply the disappointment of dashed hopes without giving up on life. Of these characters it has been said that they are "overworked, underfed, poorly clad, . . . [but they] have no touch of squalor; life is to them always significant. It is the moral element in their nature, their adherence to the 'painful right' that gives them the dignity which at times approaches grandeur."

Neighbour Rosicky

Willa Cather

Like "The Revolt of Mother," this story is about a hard-working, close-knit farm family. Unlike the last story, however, the father in "Neighbour Rosicky" not only perceives his family's needs, he also delights in meeting those needs. Rosicky is an immigrant from Czechoslovakia who has learned through hardship what is important in life and what is not. His actions clearly reflect his values. Although Rosicky's character does not change in the story, he evokes change in other characters. Pay close attention to what Rosicky says, what others say about him, and what he does. What does this information reveal about his character? What are some qualities in Rosicky's character that make his influence on others believable?

I

When Doctor Burleigh told neighbour Rosicky he had a bad heart, Rosicky protested.

"So? No, I guess my heart was always pretty good. I got a little asthma, maybe. Just a awful short breath when I was pitchin' hay last summer, dat's all."

"Well now, Rosicky, if you know more about it than I do, what did you come to me for? It's your heart that makes you short of breath, I tell you. You're sixty-five years old, and you've always worked hard, and your heart's tired. You've got to be careful from now on, and you can't do heavy work any more. You've got five boys at home to do it for you."

The old farmer looked up at the Doctor with a gleam of amusement in his queer triangular-shaped eyes. His eyes were large and lively, but the lids were caught up in the middle in a curious way, so that they formed a triangle. He did not look like a sick man. His brown face was creased but not wrinkled; he had a ruddy colour in his smooth-shaven cheeks and in his lips, under his long brown moustache. His hair was thin and ragged around his ears, but very little gray. His forehead, naturally high and crossed by deep parallel lines, now ran all the way up to his pointed crown. Rosicky's face had the habit of looking interested—suggested a contented disposition and a reflective quality that was gay rather than grave. This gave him a certain detachment, the easy manner of an onlooker and observer.

"Well, I guess you ain't got no pills for a bad heart, Doctor Ed. I guess the only thing is fur me to git me a new one."

Doctor Burleigh swung round in his desk chair and frowned at the old farmer. "I think if I were you I'd take a little care of the old one, Rosicky."

Rosicky shrugged. "Maybe I don't know how. I expect you mean fur me not to drink my coffee no more."

"I wouldn't, in your place. But you'll do as you choose about that. I've never yet been able to separate a Bohemian from his coffee or his pipe. I've quit trying. But the sure thing is you've got to cut out farm work. You can feed the stock and do chores about the barn, but you can't do anything in the fields that makes you short of breath."

"How about shelling corn?"

"Of course not!"

Rosicky considered with puckered brows.

"I can't make my heart go no longer'n it

wants to, can I, Doctor Ed?"

"I think it's good for five or six years yet, maybe more, if you'll take the strain off it. Sit around the house and help Mary. If I had a good wife like yours, I'd want to stay around the house."

His patient chuckled. "It ain't no place fur a man. I don't like no old man hanging round the kitchen too much. An' my wife, she's a awful hard worker her own self."

"That's it; you can help her a little. Rosicky, you are one of the few men I know who has a family he can get some comfort out of; happy dispositions, never quarrel among themselves, and they treat you right. I want to see you live a few years and enjoy them."

"Oh, they're good kids, all right," Rosicky assented.

The Doctor wrote him a prescription and asked him how his oldest son, Rudolph, who had married in the spring, was getting on. Rudolph had struck out for himself, on rented land. "And how's Polly? I was afraid Mary mightn't like an American daughter-in-law, but it seems to be working out all right."

"Yes, she's a fine girl. Dat widder woman bring her daughters up very nice. Polly got lots of spunk, an' she got some style, too. Da's nice, for young folks to have some style." Rosicky inclined his head gallantly. His voice and his twinkly smile were an affectionate compliment to his daughter-in-law.

"It looks like a storm, and you'd better be getting home before it comes. In town in the car?" Doctor Burleigh rose.

"No, I'm in de wagon. When you got five boys, you ain't got much chance to ride round in de Ford. I ain't much for cars, noway."

"Well, it's a good road out to your place; but I don't want you bumping around in a wagon much. And never again on a hay-rake, remember!"

Rosicky placed the Doctor's fee delicately

behind the desk-telephone, looking the other way, as if this were an absent-minded gesture. He put on his plush cap and his corduroy jacket with a sheepskin collar, and went out.

The Doctor picked up his stethoscope and frowned at it as if he were seriously annoyed with the instrument. He wished it had been telling tales about some other man's heart, some old man who didn't look the Doctor in the eye so knowingly, or hold out such a warm brown hand when he said good-bye. Doctor Burleigh had been a poor boy in the country before he went away to medical school; he had known Rosicky almost ever since he could remember, and he had a deep affection for Mrs. Rosicky.

Only last winter he had had such a good breakfast at Rosicky's, and that when he needed it. He had been out all night on a long, hard confinement case at Tom Marshall's—a big rich farm where there was plenty of stock and plenty of feed and a great deal of expensive farm machinery of the newest model, and no comfort whatever. The woman had too many children and too much work, and she was no manager. When the baby was born at last, and handed over to the assisting neighbour woman, and the mother was properly attended to, Burleigh refused any breakfast in that slovenly house, and drove his buggy—the snow was too deep for a car—eight miles to Anton Rosicky's place. He didn't know another farmhouse where a man could get such a warm welcome, and such good strong coffee with rich cream. No wonder the old chap didn't want to give up his coffee!

He had driven in just when the boys had come back from the barn and were washing up for breakfast. The long table, covered with a bright oilcloth,* was set out with dishes waiting for them, and the warm kitchen was full of the smell of coffee and hot biscuits and sausage. Five big handsome boys, running from twenty to twelve, all with what Burleigh called natural good manners—they hadn't a bit of the painful self-consciousness he himself had to struggle with when he was a lad. One ran to put his horse away, another helped him off with his fur coat and hung it up, and Josephine, the youngest child and the only daughter, quickly set another place under her mother's direction.

oilcloth: a material treated with clay, oil, and pigments to make the material waterproof

With Mary, to feed creatures was the natural expression of affection—her chickens, the calves, her big hungry boys. It was a rare pleasure to feed a young man whom she seldom saw and of whom she was as proud as if he belonged to her. Some country housekeepers would have stopped to spread a white cloth over the oilcloth, to change the thick cups and plates for their best china, and the wooden-handled knives for plate ones. But not Mary.

"You must take us as you find us, Doctor Ed. I'd be glad to put out my good things for you if you was expected, but I'm glad to get you any way at all."

He knew she was glad—she threw back her head and spoke out as if she were announcing him to the whole prairie. Rosicky hadn't said anything at all; he merely smiled his twinkling smile and put some more coal on the fire. When they were all seated, he watched his wife's face from his end of the table and spoke to her in Czech. Then, with the instinct of politeness which seldom failed him, he turned to the Doctor and said slyly: "I was just tellin' her not to ask you no questions about Mrs. Marshall till you eat some breakfast. My wife, she's terrible fur to ask questions."

The boys laughed, and so did Mary. She watched the Doctor devour her biscuit and sausage, too much excited to eat anything herself. She drank her coffee and sat taking in everything about her visitor. She had known him when he was a poor country boy, and was boastfully proud of his success, always saying: "What do people go to Omaha for, to see a doctor, when we got the best one in the State right here?" If Mary liked people at all, she felt physical pleasure in the sight of them, personal exultation in any good fortune that came to them. Burleigh didn't know many women like that, but he knew she was like that.

When his hunger was satisfied, he did, of course, have to tell them about Mrs. Marshall, and he noticed what a friendly interest the boys took in the matter.

Rudolph, the oldest one (he was still living at home then), said: "The last time I was over there, she was lifting them big heavy milkcans, and I knew she oughtn't to be doing it."

"Yes, Rudolph told me about that when he come home, and I said it wasn't right," Mary put in warmly. "It was all right for me to do them things up to the last, for I was terrible strong, but that woman's weakly. And do you think she'll be able to nurse it, Ed?" She sometimes forgot to give him the title she was so proud of. "And to think of your being up all night and then not able to get a decent breakfast! I don't know what's the matter with such people."

"I wish I'd been in practice when these were getting born." The doctor looked down the row of close-clipped heads. "I missed some good breakfasts by not being."

The boys began to laugh at their mother because she flushed so red, but she stood her ground and threw up her head. "I don't care, you wouldn't have got away from this house without breakfast. No doctor ever did. I'd have had something ready fixed that Anton could warm up for you."

The boys laughed harder than ever, and

exclaimed at her: "I'll bet you would!" "She would, that!"

"Father, did you get breakfast for the doctor when we were born?"

"Yes, and he used to bring me my breakfast, too, mighty nice. I was always awful hungry!" Mary admitted with a guilty laugh.

While the boys were getting the Doctor's horse, he went to the window to examine the house plants. "What do you do to your geraniums to keep them blooming all winter, Mary? I never pass this house that from the road I don't see your windows full of flowers."

She snapped off a dark red one, and a ruffled new green leaf, and put them in his button hole. "There, that looks better. You look too solemn for a young man, Ed. Why don't you git married? I'm worried about you. Settin' at breakfast, I looked at you real hard, and I seen you've got some grey hairs already."

"Oh, yes! They're coming. Maybe they'd come faster if I married."

"Don't talk so. You'll ruin your health eating at the hotel. I could send your wife a nice loaf of nut bread, if you only had one. I don't like to see a young man getting grey. I'll tell you something, Ed; you make some strong black tea and keep it handy in a bowl, and every morning just brush it into your hair, an' it'll keep the grey from showin' much. That's the way I do!"

Sometimes the Doctor heard the gossipers in the drug-store wondering why Rosicky didn't get on faster. He was industrious, and so were his boys, but they were rather free and easy, weren't pushers, and they didn't always show good judgment. They were comfortable, they were out of debt, but they didn't get much ahead. Maybe, Doctor Burleigh reflected, people as generous and warm-hearted and affectionate as the Rosickys never got ahead much; maybe you couldn't enjoy your life and put it into the bank, too.

II

When Rosicky left Doctor Burleigh's office, he went into the farm-implement store to light his pipe and put on his glasses and read over the list Mary had given him. Then he went into the general merchandise place next door and stood about until the pretty girl with the plucked eyebrows, who always waited on him, was free. Those eyebrows, two thin India-ink strokes, amused him, because he remembered how they used to be. Rosicky always prolonged his shopping by a little joking; the girl knew the old fellow admired her, and she liked to chaff with him.

"Seems to me about every other week you buy ticking, Mr. Rosicky, and always the best quality," she remarked as she measured off the heavy bolt with red stripes.

"You see, my wife is always makin' goose-fedder pillows, an' de thin stuff don't hold in dem little down-fedders."

"You must have lots of pillows at your house."

"Sure. She makes quilts of dem, too. We sleeps easy. Now she's makin' a fedder quilt for my son's wife. You know Polly, that married my Rudolph. How much my bill, Miss Pearl?"

"Eight eighty-five."

"Chust make it nine, and put in some candy fur de women."

"As usual. I never did see a man buy so much candy for his wife. First thing you know, she'll be getting too fat."

"I'd like dat. I ain't much fur all dem slim women like what de style is now."

"That's one for me, I suppose, Mr. Bohunk!"* Pearl sniffed and elevated her India-ink strokes.

Bohunk: slang term for a laborer from east-central Europe

When Rosicky went out to his wagon, it was beginning to snow—the first snow of the season, and he was glad to see it. He rattled out of town and along the highway through a wonderfully rich stretch of country, the finest farms in the county. He admired this High Prairie, as it was called, and always liked to drive through it. His own place lay in a rougher territory, where there was some clay in the soil and it was not so productive. When he bought his land, he hadn't the money to buy on High Prairie; so he told his boys, when they grumbled, that if their land hadn't some clay in it, they wouldn't own it at all. All the same, he enjoyed looking at these fine farms, as he enjoyed looking at a prize bull.

After he had gone eight miles, he came to the graveyard, which lay just at the edge of his own hay-land. There he stopped his horses and sat still on his wagon seat, looking about at the snowfall. Over yonder on the hill he could see his own house, crouching low, with the clump of orchard behind and the windmill before, and all down the gentle hill-slope the rows of pale gold cornstalks stood out against the white field. The snow was falling over the cornfield and the pasture and the hay-land, steadily, with very little wind—a nice dry snow. The graveyard had only a light wire fence about it and was all overgrown with long red grass. The fine snow, settling into this red grass and upon the few little evergreens and the headstones, looked very pretty.

It was a nice graveyard, Rosicky reflected, sort of snug and homelike, not cramped or mournful—a big sweep all round it. A man could lie down in the long grass and see the complete arch of the sky over him, hear the wagons go by; in summer the mowing-machine rattled right up to the wire fence. And it was so near home. Over there across the cornstalks his own roof and windmill looked so good to him that he promised himself to mind the Doctor and take care of himself. He was awful

fond of his place, he admitted. He wasn't anxious to leave it. And it was a comfort to think that he would never have to go farther than the edge of his own hayfield. The snow, falling over his barnyard and the graveyard, seemed to draw things together like. And they were all old neighbours in the graveyard, most of them friends; there was nothing to feel awkward or embarrassed about. Embarrassment was the most disagreeable feeling Rosicky knew. He didn't often have it—only with certain people whom he didn't understand at all.

Well, it was a nice snowstorm; a fine sight to see the snow falling so quietly and graciously over so much open country. On his cap and shoulders, on the horses' backs and manes, light, delicate, mysterious it fell; and with it a dry cool fragrance was released into the air. It meant rest for vegetation and men and beasts, for the ground itself; a season of long nights for sleep, leisurely breakfasts, peace by the fire. This and much more went through Rosicky's mind, but he merely told himself that winter was coming, clucked to his horses, and drove on.

When he reached home, John, the youngest boy, ran out to put away his team for him, and he met Mary coming up from the outside cellar with her apron full of carrots. They went into the house together. On the table, covered with oilcloth figured with clusters of blue grapes, a place was set, and he smelled hot coffee-cake of some kind. Anton never lunched in town; he thought that extravagant, and anyhow he didn't like the food. So Mary always had something ready for him when he got home.

After he was settled in his chair, stirring his coffee in a big cup, Mary took out of the oven a pan of *kolache** stuffed with apricots, examined them anxiously to see whether they had got too dry, put them beside his plate, and then sat down opposite him.

kolache: a rich pastry with a fruit or poppyseed filling

Rosicky asked her in Czech if she wasn't going to have any coffee.

She replied in English, as being somehow the right language for transacting business: "Now what did Doctor Ed say, Anton? You tell me just what."

"He said I was to tell you some compliments, but I forgot 'em." Rosicky's eyes twinkled.

"About you, I mean. What did he say about your asthma?"

"He says I ain't got no asthma." Rosicky took one of the little rolls in his broad brown fingers. The thickened nail of his right thumb told the story of his past.

"Well, what is the matter? And don't try to put me off."

"He don't say nothing much, only I'm a little older, and my heart ain't so good like it used to be."

Mary started and brushed her hair back from her temples with both hands as if she were a little out of her mind. From the way she glared, she might have been in a rage with him.

"He says there's something the matter with your heart? Doctor Ed says so?"

"Now don't yell at me like I was a hog in de garden, Mary. You know I always did like to hear a woman talk soft. He didn't say anything de matter wid my heart, only it ain't so young like it used to be, an' he tell me not to pitch hay or run de corn-sheller."

Mary wanted to jump up, but she sat still. She admired the way he never under any circumstances raised his voice or spoke roughly. He was city-bred, and she was country-bred; she often said she wanted her boys to have their papa's nice ways.

"You never have no pain there, do you?

It's your breathing and your stomach that's been wrong. I wouldn't believe nobody but Doctor Ed about it. I guess I'll go see him myself. Didn't he give you no advice?"

"Chust to take it easy like, an' stay round de house dis winter. I guess you got some carpenter work for me to do. I kin make some new shelves for you, and I want dis long time to build a closet in de boys room and make dem two little fellers keep dere clo'es hung up."

Rosicky drank his coffee from time to time, while he considered. His moustache was of the soft long variety and came down over his mouth like the teeth of a buggy-rake over a bundle of hay. Each time he put down his cup, he ran his blue handkerchief over his lips. When he took a drink of water, he managed very neatly with the back of his hand.

Mary sat watching him intently, trying to find any change in his face. It is hard to see anyone who has become like your own body to you. Yes, his hair had got thin, and his high forehead had deep lines running from left to right. But his neck, always clean shaved except in the busiest seasons, was not loose or baggy. It was burned a dark reddish brown, and there were deep creases in it, but it looked firm and full of blood. His cheeks had a good colour. On either side of his mouth there was a half-moon down the length of his cheek, not wrinkles, but two lines that had come there from his habitual expression. He was shorter and broader than when she married him; his back had grown broad and curved, a good deal like the shell of an old turtle, and his arms and legs were short.

He was fifteen years older than Mary, but she had hardly ever thought about it before. He was her man, and the kind of man she liked. She was rough, and he was gentle—city-bred, as she always said. They had been shipmates on a rough voyage and had stood by each other in trying times. Life had gone

well with them because, at bottom, they had the same ideas about life. They agreed, without discussion, as to what was most important and what was secondary. They didn't often exchange opinions, even in Czech—it was as if they had thought the same thought together. A good deal had to be sacrificed and thrown overboard in a hard life like theirs, and they had never disagreed as to the things that could go. It had been a hard life, and a soft life, too. There wasn't anything brutal in the short, broad-backed man with the three-cornered eyes and the forehead that went on to the top of his skull. He was a city man, a gentle man, and though he had married a rough farm girl, he had never touched her without gentleness.

They had been at one accord not to hurry through life, not to be always skimping and saving. They saw their neighbours buy more land and feed more stock than they did, without discontent. Once when the creamery agent came to the Rosickys to persuade them to sell him their cream, he told them how much money the Fasslers, their nearest neighbours, had made on their cream last year.

"Yes," said Mary, "and look at them Fassler children! Pale, pinched little things, they look like skimmed milk. I'd rather put some colour into my children's faces than put money into the bank."

The agent shrugged and turned to Anton.

"I guess we'll do like she says," said Rosicky.

III

Mary very soon got into town to see Doctor Ed, and then she had a talk with her boys and set a guard over Rosicky. Even John, the youngest, had his father on his mind. If Rosicky went to throw hay down from the loft, one of the boys ran up the ladder and took the fork from him. He sometimes complained that though he was getting to be an old man, he wasn't an old woman yet.

That winter he stayed in the house in the afternoons and carpentered, or sat in the chair between the window full of plants and the wooden bench where the two pails of drinking-water stood. This spot was called "Father's corner," though it was not a corner at all. He had a shelf there, where he kept his Bohemian papers and his pipes and tobacco, and his shears and needles and thread and tailor's thimble. Having been a tailor in his youth, he couldn't bear to see a woman patching at his clothes, or at the boys'. He liked tailoring, and always patched all the overalls and jackets and work shirts. Occasionally he made over a pair of pants one of the older boys had outgrown, for the little fellow.

While he sewed, he let his mind run back over his life. He had a good deal to remember, really; life in three countries. The only part of his youth he didn't like to remember was the two years he had spent in London, in Cheapside, working for a German tailor who was wretchedly poor. Those days, when he was nearly always hungry when his clothes were dropping off him for dirt, and the sound of a strange language kept him in continual bewilderment, had left a sore spot in his mind that wouldn't bear touching.

He was twenty when he landed at Castle Garden in New York, and he had a protector who got him work in a tailor shop in Vesey Street, down near the Washington Market. He looked upon that part of his life as very happy. He became a good workman, he was industrious, and his wages were increased from time to time. He minded his own business and envied nobody's good fortune. He went to night school and learned to read English. He often did overtime work and was well paid for it, but somehow he never saved anything. He couldn't refuse a loan to a friend, and he was self-indulgent. He often stood through an opera on Saturday nights; he could get standing-room for a dollar. Those were the great days

of opera in New York, and it gave a fellow something to think about for the rest of the week. Rosicky had a quick ear, and a childish love of all the stage splendour; the scenery, the costumes, the ballet. It was a fine life; for the first five years or so it satisfied him completely. He was never hungry or cold or dirty, and everything amused him: a fire, a dog fight, a parade, a storm, a ferry ride. He thought New York the finest, richest, friendliest city in the world.

Moreover, he had what he called a happy home life. Very near the tailor shop was a small furniture-factory, where an old Austrian, Loeffler, employed a few skilled men and made unusual furniture, most of it to order, for the rich German housewives up-town. The top floor of Loeffler's five-storey factory was a loft, where he kept his choice lumber and stored the odd pieces of furniture left on his hands. One of the young workmen he employed was a Czech, and he and Rosicky became fast friends. They persuaded Loeffler to let them have a sleeping-room in one corner of the loft. They bought good beds and bedding and had their pick of the furniture kept up there. The loft was low-pitched, but light and airy, full of windows, and good-smelling by reason of the fine lumber put up there to season. Old Loeffler used to go down to the docks and buy wood from South America and the East from the sea captains. The young men were as foolish about their house as a bridal pair. Zichec, the young cabinet-maker, devised every sort of convenience, and Rosicky kept their clothes in order. At night and on Sundays, when the quiver of machinery underneath was still, it was the quietest place in the world, and on summer nights all the sea winds blew in. Zichec often practiced on his flute in the evening. They were both fond of music and went to the opera together. Rosicky thought he wanted to live like that for ever.

But as the years passed, all alike, he began to get a little restless. When spring came round, he would begin to feel fretted. He never had time to figure out what ailed him, though he knew something did. When the grass turned green in Park Place, and the lilac hedge at the back of Trinity churchyard put out its blossoms, he was tormented by a longing to run away.

Rosicky, the old Rosicky, could remember as if it were yesterday the day when the young Rosicky found out what was the matter with him. It was on a Fourth of July afternoon, and he was sitting in Park Place in the sun. The lower part of New York was empty. Wall Street, Liberty Street, Broadway, all empty. So much stone and asphalt with nothing going on, so many empty windows. The emptiness was intense, like the stillness in a great factory when the machinery stops and the belts and bands cease running. It was too great a change, it took all the strength out of one. Those blank buildings, without the stream of life pouring through them, were like empty jails. It struck young Rosicky that this was the trouble with big cities; they built you in from the earth itself, cemented you away from any contact with the ground. You lived in an unnatural world, like the fish in an aquarium, who were probably much more comfortable than they ever were in the sea.

On that very day he began to think seriously about the articles he had read in the Bohemian papers, describing prosperous Czech farming communities in the West. He believed he would like to go out there as a farm hand; it was hardly possible that he could ever have land of his own. His people had always been workmen; his father and grandfather had worked in shops. His mother's parents had lived in the country, but they rented their farm and had a hard time to get along. Nobody in his family had ever owned any land—that belonged to a different station of life altogether. Anton's mother died when he was little, and he was sent into the country to her parents. He stayed with them until he was twelve, and formed those ties with the earth and the farm animals and growing things which are never made at all unless they are made early. After his grandfather died, he went back to live with his father and stepmother, but she was very hard on him and his father helped him to get passage to London.

After that Fourth of July day in Park Place, the desire to return to the country never left him. To work on another man's farm would be all he asked; to see the sun rise and set and to plant things and watch them grow. He was a very simple man. He was like a tree that has not many roots, but one tap-root that goes down deep. He subscribed for a Bohemian paper printed in Chicago, then for one printed in Omaha. His mind got farther and farther west. He began to save a little money to buy his liberty. When he was thirty-five, there was a great meeting in New York of Bohemian athletic societies, and Rosicky left the tailor shop and went home with the Omaha delegates to try his fortune in another part of the world.

IV

Perhaps the fact that his own youth was well over before he began to have a family was one reason why Rosicky was so fond of his boys. He had almost a grandfather's indulgence for them. He had never had to worry about any of them—except, just now, a little about Rudolph.

On Saturday night the boys always piled into the Ford, took little Josephine, and went to town. One Saturday morning they were talking at the breakfast table about starting early that evening, so that they would have an hour or so to see the Christmas things in the stores. Rosicky looked down the table.

"I hope you boys ain't disappointed, but I want you to let me have de car tonight. Maybe some of you can go in with de neighbours."

Their faces fell. They worked hard all week, and they were still like children. A new jack-knife or a box of candy pleased the older ones as much as the little fellow.

"If you and Mother are going to town," Frank said, "maybe you could take a couple of us along with you, anyway."

"No, I want to take de car down to Rudolph's, and let him an' Polly go in. She don't git into town enough, an' I'm afraid she's gettin' lonesome, an' he can't afford no car yet."

That settled it. The boys were a good deal dashed. Their father took another piece of apple-cake and went on: "Maybe next Saturday night de two little fellers can go along wid dem."

"Oh, is Rudolph going to have the car every Saturday night?"

Rosicky did not reply at once; then he began to speak seriously: "Listen, boys; Polly ain't lookin' so good. I don't like to see nobody lookin' sad. It comes hard fur a town girl to be a farmer's wife. I don't want no trouble to start in Rudolph's family. When it starts, it ain't so easy to stop. An American girl don't git used to our ways all at once. I like to tell Polly she and Rudolph can have the car every Saturday night till after New Year's, if it's all right with you boys."

"Sure it's all right, Papa," Mary cut in. "And it's good you thought about that. Town girls is used to more than country girls. I lay awake nights, scared she'll make Rudolph discontented with the farm."

The boys put as good a face on it as they could. They surely looked forward to their Saturday nights in town. That evening Rosicky drove the car the half-mile down to Rudolph's

new, bare little house.

Polly was in a short-sleeved gingham dress, clearing away the supper dishes. She was a trim, slim little thing, with blue eyes and shingled yellow hair, and her eyebrows were reduced to a mere brush-stroke, like Miss Pearl's.

"Good evening, Mr. Rosicky. Rudolph's at the barn, I guess." She never called him father, or Mary mother. She was sensitive about having married a foreigner. She never in the world would have done it if Rudolph hadn't been such a handsome, persuasive fellow and such a gallant lover. He had graduated in her class in the high school in town, and their friendship began in the ninth grade.

Rosicky went in, though he wasn't exactly asked. "My boys ain't goin' to town tonight, an' I brought de car over fur you two to go."

Polly, carrying dishes to the sink, looked over her shoulder at him. "Thank you. But I'm late with my work tonight, and pretty tired.

Maybe Rudolph would like to go in with you."

"You won't feel so tired after you ride in de air a ways. It's a nice clear night, an' it ain't cold. You go an' fix yourself up, Polly, an' I'll wash de dishes an' leave everything nice fur you."

Polly blushed and tossed her bob. "I couldn't let you do that, Mr. Rosicky. I wouldn't think of it."

Rosicky said nothing. He found a bib apron on a nail behind the kitchen door. He slipped it over his head and then took Polly by her two elbows and pushed her gently toward the door of her own room. "I washed up de kitchen many times for my wife, when de babies was sick or somethin'. You go an' make yourself look nice. I like you to look prettier'n any of dem town girls when you go in. De young folks must have some fun, an' I'm goin' to look out fur you, Polly."

That kind, reassuring grip on her elbows, the old man's funny bright eyes, made Polly want to drop her head on his shoulder for a second. She restrained herself, but she lingered in his grasp at the door of her room, murmuring tearfully: "You always lived in the city when you were young, didn't you? Don't you ever get lonesome out here?"

As she turned round to him, her hand fell naturally into his, and he stood holding it and smiling into her face with his peculiar, knowing, indulgent smile without a shadow of reproach in it. "Dem big cities is all right fur de rich, but dey is terrible hard fur de poor."

"I don't know. Sometimes I think I'd like to take a chance. You lived in New York, didn't you?"

"An' London. Da's bigger still. I learned my trade dere. Here's Rudolph comin', you better hurry."

"Will you tell me about London sometime?"

"Maybe. Only I ain't no talker, Polly. Run an' dress yourself up."

The bedroom door closed behind her, and Rudolph came in from the outside, looking anxious. He had seen the car and was sorry any of his family should come just then. Supper hadn't been a very pleasant occasion. Halting in the doorway, he saw his father in a kitchen apron, carrying dishes to the sink. He flushed crimson and something flashed in his eye. Rosicky held up a warning finger.

"I brought de car over fur you an' Polly to go into town an' I made her let me finish here so you won't be late. You go put on a clean shirt, quick!"

"But don't the boys want the car, Father?"

"Not tonight dey don't." Rosicky fumbled under his apron and found his pants pocket. He took out a silver dollar and said in a hurried whisper: "You go an' buy dat girl some ice cream an' candy tonight, like you was courtin'. She's awful good friends wid me."

Rudolph was very short of cash, but he took the money as if it hurt him. There had

been a crop failure all over the county. He had more than once been sorry he'd married this year.

In a few minutes the young people came out, looking clean and a little stiff. Rosicky hurried them off, and then he took his own time with the dishes. He scoured the pots and pans and put away the milk and swept the kitchen. He put some coal in the stove and shut off the draughts, so the place would be warm for them when they got home late at night. Then he sat down and had a pipe and listened to the clock tick.

Generally speaking, marrying an American girl was certainly a risk. A Czech should marry a Czech. It was lucky that Polly was the daughter of a poor widow woman; Rudolph was proud, and if she had a prosperous family to throw up at him, they could never make it go. Polly was one of four sisters, and they all worked; one was bookkeeper in the bank, one taught music, and Polly and her younger sister had been clerks, like Miss Pearl. All four of them were musical, had pretty voices, and sang in the Methodist choir, which the eldest sister directed.

Polly missed the sociability of a store position. She missed the choir, and the company of her sisters. She didn't dislike housework, but she disliked so much of it. Rosicky was a little anxious about this pair. He was afraid Polly would grow so discontented that Rudy would quit the farm and take a factory job in Omaha. He had worked for a winter up there, two years ago, to get money to marry on. He had done very well, and they would always take him back at the stockyards. But to Rosicky that meant the end of everything for his son. To be a landless man was to be a wage-earner, a slave, all your life; to have nothing, to be nothing.

Rosicky thought he would come over and do a little carpentering for Polly after the New

Year. He guessed she needed jollying. Rudolph was a serious sort of chap, serious in love and serious about his work.

Rosicky shook out his pipe and walked home across the fields. Ahead of him the lamplight shone from his kitchen windows. Suppose he were still in a tailor shop on Vesey Street, with a bunch of pale, narrow-chested sons working on machines, all coming home tired and sullen to eat supper in a kitchen that was a parlour also; with another crowded, angry family quarrelling just across the dumb-waiter shaft, and squeaking pulleys at the windows where dirty washings hung on dirty lines above a court full of old brooms and mops and ash-cans . . . .

He stopped by the windmill to look up at the frosty winter stars and draw a long breath before he went inside. That kitchen with the shining windows was dear to him; but the sleeping fields and bright stars and the noble darkness were dearer still.

v

On the day before Christmas the weather set in very cold; no snow, but a bitter, biting wind that whistled and sang over the flat land and lashed one's face like fine wires. There was baking going on in the Rosicky kitchen all day, and Rosicky sat inside, making over a coat that Albert had outgrown into an overcoat for John. Mary had a big red geranium in bloom for Christmas, and a row of Jerusalem cherry trees, full of berries. It was the first year she had ever grown these; Doctor Ed brought her the seeds from Omaha when he went to some medical convention. They reminded Rosicky of plants he had seen in England; and all afternoon, as he stitched, he sat thinking about those two years in London, which his mind usually shrank from even after all this while.

He was a lad of eighteen when he dropped down into London, with no money and no connections except the address of a cousin who was supposed to be working at a confectioner's. When he went to the pastry shop, however, he found that the cousin had gone to America. Anton tramped the streets for several days, sleeping in doorways and on the Embankment, until he was in utter despair. He knew no English, and the sound of the strange language all about him confused him. By chance he met a poor German tailor who had learned his trade in Vienna, and could speak a little Czech. This tailor, Lifschnitz, kept a repair shop in a Cheapside basement, underneath a cobbler. He didn't much need an apprentice, but he was sorry for the boy and took him in for no wages but his keep and what he could pick up. The pickings were supposed to be coppers given you when you took work home to a customer. But most of the customers called for their clothes themselves, and the coppers that came Anton's way were very few. He had, however, a place to sleep. The tailor's family lived upstairs in three rooms; a kitchen, a bedroom, where Lifschnitz and his wife and five children slept, and a living-room. Two corners of this living-room were curtained off for lodgers; in one Rosicky slept on an old horsehair sofa, with a feather quilt to wrap himself in. The other corner was rented to a wretched, dirty boy, who was studying the violin. He actually practiced there. Rosicky was dirty, too. There was no way to be anything else. Mrs. Lifschnitz got the water she cooked and washed with from a pump in a brick court, four flights down. There were bugs in the place, and multitudes of fleas, though the poor woman did the best she could. Rosicky knew she often went empty to give another potato or a spoonful of dripping to the two hungry, sad-eyed boys who lodged with her. He used to think he would never get out of there, never get a clean shirt to his back again. What would he do, he wondered, when his clothes actually dropped to pieces and the worn cloth wouldn't hold patches any longer?

It was still early when the old farmer put aside his sewing and his recollections. The sky had been a dark grey all day, with not a gleam of sun, and the light failed at four o'clock. He went to shave and change his shirt while the turkey was roasting. Rudolph and Polly were coming over for supper.

After supper they sat round in the kitchen, and the younger boys were saying how sorry they were it hadn't snowed. Everybody was sorry. They wanted a deep snow that would lie long and keep the wheat warm, and leave the ground soaked when it melted.

"Yes, sir!" Rudolph broke out fiercely; "if we have another dry year like last year, there's going to be hard times in this country."

Rosicky filled his pipe. "You boys don't know what hard times is. You don't owe nobody, you got plenty to eat an' keep warm, an' plenty of water to keep clean. When you got them, you can't have it very hard."

Rudolph frowned, opened and shut his big right hand, and dropped it clenched upon his knee. "I've got to have a good deal more than that, Father, or I'll quit this farming gamble. I can always make good wages railroading, or at the packing house and be sure of my money."

"Maybe so," his father answered dryly.

Mary, who had just come in from the pantry and was wiping her hands on the roller towel, thought Rudy and his father were getting too serious. She brought her darning-basket and sat down in the middle of the group.

"I ain't much afraid of hard times, Rudy," she said heartily. "We've had a plenty, but we've always come through. Your father wouldn't never take nothing very hard, not even hard times. I got a mind to tell you a story on him. Maybe you boys can't hardly remember the year we had that terrible hot wind that burned everything up on the Fourth of July? All the corn an' the gardens. An' that was in the days when we didn't have alfalfa yet—I guess it wasn't invented.

"Well, that very day your father was out cultivatin' corn, and I was here in the kitchen makin' plum preserves. We had bushels of plums that year. I noticed it was terrible hot, but it's always hot in the kitchen when you're preservin', an' I was too busy with my plums to mind. Anton come in from the field about three o'clock, an' I asked him what was the matter.

" 'Nothin',' he says, 'but it's pretty hot, an' I think I won't work no more today.' He stood round for a few minutes, an' then he says:

'Ain't you near through? I want you should git up a nice supper for us tonight. It's Fourth of July.'

"I told him to git along, that I was right in the middle of preservin', but the plums would taste good on hot biscuits. 'I'm goin' to have fried chicken, too,' he says, and he went off an' killed a couple. You three oldest boys was little fellers, playin' round outside, real hot an' sweaty, an' your father took you to the horse tank down by the windmill an' took off your clothes an' put you in. Them two box-elder trees was little then, but they made shade over the tank. Then he took off all his own clothes, an' got in with you. While he was playin' in the water with you, the Methodist preacher drove into our place to say how all the neighbours was goin' to meet at the school-house that night, to pray for rain. He drove right to the windmill, of course, and there was your father and you three with no clothes on. I was in the kitchen door, an' I had to laugh, for the preacher acted like he ain't never seen a naked man before. He surely was embarrassed, an' your father couldn't git to his clothes; they was all hangin' up on the windmill to let the sweat dry out of 'em. So he laid in the tank where he was, an' put one of you boys on top of him to cover him up a little, an' talked to the preacher.

"When you got through playin' in the water, he put clean clothes on you and a clean shirt on himself, an' by that time I'd begun to get supper. He says: 'It's too hot in here to eat comfortable. Let's have a picnic in the orchard. We'll eat our supper behind the mulberry hedge, under them linden trees.'

"So he carried our supper down, an' everything tasted good, I can tell you. The wind got cooler as the sun was goin' down, and it turned out pleasant, only I noticed how the leaves was curled up on the linden trees. That made me think, an' I asked your father if that

hot wind all day hadn't been terrible hard on the gardens an' the corn.

" 'Corn,' he says, 'there ain't no corn.'

" 'What you talkin' about?' I said. 'Ain't we got forty acres?'

" 'We ain't got an ear,' he says, 'nor nobody else ain't got none. All the corn in this country was cooked by three o'clock today, like you'd roasted it in an oven.'

" 'You mean you won't get no crop at all?' I asked him. I couldn't believe it, after he'd worked so hard.

" 'No crop this year,' he says. 'That's why we're havin' a picnic. We might as well enjoy what we got.'

" 'An that's how your father behaved, when all the neighbours was so discouraged they couldn't look you in the face. An' we enjoyed ourselves that year, poor as we was, an' our neighbours wasn't a bit better off for bein' miserable. Some of 'em grieved till they got poor digestions and couldn't relish what they did have."

The younger boys said they thought their father had the best of it. But Rudolph was thinking that, all the same, the neighbours had managed to get ahead more, in the fifteen years since that time. There must be something wrong about his father's way of doing things. He wished he knew what was going on in the back of Polly's mind. He knew she liked his father, but he knew, too, that she was afraid of something. When his mother sent over coffee-cake or prune tarts or a loaf of fresh bread, Polly seemed to regard them with a certain suspicion. When she observed to him that his brothers had nice manners, her tone implied that it was remarkable they should have. With his mother she was stiff and on her guard. Mary's hearty frankness and gusts of good humor irritated her. Polly was afraid of being unusual or conspicuous in any way, of being "ordinary," as she said!

When Mary had finished her story, Rosicky laid aside his pipe.

"You boys like me to tell you about some of dem hard times I been through in London?" Warmly encouraged, he sat rubbing his forehead along the deep creases. It was bothersome to tell a long story in English (he nearly always talked to the boys in Czech), but he wanted Polly to hear this one.

"Well, you know about dat tailor shop I worked in in London? I had one Christmas dere I ain't never forgot. Times was awful bad before Christmas; de boss ain't got much work, an' have it awful hard to pay his rent. It ain't so much fun, bein' poor in a big city like London, I'll say! All de windows is full of good t'ings to eat, an' all de pushcarts in de streets is full, an' you smell 'em all de time, an' you ain't got no money—not a bit. I didn't mind de cold so much, though I didn't have no overcoat, chust a short jacket I'd outgrowed so it wouldn't meet on me, an' my hands was chapped raw. But I always had a good appetite, like you all know, an' de sight of dem pork pies in de windows was awful fur me!

"Day before Christmas was terrible foggy dat year, an' dat fog gits into your bones and makes you all damp like. Mrs. Lifschnitz didn't give us nothin' but a little bread an' drippin' for supper, because she was savin' to try for to give us a good dinner on Christmas Day. After supper de boss say I can go an' enjoy myself, so I went into de streets to listen to de Christmas singers. Dey sing old songs an' make very nice music, an' I run round after dem a good ways, till I got awful hungry. I t'ink maybe if I go home, I can sleep till morning an' forget my belly.

"I went into my corner real quiet, and roll up in my fedder quilt. But I ain't got my head down, till I smell somet'ing good. Seem like it git stronger an' stronger, an' I can't git to sleep noway. I can't understand dat smell. Dere

was a gas light in a hall across de court, dat always shine in at my window a little. I got up an' look around. I got a little wooden box in my corner fur a stool, 'cause I ain't got no chair. I picks up dat box, and under it dere is a roast goose on a platter! I can't believe my eyes. I carry it to de window where de light comes in, an' touch it and smell it to find out, an' den I taste it to be sure. I say, I will eat chust one little bite of dat goose, so I can go to sleep, and tomorrow I won't eat none at all. But I tell you, boys, when I stop, one half of dat goose was gone!"

The narrator bowed his head, and the boys shouted. But little Josephine slipped behind his chair and kissed him on the neck beneath his ear.

"Poor little Papa, I don't want him to be hungry!"

"Da's long ago, child. I ain't never been hungry since I had your mudder to cook fur me."

"Go on and tell us the rest, please," said Polly.

"Well, when I come to realize what I done, of course, I felt terrible. I felt better in de stomach, but very bad in de heart. I set on my bed wid dat platter on my knees, an' it all come to me; how hard dat poor woman save to buy dat goose, and how she get some neighbour to cook it dat got more fire, an' how she put it in my corner to keep it away from dem hungry children. Dey was a old carpet hung up to shut my corner off, an' de children wasn't allowed to go in dere. An' I know she put it in my corner because she trust me more'n she did de violin boy. I can't stand it to face her after I spoil de Christmas. So I put on my shoes and go out into de city. I tell myself I better throw myself in de river; but I guess I ain't dat kind of a boy.

"It was after twelve o'clock, an terrible cold, an' I start out to walk about London all night.

I walk along de river awhile, but dey was lots of drunks all along; men, and women too. I chust move along to keep away from de police. I git onto de Strand, an' den over to New Oxford Street, where dere was a big German restaurant on de ground floor, wid big windows all fixed up fine, an' I could see de people having' parties inside. While I was lookin' in, two men and two ladies come out, laughin' and talkin' and feelin' happy about all dey been eatin' and drinkin', and dey was speakin' Czech—not like de Austrians, but like de home folks talk it.

"I guess I went crazy, an' I done what I ain't never done before nor since. I went right up to dem gay people an' begun to beg dem. 'Fellow-countrymen, give me money enough to buy a goose!'

"Dey laugh, of course, but de ladies speak awful kind to me, an dey take me back into de restaurant and give me hot coffee and cakes, an' make me tell all about how I happened to come to London, an what I was doin' dere.

Dey take my name and where I work down on paper, an' both of dem ladies give me ten shillings.

"De big market at Covent Garden ain't very far away, an' by dat time it was open. I go dere an' buy a big goose an' some pork pies, an' potatoes and onions, an' cakes an' oranges fur de children—all I could carry! When I git home, everybody is still asleep. I pile all I bought on de kitchen table, an' go in an' lay down on my bed, an' I ain't waken up till I hear dat woman scream when she comes out into her kitchen. My goodness, but she was surprise! She laugh an' cry at de same time, an' hug me and waken all de children. She ain't stop fur no breakfast; she git de Christmas dinner ready dat morning, and we all sit down an' eat all we can hold. I ain't never seen dat violin boy have all he can hold before.

"Two three days after dat, de two men come to hunt me up, an' dey ask my boss, and he give me a good report an' tell dem I was a steady boy all right. One of dem Bohemians

was very smart an' run a Bohemian newspaper in New York, an' de odder was a rich man, in de importing business, an' dey been traveling togedder. Dey told me how t'ings was easier in New York, an' offered to pay my passage when dey was goin' home soon on a boat. My boss say to me: 'You go. You ain't got no chance here, an' I like to see you git ahead, fur you always been a good boy to my woman, and fur dat fine Christmas dinner you give us all.' An' da's how I got to New York."

That night when Rudolph and Polly, arm in arm, were running home across the fields with the bitter wind at their backs, his heart leaped for joy when she said she thought they might have his family come over for supper on New Year's Eve. "Let's get up a nice supper, and not let your mother help at all; make her be company for once."

"That would be lovely of you, Polly," he said humbly. He was a very simple, modest boy, and he, too, felt vaguely that Polly and her sisters were more experienced and worldly than his people.

VI

The winter turned out badly for farmers. It was bitterly cold, and after the first light snows before Christmas there was no snow at all—and no rain. March was as bitter as February. On those days when the wind fairly punished the country, Rosicky sat by his window. In the fall he and the boys had put in a big wheat planting, and now the seed had frozen in the ground. All that land would have to be ploughed up and planted over again, planted in corn. It had happened before, but he was younger then, and he never worried about what had to be. He was sure of himself and of Mary; he knew they could bear what they had to bear, that they would always pull through somehow. But he was not so sure

about the young ones, and he felt troubled because Rudolph and Polly were having such a hard start.

Sitting beside his flowering window while the panes rattled and the wind blew in under the door, Rosicky gave himself to reflection as he had not done since those Sundays in the loft of the furniture-factory in New York, long ago. Then he was trying to find what he wanted in life for himself; now he was trying to find what he wanted for his boys, and why it was he so hungered to feel sure they would be here, working this very land, after he was gone.

They would have to work hard on the farm, and probably they would never do much more than make a living. But if he could think of them as staying here on the land, he wouldn't have to fear any great unkindness for them. Hardships, certainly; it was a hardship to have the wheat freeze in the ground when seed was so high; and to have to sell your stock because you had no feed. But there would be other years when everything came along right, and you caught up. And what you had was your own. You didn't have to do with dishonest and cruel people. They were the only things in his experience he had found terrifying and horrible; the look in the eyes of a dishonest and crafty man, of a scheming and rapacious woman.

In the country, if you had a mean neighbour, you could keep off his land and make him keep off yours. But in the city, all the foulness and misery and brutality of your neighbours was part of your life. The worst things he had come upon in his journey through the world were human—depraved and poisonous specimens of man. To this day he could recall certain terrible faces in the London streets. There were mean people everywhere, to be sure, even in their own country town here. But they weren't tempered, hardened, sharpened, like the treacherous people in cities who live by grinding or cheating or poisoning their fellow-men. He had helped to bury two of his fellow-workmen in the tailoring trade, and he was distrustful of the organized industries that see one out of the world in big cities. Here, if you were sick, you had Doctor Ed to look after you; and if you died, fat Mr. Haycock, the kindest man in the world, buried you.

It seemed to Rosicky that for good, honest boys like his, the worst they could do on the farm was better than the best they would be likely to do in the city. If he'd had a mean boy, now, one who was crooked and sharp and tried to put anything over on his brothers, then town would be the place for him. But he had no such boy. As for Rudolph, the discontented one, he would give the shirt off his back to anyone who touched his heart. What Rosicky really hoped for his boys was that they could get through the world without ever knowing much about the cruelty of human beings. "Their mother and me ain't prepared them for that," he sometimes said to himself.

These thoughts brought him back to a grateful consideration of his own case. What an escape he had had, to be sure! He, too, in his time, had had to take money for repair work from the hand of a hungry child who let it go so wistfully; because it was money due his boss. And now, in all these years, he had never had to take a cent from anyone in bitter need—never had to look at the face of a woman become like a wolf's from struggle and famine. When he thought of these things, Rosicky would put on his cap and jacket and slip down to the barn and give his work-horses a little extra oats, letting them eat it out of his hand in their slobbery fashion. It was his way of expressing what he felt, and made him chuckle with pleasure.

The spring came warm, with blue skies—but dry, dry as a bone. The boys began ploughing up the wheat-fields to plant them over in corn. Rosicky would stand at the fence corner and watch them, and the earth was so dry it blew up in clouds of brown dust that hid the horses and the sulky plough and the driver. It was a bad outlook.

The big alfalfa field that lay between the home place and Rudolph's came up green, but Rosicky was worried because during that open windy winter a great many Russian thistle plants had blown in there and lodged. He kept asking the boys to rake them out; he was afraid their seed would root and "take the alfalfa." Rudolph said that was nonsense. The boys were working so hard planting corn, their father felt he couldn't insist about the thistles, but he set great store by that big alfalfa field. It was a feed you could depend on—and there was some deeper reason, vague, but strong. The peculiar green of that clover woke early memories in old Rosicky, went back to something in his childhood in the old world. When he was a little boy, he had played in fields of that strong blue-green colour.

One morning, when Rudolph had gone to town in the car, leaving a work-team idle in his barn, Rosicky went over to his son's place, put the horses to the buggy-rake, and set about quietly raking up those thistles. He behaved with guilty caution, and rather enjoyed stealing a march on Doctor Ed, who was just then taking his first vacation in seven years of practice and was attending a clinic in Chicago. Rosicky got the thistles raked up, but did not stop to burn them. That would take some time, and his breath was pretty short, so he thought he had better get the horses back to the barn.

He got them into the barn and to their stalls, but the pain had come on so sharp in his chest that he didn't try to take the harness off. He started for the house, bending lower with every step. The cramp in his chest was

shutting him up like a jack-knife. When he reached the windmill, he swayed and caught at the ladder. He saw Polly coming down the hill, running with the swiftness of a slim greyhound. In a flash she had her shoulder under his armpit.

"Lean on me, Father, hard! Don't be afraid. We can get to the house all right."

Somehow they did, though Rosicky became blind with pain; he could keep on his legs, but he couldn't steer his course. The next thing he was conscious of was lying on Polly's bed, and Polly bending over him wringing out bath towels in hot water and putting them on his chest. She stopped only to throw coal into the stove, and she kept the tea-kettle and the black pot going. She put these hot applications on him for nearly an hour, she told him afterwards, and all that time he was drawn up stiff and blue, with the sweat pouring off him.

As the pain gradually loosed its grip, the stiffness went out of his jaws, the black circles round his eyes disappeared, and a little of his natural colour came back. When his daughter-in-law buttoned his shirt over his chest at last, he sighed.

"Da's fine, de way I feel now, Polly. It was a awful bad spell, an' I was so sorry it all come on you like it did."

Polly was flushed and excited. "Is the pain really gone? Can I leave you long enough to telephone over to your place?"

Rosicky's eyelids fluttered. "Don't telephone, Polly. It ain't no use to scare my wife. It's nice and quiet here, an' if I ain't too much trouble to you, just let me lay still till I feel like myself. I ain't got no pain now. It's nice here."

Polly bent over him and wiped the moisture from his face. "Oh, I'm so glad it's over!" she broke out impulsively. "It just broke my heart to see you suffer so, Father."

Rosicky motioned her to sit down on the chair where the tea-kettle had been, and looked up at her with that lively affectionate gleam in his eyes. "You was awful good to me, I won't never forgit dat. I hate it to be sick on you like dis. Down at de barn I say to myself, dat young girl ain't had much experience in sickness, I don't want to scare her, an' maybe she's got a baby comin' or somet'ing."

Polly took his hand. He was looking at her so intently and affectionately and confidingly; his eyes seemed to caress her face, to regard it with pleasure. She frowned with her funny streaks of eyebrows, and then smiled back at him.

"I guess maybe there is something of that kind going to happen. But I haven't told anyone yet, not my mother or Rudolph. You'll be the first to know."

His hand pressed hers. She noticed that it was warm again. The twinkle in his yellow-brown eyes seemed to come nearer.

"I like mighty well to see dat little child, Polly," was all he said. Then he closed his eyes and lay half-smiling. But Polly sat still, thinking hard. She had a sudden feeling that nobody in the world, not her mother, not Rudolph, or anyone, really loved her as much as old Rosicky did. It perplexed her. She sat frowning and trying to puzzle it out. It was as if Rosicky had a special gift for loving people, something that was like an ear for music or an eye for colour. It was quiet, unobtrusive; it was merely there. You felt it in his hands, too. After he dropped off to sleep, she sat holding his warm, broad, flexible brown hand. She had never seen another in the least like it. She wondered if it wasn't a kind of gypsy hand, it was so alive and quick and light in its communications— very strange in a farmer. Nearly all the farmers she knew had huge lumps of fists, like mauls, or they were knotty and bony and uncomfortable-looking, with stiff fingers. But

Rosicky's was like quicksilver, flexible, muscular, about the colour of a pale cigar, with deep, deep creases across the palm. It wasn't nervous, it wasn't a stupid lump; it was a warm brown human hand, with some cleverness in it, a great deal of generosity, and something else which Polly could only call "gypsy-like"—something nimble and lively and sure, in the way that animals are.

Polly remembered that hour long afterwards; it had been like an awakening to her. It seemed to her that she had never learned so much about life from anything as from old Rosicky's hand. It brought her to herself; it communicated some direct and untranslatable message.

When she heard Rudolph coming in the car, she ran out to meet him.

"Oh, Rudy, your father's been awful sick! He raked up those thistles he's been worrying about, and afterwards he could hardly get to the house. He suffered so I was afraid he was going to die."

Rudolph jumped to the ground. "Where is he now?"

"On the bed. He's asleep. I was terribly scared, because, you know, I'm so fond of your father." She slipped her arm through his and they went into the house. That afternoon they took Rosicky home and put him to bed, though he protested that he was quite well again.

The next morning he got up and dressed and sat down to breakfast with his family. He told Mary that his coffee tasted better than usual to him, and he warned the boys not to bear any tales to Doctor Ed when he got home. After breakfast he sat down by his window to do some patching and asked Mary to thread several needles for him before she went to feed her chickens—her eyes were better than his, and her hands steadier. He lit his pipe and took up John's overalls. Mary had been watching him anxiously all morning, and as she went out of the door with her bucket of scraps, she saw that he was smiling. He was thinking, indeed, about Polly, and how he might never have known what a tender heart she had if he hadn't got sick over there. Girls nowadays didn't wear their heart on their sleeve. But now he knew Polly would make a fine woman after the foolishness wore off. Either a woman had that sweetness at her heart or she hadn't. You couldn't always tell by the look of them; but if they had that, everything came out right in the end.

After he had taken a few stitches, the cramp began in his chest, like yesterday. He put his pipe cautiously down on the window-sill and bent over to ease the pull. No use—he had better try to get to his bed if he could. He rose and groped his way across the familiar floor, which was rising and falling like the deck of a ship. At the door he fell. When Mary came in, she found him lying there, and the moment she touched him she knew that he was gone.

Doctor Ed was away when Rosicky died, and for the first few weeks after he got home he was hard driven. Every day he said to himself that he must get out to see that family that had lost their father. One soft, warm moonlight night in early summer he started for the farm. His mind was on other things, and not until his road ran by the graveyard did he realize that Rosicky wasn't over there on the hill where the red lamplight shone, but here, in the moonlight. He stopped his car, shut off the engine, and sat there for a while.

A sudden hush had fallen on his soul. Everything here seemed strangely moving and significant, though signifying what, he did not know. Close by the wire fence stood Rosicky's mowing-machine, where one of the boys had been cutting hay that afternoon; his own work-horses had been going up and down there. The new-cut hay perfumed all the night air.

The moonlight silvered the long, billowy grass that grew over the graves and hid the fence; the few little evergreens stood out black in it, like shadows in a pool. The sky was very blue and soft, the stars rather faint because the moon was full.

For the first time it struck Doctor Ed that this was really a beautiful graveyard. He thought of city cemeteries; acres of shrubbery and heavy stone, so arranged and lonely and unlike anything in the living world. Cities of the dead, indeed; cities of the forgotten, of the "put away." But this was open and free, this little square of long grass which the wind for ever stirred. Nothing but the sky overhead, and the many-coloured fields running on until they met that sky. The horses worked here in summer; the neighbours passed on their way to town; and over yonder, in the cornfield, Rosicky's own cattle would be eating fodder as winter came on. Nothing could be more undeathlike than this place; nothing could be more right for a man who had helped to do the work of great cities and had always longed for the open country and had got to it at last. Rosicky's life seemed to him complete and beautiful.

About the Story

1. Find at least three quotations or statements from the story which demonstrate that Rosicky is patient, kind, and unselfish.
2. What does Rosicky value most for his children?
3. Why does Rosicky like country life more than city life? Do you agree with Rosicky or disagree? Explain why.
4. How do Mr. and Mrs. Rosicky compare with Mr. and Mrs. Penn in "The Revolt of Mother"?

About the Author

As a young girl growing up on the plains of Nebraska, Willa Cather (1873-1947) was a vibrant, imaginative tomboy who read voraciously, loved adventure, and dreamed of becoming a medical doctor. Among her favorite summer activities were "slicing toads" for her scientific experiments and pursuing her double hobby of "snakes and Shakespeare."

The inspiration for most of Willa Cather's writing came from the impressions and experiences of her youth and childhood. When her family moved from the gently rolling hills of Virginia to the unbroken plains of Nebraska, Willa was only ten years old, yet the extreme change powerfully affected her; especially influential were the numerous immigrants from Europe who became neighbors and friends. They introduced Willa to European culture, language, and literature, and they appeared later as characters in her works.

The dreams and frustrations of such people are a favorite theme of Cather's, as is the conflict between the need to make a living and the need for the purely pleasurable rewards of being artistic and creative. Many of Cather's characters have lives that are full of hard work and duties yet richly rewarding. For them every task becomes a work of art given to oneself and one's family, and every small and natural beauty appreciated is an act of artistic expression. Rosicky is an excellent example of this type of character. The main characters in "Neighbour Rosicky" are based on a Bohemian couple whom Cather knew. Like his real-life counterpart, Rosicky values his family's happiness more than material wealth, and the simple joys of life in the country more than the attractions of city life. Cather presents Rosicky as sympathetic to the restlessness of his daughter-in-law from the city, for Cather as a young woman felt the powerful lure of culture in the city of Chicago. But she, like Rosicky, learned the joy of contentment found in country life.

My Last Duchess

Robert Browning

> *In Browning's dramatic monologue the speaker is the Duke of Ferrara,*
> *an Italian Renaissance nobleman. The Duke is describing a painting of his*
> *last Duchess to an envoy of the count whose daughter the Duke now wishes*
> *to wed. Browning does a masterful job of creating a well-rounded character*
> *through one simple speech. What does the Duke's speech reveal about how*
> *he views himself and his former wife? What do you think of the Duke by*
> *the end of the poem? Is your view of him consistent with his view of himself?*
> *Knowing what you do of his character, what do you think he means when*
> *he says: "I gave commands; then all smiles stopped together"?*

That's my last Duchess painted on the wall,
Looking as if she were alive; I call
That piece a wonder, now; Fra Pandolf's* hands
Worked busily a day, and there she stands.
Will 't please you sit and look at her? I said   5
"Fra Pandolf" by design, for never read
Strangers like you that pictured countenance,
The depth and passion of its earnest glance,
But to myself they turned (since none puts by
The curtain I have drawn for you, but I)   10
And seemed as they would ask me, if they durst,
How such a glance came there; so, not the first
Are you to turn and ask thus. Sir, 'twas not
Her husband's presence only, called that spot
Of joy into the Duchess' cheek: perhaps   15
Fra Pandolf chanced to say, "Her mantle laps
Over my lady's wrist too much," or, "Paint
Must never hope to reproduce the faint
Half flush that dies along her throat"; such stuff
Was courtesy, she thought, and cause enough   20
For calling up that spot of joy. She had
A heart . . . how shall I say? . . . too soon made glad,
Too easily impressed; she liked whate'er
She looked on, and her looks went everywhere.

Fra Pandolf: Brother Pandolf, an imaginary monk and painter of the Italian Renaissance period

Sir, 'twas all one! My favor at her breast,   25
The dropping of the daylight in the West,
The bough of cherries some officious* fool
Broke in the orchard for her, the white mule
She rode with round the terrace—all and each
Would draw from her alike the approving speech,   30
Or blush, at least. She thanked men—good; but thanked
Somehow . . . I know not how . . . as if she ranked
My gift of a nine-hundred-year-old name
With anybody's gift. Who'd stoop to blame
This sort of trifling? Even had you skill   35
In speech—which I have not—to make your will
Quite clear to such an one, and say, "Just this
Or that in you disgusts me; here you miss
Or there exceed the mark"—and if she let
Herself be lessoned so, nor plainly set   40
Her wits to yours, forsooth, and made excuse
—E'en then would be some stooping, and I choose
Never to stoop. Oh, sir, she smiled, no doubt,
Whene'er I passed her; but who passed without
Much the same smile? This grew; I gave commands;   45
Then all smiles stopped together. There she stands
As if alive. Will 't please you rise? We'll meet
The company below, then. I repeat,
The Count your Master's known munificence*
Is ample warrant that no just pretense   50
Of mine for dowry will be disallowed;
Though his fair daughter's self, as I avowed
At starting, is my object. Nay, we'll go
Together down,* sir! Notice Neptune,* though,
Taming a sea horse, thought a rarity,   55
Which Claus of Innsbruck* cast in bronze for me.

officious: extremely forward in offering one's services to other people

munificence: liberality in giving

we'll . . . down: The Duke calls the envoy forward to a position of equality.
Neptune: the Greek god of the sea
Claus of Innsbruck: an imaginary sculptor

About the Poem

1. Who is speaking in the poem? To whom is he speaking?
2. What does the title of the poem suggest about the Duke?
3. Notice the words of the Duke. What do his own words reveal about his character?
4. By the end of the poem do you like or dislike the Duke?
5. Is the Duke pleased with his own character? Why do you think he is or is not?

About the Author

Robert Browning (1812-1889) was born in London into a well-to-do and happy family who appreciated and encouraged his natural talent. Browning's father was a man of letters and himself a poet. His mother was a devout woman whose religious outlook powerfully colored her son's work: from her, Browning inherited a profound spiritual optimism which permeated his writing. As William Lyon Phelps, one of Browning's biographers, states: "He always tried to see what was good."

Browning was largely self-educated. His father's vast library helped develop an early love of reading and writing. His reading was far-reaching, but he learned thoroughly the subjects he studied. In his writing he did not strive to please his readers but rather to teach them, to show them his observations and beliefs about mankind. Browning's insight into human character is valuable for the Christian reader, for he shows how men reveal their hearts, whether they intend to or not. "My Last Duchess" is an exquisite example of Browning's ability to expose the true character of a man.

Many of Browning's contemporaries equated beauty (especially the beauty of the natural world) with ultimate truth. Browning, however, felt that love must be added to beauty if we would understand ultimate truth. Although Browning acknowledged that creation showed the Creator's power and wisdom, it was Christ, the Incarnate Son, who revealed the Father's greatest attribute— His love. Unfortunately, Browning, as many others, saw such love only as an abstract, noble quality. He never recognized his need of a personal Saviour, never understood the true purpose behind God's great love.

3

UNIT THREE

Theme

Theme

Having learned how to analyze conflict and character, we are now ready to tackle the main goal of interpretation—discerning theme. A theme is not to be confused with a moral (although a theme may sometimes contain a moral). A **moral** is a simple statement that *teaches* a simple truth. "Those who complain the most suffer the least" (Aesop) is an example of a moral. A theme, however, is more than a statement of what a story teaches; it is a summary of what the details of the story *reveal.* A **theme** is the recurring idea or central insight mirrored in the story's conflict and characters.

An author may reveal the theme either **explicitly,** by stating it outright, or **implicitly,** by subtly weaving it into the elements of the story; or he may use both techniques. We find examples of these two methods in the parables of the lost sheep and of the prodigal son recorded in Luke 15. Although the conflict and the characters differ in these two narratives, the theme is the same in both.

The first parable, the parable of the lost sheep, is an example of the explicit method. Christ concludes this story with the statement: "I say unto you, that likewise joy shall be in heaven over one sinner that repenteth, more than over ninety and nine just persons, which need no repentance" (Luke 15:7). This verse, at first glance, may seem to be a moral. A careful reading, however, confirms that it does more than tell us what the parable teaches; it summarizes how the story's conflict and characters reflect the theme. Notice, for example, that the shepherd and his sheep mirror God's loving nature and man's complete helplessness. These characters concretely illustrate God's (the shepherd's) unwavering desire to rescue the weak and the base (the wandering sheep / the lost sinner). The parable's conflict (an unprotected lamb lost in a hostile environment) also serves to reinforce the recurring idea of God's persistent, personal love. The shepherd willingly leaves the "ninety and nine" to rescue the "one." Finally, the story's joyful resolution confirms all that we have learned thus far and assures us that God views forgiving and restoring the penitent not as an obligation but as a delight. This verse gives us much insight into God's nature and His attitude toward sinful men. It is more than a moral; it is an explicit revelation of theme.

This same thematic statement could have concluded the parable of the prodigal son. For this story, however, Christ chose to use the more subtle implicit approach and to rely solely on the story elements to communicate His theme. Although the Lord provides no direct statement to guide us, He does provide a stronger, more detailed conflict in this narrative than He does in the previous one. We learn not only what the conflict is but also what its cause and effects are. Christ also creates more vivid central characters that readily draw us into the narrative. This is a story, not of a shepherd and a sheep, but of a father and his sons. Notice, too, that these characters are more carefully developed than those in the first story. We know, for example, that the father is wealthy, loving, and wise. In contrast to the father is the elder brother who, though dutiful, is uncompassionate and unforgiving. Finally, this narrative, unlike the preceding one, has a dynamic or changing character. The prodigal who is initially corrupt, proud, and rebellious becomes penitent, humble, and obedient. These added details not only make this story more exciting but also help us grasp its central idea without the aid of an explicit thematic statement. Such details also make the story more sophisticated in structure and more poignant in effect.

Most of the stories we have read thus far have been interpretive or sophisticated works, and they have, like the parable of the prodigal son, used the implicit approach. The stories in this unit do likewise. We must, therefore, examine the details of each story if we are to discern each theme accurately. After a careful examination, ask yourself: "What one idea do the conflict, the characters, and the resolution support?" Once you can summarize this idea in one or two sentences, you will have mastered the story's theme.

The Silver Mine

Selma Lagerlöf

For this story, Selma Lagerlöf drew on the folklore of her native Sweden. "The Silver Mine," though fictional, has an actual geographical and historical setting. The narrative is laid in Dalecarlia, a region of west central Sweden, during the reign of Gustaf III (1771-1792).

Like "Marjorie Daw," it is a story within a story. It begins with an account of King Gustaf's visit to the Dalecarlian village. This narrative is the frame for the parson's tale about the discovery of a silver mine and its effects on the villagers. As you read, notice both the similarities and the differences between the king and his army and the parson and his parishioners.

King Gustaf III was traveling through Dalecarlia. He was pressed for time, and all the way he wanted to drive like lightning. Although they drove with such speed that the horses were extended like stretched rubber bands and the coach cleared the turns on two wheels, the king poked his head out of the window and shouted to the postilion,* "Why don't you go ahead? Do you think you are driving over eggs?"

---

postilion: rider on a leading horse of a coach team

Since they had to drive over poor country roads at such a mad pace, it would have been almost a miracle had the harness and wagon held together! And they didn't, either; for at the foot of a steep hill the pole broke—and there the king sat! The courtiers sprang from the coach and scolded the driver, but this did not lessen the damage done. There was no possibility of continuing until the coach was mended.

When the courtiers looked around to try to find something with which the king could amuse himself while he waited, they noticed a church spire looming high above the trees in a grove a short distance ahead. They intimated to the king that he might step into one of the coaches in which the attendants were riding and drive up to the church. It was a Sunday, and the king might attend services to pass the time until the royal coach was ready.

The king accepted the proposal and drove toward the church. He had been traveling for hours through dark forest regions; but here it looked more cheerful, with fairly large meadows and villages, and with the Dal River gliding on light and pretty, between thick rows of alder bushes.

But the king had ill luck to this extent: the bell ringer took up the recessional chant just as the king was stepping from the coach on the church knoll and the people were coming out from the service. But when they came walking past him, the king remained standing, with one foot in the wagon and the other on the footstep. He did not move from the spot—only stared at them. They were the finest lot of folk he had ever seen. All the men were above the average height, with intelligent and earnest faces, and the women were

dignified and stately, with an air of Sabbath peace about them.

The whole of the preceding day the king had talked only of the desolate tracts he was passing through, and had said to his courtiers again and again, "Now I am certainly driving through the very poorest part of my kingdom!" But now, when he saw the people, garbed in the picturesque dress of this section of the country, he forgot to think of their poverty; instead his heart warmed, and he remarked to himself, "The king of Sweden is not so badly off as his enemies think. So long as my subjects look like this, I shall probably be able to defend both my faith and my country."

He commanded the courtiers to make known to the people that the stranger who was standing among them was their king and that they should gather around him, so he could talk to them.

And then the king made a speech to the people. He spoke from the high steps outside the vestry,* and the narrow step upon which he stood is there even today.

---

vestry: wardrobe room in churches whose clergy wear vestments

---

The king gave an account of the sad plight in which the kingdom was placed. He said that the Swedes were threatened with war by both Russians and Danes. Under ordinary circumstances it would not be such a serious matter; but now the army was filled with traitors, and he did not dare depend upon it. Therefore there was no other course for him to take than to go himself into the country settlements and ask his subjects if they would be loyal to their king and help him with men and money, so he could save the fatherland.

The peasants stood quietly while the king was speaking to them, and when he had finished they gave no sign either of approval or disapproval.

The king himself thought that he had spoken well. The tears had sprung to his eyes several times while he was speaking. But when the peasants stood there all the while, troubled and undecided, and could not make up their minds to answer him, the king frowned and looked displeased.

The peasants understood that it was becoming monotonous for the king to wait, and finally one of them stepped out from the crowd.

"Now, you must know, King Gustaf, that we were not expecting a royal visit in the parish today," said the peasant, "and therefore we are not prepared to answer you at once. I advise you to go into the vestry and speak with our pastor, while we discuss among ourselves this matter which you have laid before us."

When he came into the vestry, he found no one there but a man who looked like a peasant. He was tall and rugged, with big hands toughened by labor, and he wore neither cassock* nor collar but leather breeches and a long white homespun coat like all the other men.

---

cassock: clerical robe

He rose and bowed to the king when the latter entered.

"I thought I should find the parson in here," said the king.

The man grew somewhat red in the face. He thought it annoying to mention the fact that he was the parson of this parish, when he saw that the king had mistaken him for a peasant. "Yes," said he, "the parson is usually on hand in here."

The king dropped into a large armchair which stood in the vestry at that time and which stands there today, looking exactly like itself, with this difference: the congregation has had a gilded crown attached to the back of it.

"Have you a good parson in this parish?" asked the king, who wanted to appear interested in the welfare of the peasants.

When the king questioned him in this manner, the parson felt that he couldn't possibly tell who he was. "It's better to let him go on believing that I'm only a peasant," thought he, and replied that the parson was good enough. He preached a pure and clear gospel and tried to live as he taught.

The king thought that this was a good commendation, but he had a sharp ear and marked a certain doubt in the tone. "You sound as if you were not quite satisfied with the parson," said the king.

"He's a bit arbitrary," said the man, thinking that, if the king should find out later who he was, he would not think that the parson had been standing here and blowing his own horn; therefore he wished to come out with a little faultfinding also. "There are some, no doubt, who say the parson wants to be the only one to counsel and rule in this parish," he continued.

"Then, at all events, he has led and managed in the best possible way," said the king. He didn't like it that the peasant complained of one who was placed above him. "To me it appears as though good habits and old-time simplicity were the rule here."

"The people are good enough," said the curate,* "but then they live in poverty and isolation. Human beings here would certainly be no better than others if this world's temptations came closer to them."

---

curate: clergyman in charge of a parish district served by a church

---

"But there's no fear of anything of the sort happening," said the king, with a shrug.

He said nothing further but began thrumming on the table with his fingers. He thought he had exchanged a sufficient number of gracious words with this peasant and wondered when the others would be ready with their answer.

"These peasants are not very eager to help their king," thought he. "If I only had my coach, I would drive away from them and their palaver!"*

---

palaver: tedious talk

The pastor sat there troubled, debating with himself as to how he should decide an important matter which he must settle. He was beginning to feel happy because he had not told the king who he was. Now he felt that he could speak with him about matters which otherwise he could not have placed before him.

After a while the parson broke the silence and asked the king if it was an actual fact that enemies were upon them and that the kingdom was in danger.

The king thought this man ought to have sense enough not to trouble him further. He simply glared at him and said nothing.

"I ask because I was standing in here and could not hear very well," said the parson. "But if this is really the case, I want to say to you that the pastor of this congregation might perhaps be able to procure for the king as much money as he will need."

"I thought that you said just now that everyone here was poor," said the king, thinking that the man did not know what he was talking about.

"Yes, that's true," replied the rector,* "and the parson has no more than any of the others. But if the king would condescend to listen to me for a moment, I will explain how the pastor happens to have the power to help him."

---

rector: clergyman in charge of a parish

"You may speak," said the king. "You seem to find it easier to get the words past your lips than your friends and neighbors out there, who never will be ready with what they have to tell me."

"It is not so easy to reply to the king! I'm afraid that, in the end, it will be the parson who must undertake this on behalf of the others."

The king crossed his legs, folded his arms, and let his head sink down upon his breast. "You may begin now," he said, in the tone of one already asleep.

"Once upon a time there were five men from this parish who were out on a moose hunt," began the clergyman. "One of them was the parson of whom we are speaking. Two of the others were soldiers, named Olaf and Eric Svärd; the fourth man was the innkeeper in this settlement, and the fifth was a peasant named Israel Per Persson."

"Don't go to the trouble of mentioning so many names," muttered the king, letting his head droop to one side.

"Those men were good hunters," continued the parson, "who usually had luck with them, but that day they had wandered long and far without getting anything. Finally they gave up the hunt altogether and sat down on the ground to talk. They said there was not a spot in the whole forest fit for cultivation; all of it was only mountain and swampland. 'Our Lord has not done right by us in giving us such a poor land to live in,' said one. 'In other localities people can get riches for themselves in abundance, but here, with all our toil and drudgery we can scarcely get our daily bread.' "

The pastor paused a moment, as if uncertain that the king heard him, but the latter moved his little finger to show that he was awake.

"Just as the hunters were discussing this matter, the parson saw something that glittered at the base of the mountain where he had kicked away a moss tuft. 'This is a queer mountain,' he thought, as he kicked off another

moss tuft. He picked up a sliver of stone that came with the moss and which shone exactly like the other. 'It can't be possible that this stuff is lead,' said he.

"Then the others sprang up and scraped away the turf with the butt ends of their rifles. When they did this, they saw plainly that a broad vein of ore followed the mountain.

" 'What do you think this might be?' asked the parson.

"The men chipped off bits of stone and bit into them. 'It must be lead or zinc, at least,' said they.

" 'And the whole mountain is full of it,' added the innkeeper."

When the parson had got thus far in his narrative, the king's head was seen to straighten up a little and one eye opened. "Do you know if any of these persons knew anything about ore and minerals?" he asked.

"They did not," replied the parson.

Then the king's head sank and both eyes closed.

"The clergyman and his companions were very happy," continued the speaker, without letting himself be disturbed by the king's indifference; "they fancied that now they had found that which would give them and their descendants wealth. 'I'll never have to do any more work,' said one. 'Now I can afford to do nothing at all the whole week through, and on Sundays I shall drive to church in a golden chariot!' They were otherwise sensible men, but the great find had gone to their heads, and they talked like children. Still they had enough presence of mind to put back the moss tufts and conceal the vein of ore. Then they carefully noted the place where it was and went home. Before they parted company, they agreed that the parson should travel to Falun and ask the mining expert what kind of ore this was. He was to return as soon as possible, and until then they promised one another on oath not

to reveal to a soul where the ore was to be found."

The king's head was raised again a trifle, but he did not interrupt the speaker with a word. It appeared as though he was beginning to believe that the man actually had something of importance he wished to say to him, since he didn't allow himself to be disturbed by his indifference.

"Then the parson departed with a few samples of ore in his pocket. He was just as happy in the thought of becoming rich as were the others. He was thinking of rebuilding the parsonage, which at present was no better than a peasant's cottage, and then he would marry a dean's daughter whom he liked. He had thought that he might have to wait for her many years. He was poor and obscure and knew that it would be a long while before he should get any post that would enable him to marry.

"The parson drove over to Falun in two days, and there he had to wait another whole day because the mining expert was away. Finally he ran across him and showed him the bits of ore. The mining expert took them in his hand. He looked at them first, then at the parson. The parson related how he had found them in a mountain at home in his parish and wondered if it might not be lead.

" 'No, it's not lead,' said the mining expert.

" 'Perhaps it is zinc then?' asked the parson.

" 'Nor is it zinc,' said the mineralogist.

"The parson thought that all the hope within him sank. He had not been so depressed in many a long day.

" 'Have you many stones like this in your parish?' asked the mineralogist.

" 'We have a whole mountainful,' said the parson.

"Then the mineralogist came up closer, slapped the parson on the shoulder, and said, 'Let us see that you make such good use of this that it will prove a blessing both to yourselves and to the country, for this is silver.'

" 'Indeed?' said the parson, feeling his way. 'So it is silver.'

"The mineralogist began telling him how he should go to work to get legal rights to the mine and gave him many valuable suggestions; but the parson stood there dazed and did not listen to what the mineralogist was saying. He was thinking how wonderful it was that at home in his poor parish stood a whole mountain of silver ore, waiting for him."

The king raised his head so suddenly that the parson stopped short in his narrative. "It turned out, of course, that when he got home and began working the mine, he saw that the mineralogist had only been fooling him," said the king.

"Oh, no, the mineralogist had not fooled him," said the parson.

"You may continue," said the king as he settled himself more comfortably in the chair to listen.

"When the parson was at home again and was driving through the parish," continued the clergyman, "he thought that first of all he should inform his partners of the value of their find. And as he drove alongside the innkeeper Sten Stensson's place, he intended to drive up to the house to tell him they had found silver. But when he stopped outside the gate, he noticed that a broad path of evergreen was strewn all the way up to the doorstep.

" 'Who had died in this place?' asked the parson of a boy who stood leaning against the fence.

" 'The innkeeper himself,' answered the boy. Then he let the clergyman know that the innkeeper had drunk himself full every day for a week. 'Oh, so much brandy, so much brandy, has been drunk here!'

" 'How can that be?' asked the parson. 'The innkeeper used never to drink himself full.'

" 'Oh,' said the boy, 'he drank because he said he had found a mine. He was very rich. He should never have to do anything now but drink, he said. Last night he drove off, full as he was, and the wagon turned over and he was killed.'

"When the parson heard this, he drove homeward, distressed over what he had heard. He had come back so happy, rejoicing because he could tell the great news.

"When the parson had driven a few paces, he saw Israel Per Persson walking along. He looked about as usual, and the parson thought it was well that fortune had not gone to his head too. Him he would cheer at once with the good news that he was a rich man.

" 'Good day!' said Per Persson. 'Do you come from Falun now?'

" 'I do,' said the parson. 'And now I must tell you that it has turned out even better than we had imagined. The mineralogist said it was silver ore that we had found.'

"That instant Per Persson looked as though the ground had opened under him. 'What are you saying, what are you saying? Is it silver?'

" 'Yes,' answered the parson. 'We'll all be rich men now, all of us, and can live like gentlemen.'

" 'Oh, is it silver?' said Per Persson, looking more and more mournful.

" 'Why, of course it is silver,' replied the parson. 'You mustn't think that I want to deceive you. You mustn't be afraid to be happy.'

" 'Happy!' said Per Persson. 'Should I be happy? I believed it was only glitter that we had found, so I thought it would be better to take the certain for the uncertain; I have sold my share in the mine to Olaf Svärd for a hundred dollars.' He was desperate and, when the parson drove away from him, he stood on the highway and wept.

"When the clergyman got back to his home,

he sent a servant to Olaf Svärd and his brother to tell them that it was silver they had found. He thought that he had had quite enough of driving around and spreading the good news.

"But in the evening, when the parson sat alone, his joy asserted itself again. He went out in the darkness and stood on a hillock upon which he contemplated building the new parsonage. It should be imposing, of course, as fine as a bishop's palace. He stood there long that night, nor did he content himself with rebuilding the parsonage! It occurred to him that, since there were such riches to be found in the parish, throngs of people would pour in and, finally, a whole city would be built around the mine. And then he would have to erect a new church in place of the old one. Toward this object a large portion of his wealth would probably go. And he was not content with this, either, but fancied that, when his church was ready, the king and many bishops would come to the dedication. Then

the king would be pleased with the church; but he would remark that there was no place where a king might put up, and then he would have to erect a castle in the new city."

Just then one of the king's courtiers opened the door of the vestry and announced that the big royal coach was mended.

At the first moment the king was ready to withdraw, but on second thought he changed his mind. "You may tell your story to the end," he said to the parson. "But you can hurry it a bit. We know all about how the man thought and dreamed. We want to know about how he acted."

"But while the parson was still lost in his dreams," continued the clergyman, "word came to him that Israel Per Persson had made away with himself. He had not been able to bear the disappointment of having sold his share in the mine. He had thought, no doubt, that he could not endure to go about every day seeing another enjoying the wealth that might have been his."

The king straightened up a little. He kept both eyes open. "Upon my word," he said, "if I had been that parson, I should have had enough of the mine!"

"The king is a rich man," said the parson. "He has quite enough, at all events. It is not the same thing with a poor curate who possesses nothing. The unhappy wretch thought instead, when he saw that God's blessing was not with his enterprise, 'I will dream no more of bringing glory and profit to myself with these riches, but I can't let the silver lie buried in the earth! I must take it out, for the benefit of the poor and needy. I will work the mine, to put the whole parish on its feet.'

"So one day the parson went out to see Olaf Svärd, to ask him and his brother as to what should be done immediately with the silver mountain. When he came in the vicinity of the barracks he met a cart surrounded by armed peasants, and in the cart sat a man with his hands tied behind him and a rope around his ankles.

"When the parson passed by, the cart stopped and he had time to regard the prisoner, whose head was tied up so it was not easy to see who he was. But the parson thought he recognized Olaf Svärd. He heard the prisoner beg those who guarded him to let him speak a few words with the parson.

"The parson drew nearer, and the prisoner turned toward him. 'You will soon be the only one who knows where the silver mine is,' said Olaf.

" 'What are you saying, Olaf?' asked the parson.

" 'Well, you see, parson, since we have learned that it was a silver mine we had found, my brother and I could no longer be as good friends as before. We were continually quarreling. Last night we got into a controversy over which one of us five it was who first discovered the mine. It ended in strife between us, and we came to blows. I have killed my brother and he has left me with a souvenir across the forehead to remember him by. I must hang now, and then you will be the only one who knows about the mine; therefore I wish to ask something of you.'

" 'Speak out!' said the parson. 'I'll do what I can for you.'

" 'You know that I am leaving several little children behind me,' began the soldier, but the parson interrupted him.

" 'As regards this, you can rest easy. That which comes to your share in the mine they shall have, exactly as if you yourself were living.'

" 'No,' said Olaf Svärd, 'it was another thing I wanted to ask of you. Don't let them have any portion of that which comes from the mine!'

"The parson staggered back a step. He stood there dumb and could not answer.

" 'If you do not promise me this, I cannot die in peace,' said the prisoner.

" 'Yes,' said the parson slowly and painfully. 'I promise you what you ask of me.'

"Thereupon the murderer was taken away, and the parson stood on the highway thinking how he should keep the promise he had given him. On the way home he thought of the wealth which he had been so happy over. What if it really were true that the people in this community could not stand riches? Already four were ruined who hitherto had been dignified and excellent men. He seemed to see the whole community before him, and he pictured to himself how this silver mine would destroy one after another. Was it befitting that he, who had been appointed to watch over these poor human beings' souls, should let loose upon them that which would be their destruction?"

All of a sudden the king sat bolt upright in his chair. "I declare!" said he, "you'll make me understand that a parson in this isolated settlement must be every inch a man."

"Nor was it enough with what had already happened," continued the parson, "for as soon as the news about the mine spread among the parishioners, they stopped working and went about in idleness, waiting for the time when great riches should pour in on them. All the ne'er-do-wells there were in this section streamed in, and drunkenness and fighting were what the parson heard talked of continually. A lot of people did nothing but tramp round in the forest searching for the mine, and the parson marked that as soon as he left the house people followed him stealthily to find out if he wasn't going to the silver mountain and to steal the secret from him.

"When matters were come to this pass, the parson called the peasants together to vote. To start with he reminded them of all the misfortunes which the discovery of the mountain had brought upon them, and he asked them if they were going to let themselves be ruined or if they would save themselves. Then he told them that they must not expect him, who was their spiritual adviser, to help on their destruction. Now he had declared not to reveal to anyone where the silver mine was, and never would he himself take riches from it. And then he asked the peasants how they would have it henceforth. If they wished to continue their search for the mine and wait upon riches, then he would go so far away that no word of their misery could reach him; but if they would give up thinking about the silver mine and be as heretofore, he would remain with them. 'Whichever way you may choose,' said the parson, 'remember this, that from me no one shall ever know anything about the silver mountain.' "

"Well," said the king, "how did they decide?"

"They did as their pastor wished," said the parson. "They understood that he meant well by them when he wanted to remain poor for their sakes. And they commissioned him to go to the forest and conceal the vein of ore with evergreen and stone, so that no one would be able to find it—neither they nor their posterity."

"And ever since the parson has been living here just as poor as the rest?"

"Yes," answered the curate, "he has lived here just as poor as the rest."

"He has married, of course, and built a new parsonage?" said the king.

"No, he couldn't afford to marry and he lives in the old cabin."

"It's a pretty story that you have told me," said the king. After a few seconds he resumed, "Was it of the silver mountain that you were thinking when you said that the parson here would be able to procure for me as much

money as I need?"

"Yes," said the other.

"But I can't put the thumbscrews on him," said the king. "Or how would you advise that I get such a man to show me the mountain— a man who has renounced his sweetheart and the allurements of life?"

"Oh, that's a different matter," said the parson. "But if it's the fatherland that is in need of the fortune, he will probably give in."

"Will you answer for that?" asked the king.

"Yes, that I will answer for," said the clergyman.

"Doesn't he care, then, what becomes of his parishioners?"

"That can rest in God's hands."

The king rose from his chair and walked over to the window. He stood for a moment and looked upon the group of people outside. The longer he looked, the clearer his large eyes shone; and his figure seemed to grow. "You may greet the pastor of this congregation and say that for Sweden's king there is no sight more beautiful than to see a people such as this!"

Then the king turned from the window and looked at the clergyman. He began to smile. "Is it true that the pastor of this parish is so poor that he removes his black clothes as soon as the service is over and dresses himself like a peasant?" asked the king.

"Yes, so poor is he," said the curate, and a crimson flush leaped into his rough-hewn face.

The king went back to the window. One could see that he was in his best mood. All that was noble and great within him had been quickened into life. "You must let that mine lie in peace," said the king. "Inasmuch as you have labored and starved a lifetime to make this people such as you would have it, you may keep it as it is."

"But if the kingdom is in danger?" said the parson.

"The kingdom is better served with men than with money," remarked the king. When he had said this, he bade the clergyman farewell and went out from the vestry.

Without stood the group of people, as quiet and taciturn as they were when he went in. As the king came down the steps, a peasant stepped up to him.

"Have you had a talk with our pastor?" said the peasant.

"Yes," said the king. "I have."

"Then of course you have our answer," said the peasant. "We asked you to go in and talk with our parson, that he might give you an answer from us."

"I have the answer," said the king.

About the Story

1. List some of the similarities and differences you found between the peasants (the parson and his parishoners) and the king.
2. Considering these similarities and differences, why do you think the parson told the story to the king?
3. What character in the story is a sort of companion for you, the reader, one with whom you can identify and with whom you can progressively learn?
4. In one sentence, state what you think is the central theme of the story.

About the Author

Selma Lagerlöf (1858-1940) had a special gift for creative storytelling. Throughout her life she shared with the world modern versions of old Swedish folktales and delightful creations of her own vivid imagination. Her works were infused with childlike optimism and a deep appreciation for integrity, honesty, and selflessness. One recurrent theme in her literature is the reconciliation of the desire to be happy with the need to be virtuous and noble. Her short story "The Silver Mine" is an excellent example of her approach to storytelling and her method of expressing truth to make it appealing to the reader.

Although she had the honor of being both the first woman to receive the Nobel Prize for Literature and Sweden's foremost storyteller, Lagerlöf lived a quiet and uneventful life. Her imagination, however, was always active, sustained from childhood by the wealth of Swedish folklore that she knew well. She grew up on a farm in Sweden, and as an adult she purchased the estate and ran it with the help of Swedish peasants. The Swedish school system commissioned Lagerlöf to write a reader for use in grade schools. The resulting two books, *The Wonderful Adventures of Nil* and *The Further Adventures of Nil*, tell the adventures of a young boy who magically flies about Sweden. These enchanting stories richly portray the country and customs of the Swedish countryside.

Quality

John Galsworthy

The details of both conflict and character are important in helping us crystallize a story's theme. An author, however, may choose to emphasize one of these elements above the other. For example, in Treasure Island, *the characters are subordinate to the conflict. Though Jim Hawkins and his fellow sailors are round characters, it is the dynamic action growing out of an exciting conflict that keeps us turning the page. In Galsworthy's story, however, conflict is subservient to character. The intriguing characters of the Gessler brothers* create *the conflict. They are the embodiment of a particular set of values, values that can find no place in a world of growing industrialization and materialism.*

As you read, try to discern what the author's attitude is toward the central characters he creates. Does he sympathize with the Gessler brothers? Or does he view them as old-fashioned and eccentric? What elements of the story help you decide Galsworthy's attitude toward his characters? Does the title of the story give you a clue?

I knew him from the days of my extreme youth, because he made my father's boots; inhabiting with his elder brother two little shops let into one, in a small by-street—now no more, but then most fashionably placed in the West End.

That tenement had a certain quiet distinction; there was no sign upon its face that he made for any of the Royal Family—merely his own German name of Gessler Brothers; and in the window a few pairs of boots. I remember that it always troubled me to account for those unvarying boots in the window, for he made only what was ordered, reaching nothing down, and it seemed so inconceivable that what he made could ever have failed to fit. Had he bought them to put there? That, too, seemed inconceivable. He would never have tolerated in his house leather on which he had not worked himself. Besides, they were too beautiful—the pair of pumps, so inexpressibly slim; the patent leathers with cloth tops, making water come into one's mouth; the tall brown riding boots with marvelous sooty glow, as if, though new, they had been worn a hundred years. Those pairs could have been made only by one who saw before him the Soul of Boot—so truly were they prototypes incarnating the very spirit of all footgear. These thoughts, of course, came to me later, though even when I was promoted to him, at the age of perhaps fourteen, some inkling haunted me of the dignity of himself and his brother. For to make boots—such boots as he made—seemed to me then, and still seems to me, mysterious and wonderful.

I remember well my shy remark, one day, while stretching out to him my youthful foot.

"Isn't it awfully hard to do, Mr. Gessler?"

And his answer, given with a sudden smile from out of the sardonic* redness of his beard: "Id is an ardt!"

---

sardonic: mocking with scorn

Himself, he was a little as if made from leather, with his yellow crinkly face, and crinkly reddish hair and beard, and neat folds slanting down his cheeks to the corners of his mouth, and his guttural and one-toned voice, for leather is a sardonic substance, and stiff and slow of purpose. And that was the character of his face, save that his eyes, which were grey-blue, had in them the simple gravity of one secretly possessed by the Ideal. His elder brother was so very like him—though watery, paler in every way, with a great industry—that sometimes in early days I was not quite sure of him until the interview was over. Then I knew that it was he, if the words, "I will ask my brudder," had not been spoken; and that if they had, it was his elder brother.

When one grew old and wild and ran up bills, one somehow never ran them up with Gessler Brothers. It would not have seemed becoming to go in there and stretch out one's foot to that blue iron-spectacled glance, owing him for more than—say—two pairs, just the comfortable reassurance that one was still his client.

For it was not possible to go to him very often—his boots lasted terribly, having something beyond the temporary—some, as it were, essence of boot stitched into them.

One went in, not as into most shops, in the mood of: "Please serve me, and let me go!" but restfully, as one enters a church; and, sitting on the single wooden chair, waited—for there was never anybody there. Soon, over the top edge of that sort of well—rather dark, and smelling soothingly of leather—which formed the shop, there would be seen his face, or that of his elder brother, peering down. A guttural sound, and the narrow wooden stairs, and he would stand before one without coat, a little bent, in leather apron, with sleeves turned back, blinking—as if awakened from some dream of boots, or like an owl surprised in daylight and annoyed at this interruption.

And I would say: "How do you do, Mr. Gessler? Could you make me a pair of Russian leather boots?"

Without a word he would leave me, retiring whence he came, or into the other portion of the shop, and I would continue to rest in the wooden chair, inhaling the incense of his trade. Soon he would come back, holding in his thin, veined hand a piece of gold-brown leather.

With eyes fixed on it, he would remark: "What a beaudiful biece!" When I, too, had admired it, he would speak again. "When do you wand dem?" And I would answer: "Oh! As soon as you conveniently can." And he would say: "Tomorrow fordnighd?"* Or if he were his elder brother: "I will ask my brudder!"

---

fordnighd (fortnight): two weeks

Then I would murmur: "Thank you! Good morning, Mr. Gessler." "Goot morning!" He would reply, still looking at the leather in his hand. And as I moved to the door, I would hear the tip-tap of his bast* slippers restoring him, up the stairs, to his dream of boots. But if it were some new kind of footgear that he had not yet made me, then indeed he would observe ceremony—divesting me of my boot and holding it long in his hand, looking at it with eyes at once critical and loving, as if recalling the glow with which he had created it, and rebuking the way in which one had disorganized this masterpiece. Then placing my foot on a thin piece of paper, he would two or three times tickle the outer edges with a pencil and pass his nervous fingers over my toes, feeling himself into the heart of my requirements.

---

bast: flexible fibrous material used to make textiles

I cannot forget that day on which I had occasion to say to him: "Mr. Gessler, that last pair of town walking-boots creaked, you know."

He looked at me for a time without replying, as if expecting me to withdraw or qualify the statement, then said:

"Id shouldn't 'ave greaked."

"It did, I'm afraid."

"You god dem wed before dey found demselves?"

"I don't think so."

At that he lowered his eyes, as if hunting for memory of those boots, and I felt sorry I had mentioned this grave thing.

"Zend dem back!" he said; "I will look at dem."

A feeling of compassion for creaking boots surged up in me, so well could I imagine the sorrowful long curiosity of regard which he would bend on them.

"Zome boods," he said slowly, "are bad from birdt. If I can do noding wid dem, I dake dem off your bill."

Once (once only) I went absent-mindedly into his shop in a pair of boots bought in an emergency at some large firm. He took my order without showing me any leather, and I could feel his eyes penetrating the inferior covering of my foot. At last he said:

"Dose are nod my boods."

The tone was not one of anger, nor of sorrow, not even of contempt, but there was in it something quiet that froze the blood. He put his hand down and pressed a finger on the place where the left boot, endeavoring to be fashionable, was not quite comfortable.

"Id 'urds you dere," he said. "Dose big virms 'ave no self-respect. Drash!" And then as if something had given way within him, he spoke long and bitterly. It was the only time I ever heard him discuss the conditions and hardships of his trade.

"Dey ged id all," he said, "dey ged id by adverdisement, nod by work. Dey dake id away from us, who lofe our boods. Id gomes to dis—bresently I haf no work. Every year id gets less—you will see." And looking at his lined face I saw things I had never noticed before, bitter things and bitter struggle—and what a lot of grey hairs there seemed suddenly in his red beard!

As best I could, I explained the circumstances of the purchase of those ill-omened boots. But his face and voice made so deep

an impression that during the next few minutes I ordered many pairs. Nemesis* fell! They lasted more terribly than ever. And I was not able conscientiously to go to him for nearly two years.

---

nemesis: retributive justice

When at last I went I was surprised to find that outside one of the two little windows of his shop another name was painted, also that of a boot-maker—making, of course, for the Royal Family. The old familiar boots, no longer in dignified isolation, were huddled in the single window. Inside, the now contracted well of the one little shop was more scented and darker than ever. And it was longer than usual, too, before a face peered down, and the tip-tap of the bast slippers began. At last he stood before me, and, gazing through those rusty iron spectacles, said:

"Mr. ——, isn'd id?"

"Ah, Mr. Gessler," I stammered. "But your boots are really *too* good, you know! See, these are quite decent still!" And I stretched out to him my foot. He looked at it.

"Yes," he said, "beoble do nod wand good boods, id seems."

To get away from his reproachful eyes and voice I hastily remarked: "What have you done to your shop?"

He answered quietly. "Id was too exbensif. Do you wand some boods?"

I ordered three pairs, though I had wanted only two, and quickly left. I had, I do not know quite what feeling of being part, in his mind, of a conspiracy against him; or not perhaps so much against him as against his idea of boot. One does not, I suppose, care to feel like that; for it was again many months before my next visit to his shop, paid, I remember, with the feeling: "Oh, well, I can't leave the old boy—so here goes! Perhaps it will be his elder brother!"

For his elder brother, I knew, had not character enough to reproach me, even dumbly.

And, to my relief, in the shop there did appear to be his elder brother, handling a piece of leather.

"Well, Mr. Gessler," I said, "How are you?"

He came close and peered at me.

"I am breddy well," he said slowly; "but my elder brudder is dead."

And I saw that he was indeed himself—but how aged and wan! And never before had I heard him mention his brother. Much shocked, I murmured: "Oh! I am sorry!"

"Yes," he answered, "he was a good man, he made a good bood; but he is dead." And he touched the top of his head, where the hair had suddenly gone as thin as it had been on that of his poor brother, to indicate, I suppose, the cause of death. "He could nod ged over losing de oder shop. Do you wand any boods?" And he held up the leather in his hand: "Id's a beaudiful biece."

I ordered several pairs. It was not very long before they came—but they were better than ever. One simply could not wear them out. And soon after that I went abroad.

It was over a year before I was again in London. And the first shop I went to was my old friend's. I had left a man of sixty; I came back to one of seventy-five, pinched and worn and tremulous, who genuinely, this time, did not at first know me.

"Oh! Mr. Gessler," I said, sick at heart; "how splendid your boots are! See, I've been wearing this pair nearly all the time I've been abroad; and they're not half worn out, are they?"

He looked long at my boots—a pair of Russian leather, and his face seemed to regain steadiness. Putting his hand on my instep, he said:

"Do dey vid you here? I 'ad drouble wid

dat bair; I remember."

I assured him that they had fitted beautifully.

"Do you wand any boods?" he said. "I can make dem quickly; Id is a slack dime."

I answered: "Please, please! I want boots all around—every kind!"

"I will make a vresh model. Your foot must be bigger." And with utter slowness, he traced round my foot, and felt my toes, only once looking up to say:

"Did I dell you my brudder was dead?"

To watch him was painful, so feeble had he grown; I was glad to get away.

I had given those boots up, when one evening they came. Opening the parcel, I set the four pairs in a row. Then one by one I tried them on. There was no doubt about it. In shape and fit, in finish and quality of leather, they were the best he had ever made me. And in the mouth of one of the town walking-boots I found his bill. The amount was the same as usual, but it gave me quite a shock. He had never before sent it till quarter day. I flew downstairs, and wrote a cheque and posted it at once with my own hand.

A week later, passing the little street, I thought I would go in and tell him how splendidly the new boots fitted. But when I came to where his shop had been, his name was gone. Still there, in the window, were the slim pumps, the patent leathers with cloth tops, the sooty riding boots.

I went in, very much disturbed. In the two little shops—again made into one—was a young man with an English face:

"Mr. Gessler in?" I said.

He gave me a strange, ingratiating look.

"No, sir," he said, "no, but we can attend to anything with pleasure. We've taken the shop over. You've seen our name, no doubt, next door. We make for some very good people."

"Yes, yes," I said, "but Mr. Gessler?"

"Oh!" he answered; "dead."

"Dead! But I received these boots from him last Wednesday week."

"Ah!" he said, "a shockin' go. Poor old man starved 'imself."

"What! You mean—!"

"Slow starvation, the doctor called it! You see, he went to work in such a way! Would keep the shop on; wouldn't have a soul touch his boots except himself. When he got an order, it took him such a time. People won't wait. He lost everybody. And there he'd sit, goin' on and on—I will say that for him—not a man in London made a better boot! But look at the competition! He never advertised! Would 'ave the best leather, too, and do it all 'imself. Well, there it is. What could you expect with his ideas?"

"But starvation—!"

"That may be a bit flowery, as the sayin' is—but I know myself he was sittin' over his boots day and night, to the very last. You see, I used to watch him. Never gave himself time to eat; never had a penny in the house. All went in rent and leather. How he lived so long I don't know. He regular let his fire go out. He was a character. But he made good boots."

"Yes," I said, "he made good boots."

And I turned and went out quickly, for I did not want that youth to know that I could hardly see.

About the Story

1. What clue does the title of the story give you about the theme?
2. Who embodies the characteristic of *quality?* How is this shown in the story?
3. What is the main conflict of the story?
4. How does *quality* control the action of the story?

5. What consequences occur because of the Gessler brothers' strong belief in *quality?*
6. How is the conflict resolved?
7. How does the author feel about the Gessler brothers? How do we know his feelings?

About the Author

John Galsworthy (1867-1933), with his monocle and his ability to keep a "stiff upper lip," appeared to be the epitome of the stereotypical Englishman. His upper-middle-class family was steeped in conventional English values. Despite his characteristically English tastes and attitudes, however, Galsworthy was also markedly openhearted to children and young people, especially toward those aspiring to be writers. Throughout his life, Galsworthy displayed a compassion for the underdog. Although he always enjoyed the benefits of prosperity, he criticized any improper use of social position or advantage.

Educated at Oxford and trained to practice law, Galsworthy was inspired by his wife Ada and by his acquaintance with influential men such as Joseph Conrad and Edward Garnett to turn from that profession to writing. In his numerous short stories and novels, Galsworthy discusses the conflicts that troubled his generation: the restrictions of tradition-bound English society, the tension between social classes, and the detrimental consequences of the rising materialism of his day. His writings reflect his deepest feelings, and his characters often verbalize his own convictions about society's values and morals. His short story "Quality" illustrates Galsworthy's concerns. Here he shows that, in an industrialized society, the avarice of men may prohibit the reward of excellence and the encouragement of "quality." Galsworthy's works have always been more popular with readers than with critics. His stories have enjoyed enduring popularity in England and America.

Dr. Heidegger's Experiment

Nathaniel Hawthorne

Whether the tale be somber or fanciful, Hawthorne focuses on universal themes; and his conflicts and characters, whether simple or complex, always draw the reader's attention to a specific moral point.

"Dr. Heidegger's Experiment" is a rare blend of the somber and the fanciful, of the simple and the complex. Through the setting and characters of this story, Hawthorne poses an interesting question: "If one could be young again, would the wisdom acquired with age motivate him to correct the waywardness of his youth?" The characters' responses to their "second-chance" opportunity show you Hawthorne's answer to that question and give you the theme of his story.

That very singular man, old Dr. Heidegger, once invited four venerable friends to meet him in his study. There were three white-bearded gentlemen, Mr. Medbourne, Colonel Killigrew, and Mr. Gascoigne, and a withered gentlewoman, whose name was the Widow Wycherly. They were all melancholy old creatures, who had been unfortunate in life, and whose greatest misfortune it was that they were not long ago in their graves. Mr. Medbourne, in the vigor of his age, had been a prosperous merchant, but had lost his all by a frantic speculation, and was now little better than a mendicant.* Colonel Killigrew had wasted his best years, and his health and substance, in the pursuit of sinful pleasures which had given birth to a brood of pains, such as the gout, and divers other torments of soul and body. Mr. Gascoigne was a ruined politician, a man of evil fame, or at least had been so, till time had buried him from the knowledge of the present generation, and made him obscure instead of infamous. As for the Widow Wycherly, tradition tells us that she was a great beauty in her day; but, for a long while past, she had lived in deep seclusion, on account of certain scandalous stories which had prejudiced the gentry of the town against her. It is a circumstance worth mentioning, that each of these three old gentlemen, Mr. Medbourne, Colonel Killigrew, and Mr. Gascoigne, were early lovers of the Widow Wycherly, and had once been on the point of cutting each other's throats for her sake. And before proceeding further, I will merely hint that Dr. Heidegger and all his four guests were sometimes thought to be a little beside themselves, as is not unfrequently the case with old people, when worried either by present troubles or woeful recollections.

---

mendicant: a beggar

"My dear old friends," said Dr. Heidegger, motioning them to be seated, "I am desirous of your assistance in one of those little experiments with which I amuse myself here in my study."

If all stories were true, Dr. Heidegger's study must have been a very curious place. It was a dim, old-fashioned chamber, festooned with cobwebs, and besprinkled with antique dust. Around the walls stood several oaken bookcases, the lower shelves of which were filled with rows of gigantic folios* and black-letter quartos,* and the upper with little parchment-covered duodecimos.* Over the central bookcase was a bronze bust of Hippocrates, with which, according to some authorities, Dr. Heidegger was accustomed to hold consultations in all difficult cases of his practice. In the obscurest corner of the room stood a tall and narrow oaken closet, with its door ajar, within which doubtfully appeared a skeleton. Between two of the bookcases hung a looking glass, presenting its high and dusty plate within a tarnished gilt frame. Among many wonderful stories related of this mirror, it was fabled that the spirits of all the doctor's deceased patients dwelt within its verge, and would stare him in the face whenever he looked thitherward. The opposite side of the chamber was ornamented with the full-length portrait of a young lady, arrayed in the faded magnificence of silk, satin, and brocade, and with a visage as faded as her dress. Above half a century ago, Dr. Heidegger had been on the point of marriage with this young lady; but, being affected with some slight disorder, she had swallowed one of her lover's prescriptions, and died on the bridal evening. The greatest curiosity of the study remains to be mentioned; it was a ponderous folio volume, bound in black leather, with massive silver clasps. There were no letters on the back, and nobody could tell the title of the book. But it was well known to be a book of magic; and once, when a chambermaid had lifted it, merely to brush away the dust, the skeleton had rattled in its closet, the picture of the young lady had stepped one foot upon the floor, and several ghastly faces had peeped forth from the mirror, while the brazen head of Hippocrates frowned, and said—"Forbear!"

---

folios: books about 15 inches in height
quartos: a book wherein the page is obtained by folding a whole sheet into four leaves
duodecimos: books with each page being 5 by 7-3/4 inches

Such was Dr. Heidegger's study. On the summer afternoon of our tale, a small round table, as black as ebony, stood in the center of the room, sustaining a cut-glass vase of beautiful form and elaborate workmanship. The sunshine came through the window, between the heavy festoons* of two faded damask* curtains, and fell directly across this vase; so that a mild splendor was reflected from it on the ashen visages of the five old people who sat around. Four glasses were also on the table.

---

festoons: strings or garlands draped in a curve between two points
damask: a rich patterned fabric of cotton or other material

"My dear old friends," repeated Dr. Heidegger, "may I reckon on your aid in performing an exceedingly curious experiment?"

Now Dr. Heidegger was a very strange old gentleman, whose eccentricity had become the nucleus for a thousand fantastic stories. Some of these fables, to my shame be it spoken, might possibly be traced back to mine own veracious* self; and if any passages of the present tale should startle the reader's faith, I must be content to bear the stigma of a fiction-monger.

---

veracious: truthful

When the doctor's four guests heard him talk of his proposed experiment, they anticipated nothing more wonderful than the murder of a mouse in an air pump, or the examination of a cobweb by the microscope, or some similar nonsense, with which he was constantly in the habit of pestering his intimates. But without waiting for a reply, Dr. Heidegger hobbled across the chamber, and returned with the same ponderous folio, bound in black leather, which common report affirmed to be a book of magic. Undoing the silver clasps, he opened the volume, and took from among its black-letter* pages a rose, or what was once a rose, though now the green leaves and crimson petals had assumed one brownish hue, and the ancient flower seemed ready to crumble to dust in the doctor's hands.

black-letter: a heavy type style used in European typesetting up to the time of World War II

"This rose," said Dr. Heidegger, with a sigh, "this same withered and crumbling flower, blossomed five and fifty years ago. It was given me by Sylvia Ward, whose portrait hangs yonder; and I meant to wear it in my bosom at our wedding. Five and fifty years it has been treasured between the leaves of this old volume. Now, would you deem it possible that this rose of half a century could ever bloom again?"

"Nonsense!" said the Widow Wycherly, with a peevish toss of her head. "You might as well ask whether an old woman's wrinkled face could ever bloom again."

"See!" answered Dr. Heidegger.

He uncovered the vase, and threw the faded rose into the water which it contained. At first it lay lightly on the surface of the fluid, appearing to imbibe none of its moisture. Soon, however, a singular change began to be visible. The crushed and dried petals stirred, and assumed a deepening tinge of crimson, as if the flower were reviving from a deathlike slumber; the slender stalk and twigs of foliage became green; and there was the rose of half a century, looking as fresh as when Sylvia Ward had first given it to her lover. It was scarcely full blown; for some of its delicate red leaves curled modestly around its moist bosom, within which two or three dewdrops were sparkling.

"That is certainly a very pretty deception," said the doctor's friends; carelessly, however, for they had witnessed greater miracles at a conjurer's show; "pray how was it effected?"

"Did you never hear of the 'Fountain of Youth'?" asked Dr. Heidegger, "which Ponce de Leon, the Spanish adventurer, went in search of, two or three centuries ago?"

"But did Ponce de Leon ever find it?" said

the Widow Wycherly.

"No," answered Dr. Heidegger, "for he never sought it in the right place. The famous Fountain of Youth, if I am rightly informed, is situated in the southern part of the Floridian peninsula, not far from Lake Macaco. Its source is overshadowed by several gigantic magnolias, which, though numberless centuries old, have been kept as fresh as violets by the virtues of this wonderful water. An acquaintance of mine, knowing my curiosity in such matters, has sent me what you see in the vase."

"Ahem!" said Colonel Killigrew, who believed not a word of the doctor's story; "and what may be the effect of this fluid on the human frame?"

"You shall judge for yourself, my dear colonel," replied Dr. Heidegger; "and all of you, my respected friends, are welcome to so much of this admirable fluid as may restore to you the bloom of youth. For my own part, having had much trouble in growing old, I am in no hurry to grow young again. With your permission, therefore, I will merely watch the progress of the experiment."

While he spoke, Dr. Heidegger had been filling the four glasses with the water of the Fountain of Youth. It was apparently impregnated with an effervescent gas, for little bubbles were continually ascending from the depths of the glasses, and bursting in silvery spray at the surface. As the liquor diffused a pleasant perfume, the old people doubted not that it possessed cordial and comfortable properties; and, though utter skeptics as to its rejuvenescent power, they were inclined to swallow it at once. But Dr. Heidegger besought them to stay a moment.

"Before you drink, my respectable old friends," said he, "it would be well that, with the experience of a lifetime to direct you, you should draw up a few general rules for your guidance, in passing a second time through the perils of youth. Think what a sin and a shame it would be, if with your peculiar advantages, you should not become patterns of virtue and wisdom to all the young people of the age!"

The doctor's four venerable friends made him no answer, except by a feeble and tremulous laugh; so very ridiculous was the idea, that, knowing how closely repentance treads behind the steps of error, they should ever go astray again.

"Drink, then," said the doctor, bowing; "I rejoice that I have so well selected the subjects of my experiment."

With palsied hands they raised the glasses to their lips. The liquid, if it really possessed such virtues as Dr. Heidegger imputed to it, could not have been bestowed on four human beings who needed it more woefully. They looked as if they had never known what youth or pleasure was, but had been the offspring of Nature's dotage, and always the gray, decrepit, sapless, miserable creatures, who now sat stooping round the doctor's table, without life enough in their souls or bodies to be animated even by the prospect of growing young again. They drank off the water, and replaced their glasses on the table.

Assuredly, there was an almost immediate improvement in the aspect of the party, with a sudden glow of cheerful sunshine, brightening over all their visages at once. There was a healthful suffusion on their cheeks, instead of the ashen hue that had made them look so corpselike. They gazed at one another, and fancied that some magic power had really begun to smooth away the deep and sad inscription which Father Time had been so long engraving on their brows. The Widow Wycherly adjusted her cap, for she felt almost like a woman again.

"Give us more of this wondrous water!" cried they eagerly.

"We are younger—but we are still too old! Quick—give us more!"

"Patience, patience!" quoth Dr. Heidegger, who sat watching the experiment with philosophic coolness. "You have been a long time growing old. Surely you might be content to grow young in half an hour! But the water is at your service."

Again he filled their glasses with the water of youth, enough of which still remained in the vase to turn half the old people in the city to the age of their own grandchildren. While the bubbles were yet sparkling on the brim, the doctor's four guests snatched their glasses from the table, and swallowed the contents at a single gulp. Was it delusion? Even while the draught was passing down their throats, it seemed to have wrought a change on their whole systems. Their eyes grew clear and bright; a dark shade deepened among their silvery locks; they sat around the table, three gentlemen of middle age, and a woman hardly beyond her buxom prime.

"My dear widow, you are charming!" cried Colonel Killigrew, whose eyes had been fixed upon her face, while the shadows of age were flitting from it like darkness from the crimson daybreak.

The fair widow knew, of old, that Colonel Killigrew's compliments were not always measured by sober truth; so she started up and ran to the mirror, still dreading that the ugly visage of an old woman would meet her gaze. Meanwhile, the three gentlemen behaved in such a manner as proved that the water of the Fountain of Youth possessed some intoxicating qualities; unless, indeed, their exhilaration of spirits were merely a lightsome dizziness, caused by the sudden removal of the weight of years. Mr. Gascoigne's mind seemed to run on political topics, but whether relating to the past, present, or future, could not easily be determined, since the same ideas and phrases have been in vogue these fifty years. Now he rattled forth full-throated sentences about patriotism, national glory, and the people's rights; now he muttered some perilous stuff or other, in a sly and doubtful whisper, so cautiously that even his own conscience could scarcely catch the secret; and now again he spoke in measured accents, and a deeply deferential tone, as if a royal ear were listening to his well-turned periods.* Colonel Killigrew all this time had been trolling forth a jolly bottle song, and ringing his glass in symphony with the chorus, while his eyes wandered towards the figure of the Widow Wycherly. On the other side of the table, Mr. Medbourne was involved in a calculation of dollars and cents, with which was strangely intermingled a project for supplying the East Indies with ice, by harnessing a team of whales to the polar icebergs.

well-turned periods: clever phrases or sentences

As for the Widow Wycherly, she stood before the mirror curtsying and simpering to her own image, and greeting it as the friend whom she loved better than all the world beside. She thrust her face close to the glass, to see whether some long-remembered wrinkle or crow's-foot had indeed vanished. She examined whether the snow had so entirely melted from her hair, that the venerable* cap could be safely thrown aside. At last, turning briskly away, she came with a sort of dancing step to the table.

venerable: worthy of respect because of character, position, or age

"My dear old doctor," cried she, "pray favor me with another glass!"

"Certainly, my dear madam, certainly!" replied the complaisant doctor; "See! I have already filled the glasses."

There, in fact, stood the four glasses, brimful of this wonderful water, the delicate spray of which, as it effervesced from the surface, resembled the tremulous glitter of diamonds. It was now so nearly sunset that the chamber had grown duskier than ever; but a mild and moonlike splendor gleamed from within the vase, and rested alike on the four guests, and on the doctor's venerable figure. He sat in a high-backed, elaborately carved, oaken armchair, with a gray dignity of aspect that might have well befitted that very Father Time whose power had never been disputed save by this fortunate company. Even while quaffing the third draught of the Fountain of Youth, they were almost awed by the expression of his mysterious visage.

But, the next moment, the exhilarating gush of young life shot through their veins. They were now in the happy prime of youth. Age, with its miserable train of cares, and sorrows, and diseases, was remembered only as the trouble of a dream from which they had joyously awoke. The fresh gloss of the soul, so early lost, and without which the world's successive scenes had been but a gallery of faded pictures, again threw its enchantment over all their prospects. They felt like new-created beings, in a new-created universe.

"We are young! We are young!" they cried, exultingly.

Youth, like the extremity of age, had effaced* the strongly marked characteristics of middle life, and mutually assimilated them all. They were a group of merry youngsters, almost maddened with the exuberant frolicsomeness of their years. The most singular effect of their gaiety was an impulse to mock the infirmity and decrepitude of which they had so lately been the victims. They laughed loudly at their old-fashioned attire, the wide-skirted coats and flapped waistcoats of the young men, and the ancient cap and gown of the blooming girl.

One limped across the floor, like a gouty grandfather; one set a pair of spectacles astride of his nose, and pretended to pore over the black-letter pages of the book of magic; a third seated himself in an armchair, and strove to imitate the venerable dignity of Dr. Heidegger. Then all shouted mirthfully, and leaped about the room. The Widow Wycherly—if so fresh a damsel could be called a widow—tripped up to the doctor's chair, with a mischievous merriment in her rosy face.

effaced: erased

"Doctor, you dear old soul," cried she, "get up and dance with me!" And then the four young people laughed louder than ever, to think what a queer figure the poor old doctor would cut.

"Pray excuse me," answered the doctor quietly. "I am old and rheumatic, and my dancing days were over long ago. But either of these gay young gentlemen will be glad of so pretty a partner."

"Dance with me, Clara!" cried Colonel Killigrew.

"No, no, I will be her partner!" shouted Mr. Gascoigne.

"She promised me her hand, fifty years ago!" exclaimed Mr. Medbourne.

They all gathered round her. One caught both her hands in his passionate grasp—another threw his arm about her waist—the third buried his hand among the glossy curls that clustered beneath the widow's cap. Blushing, panting, struggling, chiding, laughing, her warm breath fanning each of their faces by turns, she strove to disengage herself, yet still remained in their triple embrace. Never was there a livelier picture of youthful rivalship, with bewitching beauty for the prize. Yet, by a strange deception, owing to the duskiness of the chamber, and the antique dresses which they still wore, the tall mirror is said to have reflected the figures of the three old, gray, withered grandsires, ridiculously contending for the skinny ugliness of a shriveled grandam.

But they were young: their burning passions proved them so. Inflamed to madness by the coquetry of the girl-widow, who neither granted nor quite withheld her favors, the three rivals began to interchange threatening glances. Still keeping hold of the fair prize, they grappled fiercely at one another's throats. As they struggled to and fro, the table was overturned, and the vase dashed into a thousand fragments. The precious Water of Youth flowed in a bright stream across the floor, moistening the wings of a butterfly, which, grown old in the decline of summer, had alighted there to die. The insect fluttered lightly through the chamber, and settled on the snowy head of Dr. Heidegger.

"Come, come, gentlemen!—Come, Madam Wycherly," exclaimed the doctor, "I really must protest against this riot."

They stood still, and shivered; for it seemed as if gray Time were calling them back from their sunny youth, far down into the chill and darksome vale of years. They looked at old Dr. Heidegger, who sat in his carved armchair, holding the rose of half a century, which he had rescued from among the fragments of the shattered vase. At the motion of his hand, the four rioters resumed their seats; the more readily, because their violent exertions had wearied them, youthful though they were.

"My poor Sylvia's rose!" ejaculated Dr. Heidegger, holding it in the light of the sunset clouds; "It appears to be fading again."

And so it was. Even while the party were looking at it, the flower continued to shrivel up, till it became as dry and fragile as when the doctor had first thrown it into the vase. He shook off the few drops of moisture which clung to its petals.

"I love it as well thus as in its dewy freshness," observed he, pressing the withered rose to his withered lips. While he spoke, the butterfly fluttered down from the doctor's snowy head, and fell upon the floor.

His guests shivered again. A strange chillness, whether of the body or spirit they could not tell, was creeping gradually over them all. They gazed at one another, and fancied that each fleeting moment snatched away a charm, and left a deepening furrow where none had been before. Was it an illusion? Had the changes of a lifetime been crowded into so brief a space, and were they now four aged people, sitting with their old friend, Dr. Heidegger?

"Are we grown old again, so soon?" cried they dolefully.

In truth, they had. The Water of Youth possessed merely a virtue more transient than that of wine. The delirium which it created had effervesced away. Yes! they were old again. With a shuddering impulse that showed her a woman still, the widow clasped her skinny hands before her face, and wished that the coffin lid were over it, since it could be no longer beautiful.

"Yes, friends, ye are old again," said Dr. Heidegger; "and lo! the Water of Youth is all lavished on the ground. Well—I bemoan it not; for if the fountain gushed at my very doorstep, I would not stoop to bathe my lips in it— no, though its delirium were for years instead of moments. Such is the lesson ye have taught me!"

But the doctor's four friends had taught no such lesson to themselves. They resolved forthwith to make a pilgrimage to Florida, and quaff at morning, noon, and night, from the Fountain of Youth.

About the Story

1. Who is the central character?
2. Notice the doctor's advice to his companions before they drink the liquid (page 179). How would you describe their reactions to his advice?
3. Now look at their non-physical characteristics after the experiment (pages 180-83). Have they changed as a result of drinking the Water of Youth? How do they act?

4. After the experiment how does each character respond?
5. Which of the following best describes the central conflict?
   man *vs.* man
   man *vs.* a force greater than himself
   man *vs.* himself
6. How is the conflict resolved?
7. What does Dr. Heidegger learn from his experiment?

About the Author

Nathaniel Hawthorne (1804-1864) was born in Salem, Massachusetts, and acquired his love of books as a boy while living with his widowed mother. After attending college, Hawthorne returned to Salem and later began his literary career while working at a number of jobs, including the position of surveyor of Salem's port. Although never a rich man, Hawthorne enjoyed an especially happy family life. He enjoyed reading the Bible and works on theology but maintained that *Pilgrim's Progress* was his favorite book.

Hawthorne's timeless short stories and novels reflect the heritage of his New England ancestors. His acute consciousness of his Puritan background pervades his writings. Because of his insight into the human heart, Hawthorne is regarded as one of the greatest moralistic writers in American literature. Among his masterpieces are *The Scarlet Letter,* a classic allegory of human sin and suffering, and *The House of the Seven Gables,* both of which draw heavily on Hawthorne's rich family history and the influence of life in nineteenth-century New England. Fellow-writer Herman Melville greatly admired Hawthorne for maintaining a depth and balance in his viewpoint of man. Hawthorne did not give in to the groundless optimism of contemporary Romantic writers. While he did not condone the flaws of his Puritan forefathers, neither did he condemn their concern with morality and the consequences of man's fallen nature.

Beauty and the Beast

*Susanne Barbot de Gallos de Villeneuve
(retold by Andrew Lang)*

*The French vogue of fairy-tale writing began in the court of Louis XIV
(1638-1715) and continued until the Revolution (1789). In 1697 a lawyer
connected with the court, Charles Perrault, offered for publication a volume
of fairy tales containing "The Sleeping Beauty," "Red Riding Hood," "Blue
Beard," "Puss in Boots," "Cinderella," and several others that have become
world classics. Efforts by later participants in the vogue produced little that
is noteworthy. An exception is "Beauty and the Beast." This story gives classic
form to the theme of love's power to redeem ugliness. The heroine is named
Beauty; is her name appropriate in more ways than one?*

Once upon a time, in a very far-off country, there lived a merchant who had been so fortunate in all his undertakings that he was enormously rich. As he had, however, six sons and six daughters, he found that his money was not too much to let them all have everything they fancied, as they were accustomed to do.

But one day a most unexpected misfortune befell them. Their house caught fire and was speedily burnt to the ground, with all the splendid furniture, the books, pictures, gold, silver, and precious goods it contained; and this was only the beginning of their troubles. Their father, who had until this moment prospered in all ways, suddenly lost every ship he had upon the sea, either by dint of* pirates, shipwreck, or fire. Then he heard that his clerks in distant countries, whom he trusted entirely, had proved unfaithful; and at last from great wealth he fell into the direst poverty.

All that he had left was a little house in a desolate place at least a hundred leagues* from the town in which he had lived, and to this he was forced to retreat with his children, who were in despair at the idea of leading such a different life. Indeed, the daughters at first hoped that their friends, who had been so numerous while they were rich, would insist on their staying in their houses now they no longer possessed one. But they soon found that they were left alone, and that their former friends even attributed their misfortunes to their own extravagance, and showed no intention of offering them any help. So nothing was left for them but to take their departure to the cottage, which stood in the midst of a dark forest, and seemed to be the most dismal place upon the face of the earth. As they were too poor to have any servants, the girls had to work hard, like peasants, and the sons, for their part, cultivated the fields to earn their living. Roughly clothed, and living in the simplest way, the girls regretted unceasingly

---

by dint of: by force of

the luxuries and amusements of their former life; only the youngest tried to be brave and cheerful. She had been as sad as anyone when misfortune first overtook her father, but, soon recovering her natural gaiety, she set to work to make the best of things, to amuse her father and brothers as well as she could, and to try to persuade her sisters to join her in dancing and singing. But they would do nothing of the sort, and, because she was not as doleful* as themselves, they declared that this miserable life was all she was fit for. But she was really far prettier and cleverer than they were; indeed, she was so lovely that she was always called Beauty. After two years, when they were all beginning to get used to their new life, something happened to disturb their tranquillity. Their father received the news that one of his ships, which he had believed to be lost, had come safely into port with a rich cargo. All the sons and daughters at once thought that their poverty was at an end, and wanted to set out directly for the town; but their father, who was more prudent, begged them to wait a little, and, though it was harvest-time, and he could ill be spared, determined to go himself first, to make inquiries. Only the youngest daughter had any doubt but that they would soon again be as rich as they were before, or at least rich enough to live comfortably in some town where they would find amusement and gay companions once more. So they all loaded their father with commissions for jewels and dresses which it would have taken a fortune to buy; only Beauty, feeling sure that it was of no use, did not ask for anything. Her father, noticing her silence, said: "And what shall I bring for you, Beauty?"

---

a hundred leagues: three-hundred miles
doleful: melancholy

"The only thing I wish for is to see you come home safely," she answered.

But this reply vexed her sisters, who fancied she was blaming them for having asked for such costly things. Her father, however, was pleased, but as he thought that at her age she certainly ought to like pretty presents, he told her to choose something.

"Well, dear father," she said, "as you insist upon it, I beg that you will bring me a rose. I have not seen one since we came here, and I love them so much."

So the merchant set out and reached the town as quickly as possible, but only to find that his former companions, believing him to be dead, had divided between them the goods which the ship had brought; and after six months of trouble and expense he found himself as poor as when he started, having been able to recover only just enough to pay the cost of his journey. To make matters worse, he was obliged to leave the town in the most terrible weather, so that by the time he was within a few leagues of his home he was almost exhausted with cold and fatigue. Though he knew it would take some hours to get through the forest, he was so anxious to be at his journey's end that he resolved to go on; but night overtook him, and the deep snow and bitter frost made it impossible for his horse to carry him any farther. Not a house was to be seen; the only shelter he could get was the hollow trunk of a great tree, and there he crouched all the night, which seemed to him the longest he had ever known. In spite of his weariness the howling of the wolves kept him awake, and even when at last the day broke he was not much better off, for the falling snow had covered up every path, and he did not know which way to turn.

At length he made out some sort of track, and though at the beginning it was so rough and slippery that he fell down more than once, it presently became easier, and led him into an avenue of trees which ended in a splendid castle. It seemed to the merchant very strange that no snow had fallen in the avenue, which was entirely composed of orange trees, covered with flowers and fruit. When he reached the first court of the castle he saw before him a flight of agate* steps, and went up them, and passed through several splendidly furnished rooms. The pleasant warmth of the air revived him, and he felt very hungry; but there seemed to be nobody in all this vast and splendid palace whom he could ask to give him something to eat. Deep silence reigned everywhere, and at last, tired of roaming through empty rooms and galleries, he stopped in a room smaller than the rest, where a clear fire was burning and a couch was drawn up cosily close to it. Thinking that this must be prepared for someone who was expected, he sat down to wait till he should come, and very soon fell into a sweet sleep.

---

agate: a fine-grained variety of grayish quartz with colored bands

---

When his extreme hunger wakened him after several hours, he was still alone; but a little table, upon which was a good dinner, had been drawn up close to him, and, as he had eaten nothing for twenty-four hours, he lost no time in beginning his meal, hoping that he might soon have an opportunity of thanking his considerate entertainer, whoever it might be. But no one appeared, and even after another long sleep, from which he awoke completely refreshed, there was no sign of anybody, though a fresh meal of dainty cakes and fruit was prepared upon the little table at his elbow. Being naturally timid, the silence began to terrify him, and he resolved to search once more through all the rooms; but it was of no use. Not even a servant was to be seen; there was no sign of life in the palace! He began to wonder what he should do, and to amuse himself by pretending that all the treasures he saw were his own, and considering how he would divide them among his children. Then he went down into the garden, and though it was winter everywhere else, here the sun shone, and the birds sang, and the flowers bloomed, and the air was soft and sweet. The merchant, in ecstasies with all he saw and heard, said to himself:

"All this must be meant for me. I will go this minute and bring my children to share all these delights."

In spite of being so cold and weary when he reached the castle, he had taken his horse to the stable and fed it. Now he thought he would saddle it for his homeward journey, and he turned down the path which led to the stable. This path had a hedge of roses on each side of it, and the merchant thought he had never seen or smelt such exquisite flowers. They reminded him of his promise to Beauty, and he stopped and had just gathered one to take to her when he was startled by a strange noise behind him. Turning round, he saw a frightful Beast, which seemed to be very angry and said, in a terrible voice:

"Who told you that you might gather my roses? Was it not enough that I allowed you to be in my palace and was kind to you? This is the way you show your gratitude, by stealing my flowers! But your insolence shall not go unpunished."

The merchant, terrified by these furious words, dropped the fatal rose, and, throwing himself on his knees, cried: "Pardon me, noble sir. I am truly grateful to you for your hospitality, which was so magnificent that I could not imagine that you would be offended by my taking such a little thing as a rose." But the Beast's anger was not lessened by this speech.

"You are very ready with excuses and flattery," he cried; "but that will not save you from the death you deserve."

"Alas!" thought the merchant, "if my daughter Beauty could only know what danger her rose has brought me into!"

And in despair he began to tell the Beast all his misfortunes, and the reason of his journey, not forgetting to mention Beauty's request.

"A king's ransom would hardly have procured all that my other daughters asked," he said; "but I thought that I might at least take Beauty her rose. I beg you to forgive me,

for you see I meant no harm."

The Beast considered for a moment, and then he said, in a less furious tone:

"I will forgive you on one condition—that is, that you will give me one of your daughters."

"Ah!" cried the merchant, "if I were cruel enough to buy my own life at the expense of one of my children's, what excuse could I invent to bring her here?"

"No excuse would be necessary," answered the Beast. "If she comes at all she must come willingly. On no other condition will I have her. See if any one of them is courageous enough, and loves you well enough to come and save your life. You seem to be an honest man, so I will trust you to go home. I give you a month to see if either of your daughters will come back with you and stay here, to let you go free. If neither of them is willing, you must come alone, after bidding them good-bye forever, for then you will belong to me. And do not imagine that you can hide from me, for if you fail to keep your word I will come and fetch you!" added the Beast grimly.

The merchant accepted this proposal, though he did not really think any of his daughters would be persuaded to come. He promised to return at the time appointed, and then, anxious to escape from the presence of the Beast, he asked permission to set off at once.

But the Beast answered that he could not go until the next day. "Then you will find a horse ready for you," he said. "Now go and eat your supper, and await my orders."

The poor merchant, more dead than alive, went back to his room, where the most delicious supper was already served on the little table which was drawn up before a blazing fire. But he was too terrified to eat, and tasted only a few of the dishes, for fear the Beast should be angry if he did not obey his orders. When he had finished he heard a great noise in the next room, which he knew meant that the Beast was coming. As he could do nothing to escape his visit, the only thing that remained was to seem as little afraid as possible; so when the Beast appeared and asked roughly if he had supped well, the merchant answered humbly that he had, thanks to his host's kindness. Then the Beast warned him to remember their agreement, and to prepare his daughter exactly for what she had to expect.

"Do not get up tomorrow," he added, "until you see the sun and hear a golden bell ring. Then you will find your breakfast waiting for you here, and the horse you are to ride will be ready in the courtyard. He will also bring you back again when you come with your daughter a month hence. Farewell. Take a rose to Beauty, and remember your promise!"

The merchant was only too glad when the Beast went away, and though he could not sleep for sadness, he lay down until the sun rose. Then, after a hasty breakfast, he went to gather Beauty's rose, and mounted his horse, which carried him off so swiftly that in an instant he had lost sight of the palace, and he was still wrapped in gloomy thoughts when it stopped before the door of the cottage.

His sons and daughters, who had been very uneasy at his long absence, rushed to meet him, eager to know the result of his journey, which, seeing him mounted upon a splendid horse and wrapped in a rich mantle, they supposed to be favorable. But he hid the truth from them at first, only saying sadly to Beauty as he gave her the rose:

"Here is what you asked me to bring you; you little know what it has cost."

But this excited their curiosity so greatly that presently he told them his adventures from beginning to end, and then they were all very unhappy. The girls lamented loudly over their lost hopes, and the sons declared that their father should not return to this terrible castle,

and began to make plans for killing the Beast if it should come to fetch him. But he reminded them that he had promised to go back. Then the girls were very angry with Beauty, and said it was all her fault, and that if she had asked for something sensible this would never have happened, and complained bitterly that they should have to suffer for her folly.

Poor Beauty, much distressed, said to them:

"I have indeed caused this misfortune, but I assure you I did it innocently. Who could have guessed that to ask for a rose in the middle of summer would cause so much misery? But as I did the mischief it is only just that I should suffer for it. I will therefore go back with my father to keep his promise."

At first nobody would hear of this arrangement, and her father and brothers, who loved her dearly, declared that nothing should make them let her go; but Beauty was firm. As the time drew near she divided all her little possessions between her sisters, and said good-bye to everything she loved, and when the fatal day came she encouraged and cheered her father as they mounted together the horse which had brought him back. It seemed to fly rather than gallop, but so smoothly that Beauty was not frightened; indeed, she would have enjoyed the journey if she had not feared what might happen to her at the end of it. Her father still tried to persuade her to go back, but in vain. While they were talking the night fell, and then, to their great surprise, wonderful colored lights began to shine in all directions, and splendid fireworks blazed out before them; all the forest was illuminated by them, and even felt pleasantly warm, though it had been bitterly cold before.

This lasted until they reached the avenue of orange trees, where were statues holding flaming torches, and when they got nearer to the palace they saw that it was illuminated from the roof to the ground, and music sounded softly from the courtyard. "The Beast must be very hungry," said Beauty, trying to laugh, "if he makes all this rejoicing over the arrival of his prey."

But, in spite of her anxiety, she could not help admiring all the wonderful things she saw.

The horse stopped at the foot of the flight of steps leading to the terrace; and when they had dismounted, her father led her to the little room he had been in before, where they found a splendid fire burning and the table daintily spread with a delicious supper.

The merchant knew that this was meant for them, and Beauty, who was rather less frightened now that she had passed through so many rooms and seen nothing of the Beast, was quite willing to begin, for her long ride had made her very hungry. But they had hardly finished their meal when the noise of the Beast's footsteps was heard approaching and Beauty clung to her father in terror, which became all the greater when she saw how frightened he was. But when the Beast really appeared, though she trembled at the sight of him, she made a great effort to hide her horror, and saluted him respectfully.

This evidently pleased the Beast. After looking at her he said, in a tone that might have struck terror into the boldest heart, though he did not seem to be angry:

"Good evening, old man. Good evening, Beauty."

The merchant was too terrified to reply, but Beauty answered sweetly:

"Good evening, Beast."

"Have you come willingly?" asked the Beast. "Will you be content to stay here when your father goes away?"

Beauty answered bravely that she was quite prepared to stay.

"I am pleased with you," said the Beast. "As for you, old man," he added, turning to the merchant, "at sunrise tomorrow you will take your departure. When the bell rings, get up quickly and eat your breakfast, and you will find the same horse waiting to take you home; but remember that you must never expect to see my palace again."

Then turning to Beauty, he said:

"Take your father into the next room, and help him to choose everything you think your brothers and sisters would like to have. You will find two traveling-trunks there; fill them as full as you can. It is only just that you should send them something very precious as a remembrance of yourself."

Then he went away, after saying, "Good-bye, Beauty; good-bye, old man"; and though Beauty was beginning to think with great dismay of her father's departure, she was afraid to disobey the Beast's orders; and they went into the next room, which had shelves and cupboards all round it. They were greatly surprised at the riches it contained. There were splendid dresses fit for a queen, with all the ornaments that were to be worn with them; and when Beauty opened the cupboards she was quite dazzled by gorgeous jewels that lay in heaps upon every shelf. After choosing a vast quantity, which she divided between her sisters—for she had made a heap of the wonderful dresses for each of them—she opened the last chest, which was full of gold.

"I think, father," she said, "that, as the gold will be more useful to you, we had better take out the other things again, and fill the trunks with it." So they did this; but the more they put in, the more room there seemed to be, and at last they put back all the jewels and dresses they had taken out, and Beauty even added as many more of the jewels as she could carry at once; and then the trunks were not too full, but they were so heavy that an elephant could not have carried them!

"The Beast was mocking us," cried the merchant; "he must have pretended to give us all these things, knowing that I could not carry them away."

"Let us wait and see," answered Beauty. "I cannot believe that he meant to deceive us. All we can do is to fasten them up and leave them ready."

So they did this and returned to the little room, where, to their astonishment, they found breakfast ready. The merchant ate his with a good appetite, as the Beast's generosity made him believe that he might perhaps venture to come back soon and see Beauty. But she felt sure that her father was leaving her forever, so she was very sad when the bell rang sharply for the second time and warned them that the time was come for them to part. They went down into the courtyard, where two horses were waiting, one loaded with the two trunks, the other for him to ride. They were pawing the ground in their impatience to start, and the merchant was forced to bid Beauty a hasty farewell; and as soon as he was mounted he went off at such a pace that she lost sight of him in an instant. Then Beauty began to cry, and wandered sadly back to her own room. But she soon found that she was very sleepy, and as she had nothing better to do she lay down and instantly fell asleep. And then she dreamed that she was walking by a brook bordered with trees, and lamenting her sad fate, when a young prince, handsomer than anyone she had ever seen, and with a voice that went straight to her heart, came and said to her, "Ah, Beauty! you are not so unfortunate as you suppose. Here you will be rewarded for all you have suffered elsewhere. Your every wish shall be gratified. Only try to find me out, no matter how I may be disguised, as I love you dearly, and in making me happy you will find your own happiness. Be as true hearted as you are beautiful, and we shall have nothing left to wish for."

"What can I do, Prince, to make you happy?" said Beauty.

"Only be grateful," he answered, "and do not trust too much to your eyes. And, above all, do not desert me until you have saved me from my cruel misery."

After this she thought she found herself in a room with a stately and beautiful lady, who said to her:

"Dear Beauty, try not to regret all you have left behind you, for you are destined to a better fate. Only do not let yourself be deceived by appearances."

Beauty found her dreams so interesting that she was in no hurry to awake, but presently the clock roused her by calling her name softly twelve times, and then she got up and found her dressing table set out with everything she could possibly want; and when her toilette* was finished she found dinner was waiting in the room next to hers. But dinner does not take very long when you are all by yourself, and very soon she sat down cozily in the corner of a sofa and began to think about the charming Prince she had seen in her dream.

---

toilette: grooming

"He said I could make him happy," said Beauty to herself. "It seems, then, that this horrible Beast keeps him a prisoner. How can I set him free? I wonder why they both told me not to trust to appearances? I don't understand it. But, after all, it was only a dream, so why should I trouble myself about it? I had better go and find something to do to amuse myself."

So she got up and began to explore some of the many rooms of the palace.

The first she entered was lined with mirrors, and Beauty saw herself reflected on every side, and thought she had never seen such a charming room. Then a bracelet which was hanging from a chandelier caught her eye, and on taking it down she was greatly surprised to find that it held a portrait of her unknown admirer, just as she had seen him in her dream. With great delight she slipped the bracelet on her arm, and went on into a gallery of pictures, where she soon found a portrait of the same handsome Prince, as large as life, and so well painted that as she studied it he seemed to smile kindly at her. Tearing herself away from the portrait at last, she passed through into a room which contained every musical instrument under the sun, and here she amused herself for a long while in trying some of them, and singing until she was tired. The next room was a library, and she saw everything she had ever wanted to read, as well as everything she had read, and it seemed to her that a whole lifetime would not be enough even to read the names of the books, there were so many. By this time it was growing dusk, and wax candles in diamond and ruby candlesticks were beginning to light themselves in every room.

Beauty found her supper served just at the time she preferred to have it, but she did not see anyone or hear a sound; and, though her father had warned her that she would be alone, she began to find it rather dull.

But presently she heard the Beast coming, and wondered tremblingly if he meant to eat her up now.

However, as he did not seem at all ferocious, and only said gruffly: "Good evening, Beauty," she answered cheerfully and managed to conceal her terror. Then the Beast asked her how she had been amusing herself, and she told him all the rooms she had seen.

Then he asked if she thought she could be happy in his palace; and Beauty answered that everything was so beautiful that she would be very hard to please if she could not be happy. And after about an hour's talk Beauty began to think that the Beast was not nearly so terrible as she had supposed at first. Then he got up to leave her, and said in his gruff voice:

"Do you love me, Beauty? Will you marry me?"

"Oh! what shall I say?" cried Beauty, for she was afraid to make the Beast angry by refusing.

"Say 'yes' or 'no' without fear," he replied.

"Oh! no, Beast," said Beauty hastily.

"Since you will not, good-night, Beauty," he said. And she answered: "Good-night, Beast," very glad to find that her refusal had not provoked him. And after he was gone she was very soon in bed and asleep, and dreaming of her unknown Prince. She thought he came and said to her:

"Ah, Beauty! why are you so unkind to me? I fear I am fated to be unhappy for many a long day still."

And then her dreams changed, but the charming Prince figured in them all; and when morning came her first thought was to look at the portrait and see if it was really like him, and she found that it certainly was.

This morning she decided to amuse herself in the garden, for the sun shone, and all the fountains were playing; but she was astonished to find that every place was familiar to her, and presently she came to the brook where the myrtle trees were growing where she had first met the Prince in her dream, and that made her think more than ever that he must be kept a prisoner by the Beast. When she was tired she went back to the palace, and found a new room full of materials for every kind of work—ribbons to make into bows, and silks to work into flowers. Then there was an aviary full of rare birds, which were so tame that they flew to Beauty as soon as they saw her, and perched upon her shoulders and her head.

"Pretty little creatures," she said, "how I wish that your cage was nearer to my room that I might often hear you sing!"

So saying she opened a door, and found

to her delight that it led into her own room, though she had thought it was quite the other side of the palace.

There were more birds in a room farther on, parrots and cockatoos that could talk, and they greeted Beauty by name; indeed, she found them so entertaining that she took one or two back to her room, and they talked to her while she was at supper; after which the Beast paid her his usual visit, and asked the same questions as before, and then with a gruff "good-night" he took his departure, and Beauty went to bed to dream of her mysterious Prince. The days passed swiftly in different amusements, and after a while Beauty found out another strange thing in the palace, which often pleased her when she was tired of being alone. There was one room which she had not noticed particularly; it was empty, except that under each of the windows stood a very comfortable chair; and the first time she had looked out of the window it had seemed to her that a black curtain prevented her from seeing anything outside. But the second time she went into the room, happening to be tired, she sat down in one of the chairs, when instantly the curtain was rolled aside, and a most amusing pantomime was acted before her; there were dances, and colored lights, and music, and pretty dresses, and it was all so gay that Beauty was in ecstasies. After that she tried the other seven windows in turn, and there was some new and surprising entertainment to be seen from each of them, so that Beauty never could feel lonely any more. Every evening after supper the Beast came to see her, and always before saying good-night asked her in his terrible voice:

"Beauty, will you marry me?"

And it seemed to Beauty, now she understood him better, that when she said, "No, Beast," he went away quite sad. But her happy dreams of the handsome young prince soon made her forget the poor Beast, and the only thing that at all disturbed her was to be constantly told to distrust appearances, to let her heart guide her, and not her eyes, and many other equally perplexing things, which, consider as she would, she could not understand.

So everything went on for a long time, until at last, happy as she was, Beauty began to long for the sight of her father and her brothers and sisters; and one night, seeing her look very sad, the Beast asked her what was the matter. Beauty had quite ceased to be afraid of him. Now she knew that he was really gentle in spite of his ferocious looks and his dreadful voice.

So she answered that she was longing to see her home once more. Upon hearing this the Beast seemed sadly distressed, and cried miserably.

"Ah! Beauty, have you the heart to desert an unhappy Beast like this? What more do you want to make you happy? Is it because you hate me that you want to escape?"

"No, dear Beast," answered Beauty softly, "I do not hate you, and I should be very sorry never to see you anymore, but I long to see my father again. Only let me go for two months, and I promise to come back to you and stay for the rest of my life."

The Beast, who had been sighing dolefully while she spoke, now replied:

"I cannot refuse you anything you ask, even though it should cost me my life. Take the four boxes you will find in the room next to your own, and fill them with everything you wish to take with you. But remember your promise and come back when the two months are over, or you may have cause to repent it, for if you do not come in good time, you will find your faithful Beast dead. You will not need any chariot to bring you back. Only say good-bye to all your brothers and sisters the night before you come away, and when you have gone to bed, turn this ring round upon your finger and say firmly: 'I wish to go back to my palace and see my Beast again.' Good-night, Beauty. Fear nothing, sleep peacefully, and before long you shall see your father once more."

As soon as Beauty was alone she hastened to fill the boxes with all the rare and precious things she saw about her, and only when she was tired of heaping things into them did they seem to be full.

Then she went to bed, but could hardly sleep for joy. And when at last she did begin to dream of her beloved prince she was grieved to see him stretched upon a grassy bank sad and weary, and hardly like himself.

"What is the matter?" she cried.

But he looked at her reproachfully, and said:

"How can you ask me, cruel one? Are you not leaving me to my death perhaps?"

"Ah! don't be so sorrowful," cried Beauty; "I am only going to assure my father that I am safe and happy. I have promised the Beast faithfully that I will come back, and he would die of grief if I did not keep my word!"

"What would that matter to you?" said the prince. "Surely you would not care?"

"Indeed I should be ungrateful if I did not care for such a kind Beast," cried Beauty indignantly. "I would die to save him from pain. I assure you it is not his fault that he is so ugly."

Just then a strange sound woke her—someone was speaking not very far away; and opening her eyes she found herself in a room she had never seen before, which was certainly not nearly so splendid as those she was used to in the Beast's palace. Where could she be? She got up and dressed hastily, and then saw that the boxes she had packed the night before were all in the room. While she was wondering by what magic the Beast had transported them and her to this strange place, she suddenly heard her father's voice and rushed out and greeted him joyfully. Her brothers and sisters were all astonished at her appearance, since they had never expected to see her again, and there was no end to the questions they asked her. She had also much to hear about what had happened to them while she was away, and of her father's journey home. But when they heard that she had only come to be with them for a short time, and then must go back to the Beast's palace forever, they lamented loudly. Then Beauty asked her father what he thought could be the meaning of her strange

dreams, and why the Prince constantly begged her not to trust to appearances. After much consideration he answered: "You tell me yourself that the Beast, frightful as he is, loves you dearly, and deserves your love and gratitude for his gentleness and kindness; I think the prince must mean you to understand that you ought to reward him by doing as he wishes you to, in spite of his ugliness."

Beauty could not help seeing that this seemed very probable; still, when she thought of her dear prince who was so handsome, she did not feel at all inclined to marry the Beast. At any rate, for two months she need not decide but could enjoy herself with her sisters. But though they were rich now, and lived in a town again, and had plenty of acquaintances, Beauty found that nothing amused her very much; and she often thought of the palace, where she was so happy, especially as at home she never once dreamed of her dear Prince, and she felt quite sad without him.

Then her sisters seemed to have got quite used to being without her, and even found her rather in the way, so she would not have been sorry when the two months were over, but for her father and brothers, who begged her to stay and seemed so grieved at the thought of her departure that she had not the courage to say good-bye to them. Every day when she got up she meant to say it at night, and when night came she put it off again, until at last she had a dismal dream which helped her to make up her mind. She thought she was wandering in a lonely path in the palace gardens when she heard groans which seemed to come from some bushes hiding the entrance of a cave, and running quickly to see what could be the matter, she found the Beast stretched out upon his side, apparently dying. He reproached her faintly with being the cause of his distress, and at the same moment a stately lady appeared, and said very gravely:

"Ah! Beauty, you are only just in time to save his life. See what happens when people do not keep their promises! If you had delayed one day more, you would have found him dead."

Beauty was so terrified by this dream that the next morning she announced her intention of going back at once, and that very night she said good-bye to her father and all her brothers and sisters, and as soon as she was in bed she turned her ring round upon her finger, and said firmly:

"I wish to go back to my palace and see my Beast again," as she had been told to do.

Then she fell asleep instantly, and only woke up to hear the clock saying, "Beauty, Beauty," twelve times in its musical voice, which told her at once that she was really in the palace once more. Everything was just as before, and her birds were so glad to see her! But Beauty thought she had never known such a long day, for she was so anxious to see the Beast again that she felt as if supper time would never come.

But when it did come and no Beast appeared, she was really frightened; so, after listening and waiting for a long time, she ran down into the garden to search for him. Up and down the paths and avenues ran poor Beauty, calling him in vain, for no one answered, and not a trace of him could she find; until at last, quite tired, she stopped for a minute's rest, and saw that she was standing opposite the shady path she had seen in her dream. She rushed down it, and sure enough, there was the cave, and in it lay the Beast— asleep, as Beauty thought. Quite glad to have found him, she ran up and stroked his head, but to her horror he did not move or open his eyes.

"Oh! He is dead; and it is all my fault," said Beauty, crying bitterly.

But then, looking at him again, she fancied

he still breathed, and, hastily fetching some water from the nearest fountain, she sprinkled it over his face, and to her great delight he began to revive.

"Oh! Beast, how you frightened me!" she cried. "I never knew how much I loved you until just now, when I feared I was too late to save your life."

"Can you really love such an ugly creature as I am?" said the Beast faintly. "Ah! Beauty, you only came just in time. I was dying because I thought you had forgotten your promise. But go back now and rest, I shall see you again by and by."

Beauty, who had half expected that he would be angry with her, was reassured by his gentle voice and went back to the palace, where supper was awaiting her; and afterwards the Beast came in as usual, and talked about the time she had spent with her father, asking if she had enjoyed herself, and if they had all been very glad to see her.

Beauty answered politely, and quite enjoyed telling him all that had happened to her. And when at last the time came for him to go, and he asked, as he had so often asked before:

"Beauty, will you marry me?" she answered softly: "Yes, dear Beast."

As she spoke a blaze of light sprang up before the windows of the palace; fireworks crackled and guns banged, and across the avenue of orange trees, in letters all made of fire-flies, was written: "Long Live the Prince and His Bride."

Turning to ask the Beast what it could all mean, Beauty found that he had disappeared, and in his place stood her long-loved prince! At the same moment the wheels of a chariot were heard upon the terrace, and two ladies entered the room. One of them Beauty recognized as the stately lady she had seen in her dreams; the other was also so grand and queenly that Beauty hardly knew which to greet first.

But the one she already knew said to her companion:

"Well, Queen, this is Beauty, who has had the courage to rescue your son from the terrible enchantment. They love one another, and only your consent to their marriage is wanting to make them perfectly happy."

"I consent with all my heart," cried the Queen. "How can I ever thank you enough, charming girl, for having restored my dear son to his natural form?"

And then she tenderly embraced Beauty and the Prince, who had meanwhile been greeting the Fairy and receiving her congratulations.

"Now," said the Fairy to Beauty, "I suppose you would like me to send for all your brothers and sisters to dance at your wedding?"

And so she did, and the marriage was celebrated the very next day with the utmost splendor, and Beauty and the Prince lived happily ever after.

About the Editor

Andrew Lang (1844-1912) wrote on such a wide range of topics that he acquired the nickname " 'editor-in-chief' to the British nation." The title was well deserved, for Lang's scholarly interests were diverse, and his sense of the flow and beauty of language was keen.

An expert in historical research, Lang developed a number of concepts concerning the ultimate sources of fairy tales and folk literature. He promoted the idea that the original plots of such literature stemmed from "the worship of an ancient tribe for one God." From this initial concept, however, he went on to present Scripture as myth and to categorize the Lord of the Judeo-Christian religion with gods such as Apollo and Hyperion. He defined Judaism as "probably a revival and purification of the old conception of a moral, beneficent creator, whose creed had been involved in sacrifice and anthropological myth." Lang's anthropological works also evidence his habitual twisting of Scripture in an attempt to make it agree with Darwinism.

Apart from his anthropological work, however, Lang's accomplishments as a scholar are admirable. For many years he enjoyed great respect as a journalist. He also edited and translated Greek literature such as Homer's works and fairy tales from many sources. These enchanting stories were not just a scholarly pursuit for Lang; a genuine love of their literary beauty inspired him to re-popularize the genre in a series of fairy-tale collections. Each volume is designated by a different color, such as *The Blue Fairy Book* and *The Red Fairy Book*. Lang is best known, not for his own writing, but for the stories he edited, tales that continue to delight adults and children alike.

When You Are Old

William Butler Yeats

The last two stories dealt with two universal themes: the wisdom of age and the essence of true beauty. Yeats, through artful compression of thought and statement, merges these two themes in his poem "When You Are Old." Who is the speaker of this poem? To whom is he speaking? What do you think prompted his speech?

When you are old and gray and full of sleep,
And nodding by the fire, take down this book,
And slowly read, and dream of the soft look
Your eyes had once, and of their shadows deep;

How many loved your moments of glad grace,   5
And loved your beauty with love false or true;
But one man loved the pilgrim soul in you,
And loved the sorrows of your changing face.

And bending down beside the glowing bars,
Murmur, a little sadly, how Love fled   10
And paced upon the mountains overhead
And hid his face amid a crowd of stars.

About the Story
and the Poem

1. What two types of beauty are described in "Beauty and the Beast" and "When You Are Old"?
2. Which type do the authors portray as more enduring and valuable?
3. Do the prince and the speaker of the poem have any characteristics in common? If so, what are these characteristics?
4. What characteristics of true beauty are found in the following passages of Scripture?

   I Chronicles 16:29
   Psalm 90:17
   Proverbs 20:29
   I Peter 3:4

About the Author

William Butler Yeats (1865-1939) was born in Dublin, Ireland, and his lifelong love for his native country provided the inspiration for much of his work. As a boy, Yeats showed more interest in his bug collection than in his books; in fact, literature proved to be his worst subject. His family, nevertheless, was convinced of his creative abilities and felt certain that he would someday write.

While he was an art student in Dublin, Yeats's interest in the literary world grew, and at twenty-one he decided to make literature his profession. In addition to his work as a writer and editor, Yeats contributed to the Irish cultural revival by writing and promoting drama. As a young man, Yeats fell deeply in love with Maude Gonne, a strong-willed and elegant actress who was preoccupied with the Irish nationalist movement and other prevalent political and social causes. Yeats's devotion was unreturned, and their relationship remained purely platonic. Still, her influence on the young poet and future Irish statesman was considerable. Along with his continuing interest in Irish folklore and politics, Yeats's unrequited love for the beautiful Maude Gonne strongly influenced his writing.

In the poem "When You Are Old," Yeats demonstrates his ability to create the beautiful lyric poetry for which he is famous. Much of his poetry reflects his study of Celtic folklore and Irish fairy tales. By his generous use of symbolic imagery, Yeats sought to express his thoughts and feelings as a means of expressing reality.

Many Waters

Margaret Deland

Margaret Deland, a twentieth-century American author, often received letters about the stories she wrote. These letters were a source of knowledge and encouragement, for they were like the themes in her fiction. They referred to "the permanent emotions, the unchanging human passions; they rarely spoke of transient things, like the fashions of the time."

"Many Waters" is representative of Deland's work. Like "Beauty and the Beast," it is a picture of the power of love. Unlike the fairy tale, however, the setting is starkly realistic, the struggles vigorous, and the victories costly. What are some of the "permanent emotions" dealt with in this story? What "transient things" are eventually cast aside when the conflict is resolved?

I

"Well?"

"It's true; I'm awfully sorry."

Thomas Fleming did not speak. The other man, his lawyer, who had brought him the unwelcome news, began to make the best of it.

"Of course, it's an annoyance; but—"

"Well, yes. It's an annoyance," Fleming said, dryly.

Bates chuckled. "It strikes me, Tom, considering the difference between this and the *real thing,* that 'annoyance' is just the right word to use! As for Hammond, he won't have a leg to stand on. I don't know what Ellis & Grew meant by letting him take the case before the Grand Jury. He won't have a leg to stand on!"

Fleming was silent.

"What has Hammond got, anyhow? What's he got to support his opinion that you pinched $3,000 from the Hammond estate? His memory of something somebody said twelve years ago, and an old check. Well, we won't do a thing to 'em!"

Fleming got up and began to pull down his desk top with a slow clatter. "Hammond's a fool," he said; "and you'll punch a hole in his evidence in five minutes. But it's—well, as you say, it's 'annoying.' "

The lawyer rose briskly and reached for his hat. "What we want now is to get the case up near the head of the list as soon as we can. Get it over! Then, if you want revenge, we can turn round and hit back with 'malicious prosecution'!" He laughed, good-naturedly, and shrugged himself into his overcoat.

His client stood absently locking and unlocking his desk. "I suppose it will be in the evening papers?" he said.

"Oh, I guess so," the younger man said, easily; "the findings of the Grand Jury were reported at eleven this morning. Plenty of time for the first editions."

"Then I'll take an early train home," Thomas Fleming said, quickly; "my wife—" he paused.

"Doesn't Mrs. Fleming know about it?" the lawyer said, with a surprised look.

"No," the other man said, gloomily; "I didn't want her to worry over it, so I didn't say anything. But, of course, now she's got to know."

"Yes," Bates said, sympathetically; "but after all, Fleming, it's a small matter, except for the nuisance of it. You tell her I say it's a sure thing."

Fleming let his key-ring drop, jingling, into his pocket. Except for the occasional faint clangor of cars far down in the streets, the room, high up in the big office building, was quiet; but its quiet was the muffled, inarticulate, never-ending roar of living rising from below. Fleming sighed, and, turning his back to his lawyer, stared absently out of the window. Before him, in the afternoon dusk, lay the struggling, panting city. Far off to the south he could see the water, and ferryboats crawling like beetles back and forth. Below, the deep canyons of the streets were blurred with creeping yellow fog; but higher up, above the crowding roofs and chimneys and occasional spires, the air was clearer; it was full of tumultuous movement—sudden jets of white steam ballooning from hundreds of escape pipes; shuffling, shifting coils of black smoke; here and there the straining quiver of flags, whipping out from their masts. Fleming, his hands in his pockets, stood staring and listening—with unseeing eyes, unhearing ears. The lawyer behind him, at the office door, hesitated.

"Fleming, really, it isn't going to amount to anything. Of course, I know how you feel about Mrs. Fleming, but—"

The man at the window turned round. "Rather than have her disturbed, I'd compromise on it. I'd pay him. I'd—"

The lawyer raised his eyebrows. "This time, I think, Hammond is honest. I guess he really believes he has a case; but Ellis & Grew are sharks, and you'd be encouraging blackmail

to compromise. Anyway, you couldn't do it. Grew volunteered the information that their man 'couldn't be bought off'; he meant to put it through, Grew said. I told him they'd got the wrong pig by the ear. I told him that Thomas Fleming wasn't the kind of man who purchases peace at the cost of principle. They're shysters, and I gave 'em plain talk. Now, don't let Mrs. Fleming take it to heart. Tell her I say it will be a triumph!"

He went off, laughing; and a minute later Fleming heard his step in the corridor, and then the clang of the elevator door. He took up his black cloth bag and poked about in it among some papers; then unlocked his desk and found what he had been looking for— a box of candy for his wife. He slipped it into his bag, and a minute or two later he was down in the muddy dusk of the street. As he moved along with the steady surge of the homeward-bound crowd, he looked doubtfully into the flower stores; he wished he had bought violets for Amy instead of candy; he had taken her candy last Saturday. He debated whether he had not better get the violets too, but decided against them, because Amy was stern with him when he was extravagant for her sake. She never saw extravagance in any purchase he made on his own account! He smiled to himself at the thought of her sweet severity.

"Amy keeps me in order," he used to say, whimsically; "she insists that I shall be *her* best; it appears that my own best isn't good enough for her!" This she would always deny, indignantly, and indeed justly; for Thomas Fleming stood on his own legs, morally, in his community. But in the ten years of their married life no doubt her ideals, in small matters, had created his. With his indolent good-nature, he had found it easier to agree with Amy's delicate austerities of thought than to dispute them. Her hair-splitting in matters of conscience always amused him, and

sometimes touched him, but he accepted her standards of duty with real tenderness—which, for all practical purposes, was as good as conviction. Gradually, too, she pushed him, gently, before he knew it, into civic affairs; not in any very large way; perhaps hardly more than in a readiness to do his part as a citizen; but such readiness was sincere, and had given him a reputation for public-spiritedness in which Amy took a quiet pride. He had never had time, though he had had opportunity, to hold office, because his business demanded his entire energy; and, in fact, he had to be energetic, for he had hardly any capital, his income being almost entirely dependent upon his earnings; so he was not at all a rich man—except, indeed, as he was rich in the honor and respect of the community, and the love of a woman like Amy.

But then, if they were not rich in this world's goods, neither were they poor. There had been happy, anxious years, when they were first married, when they had ridiculously little to live on; but in those days Amy had steered their house-keeping bark between all rocks of hardship, as well as past breakers of extravagance. Even now, when things were easier each year, Amy was still prudent and economical, at least where she herself was concerned.

So Fleming, smiling, forbore to add a bunch of violets to his box of candy. After all, it was his thought that would bring the delicate and happy color up into her face, not the gift itself. They were very happy, these two; perhaps because they were only two. There had been a baby, but it had only lived long enough to draw them very close together, and not, as sometimes happens, to push them apart again; and there were many friends. But they were alone in their household and in the real heart of life. Naturally, all the thwarted maternity of the woman was added to the wife's love; and the paternal instinct of the man (which is, for the most part, only amusement, and the sense of protecting and giving joy) was centered in his wife.

So it was no wonder that that night, going home on the train, he winced at the thought of telling her that that "fool Hammond," who "would not have a leg to stand on," had prosecuted him criminally for misappropriation of funds as trustee of old Mrs. Hammond's estate. The trusts had been closed at her death a month or two before, and the estate handed over to her son—this same Hammond who "thought he remembered" hearing old Smith say, twelve years before, that he, Smith, had paid the Hammond estate $17,400 for a parcel of land; whereas Fleming's trustee account put the sum received at $14,400.

Amy's husband set his teeth as he sat there in the train, planning how he should tell her. Her incredulous anger he foresaw; and her anxiety—the anxiety of the woman unversed in legal matters. He pulled out his evening paper. There it was, in all the shamelessness of the flaring headline: "A Leading Citizen Indicted!" and so on. The big black letters were like a blow in the face. Fleming felt that every commuter on the train was looking over the top of his newspaper at him. He found himself glancing furtively across the aisle to see what page of the paper another passenger was reading; he was thankful that none of the men he knew well were on the five o'clock, so he would not have to listen to friendly assurances of astonishment at Hammond's impudence. His skin was prickly over his whole body; his ears were hot. And he had to tell Amy! He sank his head down between his shoulders and pulled his hat over his eyes, in pretense of a nap; then, suddenly, sat bolt upright. The fact was, Thomas Fleming had no experience in disgrace, and did not know how to conduct himself. When the door banged open at his station, he swung off on to the rainy platform, and plodded slowly up the lane in the darkness to his own house. It seemed to him as though his very feet hung back!

As the gate closed behind him, he saw an instant crack of light at the front door; and when his foot touched the lowest step of the porch, the door opened wide, and Amy stood there—it was rarely Jane who let him in or even his own latchkey!

"Go right into the house! You'll take cold," he commanded.

But she drew him inside with eager welcome. "Why, how *did* you manage to get the five o'clock? I heard the gate shut, and could hardly believe my ears! Oh, your coat is damp; has it begun to rain? Hurry! take it off. Then come into the library and get warm." She possessed herself of one of his hands, so that he had to dive into his bag as best he could with the other, to fish out her box of candy. She took it, smiling, with gay pretense of scolding, and then checked herself. "You look tired, Tom. When you've had your dinner (we have a good dinner tonight: I wish you had brought some man home with you!) you'll feel better."

He dropped down into his chair by the fire in silence, frowning slightly, and drawing impatiently away from her. Thomas Fleming did not always like to be fussed over; there were times when, perhaps, he endured it with a mildly obvious patience. Every tender woman knows this patience of a good and bored man. Amy Fleming knew it, and smiled to herself, quite unoffended. Something had bothered him? Well, he should not be talked to! But she looked at him once or twice. In her soft gray dress, with her gray eyes, and the sweet color in her cheeks, she brooded over him like a dove. At dinner his silence continued. Amy, being wise beyond her sex, fell into a silence of her own—the blessed, comprehending silence of love. When they came back from the dining-room to the library fireside, she let him sit uninterruptedly, while she sewed. Sometimes her eyes rested on him, quietly content with his mere presence. But she asked no question. Suddenly, with a half-embarrassed cough, he said:

"Ah, Amy—"

"Yes? Tell me; I knew you hadn't had a good day."

* * *

When he had told her, she sat dumb before him. Her face was white, and her eyes terror-stricken. But that was only for the first moment. Almost instantly there was the relief of anger.

She stood up, her delicate face red, her voice strained.

"To accuse you! *You!*"

It was just what Bates had said. The first thought everywhere would be of the absurdity of such a charge against Thomas Fleming.

"It's blackmail," Amy said, trembling very much.

"Of course, we shall have no difficulty in throwing them down," he said. "They bring their case, really, on Smith's old check to me for $17,400."

"I don't understand," Amy said. It had always been a joke between them that Amy did not know anything about business, so she tried to smile when she asked him to explain.

"Oh," he said, impatiently, "it's simple enough. L.H. Smith owed me $3,000—a personal matter. I once sold him some stock; he gave me his note; had to renew two or three times; thing sort of hung fire. You wouldn't understand it, Amy. But when he bought this Hammond property for $14,400, he made out the check for $17,400;—he'd had a windfall, so he could pay me what he owed me, see? I got my money. Understand?"

"Perfectly," she said; "what a rascal Hammond is!"

"Oh, well, I suppose this time he really thinks he has a case; though on general principles I believe he's equal to blackmail! But he has succeeded in getting from the Smith heirs that old check for the total amount, and I suppose he thinks he has me. He'll find himself mistaken. But it's a nasty business," he ended, moodily; "there will always be people who will think—"

"What do we care what such people think?" she said, passionately.

Her husband was silent. Amy's knees were shaking under her. "Oh, I could kill that man, I could kill him!"

Well as he knew her, he looked at her with astonishment—this mild creature to speak with such deadly, vindictive passion! She came and knelt down beside him; he felt her heart pounding in her side.

"Oh," she said, brokenly, "I know—"

"You know what?"

She spoke very softly. "I know how they felt; those women, 'looking on, afar off.' "

"Looking on?" he said, vaguely. And Amy, her face still hidden on his breast, said in a whisper:

"It must have been easier for—for Him, on the cross, than for them to see Him there."

He moved abruptly in his chair; then, with a faint impatience, said she mustn't talk that way. "It's foolish!" he said, irritably. She kissed him, silently; and went back to her seat by the fire.

"I'll get out of it all right," Fleming said; "Bates says so. It's annoying"—he found himself falling back on Bates's word—"but there's nothing to it. You mustn't worry. Bates says Hammond is crazy to undertake it; Smith being dead, and—" Then he stopped.

"I don't worry; in the sense of being afraid that—" she could not even put into words the fear that she did not have. "But to have your name mixed up with anything dishonorable— even though it will come out clear and shining as heaven!"

He made no answer. The fatigue of the day was showing in his face—a heavy, handsome face, with a somewhat hard mouth. His wife, looking at him, said, quietly:

"Don't let's talk about it, dearest, any more tonight. It's only on the surface; it isn't a real trouble."

He nodded, gratefully; and they did not speak of it again.

But that night Amy Fleming, lying motionless in her bed, stared into the darkness until the glimmering oblong of the window told her that dawn had come.

II

"Trouble shows us our friends," Amy said, smiling. And indeed it did, in the Flemings' case. When the news of the indictment of Thomas Fleming fell upon his community, there was a moment of stunned astonishment; then of protest and disbelief.

"Hammond is up against it," men said to each other; "Fleming? What nonsense!"

The first day or two, while it was still a nine days' wonder, public confidence was almost an ovation. The small house behind the trim hedges was crowded with Amy's women friends, coming and going, and quoting (after the fashion of women friends) what their respective husbands said:

"*Of course* Mr. Hammond has no case, Amy, darling! My Tom—or Dick or Harry—says so."

Amy did not need such assurances. She knew her husband! So she held her head proudly, and with certainty. Not certainty of the outcome of the trial—because, secretly, she had the unreasoning terror of most women of sheltered lives for the very word *law;* it meant power; wicked power, even! The opportunity of evil to get the better of goodness. But her pride and certainty were for Thomas Fleming's honor, and goodness, and courage. She was a little cold when these tender women friends tried to reassure her, quoting the opinion of their menfolk; she did not want, by eager agreement, to imply that she needed reassurance. She said, with gentle dignity, that she was sorry Mr. Hammond was so—foolish. Tom had been trustee of the Hammond estate for nearly twenty years, and he had given time and service—"service," she said, the color rising faintly in her face, "that money could not have paid for." And to have the Hammonds turn upon him now!—"Though, of course, it is only Mr. Hammond," Amy corrected herself, carefully just; "the rest of the family are nice

people. His mother was such an honorable woman. And his wife—I am sorry for his wife." Amy thought a great deal about this wife. "She must know what he is, poor soul!" she said to herself. And knowing, she could not respect him. And without respect, love must have crumbled away. She said something like this to her most intimate friend, almost in a whisper, because expression was not easy to Amy. "When Mrs. Hammond realizes that he is a blackmailer, what *will* she do!"

"Poor thing!" said the other woman; "but, Amy, I suppose she is fond of him?"

"Fond of him! When she can't respect him? Oh, no, no!"

"Perhaps she doesn't know how bad he is," the other said, thoughtfully.

"What!" said Amy, "when she has lived with him for fifteen years? Of course she knows him. And I truly pity her," she ended simply.

So in spite of her deep resentment at Hammond, Amy felt something like tenderness for Hammond's wife—losing both respect and love, poor soul!

As the weeks passed before the day set for the trial, Amy grew perceptibly thinner and whiter. For beneath all her certainties, the fear of the Law remained. She brooded over instances of goodness suspected, of innocent men condemned, of the blunders and mistakes of Justice. It was not until three or four days before the trial that Bates realized what even Thomas Fleming had not understood, that she was consumed with *fear.* Fear of prison walls, of unmerited disgrace, of her house left unto her desolate.* When the lawyer penetrated the tense cheerfulness with which she held herself in Tom's presence, and saw the fright below, he roared with laughter; which, though ill-mannered, was the best thing he could have done.

---

her house left unto her desolate: an allusion to the judgment of Jerusalem prophesied by Christ in Matthew 23:38

"You think I'm a fool?" she said, with a quivering smile.

"My dear lady, it would not be polite for me to use such a word; but certainly you— well, you are mistaken."

"Oh, *say* I am a fool," she pleaded; "I would like to think I was a fool! But, Mr. Bates, the Law can be made to do such dreadful things. Innocent people have been put into jail; oh, you know they have," she said, her face trembling; "and at night I lie awake and think—" He saw her hands grip each other to keep steady.

"Now let me explain it to you," he said kindly; "and then you won't be frightened; why, you'll be so sure you'll send out invitations for a dinner party on the nineteenth, so we can celebrate!"

Then, very explicitly, he laid before her the grounds of his confidence. Hammond, to start with, was a fool. "He always has been a cheap fellow; a sort of smart Aleck, you know; but this time he's just a fool." He had fallen into the hands of a shyster firm, who were milking him—"If you'll forgive the slang."

"Oh, go on, go on!" she entreated.

Hammond, being a fool, and having this vague idea about the price paid by Smith for the land, and having secured the old check to prove (as he thinks) that such a price was paid, falls into the hands of these sharks. "They know there is nothing to it, but they think they can pull out a plum somehow," said Mr. Bates. Then, carefully, he told her the story point by point. Briefly, it was, that while there was no question that $17,400 had been paid to Thomas Fleming, Hammond could not disprove Fleming's defense that only $14,400 of it was to go to the Trust; and that the remaining $3,000 was in payment of Smith's debt to him. "See?" said Bates, kindly. As he spoke, the drawn look in her face lessened, and she drew one or two long breaths; and

then, suddenly, she put her hands over her eyes, and he knew she wept. This sobered the rather voluble* man. He protested, with friendly vociferation,* that she must promise him not to give the matter another thought. And she, still trembling a little, looked up, smiling, and promised.

---

voluble: characterized by a steady flow of words
vociferation: outcry; strong protest

And, such being her temperament, she kept her promise. Perhaps it was the rebound from having gone down to the depths of fear; but certainly there was almost bravado* in the reaction. She made up her mind to have the dinner party! Tom would come home, cleared, crowned with the vindication of his own integrity; and he would find love, and friendship, and respect ready to exult with him. Tom, however, objected to her project.

---

bravado: a false appearance of courage

"It's all right," he said; "it's perfectly safe, as far as the verdict goes; but—" he stopped and frowned. It was evident that the plan did not please him. But for the once Amy did not consult his pleasure. She had her own views; and she did actually invite a party of old friends to dine with them on the evening when it was expected that the verdict would be given.

III

Amy, in her dove-colored dress, entered the court-room with her husband. During the trial, very quietly, and with a beautiful serenity, she kept her place at his side. If the proceedings troubled her, there was no indication of it. She looked a little tired, and once or twice a little amused. Sometimes she smiled at Thomas Fleming, and sometimes exchanged a word or two with Mr. Bates. But for the most part she was silent; and her repose was a spot of

refreshment and beauty in the dingy court-
room. Bates looked at her occasionally, with
rather jovial encouragement; but she displayed
no need of encouragement, and returned his
smile cheerfully. Once he leaned over and said:

"You make me think of a poem I read
somewhere; now, what was the name of it?
I can only remember two lines:

" 'In the fell clutch of circumstance,
I have not winched or cried aloud!'

That's as far as I can go; but that's what you
make me think of."

She turned, smiling, and finished the verse.
"It's Henley's 'I am the captain of my soul,' "
she said. "I have it somewhere: I copied it once,
because I cared so much for it. I'll read it to
you tonight, after dinner."

"Do!" Bates said heartily, and turned away
to listen to Fleming, who was on the stand.
Fleming's evidence was as straightforward as
the man himself. Yes, Smith (now deceased)
had paid him in March, 1887, the sum of
$17,400. Of this, $3,000 was on a personal
account; $14,400 was for a parcel of land
belonging to the Hammond estate. The check
was made to his order; he deposited it in his
own bank account and immediately drew
against it a check for $14,400 to the order of
the Trust. Then followed a very clear and
definite statement of that money Smith owed
him; a debt which he was unable to corroborate
by his books, for the simple reason that his
books had been burned in the great fire of
that year. Over and over, back and forth, round
and round, the prosecution went, gaining not
an inch.

Indeed, the end was obvious from the
beginning. To assert that Thomas Fleming was
an honest man was, so Bates told the jury,
to utter a commonplace. He was so cheerful
and kindly, in his reference to the unfortunate

Mr. Hammond, that the jury grinned. The
verdict, Bates declared, was a foregone
conclusion. And so, in fact it was, being
rendered fifteen minutes after the jury had been
charged.

"And now," said the good Bates, shaking
hands with his client, "let's go and get
something to eat! Come, Mrs. Fleming, you'll
go with us? You look like an army with
banners!"

But Amy, with proud eyes, said no; she
must go home. "You will come out with Tom
this evening?" she said. "Dinner is at half-past
seven; you can dress at our house; and, of
course, you must stay all night." Bates
promised, and Fleming silently squeezed his
wife's hand. Amy's heart was beating so that
her words were a little breathless, but her eyes
spoke to him.

She did not want to lunch with the two
men; she had it in mind to go into a church
which was near the courthouse, and there,
alone, in the silence and sacred dusk, return
thanks upon her knees. And deep human
experience gives the soul a chance to see God;
and when Amy came out afterward into the
roar of the street, her face shone like the face
of one who has touched the garment hem of
the Eternal, and bears back the Tables of
Law. . . .

The joyous and beautiful day passed; the
afternoon was gay with congratulations; but
the succession of friendly calls was fatiguing
and at half-past five she said, courageously,
"Now, dear friends, I'll have to leave you! It's
delightful to hear all these nice things about
Tom, but I must go and lie down, or I shall
go to sleep at dinner."

So there was more handshaking and gaiety,
and then, at last, she had the house to herself.
She reflected that it would be well to have
a little nap, so that she might be bright and
rested for the jubilant evening—oh, that poem

Mr. Bates wanted to see! She had forgotten all about it; she must find it before she went upstairs. But she must first look into the dining-room to be sure about the candles and flowers! The dinner, she knew, would be good. She had picked out the partridges herself, knowing well, under her calm exterior, that her market man, looking at her with sidewise, curious eyes, was thinking to himself, "My! and her husband to be tried for a state's prison offense!" The partridges were superb; and the salmon—Amy's eyes sparkled with joy at the thought of such extravagance—salmon in February! the salmon was perfect; and the salad, the ices, the coffee—well, they would be worthy of the occasion!

The dining-room was satisfactory, with its ten friendly chairs drawn up about the sparkling table. And her best dress was upstairs spread out on the bed, with her slippers and gloves; her flowers—Tom would bring her her flowers! She thought to herself that she would wear them, and then put them away with her wedding bouquet, that had been lying, dry and fragrant, for all these years, with her wedding dress and veil. Sighing with the joy of it all, she climbed wearily half-way upstairs; then remembered Mr. Bates's poem again, and went back to the library, with an uneasy look at the hall clock. She would not get much of a nap! And the chances of the nap lessened still more, because she could not at once find her Commonplace Book, in which she had copied the poem. Taking out one book after another, she shook her head and looked at her hands—these shelves were very dusty; that told a housekeeping story that was disgraceful, she said to herself, gaily. Well, she would look after Jane, now that she could think and breathe again! So, poking about, pulling out one flexible, leather-covered volume after another, her fate fell upon her. . . .

The book looked like her own Common-place Book; Tom had more than once given her blank books just like his own—bound in red morocco, with mottled edges, and stamped, "*Diary,* 18—." There was a whole row of these books on one of the bottom shelves of the bookcase that ran round three sides of the room, and she had been looking at them, one by one, hurriedly, for she knew she needed that rest upstairs before the company came. She pulled the books out, impatiently, fluttering the leaves over, and putting them back. One or two were her own notebooks; but the rest were Tom's memoranda—accounts, notes, etc., etc., back to—"Why, dear me!" said Amy to herself, "they go back to before we were married!"

There was one date that caught her eye; she had heard it repeated and repeated in the last few weeks; she had heard it that very morning in court, when Thomas Fleming had said: "In March, 1887, L. F. Smith paid me in one check $17,400; $14,400 for a piece of land belonging to the Hammond estate, and $3,000 which he owed my personal account."

The flexible, red-covered diary marked 1887 drew her hand with the fascination which comes with remembered pain. Ah! how she had suffered every time that date fell like a scalding drop of fear upon her heart! It is not true of spiritual pain that one remembereth no more the anguish for joy that a blessing has been born into the soul! She shivered as she opened the book. It occurred to her, with vague surprise, that this book would probably have settled the whole matter, if Tom had only remembered it. He had shown in court that records of that year had been among certain office books burned in the great March fire, when the building in which he had his office had been destroyed. Yes, this book might have cleared the whole matter up, easily and quickly, for, as she saw at a glance, here were entries about the Hammond Trust. She forgot her fatigue, and the nap she ought to have; she forgot the poem altogether; she sat down on the floor, running the pages over eagerly. It occurred to her, as a climax of the successful day, that she would bring this book out at dinner (if she could only find something about the $14,400) and show it as her final triumph. Then her eyes fell on the figures $17,400.

"Received from L. H. Smith, to-day, $17,400 for Hammond property, in Linden Hill." Then the comment, "A whacking good price. I hardly expected to get so much." The significance of this brief statement did not penetrate her joy. She began eagerly to look again for the other figures—and then turned back, perplexed. $17,400 for the Hammond property? Suddenly her eye caught another familiar sum—$3,000. Ah, now she would find it! Yes, verily, so she did. . . . "Borrowed $3,000 from the Hammond Estate to pay back money borrowed from Ropes Estate."

Suddenly it seemed to this poor woman, sitting on the floor in the dark corner of the library, her fingers dusty, her whole slender body tingling with fatigue—it seemed as if something fell, shuddering, down and down, and down in her breast. Strangely enough, this physical recognition informed her soul. She heard herself speak, as one falling into the unconsciousness of an anaesthetic hears, with vague astonishment, words faltering unbidden from the lips. "No. No. No," came the body's frightened denial.

Then, in silence, the Soul: "He—did it. He did it."

It was characteristic of Amy that she sought no loophole of escape. It never occurred to her that there could be an explanation. There were the figures; and the figures meant the facts. *"A certain man named Ananias"* (so suddenly, the words ran in her mind) *"sold a possession . . . and kept back part of the price."*

Out in the hall the half-hour struck, muffled and mellow. Then silence.

"God, if he did it, I can't live—can't live. *God?"*

Suddenly the happenings of the day seemed

to blur and run together, and there was a moment, not of unconsciousness, but of profound indifference. Her capacity for feeling snapped. But when she tried to rise, her whole being was sick; so sick that again the soul forgot or did not understand, and heard, with dull curiosity, the body saying, "No. No." She steadied herself by holding on to the bookshelves; and then, somehow, she got upstairs. It was the sight of the soft, gray dress, with its pretty laces, that stung her awake. That dress: was it hers? Was she to put it on? Was she to go and sit at the head of that shining table down in the dining-room?

"But, you know, I—*can't,*" she said aloud, her voice hoarse and falling.

* * *

But she did.

By the time Fleming and his counsel came tramping up from the gate, at a quarter past seven, and stopped hilariously, to kick the snow off their boots before entering the hall, Amy Fleming had arisen to meet the summons of life. She called Jane to fasten her dress, and when the woman, startled and shocked at the shrunken face, cried out:

"Oh, good land! what's wrong wi' ye, Mrs. Fleming?" she was able to say, quietly:

"Jane, when Mr. Fleming comes in, tell him I've had to go down to the kitchen to see about some things. And say I put his dress suit out on the sofa in my room. Tell him the studs are in his shirt."

Jane, silenced, went back to the kitchen. "Say, Mary Ann," she said, "look a-here; there's something the matter upstairs." The presence of the accommodating waitress checked further confidences; but, indeed, when Amy Fleming, ghastly, in her pretty dinner dress, sought refuge in the kitchen (the spot where her husband would not be apt to pursue her), and

stood listening to the voices of the two men going upstairs, Mary Ann needed no information that there was "something the matter."

"She looks like she was dead," the frightened women told each other.

"Jane," her mistress said, "there's the door bell! I'll go into the library." And when the two rather early comers had taken off their wraps and made their way downstairs again, they found their hostess smiling whitely at them from the hearthrug.

"Oh, Amy *dear!*" the wife said, dismayed, "what is the matter?" And the husband protested in a friendly way that he was afraid Mrs. Fleming was tired out. "Of course it has been a wearing week for you, in spite of its triumph," he said, delicately.

Then Thomas Fleming and his lawyer came downstairs, and there was more handshaking and congratulations, and it was not until he looked at his wife at dinner that Fleming really saw her face; its haggard pallor struck him dumb in the midst of some gay story to the pretty neighbor on his right. He had been dull, just at first, and his gaiety was a little forced, but he brightened up very much, and had begun to tell a funny story. "And so the automobilist," he was saying—and broke off, staring blankly at Amy. "I'm afraid my wife is not well," he said, anxiously. But the pretty neighbor reassured him.

"Oh, it's the reaction, Mr. Fleming. Amy has been perfectly splendid; but now, naturally, she feels the reaction."

Somehow or other, with its gaiety and good fellowship, that dreadful evening passed. When the friendly folk streamed out into the starry winter night, there was some anxious comment.

"How badly she looked!"

"My dear, can you wonder? Think what she's been through!"

But one woman, on her husband's arm, murmured a question: "You don't suppose he *could* have—done anything?"

"Twelve good men and true have said he didn't; your remark is out of order."

"But tell me, honestly, do you suppose it is possible that—that?"

"I don't know anything about it, Helen. I would bank on Tom Fleming as soon as on any man I know. But I don't know any man (myself included) who is not human. So, if you ask about 'possibilities'—but no! honestly, as you say, I'm sure Fleming is all right. And his wife is a noble woman. I've always admired Mrs. Fleming."

"She is the best woman in the world!" Amy's friend said, warmly. But in her own heart she was thinking that if it came to possibilities, she knew *one* man to whom wrongdoing was impossible! And, happily, she squeezed his arm, and brushed her cold, rosy cheek against his shoulder.

IV

When Fleming closed the door upon the last lingering guest, he turned anxiously to his wife. "Amy, I haven't had a chance to speak to you! You are worn out. Bates, look at her—she's worn out!"

Bates, lounging in the library doorway, agreed. "Indeed she is; Mrs. Fleming, you ought not to have attempted a dinner party. I believe it's all my fault, because I suggested it."

"It's your fault because you got me off," Fleming said, jocosely.* The dullness of the first part of the evening had quite disappeared; he was rather flushed and inclined to laugh buoyantly at everything; but his face was anxious when he looked at his wife. "Amy, you must go right straight to bed!"

---

jocosely: characterized by humor

"I am going now," she said, pulling and straightening the fingers of her long gloves. "Good-night, Mr. Bates. I—will copy that poem for you—sometime," she ended faintly.

Her husband put his arm about her to help her upstairs, but she drew away. "No; stay down with Mr. Bates." Then, as he insisted on coming up with her, she stopped on the first landing, and pushed his arm away, sharply. "Please—*don't?* My head aches. Please—go away."

Thomas Fleming, dumfounded, could not find his wits for a reply before she had slipped away from him, and he heard the door of their bedroom close behind her. He stood blankly upon the stairs for a moment, and then went back to Bates.

"I never knew Amy so upset," he said, stupidly. And, indeed, there are few things more bewildering than sudden irrational irritation in a sweet and reasonable soul.

"It's been a hard week for her," Bates explained, easily. But Fleming was morose;* he was plainly relieved when his guest said he thought he would go to bed. He arose with alacrity* to conduct the sleepy lawyer to the spare-room door.

---

morose: especially melancholy in nature
alacrity: quickness

"We'll take the eight-fifteen in the morning, Bates," he said; and Bates, yawning, agreed.

Fleming went softly into his own room, and was half disappointed, half relieved, to find his wife lying motionless, with closed eyes. "A good night's sleep will set her up," he thought, tenderly. For himself, he stopped in the process of pulling off his boots, and, shutting his lips hard together, stared at the floor. . . After a while he drew a long breath—"Well, thank the eternal Powers," he said; and pulled off his boots softly—Amy must have a good night's sleep. Fleming himself had a good night's sleep. That Amy's eyes opened painfully to the dark, when all the house had sunk into silence, of course he did not know. She seemed to be sleeping soundly when he awoke the next morning; and again he crept about, not even daring to kiss her, lest she might be disturbed. Just before he and Bates made a dash for the eight-fifteen, he told Jane to ask Mrs. Fleming to call him up on the telephone when she came downstairs, so he might know how she was.

As for Amy, when she heard the front door close behind the two hurrying men, she got up and sat wearily on the side of the bed.

"Now, I've got time to think," she said. There was a certain relief in the consciousness of silence and of time. She could think all day; she could think until half-past six; how many hours? Ten! Ten hours—in which to take up a new life. Ten hours in which to become acquainted with her husband.

"I have never known him," she said feebly to herself. Well, now she must think. . . . No doubt he had loved her; she was not questioning that. She was dully indifferent to the whole matter of love. The question was, what was she going to do? After restitution was made, what was she going to do? How were they to go on living? Mere restitution—(which must be made on Monday. No, Monday was a holiday; they would have to wait until Tuesday. Oh, how could she bear the delay?) Well, on Tuesday, then, the money would be given to Mr. Hammond. But mere restitution would not change the fact of what he was. She dropped back against her pillows, hiding her face. "I never knew him."

Oh, this would *not* do! She must think.

Poor soul! She had no thoughts but that one. Over and over the words repeated themselves, until her very mind was sore. But she did her best; the habit of common sense was a great help. She had some coffee, and

dressed and went down to the library— recoiling, involuntarily, at the sight of that corner where the books were still in some slight disorder. She even called Jane and bade her bring her duster. When the dusting was done, she told the woman that she would not see anyone, all day. "I have a headache," she explained; "don't let anyone in." And when Jane left her, she drew her little chair up to the hearth; "Now, I'll think," she said. But her eye caught the flash of sunlight on a crystal ball on the mantelpiece, and it seemed as if her mind broke into a glimmering kaleidoscope: those partridges had been a little overcooked last night . . . the gilt on the narrow, old-fashioned mirror over the mantel was tarnishing . . . the $3,000 had been "borrowed" from one trust to pay another. . . . Borrowing from Peter to pay Paul. . . . How clear the crystal was. . . . Two thefts. . . . Jane must dust those shelves better. . . . Then she started with dismay—she was not thinking! Well, restitution, first of all;—on Tuesday. They would sell a bond, and take some money out of the bank. But after restitution they must go on living. She must try to understand him, to help him to be good, to be patient with him. "But I don't know him," came over and over the dreadful refrain, checked by the instant determination: "Oh, I *must* think!"

So the day passed. She told Jane to telephone her husband that she was up and feeling better; and he sent back some anxious message—she must rest, she must not overdo. He could not, unfortunately, come out on an early train, as he had hoped to do, being detained by some business matters, so he would have to dine in town. He would come out on the eight-thirty. She grasped at the delay with passionate relief; two hours more to think. Then it came over her that she was glad not to see him. What did that mean? She wondered, vaguely, if she had stopped loving him? Not that it made any difference whether she loved him or not. Love had no meaning to her. "Perhaps this is the way people who are dead feel about us," she thought. Then she wondered if she hated him, this stranger, this—thief? No, she did not hate him either. But when respect, upon which love is built, is wrenched away, what happens? There is no love, of course. She thought, vaguely, that she had pitied Mrs. Hammond. And yet she herself did not care, apparently. How strange not to care! Pulling her wedding-ring off, slipping it on, pulling it off again, she said to herself, numbly, that she did not understand why she did not care. However, she could not go into this question of love and hate. Neither mattered. She beat her poor mind back to its task of "thinking."

The long, sunny winter afternoon faded into the dusk; a gleam of sunset broke yellow across the pleasant room, and catching with a glimmering flash on the crystal, melted into a bloom of gray, with the fire, like the spark of an opal, shifting and winking on the hearth.

When Fleming came hurriedly up the garden path to his own door, he had to pull out his latch-key to let himself into the house. This slight happening made him frown; so she was not well enough to come down? He took off his coat and started immediately upstairs, then he caught sight of her in the library, standing motionless, her back to the door, one hand resting on the mantelpiece, the other drooping at her side, the fingers between the pages of a book. He came in quickly, with a gaily derisive laugh.

"You didn't hear me!" Then, as she did not turn, he sobered. "Amy, what is it? Why, Amy! Is there anything the matter? Is anything wrong?" His face was keenly disturbed, and he put his hand on her shoulder to make her look at him, but she lifted it away, gently, still keeping her eyes fastened on the fire.

"Yes. There is something—wrong."

"Amy! he said, now thoroughly alarmed, "what is the matter? Tell me!"

"I will tell you. Sit down. There: at the library table. I will—show you."

He sat down, blankly, his lower-lip falling open with perplexity. She sighed once, and brushed her hand over her eyes; then came, quietly, away from the hearth, and, going around the table, stood behind him and laid the book down beside him. She pressed it open, and in silence ran her finger down the page.

V

The fire sputtered a little; then everything was still. She had left him, and had gone back to the hearthrug, and stood as before, one hand on the mantelpiece, the other, listless, at her side. The silence was horrible.

Then, suddenly, Thomas Fleming ripped and tore the pages out of the book, and threw them on the logs: the quick leap of the flames shone on his white face and his furious eyes. A minute afterward he spoke. . . . Under that storm of outrageous words she bent and shrunk a little, silently. Once she looked at him with a sort of curiosity. So this was her husband? Then she looked at the fire.

When, choking with anger, he paused, she said, briefly, that she had been hunting for her Commonplace Book, down on that lower shelf, and had found—this.

"What were my diaries doing on your lower shelf? One of those women of yours poking—"

"When we moved they were put there. They had been in your old desk in the other house. They were locked up there. I suppose you forgot to lock them up here," she ended, simply.

That next hour left its permanent mark on those two faces; agony and shame were cut into the wincing flesh, as by some mighty die. At first Fleming was all rage; then rage turned into sullenness, and sullenness to explanation and excuse. But as he calmed down, shame, an old, old shame, that he had loathed and lived with for a dozen years, a shame that, except when Amy was too tenderly proud of him, he was sometimes able for days, or even weeks, to forget—this old shame reared its deadly head, and looked out of his abased and shifting eyes. Yet he had his glib excuses and explanations. Amy, in the midst of them, sat down in her little low chair by the fire. She did not speak. She had her handkerchief in her hand, and kept pulling it out on her knee; smoothing it; then folding it; and a minute later, spreading it out again. At last, after a labored statement—how he had only borrowed it; how it had been at a time when he had been horribly pressed; how he had always meant to return it, of course; how, in fact, he had returned it by giving an enormous amount of work for which he had never had any credit, or any money, either! (though, as it happened, he had never been in a position to pay it back in actual cash); after this miserable and futile explanation had been repeated and repeated, he stopped to get his breath; and then, still pulling the hem of her handkerchief straight on her knee, his wife said, in a lifeless voice:

"Need we talk about it any more? On Tuesday we will send it back. (Monday is a holiday. You can't send it until Tuesday.) Then we will never talk about it any more."

"Send what back?"

"The money. To Mr. Hammond!"

"Are you out of your senses?" he said roughly.

She looked up, confusedly. "You can't send it until Tuesday," she repeated, mechanically.

He brought his fist down violently on the table. "I will never send it back! Never! You are insane! Why, it would be acknowledging—"

"It would be confession," she agreed.

"Well! that would be ruin."

"Ruin?"

"Why, if people knew—" he began.

"It is ruin, anyhow," she said, dully. "Don't you see? The only thing left is restitution."

"I can't make what you call—'restitution,' without—ruin; absolute ruin! Do you realize what it would mean to me, in this town, to have it known that I—borrowed from the Trust, and—and had not yet returned it? On the stand, of course, I had to protect myself; and that would be—against me. And it *would* be known. Hammond would never let it be settled privately! He couldn't prosecute me on the old charge; but I suppose he might make a claim of—of perjury.* Anyhow, just the publicity would ruin me. And he would make it public. Trust Hammond! Besides, I've given it back ten times over in unpaid-for work to the Estate—" He stopped abruptly. Amy had fainted. . . .

---

perjury: A deliberate false testimony while under oath

Sunday was a long day of struggle. The immediate hour of violence was over; he was ashamed; and he loved her; and he was frightened. But he was immovable. His hardness was worse than his violence.

"I can not do it, Amy; I will not do it. The thing is done. It's over. It's settled. I'm sorry; I—regret it; nobody regrets it as much as I do. But I will not destroy myself, and destroy you—you, too!—by returning it." Then, sullenly, "Anyway, I don't owe it, morally. I've more than made it up to them."

Monday, the holiday (and holidays had always been such joy to them; a whole day at home together!)—Monday, they struggled to the death.

It was in the afternoon that she suddenly flagged. She had been kneeling beside him, entreating him; and he had been hard and violent and childish by turns; but he would not. And toward dusk there came a dreadful pause. Partly, no doubt, it was because she was exhausted; but it was more than that. It was a sudden blasting consciousness that the man must save or lose his own soul. If she forced him to make restitution, the restitution would not be his, but hers. If she pushed him into honesty, he would still be dishonest. If he preferred the mire, he would be filthy if plucked out against his will and set on clean ground. A prisoner in heaven is in hell! No, he must save himself. She could not save him.

She drew away and looked at him; then

she covered her face with her hands. "I am done," she said, faintly.

The suddenness of her capitulation left him open-mouthed. But before he could speak she went away and left him. He heard her slip the bolt of their bedroom door; and then he heard her step overhead. After that all was still.

The afternoon was very long; once he went and walked drearily about the snowy lanes, avoiding passersby as well as he could. But for the most part he sat in the library and tried to read; but he forgot to turn over the pages. He said to himself that his life was over. Amy would leave him, of course; she had said as much. Well, he couldn't help it. Better the misery of a broken home than public shame, and disgrace, and ruin. And he had made restitution (as she called it); he had made it many times over!

It was late at night, as he was saying something like this to himself for the hundredth time, that his wife came back into the room. She stood up in the old place, on the hearthrug. Very gently she told him what she had to say. She did not look at him; her eyes were fixed on the Japanese crystal resting in its jade bowl on the mantelpiece; once she took it up, and turned it over and over in the palm of her hand, looking at it intently as she spoke. But probably she did not even see it.

"I have thought it all out," she began in a low voice; "and I see I was wrong—" He started. "I was wrong. You must save your own soul. I can't do it for you. Oh, I would! but I can't. I shall not ever again insist. Yes, the Kingdom of God must be within you. I never understood that before."

"Amy," he began, but she checked him.

"Please!—I am not through yet. I shall pay the money back, somehow, sometime. (Oh, wait—wait; *don't* interrupt me!) Of course, I shall not betray you. My paying it shall not

tell the truth, because, unless the truth is from you, it can not help you. It must be your truth, not mine. But I shall save, and save, and save, and pay it back—to clear my own soul. For I—I have lived on that three thousand dollars too," she said with a sick look. She put the crystal back into its bowl. "It will take—a long time," she said, faintly.

She stopped, trembling from the effort of so many calm words. Thomas Fleming, looking doggedly at the floor, said: "I suppose you'll get a separation?"

"Get a separation?" she glanced at him for an instant. "Why, we are separated," she said. "We can't be any more separated than we are. I suppose we have never been together. But I won't leave you, if that is what you mean."

"You'll stay with me?" he burst out; "I thought you despised me!"

"Why, no," she said, slowly; "I don't think I despise you. I don't think I do. But of course—" She looked away, helplessly. "Of course, I have no respect for you."

"Well," he said, "I'm sorry. But there's nothing I can do about it."

Amy turned, listlessly, as if to go upstairs again; but he caught her dress.

"You really mean you won't—leave me?"

"No, I won't leave you."

"Of course," he said, roughly, "you don't love me; but—" His voice faltered into a sort of question.

She turned sharply from him, hiding her face in her arm, moving blindly, with one hand stretched out to feel her way, toward the door. "Oh," she said; "oh—I'm afraid—I—"

And at that he broke. . . . Poor, weak Love, poor Love that would have denied itself for very shame; Love brought him to his knees; his arms around her waist, his head against her breast, his tears on her hand.

"Amy! *I will do it. I will give it back.* Oh, Amy, Amy—"

About the Author

Margaret Deland (1857-1945) is best known for her insightful character studies. She was particularly adept in creating believable characters who had to make difficult personal choices. Man's wrestling with his conscience is a frequent conflict in Deland's writing, and her themes often reflect traditional values. For example, in her story "Many Waters," honesty and respect are the cornerstone of love between husband and wife. The story also shows the ennobling power of true love. Although the goodness and sincerity of one partner cannot atone for evil in the other, Deland demonstrated that the power of self-sacrificing love can stir even a seared conscience to honesty, however painful the consequences of that honesty prove to be.

These attitudes in Deland's writing are also seen in her personal life. Although neither she nor her husband was considered a social reformer, they did regularly participate in projects that helped people in difficult circumstances. In life as well as in literature, she reflected a generous, openhearted spirit.

On Seeing Weather-beaten Trees

Adelaide Crapsey

This unit's stories dealt with such themes as wisdom, love, integrity and beauty. Conversely they have exposed such vices as foolishness, selfishness, and falsehood. The characters, through their conflicts, have shown us "by slant and twist, which way the wind hath blown." But let us leave literature and turn to ourselves. What would your answer be to the simple but poignant question posed in the following couplet?

Is it as plainly in our living shown,
By slant and twist, which way the wind hath blown?

About the Author

Adelaide Crapsey's (1878-1914) contribution to poetry, though small in volume, is significant because of her invention of the cinquain, a compact yet highly expressive verse form. Echoing the finest elements of Japanese haiku and tanka poetry, the cinquain is terse, elegant, and beautiful. In this verse form the first line contains one stress, or emphasized syllable; the second, two stresses; the third, three stresses; and the fourth, four stresses. The fifth line resembles the first, having only one stressed syllable. Her structure demands careful selection of words and word placement so that no surplus syllables break the form or the flow of the desired mental picture from the poet to the reader, who must often finish the thought and complete the imagery in his own mind.

Instead of explicitly presenting her emotions on themes such as life, death, and change, Crapsey chose to organize sensory images into a compressed verse form which expresses her world view. In her poem "On Seeing Weather-beaten Trees," for example, she conjured up a visual image of trees stoically resisting destruction by the elements but unable to avoid showing the results of that resistance. Crapsey is perhaps thinking of the effects of the choices and challenges of life on man's character and even on his physical appearance.

Adelaide Crapsey's life was as brief and concise as her poetry. She died when only thirty-six years old, after having taught English literature and history at a girls' school and also at Smith College. She followed her interests in archeology and English prosody until tuberculosis made these hobbies impossible. She devoted her later years to writing her own highly personalized cinquains. Most of these have been included in the collection of her poems entitled *Verse,* published after her death. She also left an unfinished scholarly work, *Analysis of English Metrics.*

About the Story and the Poem

1. Read Song of Solomon 8:7. What is the significance of the title of Margaret Deland's story?
2. List the "permanent" emotions dealt with in "Many Waters."
3. List some of the "transient" things that are dealt with in the story.
4. How is the conflict resolved?
5. What facets of Amy's character are "plainly in [her] living shown"?
6. What do Tom's actions and reactions show us about him?
7. What eventually prompts Tom to repent of his crime and to offer restitution?
8. How does the idea expressed in Adelaide Crapsey's couplet apply to the character of Thomas Fleming in "Many Waters"?

UNIT FOUR

Structure

Structure

"Many waters cannot quench love, neither can the floods drown it: if a man would give all the substance of his house for love, it would utterly be contemned" (Song of Solomon 8:7). This passage could be a summary for the theme of the last story, "Many Waters." Although myriad short stories supporting this theme have been written, few are as clear or as powerful as Margaret Deland's narrative. What gives her story such force? Strong conflict and vivid characters, of course, contribute to the story's success. Just as important, however, is the way that Deland moves her characters through the conflict—the way she structures her story.

In most prose narratives as well as dramas, the plot, or action, determines the structure. **Plot,** simply defined, is a series of events arranged to produce a definite sense of movement toward a specific goal. Notice the following diagram of a traditional plot structure.

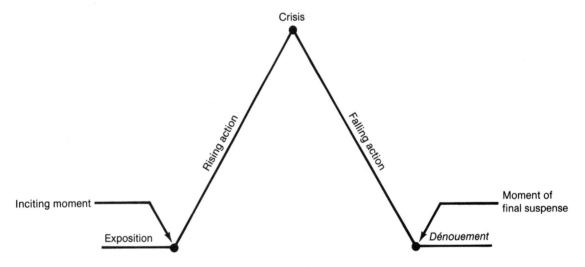

The purpose of the opening **exposition** is to introduce us to the setting, the characters, and the situation and to provide an **inciting moment,** an event that sets the conflict in motion. Following this inciting moment is the **rising action.** During this stage, the author keeps the story's conflict alive by creating various obstacles or *complications* that the central character must overcome. At this time, the writer will also carefully dole out bits of significant information, telling us just enough to move the story forward but not enough to disclose its outcome. This supplying of information is called *foreshadowing.* There are also, however, certain details the author will withhold from us, creating the *suspense* necessary for building toward the **crisis,** the moment of greatest suspense. Following the crisis is the **falling action,** during which the details of the story come together, preparing us for that **final moment of suspense**

that immediately precedes the ***dénouement.*** In a tragic story or drama, the *dénouement* may be the final catastrophe; in a comic story or drama it may be the clearing up of misconceptions, mistaken identities, and/or unfortunate situations.

Having discussed plot structure generally, let us return to Margaret Deland's story to see how she uses this traditional structure in creating "Many Waters."

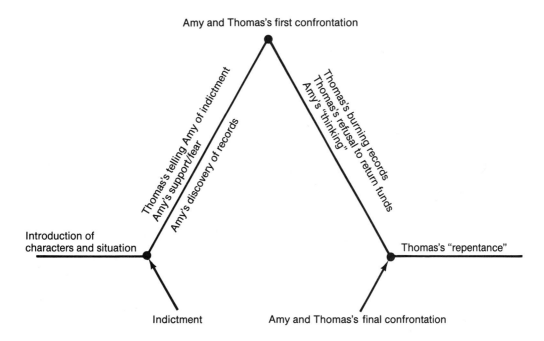

As the diagram shows, Deland gave painstaking attention to the **structure** or the organizational framework of her story. She was a careful artist, and the clarity and force of her theme are a result of this diligent artistry.

Poetry, like prose, must be carefully structured if it is to communicate a message effectively. The structural framework for poetry, however, is more complex than it is for prose. **Meter, verse forms, stanza forms,** and **shape** are four poetic structural devices that will be specifically defined and illustrated in this unit.

As you read each unit selection, whether story or poem, pay close attention to the information in the headnotes and end questions. This information will guide your understanding of the structure of each piece, an understanding that will give you not only a greater appreciation for the writer's artistry but also a greater confidence in your ability to accurately discern a story's message.

The Gold-Bug

Edgar Allan Poe

Edgar Allan Poe is often called the father of the modern detective story, for his tales of mystery and intrigue laid the groundwork for this minor fictional genre. In his three Dupin stories, for example, Poe creates the classic duo of the brilliant sleuth and his faithful but less perceptive companion. Arthur Conan Doyle's Holmes and Watson and Agatha Christie's Poirot and Hastings as well as many others are "descendants" of Poe's original characters. Poe is also responsible for developing two distinctive types of detective stories. One, the analytical type, relies heavily on careful deduction and foreshadowing. "The Purloined Letter" is an example of this type of story. The second, the sensational type, relies on dramatic action and high suspense. "The Gold-Bug" is considered by many to be the finest example of a sensational detective story. As you read, notice how Poe carefully doles out his information to the reader. What facts does he specifically withhold until the end of the story? Why do you think he chose to withhold these facts until after the crisis?

What ho! what ho! this fellow is dancing mad!
He hath been bitten by the Tarantula.

—All in the Wrong

Many years ago, I contracted an intimacy with a Mr. William Legrand. He was of an ancient Huguenot family, and had once been wealthy; but a series of misfortunes had reduced him to want. To avoid the mortification* consequent upon his disasters, he left New Orleans, the city of his forefathers, and took up his residence at Sullivan's Island, near Charleston, South Carolina.

---

mortification: shame or humiliation

This Island is a very singular one. It consists of little else than the sea sand, and is about three miles long. Its breadth at no point exceeds a quarter of a mile. It is separated from the mainland by a scarcely perceptible creek, oozing its way through a wilderness of reeds and slime, a favorite resort of the marsh-hen. The vegetation, as might be supposed, is scant, or at least dwarfish. No trees of any magnitude are to be seen. Near the western extremity, where Fort Moultrie stands, and where are some miserable frame buildings, tenanted, during the summer by the fugitives from Charleston dust and fever, may be found, indeed, the bristly palmetto; but the whole island, with the exception of this western point, and a line of hard, white beach on the seacoast, is covered with a dense undergrowth of the sweet myrtle, so much prized by the horticulturists of England. The shrub here often attains the height of fifteen or twenty feet, and forms an almost impenetrable coppice,* burthening* the air with its fragrance.

---

coppice: thicket
burthening: burdening

In the inmost recesses of this coppice, not far from the eastern or more remote end of the island, Legrand had built himself a small hut, which he occupied when I first, by mere accident, made his acquaintance. This soon ripened into friendship—for there was much in the recluse to excite interest and esteem. I found him well educated, with unusual powers of mind, but infected with misanthropy,* and subject to perverse moods of alternate enthusiasm and melancholy. He had with him many books, but rarely employed them. His chief amusements were gunning and fishing, or sauntering along the beach and through the myrtles, in quest of shells or entomological* specimens—his collection of the latter might have been envied by a Swammerdamm. In these excursions he was usually accompanied by an old Negro, called Jupiter, who had been manumitted* before the reverses of the family, but who could be induced, neither by threats nor by promises, to abandon what he considered his right of attendance upon the footsteps of his young "Massa Will." It is not improbable that the relatives of Legrand, conceiving him to be somewhat unsettled in intellect, had contrived to instil this obstinacy into Jupiter, with a view to the supervision and guardianship of the wanderer.

misanthropy: hatred of men
entomological: relating to the scientific study of insects
manumitted: freed from slavery

The winters in the latitude of Sullivan's Island are seldom very severe, and in the fall of the year it is a rare event indeed when a fire is considered necessary. About the middle of October, 18—, there occurred, however, a day of remarkable chilliness. Just before sunset I scrambled my way through the evergreens to the hut of my friend, whom I had not visited for several weeks—my residence being, at that time, in Charleston, a distance of nine miles from the Island, while the facilities of passage and repassage were very far behind those of the present day. Upon reaching the hut I rapped, as was my custom, and getting no reply, sought for the key where I knew it was secreted, unlocked the door and went in. A fine fire was blazing upon the hearth. It was a novelty, and by no means an ungrateful one. I threw off an overcoat, took an arm-chair by the crackling logs, and awaited patiently the arrival of my hosts.

Soon after dark they arrived, and gave me a most cordial welcome. Jupiter, grinning from ear to ear, bustled about to prepare some marsh-hens for supper. Legrand was in one of his fits—how else shall I term them?—of enthusiasm. He had found an unknown bivalve,* forming a new genus, and, more than this, he had hunted down and secured, with Jupiter's assistance, a *scarabaeus* which he believed to be totally new, but in respect to which he wished to have my opinion on the morrow.

bivalve: any of the species which has a shell with two hinged parts

"And why not to-night?" I asked, rubbing my hands over the blaze.

"Ah, if I had only known you were here!" said Legrand, "but it's so long since I saw you; and how could I foresee that you would pay me a visit this very night of all others? As I was coming home I met Lieutenant G—, from the fort, and, very foolishly, I lent him the bug; so it will be impossible for you to see it until morning. Stay here to-night, and I will send Jup down for it at sunrise. It is the loveliest thing in creation!"

"What?—sunrise?"

"Nonsense! no!—the bug. It is of a brilliant gold color—about the size of a large hickory-nut—with two jet black spots near one extremity of the back, and another, somewhat longer, at the other. The *antennae* are—"

"Dey aint *no* tin in him, Massa Will, I keep a tellin on you," here interrupted Jupiter; "de bug is a goole bug, solid, ebery bit of him, inside and all, sep him wing—neber feel half so hebby a bug in my life."

"Well, suppose it is, Jup," replied Legrand, somewhat more earnestly, it seemed to me, than the case demanded, "is that any reason for your letting the birds burn? The color"— here he turned to me—"is really almost enough to warrant Jupiter's idea. You never saw a more brilliant metallic lustre than the scales emit— but of this you cannot judge till to-morrow. In the mean time I can give you some idea of the shape." Saying this, he seated himself at a small table, on which were a pen and ink, but no paper. He looked for some in a drawer, but found none.

"Never mind," said he at length, "this will answer"; and he drew from his waistcoat pocket a scrap of what I took to be very dirty foolscap,* and made upon it a rough drawing with the pen. While he did this, I retained my seat by the fire, for I was still chilly. When the design was complete, he handed it to me without rising. As I received it, a loud growl was heard, succeeded by a scratching at the door. Jupiter opened it, and a large Newfoundland, belonging to Legrand, rushed in, leaped upon my shoulders, and loaded me with caresses; for I had shown him much attention during previous visits. When his gambols* were over, I looked at the paper, and, to speak the truth, found myself not a little puzzled at what my friend had depicted.

---

foolscap: large piece of writing paper
gambols: playful antics

"Well!" I said, after contemplating it for some minutes, "this *is* a strange *scarabaeus,* I must confess: new to me: never saw anything like it before—unless it was a skull, or a death's-head—which it more nearly resembles than anything else that has come under *my* observation."

"A death's-head!" echoed Legrand—"Oh— yes—well, it has something of that appearance upon paper, no doubt. The two upper black spots look like eyes, eh? And the longer one at the bottom like a mouth—and then the shape of the whole is oval."

"Perhaps so," said I; "but, Legrand, I fear you are no artist. I must wait until I see the beetle itself, if I am to form any idea of its personal appearance."

"Well, I don't know," said he, a little nettled, "I draw tolerably—*should* do it at least—have had good masters, and flatter myself that I am not quite a blockhead."

"But, my dear fellow, you are joking then," said I, "this is a very passable *skull*—indeed, I may say that it is a very excellent skull, according to the vulgar notions about such specimens of physiology—and your *scarabaeus* must be the queerest *scarabaeus* in the world if it resembles it. But where are the antennae you spoke of?"

"The *antennae!*" said Legrand, who seemed to be getting unaccountably warm upon the subject; "I am sure you must see the *antennae.* I made them as distinct as they are in the original insect, and I presume that is sufficient."

"Well, well," I said, "perhaps you have— still I don't see them;" and I handed him the paper without additional remark, not wishing to ruffle his temper; but I was much surprised at the turn affairs had taken; his ill humor puzzled me—and, as for the drawing of the beetle, there were positively *no antennae* visible, and the whole *did* bear a very close resemblance to the ordinary cuts of a death's-head.

He received the paper very peevishly, and was about to crumple it, apparently to throw

it in the fire, when a casual glance at the design seemed suddenly to rivet his attention. In an instant his face grew violently red—in another as excessively pale. For some minutes he continued to scrutinize the drawing minutely where he sat. At length he arose, took a candle from the table, and proceeded to seat himself upon a sea-chest in the farthest corner of the room. Here again he made an anxious examination of the paper; turning it in all directions. He said nothing, however, and his conduct greatly astonished me; yet I thought it prudent not to exacerbate* the growing moodiness of his temper by any comment. Presently he took from his coat pocket a wallet, placed the paper carefully in it, and deposited both in a writing-desk, which he locked. He now grew more composed in his demeanor; but his original air of enthusiasm had quite disappeared. Yet he seemed not so much sulky as abstracted. As the evening wore away he became more and more absorbed in reverie, from which no sallies of mine could arouse him. It had been my intention to pass the night at the hut, as I had frequently done before, but, seeing my host in this mood, I deemed it proper to take leave. He did not press me to remain, but, as I departed, he shook my hand with even more than his usual cordiality.

exacerbate: aggravate

It was about a month after this (and during the interval I had seen nothing of Legrand) when I received a visit, at Charleston, from his man, Jupiter. I had never seen the good old Negro look so dispirited, and I feared that some serious disaster had befallen my friend.

"Well, Jup," said I, "what is the matter now?—how is your master?"

"Why, to speak de troof, massa, him not so berry well as mought be."

"Not well! I am truly sorry to hear it. What does he complain of?"

"Dar! dat's it!—him neber plain of notin—but him berry sick for all dat."

"_Very_ sick, Jupiter!—why didn't you say so at once? Is he confined to bed?"

"No, dat he aint!—he aint find nowhar—dat's just whar de shoe pinch—my mind is got to be berry hebby bout poor Massa Will."

"Jupiter, I should like to understand what it is you are talking about. You say your master is sick. Hasn't he told you what ails him?"

"Why, massa, taint worf while for to git mad bout de matter—Massa Will say noffin at all aint de matter wid him—but den what make him go about looking dis here way, wid he head down and he soldiers up, and as white as a gose? And den he keep a syphon all de time—"

"Keeps a what, Jupiter?"

"Keeps a syphon wid de figgurs on de slate—de queerest figgurs I ebber did see. Ise gittin to be skeered, I tell you. Hab for to keep mighty tight eye pon him noovers. Todder day he gib me slip fore de sun up and was gone de whole ob de blessed day. I had a big stick ready cut for to gib him a good beating when he did come—but Ise sich a fool dat I hadn't de heart arter all—he look so berry poorly."

"Eh?—what?—ah yes!—upon the whole I think you had better not be too severe with the poor fellow—don't flog him, Jupiter—he can't very well stand it—but can you form no idea of what has occasioned this illness, or rather this change of conduct? Has anything unpleasant happened since I saw you?"

"No, massa, day aint bin noffin onpleasant *since* den—'t was *fore* den I'm feared—'t was de berry day you was dare."

"How? what do you mean?"

"Why massa, I mean de bug—dare now."

"The what?"

"De bug—I'm berry sartain dat Massa Will bin bit somewhere bout de head by dat goole-bug."

"And what cause have you, Jupiter, for such a supposition?"

"Claws enuff, massa, and mouff too. I nebber did see sich a bug—he kick and he bite ebery ting what cum near him. Massa Will cotch him fuss, but had for to let him go gin mighty quick, I tell you—den was de time he must ha got de bite. I didn't like de look ob de bug mouff, myself, no how, so I wouldn't take hold ob him wid my finger, but I cotch him wid a piece ob paper dat I found. I rap him up in de paper and stuff piece ob it in he mouff—dat was de way."

"And you think, then, that your master was really bitten by the beetle, and that the bite made him sick?"

"I don't tink noffin about it—I nose it.

What make him dream bout de goole so much, if taint cause he bit by de goole-bug? Ise heerd bout dem goole-bugs fore dis."

"But how do you know he dreams about gold?"

"How I know? why cause he talk about it in he sleep—dat's how I nose."

"Well, Jup, perhaps you are right; but to what fortunate circumstance am I to attribute the honor of a visit from you to-day?"

"What de matter, massa?"

"Did you bring any message from Mr. Legrand?"

"No, massa, I bring dis here pissel"; and here Jupiter handed me a note which ran thus:

My Dear—

Why have I not seen you for so long a time? I hope you have not been so foolish as to take offence at any little *brusquerie* of mine; but no, that is improbable.

Since I saw you I have had great cause for anxiety. I have something to tell you, yet scarcely know how to tell it, or whether I should tell it at all.

I have not been quite well for some days past, and poor old Jup annoys me, almost beyond endurance, by his well-meant attentions. Would you believe it?—he had prepared a huge stick, the other day, with which to chastise me for giving him the slip, and spending the day, *solus,* among the hills on the main land. I verily believe that my ill looks alone saved me a flogging.

I have made no addition to my cabinet since we met.

If you can, in any way, make it convenient, come over with Jupiter. *Do* come. I wish to see you *to-night,* upon business of importance. I assure you that it is of the *highest* importance.

Ever yours,
William Legrand

There was something in the tone of this note which gave me great uneasiness. Its whole style differed materially from that of Legrand. What could he be dreaming of? What new crotchet* possessed his excitable brain? What "business of the highest importance" could *he* possibly have to transact? Jupiter's account of him boded no good. I dreaded lest the continued pressure of misfortune had, at length, fairly unsettled the reason of my friend. Without a moment's hesitation, therefore, I prepared to accompany the Negro.

crotchet: whimsical notion

Upon reaching the wharf, I noticed a scythe and three spades, all apparently new, lying in the bottom of the boat in which we were to embark.

"What is the meaning of all this, Jup?" I inquired.

"Him syfe, massa, and spade."

"Very true; but what are they doing here?"

"Him de syfe and de spade what Massa Will sis pon my buying for him in de town."

"But what, in the name of all that is mysterious, is your 'Massa Will' going to do with scythes and spades?"

"Dat's more dan I know, and I believe 't is more dan he know, too. But it's all cum ob de bug."

Finding that no satisfaction was to be obtained of Jupiter, whose whole intellect seemed to be absorbed by "de bug," I now stepped into the boat and made sail. With a fair and strong breeze we soon ran into the little cove to the northward of Fort Moultrie, and a walk of some two miles brought us to the hut. It was about three in the afternoon when we arrived. Legrand had been awaiting us in eager expectation. He grasped my hand with a nervous *empressement* which alarmed me and strengthened the suspicions already entertained. His countenance was pale even to ghastliness, and his deep-set eyes glared with unnatural lustre. After some inquiries respecting his health, I asked him, not knowing what better to say, if he had yet obtained the *scarabaeus* from Lieutenant G—.

"Oh yes," he replied, coloring violently, "I got it from him the next morning. Nothing should tempt me to part with that *scarabaeus*. Do you know that Jupiter is quite right about it?"

"In what way?" I asked, with a sad foreboding at heart.

"In supposing it to be a bug of *real gold.*" He said with an air of profound seriousness, and I felt inexpressibly shocked.

"This bug is to make my fortune," he continued, with a triumphant smile, "to reinstate me in my family possessions. Is it any wonder, then, that I prize it? Since Fortune has thought fit to bestow it upon me, I have only to use it properly and I shall arrive at the gold of which it is the index. Jupiter, bring me that *scarabaeus!*"

"What! De bug, massa? I'd rudder not go fer trubble dat bug—you mus git him for your own self." Hereupon Legrand arose, with a grave and stately air, and brought me the beetle from a glass case in which it was enclosed. It was a beautiful *scarabaeus,* and, at that time, unknown to naturalists—of course a great prize in a scientific point of view. There were two round, black spots near one extremity of the back, and a long one near the other. The scales were exceedingly hard and glossy, with all the appearance of burnished gold. The weight of the insect was very remarkable, and, taking all things into consideration, I could hardly blame Jupiter for his opinion respecting it; but what to make of Legrand's agreement with that opinion, I could not, for the life of me, tell.

"I sent for you," said he, in a grandiloquent tone, when I had completed my examination of the beetle, "I sent for you, that I might have your counsel and assistance in furthering the views of Fate and of the bug"—

"My dear Legrand," I cried, interrupting him, "you are certainly unwell, and had better use some little precautions. You shall go to bed, and I will remain with you a few days, until you get over this. You are feverish and"—

"Feel my pulse," said he.

I felt it, and, to say the truth, found not the slightest indication of fever.

"But you may be ill and yet have no fever. Allow me this once to prescribe for you. In the first place, go to bed. In the next"—

"You are mistaken," he interposed, "I am as well as I can expect to be under the excitement which I suffer. If you really wish me well, you will relieve this excitement."

"And how is this to be done?"

"Very easily. Jupiter and myself are going upon an expedition into the hills, upon the main land, and, in this expedition, we shall need the aid of some person in whom we can confide. You are the only one we can trust. Whether we succeed or fail, the excitement which you now perceive in me will be equally allayed."

"I am anxious to oblige you in any way," I replied; "but do you mean to say that this infernal beetle has any connection with your expedition into the hills?"

"It has."

"Then, Legrand, I can become a party to no such absurd proceeding."

"I am sorry—very sorry—for we shall have to try it by ourselves."

"Try it by yourselves! The man is surely mad!—but stay!—how long do you propose to be absent?"

"Probably all night. We shall start immediately, and be back, at all events, by sunrise."

"And will you promise me, upon your honor, that when this freak of yours is over, and the bug business settled to your satisfaction, you will then return home and follow my advice implicitly, as that of your physician?"

"Yes; I promise; and now let us be off, for we have no time to lose."

With a heavy heart I accompanied my friend. We started about four o'clock—Legrand, Jupiter, the dog, and myself. Jupiter had with him the scythe and spades—the whole of which he insisted upon carrying—more through fear, it seemed to me, of trusting either of the implements within reach of his master, than from any excess of industry or complaisance. His demeanor was dogged in the extreme, and "dat bug" were the sole words which escaped his lips during the journey. For my own part, I had charge of a couple of dark lanterns, while Legrand contented himself with the *scarabaeus,* which he carried attached to the end of a bit of whip-cord; twirling it to and fro, with the air of a conjuror, as he went. When I observed this last, plain evidence of my friend's aberration of mind, I could scarcely refrain from tears. I thought it best, however, to humor his fancy, at least for the present, or until I could adopt some more energetic measures with a chance of success. In the mean time I endeavored, but all in vain, to sound him in regard to the object of the expedition. Having succeeded in inducing me to accompany him, he seemed unwilling to hold conversation upon any topic of minor importance, and to all my questions vouchsafed no other reply than "we shall see!"

We crossed the creek at the head of the island by means of a skiff, and, ascending the high grounds on the shore of the main land, proceeded in a northwesterly direction, through a tract of country excessively wild and desolate, where no trace of a human footstep was to be seen. Legrand led the way with decision; pausing only for an instant, here and there, to consult what appeared to be certain

landmarks of his own contrivance upon a former occasion.

In this manner we journeyed for about two hours, and the sun was just setting when we entered a region infinitely more dreary than any yet seen. It was a species of table land, near the summit of an almost inaccessible hill, densely wooded from base to pinnacle, and interspersed with huge crags that appeared to lie loosely upon the soil, and in many cases were prevented from precipitating themselves into the valleys below, merely by the support of the trees against which they reclined. Deep ravines, in various directions, gave an air of still sterner solemnity to the scene.

The natural platform to which we had clambered was thickly overgrown with brambles, through which we soon discovered that it would have been impossible to force our way but for the scythe; and Jupiter, by direction of his master, proceeded to clear for us a path to the foot of an enormously tall tulip-tree, which stood, with some eight or ten oaks, upon the level, and far surpassed them all, and all other trees which I had then ever seen, in the beauty of its foliage and form, in the wide spread of its branches, and in the general majesty of its appearance. When we reached this tree, Legrand turned to Jupiter, and asked him if he thought he could climb it. The old man seemed a little staggered by the question, and for some moments made no reply. At length he approached the huge trunk, walked slowly around it, and examined it with minute attention. When he had completed his scrutiny, he merely said,

"Yes, massa, Jup climb any tree he ebber see in he life."

"Then up with you as soon as possible, for it will soon be too dark to see what we are about."

"How far mus go up, massa?" inquired Jupiter.

"Get up the main trunk first, and then I will tell you which way to go—and here—stop! take this beetle with you."

"De bug, Massa Will!—de goole bug!" cried the Negro, drawing back in dismay—"what for mus tote de bug way up de tree?"

"If you are afraid, Jup, to take hold of a harmless little dead beetle, why you can carry it up by this string—but, if you do not take it up with you in some way, I shall be under the necessity of breaking your head with this shovel."

"What de matter now, massa?" said Jup, evidently shamed into compliance; "always want for to raise fuss. Was only funnin any how. *Me* feered de bug! what I keer for de bug?" Here he took cautiously hold of the extreme end of the string, and, maintaining the insect as far from his person as circumstances would permit, prepared to ascend the tree.

In youth the tulip-tree, or *Liriodendron Tulipiferum,* the most magnificent of American foresters, has a trunk peculiarly smooth, and often rises to a great height without lateral branches; but, in its riper age, the bark becomes gnarled and uneven, while many short limbs make their appearance on the stem. Thus the difficulty of ascension, in the present case, lay more in semblance than in reality. Embracing the huge cylinder, as closely as possible, with his arms and knees, seizing with his hands some projections, and resting his naked toes upon others, Jupiter, after one or two narrow escapes from falling, at length wriggled himself into the first great fork, and seemed to consider the whole business as virtually accomplished. The *risk* of the achievement was, in fact, now over, although the climber was some sixty or seventy feet from the ground.

"Which way mus go now, Massa Will?" he asked.

"Keep up the largest branch—the one on this side," said Legrand. The Negro obeyed him promptly, and apparently with but little trouble; ascending higher and higher, until no glimpse of his squat figure could be obtained through the dense foliage which enveloped it. Presently his voice was heard in a sort of halloo.

"How much fudder is got for go?"

"How high up are you?" asked Legrand.

"Ebber so fur," replied the Negro; "can see de sky fru de top ob de tree."

"Never mind the sky, but attend to what I say. Look down the trunk and count the limbs below you on this side. How many limbs have you passed?"

"One, two, tree, four, fibe—I done pass fibe big limb, massa, pon dis side."

"Then go one limb higher."

In a few minutes the voice was heard again, announcing that the seventh limb was attained.

"Now, Jup," cried Legrand, evidently much excited, "I want you to work your way out upon that limb as far as you can. If you see anything strange, let me know."

By this time what little doubt I might have entertained of my poor friend's insanity, was put finally at rest. I had no alternative but to conclude him stricken with lunacy, and I became seriously anxious about getting him home. While I was pondering upon what was best to be done, Jupiter's voice was again heard.

"Mos feered for to ventur pon dis limb berry far—tis dead limb putty much all de way."

"Did you say it was a *dead* limb, Jupiter?" cried Legrand in a quavering voice.

"Yes, massa, him dead as de door-nail—done up for sartian—done departed dis here life."

"What in the name of heaven shall I do?" asked Legrand, seemingly in the greatest distress.

"Do!" said I, glad of an opportunity to interpose a word, "why come home and go to bed. Come now!—that's a fine fellow. It's getting late, and, besides, you remember your promise."

"Jupiter," cried he, without heeding me in the least, "do you hear me?"

"Yes, Massa Will, hear you ebber so plain."

"Try the wood well, then, with your knife, and see if you think it *very* rotten."

"Him rotten, massa, sure nuff," replied the Negro in a few moments, "but not so berry rotten as mought be. Mought ventur out leetle way pon de limb by myself, dat's true."

"By yourself!—what do you mean?"

"Why I mean de bug. 'Tis *berry* hebby bug. Spose I drop him down fuss, and den de limb won't break wid just de weight ob me."

"You scoundrel!" cried Legrand, apparently much relieved, "what do you mean by telling me such nonsense as that? As sure as you let that beetle fall!—I'll break your neck. Look here, Jupiter! Do you hear me?"

"Yes massa, needn't hollo at poor Jupiter dat style."

"Well! Now listen!—if you will venture out on the limb as far as you think safe, and not let go the beetle, I'll make you a present of a silver dollar as soon as you get down."

"I'm gwine, Massa Will—deed I is," replied Jupiter very promptly—"mos out to the end now."

"Out to the end!" here fairly screamed Legrand, "do you say you are out to the end of that limb?"

"Soon be to de eend, massa,—o-o-o-o-oh! What *is* dis here pon de tree?"

"Well!" cried Legrand, highly delighted, "what is it?"

"Why taint noffin but a skull—somebody bin lef him head up de tree, and de crows done gobble ebery bit ob de meat off."

"A skull, you say!—very well!—how is it fastened to the limb?—what holds it on?"

"Sure nuff, massa; mus look. Why dis berry curous sarcumstance, pon my word—dare's a great big nail in de skull, what fastens ob it on to de tree."

"Well now, Jupiter, do exactly as I tell you—do you hear?"

"Yes, massa."

"Pay attention, then!—find the left eye of the skull."

"Hum! Hoo! Dat's good! Why dar aint no eye lef at all."

"Curse your stupidity! Do you know your right hand from your left?"

"Yes, I nose dat—nose all bout dat—tis my left hand what I chops de wood wid."

"To be sure! You are left-handed; and your left eye is on the same side as your left hand. Now, I suppose, you can find the left eye of the skull, or the place where the left eye has been. Have you found it?"

Here was a long pause. At length Jupiter asked,

"Is de lef eye of de skull pon de same side as de lef hand of de skull, too?—cause de skull aint got not a bit of a hand at all—nebber mind! I got de lef eye now—here the lef eye! What mus do wid it?"

"Let the beetle drop through it, as far as the string will reach—but be careful and not let go your hold of the string."

"All dat done, Massa Will; mighty easy ting for to put de bug fru de hole—look out for him dar below!"

During this colloquy no portion of Jupiter's person could be seen; but the beetle, which he had suffered to descend, was now visible at the end of the string, and glistened, like a globe of burnished gold, in the last rays of the setting sun, some of which still faintly illumined the eminence upon which we stood. The *scarabaeus* hung quite clear of any branches, and, if allowed to fall, would have fallen at our feet. Legrand immediately took the scythe, and cleared with it a circular space, three or four yards in diameter, just beneath the insect, and, having accomplished this, ordered Jupiter to let go the string and come down from the tree.

Driving a peg, with great nicety, into the ground, at the precise spot where the beetle fell, my friend now produced from his pocket a tape-measure. Fastening one end of this at that point of the trunk of the tree which was nearest the peg, he unrolled it till it reached the peg, and thence farther unrolled it, in the direction already established by the two points of the tree and the peg, for the distance of fifty feet—Jupiter clearing away the brambles with the scythe. At the spot thus attained a second peg was driven, and about this, as a centre, a rude circle, about four feet in diameter, described. Taking now a spade himself, and giving one to Jupiter and one to me, Legrand begged us to set about digging as quickly as possible.

To speak the truth, I had no especial relish for such amusement at any time, and, at that particular moment, would most willingly have declined it; for the night was coming on, and I felt much fatigued with the exercise already taken; but I saw no mode of escape, and was fearful of disturbing my poor friend's equanimity by a refusal. Could I have depended, indeed, upon Jupiter's aid, I would have had no hesitation in attempting to get the lunatic home by force; but I was too well assured of the old Negro's disposition, to hope that he would assist me, under any circumstances, in a personal contest with his master. I made no doubt that the latter had been infected with some of the innumerable Southern superstitions about money buried, and that his phantasy had received confirmation by the finding of the *scarabaeus,* or, perhaps, by Jupiter's obstinacy in maintaining it to be "a bug of real gold." A mind disposed to lunacy would readily be led away by such suggestions—especially if chiming in with favorite preconceived ideas—and then I called to mind the poor fellow's speech about the beetle's being "the index of his fortune." Upon the whole, I was sadly vexed and puzzled, but, at length, I concluded to make a virtue of necessity— to dig with a good will, and thus the sooner to convince the visionary, by ocular*

demonstration, of the fallacy of the opinions he entertained.

ocular: pertaining to the eye or eyesight

The lanterns having been lit, we all fell to work with a zeal worthy a more rational cause; and, as the glare fell upon our persons and implements, I could not help thinking how picturesque a group we composed, and how strange and suspicious our labors must have appeared to any interloper who, by chance, might have stumbled upon our whereabouts.

We dug very steadily for two hours. Little was said; and our chief embarrassment lay in the yelpings of the dog, who took exceeding interest in our proceedings. He, at length, became so obstreperous* that we grew fearful of his giving the alarm to some stragglers in the vicinity—or, rather, this was the apprehension of Legrand—for myself, I should have rejoiced at any interruption which might have enabled me to get the wanderer home. The noise was, at length, very effectually silenced by Jupiter, who, getting out of the hole with a dogged air of deliberation, tied the brute's mouth up with one of his suspenders, and then returned, with a grave chuckle, to his task.

obstreperous: stubborn

When the time mentioned had expired, we had reached a depth of five feet, and yet no signs of any treasure became manifest. A general pause ensued, and I began to hope that the farce was at an end. Legrand, however, although evidently much disconcerted, wiped his brow thoughtfully and recommenced. We had excavated the entire circle of four feet diameter, and now we slightly enlarged the limit, and went to the farther depth of two feet. Still nothing appeared. The goldseeker, whom I sincerely pitied, at length clambered from the pit, with the bitterest disappointment imprinted upon every feature, and proceeded, slowly and reluctantly, to put on his coat, which he had thrown off at the beginning of his labor. In the mean time I made no remark. Jupiter, at a signal from his master, began to gather up his tools. This done, and the dog having been unmuzzled, we turned in profound silence towards home.

We had taken, perhaps, a dozen steps in this direction, when Legrand strode up to Jupiter, and seized him by the collar. The astonished Negro opened his eyes and mouth to the fullest extent, let fall the spades, and fell upon his knees.

"You scoundrel," said Legrand, hissing out the syllables from between his clenched teeth—"you villain!—speak, I tell you!—answer me this instant, without prevarication!*—which—which is your left eye?"

---

prevarication: lying

"Oh, Massa Will! Aint dis here my lef eye for sartin?" roared the terrified Jupiter, placing his hand upon his *right* organ of vision, and holding it there with a desperate pertinacity,* as if in immediate dread of his master's attempt at a gouge.

---

pertinacity: persistency

"I thought so!—I knew it!—hurrah!" vociferated* Legrand, letting Jupiter go, and executing a series of curvets and caracols,* much to the astonishment of his valet, who, arising from his knees, looked, mutely, from his master to myself, and then from myself to his master.

---

vociferated: exclaimed vehemently
curvets and caracols: leaps and half turns

"Come! We must go back," said the latter, "the game's not up yet;" and he again led the way to the tulip-tree.

"Jupiter," said he, when we reached its foot, "come here! Was the skull nailed to the limb with the face outward or with the face to the limb?"

"De face was out, massa, so dat de crows could get at de eyes good, widout any trouble."

"Well, then, was it this eye or that through which you let the beetle fall?"—here Legrand touched each of Jupiter's eyes.

" 'Twas dis eye, massa—de lef eye—jis as you tell me," and here it was his right eye that the Negro indicated.

"That will do—we must try again."

Here my friend, about whose madness I now saw, or fancied that I saw, certain indications of method, removed the peg which marked the spot where the beetle fell, to a spot about three inches to the west-ward of its former position. Taking, now, the tape-measure from the nearest point of the trunk to the peg, as before, and continuing the extension in a straight line to the distance of fifty feet, a spot was indicated, removed, by several yards, from the point at which we had been digging.

Around the new position a circle, somewhat larger than in the former instance, was now described, and we again set to work with the spades. I was dreadfully weary, but, scarcely understanding what had occasioned the change in my thoughts, I felt no longer any great aversion from the labor imposed. I had become most unaccountably interested—nay, even excited. Perhaps there was something, amid all the extravagant demeanor of Legrand— some air of forethought, or of deliberation, which impressed me. I dug eagerly, and now and then caught myself actually looking, with something that very much resembled expectation, for the fancied treasure, the vision of which had demented* my unfortunate companion. At a period when such vagaries* of thought most fully possessed me, and when we had been at work perhaps an hour and a half, we were again interrupted by the violent howlings of the dog. His uneasiness, in the first instance, had been, evidently, but the result of playfulness or caprice,* but he now assumed a bitter and serious tone. Upon Jupiter's again attempting to muzzle him, he made furious resistance, and, leaping into the hole, tore up the mould frantically with his claws. In a few seconds he had uncovered a mass of human bones, forming two complete skeletons, intermingled with several buttons of metal, and what appeared to be the dust of decayed woollen. One or two strokes of a spade upturned the blade of a large Spanish knife, and, as we dug farther, three or four pieces of gold and silver coin came to light.

---

demented: made insane
vagaries: flights of fancy
caprice: impulsiveness

At sight of these the joy of Jupiter could scarcely be restrained, but the countenance of his master wore an air of extreme disappointment. He urged us, however, to continue our exertions, and the words were hardly uttered when I stumbled and fell forward, having caught the toe of my boot in a large ring of iron that lay half buried in the loose earth.

We now worked in earnest, and never did I pass ten minutes of more intense excitement. During this interval we had fairly unearthed an oblong chest of wood, which, from its perfect preservation, and wonderful hardness, had plainly been subjected to some mineralizing process—perhaps that of the Bi-chloride of Mercury. This box was three feet and a half long, three feet broad, and two and a half feet deep. It was firmly secured by bands of wrought iron, riveted, and forming a kind of trellis-work over the whole. On each side of the chest, near the top, were three rings of iron—six in all—by means of which a firm hold could be obtained by six persons. Our utmost united endeavors served only to disturb the coffer very slightly in its bed. We at once saw the impossibility of removing so great a weight. Luckily, the sole fastenings of the lid consisted of two sliding bolts. These we drew back—trembling and panting with anxiety. In an instant, a treasure of incalculable value lay gleaming before us. As the rays of the lanterns fell within the pit, there flashed upwards, from the confused heap of gold and of jewels, a glow and a glare that absolutely dazzled our eyes.

I shall not pretend to describe the feelings with which I gazed. Amazement was, of course, predominant. Legrand appeared exhausted with excitement, and spoke very few words. Jupiter's countenance wore, for some minutes, as deadly a pallor as it is possible, in the nature of things, for any Negro's visage to assume. He seemed stupefied—thunderstricken. Presently he fell upon his knees in the pit, and, burying his naked arms up to the elbows in gold, let them there remain, as if enjoying the luxury of a bath. At length, with a deep sigh, he exclaimed, as if in a soliloquy,

"And dis all cum ob de goole-bug! De putty goole-bug! De poor little goole-bug, what I boosed in dat sabage kind ob style! Ain't you shamed ob yourself, Jup?—answer me dat!"

It became necessary, at last, that I should arouse both master and valet to the expediency of removing the treasure. It was growing late, and it behooved us to make exertion, that we might get every thing housed before daylight. It was difficult to say what should be done; and much time was spent in deliberation—so confused were the ideas of all. We, finally, lightened the box by removing two thirds of its contents, when we were enabled, with some trouble, to raise it from the hole. The articles taken out were deposited among the brambles, and the dog left to guard them, with strict orders from Jupiter neither, upon any pretense, to stir from the spot, nor to open his mouth until our return. We then hurriedly made for home with the chest; reaching the hut in safety, but after excessive toil, at one o'clock in the morning. Worn out as we were, it was not in human nature to do more just then. We rested until two, and had supper; starting for the hills immediately afterwards, armed with three stout sacks, which, by good luck, were upon the premises. A little before four we arrived at the pit, divided the remainder of the booty, as equally as might be, among us, and, leaving the holes unfilled, again set out for the hut, at which, for the second time, we deposited our golden burthens, just as the first streaks of the dawn gleamed from over the tree-tops in the East.

We were now thoroughly broken down; but the intense excitement of the time denied us repose. After an unquiet slumber of some three or four hours' duration, we arose, as if by preconcert, to make examination of our treasure.

The chest had been full to the brim, and we spent the whole day, and the greater part of the next night, in a scrutiny of its contents. There had been nothing like order or arrangement. Every thing had been heaped in promiscuously. Having assorted all with care, we found ourselves possessed of even vaster wealth than we had at first supposed. In coin there was rather more than four hundred and fifty thousand dollars—estimating the value of the pieces, as accurately as we could, by the tables of the period. There was not a particle of silver. All was gold of antique date and of great variety—French, Spanish, and German money, with a few English guineas, and some counters, of which we had never seen specimens before. There were several very large and heavy coins, so worn that we could make nothing of their inscriptions. There was no American money. The value of the jewels we found more difficulty in estimating. There were diamonds—some of them exceedingly large and fine—a hundred and ten in all, and not one of them small; eighteen rubies of remarkable brilliancy—three hundred and ten emeralds, all very beautiful; and twenty-one sapphires, with an opal. These stones had all been broken from their settings and thrown loose in the chest. The settings themselves, which we picked out from among the other gold, appeared to have been beaten up with hammers, as if to prevent identification. Besides all this, there was a vast quantity of solid gold ornaments;—nearly two hundred massive finger and ear rings—rich chains—thirty of these, if I remember—five gold censers of great value—a prodigious golden punch-bowl, ornamented with richly chased vine-leaves; with two sword-handles exquisitely embossed, and many other smaller articles which I cannot recollect. The weight of these valuables exceeded three hundred and fifty pounds avoirdupois;* and in this estimate I have not included one hundred and ninety-seven superb gold watches; three of the number being worth each five hundred dollars, if one. Many of them were very old, and as time keepers valueless; the works having suffered, more or less, from corrosion—but all were richly jewelled and in cases of great worth. We estimated the entire contents of the chest, that night, at a million and a half dollars; and, upon the subsequent disposal of the trinkets and jewels (a few being retained for our own use), it was found that we had greatly undervalued the treasure.

avoirdupois: weight

When, at length we had concluded our examination, and the intense excitement of the time had, in some measure, subsided, Legrand, who saw that I was dying with impatience for

a solution of this most extraordinary riddle, entered into a full detail of all the circumstances connected with it.

"You remember," said he, "the night when I handed you the rough sketch I had made of the *scarabaeus*. You recollect also, that I became quite vexed at you for insisting that my drawing resembled a death's-head. When you first made this assertion I thought you were jesting; but afterwards I called to mind the peculiar spots on the back of the insect, and admitted to myself that your remark had some little foundation in fact. Still, the sneer at my graphic powers irritated me—for I am considered a good artist—and, therefore, when you handed me the scrap of parchment, I was about to crumple it up and throw it angrily into the fire."

"The scrap of paper, you mean," said I.

"No; it had much of the appearance of paper, and at first I supposed it to be such, but when I came to draw upon it, I discovered it, at once, to be a piece of very thin parchment. It was quite dirty, you remember. Well, as I was in the very act of crumpling it up, my glance fell upon the sketch at which you had been looking, and you may imagine my astonishment when I perceived, in fact, the figure of a death's-head just where, it seemed to me, I had made the drawing of the beetle. For a moment I was too much amazed to think with accuracy. I knew that my design was very different in detail from this—although there was a certain similarity in general outline. Presently I took a candle, and seating myself at the other end of the room, proceeded to scrutinize the parchment more closely. Upon turning it over, I saw my own sketch upon the reverse, just as I had made it. My first idea, now, was mere surprise at the really remarkable similarity of outline—at the singular coincidence involved in the fact, that unknown to me, there should have been a skull upon the other side of the parchment, immediately beneath my figure of the *scarabaeus,* and that this skull, not only in outline, but in size, should so closely resemble my drawing. I say the singularity of this coincidence absolutely stupefied me for a time. This is the usual effect of such coincidences. The mind struggles to establish a connection—a sequence of cause and effect—and, being unable to do so, suffers a species of temporary paralysis. But, when I recovered from this stupor, there dawned upon me gradually a conviction which startled me even far more than the coincidence. I began distinctly, positively, to remember that there had been *no* drawing on the parchment when I made my sketch of the *scarabaeus.* I became perfectly certain of this; for I recollected turning up first one side and then the other, in search of the cleanest spot. Had the skull been then there, of course I could not have failed to notice it. Here was indeed a mystery which I felt it impossible to explain; but, even at that early moment, there seemed to glimmer, faintly, within the most remote and secret chambers of my intellect, a glow-worm-like conception of that truth which last night's adventure brought to so magnificent a demonstration. I arose at once, and putting the parchment securely away, dismissed all farther reflection until I should be alone.

"When you had gone, and when Jupiter was fast asleep, I betook myself to a more methodical investigation of the affair. In the first place I considered the manner in which the parchment had come into my possession. The spot where we discovered the *scarabaeus* was on the coast of the main land, about a mile eastward of the island, and but a short distance above high water mark. Upon my taking hold of it, it gave me a sharp bite, which caused me to let it drop. Jupiter, with his accustomed caution, before seizing the insect, which had flown towards him, looked about him for a leaf, or something of that nature, by which to take hold of it. It was at this moment that his eyes, and mine also, fell upon the scrap of parchment, which I then supposed to be paper. It was lying half buried in the sand, a corner sticking up. Near the spot where we found it, I observed the remnants of the hull of what appeared to have been a ship's long boat. The wreck seemed to have been there for a very great while; for the resemblance to boat timbers could scarcely be traced.

"Well, Jupiter picked up the parchment, wrapped the beetle in it, and gave it to me. Soon afterwards we turned to go home, and on the way met Lieutenant G—. I showed him the insect, and he begged me to let him take it to the fort. On my consenting, he thrust it forthwith into his waistcoat pocket, without the parchment in which it had been wrapped, and which I had continued to hold in my hand during his inspection. Perhaps he dreaded my changing my mind, and thought it best to make sure of the prize at once—you know how enthusiastic he is on all subjects connected with Natural History. At the same time, without being conscious of it, I must have deposited the parchment in my own pocket.

"You remember that when I went to the table, for the purpose of making a sketch of the beetle, I found no paper where it was usually kept. I looked in the drawer, and found none there. I searched my pockets, hoping to find an old letter—and then my hand fell upon the parchment. I thus detail the precise mode in which it came into my possession; for the circumstances impressed me with peculiar force.

"No, doubt you will think me fanciful—but I had already established a kind of *connection.* I had put together two links of a great chain. There was a boat lying on a sea-coast, and not far from the boat was a parchment—*not a paper*—with a skull depicted on it. You will, of course, ask 'where is the connection?' I reply that the skull, or death's-head, is the well-known emblem of the pirate. The flag of the death's-head is hoisted in all engagements.

"I have said that the scrap was parchment, and not paper. Parchment is durable—almost imperishable. Matters of little moment are rarely consigned to parchment; since, for the mere ordinary purposes of drawing or writing, it is not nearly so well adapted as paper. This reflection suggested some meaning—some relevancy—in the death's-head. I did not fail to observe, also, the *form* of the parchment. Although one of its corners had been, by some accident, destroyed, it could be seen that the original form was oblong. It was just such a slip, indeed, as might have been chosen for a memorandum—for a record of something to be long remembered and carefully preserved."

"But," I interposed, "you say that the skull was *not* upon the parchment when you made the drawing of the beetle. How then do you trace any connection between the boat and the skull—since this latter, according to your own admission, must have been designed at some period subsequent to your sketching the *scarabaeus?*"

"Ah, hereupon turns the whole mystery; although the secret, at this point, I had comparatively little difficulty in solving. My steps were sure, and could afford but a single result. I reasoned, for example, thus: When I drew the *scarabaeus,* there was no skull apparent on the parchment. When I had completed the drawing, I gave it to you, and observed you narrowly until you returned it. *You,* therefore, did not design the skull, and no one else was present to do it. Then it was not done by human agency. And nevertheless it was done.

"At this stage of my reflections I endeavored to remember, and *did* remember, with entire distinctness, every incident which occurred about the period in question. The weather was chilly (oh rare and happy accident!), and a fire was blazing on the hearth. I was heated with exercise and sat near the table. You, however, had drawn a chair close to the chimney. Just as I placed the parchment in your hand, and as you were in the act of inspecting it, Wolf, the Newfoundland, entered, and leaped upon your shoulders. With your left hand you caressed him and kept him off, while your right, holding the parchment, was permitted to fall listlessly between your knees, and in close proximity to the fire. At one moment I thought the blaze had caught it, and was about to caution you, but, before I could speak, you had withdrawn it, and were engaged in its examination. When I considered all these particulars, I doubted not for a moment that *heat* had been the agent in bringing to light, on the parchment, the skull which I saw designed on it. You are well aware that chemical preparations exist, and have existed time out of mind, by means of which it is possible to write on either paper or vellum,* so that the characters shall become visible only when subjected to the action of fire. Zaffre, digested in *aqua regia,* and diluted with four times its weight of water, is sometimes employed; a green tint results. The regulus of cobalt, dissolved in spirit of nitre, gives a red. These colors disappear at longer or shorter intervals after the material written on cools, but again become apparent upon the reapplication of heat.

---

vellum: type of fine parchment

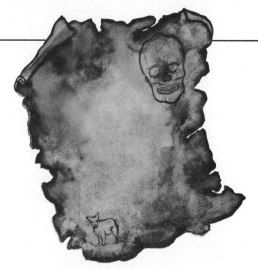

"I now scrutinized the death's-head with care. Its outer edges—the edges of the drawing nearest the edge of the vellum—were far more *distinct* than the others. It was clear that the action of the caloric had been imperfect or unequal. I immediately kindled a fire, and subjected every portion of the parchment to a glowing heat. At first, the only effect was the strengthening of the faint lines in the skull; but, on persevering in the experiment, there became visible, at the corner of the slip, diagonally opposite to the spot in which the death's-head was delineated, the figure of what I at first supposed to be a goat. A closer scrutiny, however, satisfied me that it was intended for a kid."

"Ha! ha!" said I, "to be sure I have no right to laugh at you—a million and a half of money is too serious a matter for mirth—but you are not about to establish a third link in your chain—you will not find any especial connexion between your pirates and a goat—pirates, you know, have nothing to do with goats; they appertain to the farming interest."

"But I have just said that the figure was *not* that of a goat."

"Well, a kid then—pretty much the same thing."

"Pretty much, but not altogether," said Legrand. "You may have heard of one *Captain Kidd*. I at once looked on the figure of the animal as a kind of punning or hieroglyphical signature. I say signature, because its position on the vellum suggested this idea. The death's-head at the corner diagonally opposite, had, in the same manner, the air of a stamp, or seal. But I was sorely put out by the absence of all else—of the body to my imagined instrument—of the text for my context."

"I presume you expected to find a letter between the stamp and the signature."

"Something of that kind. The fact is, I felt irresistibly impressed with a presentiment of some vast good fortune impending. I can scarcely say why. Perhaps, after all, it was rather a desire than an actual belief;—but do you know that Jupiter's silly words about the bug being of solid gold, had a remarkable effect on my fancy? And then the series of accidents and coincidences—these were so *very* extraordinary. Do you observe how mere an accident it was that these events should have occurred on the *sole* day of all the year in which it has been, or may be, sufficiently cool for fire, and that without the fire, or without the intervention of the dog at the precise moment in which he appeared, I should never have become aware of the death's-head, and so never the possessor of the treasure?"

"But proceed—I am all impatience."

"Well; you have heard, of course, the many stories current—the thousand vague rumors afloat about money buried, somewhere on the Atlantic coast, by Kidd and his associates. These rumors must have had some foundation in fact. And that the rumors have existed so long and so continuously could have resulted, it appeared to me, only from the circumstance of the buried treasure still *remaining* entombed. Had Kidd concealed his plunder for a time, and afterwards reclaimed it, the rumors would scarcely have reached us in their present unvarying form. You will observe that the stories told are all about money-seekers, not about money-finders. Had the pirate recovered his money, there the affair would have dropped. It seemed to me that some accident—say the loss of a memorandum indicating its locality—had deprived him of the means of recovering it, and that this accident had become known to his followers, who otherwise might never have heard that treasure had been concealed at all, and who, busying themselves in vain, because unguided attempts, to regain it, had given first birth, and then universal currency, to the reports which are now so common. Have you ever heard of any important treasure being unearthed along the coast?"

"Never."

"But that Kidd's accumulations were immense is well known. I took it for granted, therefore, that the earth still held them; and you will scarcely be surprised when I tell you that I felt a hope, nearly amounting to certainty, that the parchment so strangely found, involved a lost record of the place of deposit."

"But how did you proceed?"

"I held the vellum again to the fire, after increasing the heat; but nothing appeared. I now thought it possible that the coating of dirt might have something to do with the failure; so I carefully rinsed the parchment by pouring warm water over it, and, having done this, I placed it in a tin pan, with the skull downwards, and put the pan upon a furnace of lighted charcoal. In a few minutes, the pan having become thoroughly heated, I removed the slip, and, to my inexpressible joy, found it spotted, in several places, with what appeared to be figures arranged in lines. Again I placed it in the pan, and suffered it to remain another minute. On taking it off, the whole was just as you see it now."

Here Legrand, having re-heated the parchment, submitted it to my inspection. The following characters were rudely traced, in a red tint, between the death's-head and the goat:

53‡‡†305))6* ;4826)4‡.)4‡) ;806*
;48†8¶60))85;]3* ;:‡*8†83 (88) 5*†
;46(;88*96*?;8) *‡(;485)
;5*†2:*‡(;4956*2(5*—4) 8¶8* ;4069285)
;)6†8)4‡‡;1 (‡9;48081 ;8:8‡1
;48†85;4)485†528806*81 (‡9;48;(88;4
(‡?34;48)4‡;161;:188;‡?;

"But," said I, returning him the slip, "I am as much in the dark as ever. Were all the jewels of Golconda awaiting me on my solution of this enigma, I am quite sure that I should be unable to earn them."

"And yet," said Legrand, "the solution is by no means so difficult as you might be led to imagine from the first hasty inspection of the characters. These characters, as any one might readily guess, form a cipher—that is to say, they convey a meaning; but then, from what is known of Kidd, I could not suppose him capable of constructing any of the more abstruse cryptographs. I made up my mind, at once, that this was of a simple species—such, however, as would appear, to the crude intellect of the sailor, absolutely insoluble without the key."

"And you really solved it?"

"Readily; I have solved others of an abstruseness ten thousand times greater. Circumstances, and a certain bias of mind, have led me to take interest in such riddles, and it may be doubted whether human ingenuity can construct an enigma of the kind which human ingenuity may not, by proper application, resolve. In fact, having once established connected and legible characters, I scarcely gave thought to the mere difficulty of developing their import.

"In the present case—indeed in all cases of secret writing—the first question regards the *language* of the cipher; for the principles of solution, so far, especially, as the more simple ciphers are concerned, depend on, and are varied by, the genius of the particular idiom. In general, there is no alternative but experiment (directed by probabilities) of every tongue known to him who attempts the solution, until the true one be attained. But, with the cipher now before us, all difficulty is removed by the signature. The pun on the word 'Kidd' is appreciable in no other language than the English. But for this consideration I should have begun my attempts with the Spanish and French, as the tongues in which a secret of this kind would most naturally have been written by a pirate of the Spanish main. As it was, I assumed the cryptograph to be English.

"You observe there are no divisions between the words. Had there been divisions, the task would have been comparatively easy. In such case I should have commenced with a collation and analysis of the shorter words, and, had a word of a single letter occurred, as is most likely, (*a* or *I,* for example,) I should have considered the solution as assured. But, there being no division, my first step was to ascertain the predominant letters, as well as the least frequent. Counting all, I constructed a table, thus:

Of the character 8 there are 33.

;	26.
4	19.
‡ and)	16.
*	13.
5	12.
6	11.
† and 1	8.
0	6.
9 and 2	5.
: and 3	4.
?	3.
¶	2.
], —, and .	1.

"Now, in English, the letter which most frequently occurs is *e.* Afterwards, the succession runs thus: *a o i d h n r s t u y c f g l m w b k p q x z. E* however predominates so remarkably that an individual sentence of any length is rarely seen, in which it is not the prevailing character.

"Here, then, we have, in the very beginning, the groundwork for something more than a mere guess. The general use which may be made of the table is obvious—but, in this particular cipher, we shall only very partially require its aid. As our predominant character is 8, we will commence by assuming it as the *e* of the natural alphabet. To verify the supposition, let us observe if the 8 be seen often in couples—for *e* is doubled with great frequency in English—in such words, for example, as *meet, fleet, speed, seen, been, agree,* etc. In the present instance we see it doubled no less than five times, although the cryptograph is brief.

"Let us assume *8,* then, as *e.* Now, of all *words* in the language, *the* is most usual; let us see, therefore, whether there are not repetitions of any three characters, in the same order of collocation, the last of them being 8. If we discover repetitions of such letters, so arranged, they will most probably represent the word *the.* On inspection we find no less than seven such arrangements, the characters being *;48.* We may, therefore, assume that the semicolon represents *t,* that 4 represents *h,* and that *8* represents *e*—the last being now well confirmed. Thus a great step has been taken.

"But, having established a single word, we are enabled to establish a vastly important point; that is to say, several commencements and terminations of other words. Let us refer, for example, to the last instance but one, in which the combination *;48* occurs—not far from the end of the cipher. We know that the semicolon immediately ensuing is the commencement of a word, and, of the six characters succeeding this *the,* we are cognizant of no less than five. Let us set these characters down, thus, by the letters we know them to represent, leaving a space for the unknown—

t eeth.

"Here we are enabled, at once, to discard the *th,* as forming no portion of the word commencing with the first *t;* since, by experiment of the entire alphabet for a letter adapted to the vacancy we perceive that no word can be formed of which this *th* can be a part. We are thus narrowed into

t ee,

and, going through the alphabet, if necessary, as before, we arrive at the word *tree,* as the sole possible reading. We thus gain another letter, *r,* represented by *(,* with the words 'the tree' in juxtaposition.

"Looking beyond these words, for a short distance, we again see the combination of *;48,* and employ it by way of *termination* to what immediately precedes. We have thus this arrangement:

the tree;4 (‡?34 the,

or, substituting the natural letters, where known, it reads thus:

the tree thr ‡?3h the.

"Now, if, in place of the unknown characters, we leave blank spaces, or substitute dots, we read thus:

the tree thr . . . h the,

when the word *through* makes itself evident at once. But this discovery gives us three new letters, *o, u,* and *g,* represented by ‡, ?, and *3.*

"Looking now, narrowly, through the cipher for combinations of known characters, we find, not very far from the beginning, this arrangement,

83(88, or egree,

which, plainly, is the conclusion of the word *degree,* and gives us another letter, *d,* represented by †.

"Four letters beyond the word *degree,* we perceive the combination

;46(;88*.

"Translating the known characters, and representing the unknown by dots, as before, we read thus:

th.rtee.

an arrangement immediately suggestive of the word *thirteen,* and again furnishing us with two new characters, *i* and *n,* represented by *6* and *.*

"Referring, now, to the beginning of the cryptograph, we find the combination,

53‡‡†.

"Translating, as before, we obtain

.good,

which assures us that the first letter is A, and that the first two words are *A good.*

"To avoid confusion, it is now time that we arrange our key, as far as discovered, in a tabular form. It will stand thus:

5 represents	a.
†	d.
8	e.
3	g.
4	h.
6	i.
*	n.
‡	o.
(	r.
;	t.

"We have, therefore, no less than ten of the most important letters represented, and it will be unnecessary to proceed with the details of the solution. I have said enough to convince you that ciphers of this nature are readily soluble, and to give you some insight into the *rationale* of their development. But be assured that the specimen before us appertains to the very simplest species of cryptograph. It now only remains to give you the full translation of the characters upon the parchment, as unriddled. Here it is:

"A good glass in the bishop's hostel in the devil's seat twenty-one degrees and thirteen minutes northeast and by north main branch seventh limb east side shoot from the left eye of the death's-head a bee line from the tree through the shot fifty feet out."

"But," said I, "the enigma seems still in as bad a condition as ever. How is it possible to extort a meaning from all this jargon about 'devil's seats,' 'death's-heads,' and 'bishop's hotels?' "

"I confess," replied Legrand, "that the matter still wears a serious aspect, when regarded with a casual glance. My first endeavor was to divide the sentence into the natural division intended by the cryptographist."

"You mean, to punctuate it?"

"Something of that kind."

"But how was it possible to effect this?"

"I reflected that it had been a *point* with the writer to run his words together without division, so as to increase the difficulty of solution. Now, a not over-acute man, in pursuing such an object, would be nearly certain to overdo the matter. When, in the course of his composition, he arrived at a break in his subject which would naturally require a pause, or a point, he would be exceedingly apt to run his characters, at this place, more than usually close together. If you will observe the MS., in the present instance, you will easily detect five such cases of unusual crowding. Acting on this hint, I made the division thus:

"A good glass in the Bishop's hostel in the Devil's seat—twenty-one degrees and thirteen minutes—northeast and by north—main branch seventh limb east side—shoot from the left eye of the death's-head—a bee-line from the tree through the shot fifty feet out."

"Even this division," said I, "leaves me still in the dark."

"It left me also in the dark," replied Legrand, "for a few days; during which I made diligent inquiry, in the neighborhood of Sullivan's Island, for any building which went by the name of the 'Bishop's Hotel'; for, of course, I dropped the obsolete word 'hostel,' Gaining no information on the subject, I was on the point of extending my sphere of search, and proceeding in a more systematic manner, when, one morning, it entered into my head, quite suddenly, that this 'Bishop's Hostel' might have some reference to an old family, of the name of Bessop, which, time out of mind, had held possession of an ancient manor-house, about four miles to the northward of the Island. I accordingly went over to the plantation, and re-instituted my inquiries among the older Negroes of the place. At length one of the most aged of the women said that she had heard of such a place as *Bessop's Castle,* and thought that she could guide me to it, but that it was not a castle, nor a tavern, but a high rock.

"I offered to pay her well for her trouble, and, after some demur, she consented to accompany me to the spot. We found it without much difficulty, when, dismissing her, I proceeded to examine the place. The 'castle' consisted of an irregular assemblage of cliffs and rocks—one of the latter being quite remarkable for its height as well as for its insulated and artificial appearance. I clambered to its apex, and then felt much at a loss as to what should be next done.

"While I was busied in reflection, my eyes fell upon a narrow ledge in the eastern face of the rock, perhaps a yard below the summit on which I stood. This ledge projected about eighteen inches, and was not more than a foot wide, while a niche in the cliff just above it, gave it a rude resemblance to one of the hollow-backed chairs used by our ancestors. I made no doubt that here was the 'devil's seat' alluded to in the MS., and now I seemed to grasp the full secret of the riddle.

"The 'good glass,' I knew, could have reference to nothing but a telescope; for the word *glass* is rarely employed in any other sense by seamen. Now here, I at once saw, was a telescope to be used, and a definite point of view, *admitting no variation,* from which to use it. Nor did I hesitate to believe that the phrases, 'twenty-one degrees and thirteen minutes,' and 'northeast and by north,' were intended as directions for the levelling of the glass. Greatly excited by these discoveries, I hurried home, procured a telescope, and returned to the rock.

"I let myself down to the ledge, and found that it was impossible to retain a seat on it unless in one particular position. This fact confirmed my preconceived idea. I proceeded to use the glass. Of course, the 'twenty-one degrees and thirteen minutes' could allude to nothing but elevation above the visible horizon, since the horizontal direction was clearly indicated by the words, 'northeast and by north.' This latter direction I at once established by means of a pocket-compass; then, pointing the glass as nearly at an angle of twenty-one degrees of elevation as I could do it by guess, I moved it cautiously up or down, until my attention was arrested by a circular rift or opening in the foliage of a large tree that overtopped its fellows in the distance. In the centre of this rift I perceived a white spot, but could not, at first, distinguish what it was. Adjusting the focus of the telescope, I again looked, and now made it out to be a human skull.

"On this discovery I was so sanguine* as to consider the enigma solved for the phrase 'main branch, seventh limb, east side,' could refer only to the position of the skull on the tree, while 'shoot from the left eye of the death's-head' admitted, also, of but one interpretation, in regard to a search for buried treasure. I perceived that the design was to drop a bullet from the left eye of the skull, and that a bee-line, or, in other words, a straight line, drawn from the nearest point of the trunk through 'the shot,' (or the spot where the bullet fell,) and thence extended to a distance of fifty feet, would indicate a definite point—and beneath this point I thought it at least possible that a deposit of value lay concealed."

sanguine: optimistic or confident

"All this," I said, "is exceedingly clear, and, although ingenious, still simple and explicit. When you left the Bishop's Hotel, what then?"

"Why, having carefully taken the bearings of the tree, I turned homewards. The instant that I left 'the devil's seat,' however, the circular rift vanished; nor could I get a glimpse of it afterwards, turn as I would. What seems to me the chief ingenuity in this whole business, is the fact (for repeated experiment has convinced me it *is* a fact) that the circular opening in question is visible from no other attainable point of view than that afforded by the narrow ledge on the face of the rock.

"In this expedition to the 'Bishop's Hotel' I had been attended by Jupiter, who had, no doubt, observed, for some weeks past, the abstraction of my demeanor, and took especial care not to leave me alone. But, on the next day, getting up very early, I contrived to give him the slip, and went into the hills in search of the tree. After much toil I found it. When I came home at night my valet proposed to give me a flogging. With the rest of the adventure I believe you are as well acquainted as myself."

"I suppose," said I, "you missed the spot, in the first attempt at digging, through Jupiter's stupidity in letting the bug fall through the right instead of through the left eye of the skull."

"Precisely. This mistake made a difference of about two inches and a half in the 'shot'— that is to say, in the position of the peg nearest the tree; and had the treasure been *beneath* the 'shot,' the error would have been of little moment; but 'the shot,' together with the nearest point of the tree, were merely two points for the establishment of a line of direction; of course the error, however trivial in the beginning, increased as we proceeded with the line, and by the time we had gone fifty feet, threw us quite off the scent. But for my deep-seated convictions that treasure was here somewhere actually buried, we might have had all our labor in vain."

"I presume the fancy of *the skull,* of letting fall a bullet through the skull's eye—was suggested to Kidd by the piratical flag. No doubt he felt a kind of poetical consistency in recovering his money through this ominous insignium."

"Perhaps so; still I cannot help thinking that common-sense had quite as much to do with the matter as poetical consistency. To be visible from the devil's seat, it was necessary that the object, if small, should be white; and there is nothing like your human skull for retaining and even increasing its whiteness under exposure to all vicissitudes of weather."

"But your grandiloquence, and your conduct in swinging the beetle—how excessively odd! I was sure you were mad. And why did you insist on letting fall the bug, instead of a bullet, from the skull?"

"Why, to be frank, I felt somewhat annoyed by your evident suspicions touching my sanity, and so resolved to punish you quietly, in my own way, by a little bit of sober mystification. For this reason I swung the beetle, and for this reason I let it fall from the tree. An observation of yours about its great weight suggested the latter idea."

"Yes, I perceive; and now there is only one point which puzzles me. What are we to make of the skeletons found in the hole?"

"That is a question I am no more able to answer than yourself. There seems, however, only one plausible way of accounting for them—and yet it is dreadful to believe in such atrocity as my suggestion would imply. It is clear that Kidd—if Kidd indeed secreted this treasure, which I doubt not—it is clear that he must have had assistance in the labor. But, the worst of this labor concluded, he may have thought it expedient to remove all participants in his secret. Perhaps a couple of blows with a mattock were sufficient, while his coadjutors* were busy in the pit; perhaps it required a dozen—who shall tell?"

---

coadjutors: assistants or coworkers

About the Story

1. What incident proves to be the inciting moment of the story?
2. How does Legrand change following this incident?
3. To what does Jupiter attribute this change?
4. Describe each of the following characters with a single word or phrase:
   Legrand
   the physician (narrator)
   Jupiter
5. The peculiarities of each character contribute to the complications in the story's rising action. Choose one of the characters you described above and list one specific complication created by that character.
6. List one specific method Poe uses to create an atmosphere of tension in the story.
7. Why did Legrand use the *scarabaeus* in his treasure hunt?
8. With which of the following characters do you think Poe wanted you to feel the greatest empathy: Legrand, the physician, or Jupiter?

About the Author

Edgar Allan Poe (1809-1849)—American poet, critic, and short story writer—was orphaned as a small boy and reared by a well-to-do Virginia businessman, John Allan, whose name Poe added to his own. The indulgent Mrs. Allan pampered the young boy, but Mr. Allan refused to adopt him officially, although he did pay for Poe's attendance at the University of Virginia for one year.

Poe joined the United States Army after a year at the university, leaving behind him a large number of unpaid bills and unsettled gambling debts, which his foster father refused to pay. By this time Poe was already writing and had managed to pay for the publication of his first collection of poems. In the service he was stationed off the coast of South Carolina at Sullivan's Island. This experience later furnished the locale for the story "The Gold-Bug," written in 1843.

After expulsion from West Point Military Academy, Poe continued to write poems, such as "the Raven," while working as a journalist and editor. Poe also began to compose and publish his unusual stories of terror and mystery. His work, however, never brought him financial stability. After his young wife, Virginia, died, Poe's already fragile mental and physical health (worsened by his addiction to drugs and alcohol) declined drastically. Poe died, amid mysterious circumstances, at forty years of age. Though his works were never well known during his lifetime, they became increasingly popular after his death, and his detective and mystery stories continue to fascinate modern readers.

The Adventure of the Beryl Coronet

Sir Arthur Conan Doyle

Although Sir Arthur Conan Doyle did not invent the detective story, his novels and tales of Sherlock Holmes helped to define the essentials. Baffling crime, dull-witted inspectors, false leads, ambiguous clues, and solutions by keen observation and rigorous logic—these all appear in story after story of the master detective Holmes and his friend Watson. The bachelors Holmes and Watson share a suite of rooms (until Watson marries) which furnishes them living quarters, a reception area for Watson's patients and Holmes's customers, and a laboratory for Watson's medical practice and Holmes's investigations. Holmes is an eccentric genius who lives for his work. He drives himself hard for justice and for the relief of his client-victims, but even harder for the exhiliration of a mental challenge. Holmes's obsession with solving difficult cases affects Watson, who will drop his own work any time and allow it to suffer neglect in order to accompany his friend. Watson, the narrator, is both Holmes's confidant and chronicler.

As a hero, Holmes has ample physical courage, strength, and agility. But he relies mainly on his brainpower: his ability to see significance in details that everyone else overlooks and to reason accurately from them. He is also a student of human nature and can construct hypotheses on the basis of normal human behavior. Where do these qualities occur in Holmes in this story? What moral lessons are hinted in the conclusion?

"Holmes," said I, as I stood one morning in our bow-window* looking down the street, "here is a madman coming along. It seems rather sad that his relatives should allow him to come out alone."

---
bow-window: curved bay window

My friend rose lazily from his arm-chair and stood with his hands in the pockets of his dressing-gown, looking over my shoulder. It was a bright, crisp February morning, and the snow of the day before still lay deep upon the ground, shimmering brightly in the wintry sun. Down the center of Baker Street it had been plowed in a brown crumbly band by the traffic, but at either side and on the heaped-up edges of the foot-paths it still lay as white as when it fell. The gray pavement had been cleaned and scraped, but was still dangerously slippery, so that there were fewer passengers than usual. Indeed, from the direction of the Metropolitan Station no one was coming save the single gentleman whose eccentric conduct had drawn my attention.

He was a man of about fifty, tall, portly,* and imposing, with a massive, strongly marked

face and a commanding figure. He was dressed in a sombre yet rich style, in black frock-coat, shining hat, neat brown gaiters,* and well-cut pearl-gray trousers. Yet his actions were in absurd contrast to the dignity of his dress and features, for he was running hard, with occasional little springs, such as a weary man gives who is little accustomed to set any tax* upon his legs. As he ran he jerked his hands up and down, waggled his head, and writhed his face into the most extraordinary contortions.

---

portly: stout
gaiters: buttoned coverings for instep and ankle
tax: strain

"What on earth can be the matter with him?" I asked. "He is looking up at the numbers of the houses."

"I believe that he is coming here," said Holmes, rubbing his hands.

"Here?"

"Yes; I rather think he is coming to consult me professionally. I think that I recognize the symptoms. Ha! did I not tell you?" As he spoke, the man, puffing and blowing, rushed at our door and pulled at our bell until the whole house resounded with the clanging.

A few moments later he was in our room, still puffing, still gesticulating, but with so fixed a look of grief and despair in his eyes that our smiles were turned in an instant to horror and pity. For a while he could not get his words out, but swayed his body and plucked at his hair like one who has been driven to the extreme limits of his reason. Then, suddenly springing to his feet, he beat his head against the wall with such force that we both rushed upon him and tore him away to the center of the room. Sherlock Holmes pushed him down into the easy-chair, and, sitting beside him, patted his hand, and chatted with him in the easy, soothing tones which he knew so well how to employ.

"You have come to me to tell your story, have you not?" said he. "You are fatigued with your haste. Pray wait until you have recovered yourself, and then I shall be most happy to look into any little problem which you may submit to me."

The man sat for a minute or more with a heaving chest, fighting against his emotion. Then he passed his handkerchief over his brow, set his lips tight, and turned his face towards us.

"No doubt you think me mad?" said he.

"I see that you have had some great trouble," responded Holmes.

"I have!—a trouble which is enough to unseat my reason, so sudden and so terrible is it. Public disgrace I might have faced, although I am a man whose character has never yet borne a stain. Private affliction also is the lot of every man; but the two coming together, and in so frightful a form, have been enough to shake my very soul. Besides, it is not I alone. The very noblest in the land may suffer, unless some way be found out of this horrible affair."

"Pray compose yourself, sir," said Holmes, "and let me have a clear account of who you are, and what it is that has befallen you."

"My name," answered our visitor, "is probably familiar to your ears. I am Alexander Holder, of the banking firm of Holder & Stevenson, of Threadneedle Street."

The name was indeed well known to us as belonging to the senior partner in the second largest private banking concern in the City of London. What could have happened, then, to bring one of the foremost citizens of London to this most pitiable pass? We waited, all curiosity, until with another effort he braced himself to tell his story.

"I feel that time is of value," said he; "that is why I hastened here when the police inspector suggested that I should secure your cooperation. I came to Baker Street by the Underground,* and hurried from there on foot, for the cabs go slowly through this snow. That is why I was so out of breath, for I am a man who takes very little exercise. I feel better now, and I will put the facts before you as shortly and yet as clearly as I can.

Underground: subway

"It is, of course, well known to you that in a successful banking business as much depends upon our being able to find remunerative* investments for our funds as upon our increasing our connection and the number of our depositors. One of our most lucrative means of laying out money is in the shape of loans, where the security is unimpeachable.* We have done a good deal in this direction during the last few years, and there are many noble families to whom we have advanced large sums upon the security of their pictures, libraries, or plate.*

---

remunerative: well-paying
unimpeachable: unquestionable
plate: silver

"Yesterday morning I was seated in my office at the bank when a card was brought in to me by one of the clerks. I started* when I saw the name, for it was that of none other than—well, perhaps even to you I had better say no more than that it was a name which is a household word all over the earth—one of the highest, noblest, most exalted names in England. I was overwhelmed by the honor, and attempted, when he entered, to say so, but he plunged at once into business with the air of a man who wishes to hurry quickly through a disagreeable task.

---

started: jumped

" 'Mr. Holder,' said he, 'I have been informed that you are in the habit of advancing money.'

" 'The firm does so when the security is good,' I answered.

" 'It is absolutely essential to me,' said he, 'that I should have £50,000 at once. I could of course borrow so trifling a sum ten times over from my friends, but I much prefer to make it a matter of business, and to carry out that business myself. In my position you can readily understand that it is unwise to place one's self under obligations.'

" 'For how long, may I ask, do you want this sum?' I asked.

" 'Next Monday I have a large sum due to me, and I shall then most certainly repay what you advance, with whatever interest you think it right to charge. But it is very essential to me that the money should be paid at once.'

" 'I should be happy to advance it without further parley from my own private purse,' said I, 'were it not that the strain would be rather more than it could bear. If, on the other hand, I am to do it in the name of the firm, then in justice to my partner I must insist that, even in your case, every business-like precaution should be taken.'

" 'I should much prefer to have it so,' said he, raising up a square, black morocco case which he had laid beside his chair. 'You have doubtless heard of the Beryl Coronet?' "

" 'One of the most precious public possessions of the empire,' " said I.

" 'Precisely.' He opened the case, and there, imbedded in soft, flesh-colored velvet, lay the magnificent piece of jewelry which he had named. 'There are thirty-nine enormous beryls,' said he, 'and the price of the gold chasing is incalculable. The lowest estimate would put the worth of the coronet at double the sum which I have asked. I am prepared to leave it with you as my security.'

"I took the precious case into my hands and looked in some perplexity from it to my illustrious client.

" 'You doubt its value?' he asked.

" 'Not at all. I only doubt—'

" 'The propriety of my leaving it. You may set your mind at rest about that. I should not dream of doing so were it not absolutely certain that I should be able in four days to reclaim it. It is a pure matter of form. Is the security sufficient?'

" 'Ample.'

" 'You understand, Mr. Holder, that I am giving you a strong proof of the confidence which I have in you, founded upon all that I have heard of you. I rely upon you not only to be discreet and to refrain from all gossip upon the matter, but, above all, to preserve this coronet with every possible precaution, because I need not say that a great public scandal would be caused if any harm were to befall it. Any injury to it would be almost as serious as its complete loss, for there are no beryls in the world to match these, and it would be impossible to replace them. I leave it with you, however, with every confidence, and I shall call for it in person on Monday morning.'

"Seeing that my client was anxious to leave, I said no more; but, calling for my cashier, I ordered him to pay over fifty £1000 notes. When I was alone once more, however, with the precious case lying upon the table in front of me, I could not but think with some misgivings of the immense responsibility which it entailed upon me. There could be no doubt that, as it was a national possession, a horrible scandal would ensue if any misfortune should occur to it. I already regretted having ever consented to take charge of it. However, it was too late to alter the matter now, so I locked it up in my private safe, and turned once more to my work.

"When evening came I felt that it would

be an imprudence to leave so precious a thing in the office behind me. Bankers' safes had been forced before now, and why should not mine be? If so, how terrible would be the position in which I should find myself! I determined, therefore, that for the next few days I would always carry the case backward and forward with me, so that it might never be really out of my reach. With this intention, I called a cab, and drove out to my house at Streatham, carrying the jewel with me. I did not breathe freely until I had taken it upstairs and locked it in the bureau of my dressing-room.

"And now a word as to my household, Mr. Holmes, for I wish you to thoroughly understand the situation. My groom and my page sleep out of the house, and may be set aside altogether. I have three maid-servants who have been with me a number of years, and whose absolute reliability is quite above suspicion. Another, Lucy Parr, the second waiting-maid, has only been in my service a few months. She came with an excellent character, however, and has always given me satisfaction. She is a very pretty girl, and has attracted admirers who have occasionally hung about the place. That is the only drawback which we have found to her, but we believe her to be a thoroughly good girl in every way.

"So much for the servants. My family itself is so small that it will not take me long to describe it. I am a widower, and have an only son, Arthur. He has been a disappointment to me, Mr. Holmes—a grievous disappointment. I have no doubt that I am myself to blame. People tell me that I have spoiled him. Very likely I have. When my dear wife died I felt that he was all I had to love. I could not bear to see the smile fade even for a moment from his face. I have never denied him a wish. Perhaps it would have been better for both of us had I been sterner, but I meant it for the best.

"It was naturally my intention that he should succeed me in my business, but he was not of a business turn. He was wild, wayward, and, to speak the truth, I could not trust him in the handling of large sums of money. When he was young he became a member of an aristocratic club, and there, having charming manners, he was soon the intimate of a number of men with long purses and expensive habits. He learned to play heavily at cards and to squander money on the turf,* until he had again and again to come to me and implore me to give him an advance upon his allowance, that he might settle his debts of honor. He tried more than once to break away from the dangerous company which he was keeping, but each time the influence of his friend Sir George Burnwell was enough to draw him back again.

turf: horseracing

"And, indeed, I could not wonder that such a man as Sir George Burnwell should gain an influence over him, for he has frequently brought him to my house, and I have found myself that I could hardly resist the fascination of his manner. He is older than Arthur, a man of the world to his finger-tips, one who had been everywhere, seen everything, a brilliant talker, and a man of great personal beauty. Yet when I think of him in cold blood, far away from the glamor of his presence, I am convinced from his cynical speech, and the look which I have caught in his eyes, that he is one who should be deeply distrusted. So I think, and so, too, thinks my little Mary, who has a woman's quick insight into character.

"And now there is only she to be described. She is my niece; but when my brother died five years ago and left her alone in the world I adopted her, and have looked upon her ever since as my daughter. She is a sunbeam in my house—sweet, loving, beautiful, a wonderful manager and housekeeper, yet as tender and quiet and gentle as a woman could be. She is my right hand. I do not know what I could do without her. In only one matter has she ever gone against my wishes. Twice my boy has asked her to marry him, for he loves her devotedly, but each time she has refused him. I think that if any one could have drawn him into the right path it would have been she, and that his marriage might have changed his whole life; but now, alas! it is too late—for ever too late!

"Now, Mr. Holmes, you know the people who live under my roof, and I shall continue with my miserable story.

"When we were taking coffee in the drawing-room that night, after dinner, I told Arthur and Mary my experience, and of the precious treasure which we had under our roof, suppressing only the name of my client. Lucy Parr, who had brought in the coffee, had, I am sure, left the room; but I cannot swear that the door was closed. Mary and Arthur were much interested, and wished to see the famous coronet, but I thought it better not to disturb it.

" 'Where have you put it?' asked Arthur.

" 'In my own bureau.'

" 'Well, I hope to goodness the house won't be burgled during the night,' said he.

" 'It is locked up,' I answered.

" 'Oh, any old key will fit that bureau. When I was a youngster I have opened it myself with the key of the box-room* cupboard.'

---

box-room: storeroom

"He often had a wild way of talking, so that I thought little of what he said. He followed me to my room, however, that night with a very grave face.

" 'Look here, Dad,' said he, with his eyes cast down, 'can you let me have £200?'

" 'No, I cannot!' I answered sharply. 'I have been far too generous with you in money matters.'

" 'You have been very kind,' said he: 'but I must have this money, or else I can never show my face inside the club again.'

" 'And a very good thing, too!' I cried.

" 'Yes, but you would not have me leave it a dishonored man,' said he. 'I could not bear the disgrace. I must raise the money in some way, and if you will not let me have it, then I must try other means.'

"I was very angry, for this was the third demand during the month. 'You shall not have a farthing from me,' I cried; on which he bowed and left the room without another word.

"When he was gone I unlocked my bureau, made sure that my treasure was safe, and locked it again. Then I started to go round the house to see that all was secure—a duty which I usually leave to Mary, but which I thought it well to perform myself that night. As I came down the stairs I saw Mary herself at the side window of the hall, which she closed and fastened as I approached.

" 'Tell me, Dad,' said she, looking, I thought, a little disturbed, 'did you give Lucy, the maid, leave to go out tonight?'

" 'Certainly not.'

" 'She came in just now by the back door. I have no doubt that she has only been to the side gate to see someone; but I think that it is hardly safe, and should be stopped.'

" 'You must speak to her in the morning, or I will, if you prefer it. Are you sure that everything is fastened?'

" 'Quite sure, Dad.'

" 'Then, good-night.' I kissed her, and went up to my bedroom again, where I was soon asleep.

"I am endeavoring to tell you everything, Mr. Holmes, which may have any bearing upon the case, but I beg that you will question me upon any point which I do not make clear."

"On the contrary, your statement is singularly lucid."

"I come to a part of my story now in which I should wish to be particularly so. I am not a very heavy sleeper, and the anxiety in my mind tended, no doubt, to make me even less so than usual. About two in the morning, then, I was awakened by some sound in the house. It had ceased ere I was wide awake, but it had left an impression behind it as though a window had gently closed somewhere. I lay listening with all my ears. Suddenly, to my horror, there was a distinct sound of footsteps moving softly in the next room. I slipped out of bed, all palpitating with fear, and peeped round the corner of my dressing-room door.

" 'Arthur!' I screamed, 'you villain! you thief! How dare you touch that coronet?'

"The gas was half up, as I had left it, and my unhappy boy, dressed only in his shirt and trousers, was standing beside the light, holding the coronet in his hands. He appeared to be wrenching at it, or bending it with all his strength. At my cry he dropped it from his grasp, and turned as pale as death. I snatched it up and examined it. One of the gold corners, with three of the beryls in it, was missing.

" 'You blackguard!'* I shouted, beside myself with rage. 'You have destroyed it! You have dishonored me for ever! Where are the jewels which you have stolen?'

---

blackguard: villain

" 'Stolen!' he cried.

" 'Yes, you thief!' I roared, shaking him by the shoulder.

" 'There are none missing. There cannot be any missing,' said he.

" 'There are three missing. And you know where they are. Must I call you a liar as well as a thief? Did I not see you trying to tear off another piece?'

" 'You have called me names enough,' said

he; 'I will not stand it any longer. I shall not say another word about this business since you have chosen to insult me. I will leave your house in the morning and make my own way in the world.'

" 'You shall leave it in the hands of the police!' I cried, half-mad with grief and rage. 'I shall have this matter probed to the bottom.'

" 'You shall learn nothing from me,' said he, with a passion such as I should not have thought was in his nature. 'If you choose to call the police, let the police find what they can.'

"By this time the whole house was astir, for I had raised my voice in my anger. Mary was the first to rush into my room, and, at the sight of the coronet and of Arthur's face, she read the whole story, and, with a scream, fell down senseless on the ground. I sent the housemaid for the police, and put the investigation into their hands at once. When the inspector and a constable entered the house, Arthur, who had stood sullenly with his arms folded, asked me whether it was my intention to charge him with theft. I answered that it had ceased to be a private matter, but had become a public one, since the ruined coronet was national property. I was determined that the law should have its way in everything.

" 'At least,' said he, 'you will not have me arrested at once. It would be to your advantage as well as mine if I might leave the house for five minutes.'

" 'That you may get away, or perhaps that you may conceal what you have stolen,' said I. And then realizing the dreadful position in which I was placed, I implored him to remember that not only my honor, but that of one who was far greater than I was at stake; and that he threatened to raise a scandal which would convulse the nation. He might avert* it all if he would but tell me what he had done with the three missing stones.

---

avert: avoid

" 'You may as well face the matter,' said I; 'you have been caught in the act, and no confession could make your guilt more heinous.* If you but make reparation as is in your power, by telling us where the beryls are, all shall be forgiven and forgotten.'

---

heinous: evil

" 'Keep your forgiveness for those who ask for it,' he answered, turning away from me, with a sneer. I saw that he was too hardened for any words of mine to influence him. There was but one way for it. I called in the inspector, and gave him into custody. A search was made at once, not only of his person, but of his room, and of every portion of the house where he could possibly have concealed the gems; but no trace of them could be found, nor would the wretched boy open his mouth for all our persuasions and our threats. This morning he was removed to a cell, and I, after going through all the police formalities, have hurried round to you, to implore you to use your skill in unraveling the matter. The police have openly confessed that they can at present make nothing of it. You may go to any expense which you think necessary. I have already offered a reward of £1000. What shall I do! I have lost my honor, my gems, and my son in one night. Oh, what shall I do!"

He put a hand on either side of his head, and rocked himself to and fro, droning to himself like a child whose grief has got beyond words.

Sherlock Holmes sat silent for some few minutes, with his brows knitted and his eyes fixed upon the fire.

"Do you receive much company?" he asked.

"None, save my partner with his family, and an occasional friend of Arthur's. Sir George Burnwell has been several times lately. No one else, I think."

"Do you go out much in society?"

"Arthur does. Mary and I stay at home. We neither of us care for it."

"That is unusual in a young girl."

"She is of a quiet nature. Besides, she is not so very young. She is four and twenty."

"This matter, from what you say, seems to have been a shock to her also."

"Terrible! She is even more affected than I."

"You have neither of you any doubt as to your son's guilt?"

"How can we have, when I saw him with my own eyes with the coronet in his hands."

"I hardly consider that a conclusive proof. Was the remainder of the coronet at all injured?"

"Yes, it was twisted."

"Do you not think, then, that he might have been trying to straighten it?"

"God bless you! You are doing what you can for him and for me. But it is too heavy a task. What was he doing there at all? If his purpose were innocent, why did he not say so?"

"Precisely. And if it were guilty, why did he not invent a lie? His silence appears to me to cut both ways. There are several singular points about the case. What did the police think of the noise which awoke you from your sleep?"

"They considered that it might be caused by Arthur's closing his bedroom door."

"A likely story! As if a man bent on felony would slam his door so as to wake a household. What did they say, then, of the disappearance of these gems?"

"They are still sounding the planking and probing the furniture in the hope of finding them."

"Have they thought of looking outside the house?"

"Yes, they have shown extraordinary energy. The whole garden has already been minutely examined."

"Now, my dear sir," said Holmes, "is it

not obvious to you now that this matter really strikes very much deeper than either you or the police were at first inclined to think? It appeared to you to be a simple case; to me it seems exceedingly complex. Consider what is involved by your theory. You suppose that your son came down from his bed, went, at great risk, to your dressing-room, opened your bureau, took out your coronet, broke off by main force a small portion of it, went off to some other place, concealed three gems out of the thirty-nine, with such skill that nobody can find them, and then returned with the other thirty-six into the room in which he exposed himself to the greatest danger of being discovered. I ask you now, is such a theory tenable?"*

---

tenable: reasonable

"But what other is there?" cried the banker, with a gesture of despair. "if his motives were innocent, why does he not explain them?"

"It is our task to find that out," replied Holmes; "so now, if you please, Mr. Holder, we will set off for Streatham together, and devote an hour to glancing a little more closely into details."

My friend insisted upon my accompanying them in their expedition, which I was eager enough to do, for my curiosity and sympathy were deeply stirred by the story to which we had listened. I confess that the guilt of the banker's son appeared to me to be as obvious as it did to his unhappy father, but still I had such faith in Holmes's judgment that I felt that there must be some grounds for hope as long as he was dissatisfied with the accepted explanation. He hardly spoke a word the whole way out to the southern suburb, but sat with his chin upon his breast and his hat drawn over his eyes, sunk in the deepest thought. Our client appeared to have taken fresh heart at the little glimpse of hope which had been presented to him, and he even broke into a desultory* chat with me over his business affairs. A short railway journey and a shorter walk brought us to Fairbank, the modest residence of the great financier.

---

desultory: rambling

Fairbank was a good-sized square house of white stone, standing back a little from the road. A double carriage-sweep,* with a snow-clad lawn, stretched down in front to two large iron gates which closed the entrance. On the right side was a small wooden thicket, which led into a narrow path between two neat hedges stretching from the road to the kitchen door, and forming the tradesmen's entrance. On the left ran a lane which led to the stables, and was not itself within the grounds at all, being a public, though little used, thoroughfare. Holmes left us standing at the door, and walked slowly all round the house, across the front, down the tradesmen's path, and so round by the garden behind into the stable lane. So long was he that Mr. Holder and I went into the dining-room and waited by the fire until he should return. We were sitting there in silence when the door opened and a young lady came in. She was rather above the middle height, slim, with dark hair and eyes, which seemed the darker against the absolute pallor of her skin. I do not think that I have ever seen such deadly paleness in a woman's face. Her lips, too, were bloodless, but her eyes were flushed with crying. As she swept silently into the room she impressed me with a greater sense of grief than the banker had done in the morning, and it was the more striking in her as she was evidently a woman of strong character, with immense capacity for self-restraint. Disregarding my presence, she went straight to her uncle, and passed her hand over his head with a sweet womanly caress.

double carriage-sweep: circular drive

"You have given orders that Arthur should be liberated, have you not, Dad?" she asked.

"No, no, my girl, the matter must be probed to the bottom."

"But I am so sure that he is innocent. You know what women's instincts are. I know that he has done no harm and that you will be sorry for having acted so harshly."

"Why is he silent, then, if he is innocent?"

"Who knows? Perhaps because he was so angry that you should suspect him."

"How could I help suspecting him, when I actually saw him with the coronet in his hand?"

"Oh, but he had only picked it up to look at it. Oh do, do take my word for it that he is innocent. Let the matter drop and say no more. It is so dreadful to think of our dear Arthur in prison!"

"I shall never let it drop until the gems are found—never, Mary! Your affection for Arthur blinds you as to the awful consequences to me. Far from hushing the thing up, I have brought a gentleman down from London to inquire more deeply into it."

"This gentleman?" she asked, facing round to me.

"No, his friend. He wished us to leave him alone. He is round in the stable lane now."

"The stable lane?" She raised her dark eyebrows. "What can he hope to find there? Ah! this, I suppose, is he. I trust, sir, that you will succeed in proving, what I feel sure is the truth, that my cousin Arthur is innocent of this crime."

"I fully share your opinion, and I trust, with you, that we may prove it," returned Holmes, going back to the mat to knock the snow from his shoes. "I believe I have the honor of addressing Miss Mary Holder. Might I ask you a question or two?"

"Pray do, sir, if it may help to clear this horrible affair up."

"You heard nothing yourself last night?"

"Nothing, until my uncle began to speak loudly. I heard that, and I came down."

"You shut up the windows and doors the night before. Did you fasten all the windows?"

"Yes."

"Were they all fastened this morning?"

"Yes."

"You have a maid who has a sweetheart? I think that you remarked to your uncle last night that she had been out to see him?"

"Yes, and she was the girl who waited in the drawing-room, and who may have heard uncle's remarks about the coronet."

"I see. You infer that she may have gone out to tell her sweetheart, and that the two may have planned the robbery."

"But what is the good of all these vague theories," cried the banker, impatiently, "when I have told you that I saw Arthur with the coronet in his hands?"

"Wait a little, Mr. Holder. We must come back to that. About this girl, Miss Holder. You saw her return by the kitchen door, I presume?"

"Yes; when I went to see if the door was fastened for the night I met her slipping in. I saw the man, too, in the gloom."

"Do you know him?"

"Oh yes; he is the green-grocer* who brings our vegetables round. His name is Francis Prosper."

---

green-grocer: produce man

"He stood," said Holmes, "to the left of the door—that is to say, farther up the path than is necessary to reach the door?"

"Yes, he did."

"And he is a man with a wooden leg?"

Something like fear sprang up in the young lady's expressive black eyes. "Why, you are like a magician," said she. "How do you know that?" She smiled, but there was no answering smile in Holmes's thin, eager face.

"I should be very glad now to go upstairs," said he. "I shall probably wish to go over the outside of the house again. Perhaps I had better take a look at the lower windows before I go up."

He walked swiftly round from one to the other, pausing only at the large one which looked from the hall onto the stable lane. This he opened, and made a very careful examination of the sill with his powerful magnifying lens. "Now we shall go upstairs," said he, at last.

The banker's dressing-room was a plainly furnished little chamber, with a gray carpet, a large bureau, and a long mirror. Holmes went to the bureau first and looked hard at the lock.

"Which key was used to open it?" he asked.

"That which my son himself indicated— that of the cupboard of the lumber-room."*

---

lumber-room: storeroom

"Have you it here?"

"That is it on the dressing-table."

Sherlock Holmes took it up and opened the bureau.

"It is a noiseless lock," said he. "It is no wonder that it did not wake you. This case, I presume, contains the coronet. We must have a look at it." He opened the case, and, taking out the diadem, he laid it upon the table. It was a magnificent specimen of the jeweler's art, and the thirty-six stones were the finest that I have ever seen. At one side of the coronet was a cracked edge, where a corner holding three gems had been torn away.

"Now, Mr. Holder," said Holmes, "here is the corner which corresponds to that which has been so unfortunately lost. Might I beg that you will break it off."

The banker recoiled in horror. "I should not dream of trying." said he.

"Then I will." Holmes suddenly bent his strength upon it, but without result. "I feel it give a little," said he; "but, though I am exceptionally strong in the fingers, it would take me all my time to break it. An ordinary man could not do it. Now, what do you think would happen if I did break it, Mr. Holder? There would be a noise like a pistol shot. Do you tell me that all this happened within a few yards of your bed, and that you heard nothing of it?"

"I do not know what to think. It is all dark to me."

"But perhaps it may grow lighter as we go. What do you think, Miss Holder?"

"I confess that I still share my uncle's perplexity."

"Your son had no shoes or slippers on when you saw him?"

"He had nothing on save only his trousers and shirt."

"Thank you. We have certainly been favored with extraordinary luck during this inquiry, and it will be entirely our own fault if we do not succeed in clearing the matter up. With your permission, Mr. Holder, I shall now continue my investigations outside."

He went alone, at his own request, for he explained that any unnecessary footmarks might make his task more difficult. For an hour or more he was at work, returning at last with his feet heavy with snow and his features as inscrutable* as ever.

---

inscrutable: difficult to understand or fathom

"I think that I have seen now all that there is to see, Mr. Holder," said he; "I can serve you best by returning to my rooms."

"But the gems, Mr Holmes. Where are they?"

"I cannot tell."

The banker wrung his hands. "I shall never see them again!" he cried. "And my son? You give me hopes?"

"My opinion is in no way altered."

"Then, what was this dark business which was acted in my house last night?"

"If you can call upon me at my Baker Street rooms tomorrow morning between nine and ten I shall be happy to do what I can to make it clearer. I understand that you give me *carte blanche** to act for you, provided only that I get back the gems, and that you place no limit on the sum I may draw."

---

carte blanche: unrestricted power

"I would give my fortune to have them back."

"Very good. I shall look into the matter between this and then. Good-bye; it is just possible that I may have to come over here again before evening."

It was obvious to me that my companion's mind was now made up about the case, although what his conclusions were was more than I could even dimly imagine. Several times during our homeward journey I endeavored to sound* him upon the point, but he always glided away to some other topic, until at last I gave it over in despair. It was not yet three when we found ourselves in our room once more. He hurried to his chamber, and was down again in a few minutes dressed as a common loafer.* With his collar turned up, his shiny, seedy coat, his red cravat,* and his worn boots, he was a perfect sample of the class.

---

sound: probe
loafer: vagrant
cravat: necktie

"I think that this should do," said he, glancing into the glass above the fireplace. "I only wish that you could come with me, Watson, but I fear that it won't do. I may be on the trail in this matter, or I may be following a will-of-the-wisp, but I shall soon know which it is. I hope that I may be back in a few hours." He cut a slice of beef from the joint upon the sideboard,* sandwiched it between two rounds of bread, and, thrusting this rude* meal into his pocket, he started off upon his expedition.

sideboard: buffet
rude: simple

I had just finished my tea when he returned, evidently in excellent spirits, swinging an old elastic-sided boot in his hand. He chucked it down into a corner and helped himself to a cup of tea.

"I only looked in as I passed," said he. "I am going right on."

"Where to?"

"Oh, to the other side of the West End. It may be some time before I get back. Don't wait up for me in case I should be late."

"How are you getting on?"

"Oh, so-so. Nothing to complain of. I have been out to Streatham since I saw you last, but I did not call at the house. It is a very sweet little problem, and I would not have missed it for a good deal. However, I must not sit gossiping here, but must get these disreputable clothes off and return to my highly respectable self."

I could see for his manner that he had stronger reasons for satisfaction than his words alone would imply. His eyes twinkled, and there was even a touch of color upon his sallow cheeks. He hastened upstairs, and a few minutes later I heard the slam of the hall door, which told me he was off once more upon his congenial hunt.

I waited until midnight, but there was no sign of his return, so I retired to my room. It was no uncommon thing for him to be away for days and nights on end when he was hot upon a scent, so that his lateness caused me no surprise. I do not know at what hour he came in, but when I came down to breakfast in the morning, there he was with a cup of coffee in one hand and the paper in the other, as fresh and trim as possible.

"You will excuse my beginning without you, Watson," said he; "but you remember that our client has rather an early appointment this morning."

"Why, it is after nine now," I answered. "I should not be surprised if that were he. I thought I heard a ring."

It was, indeed, our friend the financier. I was shocked by the change which had come over him, for his face, which was naturally of a broad and massive mould, was now pinched and fallen in, while his hair seemed to me at least a shade whiter. He entered with a weariness and lethargy* which was even more painful than his violence of the morning before, and he dropped heavily into the armchair which I pushed forward for him.

lethargy: dullness

"I do not know what I have done to be so severely tried," said he. "Only two days ago I was a happy and prosperous man, without a care in the world. Now I am left to a lonely and dishonored age. One sorrow comes close upon the heels of another. My niece, Mary, has deserted me."

"Deserted you?"

"Yes. Her bed this morning had not been slept in, her room was empty, and a note for me lay upon the hall table. I had said to her last night, in sorrow and not in anger, that if she had married my boy all might have been well with him. Perhaps it was thoughtless of me to say so. It is to that remark that she refers in this note:

" 'My dearest Uncle,
I feel that I have brought trouble upon you, and that if I had acted differently this terrible misfortune might never have occurred. I cannot, with this thought in my mind, ever again be happy under your roof, and I feel that I must leave you for ever. Do not worry about my future, for that is provided for; and, above all, do not search for me, for it will be fruitless labor and an ill-service to me. In life or in death, I am ever your loving
                                          Mary.'

"What could she mean by that note, Mr. Holmes? Do you think it points to suicide?"

"No, no, nothing of the kind. It is perhaps the best possible solution. I trust, Mr. Holder, that you are nearing the end of your troubles."

"Ha! You say so! You have heard something, Mr. Holmes; you have learned something! Where are the gems?"

"You would not think £1000 apiece an excessive sum for them?"

"I would pay ten."

"That would be unnecessary. Three thousand will cover the matter. And there is a little

reward, I fancy. Have you your checkbook? Here is a pen. Better make it out for £3000."

With a dazed face the banker made out the required check. Holmes walked over to his desk, took out a little triangular piece of gold with three gems in it, and threw it down upon the table.

With a shriek of joy our client clutched it up.

"You have it!" he gasped. "I am saved! I am saved!"

The reaction of joy was as passionate as his grief had been, and he hugged his recovered gems to his bosom.

"There is one other thing you owe, Mr. Holder," said Sherlock Holmes, rather sternly.

"Owe!" He caught up a pen. "Name the sum, and I will pay it."

"No, the debt is not to me. You owe a very humble apology to that noble lad, your son, who has carried himself in this matter as I should be proud to see my own son do, should I ever chance to have one."

"Then it was not Arthur who took them?"

"I told you yesterday, and I repeat today, that it was not."

"You are sure of it! Then let us hurry to him at once, to let him know that the truth is known."

"He knows already. When I had cleared it all up I had an interview with him, and, finding that he would not tell me the story, I told it to him, on which he had to confess that I was right, and to add the very few details which were not yet quite clear to me. Your news of this morning, however, may open his lips."

"For Heaven's sake, tell me, then, what is this extraordinary mystery!"

"I will do so, and I will show you the steps by which I reached it. And let me say to you, first, that which it is hardest for me to say and for you to hear: there has been an understanding between Sir George Burnwell and your niece Mary. They have now fled together."

"My Mary? Impossible!"

"It is, unfortunately, more than possible; it is certain. Neither you nor your son knew the true character of this man when you admitted him into your family circle. He is one of the most dangerous men in England—a ruined gambler, an absolutely desperate villain, a man without heart or conscience. Your niece knew nothing of such men. When he breathed his vows to her, as he had done to a hundred before her, she flattered herself that she alone had touched his heart. The devil knows best what he said, but at least she became his tool, and was in the habit of seeing him nearly every evening."

"I cannot, and I will not, believe it!" cried the banker, with an ashen face.

"I will tell you, then, what occurred in your house last night. Your niece, when you had, as she thought, gone to your room, slipped down and talked to her lover through the window which leads into the stable lane. His footmarks had pressed right through the snow, so long had he stood there. She told him of the coronet. His wicked lust for gold kindled at the news, and he bent her to his will. I have no doubt that she loved you, but there are women in whom the love of a lover extinguishes all other loves, and I think that she must have been one. She had hardly listened to his instructions when she saw you coming downstairs, on which she closed the window rapidly, and told you about one of the servants' escapade with her wooden-legged lover, which was all perfectly true.

"Your boy, Arthur, went to bed after his interview* with you, but he slept badly on account of his uneasiness about his club debts. In the middle of the night he heard a soft tread pass his door, so he rose, and looking out, was surprised to see his cousin walking very stealthily along the passage, until she disappeared into your dressing-room. Petrified with astonishment, the lad slipped on some clothes, and waited there in the dark to see what would come of this strange affair. Presently she emerged from the room again, and in the light of the passage-lamp your son saw that she carried the precious coronet in her hands. She passed down the stairs, and he, thrilling* with horror, ran along and slipped behind the curtain near your door, whence he could see what passed in the hall beneath. He saw her stealthily open the window, hand out the coronet to some one in the gloom, and then closing it once more hurry back to her room, passing quite close to where he stood hid behind the curtain.

---

interview: conversation
thrilling: shuddering

As long as she was on the scene he could not take any action without a horrible exposure of the woman whom he loved. But the instant that she was gone he realized how crushing a misfortune this would be for you, and how all-important it was to set it right. He rushed down, just as he was, in his bare feet, opened the window, sprang out into the snow, and ran down the lane, where he could see a dark figure in the moonlight. Sir George Burnwell tried to get away, but Arthur caught him, and there was a struggle between them, your lad tugging at one side of the coronet, and his opponent at the other. In the scuffle, your son struck Sir George, and cut him over the eye. Then something suddenly snapped, and your son, finding that he had the coronet in his hands, rushed back, closed the window, ascended to your room, and had just observed that the coronet had been twisted in the struggle and was endeavoring to straighten it when you appeared upon the scene."

"Is it possible?" gasped the banker.

"You then roused his anger by calling him names at a moment when he felt that he had deserved your warmest thanks. He could not explain the true state of affairs without betraying one who certainly deserved little enough consideration at his hands. He took the more chivalrous view, however, and preserved her secret."

"And that was why she shrieked and fainted when she saw the coronet," cried Mr. Holder. "Oh, what a blind fool I have been! And his asking to be allowed to go out for five minutes! The dear fellow wanted to see if the missing piece were at the scene of the struggle. How cruelly I have misjudged him!"

"When I arrived at the house," continued Holmes, "I at once went very carefully round it to observe if there were any traces in the snow which might help me. I knew that none had fallen since the evening before, and also that there had been a strong frost to preserve impressions. I passed along the tradesmen's path, but found it all trampled down and indistinguishable. Just beyond it, however, at the far side of the kitchen door, a woman had stood and talked with a man, whose round impressions on one side showed that he had a wooden leg. I could even tell that they had been disturbed, for the woman had run back swiftly to the door, as was shown by the deep toe and light heel marks, while Wooden-Leg had waited a little, and then had gone away. I thought at the time that this might be the maid and her sweetheart of whom you had already spoken to me, and inquiry showed it was so. I passed round the garden without seeing anything more than random tracks, which I took to be the police; but when I got into the stable lane a very long and complex story was written in the snow in front of me.

"There was a double line of tracks of a booted man, and a second double line which

I saw with delight belonged to a man with naked feet. I was at once convinced from what you had told me that the latter was your son. The first had walked both ways, but the other had run swiftly, and, as his tread was marked in places over the depression of the boot, it was obvious that he had passed after the other. I followed them up, and found that they led to the hall window, where Boots had worn all the snow away while waiting. Then I walked to the other end, which was a hundred yards or more down the lane. I saw where Boots had faced round, where the snow was cut up as though there had been a struggle, and, finally, where a few drops of blood had fallen, to show me that I was not mistaken. Boots had then run down the lane, and another little smudge of blood showed that it was he who had been hurt. When he came to the highroad at the other end, I found that the pavement had been cleared, so there was an end to that clue.

"On entering the house, however, I examined, as you remember, the sill and framework of the hall window with my lens, and I could at once see that someone had passed out. I could distinguish the outline of an instep where the wet foot had been placed in coming in. I was then beginning to be able to form an opinion as to what had occurred. A man had waited outside the window, someone had brought the gems; the deed had been overseen by your son, he had pursued the thief, had struggled with him, they had each tugged at the coronet, their united strength causing injuries which neither alone could have effected. He had returned with the prize, but had left a fragment in the grasp of his opponent. So far I was clear. The question now was, who was the man, and who was it brought him the coronet?

"It is an old maxim of mine that when you have excluded the impossible, whatever remains, however improbable, must be the truth. Now, I knew that it was not you who had brought it down, so there only remained your niece and the maids. But if it were the maids, why should your son allow himself to be accused in their place? There could be no possible reason. As he loved his cousin, however, there was an excellent explanation why he should retain her secret—the more so as the secret was a disgraceful one. When I remembered that you had seen her at that window, and how she had fainted on seeing the coronet again, my conjecture became a certainty.

"And who could it be who was her confederate? A lover evidently, for who else could outweigh the love and gratitude which she must feel to you? I knew that you went out little, and that your circle of friends was a very limited one. But among them was Sir George Burnwell. I had heard of him before as being a man of evil reputation among women. It must have been he who wore those

boots and retained the missing gems. Even though he knew that Arthur had discovered him, he might still flatter himself that he was safe, for the lad could not say a word without compromising* his own family.

---

compromising: implicating

"Well, your own good sense will suggest what measures I took next. I went in the shape of a loafer to Sir George's house, managed to pick up an acquaintance with his valet, learned that his master had cut his head the night before, and, finally, at the expense of six shillings, made all sure by buying a pair of his cast-off shoes. With these I journeyed down to Streatham, and saw that they exactly fitted the tracks."

"I saw an ill-dressed vagabond in the lane yesterday evening," said Mr. Holder.

"Precisely. It was I. I found that I had my man, so I came home and changed my clothes. It was a delicate part which I had to play then, for I saw that a prosecution must be avoided to avert scandal, and I knew that so astute a villain would see that our hands were tied in the matter. I went and saw him. At first, of course, he denied everything. But when I gave him every particular that had occurred, he tried to bluster, and took down a life-preserver* from the wall. I knew my man, however, and I clapped a pistol to his head before he could strike. Then he became a little more reasonable. I told him that we would give him a price for the stones he held—£1000 apiece. That brought out the first signs of grief that he had shown. 'Why, dash it all!' said he, 'I've let them go at six hundred for the three!' I soon managed to get the address of the receiver who had them, on promising him that there would be no prosecution. Off I set to him, and after much chaffering* I got our stones at £1000 a piece. Then I looked in upon your son, told him that all was right, and eventually got to my bed about two o'clock, after what I may call a really hard day's work."

---

life-preserver: blackjack
chaffering: haggling

"A day which has saved England from a great public scandal," said the banker, rising. "Sir, I cannot find words to thank you, but you shall not find me ungrateful for what you have done. Your skill has indeed exceeded all that I have heard of it. And now I must fly to my dear boy to apologize to him for the wrong which I have done him. As to what you tell me of poor Mary, it goes to my very heart. Not even your skill can inform me where she is now."

"I think that we may safely say," returned Holmes, "that she is wherever Sir George Burnwell is. It is equally certain, too, that whatever her sins are, they will soon receive a more than sufficient punishment."

About the Story

1. Would you say that "The Adventure of the Beryl Coronet" is a more analytical or sensational type of detective story?
2. When Watson first sees Mr. Holder on Baker street, what does he deduce about the man?
3. Does Holmes agree with Watson's deduction?
4. What is the cause of Mr. Holder's frenzied condition?
5. Who does Mr. Holder believe is responsible for stealing the jewels from the beryl coronet?
6. What specific details of Mr. Holder's story convince Holmes that Mr. Holder's son is innocent?
7. What incident brings the story to a crisis?
8. Was the resolution satisfying? Why or why not?

About the Author

Sir Arthur Conan Doyle (1859-1930), the creator of the fictional detective Sherlock Holmes, was an amateur sleuth himself. Though Doyle solved several intricate cases, he did not make his living as a detective. He was rather like the famous Watson in his stories, a medical doctor who also became a respected author. Finding that his fledgling medical practice was slow to develop, the young Doyle took to writing stories to fill spare time and bring in much-needed income. The popularity of the Holmes stories surprised and encouraged Doyle, who viewed the stories only as entertaining and profitable. He considered his more serious writings to be more important. These include several fine historical novels such as the enduringly popular *The White Company,*

Throughout his life, Doyle proved his reputation for being a man of great character and honor, especially in his work as a military doctor. For his loyal service, which included the writing of a pamphlet and several historical works, King Edward VII knighted Doyle in 1902. Sir Arthur Conan Doyle's popularity, both personal and literary, remains high today. His unforgettable Holmes, accompanied by the faithful Watson, is recognized worldwide. Even to those who have never actually read Doyle's stories, Sherlock Holmes is the epitome of the private detective.

In the Ring
with Jack Dempsey

Paul Gallico

The American journalist and short-story writer Paul Gallico began as a sportswriter and remained interested in sports. Like other writers, he thought he needed to have firsthand experience in the subjects he was writing about. His autobiographical essay "The Feel," from which this excerpt is taken, tells of his participation in various sports he was assigned to cover. Notice that this excerpt is organized according to what he learns.

It all began back in 1922 when I was a cub sportswriter and consumed with more curiosity than was good for my health. I had seen my first professional prizefights and wondered at the curious behavior of men under the stress of blows, the sudden checking and the beginning of a little fall forward after a hard punch, the glazing of eyes and the loss of locomotor control, the strange actions of men on the canvas after a knockdown as they struggled to regain their senses and arise on legs that seemed to have turned into rubber.

I had never been in any bad fist fights as a youngster, though I had taken a little physical punishment in football, but it was not enough to complete the picture. Could one think under those conditions?

I had been assigned to my first training-camp coverage, Dempsey's at Saratoga Springs, where he was preparing for his famous fight with Luis Firpo. For days I watched him sag a spar boy with what seemed to be no more than a light cuff on the neck, or pat his face with what looked like no more than a caressing stroke of his arm, and the fellow would come all apart at the seams and collapse in a useless heap, grinning vacuously* or twitching strangely. My burning curiosity got the better of prudence and a certain reluctance to expose myself to physical pain. I asked Dempsey to permit me to box a round with him. I had never boxed before, but I was in good physical shape, having just completed a four-year stretch as a galley slave in the Columbia eight-oared shell.

vacuously: stupidly, without meaning

When it was over and I escaped through the ropes, shaking, bleeding a little from the mouth, with rosin dust on my pants and a vicious throbbing in my head, I knew all that there was to know about being hit in the prize-ring. It seems that I had gone to an expert for tuition. I knew the sensation of being stalked and pursued by a relentless, truculent* professional destroyer whose trade and business it was to injure men. I saw the quick flash of the brown forearm that precedes the stunning shock as a bony, leather-bound fist lands on cheek or mouth. I learned more (partly from photographs of the lesson, viewed afterwards, one of which shows me ducked under a vicious left hook, an act of which I never had the slightest recollection) about

instinctive ducking and blocking than I could have in ten years of looking at prizefights, and I learned, too, that as the soldier never hears the bullet that kills him, so does the fighter rarely, if ever, see the punch that tumbles blackness over him like a mantle, with a tearing rip as though the roof of his skull were exploding, and robs him of his senses.

truculent: savage, cruel

There was just that—a ripping in my head and then sudden blackness, and the next thing I knew, I was sitting on the canvas covering of the ring floor with my legs collapsed under me, grinning idiotically. How often since have I seen that same silly, goofy look on the faces of dropped fighters—and understood it. I held onto the floor with both hands, because the ring and the audience outside were making a complete clockwise revolution, came to a stop, and then went back again counterclockwise. When I struggled to my feet, Jack Kearns, Dempsey's manager, was counting over me, but I neither saw nor heard him and was only conscious that I was in a ridiculous position and that the thing to do was to get up and try to fight back. The floor swayed and rocked beneath me like a fishing dory in an off-shore swell, and it was a welcome respite when Dempsey rushed into a clinch, held me up, and whispered into my ear: "Wrestle around a bit, son, until your head clears." And then it was that I learned what those little lovetaps to the back of the neck and the short digs to the ribs can mean to the groggy pugilist* more than half knocked out. It is a murderous game, and the fighter who can escape after having been felled by a lethal blow has my admiration. And there, too, I learned that there can be no sweeter sound than the bell that calls a halt to hostilities.

pugilist: boxer

From that afternoon, also, dated my antipathy* for the spectator at prizefights who yells: "Come on, you bum, get up and fight! Oh, you big quitter! Yah yellow, yah yellow!" Yellow, eh? It is all a man can do to get up after being stunned by a blow, much less fight back. But they do it. And how a man is able to muster any further interest in a combat after being floored with a blow to the pit of the stomach will always remain to me a miracle of what the human animal is capable of under stress.

antipathy: extreme dislike

About the Essay

1. Though Gallico's piece is an essay rather than a short story, is there an incident that could serve as an "inciting moment"?
2. List several misconceptions Gallico held about fighting before he entered the ring with Dempsey.
3. How did Gallico's attitude as a spectator change after his encounter in the ring?
4. Gallico compares his experience in the ring to that of a man being stalked by a professional destroyer and that of a soldier in his last battle. Why do you think Gallico chose these two specific comparisons? Which of these comparisons did you think was stronger? Why?
5. Through vivid description, Gallico makes you almost *feel* Dempsey's blows. List three specific phrases that were especially effective in making you empathize with Gallico.

About the Author

Paul Gallico's (1894-1976) interest in sports began during his college days when he distinguished himself as a college cheerleader and captain of the crewing (rowing) team. Following a tour of duty as a sailor in World War I, Gallico finished his college work and took a position with the New York *Daily News.* After working as sports editor for that newspaper for twelve years, Gallico decided to limit himself to free-lance work. His short stories and novels became popular. In addition, he served as a war correspondent during the Second World War.

Gallico's greatest gift is his keen observance of minute detail and his ability to transfer his careful study of people and places into well-narrated stories. In his first-person narration "In the Ring with Jack Dempsey," Gallico uses his gifts to help the reader "feel" the rigors of prizefighting. It is not only Gallico who, through his experience with a professional boxer, has learned lessons about human determination and bravery. His readers, too, have been "in the ring," thanks to his story-telling ability.

A Bit of String

Guy de Maupassant

Maupassant is a master at didactic writing. His style is characterized by classical simplicity, clarity, and reserve that gives force to his theme. In this story Maupassant shows the diabolical effects of gossip. Notice the tone of the story. What does this tone reveal about the author's attitude toward those who destroy the old Master Hauchecorne?

Along all the roads leading to Goderville the peasants and their wives were going toward the town, for it was market day. The men walked at an easy pace, the whole body thrown ahead at each movement of the long, crooked legs, men deformed by rude labor, by guiding the plow, which at once forces the right shoulder upward and twists the waist; by reaping, which spreads the knees, for solid footing; by all the patient and painful toil of the country. Their blue blouses, glossy with starch, as though varnished, ornamented at the neck and wrists by a simple pattern in white, swelled out round their bony chests, like captive balloons from which heads, arms, and legs were protruding.

Some were leading by a cord a cow or calf, and their wives behind the animals were hastening their pace by the strokes of branches stripped of their leaves. The women carried on their arms great baskets, out of which hung, here and there, heads of chickens or ducks. They walked with shorter steps than their husbands, and at a more rapid pace, spare, erect and wrapped in scant shawls pinned across their flat chests, their heads enveloped in white linen drawn closely over the hair and surmounted by a bonnet.

Now a pleasure wagon passed at a jerky pony trot, shaking fantastically two men seated side by side, and a woman at the back of the vehicle, holding on to its sides to soften the hard jolts.

In the square of Goderville was a crowd— a jam of mingled human beings and beasts. The horns of cattle, the high hats of the rich farmers and the head-dresses of the women, emerged from the surface of the assembly; and discordant voices, clamorous, bawling, kept up a continuous and savage babel, overtopped now and then by a shout from the robust lungs of a merry countryman, or the lowing of a cow attached to the wall of a house. All this mass was redolent* of the stable and soilure, of milk, of hay, of sweat, and diffused that rank, penetrating odor, human and bestial, peculiar to people of the fields.

---

redolent: having or emitting an odor

Master Hauchecorne of Bréauté had just arrived at Goderville, and was going toward the square when he saw on the ground a bit of string. Master Hauchecorne, economist, like every true Norman, thought that anything of use might be worth picking up, and he bent down painfully, for he suffered from rheumatism. He took up the piece of string, and was winding it carefully, when he noticed Malandin, the harness-maker, watching him from his doorway. The two men had long ago had a quarrel about a halter, and both being vindictive, had remained unfriendly. Hauchecorne was seized with a kind of shame, at thus being seen by his enemy picking a bit of twine out of the mud. He quickly hid his prize under his blouse, then in his breeches pocket; then he pretended to search the ground again for something which he did not find, and he went off toward the market, his head in advance, bent double by his infirmities.

He was forthwith lost in the noisy, shuffling crowd everywhere in motion from innumerable buyings and sellings. The peasants examined the cows, went away, came back, hesitated, always fearful of being outwitted, never daring to decide, peering into the face of the vendor, endlessly searching to discover the ruse* in the man and the fault in the beast.

---

ruse: action or device used to confuse or mislead

The women, putting their great baskets down at their feet, had drawn out their fowls, which were lying on the ground, legs bound, eyes wild, combs scarlet. They listened to offers, held to their prices unmoved, their faces inscrutable; or suddenly deciding to accept an offer, cried out to the would-be purchaser slowly moving away:

"Agreed, Master Hutine; I will give it at your price."

Then little by little the square emptied, and the Angelus* sounding noon, those who lived too far to go home dispersed in the various public houses.

Angelus: a bell rung for a call to prayer

At Jourdain's the great dining-room was full of feasters, as the vast court was full of vehicles of every pedigree—carts, gigs, tilburies,* pleasure vans, carioles* innumerable, yellow with mud, mended, out of order, lifting to heaven their shafts, like two arms, or nosing the ground, rear in the air.

---

tilburies: open carriages with two wheels and a seat for two persons
carioles: small open one-horse carriages that have two wheels

---

Opposite the tables of diners the great chimney-piece, full of bright flame, threw a lively warmth on the backs of the row at the right. Three spits were turning, weighted with chickens, pigeons, and legs of mutton, and a delectable odor of roast flesh and of juice streaming over its golden brown skin, escaped from the hearth, put every one in gay humor, and made mouths water. All the aristocracy of the plow dined there with Master Jourdain, innkeeper and horse-dealer, a shrewd fellow, who had his dollars.

The platters were passed and emptied as were the tankards of yellow cider. Each one talked of his affairs, his purchases, his sales. The harvest was discussed. The weather was good for grass, but a little sharp for grain.

All at once the drum sounded in the court before the house. All save a few indifferent fellows were quickly on their feet, and running to the door or the windows, their mouths full, their napkins in their hands.

When he had finished his roulade* the public crier held fourth in a jerky voice, cutting his phrases at the wrong place:

---

roulade: drum roll

"It is made known to the inhabitants of Goderville and in general to all—the people present at market, that there was lost this morning, on the Benzeville road between—nine and ten o'clock, a wallet containing five hundred francs and important papers. You are asked to return—it to the town hall, without delay, or to the house of Master Fortuné Houlèbreque, of Manneville. There will be twenty francs reward."

Then the crier went on. One heard once more far off the muffled beating of his drum, and his voice enfeebled by the distance. Then they all began to talk of the event, estimating Master Houlèbreque's chances of finding or not finding his wallet.

And the meal went on.

They were finishing the coffee when the chief of police appeared at the door.

"Where is Master Hauchecorne of Bréauté?" he asked.

Hauchecorne, seated at the farther end of the table, replied:

"I'm here."

The chief proceeded:

"Master Hauchecorne, will you have the kindness to accompany me to the town hall? The mayor wishes to speak with you."

The countryman, surprised and disquieted, emptied at a draft his little glass of cider, arose, and, still more bent than in the morning, for the first movement after each relaxation was particularly difficult, he set out, repeating:

"I'm here, I'm here."

And he followed the chief.

The mayor was waiting for him, seated in his fauteuil.* He was the notary of the vicinity, a big, solemn man, of pompous phrases.

fauteuil: armchair

"Master Hauchecorne," said he, "you were seen to pick up, on the Benzeville road, this morning, the wallet lost by Master Houlèbreque, of Manneville."

The peasant, astonished, looked at the mayor, frightened already, without knowing why, by this suspicion which had fallen on him.

"What! What! I picked up the wallet?"

"Yes; you yourself."

"Word of honor, I didn't even know of it."

"You were seen."

"Seen? What? Who saw me?"

"Monsieur Malandin, the harness-maker."

Then the old man remembered, understood, reddened with anger.

"He saw meh, th' lout? He saw meh pick up that string! See here, m'sieu mayor," and feeling in his pocket, he drew out the bit of cord.

But the mayor, incredulous, shook his head.

"You won't make me believe, Master Hauchecorne, that Malandin, who is a man worthy of credence,* took that thread for a wallet."

---

credence: belief

The peasant, furious, raised his hand, spit, to attest his innocence, and declared:

"Yet it's the truth of God, the sacred truth, m'sieu mayor. On my soul and my salvation, I repeat it."

The mayor continued:

"After picking up the object you went on searching in the mud a long time to see if some piece of money mightn't have escaped you."

The old man gasped with indignation and fear.

"May one tell—may one tell lies like that to injure an honest man? May one say—"

His protest was vain. He was not believed. He was confronted with Monsieur Malandin, who repeated and sustained his former affirmation. For an hour the two men hurled insults at each other. Hauchecorne was searched, at his demand, and nothing was found on him. Finally the mayor, greatly perplexed, sent him away, warning him that he should inform the council and await orders.

The news spread. When he came out of the town hall the old man was surrounded and questioned with a curiosity serious or mocking, but with no ill-will in it.

He began to recount the story of the string, but no one believed him—they only laughed.

He went on, stopped by everybody, stopping his acquaintances, beginning anew his tale and his protestations, turning his pockets inside out to prove that he had nothing.

"Move on, old quibbler," they said to him.

And he became angry, exasperated, feverish, sick at heart, at not being believed. He did not know what to do, but told his story over and over.

Night came. It was time to go home. He set out with three of his neighbors, to whom he pointed out the place where he had picked up the bit of cord, and all the way home he talked of his adventure. In the evening he made a circuit of the village of Bréauté to tell it to everybody. He met only incredulity. He was ill all night from his trouble.

The next day, toward one o'clock in the afternoon, Marius Paumelle, a farm hand, of Ymanville, returned the wallet and its contents to Monsieur Houlèbreque, of Manneville. The man stated, in effect, that he had found the wallet in the road, but not knowing how to read, had taken it home to his employer.

The news spread all about. Master Hauchecorne was told of it. He at once set out again on his travels, and began to narrate his story, completed by the dénouement. He was triumphant.

"It's not the thing 'at grieved me most, you understand," he said, "but it's the lie. Nothing harms you like being charged with a lie."

All day long he talked of his adventure. He told it on the streets to men passing, in the taverns to men drinking, after church next Sunday. He stopped strangers to tell it to them. Now he was tranquil, yet something half disturbed him, without his knowing exactly what. People had an amused air as they listened to him. They did not appear convinced. He thought he detected whispers behind his back.

Tuesday of the following week he betook himself to the market of Goderville, driven there by the need of exploiting his case. Malandin, standing in his doorway, began to laugh when he saw him passing. Why? He accosted a farmer of Criquetot, who did not let him finish, but giving him a blow in the pit of the stomach, cried in his face:

"Go your way, humbug!"

Master Hauchecorne was dumfounded, and more and more ill at ease. Why had he been called a humbug?

When he was seated at table in Jourdain's inn he again began to explain the affair. A jockey of Montivilliers cried to him:

"Come, come, old croaker, I know about your string!"

Hauchecorne stammered:

"But since it is found—the wallet?"

The other answered:

"Hold your tongue, father. One finds, another returns. I know nothing about it, but I implicate you."

The peasant was left choking. He understood at last. He was accused of having returned the wallet through an accomplice. He tried to protest. The whole table began to laugh. He could not finish his dinner, and went out in the midst of mockeries.

He returned home, ashamed and disgraced, strangling with rage and confusion, so much more overwhelmed, in that he was capable, with his Norman duplicity, of doing the very thing of which he was accused, and even boasting of it as a good stroke. Confusedly he saw his innocence impossible to prove, his chicanery* being well known, and he felt himself cut to the heart by the injustice of the suspicion.

---

chicanery: trickery

Then he commenced again to recount his adventure, lengthening each day his story, adding each time new reasonings, more energetic protestations, more solemn oaths, which he invented and arranged in his hours of solitude, his mind occupied solely with the story of the string. He was believed the less in proportion to the complication of his defense and the subtlety of his argument.

"That's the reasoning of a liar," they said behind his back.

He felt it, spent himself, wore his life out in useless efforts. He wasted away visibly. Wags now made him tell "the string" for their amusement, as one makes a soldier who has fought recount his battle. His mind, harassed and unsettled, grew feeble.

Toward the end of December he took to his bed. He died early in January, and in the delirium of his agony he attested his innocence, repeating:

"A little string . . . a little string . . . wait, here it is m'sieu mayor!"

About the Story

1. Who is the central character in the story?
2. What is the inciting moment?
3. What is the climax?
4. Why do the villagers refuse to accept Master Hauchecorne's innocence even after the stolen wallet is returned?
5. How does the refusal of the villagers to

accept his innocence affect Hauchecorne?

6. The author does not specifically punish those who destroy Hauchecorne in the story, but the tone he creates through the tragic events in the story reveals to us how he views such people. What would you say is Maupassant's view of gossipers?

About the Author

Guy de Maupassant (1850-93) is a writer of international and timeless appeal; almost all of his works are available in English. Most popular and most artistic are his short stories, which portray life as Maupassant saw it, in all of its bleakness and disappointment. The despair of Maupassant's characters is usually a direct result of some sin or combination of sinful tendencies. Though many other sins also appear, covetousness and lying are two of the more common vices that destroy the lives and hopes of his characters.

Maupassant strongly objected to attempts to idealize reality or to give people hope in the here or the hereafter. He would, in fact, have rejected the Christian's hope in God or the realization of any absolute, reliable truths, as being absurd. Maupassant belongs to that group of writers who think that we can know only what we can perceive through our senses. This philosophy is contrary to the Christian faith. As Christians, we realize that not all that occurs around us meets God's approval; but we also realize that an ideal exists. Maupassant rejects the Christian ideal of hope, choosing instead to show a sad and hopeless reality.

Maupassant was born at the Château de Miromesnil, France, and was raised by his mother in Normandy. As a young boy, Maupassant collected many mental images of the people he met. He was exposed to all types and classes of French society but found in the middle class, or bourgeoisie, his greatest source of interest. His special art of portraying these people in short stories was a result of long years of literary apprenticeship to the famous French writer Flaubert. After Maupassant's story "Ball-of-Fat" was published in an anthology, he received the recognition that launched his writing career. At the age of forty-three Maupassant developed severe mental and physical ailments and died insane.

METER

The following group of narrative poems illustrates how **meter**—*the regular arrangement of stressed and unstressed syllables—not only gives structure to a poem but also reinforces its content. The first poem is a nonsense poem by Edward Lear. Despite a reputation for "stuffiness," Victorians such as Lear delighted in creating rollicking people, fanciful places, and zany things. As Lear himself unabashedly confessed, his poems were intended to be "nonsense pure and absolute," and he purposely chose a meter that would help communicate a playful tone.*

Unlike "The Jumblies," "The Charge of the Light Brigade" by Tennyson and "The Destruction of Sennacherib" by Byron are serious poems. They are narratives about specific historical events. Each, however, has a unique tone. Like Lear, these poets were careful to choose the meter that would best support the tone of their poems.

The Jumblies

Edward Lear

They went to sea in a sieve, they did;
  In a sieve they went to sea;
In spite of all their friends could say,
On a winter's morn, on a stormy day,
  In a sieve they went to sea.   5
And when the sieve turned round and round,
And everyone cried, "You'll be drowned!"
They called aloud, "Our sieve ain't big,
But we don't care a button; we don't care a fig—
  In a sieve we'll go to sea!"   10
    Far and few, far and few,
      Are the lands where the Jumblies live.
    Their heads are green, and their hands are blue;
      And they went to sea in a sieve.

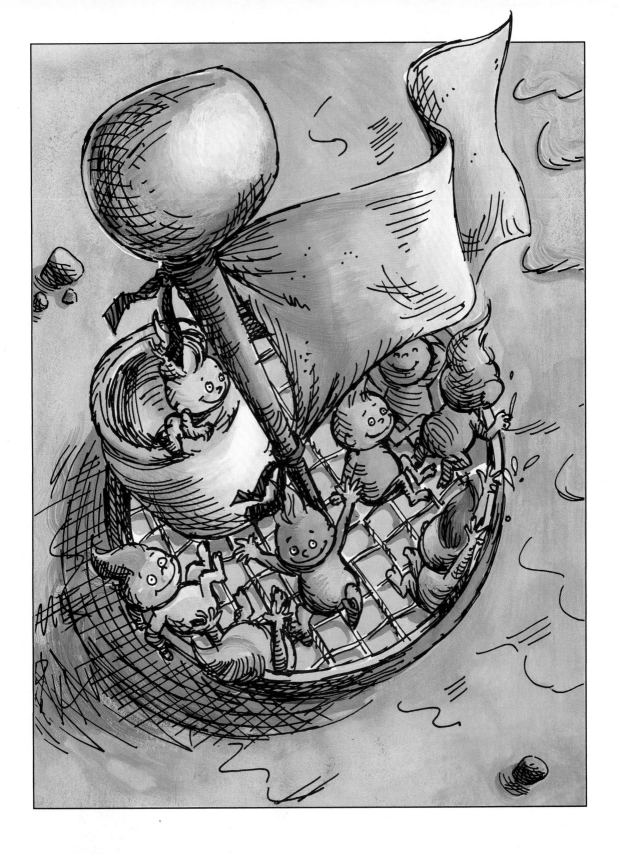

They sailed away in a sieve, they did, 15
  In a sieve they sailed so fast,
With only a beautiful pea-green veil
Tied with a ribbon, by way of a sail,
  To a small tobacco-pipe mast.
And everyone said who saw them go, 20
"Oh! won't they be soon upset, you know,
For the sky is dark, and the voyage is long;
And, happen what may, it's extremely wrong
  In a sieve to sail so fast."

The water it soon came in, it did; 25
  The water it soon came in.
So, to keep them dry, they wrapped their feet
In a pinky paper all folded neat;
  And they fastened it down with a pin.
And they passed the night in a crockery-jar; 30
And each of them said, "How wise we are!
Though the sky be dark, and the voyage be long,
Yet we never can think we were rash or wrong,
  While round in our sieve we spin."

And all night long they sailed away; 35
  And, when the sun went down,
They whistled and warbled a moony song
To the echoing sound of a coppery gong,
  In the shade of the mountains brown,
"O Timballoo! how happy we are 40
When we live in a sieve and a crockery-jar!
And all night long, in the moonlight pale,
We sail away with a pea-green sail
  In the shade of the mountains brown."

They sailed to the Western Sea, they did— 45
  To a land all covered with trees;
And they bought an owl, and a useful cart,
And a pound of rice, and a cranberry tart,
  And a hive of silvery bees;
And they bought a pig, and some green jackdaws,* 50 *jackdaws: birds resembling crows
And a lovely monkey with lollipop paws,
And seventeen bags of edelweiss tea,
And forty bottles of ring-bo-ree,
  And no end of Stilton cheese.

And in twenty years they all came back—   55
  In twenty years or more;
And everyone said, "How tall they've grown!
For they've been to the Lakes, and the Torrible Zone,
  And the hills of the Chankly Bore."
And they drank their health, and gave them a feast   60
Of dumplings made of beautiful yeast;
And everyone said, "If we only live,
We, too, will go to the sea in a sieve,
  To the hills of the Chankly Bore."
  Far and few, far and few,   65
    Are the lands where the Jumblies live.
  Their heads are green, and their hands are blue;
    And they went to sea in a sieve.

About the Author

Edward Lear (1812-1888), author of *The Book of Nonsense, More Nonsense,* and *Laughable Lyrics,* was as charming as the poetry he wrote to amuse the children of his friends. Edward, Lord Stanley, the earl of Derby, kept a large zoological garden at his home, Knowsley Hall, and he commissioned Lear to paint a large number of detailed pictures of his animals. While there, the endearing young artist enjoyed great popularity with the children, amusing them with lively drawings and witty limericks.

Lear did much to popularize the limerick form among his Victorian audience. Although his devoted readers loved his poetical and artistic nonsense, they often failed to recognize the author in public. Lear, a plain-featured man with a big, bushy beard and tiny spectacles, hardly seemed like a writer of nonsense books, and he often had to convince people of his authorship. Among his close friends, however, Lear was well loved and admired as an amusing and unusually loyal friend.

Because of his failing eyesight, Lear abandoned his natural-history artwork to concentrate on landscape painting. His friends and patrons were very generous to the talented but poor young man, and their help in financing his world travels helped him maintain his delicate health. Lear's seven travel books, full of his fine artwork, reflect his innate sense of rhythm and music in both prose and art. This rhythmic sense flowed into his nonsense poems as well. Though written purely for pleasure, these poems display an inner rhythm and often reflect Lear's feelings about himself and about people in general.

The Charge of the Light Brigade

Alfred, Lord Tennyson

Half a league, half a league,
Half a league onward,
All in the valley of Death
  Rode the six hundred.
"Forward the Light Brigade!   5
Charge for the guns!" he said.
Into the valley of Death
  Rode the six hundred.

"Forward, the Light Brigade!"
Was there a man dismay'd?   10
Not tho' the soldier knew
  Some one had blunder'd.
Theirs not to make reply,
Theirs not to reason why,
Theirs but to do and die.   15
Into the valley of Death
  Rode the six hundred.

Cannon to right of them,
Cannon to left of them,
Cannon in front of them   20
  Volley'd and thunder'd;
Storm'd at with shot and shell,
Boldly they rode and well,
Into the jaws of Death,
Into the mouth of hell   25
  Rode the six hundred.

Flash'd all their sabres bare,
Flash'd as they turn'd in air
Sabring the gunners there,
Charging an army, while   30
  All the world wonder'd.
Plunged in the battery-smoke
Right thro' the line they broke;
Cossack and Russian
Reel'd from the sabre-stroke   35
  Shatter'd and sunder'd.
Then they rode back, but not,
  Not the six hundred.

Cannon to right of them,
Cannon to left of them,   40
Cannon behind them
  Volley'd and thunder'd;
Storm'd at with shot and shell,
While horse and hero fell,
They that had fought so well   45
Came thro' the jaws of Death,
Back from the mouth of hell,
All that was left of them,
  Left of six hundred.

When can their glory fade?   50
O the wild charge they made!
  All the world wonder'd.
Honor the charge they made!
Honor the Light Brigade,
  Noble six hundred!   55

About the Author

Alfred, Lord Tennyson (1809-92) was born into a large Victorian family. Unfortunately, his father's epilepsy and drunkenness produced a very unstable family life. Tennyson himself struggled with a seizure disorder until early manhood but apparently overcame the problem by his late twenties.

Educated at Cambridge, he met many other young men interested in literature and the arts. He became a member of the Apostles, a club of intellectuals who gathered to discuss their ideas and enjoy good company. There he became close friends with Arthur H. Hallam, whose early death caused Tennyson much soul-searching. As a result of these inner struggles, Tennyson wrote his famous *In Memoriam*. After leaving the university, Tennyson traveled abroad and began his serious writing, which was well received.

Tennyson's popularity earned him the coveted position of poet laureate of England when he was only forty-one years old. Four years later, he wrote the poem "The Charge of the Light Brigade," which reflects the Victorian high esteem for the virtues of duty, patriotism, and unquestioning obedience.

Tennyson was the poetic spokesman of the Victorian Age, and much of his poetry reflects ideas and ideals admired by Christians. His works undeniably possess moral value but also reflect several anti-Biblical concepts. Attempting to bridge the gap between traditional religion and Darwinism, Tennyson created a religion of his own in his poetry—a religion of optimism. He firmly believed in Darwinian evolution. He believed in both the upward evolutionary progress of the physical world and in man's upward moral progress. Although Tennyson knew the Bible well and used many Biblical references, he rejected several essential Christian doctrines.

The Destruction of Sennacherib

George Gordon, Lord Byron

The Assyrian* came down like a wolf on the fold,
And his cohorts were gleaming in purple and gold;
And the sheen of their spears was like stars on the sea,
When the blue wave rolls nightly on deep Galilee.

Like the leaves of the forest when Summer is green,   5
That host with their banners at sunset were seen:
Like the leaves of the forest when Autumn hath blown,
That host on the morrow lay withered and strown.

For the Angel of Death spread his wings on the blast,
And breathed in the face of the foe as he passed;   10
And the eyes of the sleepers waxed deadly and chill,
And their hearts but once heaved, and for ever grew still!

And there lay the steed with his nostril all wide,
But through it there rolled not the breath of his pride:
And the foam of his gasping lay white on the turf,   15
And cold as the spray of the rock-beating surf.

And there lay the rider distorted and pale,
With the dew on his brow, and the rust on his mail;
And the tents were all silent, the banners alone,
The lances unlifted, the trumpet unblown.   20

And the widows of Ashur* are loud in their wail,
And the idols are broke in the temple of Baal;*
And the might of the Gentile,* unsmote by the sword,
Hath melted like snow in the glance of the Lord!

The Assyrian:
Sennacherib, ruler of
Assyria in the seventh century B.C.

Ashur: noted
Assyrian city on the
Tigris River
Baal: a major god in
many Near Eastern
religions
Gentile: a non-Jew,
used in reference
here to Sennacherib

About the Author

George Gordon, Lord Byron (1788-1824) led a life that was as romantic as his poetry. When he was only ten years old, he inherited a Gothic mansion and the title of baron. Unfortunately, little wealth accompanied the title, and Byron and his mother struggled against poverty for many years. In addition to financial worries, Byron was self-conscious about his lame right leg. Despite these difficulties, however, the handsome young boy was known for his determination and spirit and his inclination to read and daydream.

Byron published his first book of verse, *Hours of Idleness,* when he was nineteen. This work was so poorly received that Byron composed a satire against his critics, thus venturing into what was to become the genre he would later use.

After this first attempt at writing, Bryon traveled to the Near East with a friend, where he led a wasted life. Inspired by the exotic foreign countries, Byron wrote a collection of Spenserian stanzas entitled *Childe Harold's Pilgrimage.* The publication of this collection launched Byron's social and literary career.

Byron's popularity was not a measure of his moral uprightness. After he married, he mistreated his wife. She eventually fled to her parents, leaving Byron to face the growing disapproval of British society. In 1816 he left England permanently to escape public opinion.

Byron traveled to Switzerland, Italy, and Greece. He turned his interests to Italian politics and the struggles of the Italian revolutionaries. When this cause ceased to interest him, Bryon promoted the cause of the Greek freedom fighters. Before he had the opportunity to lend them his aid, he died of a fever at the age of thirty-six.

About the Poems

1. What word would you use to describe the tone or mood of Edward Lear's "The Jumblies"?
2. Although both Tennyson's and Byron's poems are serious narratives about specific historical events, which one would you say builds greater tension? Which one presents a mood of grandeur or awe?
3. What type of meter is used in "The Jumblies"? Why do you think Lear chose this type of meter?
4. What type of meter is used in "The Charge of the Light Brigade"? Why do you think Tennyson chose this type of meter?
5. What type of meter is used in "The Destruction of Sennacherib"? How does the effect of this meter differ from that of Tennyson's poem?

VERSE FORMS

The following poems illustrate three basic **verse forms.** *"The Eagle" by Tennyson is standard* RHYMED VERSE, *having end rhyme and regular meter. The second poem, an excerpt from Shakespeare's* Julius Caesar, *illustrates the popular* BLANK VERSE *(unrhymed iambic pentameter). Blank verse is most like the natural rhythms of our speech; thus, Shakespeare could use this verse form in his drama and still maintain a conversationlike quality in his dialogue. The last poem in the group illustrates* FREE VERSE. *Notice that in Sandburg's free-verse poem there is neither regular meter nor rhyme. Its rhythm, however, is more controlled and the line length is shorter than it would be in ordinary prose.*

The Eagle
Alfred, Lord Tennyson

He clasps the crag with crooked hands.
Close to the sun in lonely lands,
Ringed with the azure world, he stands.

azure: a purplish blue

The wrinkled sea beneath him crawls,
He watches from his mountain walls,   5
And like a thunderbolt he falls.

from *Julius Caesar*
*William Shakespeare**

Cowards die many times before their deaths;
The valiant never taste of death but once.
Of all the wonders that I yet have heard,
It seems to me most strange that men should fear;
Seeing that death, a necessary end,   5
Will come when it will come.

*For biographical information, see BRITISH LITERATURE for Christian Schools:® The Early Tradition, pp. 264-68.

Splinter

Carl Sandburg

The voice of the last cricket
across the first frost
is one kind of good-by.
It is so thin a splinter of singing.

About the Author

Carl August Sandburg (1878-1967) is called "the American bard" and "the voice of mid-America." Trained in the school of experience, Sandburg could express the dreams and desires of everyday people. He had worked as an itinerant laborer and journalist, fought in the Spanish-American War, and participated in Socialist causes. After achieving popularity as a writer, he traveled the country widely as a singer and guitarist, reciting his own poetry and becoming an American symbol.

Sandburg's writing reveals his three great passions: his faith in democracy and the working class, his delight in nature and all honest beauty, and his innate personal realism.

Sandburg held a firmly humanistic view of life. He spoke against "intolerance," especially with respect to such evangelists as Billy Sunday, of whose ministry Sandburg was highly skeptical. Although Sandburg himself claimed affiliation with no particular religious view, he placed his faith in people and in their innate goodness and capacity to adapt and succeed. Sandburg took comfort in his belief in an evolutionary cycle of life and in his membership in the "family of man," with God as the Father of all men.

About the Poems

1. How does Tennyson's description of the eagle differ from the description you may find in an encyclopedia?

2. The first five lines of Tennyson's poem are simple description. Line 6, however, adds action to the description. What does the simile "like a thunderbolt" in line 6 convey?

3. What is the meaning of Caesar's first line, "Cowards die many times before their deaths"?

4. Why do you think Sandburg chose to compare "voice of the last cricket" to "one kind of good-by"? What do you think could be the setting for the "good-by" Sandburg is describing in his poem?

STANZA FORMS

A **stanza** is a division of a poem based on thought, meter, or rhyme. It is recognized by the number of lines it contains. The basic stanza forms are couplet (two-line stanza), triplet (three-line stanza), quatrain (four-line stanza), quintet (five-line stanza), sestet (six-line stanza), septet (seven-line stanza), and octave (eight-line stanza). From these basic forms other traditional forms emerge. The following groups of poems illustrate several of these traditional stanza forms.

The first group are couplets taken from Alexander Pope's An Essay on Criticism. They are called HEROIC COUPLETS because they not only contain the typical aa rhyme scheme, but they are also written in iambic pentameter, and the couplet itself forms a complete thought.

"Bonnie George Campbell" and "Allen-a-Dale" are BALLADS, narrative poems often derived from folklore and originally intended to be sung or recited. Ballads typically use the four-line stanza or quatrain (probably the most common stanza form) and have an abcb rhyme scheme.

Donne's "Holy Sonnet 10" and Shakespeare's "Sonnet 29" represent the sonnet stanza form. A SONNET is a lyric poem of fourteen lines. The two most common types of sonnets are the Italian (or Petrarchan) and the English (or Shakespearean). In an ITALIAN SONNET the first eight lines (the octave, rhyming abbaabba) form a distinct unit of thought, and the last six lines (the sestet, rhyming variously with two or three new rhymes) form another. In an ENGLISH SONNET the thought is usually distributed over three quatrains and a concluding couplet, the whole rhyming ababcdcdefefgg.

Although the LIMERICK is used only for humorous poetry, it could also be categorized as a stanza form. It is a five-line poem with an anapestic meter and a specific pattern (lines 1, 2, and 5 have three feet; lines 3 and 4 have two feet). The two examples given represent the typical limerick structure and tone.

The last two poems in this group are HAIKU. Haiku is a Japanese form of poetry whose purpose is to create one vivid picture which will either touch the reader's heart or enlighten his mind. The haiku uses a three-line stanza form. Like the limerick, it has a specific pattern (lines 1 and 3 have five syllables; line 2 has seven). Unlike the limerick, however, its tone is serious, often melancholy.

As you read this group of poems, notice that stanza divisions are not only an organizational tool but also a means of clarifying and intensifying a poetic theme.

from *An Essay on Criticism*

Alexander Pope

Trust not yourself; but, your defects to know,
Make use of every friend—and every foe.
True wit is nature* to advantage dressed,
What oft was thought, but ne'er so well expressed.

nature: universal truth

Be not the first by whom the new are tried,   5
Nor yet the last to lay the old aside.

Words are like leaves; and where they most abound,
Much fruit of sense beneath is rarely found.
Good nature* and good sense must ever join;*
To err is human, to forgive divine.   10

nature: natural ability
join: pronounce *jine*

About the Author

Alexander Pope (1688-1744), born in London to a merchant's family, became the poet of an era known for its self-confidence and optimism. Before he became successful, however, Pope had to overcome several personal obstacles, one of which was a serious bout with a crippling disease. Because of frail health, Pope received his schooling at home. By eighteen he was writing poetry with great technical skill and wit, and at twenty-three, he published his well-known work, *An Essay on Criticism,* which outlines the art of writing.

Pope's poetry was well received by his contemporaries and won him a reputation for satiric, well-constructed verse. With the money he received for translating Homer's *Illiad* into heroic couplet, Pope bought an estate and settled there with his mother.

Over the years Pope was greatly influenced by his friend Bolingbroke, who believed in the values of patriotism and virtue. In honor of his friend, Pope wrote a long poem entitled *An Essay on Man.* The poem is a set of four letters which reflect much of Pope's philosophy. Pope's objective in the poem was to "vindicate the ways of God to man."

Although he died at fifty-six, Pope had already become the poet of his age. Later movements tended to criticize his finely tuned poetic form and didactic style; however, Pope's poetry is now admired not only for its beautiful and careful attention to form but also for its thoughtful messages.

Allen-a-Dale

Sir Walter Scott

Allen-a-Dale has no fagot* for burning,
Allen-a-Dale has no furrow for turning,
Allen-a-Dale has no fleece for the spinning,
Yet Allen-a-Dale has red gold for the winning.
Come, read me my riddle! come, hearken my tale!   5
And tell me the craft of bold Allen-a-Dale.

fagot: bundle of twigs or sticks tied together

The Baron of Ravensworth prances in pride,
And he views his domains upon Arkindale side.
The mere for his net and the land for his game,
The chase for the wild and the park for the tame;   10
Yet the fish of the lake and the deer of the vale
Are less free to Lord Dacre than Allen-a-Dale!

Allen-a-Dale was ne'er belted a knight,
Though his spur be as sharp and his blade be as bright;
Allen-a-Dale is no baron or lord,   15
Yet twenty tall yeomen will draw at his word;
And the best of our nobles his bonnet will vail,
Who at Rere-cross on Stanmore meets Allen-a-Dale!

Allen-a-Dale to his wooing is come,
The mother, she asked of his household and home: 20
'Though the castle of Richmond stand fair on the hill,
"My hall," quoth bold Allen, "shows gallanter still;
'Tis the blue vault of heaven, with its crescent so pale
And with all its bright spangles!" said Allen-a-Dale.

The father was steel and the mother was stone;   25
They lifted the latch, and they bade him begone;
But loud, on the morrow, their wail and their cry!
He had laughed on the lass with his bonny black eye,
And she fled to the forest to hear a love-tale,
And the youth it was told by was Allen-a-Dale!

About the Author

Sir Walter Scott (1771-1832) loved his native home of Scotland and was interested in its colorful past. From the time he was a small boy, Scott liked nothing better than to listen to stories of the turbulent times in Scotland's history. Because of his excellent memory and his appreciation for the exciting and dramatic in literature, Scott was able to entertain his schoolmates for hours with the stories he had heard. Encouraged at school by an excellent and capable teacher, Scott worked hard at his history lessons and even learned to read foreign languages so that he might be able to enjoy the stories of different countries.

As a boy, Scott had a serious bout with polio that permanently injured his right leg. After Scott had another serious illness, his uncle offered to care for him. While recuperating at his uncle's home, Scott took advantage of the extra time to read. Although he later became an apprentice to his father and continued in an uneventful law career, Scott's interest in literature became his true occupation. He traveled extensively in Scotland, gathering traditional songs and stories, and he eventually published *The Ministrelsy of the Scottish Border,* a collection of Scottish ballads with Scott's commentary. His next collection of traditional ballads, unlike the first, was wholly original. This second collection launched Scott's professional career, and he quickly became popular.

Scott was also adept at historical fiction. His well-known *Waverly* novels brought him a solid reputation and a steady income. They also set a literary standard for the upcoming popularity of the English novel. Scott's historical novels take for their settings places other than Scotland. Two of his more popular novels were set in Europe, *Quentin Durward* in France, and *Ivanhoe* in England during the reign of Richard the Lion-Hearted.

Though today some of Scott's works seem stilted and sentimental, we must remember that the genre of historical fiction was new, and thus, exciting for his readers. Much of his poetry, however, is as exciting today as it was when he wrote it.

Bonnie George Campbell

High upon Highlands*
  And low upon Tay,*
Bonny George Campbell
  Rade out on a day.

Saddled and bridled   5
  And gallant rade he:
Hame* cam his guid horse,
  But never cam he.

Out cam his auld mither,
  Greeting fu' sair,*   10
And out cam his bonny bride,
  Riving* her hair.

Saddled and bridled
  And booted rade he:
Toom* hame cam the saddle,   15
  But never cam he.

"My meadow lies green,
  And my corn is unshorn,*
My barn is to build,
  And my babe is unborn."   20

Saddled and bridled
  And booted rade he:
Toom hame cam the saddle,
  But never cam he.

Highlands: northern
  Scotland
Tay: a long river in
  the Scottish High-
  lands emptying into
  the North Sea

hame: home

Greeting fu' sair:
  weeping greatly

Riving: tearing

Toom: empty

unshorn: grains
  unharvested

Holy Sonnet 10

John Donne

Death, be not proud, though some have calléd thee
Mighty and dreadful, for thou art not so;
For those whom thou think'st thou dost overthrow
Die not, poor Death, nor yet canst thou kill me.
From rest and sleep, which but thy pictures be,   5
Much pleasure; then from thee much more must flow,
And soonest our best men with thee do go,
Rest of their bones, and soul's delivery.
Thou art slave to fate, chance, kings, and desperate men,
And dost with poison, war, and sickness dwell,   10
And poppy* or charms can make us sleep as well
And better than thy stroke; why swell'st thou* then?
One short sleep past, we wake eternally
And death shall be no more; Death, thou shalt die.

poppy: opium

Why swell'st thou:
Why do you become
proud

About the Author

John Donne (1573-1631), a contemporary of William Shakespeare, was for most of his life a passionate, impetuous man. Born a Catholic in Protestant England, Donne was denied the social advancement he desired, and he wrote poetry to express his frustrations. Much of his earlier poetry (often called "metaphysical" poetry) contains strained, complex comparisons.

Donne often used religious imagery to voice his central concerns: love and death. Though some critics fault Donne for his preoccupation with the latter, Donne saw death as the door through which one comes to God. Because of Donne's later conversion and because of his poetry's message, we may safely assume that Donne's view of death was not mere fancy but was firmly grounded in his faith in Christ's atonement.

Most of Donne's later works (*Holy Sonnets* and *Meditations,* for example) testify of God's grace. Even his earlier poetry shows Donne's ability to express verbally the struggles of the human soul. Christians can learn much from Donne, for his works set forth the truths of Christianity in beautiful language, showing both spiritual conflict and its resolution.

Sonnet 29

William Shakespeare

When, in disgrace with fortune and men's eyes,
I all alone beweep my outcast state,
And trouble deaf heaven with my bootless* cries,

bootless: useless

And look upon myself, and curse my fate,
Wishing me like to one more rich in hope, 5
Featured like him, like him with friends possessed,
Desiring this man's art and that man's scope,
With what I most enjoy contented least;
Yet in these thoughts myself almost despising,
Haply I think on thee—and then my state, 10
Like to the lark at break of day arising
From sullen earth, sings hymns at heaven's gate;
For thy sweet love remembered such wealth brings
That then I scorn to change my state with kings.

The Limerick

Well, it's partly the shape of the thing
That gives the old limerick wing;
 These accordion pleats
 Full of airy conceits
Take it up like a kite on a string.

The Tutor

A tutor who tooted the flute
Tried to tutor two tooters to toot.
 Said the two to the tutor,
 "Is it harder to toot or
To tutor two tooters to toot?"

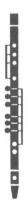

Japanese Haiku

Matsuo Bashō

The lightning flashes!
And slashing through the darkness,
A night-heron's screech.

A lightning gleam:
into darkness travels
a night heron's scream.

About the Author

Matsuo Bashō (1644-1694) is undoubtedly Japan's most highly revered poet of haiku. Bashō's poetry was instrumental in developing this unusual form of poetry. His writing was not limited to poetry, however. He also wrote literary criticism, numerous essays, and travelogues. In his travel diaries Bashō included haiku written during lengthy trips he made throughout his native Japan.

Matsuo Bashō's father was a samurai, a member of the military class in ancient Japan. Bashō initially wanted to become a samurai like his father. But while he was still young, he became the personal servant of a young noble. This young noble, along with Bashō's teacher, inspired him to write poetry. After the death of his master, Bashō spent several years in the capital of Kyoto and then in Edo (Tokyo). While there he decided to make writing and the teaching of writing his vocation. Bashō was a thoughtful, meditative, and upright person. His reputation as a teacher and poet was well established during his lifetime and remains so today.

About the Poems

1. The compactness of the heroic couplet was especially suited for displaying the intellectual ingenuity admired by the Neoclassic poets and for making important truths beautiful and memorable. Which of Alexander Pope's couplets is your favorite? Why?

2. The ballad of "Bonnie George Campbell" is about the powerful Campbell clan of the western Highlands. The Campbells were hated by all other clans; thus, they had to be fighters as well as tillers of the soil. This ballad shows clan rivalry from a woman's point of view. The facts are few but eloquently expressive. Notice the careful organization and the use of repetition with variation. What effect is produced by the repetition of the second stanza?

3. Compare Sir Walter Scott's ballad with the Robin Hood ballad on pp. 19-21. What specific characteristics does each reveal about the legendary figure of Robin Hood? Which poem has a more familiar tone?

4. "Sonnet 29" is one of the many sonnets in which Shakespeare extols a friendship. As you learned in the headnote, the thought in an English sonnet is usually distributed over three quatrains and a concluding couplet. Sometimes, however, as in "Sonnet 29," a major break occurs after the eighth line in the manner of the Italian form. What prompts this sudden shift in thought and feeling? How is it an evidence of the power of love and a compliment to his friend?

5. From the two examples given, what would you say are some characteristics of an effective limerick?

6. What are some characteristics of a well-written haiku?

SHAPE

These last poems are **shaped poems.** *In a shaped poem the author has, in addition to the normal challenge of adjusting sound and syntax to sense, the problem of arranging the sentences on the page to form a specific picture. Notice how each poet's visualization supports the subject of his poem.*

400-Meter Freestyle

by Maxine Kumin

```
The  gun  full  swing  the  swimmer  catapults  and  cracks
                                                          s
                                                           i
                                                          x
feet  away  onto  that  perfect  glass  he  catches  at
  a
 n
  d
    throws  behind  him  scoop  after  scoop  cunningly  moving
                                                                t
                                                                 h
                                                                e
    water  back  to  move  him  forward.  Thrift  is  his  wonderful
  s
 e
  c
    ret;  he  has  schooled  out  all  extravagance.  No  muscle
                                                            r
                                                             i
                                                            p
    ples  without  compensation  wrist  cock  to  heel  snap  to
  h
 i
  s
    mobile  mouth  that  siphons  in  the  air  that  nurtures
                                                           h
                                                            i
                                                           m
    at  half  an  inch  above  sea  level  so  to  speak.
  T
 h
  e
    astonishing  whites  of  the  soles  of  his  feet  rise
                                                           a
                                                            n
                                                           d
    salute  us  on  the  turns.  He  flips,  converts,  and  is  gone
  a
 l
  l
    in  one.  We  watch  him  for  signs.  His  arms  are  steady  at
                                                                   t
                                                                    h
                                                                   e
```

catch, his cadent* feet tick in the stretch, they know
t
h
  e
lesson well. Lungs know, too; he does not list for
                                              a
                                                i
                                            r
he drives along on little sips carefully expended
b
u
  t
that plum red heart pumps hard cries hurt how soon
                                              i
                                            t
                                          s
near one more and makes its final surge TIME: 4:25:9

cadent: rhythmic

About the Author

Maxine Kumin (1925-) is a talented contemporary American poet noted especially for her clear style and use of realistic imagery. Her greatest skill lies in her ability to convey a sight, a sound, or an experience in such a way that the reader is able to share that sensation.

Kumin was born in Philadelphia, Pennsylvania, and attended Radcliffe College, Cambridge, in Massachusetts. She has three children and lives in Massachusetts. Active in many scholarly and educational organizations, she has years of experience as a teacher and lecturer. In 1973 she won a Pulitzer Prize for *Up Country*. Although she has enjoyed success as a novelist and an author of children's books, she has had her greatest success as a poet. She writes best on ordinary, unsensational themes, and her work is always fresh and original.

The title of her poem "400-Meter Freestyle" refers not only to the subject matter of the poem (swimming) but also to the writing of the poem itself ("meter," "freestyle").

A Christmas Tree

William Burford

Star,

If you are

A love compassionate,

You will walk with us this year.

We face a glacial distance, who are here   5

Huddld

At your feet.

About the Author

The American poet William Burford (1927-) received an extensive education. He studied at Amherst College in Massachusetts, at the Sorbonne in Paris as a Fulbright scholar, and finished his education at Johns Hopkins in Baltimore, where he later was a professor. Burford has also held teaching positions at Southern Methodist University in Dallas, Texas; at the University of Texas, Austin; and at the University of Montana. Besides teaching, Burford also once served as an assistant to the president of an oil-refining company. Despite his rather learned background, Burford's poetry is delightfully simple.

The Altar

George Herbert

A   broken   altar,   Lord,   thy   servant   rears,
Made   of   a   heart   and   cemented   with   tears;

Whose   parts   are   as   thy   hand   did   frame;
No   workman's   tool   hath   touched   the   same.

A   heart   alone   5
Is   such   a   stone
As   nothing   but
Thy   power   doth   cut.
Wherefore   each   part
Of   my   hard   heart   10
Meets   in   this   frame
To   praise   thy   name;

That   if   I   chance   to   hold   my   peace,
These   stones   to   praise   thee   may   not   cease.

Oh,   let   thy   blessed   sacrifice   be   mine,   15
And   sanctify   this   altar   to   be   thine.

About the Author

George Herbert (1593-1632) was born into an aristocratic English family. He received his education at Cambridge, where he took the prominent position of public orator when he was twenty-seven years old. Through the guidance of his mother, who had befriended the gifted but struggling poet John Donne, Herbert chose to enter a career in the Anglican church, and he devoted the remainder of his short life to this calling. Herbert forsook his own political career and social reputation because the inner workings of Parliament and court life disappointed him. Much of the poetry Herbert later wrote reflects this surrender of personal ambition to God and the peace of mind and heart that results from such surrender.

Although Herbert died at thirty-nine, his parishioners had already come to recognize his godliness. They realized, too, that he was a man who could easily have taken a more illustrious position than that of country parson of Bemerton. After Herbert's death, a friend privately published *The Temple,* a volume of Herbert's verse. Its simple, musical style and its originality in meter and form quickly attracted attention. Herbert's poems touch every area of Christian life, especially the surrender of the individual's will to God's will. Our selection is taken from *The Temple.* Its twin themes are God's love and mercy in providing justification by faith and the proper responses of the human heart: contrition and sanctification.

About the Poems

1. What qualities of the swimmer does the poem "400-Meter Freestyle" make you admire?
2. In Kumin's poem, what is the arrangement of the lines on the page meant to show?
3. In addition to a swimming race, what might the title refer to?
4. Why do you think Burford spelled *Huddld* as he did?
5. What is the theme of Herbert's poem "The Altar"?

5

UNIT FIVE

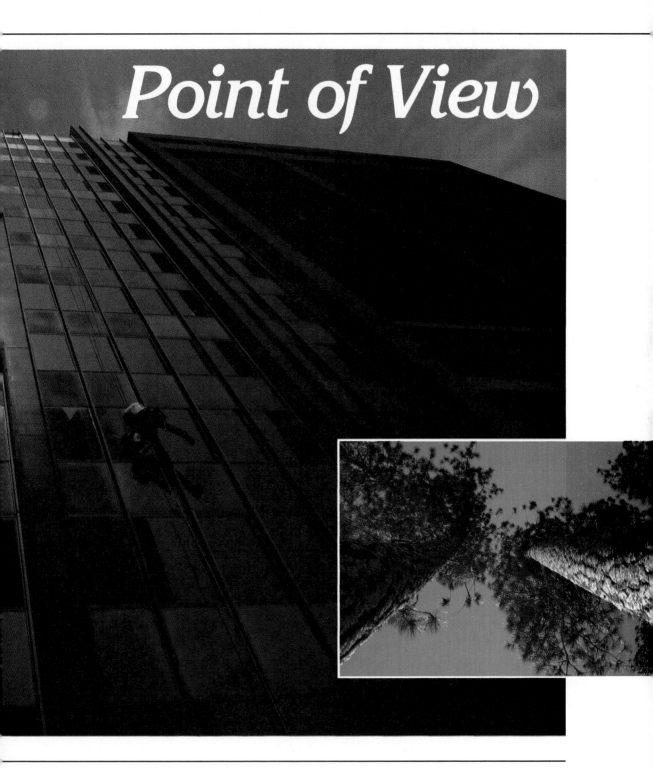

Point of View

Point of View

We have all heard such comments as, "That's not the way I remember it," or, "That's not how he told the story." Experience confirms that a single incident can be viewed in several ways. It is also true that the one who tells the story, how much the storyteller knows, and how much he reveals determine what we learn from the narrative and how we interpret what we learn. In literature, as in life, incidents can be perceived from several points of view. Essentially, there are three possible viewpoints from which a writer of fiction might tell his story.

The first viewpoint we will discuss, the **omniscient viewpoint,** is the most versatile. When using this point of view the author tells his story in third person, and as the storyteller he "knows all." He can tell us not only what the characters do but also how they think and feel. In her story "Through the Tunnel" (pp. 22-30), Doris Lessing provides a good illustration. Look, for example, at the following excerpt:

> Next morning, when it was time for the routine of swimming and sunbathing, his mother said, "Are you tired of the usual beach, Jerry? Would you like to go somewhere else?"
>
> "Oh, no!" he said quickly, *smiling at her out of that unfailing impulse of contrition—a sort of chivalry.* Yet, walking down the path with her, he blurted out, "I'd like to go down and have a look at those rocks down there."
>
> *She gave the idea her attention. It was a wild-looking place, and there was no one there;* but she said, "Of course, Jerry. When you've had enough, come to the big beach. Or just go straight back to the villa, if you like." She walked away, that bare arm, now slightly reddened from yesterday's sun, swinging. *And he almost ran after her again, feeling it unbearable that she should go by herself, but he did not.*
>
> *She was thinking, Of course he's old enough to be safe without me. Have I been keeping him too close? He mustn't feel he ought to be with me. I must be careful.*
>
> He was an only child, eleven years old. She was a widow. *She was determined to be neither possessive nor lacking in devotion. She went worrying to her beach.*

As the italicized portions show, Lessing is no mere observer. She does not simply record what her characters say and do; she reveals the thoughts that prompt their actions and the contradictory feelings that arise from those actions. She also gives us insight into why the characters are as they are.

The second viewpoint, the **limited-omniscient viewpoint,** resembles the first in that the author tells the story in third person. There is, however, an important difference between this second point of view and the first. In the limited-omniscient viewpoint, the author "gets inside" only *one* of the characters, usually the central character. Let's look again at the excerpt from Lessing's story, this time from the limited-omniscient point of view.

> Next morning, when it was time for the routine of swimming and sunbathing, his mother said, "Are you tired of the usual beach, Jerry? Would you like to go somewhere else?"
>
> "Oh, no!" he said quickly, *smiling at her out of that unfailing impulse of contrition—*

a sort of chivalry. Yet, walking down the path with her, he blurted out, "I'd like to go and have a look at those rocks down there."

"Of course, Jerry," she said. "When you've had enough, come to the big beach. Or just go straight back to the villa, if you like." She walked away, that bare arm, now slightly reddened from yesterday's sun, swinging. *And he almost ran after her again, feeling it unbearable that she should go by herself, but he did not.*

He was an only child, eleven years old. She was a widow.

Notice that Jerry's "inner life" is still revealed, but references to the mother's thoughts and feelings have been deleted. We have narrowed our scope somewhat. We do, however, still have the author's third person commentary (the last sentence in the excerpt, for example). The advantage to this viewpoint is that it draws us more completely into Jerry's world by focusing our attention on his ideas and attitudes. In other words, we have exchanged some breadth for greater intimacy.

The **first-person viewpoint** provides an even more intimate perspective than either the omniscient or limited-omniscient point of view. When using this viewpoint, the author drops his third-person persona and *becomes* one of the characters, sometimes a minor character but most often a major character.

> *Next morning, when it was time for the routine of swimming and sunbathing, my mother said, "Are you tired of the usual beach, Jerry? Would you like to go somewhere else?"*
>
> *"Oh, no!" I said quickly, smiling at her out of that unfailing impulse of contrition— a sort of chivalry. Yet, walking down the path with her, I blurted out, "I'd like to go down and have a look at those rocks down there."*
>
> *"Of course, Jerry," she said. "When you've had enough, come to the big beach. Or just go straight back to the villa, if you like." As she walked away, I watched her bare arm, now slightly reddened from yesterday's sun, swinging. And I almost ran after her again, feeling it unbearable that she should go by herself, but I did not.*

Notice that in this excerpt Jerry, the central character, tells us the story. We see only what he sees, feel only what he feels, and think only as he thinks. We have gained an even greater sense of intimacy and immediacy. At the same time, however, we have narrowed our scope considerably by removing other characters' perceptions and the author's third-person commentary.

An author may use any one or any combination of the three viewpoints discussed. In this unit's stories you will find examples of all three. To discover the point of view each author chose, ask yourself the following questions: Who is telling the story? How much does the storyteller know? How much does he reveal? How does this information influence what I consider to be the message of the story? Once you have determined the point of view, ask yourself one final question: How does the author's choice of viewpoint clarify or enhance the story's message?

The Forty Thieves

retold by Andrew Lang

"The Forty Thieves" is one of two hundred stories from the frame tale, The Thousand and One Nights, *also called* The Arabian Nights. *This oriental work became known to Europe in French translation early in the eighteenth century. Constant references to its two hundred tales indicate their popularity in England from the 1780s onward. The frame tale that links the stories is also interesting. The Sultan Shahriyar had the custom of executing each of his brides on the morning after their wedding. The beautiful and clever Scheherazade volunteered to marry him and end this cruel practice. On the evening of her wedding day, she charmed the sultan with a tale of marvels, but left it unfinished. Scheherazade was granted a one-day's stay of execution to finish her story. She finished the fascinating tale the next night, then began another, breaking off as before at the climax of the story. Again she was granted a reprieve. After granting 1,001 such reprieves, Shahriyar, who had by this time fallen in love with Scheherazade, changed his rule. Scheherazade had won his heart by first capturing his imagination.*

"The Forty Thieves," like all of The Arabian Nights, *is an exciting story; it contains, however, certain elements that are in conflict with a Christian viewpoint. As you read, notice the types of characters presented. How would you describe each? Notice, too, how the story is resolved.*

In a town in Persia there dwelt two brothers, one named Cassim, the other Ali Baba. Cassim was married to a rich wife and lived in plenty, while Ali Baba had to maintain his wife and children by cutting wood in a neighboring forest and selling it in the town. One day, when Ali Baba was in the forest, he saw a troop of men on horseback, coming towards him in a cloud of dust. He was afraid they were robbers, and climbed into a tree for safety. When they came up to him and dismounted, he counted forty of them. They unbridled their horses and tied them to trees. The finest man among them, whom Ali Baba took to be their captain, went a little way among some bushes, and said: "Open, Sesame!" so plainly that Ali Baba heard him. A door opened in the rocks, and having made the troop go in, he followed them, and the door shut again of itself. They stayed some time inside, and Ali Baba, fearing they might come out and catch him, was forced to sit patiently in the tree. At last the door opened again, and the Forty Thieves came out. As the Captain went in last he came out first, and made them all pass by him; he then closed the door, saying: "Shut, Sesame!" Every man bridled his horse and mounted, the Captain put himself at their head, and they returned as they came.

Then Ali Baba climbed down and went to the door concealed among the bushes, and said: "Open, Sesame!" and it flew open. Ali Baba, who expected a dull, dismal place, was greatly surprised to find it large and well lighted, and hollowed by the hand of man in the form of a vault, which received the light from an opening in the ceiling. He saw rich bales of merchandise—silk, stuff-brocades, all piled together, and gold and silver in heaps, and money in leather purses. He went in and the door shut behind him. He did not look at the silver, but brought out as many bags of gold as he thought his asses, which were browsing outside, could carry, loaded them with the bags, and hid it all with fagots.* Using the words: "Shut, Sesame!" he closed the door and went home.

---

fagots: a bundle of branches or twigs

Then he drove his asses into the yard, shut the gates, carried the money bags to his wife, and emptied them out before her. He bade her keep the secret, and he would go and bury the gold. "Let me first measure it," said his wife. "I will go borrow a measure of someone, while you dig the hole." So she ran to the wife of Cassim and borrowed a measure. Knowing Ali Baba's poverty, the sister was curious to find out what sort of grain his wife wished to measure, and artfully put some suet* at the bottom of the measure. Ali Baba's wife went home and set the measure on the heap of gold, and filled it and emptied it often, to her great content. She then carried it back to her sister, without noticing that a piece of gold was sticking to it, which Cassim's wife perceived directly* her back was turned. She grew very curious, and said to Cassim when he came home: "Cassim, your brother is richer than you. He does not count his money, he measures it." He begged her to explain this riddle, which she did by showing him the piece of money and telling him where she found it. Then Cassim grew so envious that he could not sleep,

and went to his brother in the morning before sunrise. "Ali Baba," he said showing him the gold piece, "you pretend to be poor and yet you measure gold." By this Ali Baba perceived that through his wife's folly Cassim and his wife knew their secret, so he confessed all and offered Cassim a share. "That I expect," said Cassim; "but I must know where to find the treasure, otherwise I will discover all, and you will lose all." Ali Baba, more out of kindness than fear, told him of the cave, and the very words to use. Cassim left Ali Baba, meaning to be beforehand with him and get the treasure for himself. He rose early next morning, and set out with ten mules loaded with great chests. He soon found the place, and the door in the rock. He said: "Open, Sesame!" and the door opened and shut behind him. He could have feasted his eyes all day on the treasures, but he now hastened to gather together as much of it as possible; but when he was ready to go he could not remember what to say for thinking of his great riches. Instead of "Sesame," he said: "Open, Barley!" and the door remained fast. He named several different sorts of grain, all but the right one, and the door still stuck fast. He was so frightened at the danger he was in that he had as much forgotten the word as if he had never heard it.

---

suet: hard fatty tissues from cattle or sheep, used in cooking or making tallow
directly: as soon as

About noon the robbers returned to their cave, and saw Cassim's mules roving about with great chests on their backs. This gave them the alarm; they drew their sabers, and went to the door, which opened on their Captain's saying: 'Open, Sesame!' Cassim, who heard the trampling of their horses' feet, resolved to sell his life dearly, so when the door opened he leaped out and threw the Captain down. In vain, however, for the robbers with their sabers soon killed him. On entering the cave they saw all the bags laid ready, and could not imagine how anyone had got in without knowing their secret. They cut Cassim's body into four quarters, and nailed them up inside the cave, in order to frighten anyone who should venture in, and went away in search of more treasure.

As night drew on Cassim's wife grew very uneasy, and ran to her brother-in-law, and told him where her husband had gone. Ali Baba did his best to comfort her, and set out to the forest in search of Cassim. The first thing he saw on entering the cave was his dead brother. Full of horror, he put the body on one of his asses, and bags of gold on the other two, and, covering all with some fagots, returned home. He drove the two asses laden with gold into his own yard, and led the other to Cassim's house. The door was opened by the slave Morgiana, whom he knew to be both brave and cunning. Unloading the ass, he said to her: "This is the body of your master, who has been murdered, but whom we must bury as though he had died in his bed. I will speak with you again, but now tell your mistress I am come." The wife of Cassim, on learning the fate of her husband, broke out into cries and tears, but Ali Baba offered to take her to live with him and his wife if she would promise to keep his counsel and leave everything to Morgiana; whereupon she agreed, and dried her eyes.

Morgiana, meanwhile, sought an apothecary and asked him for some lozenges. "My poor master," she said, "can neither eat nor speak, and no one knows what his distemper is." She carried home the lozenges and returned next day weeping, and asked for an essence only given to those just about to die. Thus, in the evening, no one was surprised to hear the wretched shrieks and cries of Cassim's wife and Morgiana, telling everyone that Cassim was dead. The day after Morgiana went to an old cobbler near the gates of the town who opened his stall early, put a piece of gold in his hand, and bade him follow her with his needle and thread. Having bound his eyes with a handkerchief, she took him to the room where the body lay, pulled off the bandage, and bade him sew the quarters together, after which she covered his eyes again and led him home. Then they buried Cassim, and Morgiana his slave followed him to the grave, weeping and tearing her hair, while Cassim's wife stayed at home uttering lamentable cries. Next day she went to live with Ali Baba, who gave Cassim's shop to his eldest son.

The Forty Thieves, on their return to the cave, were much astonished to find Cassim's body gone and some of their money-bags. "We are certainly discovered," said the Captain, "and shall be undone if we cannot find out who it is that knows our secret. Two men must have known it; we have killed one, we must now find the other. To this end one of you who is bold and artful must go into the city dressed as a traveller, and discover whom we have killed, and whether men talk of the strange manner of his death. If the messenger fails he must lose his life, lest we be betrayed." One of the thieves started up and offered to do this, and after the rest had highly commended him for his bravery he disguised himself, and happened to enter the town at daybreak, just by Baba Mustapha's stall. The thief bade him good-day, saying: "Honest man, how can you possibly see to stitch at your age?" "Old as I am," replied the cobbler, "I have very good eyes, and you will believe me when I tell you that I sewed a dead body together in a place where I had less light than I have now." The robber was overjoyed at his good fortune, and, giving him a piece of gold, desired to be shown the house where he stitched up the dead body. At first Mustapha refused, saying that he had been blindfolded; but when the robber gave him another piece of gold he began to think he might remember the turnings if blindfolded as before. This means succeeded; the robber partly led him, and was partly guided by him, right in front of Cassim's house, the door of which the robber marked with a piece of chalk. Then, well pleased, he bade farewell to Baba Mustapha and returned to the forest. By-and-by Morgiana, going out, saw the mark the robber had made, quickly guessed that some mischief was brewing, and fetching a piece of chalk marked two or three doors on each side, without saying anything to her master or mistress.

The thief, meantime, told his comrades of his discovery. The Captain thanked him, and bade him show him the house he had marked. But when they came to it they saw that five or six of the houses were chalked in the same manner. The guide was so confounded that he knew not what answer to make, and when they returned he was at once beheaded for having failed. Another robber was despatched, and, having won over Baba Mustapha, marked the house in red chalk; but Morgiana being again too clever for them, the second messenger was put to death also. The Captain now resolved to go himself, but, wiser than the others, he did not mark the house, but looked at it so closely that he could not fail to remember it. He returned, and ordered his men to go into the neighboring villages and buy nineteen mules, and thirty-eight leather jars, all empty, except one which was full of oil. The Captain put one of his men, fully armed, into each, rubbing the outside of the jars with oil from the full vessel. Then the nineteen mules were loaded with thirty-seven robbers in jars, and the jar of oil, and reached the town by dusk. The Captain stopped his mules in front of Ali Baba's house, and said to Ali Baba, who was sitting outside for coolness: "I have brought some oil from a distance to sell at tomorrow's market, but it is now so late that I know not where to pass the night, unless you will do me the favor to take me in." Though Ali Baba had seen the Captain of the robbers in the forest, he did not recognize him in the disguise of an oil merchant. He bade him welcome, opened his gates for the mules to enter, and went to Morgiana to bid her prepare a bed and supper for his guest. He brought the stranger into his hall, and after they had supped went again to speak to Morgiana in the kitchen, while the Captain went into the yard under pretense of seeing after his mules, but really to tell his men what to do. Beginning at the first jar and ending at the last, he said to each man: "As soon as I throw some stones from the window of the chamber where I lie, cut the jars open with your knives and come out, and I will be with you in a trice."* He returned to the house, and Morgiana led him to his chamber. She then told Abdallah, her fellow-slave, to set on the pot to make some broth for her master, who had gone to bed. Meanwhile her lamp went out, and she had no more oil in the house. "Do not be uneasy," said Abdallah; "go into the yard and take some out of one of those jars." Morgiana thanked him for his advice, took the oil pot, and went into the yard. When she came to the first jar the robber inside said softly: "Is it time?"

---

trice: short period of time

Any other slave but Morgiana, on finding a man in the jar instead of the oil she wanted, would have screamed and made a noise; but she, knowing the danger her master was in, bethought herself of a plan, and answered quietly: "Not yet, but presently." She went to all the jars, giving the same answer, till she came to the jar of oil. She now saw that her master, thinking to entertain an oil merchant,

had let thirty-eight robbers into his house. She filled her oil pot, sent back to the kitchen, and, having lit her lamp, went again to the oil jar and filled a large kettle full of oil. When it boiled she went and poured enough oil into every jar to stifle and kill the robber inside. When this brave deed was done she went back to the kitchen, put out the fire and the lamp, and waited to see what would happen.

In a quarter of an hour the Captain of the robbers awoke, got up, and opened the window. As all seemed quiet he threw down some little pebbles which hit the jars. He listened, and as none of his men seemed to stir he grew uneasy, and went down into the yard. On going to the first jar and saying: "Are you asleep?" he smelt the hot boiled oil, and knew at once that his plot to murder Ali Baba and his household had been discovered. He found all the gang were dead, and, missing the oil out of the last jar, became aware of the manner of their death. He then forced the lock of a door leading into a garden, and climbing over several walls made his escape. Morgiana heard and saw all this, and, rejoicing at her success, went to bed and fell asleep.

At daybreak Ali Baba arose, and, seeing the oil jars there still, asked why the merchant had not gone with his mules. Morgiana bade him look in the first jar and see if there was any oil. Seeing a man, he started back in terror. "Have no fear," said Morgiana; "the man cannot harm you: he is dead." Ali Baba, when he had recovered somewhat from his astonishment, asked what had become of the merchant. "Merchant!" said she, "He is no more a merchant than I am!" and she told him the whole story, assuring him that it was a plot of the robbers of the forest, of whom only three were left, and that the white and red chalk marks had something to do with it. Ali Baba at once gave Morgiana her freedom, saying that he owed her his life. They then buried the bodies in Ali Baba's garden, while the mules were sold in the market by his slaves.

The Captain returned to his lonely cave, which seemed frightful to him without his lost companions, and firmly resolved to avenge them by killing Ali Baba. He dressed himself carefully, and went into town, where he took lodgings in an inn. In the course of a great many journeys to the forest he carried away many rich stuffs and much fine linen, and set up a shop opposite that of Ali Baba's son. He called himself Cogia Hassan, and as he was both civil and well dressed he soon made friends with Ali Baba's son, and through him with Ali Baba, whom he was continually asking to sup with him. Ali Baba, wishing to return his kindness, invited him into his house and received him smiling, thanking him for his kindness to his son. When the merchant was about to take his leave Ali Baba stopped him, saying: "Where are you going, sir, in such haste? Will you not stay and sup with me?" The merchant refused, saying that he had a reason; and, on Ali Baba's asking him what that was, he replied: "It is, sir, that I can eat no victuals that have any salt in them." "If that is all," said Ali Baba, "let me tell you that there shall be no salt in either the meat or the bread that we eat tonight." He went to give this order to Morgiana, who was much surprised. "Who is this man," she said, "who eats no salt with his meat?" "He is an honest man, Morgiana," returned her master; "therefore do as I bid you." But she could not withstand a desire to see this strange man, so she helped Abdallah to carry up the dishes, and saw in a moment that Cogia Hassan was the robber Captain, and carried a dagger under his garment. "I am not surprised," she said to herself, "that this wicked man, who intends to kill my master, will eat no salt* with him; but I will hinder his plans."

eat no salt: make no tacit pledge of friendship

She sent up the supper by Abdallah, while she made ready for one of the boldest acts that could be thought on. When the dessert had been served, Cogia Hassan was left alone with Ali Baba and his son, whom he thought to make drunk and then to murder them. Morgiana, meanwhile, put on a headdress like a dancing-girl's, and clasped a girdle round her waist, from which hung a dagger with a silver hilt, and said to Abdallah: "Take your tabor,* and let us go and divert* our master and his guest." Abdallah took his tabor and played before Morgiana until they came to the door, where Abdallah stopped playing and Morgiana made a low courtsy. "Come in, Morgiana," said Ali Baba, and, turning to Cogia Hassan, he said: "She's my slave and my housekeeper." Cogia Hassan was by no means pleased, for he feared that his chance of killing Ali Baba was gone for the present; but he pretended great eagerness to see Morgiana, and Abdallah began to play and Morgiana to dance. After she had performed several dances she drew her dagger and made passes with it, sometimes pointing it at her own breast, sometimes at her master's, as if it were part of the dance. Suddenly, out of breath, she snatched the tabor from Abdallah with her left hand, and, holding the dagger in her right, held out the tabor to her master. Ali Baba and his son put a piece of gold into it, and Cogia Hassan, seeing that she was coming to him, pulled out his purse to make her a present, but while he was putting his hand into it Morgiana plunged the dagger into his heart.

---

tabor: small drum
divert: entertain

"Unhappy girl!" cried Ali Baba and his son, "what have you done to ruin us?" "It was to preserve you, master, not to ruin you," answered Morgiana. "See here," opening the false merchant's garment and showing the dagger; "see what an enemy you have entertained! Remember, he would eat no salt with you, and what more would you have? Look at him! he is both the false oil merchant and the Captain of the Forty Thieves."

Ali Baba was so grateful to Morgiana for thus saving his life that he offered her to his son in marriage, who readily consented, and a few days after the wedding was celebrated with great splendor. At the end of the year Ali Baba, hearing nothing of the two remaining robbers, judged they were dead, and set out to the cave. The door opened on his saying: "Open, Sesame!" He went in, and saw that nobody had been there since the Captain left it. He brought away as much gold as he could carry, and returned to town. He told his son the secret of the cave, which his son handed down in his turn, so the children and grandchildren of Ali Baba were rich to the end of their lives.

About the Story

1. Does the author desire you to have more sympathy for Cassim or Ali Baba?
2. After analyzing each character's actions, can you say that any of them are really noble? Why or why not?
3. Though the resolution of the story is in some ways satisfying, it is not completely acceptable from a moral standpoint. Explain why.
4. What is the story's point of view?
5. List at least four phrases or sentences from the story's text that support the point of view you chose.

The Open Window

Saki (H. H. Munro)

Known as Saki, *a psuedonym taken from the cupbearer in* The Rubaiyat of Omar Khayyám, *H. H. Munro is noted for his unique ability to entertain his readers with witty, ironic tales. Saki's stories are often a strange mixture of emotions. "The Open Window" is a good example of this quality in Saki's work. One moment you will find yourself amused, the next moment appalled. Saki's impersonal style, however, prevents his stories from becoming macabre and keeps them solidly in the realm of entertainment.*

"My aunt will be down presently, Mr. Nuttel," said a very self-possessed young lady of fifteen; "in the meantime you must try and put up with me."

Framton Nuttel endeavored to say the correct something which should duly flatter the niece of the moment without unduly discounting the aunt that was to come. Privately he doubted more than ever whether these formal visits on a succession of total strangers would do much toward helping the nerve cure which he was supposed to be undergoing.

"I know how it will be," his sister had said when he was preparing to migrate to this rural retreat; "you will bury yourself down there and not speak to a living soul, and your nerves will be worse than ever from moping. I shall just give you letters of introduction to all the people I know there. Some of them, as far as I can remember, were quite nice."

Framton wondered whether Mrs. Sappleton, the lady to whom he was presenting one of the letters of introduction, came into the nice division.

"Do you know many of the people round here?" asked the niece, when she judged that they had had sufficient silent communion.

"Hardly a soul," said Framton. "My sister was staying here, at the rectory, you know, some four years ago, and she gave me letters of introduction to some of the people here."

He made the last statement in a tone of distinct regret.

"Then you know practically nothing about my aunt?" pursued the self-possessed young lady.

"Only her name and address," admitted the caller. He was wondering whether Mrs. Sappleton was in the married or widowed state. An undefinable something about the room seemed to suggest masculine habitation.

"Her great tragedy happened just three years ago," said the child; "that would be since your sister's time."

"Her tragedy?" asked Framton; somehow in this restful country spot tragedies seemed out of place.

"You may wonder why we keep that window wide open on an October afternoon," said the niece, indicating a large French window that opened on to a lawn.

"It is quite warm for the time of the year," said Framton; "but has that window got anything to do with the tragedy?"

"Out through that window, three years ago to a day, her husband and her two young brothers went off for their day's shooting. They never came back. In crossing the moor to their favorite snipeshooting ground they were all three engulfed in a treacherous piece of bog. It had been that dreadful wet summer, you know, and places that were safe in other years gave way suddenly without warning. Their bodies were never recovered. That was the dreadful part of it." Here the child's voice lost its self-possessed note and became falteringly human. "Poor aunt always thinks that they will come back some day, they and the little brown spaniel that was lost with them, and walk in at that window just as they used to do. That is why the window is kept open every evening till it is quite dusk. Poor dear aunt, she has often told me how they went out, her husband with his white waterproof coat over his arm, and Ronnie, her youngest brother, singing, 'Bertie, why do you bound?' as he always did to tease her, because she said it got on her nerves. Do you know, sometimes on still, quiet evenings like this, I almost get a creepy feeling that they will all walk in through that window—"

She broke off with a little shudder. It was a relief to Framton when the aunt bustled into the room with a whirl of apologies for being late in making her appearance.

"I hope Vera has been amusing you?" she said.

"She has been very interesting," said Framton.

"I hope you don't mind the open window," said Mrs. Sappleton briskly; "my husband and brothers will be home directly from shooting, and they always come in this way. They've

been out for snipe in the marshes today, so they'll make a fine mess over my poor carpets. So like you men-folk, isn't it?"

She rattled on cheerfully about the shooting and the scarcity of birds, and the prospects for duck in the winter. To Framton it was all purely horrible. He made a desperate but only partially successful effort to turn the talk on to a less ghastly topic; he was conscious that his hostess was giving him only a fragment of her attention, and her eyes were constantly straying past him to the open window and the lawn beyond. It was certainly an unfortunate coincidence that he should have paid his visit on this tragic anniversary.

"The doctors agree in ordering me complete rest, an absence of mental excitement, and avoidance of anything in the nature of violent physical exercise," announced Framton, who labored under the tolerably wide-spread delusion that total strangers and chance acquaintances are hungry for the least detail of one's ailments and infirmities, their cause and cure. "On the matter of diet they are not so much in agreement," he continued.

"No?" said Mrs. Sappleton, in a voice which only replaced a yawn at the last moment. Then she suddenly brightened into alert attention—but not to what Framton was saying.

"Here they are at last!" she cried. "Just in time for tea, and don't they look as if they were muddy up to the eyes!"

Framton shivered slightly and turned toward the niece with a look intended to convey sympathetic comprehension. The child was staring out through the open window with dazed horror in her eyes. In a chill shock of nameless fear Framton swung around in his seat and looked in the same direction.

In the deepening twilight three figures were walking across the lawn toward the window; they all carried guns under their arms, and one of them was additionally burdened with a white coat hung over his shoulders. A tired brown spaniel kept close at their heels. Noiselessly they neared the house, and then a hoarse young voice chanted out of the dusk: "I said, Bertie, why do you bound?"

Framton grabbed wildly at his stick and hat; the hall-door, the gravel-drive, and the front gate were dimly noted stages in his headlong retreat. A cyclist coming along the road had to run into the hedge to avoid imminent collision.

"Here we are, my dear," said the bearer of the white mackintosh, coming in through the window; "fairly muddy, but most of it's dry. Who was that who bolted out as we came up?"

"A most extraordinary man, a Mr. Nuttel," said Mrs. Sappleton; "could only talk about his illnesses, and dashed off without a word of good-bye or apology when you arrived. One would think he had seen a ghost."

"I expect it was the spaniel," said the niece calmly; "he told me he had a horror of dogs. He was once hunted into a cemetery somewhere on the banks of the Ganges by a pack of pariah dogs, and had to spend the night in a newly dug grave with the creatures snarling and grinning and foaming just above him. Enough to make anyone lose their nerve."

Romance at short notice was her specialty.

About the Story

1. This story uses the limited omniscient point of view throughout most of the story. Which character does Saki use to view the events?
2. In the last four paragraphs of the story, Saki changes point of view. What is the point of view of these last four paragraphs?
3. Why do you think he chose to change viewpoint at the end of the story?
4. At what point do you begin to suspect that Mrs. Sappleton's niece was making up her story?
5. Notice the names Saki chose for his characters. What impression do the following two names give you: Framton Nuttel and Mrs. Sappleton?

About the Author

Hector Hugh Munro (1870-1916) was born in Akyab, Burma, while his father served in the British armed forces. His father returned to India after Mrs. Munro's death, leaving the boy and his older brother and sister in the care of a grandmother and two severe, complaining aunts. The three children, cloistered in a stuffy English country house, were reared in a stifling atmosphere with no encouragement to be imaginative. Thus, the three of them created their own little world and made their own adventures.

Munro wrote under the pen name of "Saki." His upbringing affected his writing profoundly, especially his characterization and moral tone. Many characters and situations are taken from childhood memories. The moral tone of Saki's writing is often said to be the result of the eccentricity and mental cruelty of his aunts. Although Saki's sister denies accusations of cruelty in the characters her brother created, even she draws startling parallels between them and their real-life counterparts. Children in Saki's writing often deal cruelly with some oppressive adult figure. They display a studied indifference to wrongdoing. S.P.B. Mais notes that "Munro's understanding of children can only be explained by the fact that he was in many ways a child himself: his sketches betray a harshness, a love of practical jokes, a craze for animals of the most exotic breeds, a lack of mellow geniality that hint very strongly at the child in the man." Saki's greatest skill seems to be his ability to present life's little miseries with ironic humor.

In 1893 Saki returned to Burma as a part of the British military police force there. His short stay (a year and one month) furnished him with creative fuel for his imaginative stories. During his youth Saki was more adept at drawing than writing; however, only a few years after his return to England, he decided to make writing his career. His first works were political satires (*Not So Stories,* 1902). Saki then began to travel widely as a newspaper correspondent in Eastern Europe. His *Reginald* sketches (1904) are humorous short stories recounting the adventures and opinions of a young Englishman. His output of short stories was enormous.

Saki readily enlisted when World War I broke out, and he displayed great character and concern for others while serving in France. He was killed there by enemy fire in 1916.

After the Battle

Joseph A. Altsheler

Like "The Open Window," the point of view of this story is limited omniscient. Its ending also has an ironic twist. The tone of the selection, however, is more melancholy than fanciful, and the theme more didactic than entertaining. What do you learn from the character of Joyce? How do his actions at the end of the story reveal the story's theme?

The falling dusk quenched the fury of the battle. The cannon glimmered but feebly on the dim horizon like the sputter of a dying fire. The shouts of combatants were unheard, and Dave Joyce concluded that the fighting was over for that day at least. In his soul he was glad of it.

"Pardner," he said to the wounded man, "the battle has passed on an' left us here like a canoe stuck on a sand bank. I think the fightin' is over, but if it ain't we're out of it anyhow, an' I don't know any law why we shouldn't make ourselves as comf'table as things will allow."

"If there's anythin' done," said the wounded man, "you'll have to do it, for I can't walk, an' I can't move, except when there's a bush for me to grab hold of and pull myself along by."

"That's mighty bad," said Joyce, sympathetically. "Where did you say that bullet took you?"

"I got it in my right leg here," the other replied, "an' I think it broke the bone. Leastways the leg ain't any more use to me than if it was dead, though it hurts like tarnation sometimes. I guess it'll be weeks before I walk again."

"Maybe I could do somethin' for you," said Joyce, "if there was a little more light. I guess I'll take a look, anyhow. I haven't been two years in the army not to know anythin' about bullet wounds."

He bent down and with his pocket-knife cut away a patch of the faded blue cloth from the wounded man's leg.

"I guess I'd better not fool with that," he said, looking critically at the wound. "The bullet's gone all the way through, but the blood's clotted up so thick over the places that the bleedin' has stopped. You won't die if you don't move too much an' start that wound to bleedin' again."

"That's consolin'," said the wounded man; "but, since I can't move, I don't know what's to become of me but to lay here on the field an' die anyway."

"Don't you fret," said Joyce, cheerfully. "I'll take care of you. You're Fed. and I'm Confed., but you're hurt an' I ain't, an' if the case was the other way I'd expect you to do as much for me. Besides, I've lost my regiment in the shuffle, and the chances are if I tried to find it again to-night I'd run right into the middle of the Yankee army, and that would mean Camp Chase for your humble servant, which is a bunk he ain't covetin' very bad just now. So I guess it'll be the safe as well as the right thing for me to do to stick by you. Listen to that! Just hear them crickets chirpin', will you!"

There was a blaze of light in the west, followed by a crash which seemed to roll around the horizon and set all the trees of the forest to trembling. When the echoes were lost beyond the hills the silence became heavy and portentous. The night was hot and sticky, and the powdery vapor that still hung over the field crept into Joyce's throat and made him cough for breath.

"Thunderation!" he said at length, still looking in the direction in which the light had blazed up. "I guess at least a dozen of the big cannon must have been fired at once then. Can't some fellows get enough fightin' in the daytime, without pluggin' away in the night-time too? Now I come of fightin' stock myself— I'm from Kentucky—but twelve hours out of the twenty-four always 'peared to me to be enough for that sort of thing. Besides, it's awful hot to-night, too."

"It was hotter than this for me a while ago," said the wounded man.

"So it was, so it was," said Joyce, apologetically, "an' I mustn't forget you, either. Let 'em fight over there if they want to, an' if they're big enough fools to spile a night that way when they might be restin'. What you need just now is water. I think there's a spring runnin' out of the side of that hill there. If you'll listen you'll hear it tricklin' away, so cool and refreshin' like. I guess it was tricklin' that same way, just as calm an' peaceful as Sunday mornin', while the battle was goin' on round here. Don't you feel as if a little water would help you mightily, pardner?"

"'Twould so," said the wounded man. "I'm burnin' up inside, an' if you'd get a big drink of it I'd think you were mighty nigh good enough to be one of the twelve apostles."

"It's easy enough for me to do it," said Joyce. "I'll be back in a minute."

He took off his big slouch hat and walked toward the source of the trickling sound. From beneath an overhanging rock in the side of the hill near by a tiny stream of water flowed. After a fall of five feet it plunged into a little basin which it had hallowed out for itself in the rock, and formed a deep and cool little pool. Around the edge of the pool the tender green grass grew. The overflow from it wandered away in a little rill through the woods.

"Thunder, but ain't this purty?" exclaimed Joyce, forgetting that the wounded man was out of hearing. "It's just like our springhouse back in old Kentuck. I've put out butter-crocks an' milk-buckets a hundred times to cool in our pool when I was a boy. Wish I had some of them things now!"

The stirring of peaceful memories caused Joyce to linger a little, in forgetfulness of the wounded man. It was cool in the shadow of the hill, and the gay little stream tinkled merrily in his ears. He would have liked to remain there, but he pulled himself together with an impatient jerk, filled the crown of his hat with the limpid water, and started back to the relief of the wounded man.

He followed the channel of the stream for a little way, and as he turned to step across it he noticed the increasing depth of its waters.

"It's dammed up," he muttered. "I wonder what's done that."

Then he started back shuddering and spilled half the water from his hat, for he had almost stepped on the body of a man that had fallen across the channel of the poor little rivulet, checking the flow of its waters and deepening the stream.

The body lay face downward, and Joyce could not see the wound that had caused death. But as he stooped down he saw again the broad red flash in the west, and heard the heavy crash of the cannon.

"Will them cannon always be hungry?" he muttered. "But I guess I must give this poor little stream which 'ain't done no harm to anybody the right of way again."

He stooped and pulled the body to one side. With a thankful rush and gurgle the waters of the recent pool sped on in their natural channel, and Joyce returned to the fountain-head to fill his hat again.

He found the wounded man waiting with patience.

"I was gone longer than I ought to have been. Did you think I had left you, pardner?" asked Joyce.

"No," said the man. "I didn't believe you'd play that kind of a trick on me."

"An' so I haven't," said Joyce, "an' for your faith in me I've brought you a hatful of the nicest an' freshest an' coolest water you ever put your lips to in all your born days. Raise your head up, there, an' drink."

The wounded man drank and drank, and then when the hat was emptied he laid his head back in the grass and sighed as if he were in heaven.

"I must say that you 'pear to like water, pardner," said Joyce.

"Like it?" said the wounded man. "Wait till you've been wounded, an' then you'll know what it is to want water. Why, till you brought it I felt as if my inside was full of hot coals an' I'd burn all up if I didn't get something mighty quick to put the fire out."

"Then I reckon I've stopped a whole conflagration," said Joyce, "an' with mighty little trouble to myself, too. But I don't wonder that you get thirsty on a night like this. Thunderation, but ain't it clammy!"

He sat down on the fallen tree and drew his coat-sleeve across his brow. Then he held up the sleeve: it was wet with sweat. There was no wind. The night had brought no coolness. The thick and heavy atmosphere hung close to the earth and coiled the throats and nostrils of the two men.

"I wish I was at home sleepin' on the hall floor," said Joyce. "I'll bet it would be cool there."

The wounded man made no answer, but turned his face up to the sky and drew in great mouthfuls of the warm air.

"Them fools over yonder 'pear to have their dander up yet," said Joyce, pointing to the west, where the alternate flashing and rumbling

showed that the battle still lingered. "I thought the battle was over long ago, but I guess it ain't. I've knowed some fools in my time, but the fellows that would keep on fightin' on a hot night like this must be the biggest fools."

Then the two lay quite still for a while, watching the uneasy rising and falling of the night battle. Had they not known so much of war, they might have persuaded themselves that the flashes they saw were flashes of heat-lightning and the rumbling but the rumbling of summer thunder. But they knew better. They knew it was men and not the elements that fought.

"It's mighty curious," said Joyce, "how the sand's all gone out of me for the time. To-day I felt as if I could whip the whole Yankee army all by myself. To-night I don't want to fight anythin'. I'm as peaceful in temper as a little lamb friskin' about in our field at home. I hope that there fightin' won't come our way; at least not to-night. How are you feelin', pardner?"

"Pretty well for a wounded man," replied

the other; "but I'd like to have some more water."

"Then I'm the man to get it for you," said Joyce, springing up. "An' I'm goin' to see if I can't get somethin' to eat, too, for my innards are cryin' cupboard mighty loud. There's dead men layin' aroun' here, an' there may be somethin' in their haversacks.* I hate to rob the dead, but if they've got grub we need it more'n they do."

---

haversacks: bags slung over the shoulder used to carry supplies

---

He returned with another hatful of water, which the wounded man drank eagerly, gratefully. Then he went back and searched in the grass and bushes for the fallen. Presently he came in great glee, and triumphantly held up two haversacks.

"Luck, pardner!" he exclaimed. "Great luck! Bully luck! One of these I got off a dead Fed. and t'other off a dead Confed., and both must have been boss foragers, for in one haversack there's a roast chicken an' in t'other there's half a b'iled ham, an' in both there's plenty of bread. I haven't had such luck before in six months. You're a Yank, pardner, and a Northerner, an' maybe you don't know much about the vanities of roast chicken an' cold b'iled ham. But it's time you did know. I've come from the field at home when I'd been plowin' all day, an' my appetite was as sharp as a razor an' as big as our barn. I'd put up old Pete, our black mule that I'd been plowin' with, an' feed him; then I'd go to the house an' kinder loosen my waist-ban', an' mother would say to me, 'Come in the kitchen, Dave; your supper's ready for you.' Say, pardner, you ought to see me then. There'd be a pitcher of cold buttermilk from the spring-house, and one dish of roast chicken, an' another of cold ham, an' all for me, too. An' say, pardner, I can taste that ham now. When you eat one piece you want another, an' then another, an' you keep on till there ain't any left on the dish, an' then you lean back in your chair an' wish that when you come to die you'd feel as happy as you do then. Pardner, I wish them times was back again."

"I wish so too," said the wounded man.

"We can't have 'em back, at least not now," said Joyce, cheerily, "but we can make believe, an' it'll be mighty good make-believe, too, for we've got the ham an' the chicken, an' we can get cold water to take the place of cold milk. I guess you can use your arms all right; so you can spread this ham an' chicken out on the grass an' I'll see if I can't find a canteen to keep the water in. Say pardner, we'll have a banquet, you an' me, that's what we'll have."

The stalwart young fellow, full of boyish delight at the idea that the thought of home had suggested to him, swung off in search of the canteen. He found not one alone, but two. Then he returned clanking them together to indicate his success. As he came up he called out, in his hearty voice:

"Pardner, is the supper-table ready? Have you got the knives an' forks? You needn't min' about the napkins. I guess we can get along without 'em just this once."

"All ready," said the wounded man; "an' I guess I can keep you company at this ham an' chicken an' bread, for I'm gettin' a mighty sharp edge on my appetite too."

"So much the better," said Joyce. "There's plenty for both, an' it wouldn't be good manners for me to eat by myself."

He sat down on the grass in front of the improvised repast, and placed one canteen beside the wounded man and the other beside himself.

"Now, pardner," he said, "we'll drink to each other's health, an' then we'll charge the ham an' chicken with more vim than either of us ever charged a breastwork."

They drank from the canteens; and then they made onslaught upon the provisions. Joyce ate for a while in deep and silent content, forgetting the heat and the battle which still lowered in the west. But presently, when his appetite was dulled, he remembered the cannonade.

"There they go again!" he said. "Boom! Boom! Boom! Won't them fellows ever get enough? I thought I was hungry, but the cannon over there 'pear to be hungrier. I suppose there ain't men enough in all this country to stop up their iron throats. But bang away! They don't bother us, do they, pardner? They can't spile this supper, for all their boomin' an' flashin'.'"

The wounded man bowed assent and took another piece of the ham.

Joyce leaned back on the grass, held up a chicken leg in his hand, and looked contemplatively at it.

"Ain't it funny, pardner," he said, "that you, a Tommy Yank, an' me, a Johnny Reb, are sittin' here, eatin' grub together, as friendly as two brothers, when we ought to be killin' each other? I don't know what Jeff Davis an' old Abe Lincoln will say about it when they hear of the way you an' me are doin'.'"

The wounded man laughed.

"You can say that I was your prisoner," he said, "when they summon you before the courtmartial. An' so I am, if you choose to make me. I can't resist."

"I'm thinkin' more about gettin' back safe to our army than makin' prisoners," said Joyce, as he flung the chicken bone, now bare, into the bushes.

"That may be hard to do," said the wounded man; "for neither you nor me can tell which way the armies will go. Listen to that boomin'! Wasn't it louder than before? That fightin' must be movin' round nearer to us."

"Let it move," said Joyce. "I tell you I've had enough of fightin' for one day. That battle can take care of itself. I won't let it bother me. I don't want to shoot anybody."

"Is that the way you feel when you go into battle?" asked the wounded man.

"I can't say exactly," replied Joyce. "Of course when I go out in a charge with my regiment I want to beat the other fellows, but I don't hate 'em, no, not a bit. I've got nothin' against the Yanks. I've knowed some of 'em that was mighty good fellows. There ain't any of 'em that I want to kill. No, I'll take that back; there is one, just one, a bloody villain that I'd like to draw a bead on an' send a bullet through his skulkin' body."

"Who is that?" asked the wounded man; "an' why do you make an exception of him?"

Joyce remained silent for a moment or two and drew a long blade of grass restlessly through his fingers.

"It's not a pleasant story," he said at last, "an' it hurts me to tell it, but I made you ask the question, an' I guess I might as well tell you, 'cause I feel friendly toward you, pardner, bein' as we are together in distress, like two Robinson Crusoes, so to speak."

The wounded man settled himself in the grass like one who is going to listen comfortably to a story.

"It's just a yarn of the Kentuck hills," said Joyce, "an' a bad enough one, too. We're a good sort of people up there, but we're hot-blooded, an' when we get into trouble, as we sometimes do, kinfolks stan' together. I guess you're from Maine, or York State, or somewhere away up North, an' you can't understand us. But it's just as I say. Sometimes two men up in our hills fight, an' one kills the other. Then the dead man's brothers, an' sons if he's got any old enough, an' cousins, an' so on, take up their guns an' go huntin' for the man that killed him. An' the livin' man's brothers

an' sons' an' cousins an' so on take up their guns an' come out to help him. An' there you've got your feud, an' there's no tellin' how many years it'll run on, an' how many people will get killed in it.—Thunderation, but wasn't them cannon loud that time! The battle is movin' round toward us sure!"

Joyce listened a moment, but heard nothing more except the echoes.

"Our family got into one of them feuds," he said. "It was the Joyces and the Ryders. I's Dave Joyce, the son of Henry Joyce. I don't remember how the feud started; about nothin' much, I guess; but it was a red-hot one, I can tell you, pardner. It was fought fair for a long time, but at last Bill Ryder shot father from ambush and killed him. Father hadn't had much to do with the feud, either; he didn't like that sort of thing—didn't think it was right. I said right then that if I ever found the chance when I got big enough I'd kill Bill Ryder."

"Did you get the chance?" asked the wounded man.

"No," replied Joyce. "Country got too hot for Ryder, and he went away. He came back after a while, an' I was big enough to go gunnin' for him then, but the war broke out, an' off he went into the Union army before I could get a chance to draw a bead on him. I ain't heard of him since. Maybe he's been killed in battle an' his bones are bleachin' somewhere in the woods."

"Most likely," said the wounded man.

"There's no tellin'," said Joyce. "Still, some day when we're comin' up against the Yanks face to face I may see him before me, an' then I'll hold my gun steady an' shoot straight at him, instead of whoopin' like mad an' firin' lickety-split into the crowd, aimin' at nothin', as I generally do."

"It's a sad story, very sad for you," said the wounded man.

"Yes," said Joyce. "You don't have such

things as feuds up North, do you?"

"No," replied the other, "an' we're well off without 'em. Hark, there's the cannon again!"

"Yes, an' they keep creepin' round toward us with their infernal racket," said Joyce. "Cannon love to chaw up people an' then brag about it. But if them fellows are bent on fightin' all night I guess we'll have to give 'em room for it. What do you say to movin'? I've eat all I want, an' I guess you have too, an' we can take what's left with us."

"I don't know," said the wounded man. "My leg's painin' me a good deal, an' the grass is soft an' long here where I'm layin'. It makes a good bed, an' maybe I'd better stay where I am."

"I think not," said Joyce, decidedly. "That night fight's still swingin' down on us, an' if we stay too long them cannon'll feed on us too. We'd better move, pardner. Let me take a look at your wound. It's gettin' lighter, an' I can see better now. The moon's up, an' she's shinin' for all she's worth through them trees. Besides, them cannon-flashes help. Raise your head, pardner, an' we'll take a look at your wound together."

"I don't think you can do any good," said the wounded man. "It would be better not to disturb it."

"But we must be movin', pardner," said Joyce, a little impatiently. "See, the fight's warmin' up, an' it's still creepin' down on us. Seems to me I can almost hear the tramp of the men an' the rollin' of the cannon-wheels. What a blaze that was! I say, it's time for us to be goin'. If we stay here we're likely to be ground to death under the cannon-wheels, if we ain't shot first. Just let me get a grip under your shoulders, pardner, an' I'll take you out of this."

The cannon flamed up again, and the deep thunder filled all the night.

"Listen how them old iron throats are growlin' an' mutterin'," said Joyce; "an' they're saying' it's time for us to be travelin'."

"I believe," said the wounded man, "that I would rather stay where I am an' take my chances. If I move I'm afraid I'll break open my wound. Besides, I think you're mistaken. It seems to me that the fight's passin' round to the right of us."

"Passin' to the right of us nothin'," said Joyce. "It's coming straight this way, with no more respect for our feelin's than if you an' me was a couple of field-mice."

The wounded man made no answer.

"Do you think, pardner," asked Joyce, slight offence showing in his voice, "that the Yanks may come this way an' pick you up an' then you won't be a prisoner? Is that your game?"

As his companion made no answer, Joyce continued:

"You don't think, pardner, that I want to hold you a prisoner, do you? an' you a wounded man, too, that I picked up on the battle-field and that I've eat and drank with? Why, that ain't my style."

He waited for an answer and as none came he was seized with a sudden alarm.

"You ain't dead, pardner?" he cried. "What if he's dead while I've been standin' here talkin' an' wastin' time!"

He bent over to take a look at the other's face, but the wounded man, with a sudden and convulsive movement, writhed away from him and struck at him with his open hand.

"Keep away!" he cried. "Don't touch me! Don't come near me! I won't have it! I won't have it!"

"Thunderation, pardner!" exclaimed Joyce; "what do you mean? I ain't goin' to harm you. I want to help you." Then he added, pityingly, "I guess he's got the fever an' gone out of his head. So I'll take him along whether he wants to go or not."

He bent over again, seized the wounded man by the shoulders, and forcibly raised him up. At the same moment the cannonade burst out afresh and with increased violence. A blaze of light played over the face of the wounded man, revealing and magnifying every line.

Joyce uttered no exclamation, but he dropped the man as if he had been a coiling serpent in his hands, and looked at him, an expression of hate and loathing creeping over his face.

"So," he said, at last, "this is the way I have found you?"

The wounded man lay as he had fallen, with his face to the earth.

"No wonder," said Joyce, "you wanted to keep your face hid in the grass! No wonder you hide it there now!"

"Oh, Dave! Dave!" exclaimed the man, springing to his knees with sudden energy, "don't kill me! Don't kill me, Dave!"

"Why shouldn't I kill you?" asked Joyce, scornfully. "What reason can you give why I shouldn't do it?"

"There ain't any. There ain't any. Oh, I know there ain't any," cried the wounded man. "But don't do it, Dave! Don't do it!"

"You murderer! You sneakin', ambushin' murderer!" said Joyce. "It's right for you to beg for your life an' then not get it! Hear them cannon! Hear how they growl, an' see the flash from their throats! They'd like to feed on you, but they won't. That sort of death is too good for the likes of you. The death for you is to be shot like a ravin' cur."

He drew the loaded pistol from his belt and cocked it with deliberate motion.

"Dave! Dave!" the man cried, dragging himself to Joyce's feet, "you won't do that! You can't! It would be murder, Dave, to shoot me here, me a wounded man that can't help myself!"

"You done it, an' worse," said Joyce. "Of all the men unburnt in hell I think the one who deserves to be there most is the man who hid in ambush and shot another in the back that had never harmed him."

"I know it, Dave, I know it!" cried the

wounded man, grasping Joyce's feet with both hands; "it was an awful thing to do, an' I've been sorry a thousand times that I done it, but all the sorrow in the world an' everythin' else that's in the world can't undo it now."

"That's so," said Joyce, "but it don't make any reason why the murderer ought to be kept on livin.' "

"It don't, Dave; you're right, I know; but I don't want to die!" cried the man. "I'm a coward, Dave, and I don't want to die by myself here in the woods an' in the dark!"

"You'll soon have light enough," said Joyce, "an' I won't shoot you."

He let down the hammer of his pistol and replaced the weapon in his belt.

"Oh, Dave! Dave!" exclaimed the man, kissing Joyce's foot. "I'm so glad you'll let me have my life. I know I ain't fit to live, but I want to live anyhow."

"I said I wouldn't shoot you," said Joyce, "but I never said I'd spare your life. See that blaze in the trees up there."

A few hundred yards away the forest had burst into flame. Sparks fell upon a tree and blazed up. Long red spirals coiled themselves around the trunk and boughs until the tree became a mass of fire, and then other tongues of flame leaped forward and seized other trees. There was a steady crackling and roaring, and the wind that had sprung up drove smoke and ashes and fiery particles before it.

"That," said Joyce, "is the wood on fire. Them cannon that's been makin' so much fuss done it. I've seen it often in battle when the cannon have been growlin'. The fire grows an' it grows, an it burns up everythin' in its way. The army is still busy fightin', an' the wounded, them that's hurt too bad to help theirselves, have to lay there on the ground an' watch the fire comin', an' sure to get 'em. By an' by it sweeps down on 'em, an' they shriek an' shriek, but that don't do you no good, for before long

the fire goes on, an' there they are, dead an' burnt to a coal. I tell you it's an awful death!"

The wounded man was silent now. He had drawn himself up a little, and was watching the fire as it leaped from tree to tree and devoured them one after another.

"That fire is comin' for us, an' the wind is bringin' it along fast," said Joyce, composedly, "but it's easy enough for me to get out of its way. All I've got to do is to go up the hill, an' the clearin's run for a long way beyond. I can stay up there an' watch the fire pass, an' you'll be down here right in its track."

"Dave!" cried the man, "you ain't goin' to let me burn to death right before your eyes?"

"That's what I mean to do," said Joyce. "I don't like to shoot a wounded man that can't help himself, an' I won't do it, but I ain't got no call to save you from another death."

"I'd rather be shot than burned to death," cried the man, in a frenzy.

"It's just the death for you," said Joyce.

Then the wounded man again dragged himself to the feet of Joyce.

"Don't do it, Dave!" he cried. "Don't leave me here to burn to death! Oh, I tell you, Dave, I ain't fit to die!"

"Take your hands off my feet," said Joyce. "I don't want 'em to touch me. There's too much blood on 'em."

"Don't leave me to the fire!" continued the man. "You've been kind to me to-night. Help me a little more, Dave, an' you'll be glad you done it when you come to die yourself!"

"I must be goin'," said Joyce, repulsing the man's detaining hands. "It's gettin' hot here now, an' that fire will soon be near enough to scorch my face. Good-by."

"For the sake of your own soul, Dave Joyce," cried the man, beating the ground with his hands, "don't leave me to be burned to a coal! Think, Dave, how we eat an' drank together to-night, like two brothers, an' how you waited on me an' brought the water an' the grub. You'll remember them things, Dave, when you come to die yourself!"

The fire increased in strength and violence. The flames ran up the trees, and whirled far above them in red coils that met and twined with each other, and then whirled triumphantly on in search of fresh fuel. A giant oak, burned through at the base and swept of all its young boughs and foliage, fell with a rending crash, a charred and shattered trunk. The flames roared, and the burning trees maintained an incessant crackling like a fire of musketry. The smoke through which the sparks of fire were sown in millions grew stifling.

"What a sight!" cried Joyce.

"Dave, you won't leave me to that?" cried Ryder.

Joyce drew down his hat over his eyes to shield them from the smoke. Then he stooped, lifted the wounded man upon his powerful shoulders, and went on over the hill.

About the Story

1. The story is told from which character's viewpoint?
2. Why do you think the author chose to view the story through this character's eyes?
3. How do Dave Joyce and Bill Ryder differ?
4. How is the story resolved?
5. What does the resolution reveal about Dave Joyce?
6. If Joyce had been the wounded man, how do you think Ryder would have treated him? Support your answer with examples from the story's text.

About the Author

At the turn of the century, Joseph A. Altsheler (1862-1919) became the most popular author of adventure stories for boys. He maintained this popularity well into the 1920s. Altsheler's stories gave his youthful readers drama, humor, and reliable history while improving their literary tastes. His well-constructed plots and skillful characterizations raised the standard of children's literature.

Altsheler's first story was written while he was editor of the New York *World,* a well-known magazine published three times weekly. One day, Altsheler needed a boy's adventure story to include in the magazine. Because none was forthcoming, Altsheler took it upon himself to fill the need. Although he had been working in journalism successfully, Altsheler found his true talent as an author of historical romances for young readers. His adventures dealt with the American West, American Indians, the Civil War, and World War I. Although Altsheler had no intention of becoming a children's author when he wrote his first story, his subsequent output (usually one or two books annually) helped him become one of America's favorite children's authors.

The Crime

Max Beerbohm

In this narrative essay Max Beerbohm pokes fun at a certain type of person. His good humor, however, makes the tone lighthearted and inoffensive. The structure of the essay, though simpler than it would be in short fiction, has a storylike quality. Notice, for example, the elements of plot in the narrative. Is there an inciting moment? Is there rising action? Where is the crisis? All of these elements serve to develop a specific idea. What is the idea Beerbohm is trying to get across?

On a bleak wet stormy afternoon at the outset of last year's Spring, I was in a cottage, all alone, and knowing that I must be all alone till evening. It was a remote cottage, in a remote county, and had been "let furnished" by its owner. My spirits are easily affected by weather, and I hate solitude. And I dislike to be master of things that are not mine. "Be careful not to break us," say the glass and china. "You'd better not spill ink on *me*," growls the carpet. "None of your dog's-earing, thumb-marking, backbreaking tricks *here!*" snarl the books.

The books in this cottage looked particularly disagreeable—horrid little upstarts of this and that scarlet or cerulean* "series" of "standard" authors. Having gloomily surveyed them, I turned my back on them, and watched the rain streaming down the latticed window, whose panes seemed likely to be shattered at any moment by the wind. I have known men who constantly visit the Central Criminal Court, visit also the scenes where famous crimes were committed, form their own theories of those crimes, collect souvenirs of those crimes, and call themselves

Criminologists. As for me, my interest in crime is, alas, merely morbid. I did not know, as those others would doubtless have known, that the situation in which I found myself was precisely of the kind most conducive to the darkest deeds. I did but bemoan it, and think of Lear in the hovel on the heath.* The wind howled in the chimney, and the rain had begun to sputter right down it, so that the fire was beginning to hiss in a very sinister manner. Suppose the fire went out! It looked as if it meant to. I snatched the pair of bellows that hung beside it. I plied them vigorously. "Now mind!—not *too* vigorously. We aren't yours!" they wheezed. I handled them more gently. But I did not release them till they had secured me a steady blaze. I sat down before that blaze. Despair had been warded off. Gloom, however, remained; and gloom grew. I felt that I should prefer any one's thoughts to mine. I rose, I returned to the books. A dozen or so of those which were on the lowest of the three shelves were full-sized, were octavo, looked as though they had been bought to be read. I would exercise my undoubted right to read one of them. Which of them? I gradually decided on a novel by a well-known writer whose works, though I had several times had the honor of meeting her, were known to me only by repute.

---

cerulean: sky blue
Lear in the hovel on the heath: an allusion to Shakespeare's *King Lear,* in which Lear, self-exiled and on the verge of madness, takes refuge from a storm in a small, miserable dwelling in the wilderness

I knew nothing of them that was not good. The lady's "output" had not been at all huge, and it was agreed that her "level" was high. I had always gathered that the chief characteristic of her work was its great "vitality." The book in my hand was a third edition of her latest novel, and at the end of it were numerous press-notices, at which I glanced for confirmation. "Immense vitality,"

yes, said one critic. "Full," said another, "of an intense vitality." "A book that will live," said a third. How on earth did he know that? I was, however, very willing to believe in the vitality of this writer for all present purposes. Vitality was a thing in which she herself, her talk, her glance, her gestures, abounded. She and they had been, I remembered, rather too much for me. The first time I met her, she said something that I lightly and mildly disputed. On no future occasion did I stem any opinion of hers. Not that she had been rude. Far from it. She had but in a sisterly, brotherly way, and yet in a way that was filially eager too, asked me to explain my point. I did my best. She was all attention. But I was conscious that my best, under her eye, was not good. She was quick to help me: she said for me just what I had tried to say, and proceeded to show me just why it was wrong. I smiled the gallant smile of a man who regards women as all the more adorable because logic is *not* their strong point, bless them! She asked—not aggressively, but strenuously, as one who dearly loves a joke—what I was smiling at. Altogether, a chastening encounter; and my memory of it was tinged with a feeble resentment. How she had scored. No man likes to be worsted in argument by a woman. And I fancy that to be vanquished by a feminine writer is the kind of defeat least of all agreeable to a man who writes. A "sex war," we are often told, is to be one of the features of the world's future—women demanding the right to do men's work, and men refusing, resisting, counter-attacking. It seems likely enough. One can believe anything of the world's future. Yet one conceives that not all men, if this particular evil come to pass, will stand packed shoulder to shoulder against all women. One does not feel that the dockers will be very bitter against such women as want to be miners, or the plumbers frown much upon the would-be steeple-jills. I myself have never had my sense of fitness jarred, nor a spark of animosity roused in me, by a woman practicing any of the fine arts—except the art of writing. That she should write a few little poems or *pensées,** or some impressions of a trip in a dahabieh* as far as (say) Biskra,* or even a short story or two, seems to me not wholly amiss, even though she do such things for publication. But that she should be an habitual, professional author, with a passion for her art, and a fountainpen and an agent, and sums down in advance of royalties on sales in Canada and Australia, and a profound knowledge of human character, and an essentially sane outlook, is somehow incongruous with my notions—my mistaken notions, if you will—of what she ought to be.

---

pensées: maxims; proverbs
dahabieh: large sailing boat used by travelers on the Nile
Biskra: a city in northeast Algeria

"Has a profound knowledge of human character, and an essentially sane outlook" said one of the critics quoted at the end of the book I had chosen. The wind and the rain in the chimney had not abated, but the fire was bearing up bravely. So would I. I would read cheerfully and without prejudice. I poked the fire and, pushing my chair slightly back, lest the heat should warp the book's covers, began Chapter I. A woman sat writing in a summer-house at the end of a small garden that overlooked a great valley in Surrey. The description of her was calculated to make her very admirable—a thorough *woman,* not strictly beautiful, but likely to be thought beautiful by those who knew her well; not dressed as though she gave much heed to her clothes, but dressed in a fashion that exactly harmonised with her special type. Her pen "travelled" rapidly across the foolscap, and while it did so she was described in more and

more detail. But at length she came to a "knotty point" in what she was writing. She paused, she pushed back the hair from her temples, she looked forth at the valley; and now the landscape was described, but not at all exhaustively, for the writer soon overcame her difficulty, and her pen travelled faster than ever, till suddenly there was a cry of "Mammy!" and in rushed a seven-year-old child, in conjunction with whom she was more than ever admirable; after which the narrative skipped back across eight years, and the woman became a girl giving as yet no token of future eminence in literature, but—I had an impulse which I obeyed almost before I was conscious of it.

Nobody could have been more surprised than I was at what I had done—done so neatly, so quietly and gently. The book stood closed, upright, with its back to me, just as on a book-shelf, behind the bars of the grate. There it was. And it gave forth, as the flames crept up the blue cloth sides of it, a pleasant though acrid smell. My astonishment had passed, giving place to an exquisite satisfaction. How pottering* and fumbling a thing was even the best kind of written criticism! I understood the contempt felt by the man of action for the man of words. But what pleased me most was that at last, actually, I, at my age, I of all people, had committed a crime—was guilty of a crime. I had power to revoke it. I might write to my bookseller for an unburnt copy, and place it on the shelf where this one had stood—this gloriously glowing one. I would do nothing of the sort. What I had done I had done. I would wear forever on my conscience the white rose of theft and the red rose of arson. If hereafter the owner of this cottage happened to miss that volume—let him! If he were fool enough to write me about it, would I share my grand secret with him? No. Gently, with his poker, I prodded that volume further among the coals. The all-but-consumed binding shot forth little tongues of bright colour—flamelets of sapphire, amethyst, emerald. Charming! Could even the author herself not admire them? Perhaps. Poor woman!—I had scored now, scored so perfectly that I felt myself to be almost a brute while I poked off the loosened black outer pages and led the fire on to pages that were but pale brown.

---

pottering: variant of *puttering*

These were quickly devoured. But it seemed to me whenever I left the fire to forage for itself it made little headway. I pushed the book over on its side. The flames closed on it, but presently, licking their lips, fell back, as though they had had enough. I took the tongs and put the book upright again, and raked it fore and aft. It seemed almost as thick as ever. With poker and tongs I carved it into two, three sections—the inner pages flashing white as when they were sent to the binders. Strange! Aforetime, a book was burnt now and again in the market-place by the common hangman. Was he, I wondered, paid by the hour? I had always supposed the thing quite easy for him—a bright little, brisk little conflagration, and so home. Perhaps other books were less resistant than this one? I began to feel that the critics were more right than they knew. Here was a book that had indeed an intense vitality, and an immense vitality. It was a book that would live—do what one might. I vowed it should not. I sub-divided it, spread it, redistributed it. Ever and anon my eye would be caught by some sentence or fragment of a sentence in the midst of a charred page before the flames crept over it. "lways loathed you, but," I remember; and "ning. Tolstoi was right." Who had always loathed whom? And what, what, had Tolstoi been right about? I had an absurd but genuine desire to know. Too late! Confound the woman!—she was scoring again. I furiously drove her pages into the yawning crimson jaws of the coals. Those jaws had lately been golden. Soon, to my horror, they seemed to be growing grey. They seemed to be closing—on nothing. Flakes of black paper, full-sized layers of paper brown and white, began to hide them from me altogether. I sprinkled a boxful of wax matches. I resumed the bellows. I lunged with the poker. I held a newspaper over the whole grate. I did all that inspiration could suggest, or skill accomplish. Vainly. The fire went out—darkly, dismally, gradually, quite out.

How she had scored again! But she did not know it. I felt no bitterness against her as I lay back in my chair, inert, listening to the storm that was still raging. I blamed only myself. I had done wrong. The small room became very cold. Whose fault was that but my own? I had done wrong hastily, but had done it and been glad of it. I had not remembered the words a wise king wrote long ago, that the lamp of the wicked shall be put out, and that the way of transgressors is hard.

About the Essay

1. Who is Beerbohm poking fun at in his essay?
2. What does Beerbohm really think of women novelists? Support your answer with specific quotations from the essay.
3. Why do you think the author chose to write the essay in first rather than third person?
4. What clues does Beerbohm give you that helped you discern that his intent is humorous?
5. What is the significance of the last sentence in the essay?

About the Author

As a youth, Max Beerbohm (1872-1956) delighted in sitting by the window observing people and noting their unique characteristics. This youthful pastime later provided valuable material for his humorous caricatures of important people. His skill in exaggerating the peculiarities of public figures was to make him famous. Though he was a drama critic for over a decade, it was as a witty artist and essayist that he achieved renown, both in his native England and in America.

Well loved for his sophisticated manners and wry humor, Beerbohm moved in social and literary circles that included such avant-garde figures as Oscar Wilde and George Bernard Shaw. He himself, however, lived an uneventful and scandal-free life; in fact, unlike the narrator of "The Crime," Beerbohm was a homebody who enjoyed solitude. He had been reared in a happy home filled with laughter and pleasant conversation. In such an atmosphere he acquired his impish sense of fun and love for jokes.

Beerbohm was a moralist who kept his homilies well mixed with humor. "The Crime" is an excellent example of his successful technique. Although we enjoy the humorous way the story's narrator mocks his own destructive act, Beerbohm does not neglect to stress the foolishness of a rash action. As the essay illustrates, his most perceptive criticisms were always the funniest; he was at his best when laughing at himself.

The Age of Miracles

Melville Davisson Post

Melville Davisson Post, like Poe and Doyle, is a master detective writer. He is outstanding not only in presenting detail and building suspense but also in capitalizing on the element of surprise. It is this surprise element that gives his stories their sensational quality, making them much like "The Gold-Bug" in style.

Like Doyle's Holmes, Post's Uncle Abner is a keen observer of detail and an avid student of human nature. Unlike Holmes, however, Abner is not eccentric, and his motive for unraveling complex problems is different from that of Holmes. It is a sense of moral responsibility, not the stimulation of a mental challenge, that motivates Abner. He is not a professional who simply enjoys his work, but rather a moral man who desires justice. Notice, for example, how the narrator views Abner. How does this narrator's view of the protagonist differ from the physician's view of Legrand in "The Gold-Bug" and Watson's view of Holmes in "The Adventure of the Beryl Coronet"?

The girl was standing apart from the crowd in the great avenue of poplars that led up to the house. She seemed embarrassed and uncertain what to do, a thing of April emerging into summer.

Abner and Randolph marked her as they entered along the gravel road.

They had left their horses at the gate, but she had brought hers inside, as though after some habit unconsciously upon her.

But half-way to the house she had remembered and got down. And she stood now against the horse's shoulder. It was a black hunter, big and old, but age marred no beauty of his lines. He was like a horse of ebony, enchanted out of the earth by some Arabian magic, but not yet by that magic awakened into life.

The girl wore a long, dark riding-skirt, after the fashion of the time, and a coat of hunter's pink. Her dark hair was in a great wrist-thick plait. Her eyes, too, were big and dark, and her body firm and lithe from the out-of-doors.

"Ah!" cried Randolph, making his characteristic gesture, "Prospero has been piping in this grove. Here is a daughter of the immortal morning! We grow old, Abner, and it is youth that the gods love."

My uncle, his hands behind him, his eyes on the gravel road, looked up at the bewitching picture.

"Poor child," he said; "the gods that love her must be gods of the valleys and not gods of the hills."

"Ruth amid the alien corn! Is it a better figure, Abner? Well, she has a finer inheritance than these lands; she has youth!"

"She ought to have both," replied my uncle. "It was sheer robbery to take her inheritance."

"It was a proceeding at law," replied the Justice. "It was the law that did the thing, and we cannot hold the law in disrespect."

"But the man who uses the law to accomplish a wrong, we can so hold," said Abner. "He is an outlaw, as the highwayman and the pirate are."

He extended his arm toward the great house sitting at the end of the avenue.

"In spite of the sanction of the law, I hold this dead man for a robber. And I would have wrested these lands from him, if I could. But your law, Randolph, stood before him."

"Well," replied the Justice, "he takes no gain from it; he lies yonder waiting for the grave."

"But his brother takes," said Abner, "and this child loses."

The Justice, elegant in the costume of the time, turned his ebony stick in his fingers.

"One should forgive the dead," he commented in a facetious note; "it is a mandate of the Scripture."

"I am not concerned about the dead," replied Abner. "The dead are in God's hands. It is the living who concern me."

"Then," cried the Justice, "you should forgive the brother who takes."

"And I shall forgive him," replied Abner, "when he returns what he has taken."

"Returns what he has taken!" Randolph laughed. "Why, Abner, the devil could not filch coins out of the clutches of old Benton Wolf."

"The devil," said my uncle, "is not an authority that I depend on."

"A miracle of Heaven, then," said the Justice. "But, alas, it is not the age of miracles."

"Perhaps," replied Abner, his voice descending into a deeper tone, "but I am not so certain."

They had come now to where the girl stood, her back against the black shoulder of the horse. The morning air moved the yellow leaves about her feet. She darted out to meet them, her face aglow.

"How do you do, Julia?" cried Randolph. "I have hardly seen you since you were no taller than my stick, and told me that your name was 'Pete-George,' and that you were a circus-horse, and offered to do tricks for me."

"I remember," she said. "it was up there on the porch!"

"And so it was!" cried Randolph, embarrassed.

He kissed the tips of the girl's fingers and the shadow in her face fled.

For the man's heart was good, and he had the manner of a gentleman. But it was Abner that she turned to in her dilemma.

"I forgot," she said, "and almost rode into the house. Do you think I could leave the horse here? He will stand if I drop the rein."

Then she went on to make her explanation. She wanted to see the old house that had been so long her home. This was the only opportunity, to-day, when all the countryside came to the dead man's burial. She thought she might come, too, although her motive was no tribute of respect.

She put her hand through Abner's arm and he looked down upon her, grave and troubled.

"My child," he said, "leave the horse where he stands and come with me, for my motive, also, is no tribute of respect; and you go with a better right than I do."

"I suppose," the girl hesitated, "that one ought to respect the dead, but this man—these men—I cannot."

"Nor can I," replied my uncle. "If I do not respect a man when he is living, I shall not pretend to when he is dead. One does not make a claim upon my honor by going out of life."

They went up the avenue among the yellow poplar leaves and the ragweed and fennel springing up along the unkept gravel.

It was a crisp and glorious morning. The frost lay on the rail fence. The spider-webs stretched here and there across the high grasses of the meadows in intricate and bewildering

lace-work. The sun was clear and bright, but it carried no oppressive heat as it drew on in its course toward noon.

The countryside had gathered to see Adam Wolf buried. It was a company of tenants, the idle and worthless mostly, drawn by curiosity. For in life the two old men who had seized upon this property by virtue of a defective acknowledgment to a deed, permitted no invasion of their boundary.

Everywhere the lands were posted; no urchin fished and no schoolboy hunted. The green perch, fattened in the deep creek that threaded the rich bottom lands, no man disturbed. But the quail, the pheasant, the robin and the meadow-lark, old Adam pursued with his fowling-piece. He trampled about with it at all seasons. One would have believed that all the birds of heaven had done the creature some unending harm and in revenge he had declared a war. And so the accident by which he met his death was a jeopardy of the old man's habits, and to be looked for when one lived with a fowling-piece in one's hands and grew careless in its use.

The two men lived alone and thus all sorts of mystery sprang up around them, gaining in grim detail at every story-teller's hand. It had the charm and thrilling interest of an adventure, then, for the countryside to get this entry.

The brothers lived in striking contrast. Adam was violent, and his cries and curses, his hard and brutal manner were the terror of the poor man who passed at night that way, or the urchin overtaken by darkness on his road home. But Benton got about his affairs in silence, with a certain humility of manner, and a mild concern for the opinion of his fellows. Still, somehow, the poor man and the urchin held him in a greater terror. Perhaps because he had got his coffin made and kept it in his house, together with his clothes for burial. It seemed uncanny thus to prepare against his dissolution and to bargain for the outfit, with anxiety to have his shilling's worth.

And yet, with this gruesome furniture at hand, the old man, it would seem, was in no contemplation of his death. He spoke sometimes with a marked savor and an unctuous kneading of the hands of that time when he should own the land, for he was the younger and by rule should have the expectancy of life.

There was a crowd about the door and filling the hall inside, a crowd that elbowed and jostled, taken with a quivering interest, and there to feed its maw of curiosity with every item.

The girl wished to remain on the portico, where she could see the ancient garden and the orchard and all the paths and byways that had been her wonderland of youth, but Abner asked her to go in.

Randolph turned away, but my uncle and the girl remained some time by the coffin. The rim of the dead man's forehead and his jaw were riddled with bird-shot, but his eyes and an area of his face below them, where the thin nose came down and with its lines and furrows made up the main identity of features, were not disfigured. And these preserved the hard stamp of his violent nature, untouched by the accident that had dispossessed him of his life.

He lay in the burial clothes and the coffin that Benton Wolf had provided for himself, all except the gloves upon his hands. These the old man had forgot. And now when he came to prepare his brother for a public burial, for no other had touched the man, he must needs take what he could find about the house, a pair of old, knit gloves with every rent and moth-hole carefully darned, as though the man had sat down there with pains to give his brother the best appearance that he could.

This little touch affected the girl to tears,

so strange is a woman's heart. "Poor thing!" she said. And for this triviality she would forget the injury that the dead man and his brother had done to her, the loss they had inflicted, and her long distress.

She took a closer hold upon Abner's arm, and dabbed her eyes with a tiny kerchief.

"I am sorry for him," she said, "for the living brother. It is so pathetic."

And she indicated the old, coarse gloves so crudely darned and patched together.

But my uncle looked down at her, strangely, and with a cold, inexorable* face.

---

inexorable: incapable of being persuaded by entreaty

"My child," he said, "there is a curious virtue in this thing that moves you. Perhaps it will also move the man whose handiwork it is. Let us go up and see him."

Then he called the Justice.

"Randolph," he said, "come with us."

The Justice turned about. "Where do you go?" he asked.

"Why, sir," Abner answered, "this child is weeping at the sight of the dead man's gloves, and I thought, perhaps, that old Benton might weep at them too, and in the softened mood return what he has stolen."

The Justice looked upon Abner as upon one gone mad.

"And be sorry for his sins! And pluck out his eye and give it to you for a bauble! Why, Abner, where is your common sense? This thing would take a miracle of God."

My uncle was undisturbed.

"Well," he said, "come with me, Randolph, and help me to perform that miracle."

He went out into the hall and up the wide old stairway, with the girl, in tears, upon his arm. And the Justice followed, like one who goes upon a patent and ridiculous fool's errand.

They came into an upper chamber, where a great bulk of a man sat in a padded chair looking down upon his avenue of trees. He looked with satisfaction. He turned his head about when the three came in and then his eyes widened in among the folds of fat.

"Abner and Mr. Randolph and Miss Julia Clayborne!" he gurgled. "You come to do honor to the dead!"

"No, Wolf," replied my uncle, "we come to do justice to the living."

The room was big, and empty but for chairs and an open secretary of some English make. The pictures on the wall had been turned about as though from lack of interest in the tenant. But there hung in a frame above the secretary— with its sheets of foolscap, its iron ink-pot and quill pens—a map in detail, and the written deed for the estate that these men had taken in their lawsuit. It was not the skill of any painter that gave pleasure to this mountain of a man; not fields or groves imagined or copied for their charm, but the fields and groves that he possessed and mastered. And he would be reminded at his ease of them and of no other.

---

foolscap: a large sheet of writing paper

The old man's eyelids fluttered an instant as with some indecision, then he replied, "It was kind to have this thought of me. I have been long neglected. A little justice of recognition, even now, does much to soften the sorrow at my brother's death." Randolph caught at his jaw to keep in the laughter. And the huge old man, his head crouched into his billowy shoulders, his little reptilian eye shining like a crum of glass, went on with his speech.

"I am the greater moved," he said, "because you have been aloof and distant with me. You, Abner, have not visited my house, nor you, Randolph, although you live at no great dis-

tance. It is not thus that one gentleman should treat another. And especially when I and my dead brother, Adam, were from distant parts and came among you without a friend to take us by the hand and bring us to your door."

He sighed and put the fingers of his hands together.

"Ah, Abner," he went on, "it was a cruel negligence, and one from which I and my brother Adam suffered. You, who have a hand and a word at every turning, can feel no longing for this human comfort. But to the stranger, alone, and without the land of his nativity, it is a bitter lack."

He indicated the chairs about him.

"I beg you to be seated, gentlemen and Miss Clayborne. And overlook that I do not rise. I am shaken at Adam's death."

Randolph remained planted on his feet, his face now under control. But Abner put the child into a chair and stood behind it, as though he were some close and masterful familiar.

"Wolf," he said, "I am glad that your heart is softened."

"My heart—softened!" cried the man. "Why, Abner, I have the tenderest heart of any of God's creatures. I cannot endure to kill a sparrow. My brother Adam was not like that. He would be for hunting the wild creatures to their death with firearms. But I took no pleasure in it."

"Well," said Randolph, "the creatures of the air got their revenge of him. It was a foolish accident to die by."

"Randolph," replied the man, "it was the very end and extreme of carelessness. To look into a fowling-piece, a finger on the hammer, a left hand holding the barrel halfway up, to see if it was empty. It was a foolish and simple habit of my brother, and one that I abhorred and begged him to forego, again and again, when I have seen him do it.

"But he had no fear of any firearms, as

though by use and habit he had got their spirit tamed—as trainers, I am told, grow careless of wild beasts, and jugglers of the fangs and poison of their reptiles. He was growing old and would forget if they were loaded."

He spoke to Randolph, but he looked at Julia Clayborne and Abner.

The girl sat straight and composed, in silence. The body of my uncle was to her a great protecting presence. He stood with his broad shoulders above her, his hands on the back of the chair, his face lifted. And he was big and dominant, as painters are accustomed to draw Michael in Satan's wars.

The pose held the old man's eye, and he moved in his chair; then he went on, speaking to the girl.

"It was kind of you, Abner, and you, Randolph, to come in to see me in my distress, but it was fine and noble in Miss Julia Clayborne. Men will understand the justice of the law and by what right it gives and takes. But a child will hardly understand that. It would be in nature for Miss Clayborne in her youth, to hold the issue of this lawsuit against me and my brother Adam, to feel that we had wronged her; had by some unfairness taken what her father bequeathed to her at his death, and always regarded as his own. A child would not see how the title had never vested, as our judges do. How possession is one thing, and the title in fee simple another and distinct. And so I am touched by this consideration."

Abner spoke then.

"Wolf," he said, "I am glad to find you in this mood, for now Randolph can write his deed, with consideration of love and affection instead of the real one I came with."

The old man's beady eye glimmered and slipped about.

"I do not understand, Abner. What deed?"

"The one Randolph came to write," replied my uncle.

"But, Abner," interrupted the Justice, "I did not come to write a deed." And he looked at my uncle in amazement.

"Oh yes," returned Abner, "that is precisely what you came to do."

He indicated the open secretary with his hand.

"And the grantor, as it happens, has got everything ready for you. Here are foolscap and quill pens and ink. And here, exhibited for your convenience, is a map of the lands with all the metes* and bounds. And here," he pointed to the wall, "in a frame, as though it were a work of art with charm, is the court's deed. Sit down, Randolph, and write." And such virtue is there in a dominant command, that the Justice sat down before the secretary and began to select a goose quill.

---

metes: a boundary line

Then he realized the absurdity of the direction and turned about.

"What do you mean, Abner?" he cried.

"I mean precisely what I say," replied my uncle. "I want you to write a deed."

"But what sort of deed," cried the astonished Justice, "and by what grantor, and to whom, and for what lands?"

"You will draw a conveyance," replied Abner, "in form, with covenants of general warranty for the manor and lands set out in the deed before you and given in the plat. The grantor will be Benton Wolf, esquire, and the grantee Julia Clayborne, infant, and mark you, Randolph, the consideration will be love and affection, with a dollar added for the form."

The old man was amazed. His head, bedded into his huge shoulders, swung about; his pudgy features worked; his expression and his manner changed; his reptilian eyes hardened; he puffed with his breath in gusts.

"Not so fast, my fine gentleman!" he gurgled. "There will be no such deed."

"Go on, Randolph," said my uncle, "let us get this business over."

"But, Abner," returned the Justice, "it is fool work, the grantor will not sign."

"He will sign," said my uncle, "when you have finished, and seal and acknowledge—go on!"

"But, Abner, Abner!" the amazed Justice protested.

"Randolph," cried my uncle, "will you write, and leave this thing to me?"

And such authority was in the man to impose his will that the bewildered Justice spread out his sheet of foolscap, dipped his quill into the ink and began to draw the instrument, in form and of the parties, as my uncle said. And while he wrote, Abner turned back to the gross old man.

"Wolf," he said, "must I persuade you to sign the deed?"

"Abner," cried the man, "do you take me for a fool?"

He had got his unwieldy body up and defiant in the chair.

"I do not," replied my uncle, "and therefore I think that you will sign."

The obese old man spat violently on the floor, his face a horror of great folds.

"Sign!" he sputtered. "Fool, idiot, madman! Why should I sign away my lands?"

"There are many reasons," replied Abner calmly. "The property is not yours. You got it by a legal trick; the Judge who heard you was bound by the technicalities of language. But you are old, Wolf, and the next Judge will go behind the record. He will be hard to face. He has expressed Himself on these affairs. 'If the widow and the orphan cry to me, I will surely hear their cry.' Sinister words, Wolf, for one who comes with a case like yours into the court of Final Equity."

"Abner," cried the old man, "begone with your little sermons!"

My uncle's big fingers tightened on the back of the chair.

"Then, Wolf," he said, "if this thing does not move you, let me urge the esteem of men and this child's sorrow, and our high regard."

The old man's jaw chattered and he snapped his fingers.

"I would not give that for the things you name," he cried, and he set off a tiny measure on his index-finger with the thumb.

"Why, sir, my whim, idle and ridiculous, is a greater power to move me than this drivel."

Abner did not move, but his voice took on depth and volume.

"Wolf," he said, "a whim is sometimes a great lever to move a man. Now, I am taken with a whim myself. I have a fancy, Wolf, that your brother Adam ought to go out of the world barehanded as he came into it."

The old man twisted his great head, as though he would get Abner wholly within the sweep of his reptilian eye.

"What?" he gurgled. "What is that?"

"Why, this," replied my uncle. "I have a whim—'idle and ridiculous,' did you say, Wolf? Well, then, idle and ridiculous, if you like, that your brother ought not to be buried in his gloves."

Abner looked hard at the man and, although he did not move, the threat and menace of his presence seemed somehow to advance him. And the effect upon the huge old man was like some work of sorcery. The whole mountain of him began to quiver and the folds of his face seemed spread over with thin oil. He sat piled up in the chair and the oily sweat gathered and thickened on him. His jaw jerked and fell into a baggy gaping and the great expanse of him shook.

Finally, out of the pudgy, undulating mass, a voice issued, thin and shaken.

"Abner," it said, "has any other man this fancy?"

"No," replied my uncle, "but I hold it, Wolf, at your decision."

"And, Abner," his thin voice trembled, "you will let my brother be buried as he is?"

"If you sign!" said my uncle.

The man reeked and grew wet in the terror on him, and one thought that his billowy body would never be again at peace. "Randolph," he quavered, "bring me the deed."

Outside, the girl sobbed in Abner's arms. She asked for no explanation. She wished to believe her fortune a miracle of God, forever—to the end of all things. But Randolph turned on my uncle when she was gone.

"Abner! Abner!" he cried. "Why in the name of the Eternal was the old creature so shaken at the gloves?"

"Because he saw the hangman behind them," replied my uncle. "Did you notice how the rim of the dead man's face was riddled by the bird-shot and the center of it clean? How could that happen, Randolph?"

"It was a curious accident of gun-fire," replied the Justice.

"It was no accident at all," said Abner. "That area of the man's face is clean because it was protected. Because the dead man put up his hands to cover his face when he saw that his brother was about to shoot him.

"The backs of old Adam's hands, hidden by the gloves, will be riddled with bird-shot like the rim of his face."

About the Story

1. Why do you think Post chose to title this story "The Age of Miracles"?
2. How does Abner's view of justice differ from Randolph's?
3. What specific significant details does Abner notice that the other characters overlook?
4. At what point in the story does Post let you know the real reason that Wolf consents to sign the deed?
5. Like Poe and Doyle, Post uses a first-person point of view, having a secondary character narrate the master sleuth's unraveling of the mystery. How does this point of view aid in building suspense?

About the Author

Melville Davisson Post (1869-1930) was a skilled defense lawyer who turned his observations of the inner workings of justice into short stories and novels. In his stories Post introduced a character called Uncle Abner, a country squire who solves mysteries through intuition and close attention to detail. This Abner is, according to Allan J. Hubin, "profoundly conscious of God's providence, His justice, of the rightness of things, and the wrongness of other things." Abner's sense of justice helped him to realize that the judicial system does not always produce true justice.

In addition to Uncle Abner, Post created the character Randolph Mason, a product of Post's advanced studies in criminology. Mason was described by John Howard as "a great legal misanthrope without moral sense, who believed that all wrongs, even murder, could be committed in such a manner that before the law they were not crimes." The later Randolph Mason stories deal with "such problems as required the return directly of an injury, in an exact measure, to the author of a wrong."

Unlike many writers of detective fiction, Post did not create a spokesman for the glorification of human reasoning. Through the character of Uncle Abner, Post presents reason as a God-given ability by which feeble man might come to know and realize the truth and thereby obey it.

UNIT SIX

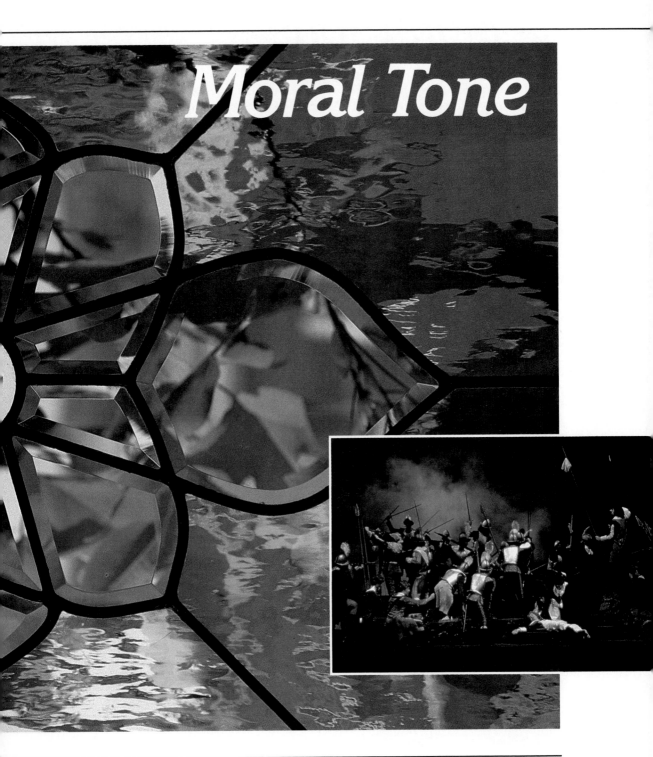

Moral Tone

Moral Tone

T. S. Eliot, a noteworthy poet and literary critic, warns that "a book is not harmless merely because no one is consciously offended by it." We are all adept at spotting flagrantly objectionable elements in literature. We understand the pitfalls of worldly behavior, and we know to reject literature that glorifies profane language and behavior. But are we as skilled in discerning harmful, and often subtle, attitudes and ideas in a work?

Our reading thus far has helped us differentiate between what is literary and what is not. But as Eliot implies in his statement, there is more to discerning literary excellence than evaluating the elements of a story. A story is *literary* if the conflict and characters are artfully developed, the plot is well structured, and the theme is significant. It is *excellent* if added to these key elements is a positive moral tone. Without a positive moral tone a work may prove harmful despite its literary merit.

As the following chart shows, **moral tone** is the overriding philosophy of a work, and it influences—even dominates—all the other elements of a story. An excellent story, however, will not necessarily be free of all negative characters and behavior. Many of the stories we have read, although they have negative characters who behave wrongly, still have a positive moral tone. The key is that these characters and their behavior were not presented as praiseworthy.

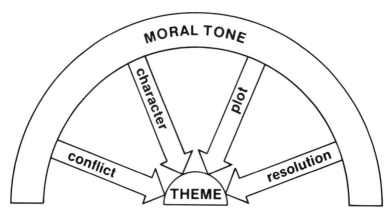

Understanding the definition and importance of moral tone is the first goal in developing discernment in reading. The second and more essential goal, however, is identifying and evaluating moral tone. Answering the following questions as we read will help us achieve this second goal. First, are the characters that we like or sympathize with noble? Second, do the actions of the story cause us to desire virtue and reject vice? Third, does the story's resolution reward good and punish evil and/or honor wisdom and scorn foolishness? Finally, does the theme or message of the story conflict with God's truth? If it does, how? Where is the flaw?

To see how these guidelines work, look at the oriental frame tale "The Forty Thieves" (pp. 308-18). We already know from reading the story that it has literary merit. Its conflict and characters are artfully developed, and the plot is well constructed. We know, too, that the story is free of flagrantly objectionable elements. But what about its moral tone? Look first at the characters. Remember the central character, Ali Baba? Although he is not a noble character, the author intends that we sympathize with him. Isn't Ali Baba a thief? It is true that he is more noble than his brother Cassim. It is also true that he steals from thieves, but these facts do not justify his theft. Look now at the story's plot. The action centers upon Ali Baba's acquisition and maintenance of stolen treasure. Although Cassim's tragic death seems to discourage us from stealing, Ali Baba's actions seem to justify this vice. And what about the story's resolution? Ali Baba is never punished for his thievery. He is instead preserved from any misfortune by his faithful servant, Morgiana. Morgiana's methods of dealing with the thieves and their leader are also questionable. We can see, then, that the message communicated through the characters and their actions and through the conflict and its resolution is contrary to a Christian viewpoint (as was stated in the story's headnote).

There are, of course, many examples of negative moral tone much more subtle and dangerous than "The Forty Thieves." This example, however, is valuable in training us to be discerning readers. Such discernment will protect us from being taken in by harmful ideas and attitudes. It will also encourage us to search God's Word for the refutation of errors. We must remember that "it is our business, as readers of literature, to know what we like. It is our business, as Christians, *as well as* readers of literature, to know what we ought to like" (T. S. Eliot).

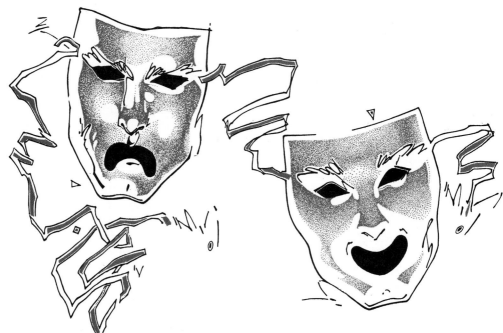

Cyrano de Bergerac
Edmond Rostand

Edmond Rostand's heroic comedy Cyrano de Bergerac *(1897) is partly based on historical fact. The real Cyrano (1619-1655) was not a Gascon, like Rostand's main character, but a native of Paris, educated in Bergerac, Gascony. A soldier for ten years, twice severely wounded, Cyrano turned to a literary career. As a writer he showed extraordinary gifts. From one of his two plays the great playwright Molière (1622-1673) borrowed heavily. Cyrano's swaggering Bohemian lifestyle, imaginative genius, and oversized nose are the main historical ingredients of Rostand's heroic character.*

On these basic elements Rostand elaborated considerably. His Cyrano excels as poet, critic, fighter, and friend. He has no equal with either sword or pen, and his poetic eloquence comes spontaneously on demand. His one defect— his ridiculously large nose—he regards with extreme sensitivity and, seemingly, with genuine pride. In only one area of his life does he let it dishearten him. Because of his face he hesitates to woo the only woman he has ever loved— his cousin, the beautiful, witty Roxane.

Cyrano de Bergerac, Edmond Rostand. Bob Jones University
Classic Players. (Each of the photographs in Unit 6 is from
this production.)

Characters

Primary

CYRANO DE BERGERAC: admired and feared Gascon, poet, and soldier
ROXANE: Cyrano's beautiful cousin
ROXANE'S DUENNA: servant, companion, and chaperon to Roxane
CHRISTIAN DE NEUVILLETTE: a cadet in love with Roxane
LE BRET: Cyrano's truest friend
RAGUENEAU: poet, pastrycook, and friend of Cyrano
LIGNIÈRE: Christian's friend
COMTE DE GUICHE: nephew of Richelieu, rival to Christian, and enemy of Cyrano
VICOMTE DE VALVERT: friend of De Guiche
MONTFLEURY: actor despised by Cyrano and in love with Roxane
LISE: wife of Ragueneau
CARBON DE CASTEL-JALOUX: Captain of Cyrano and Christian's regiment

Secondary

Actors	Meddler
Apprentice	Mother Marguérite
Bellerose	Musketeer
Bourgeoisie	Nobility
Brissaille	Old Man
Cadets	Orange Girl
Capuchin	Pages
Cavaliers	Pastrycooks
Children	Pikemen
Citizen and His Boy	Poets
Comedians	Porter
Comediennes	Proletariat
Crowd	Sentry
Cuigy	Spanish Officer
Cut-Purse	Spectators
Editor	Sister Claire
Intellectuals	Sister Marthe
Jodelet	Theatre Personnel
Marquises	Violins and Other Musicians

ACT I

A Performance at the Hôtel de Bourgogne

The theater hall of the Hôtel de Bourgogne in 1640. A sort of tennis court, arranged and decorated for theatrical productions. The audience, waiting for the play to begin, includes a young soldier, CHRISTIAN DE NEUVILLETTE, *who has come to see* ROXANE. *He has fallen in love with her from a distance and desires to meet her. Also present are his rival suitors:* COMTE DE GUICHE, *as petty in character as powerful in rank, and the actor* MONTFLEURY, *who begins the play. Concealed in the audience is* CYRANO DE BERGERAC, *who has vowed to stop any performance in which* MONTFLEURY, *whom he detests, appears on stage.*

As the curtain rises, the hall is dimly lighted and still empty. The chandeliers are lowered to the floor, in the middle of the hall, ready for lighting. There is the sound of voices outside the door. Then a CAVALIER *enters abruptly.*

PORTER	*(Follows him)* Halloa there!—Fifteen sols!*

■ **Scene i** ■

sols: French coins of little value

FIRST CAVALIER	I enter free.
PORTER	Why?
FIRST CAVALIER	Soldier of the Household of the King!
PORTER	*(Turns to a* SECOND CAVALIER *who has just entered)* You?
SECOND CAVALIER	I pay nothing.
PORTER	Why not?
SECOND CAVALIER	Musketeer!
FIRST CAVALIER	*(To the* SECOND CAVALIER*)* The play begins at two. Plenty of time— And here's the whole floor empty. Shall we try 5 Our exercise? *(They fence with the foils which they have brought.)*

CITIZEN   *(Escorting his son, a boy of sixteen)*
                        Sit here, my son . . . right here.
             —To think, my son, that in this hall they play
             Rotrou!

BOY   Yes father—and Corneille too!

PAGES   *(Dance in, holding hands and singing)*
             Tra-la-la-la-la-la-la-la-la-lére . . .

PORTER   You pages there—no nonsense!

FIRST PAGE   *(With wounded dignity)*
                                    Oh, monsieur!*   10
             Really! How could you?
             (To the SECOND CAVALIER, *the moment the* PORTER *turns
             his back)*
                           Psst!—a bit of string?

SECOND PAGE *(Shows fishline with hook)*
             Up in the gallery, and fish for wigs!

FIRST PAGE   *(Calls to other* PAGES *already in the gallery)*
             Hey! Brought your pea-shooters?

THIRD PAGE   *(From above)*
                                    And our peas, too!
             (Blows, and showers them with peas)

BOY   What is the play this afternoon?

CITIZEN   "Clorise."

BOY   Who wrote that?

CITIZEN   Balthasar Baro. What a play! . . .   15
             (He takes the BOY*'s arm and leads him upstage.)*
             Great actors we shall see to-day—Montfleury—

VOICE   *(In the gallery)*
             Lights! Light the lights!

CITIZEN   —Bellerose, Jodelet—

monsieur: title of courtesy for French nobility

PAGE   *(On the floor)*
                    Here comes the orange girl.

ORANGE GIRL   Oranges, milk,
                    Raspberry syrup—

                    (Noise at the door)

FIRST MARQUIS   *(Entering in a little group and seeing the hall half empty)*
                                How now! We enter
                    Like trades people—no crowding, no disturbance!   20
                    No treading on the toes of citizens?
                    Oh fie! Oh fie!
                    (He encounters two gentlemen who have already arrived.)
                                Cuigy! Brissaille!

                    (Great embracings)

CUIGY   The faithful!
                    (Looks around him)
                    We are here before the candles.

SECOND MARQUIS   Console yourself,
                    Marquis—the lamplighter!

CROWD   *(Applauding the appearance of the* LAMPLIGHTER*)*
                                Ah! . . .

                    *(A group gathers around the chandelier while he lights it.
                    A few people have already taken their place in the gallery.
                    LIGNIÈRE enters the hall, arm in arm with CHRISTIAN DE
                    NEUVILLETTE. LIGNIÈRE is a slightly disheveled figure,
                    dissipated and yet distinguished looking. CHRISTIAN,
                    elegantly but rather unfashionably dressed, appears
                    preoccupied and keeps looking up at the boxes.)*

CUIGY   Lignière!—

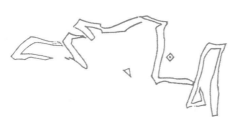

■ **Scene ii** ▰▰▰▰

LIGNIÈRE   (*To* CHRISTIAN)
May I present you?
(CHRISTIAN *assents.*)
                Baron Christian
De Neuvillette.

(*They salute.*)

LIGNIÈRE   (*To* CUIGY)
                Monsieur is recently
From the Touraine.

CHRISTIAN   Yes, I have been in Paris
Two or three weeks only. I join the Guards
Tomorrow.

FIRST MARQUIS   (*Watching the people who come into the boxes*)
                Look—Madame—la Présidente   5
Aubry!

ORANGE GIRL   Oranges, milk—

VIOLINS   (*Tuning up*)
                La . . . la . . .

CUIGY   (*To* CHRISTIAN, *calling his attention to the increasing crowd*)
                We have
An audience today!

CHRISTIAN   A brilliant one.

FIRST MARQUIS   Oh yes, all our own people: de Chavigny . . .

(*They watch as a procession of aristocrats and intelligentsia enter the boxes elaborately dressed. He trails off as the* CITIZEN *picks up.*)

CITIZEN   . . . Boissat—Porchères—Colomby—those great
        names . . . .

LIGNIÈRE   (*Draws* CHRISTIAN *aside*)
My dear boy, I came here to serve you—Well,   10
But where's the lady? I'll be going.

CHRISTIAN   Not yet—
A little longer! She is always here.
Please! I must find some way of meeting her.
I am dying of love! And you—you know
Everyone, the whole court and the whole town,   15
And put them all into your songs—at least
You can tell me her name!

LIGNIÈRE   *(Starts for the door)*
                                    I am going.

CHRISTIAN   *(Restrains him)*
No—wait!

LIGNIÈRE   *(Resigned)*
              I'll stay a little.

VOICES   *(In the crowd about the door, upon the entrance of a
              spruce little man, rather fat, with a beaming smile)*
                                    Ragueneau!

LIGNIÈRE   *(To* CHRISTIAN*)*
Poet and pastrycook—a character!

RAGUENEAU   *(Dressed like a confectioner in his Sunday clothes,
              advances quickly to* LIGNIÈRE*)*
Sir, have you seen Monsieur de Cyrano?   20

LIGNIÈRE   *(Presents him to* CHRISTIAN*)*
Permit me . . . Ragueneau, confectioner,
The chief support of modern poetry.

RAGUENEAU   *(Ignoring* LIGNIÈRE'S *compliment; looking about)*
What—Cyrano not here? Astonishing!

LIGNIÈRE   Why so?

RAGUENEAU   Why—Montfleury plays!

LIGNIÈRE   Yes, I hear
That hippopotamus assumes the role   25
Of Phédon. What is that to Cyrano?

RAGUENEAU   Have you not heard? Monsieur de Bergerac
                   So hates Montfleury, he has forbidden him
                   For three weeks to appear upon the stage.

LIGNIÈRE   Well?

RAGUENEAU   Montfleury plays!—

CUIGY   *(Strolls over to them)*
                                          Yes—what then?

RAGUENEAU   Ah! That   30
                   Is what I came to see.

FIRST MARQUIS   This Cyrano—
                   Who is he?

CUIGY   Oh, he is the lad with the long sword.

SECOND MARQUIS Noble?

CUIGY   Sufficiently; he's in the Guards.
                   *(Points to a gentleman who comes and goes about
                   the hall as though seeking for someone)*
                   His friend Le Bret can tell you more.
                   (Calls to him)
                                          Le Bret!

                   (LE BRET comes down to them.)
                   Looking for Bergerac?

LE BRET   Yes, and for trouble.   35

CUIGY   Is he not an extraordinary man?

LE BRET   The best friend and the bravest soul alive!

RAGUENEAU   Poet—

CUIGY   Swordsman—

LE BRET   Musician—

BRISSAILLE   Philosopher—

LIGNIÈRE   Such a remarkable appearance, too!

RAGUENEAU   One of those wild swashbucklers in a masque—   40
                Hat with three plumes, and doublet with six points—
                His cloak behind him over his long sword
                Cocked, like the tail of strutting Chanticleer*—
                Prouder than all the swaggering Tamburlaines*
                Hatched out of Gascony. And to complete   45
                This Punchinello* figure—such a nose!—
                My lords, there is no such nose as that nose—
                You cannot look upon it without crying: "Oh, no,
                Impossible! Exaggerated!" Then
                You smile, and say: "Of course—I might have known;   50
                Presently he will take it off." But that
                Monsieur de Bergerac will never do.

Chanticleer: rooster in Chaucer's *Canterbury Tales,* "The Nun's Priest's Tale"
Tamburlaine(s): famous medieval conqueror
Punchinello: main character in an old Italian puppet show, fat and quarrelsome with a beak-like nose

LIGNIÈRE *(Grimly)*
He keeps it—and may kill the man who smiles!

RAGUENEAU His sword is one half of the shears of Fate!*

> shears of Fate: that which cuts the thread of life

FIRST MARQUIS *(Shrugs)*
He will not come.

RAGUENEAU Will he not? Sir, I'll lay you 55
A pullet* à la Ragueneau!

> pullet: young hen

FIRST MARQUIS *(Laughing)*
'Tis done!

(Murmurs of admiration; ROXANE *has just appeared in her box. She sits at the front of the box, and her* DUENNA* *takes a seat toward the rear.* CHRISTIAN, *busy paying the* ORANGE GIRL, *does not see her at first.)*

> Duenna: elderly female; companion, protector of a young woman

CHRISTIAN *(Looks up, sees* ROXANE, *and seizes* LIGNIÈRE *by the arm)*
There! Quick—up there—

LIGNIÈRE *(Coolly)*
—Herself?

CHRISTIAN Quickly—Her name?

LIGNIÈRE Madeleine Robin, called Roxane . . . refined . . .
Intellectual . . .

CHRISTIAN Ah!—

LIGNIÈRE Unmarried . . .

CHRISTIAN Oh!—

LIGNIÈRE No title . . . rich enough . . . an orphan . . . cousin 60
To Cyrano . . . of whom we spoke just now . . .

(At this point, a very distinguished looking gentleman, the Cordon Bleu around his neck, enters the box, and stands a moment talking with ROXANE.)*

CHRISTIAN	*(Starts)* And the man?

LIGNIÈRE	Oho! That man? Comte de Guiche . . . Wishes to marry Roxane . . . she says No; Nevertheless, De Guiche is powerful, Not above persecuting. . . . I have written 65 A little song about his little game . . . Good little song too. . . . Here, I'll sing it for you . . . Make De Guiche furious . . . naughty little song . . . Not so bad, either—Listen! . . . *(He stands.)*

CHRISTIAN	No. Adieu. 70

LIGNIÈRE	Whither away?

CHRISTIAN	To that Monsieur de Guiche!

LIGNIÈRE	Careful! The man's a swordsman . . . *(Nods toward* ROXANE, *who is watching* CHRISTIAN*)* Wait! Someone Looking at you—

CHRISTIAN	Roxane! . . . *(He forgets everything and stands spellbound, gazing toward* ROXANE. *A* CUT-PURSE *and his crew, observing him transfixed, his eyes raised and his mouth half open, begin edging in his direction.)*

LIGNIÈRE	Oh! Very well, Then I'll be leaving you . . . Good day . . . Good day! *(*CHRISTIAN *remains motionless.)* Everywhere else, they like to hear me sing!— 75 *(He goes out.* LE BRET, *having made the circuit of the hall, returns to* RAGUENEAU, *somewhat reassured.)*

LE BRET	There's no sign anywhere of Cyrano!

RAGUENEAU	*(Incredulous)* Just wait and see!

LE BRET   Hmph! I hope he has not
Seen the bill.

CROWD   The play!—The play!—The play!—

FIRST MARQUIS   *(Observing* DE GUICHE, *as he descends from* ROXANE'S
*box and crosses the floor, followed by a knot of
obsequious gentlemen, the* VICOMTE DE VALVERT *among
them)*
This man De Guiche—what ostentation!

SECOND MARQUIS   Bah!—
Another Gascon!

FIRST MARQUIS   Gascon, yes—but cold
And calculating—certain to succeed—
My word for it. Come, shall we make our bow?
We shall be none the worse, I promise you. . . .   5

(They go toward DE GUICHE.*)*

CHRISTIAN   *(Starts at the name)*
De Guiche!—The Comte—that scoundrel! Quick—my
      glove—
I'll throw it in his face—
*(As he reaches into his pocket for his glove, he catches the
hand of the* CUT-PURSE *and holds it.)*
                  Oh! Who are you?
I was looking for a glove—

CUT-PURSE   *(Cringing)*
                  You found a hand.
(Hurriedly)
Let me go—I can tell you something—

CHRISTIAN   *(Still holding him)*
                        Well?

CUT-PURSE   Lignière—that friend of yours—

CHRISTIAN   *(Same business)*
                  Well?

CUT-PURSE   Good as dead—   10
Understand? Ambuscaded.* Wrote a song
About—no matter. There's a hundred men
Waiting for him tonight—I'm one of them.

Ambuscaded:
ambushed

CHRISTIAN   A hundred? Who arranged this?

CUT-PURSE   Secret.

CHRISTIAN   Oh!

CUT-PURSE   *(With dignity)*
Professional secret.

CHRISTIAN   Where are they to be?   15

CUT-PURSE   Porte de Nesle. On his way home. Tell him so.
Save his life.

CHRISTIAN   *(Starts for the door)*
                        I'll go! What swine—a hundred
Against one man!
(Stops and looks longingly at ROXANE*)*
                        Leave *her* here!—
(Savagely, turning toward DE GUICHE*)*
                                And leave *him!*—
(Decidedly)
I must save Lignière!
(Exits)

*(*DE GUICHE, VALVERT, *and all the* MARQUISES *have
disappeared through the curtains, to take their seats upon
the stage. The floor is entirely filled; not a vacant seat
remains in the gallery or in the boxes.)*

CROWD   The play! The play!
Begin the play!

CITIZEN   *(As his wig is hoisted into the air on the end of a fishline,
in the hands of the* PAGES *in the gallery)*
                        My wig!

CROWD   He's bald! Bravo,   20
You pages! Ha ha ha!

SPECTATOR   Silence!

VOICES   Hssh! . . . Hssh!

(Three raps on the stage. The curtains part. The
MARQUISES *seated on their chairs to right and left of the*
stage, insolently posed. Backdrop representing a pastoral
scene, bluish in tone. Four little crystal chandeliers light
up the stage. The violins play softly.)

LE BRET   *(In a low tone, to* RAGUENEAU*)*
Montfleury enters now?

RAGUENEAU   *(Nods)*
                                Opens the play.

LE BRET   *(Much relieved)*
Then Cyrano is not here!

RAGUENEAU   I lose. . . .

LE BRET   Humph!—
So much the better!

(The melody of a musette* is heard. MONTFLEURY *appears*   musette: a small
upon the scene, a ponderous figure in the costume of a   seventeenth- or
rustic shepherd, a hat garlanded with roses tilted over one   eighteenth-century
ear, playing upon a beribboned pastoral pipe.)   French bagpipe

CROWD   *(Applauds)*
                                Montfleury! . . . Bravo! . . .

MONTFLEURY   *(After bowing to the applause, begins the role of Phédon)*
"Thrice happy he who hides from pomp and power   25
In sylvan* shade or solitary bower;   sylvan: forest
Where balmy zephyrs* fan his burning cheeks—"   balmy zephyrs: gentle
                                                                        breezes

| VOICE | *(From the midst of the hall)* |
| | Wretch. Have I not forbade you these three weeks? |

(Sensation. Everyone turns to look. Murmurs.)

| SEVERAL VOICES | What? . . . Where? . . . Who is it? |

| CUIGY | Cyrano! |

| LE BRET | *(In alarm)* |
| | Himself! |

| VOICE | King of clowns! Leave the stage—*at once!* |

| CROWD | Oh!— |

MONTFLEURY   Now,   30
                    Now, now—

VOICE   You disobey me?

SEVERAL VOICES   *(From the floor, from the boxes)*
                                Hssh! Go on—
                    Quiet!—Go on, Montfleury!—Who's afraid?—

MONTFLEURY   *(In a voice of no great assurance)*
                    "Thrice happy he who hides from . . ."

VOICE   *(More menacingly)*
                                        Well? Well?
                        Well? . . .
                    Monarch of mountebanks!* Must I come and plant   *mountebanks:* boast-
                    A forest on your shoulders?   ful pretenders

                    *(A cane at the end of a long arm shakes above the heads
                    of the crowd.)*

MONTFLEURY   *(In a voice increasingly feeble)*
                                "Thrice hap—"

                    (The cane is violently agitated.)

VOICE   *GO!!!*   35

CROWD   Ah . . .

                                                                ■ Scene iv ■

CYRANO   *(Arises in the center of the floor, erect upon a chair, his
                arms folded, his hat cocked ferociously, his moustache
                bristling, his nose terrible)*
                    Presently I shall grow angry!

                (Sensation at his appearance)

MONTFLEURY   *(To the* MARQUISES*)*
                                    Messieurs,
                    If you protect me—

MARQUIS   *(Nonchalantly)*
                        Well—proceed!

CYRANO

Fat swine!
If you dare breathe one balmy zephyr more,
I'll fan your cheeks for you!

MARQUIS

Quiet down there!

CYRANO

Unless these gentlemen retain their seats,   5
My cane may bite their ribbons!

MARQUISES

(On their feet)

That will do!—
Montfleury—

CYRANO

Fly, goose! Shoo! Take to your wings,
Before I pluck your plumes, and draw your gorge!*

draw your gorge: cut your throat

CROWD

Montfleury! . . . Montfleury! . . . The play! The play!

CYRANO

(To those who are shouting and crowding about him)
Pray you, be gentle with my scabbard here—   10
She'll put her tongue out at you presently!—

(The circle enlarges.)

CROWD

(Recoiling)
Keep back—

CYRANO

(To MONTFLEURY*)*
Begone!

CROWD

(Pushing in closer, and chanting)
"La Clorise!" "La Clorise!"

CYRANO

(Turns on them)
Let me hear one more word of that same song,
And I destroy you all!

(They recoil again.)

CITIZEN

Who might you be?
Samson?—

CYRANO	Precisely. Would you kindly lend me Your jawbone?*	15

Samson . . . jawbone:
an allusion to
Judges 15:15, in
which Samson kills
a thousand Philis-
tines with the jaw-
bone of an ass

LADY   *(In one of the boxes)*
                                      What an outrage!

NOBLE   Scandalous!

CITIZEN   Annoying!

PAGE   What a game!

CROWD   Kss! Montfleury!
                    Cyrano!

CYRANO   *(His voice dominating the uproar)*
                        Be silent!—

(A momentary hush)

                              And I offer
One universal challenge to you all!
Approach, young heroes—I will take your names.   20
Each in his turn—no crowding! One, two, three—
Come, get your numbers—who will head the list—
You sir? No—You? Ah, no. To the first man
Who falls I'll build a monument! . . . Not one?
Will all who wish to die, please raise their hands? . . .   25
Not one name? Not one finger? . . . Very well,
Then I go on:
(Turning back toward the stage, where MONTFLEURY *waits
in despair)*
                        I'd have our theater cured
Of this carbuncle.* Or if not, why then—
(His hand on his sword hilt)
The lancet!*

carbuncle: boil

lancet: sharp, pointed
instrument used by
physicians

MONTFLEURY   I—

CYRANO   *(Descends from his chair, seats himself comfortably in the
                center of the circle which has formed around him, and
                makes himself quite at home)*
                        Attend to me—full moon!

	I clap my hands, three times—thus. At the third 30 You will eclipse yourself.
CROWD	*(Amused)* Ah!
CYRANO	Ready? One!
MONTFLEURY	I—
VOICE	*(From the boxes)* No!
CROWD	He'll go—He'll stay—
MONTFLEURY	I really think, Gentlemen—
CYRANO	Two!
MONTFLEURY	Perhaps I had better—
CYRANO	Three!

(MONTFLEURY disappears, as if through a trap door. Tempest of laughter, hoots and hisses.)

CROWD	Yah!—Coward—Come back—
CYRANO	*(Beaming, drops back in his chair and crosses his legs)* Let him—if he dare!
BOY	*(To CYRANO)* After all, Monsieur, what reason have you 35 To hate this Montfleury?
CYRANO	*(Graciously, still seated)* My dear young man, I have two reasons, either one alone Conclusive. *Primo:** A lamentable actor, Who mouths his verse and moans his tragedy, And heaves up—Ugh!—like a hod-carrier,* lines 40 That ought to soar on their wings. *Secundo:**— Well—that's my secret.

Primo: first

hod-carrier: coal scuttle
Secundo: second

OLD CITIZEN   *(Behind him)*
                             But you close the play—
               "La Clorise"—by Baro! Are we to miss
               Our entertainment, merely—

CYRANO   *(Respectfully, turns his chair toward the old man)*
                             My dear old boy,
               The poetry of Baro being worth   45
               Zero, or less, I feel that I have done
               Poetic justice!

INTELLECTUALS *(In the boxes)*
                             Really!—our Baro!—
               My dear!—Who ever?—Ah, no! The idea!—

CYRANO   *(Gallantly, turns his chair toward the boxes)*
               Fair ladies—shine upon us like the sun,
               Blossom like the flowers around us—be our songs,   50
               Heard in a dream—Make sweet the hour of death,
               Smiling upon us as you close our eyes—
               Inspire, but do not try to criticize!

               *(*BELLEROSE, *the manager, advances.)*

BELLEROSE   Quite so!—and the mere money—possibly
               You would like that returned—Yes?

CYRANO   Bellerose,   55
               You speak the first word of intelligence!
               I will not wound the mantle of the Muse—
               Here, catch!—
               (Throws him a purse of gold)
                             And hold your tongue.

CROWD   *(Astonished)*
                                          Ah! Ah!

               *(*JODELET, *a comedian, deftly intercepts the toss and
               weighs the purse in his hand.)*

JODELET   Monsieur,
               You are hereby authorized to close our play
               Every night, on the same terms.

CROWD	Boo!
JODELET	And welcome! 60
BELLEROSE	*(To the* CROWD*)* Kindly pass out quietly . . .
JODELET	*(Mimicking* BELLEROSE*)* Quietly . . .

(They begin to go out, while CYRANO *looks about him with satisfaction. But the exodus ceases presently during the ensuing scene. The* LADIES *in the boxes, who have already risen and put on their wraps, stop to listen and finally sit down again.)*

■ Scene V ▩▩▩▩▩▩

LE BRET	*(To* CYRANO*)* Idiot!
MEDDLER	*(Hurries up to* CYRANO*)* But what a scandal! Montfleury— The great Montfleury! Did you know the Duc de* Candale was his patron? Who is yours?
CYRANO	No one.
MEDDLER	No patron? But—
CYRANO	You may go now— *(Pause)* Or tell me why you're staring at my nose! 5
MEDDLER	*(In confusion)* No—I—
CYRANO	*(Stepping up to him)* Does it astonish you?
MEDDLER	*(Drawing back)* Your grace Misunderstands my—
CYRANO	Is it long and soft And dangling, like a trunk?

Duc de: duke of

MEDDLER   *(Same business)*
                                              I never said—

CYRANO   Or crooked, like an owl's beak?

MEDDLER   I—

CYRANO   Perhaps
                   A pimple ornaments the end of it?   10

MEDDLER   No—

CYRANO   Or a fly parading up and down?
                   What is this portent?* This phenomenon?

portent: sign of future ill fortune

MEDDLER   But I've been careful not to look—

CYRANO   And why
                   Not, if you please?

MEDDLER   Why—

CYRANO   It disgusts you, then?

MEDDLER   My dear sir—

CYRANO   Does its color appear to you   15
                   Unwholesome?

MEDDLER   Oh, by no means!

CYRANO   Or its form
                   Obscene?

MEDDLER   Not in the least—

CYRANO   Then why assume
                   This deprecating manner? Possibly
                   You find it just a trifle *large?*

MEDDLER   Oh no!
                   Small, very small, infinitesimal—

| CYRANO | *(Roars)* | | 20 |

                             What?
How? You accuse me of absurdity?
Small—*my nose?* Why—

| MEDDLER | *(Breathless)* |

                  Oh no!—

| CYRANO |

                             Magnificent,
My nose! . . . You pug,* you knob, you button-head,   *pug:* snub-nosed dog
Know that I glory in this nose of mine,
For a great nose indicates a great man—   25
Genial, courteous, intellectual,
Virile, courageous—as I am—and such
As you—poor wretch—will never dare to be
Even in imagination. For that face—
That blank, inglorious concavity*   30   *concavity:* curved-in
Which my right hand finds—   structure

(He strikes him.)

| MEDDLER |

                    Ow!

| CYRANO |

                       —on top of you,
Is as devoid of pride, of poetry,
Of soul, of picturesqueness, of contour,
Of character, of *NOSE* in short—as that
*(Takes him by the shoulders and turns him around, suiting
the action to the word)*
Which at the end of that limp spine of yours   35
My left foot—

| MEDDLER | *(Escaping)* |

                 Help! The Guard!

| CYRANO |

                          Take notice, all
Who find this feature of my countenance
A theme for comedy! When the humorist
Is noble, then my custom is to show
Appreciation proper to his rank—   40
More heartfelt . . . and more pointed. . . .

DE GUICHE   *(Who has come down from the stage, surrounded by the*
                   MARQUISES*)*
                                                   Presently
                   This fellow will grow tiresome.

VALVERT   *(Shrugs)*
                                                 Oh, he blows
                   His trumpet!

DE GUICHE   Well—will no one interfere?

VALVERT   No one?
                   (Looks around)
                             Observe. I myself will proceed
                   To put him in his place.

                   (He walks up to CYRANO, *who has been watching him,*
                   and stands there, looking him over with an affected air.)
                                       Ah . . . your nose . . . hem!   45
                   Your nose is . . . rather large!

CYRANO   *(Gravely)*
                                             Rather.

VALVERT   *(Simpering)*
                                                 Oh well—

CYRANO   *(Coolly)*
                   Is that all?

VALVERT   *(Turns away with a shrug)*
                             Well, of course—

CYRANO   Ah, no young sir!
                   You are too simple. Why, you might have said—
                   Oh, a great many things! Dear me, why waste
                   Your opportunity? For example, thus:—   50
                   Aggressive: I, sir, if that nose were mine,
                   I'd have it amputated—on the spot!
                   Friendly: How do you drink with such a nose?
                   You ought to have a cup made specially.
                   Descriptive: 'Tis a rock—a crag—a cape—   55
                   A cape? say rather, a peninsula!

Inquisitive: What is the receptacle—
A razor-case or a portfolio?
Eloquent: When it blows, that typhoon howls,
And the clouds darken. *Dramatic:* When it bleeds—   60
The Red Sea! *Enterprising:* What a sign
For some perfumer! *Lyric:* Hark—the horn
Of Roland* calls to summon Charlemagne!*—
Or—parodying* Faustus* in the play—
"Was this the nose that launched a thousand ships   65
And burned the topless towers of Ilium?"
These, my dear sir, are things you might have said
Had you some tinge of letters, or of wit.
Moreover—if you had the inventions, here
Before these folks to make a jest of me—   70
Be sure you would not then articulate
The twentieth part of half a syllable
Of the beginning! For I say these things
Lightly enough myself, about myself,
But I allow none else to utter them.   75

Roland: legendary
heroic nephew of
Charlemagne
Charlemagne: king of
Franks and emperor
of Rome
parodying: making
light of
Faustus: main charac-
ter of Christopher
Marlowe's play, who
conjures up Helen
of Troy

DE GUICHE   *(Tries to lead away the amazed* VALVERT*)*
              Vicomte—come.

VALVERT   *(Choking)*
                        Oh—These arrogant grand airs!—
              A clown who—look at him—not even gloves!
              No ribbons—no lace—no buckles on his shoes—

CYRANO   I carry my adornments on my soul.
              I do not dress up like a popinjay;*   80   *popinjay:* parrot; vain,
              But inwardly, I keep my daintiness.   talkative person
              I do not bear with me, by any chance,
              An insult not yet washed away—a conscience
              Yellow with unpurged bile*—an honor frayed   *unpurged bile:*
              To rags, a set of scruples badly worn.   85   uncleansed irrita-
              I go caparisoned* in gems unseen,   tion, i.e., bitterness
              Trailing white plumes of freedom, garlanded   *caparisoned:*
              With my good name—no figure of a man,   ornamented
              But a soul clothed in shining armor, hung
              With deeds for decorations, twirling—thus—   90
              A bristling wit, and swinging at my side
              Courage, and on the stones of this old town
              Making the sharp truth ring, like golden spurs!

VALVERT   But—

CYRANO   But I have no gloves! A pity too!
              I had one—the last one of an old pair—   95
              And lost that. Very careless of me. Some
              Gentleman offered me an impertinence.*   *impertinence:* insult
              I left it—in his face.

VALVERT   Dolt,* bumpkin,* fool,   *Dolt:* stupid person
              Insolent puppy, jobbernowl!*   *bumpkin:* clumsy,
                                                                               ignorant fellow
                                                                             jobbernowl:
                                                                               blockhead
CYRANO   *(Removes his hat and bows)*
                            Ah, yes?
              And I—Cyrano-Savinien-Hercule   100
              De Bergerac!

VALVERT   *(Turns away)*
                      Buffoon!*   *Buffoon:* clown

CYRANO	*(Cries out as if suddenly taken with a cramp)* Oh!
VALVERT	*(Turns back)* Well, what now?
CYRANO	*(With grimaces of anguish)* I must do something to relieve these cramps— This is what comes of lack of exercise— Ah!—
VALVERT	What is all this?
CYRANO	My sword has gone to sleep?
VALVERT	*(Draws)* So be it!
CYRANO	You shall die exquisitely. 105
VALVERT	*(Contemptuously)* Poet!
CYRANO	Why yes, a poet, if you will; So while we fence, I'll make you a Ballade Extempore.*
VALVERT	A Ballade?
CYRANO	Yes. You know What that is?
VALVERT	I—
CYRANO	The Ballade, sir, is formed Of three stanzas of eight lines each—
VALVERT	Oh, come! 110
CYRANO	And a refrain of four.
VALVERT	You—

Extempore: offhand

CYRANO

I'll compose
One, while I fight with you; and at the end
Of the last line—thrust home!*

thrust home: pierce the opponent with a sword

VALVERT

Will you?

CYRANO

I will.
(Declaims)
"Ballade of the duel at the Hôtel de Bourgogne
Between De Bergerac and a Boeotian."*   115

Boeotian: one from Boeotia; stupid person

VALVERT

(Sneering)
What do you mean by that?

CYRANO

Oh, that? The title.

(A ring of interested spectators in the center of the floor, the MARQUISES and the OFFICERS mingling with the citizens and common folk. PAGES swarming up on the men's shoulders to see better; the LADIES in the boxes standing and leaning over. To the right, DE GUICHE and his following; to the left, LE BRET, CUIGY, RAGUENEAU, and others of CYRANO's friends.)

CYRANO

(Closes his eyes for an instant)
Stop . . . Let me choose my rimes . . . Now! Here we go—

(He suits the action to the word, throughout the following:)

Lightly I toss my hat away,
  Languidly* over my arm let fall
The cloak that covers my bright array—   120
  Then out swords, and to work withal!
  A Launcelot,* in his Lady's hall . . .
A Spartacus,* at the Hippodrome!* . . .
  I dally awhile with you, dear jackal,*
Then, as I end the refrain, thrust home!   125

(The swords cross—the fight is on.)

languidly: droopingly

Launcelot: most famous knight of King Arthur's Round Table
Spartacus: famous Thracian gladiator
Hippodrome: ancient sports arena
jackal: doglike wild animal

Where shall I skewer* my peacock? . . . Nay, *skewer:* pierce with a
  Better for you to have shunned this brawl!—   metal pin
Here, in the heart, thro' your ribbons gay?
  —In the belly, under your silken shawl?
Hark, how the steel rings musical!   130
Mark how my point floats, light as the foam,
  Ready to drive you back to the wall,
Then, as I end the refrain, thrust home!

Ho, for a rime! . . .You are white as whey—
  You break, you cower, you cringe, you . . . crawl!   135
Tac!—and I parry* your last essay:* *parry:* evade
  So may the turn of a hand forestall* *essay:* attempt
  Life with its honey, death with its gall; *forestall:* keep out
So may the turn of my fancy* roam *fancy:* imagination
  Free, for a time, till the rimes recall,   140
Then, as I end the refrain, thrust home!

(He announces solemnly.)

Refrain:
      Prince! Pray God, that is Lord of all,
Pardon your soul, for your time has come!
  Beat—pass—fling you aslant,* asprawl*— *aslant:* to one side
Then, as I end the refrain . . . *asprawl:* sprawling

(He lunges; VALVERT *staggers back and falls into
the arms of his friends.* CYRANO *recovers and
salutes.)*
          —Thrust home!   145

*(Shouts. Applause from the boxes. Flowers and
handkerchiefs come fluttering down. The officers surround*
CYRANO *and congratulate him.* RAGUENEAU *dances for
joy.* LE BRET *is unable to conceal his enthusiasm. The
friends of* VALVERT *hold him up and help him away.)*

CROWD   *(In one long cry)*
             Ah-h!

CAVALIER   Superb!

WOMAN   Simply sweet!

RAGUENEAU   Magnelephant!

MARQUIS   A novelty!

LE BRET   Bah!

CROWD   *(Thronging around* CYRANO*)*
                        Compliments—regards—
              Bravo!—

WOMAN'S VOICE   Why, he's a hero!

MUSKETEER   *(Advances quickly to* CYRANO, *with outstretched hands)*
                        Monsieur, will you
              Permit me?—It was altogether fine!
              I think I may appreciate these things—   150
              Moreover, I have been stamping for pure joy!

              (He retires quickly.)

CYRANO   *(To* CUIGY*)*
              What was that gentleman's name?

CUIGY   Oh . . . D'Artagnan.*   *D'Artagnan:* one of the
                                                                 Three Musketeers

LE BRET   *(Takes* CYRANO'S *arm)*
              Come here and tell me—

CYRANO   Let this crowd go first—
              (To BELLEROSE*)*
              May we stay?

BELLEROSE   *(With great respect)*
                        Certainly!

              (Cries off-stage)

JODELET   *(Comes down from the door where he has been looking
              out)*
                        Hark!—Montfleury—
              They are hooting him.

BELLEROSE	*(Solemnly)*

"Sic transit gloria!"*

Sic transit gloria: Latin: "thus the glory passes away"

155

(Changes his tone and shouts to the PORTER *and the* LAMPLIGHTER*)*
Strike! . . . Close the house! . . . Leave the lights—
    We rehearse
The new farce* after dinner.

farce: ludicrous entertainment

*(*JODELET *and* BELLEROSE *go out after elaborately saluting* CYRANO.*)*

PORTER   *(To* CYRANO*)*

You do not dine?

CYRANO   I?—No!

(The PORTER *turns away.)*

LE BRET   Why not?

CYRANO   *(Haughtily)*

Because—

(Changing his tone when he sees the PORTER *has gone)*

Because I have

No money.

LE BRET   *(Gesture of tossing)*

But—the purse of gold?

CYRANO

Farewell,

Paternal* pension!

paternal: from a father

LE BRET

So you have, until   160

The first of next month—?

CYRANO

Nothing.

LE BRET

What a fool!—

CYRANO   But—what a gesture!

ORANGE GIRL   *(Behind her little counter; coughs)*

Hem!

(CYRANO and LE BRET look around; she advances timidly.)

                                Pardon, monsieur . . .
A man ought never to go hungry . . .
(Indicating the sideboard)
                                See,
I have everything here . . .
(Eagerly)
                    Please!

CYRANO   *(Uncovers)*
                                My dear child,
I cannot bend this Gascon pride of mine   165
To accept such a kindness—Yet, for fear
That I may give you pain if I refuse,
I will take . . .
(He goes to the sideboard and makes his selection.)
                Oh, not very much! A grape . . .
(She gives him the bunch; he removes a single grape.)
One only! And a glass of water . . .
(She starts to pour him another beverage; he stops her.)
                                Clear!
(She gets out another glass and pours water.)
And half a macaroon!
(He gravely returns the other half.)

LE BRET   Old idiot!   170

ORANGE GIRL   Please!—Nothing more?

CYRANO   Why yes—Your hand to kiss.

(He kisses the hand which she holds out, as he would the hand of a princess.)

ORANGE GIRL   Thank you, sir.
(She curtsies.)
                    Good-night.
(She goes out.)

CYRANO   *(To LE BRET as he dines)*
                                Now, I am listening.

LE BRET	These fatheads with the bellicose* grand airs Will have you ruined if you listen to them; Talk to a man of sense and hear how all 175 Your swagger impresses him.
CYRANO	*(Finishes his macaroon)* Enormously.
LE BRET	But look at all the enemies you have made!
CYRANO	*(Begins on the grape)* How many—do you think?
LE BRET	Just forty-eight Without the women.
CYRANO	Count them.
LE BRET	Montfleury, Baro, De Guiche, the Vicomte, the Old Man, 180 All the Academy*—
CYRANO	Enough! You make me Happy!
LE BRET	But where is all this leading you? What is your plan?
CYRANO	I have been wandering— Wasting my force upon too many plans. Now I have chosen one.
LE BRET	What one?
CYRANO	The simplest— 185 To make myself in all things admirable!
LE BRET	Hmph!—Well, then, the real reason why you hate Montfleury—Come, the truth, now!
CYRANO	*(Rises)* That Silenus*—

bellicose: warlike

Academy: prestigious organization of French writers, churchmen, and military heroes who governed literary effort

Silenus: mythological satyr, jovial, fat, and drunken

Who cannot hold his belly in his arms,
Still dreams of being sweetly dangerous   190
Among the women—sighs and languishes,
Making sheeps' eyes out of his great frog's face—
I hate him ever since one day he dared
Smile upon—
        Oh, my friend, I seemed to see
Over some flower a great snail crawling!

LE BRET   *(Amazed)*

                            How,   195
What? Is it possible?—

CYRANO   *(With a bitter smile)*
                    For me to love? . . .
(Changing his tone; seriously)
I love.

LE BRET   May I know? You have never said—

CYRANO   Whom I love? Think a moment. Think of me—
Me, whom the plainest woman would despise—
Me, with this nose of mine that marches on   200
Before me by a quarter of an hour!
Whom should I love? Why—of course—it must be
The woman in the world most beautiful.

LE BRET   Most beautiful?

CYRANO   In all this world—most sweet;
Also most wise; most witty; and most fair!   205

LE BRET   Who and what is this woman?

CYRANO   Dangerous
Mortally, without meaning; exquisite
Without imagining. Nature's own snare
To allure manhood. A white rose wherein
Love lies in ambush for his natural prey.   210
Who knows her smile has known a perfect thing.
She creates grace in her own image, brings
Heaven to earth in one movement of her hand—

LE BRET   —That makes everything clear!

CYRANO   Transparently.

LE BRET   Madeleine Robin—your cousin?

CYRANO   Yes; Roxane.   215

LE BRET   And why not? If you love her, tell her so!
             You have covered yourself with glory in her eyes
             This very day.

CYRANO   My old friend—look at me,
             And tell me how much hope remains for me
             With this protuberance!* Oh I have no more   220
             Illusions! Now and then—bah! I may grow
             Tender, walking alone in the blue cool
             Of evening, through some garden fresh with flowers
             After the benediction of the rain;
             My poor big devil of a nose inhales   225
             April . . . and so I follow with my eyes
             Where some boy, with a girl upon his arm,
             Passes a patch of silver . . . and I feel
             Somehow, I wish I had a woman too,
             Walking with little steps under the moon,   230
             And holding my arm so, and smiling. Then
             I dream—and I forget. . . .
                               And then I see
             The shadow of my profile on the wall!

protuberance: something that is bulging or swollen

LE BRET   My friend! . . .

CYRANO   My friend, I have my bitter days,
             Knowing myself so ugly, so alone.   235
             Sometimes—

LE BRET   You weep?

CYRANO   *(Quickly)*
                          Oh, not that ever! No.
             That would be too grotesque—tears trickling down
             All the long way along this nose of mine?
             I will not so profane* the dignity
             Of sorrow. Never any tears for me!   240
             Why, there is nothing more sublime than tears,

profane: treat with irreverence

Nothing!—Shall I make them ridiculous
In my poor person?

LE BRET   Love's no more than chance!

CYRANO   *(Shakes his head)*
                No. I love Cleopatra;* do I appear
                Caesar?* I adore Beatrice;* have I   245
                The look of Dante?

LE BRET   But your wit—your courage—
                Why, that poor child who offered you just now
                Your dinner! She—you saw with your own eyes,
                Her eyes did not avoid you.

CYRANO   *(Thoughtful)*
                                        That is true. . . .

LE BRET   Well then! Roxane herself, watching your duel,   250
                Paler than—

CYRANO   Pale?—

LE BRET   Her lips parted, her hand
                Thus, at her breast—I saw it! Speak to her!
                Speak, man!

CYRANO   Through my nose? She might laugh at me;
                That is the one thing in this world I fear!

PORTER   *(Followed by the* DUENNA, *approaches* CYRANO
                respectfully)
                A lady asking for Monsieur.

CYRANO   Look here . . . !   255
                Her Duenna!—

DUENNA   *(A sweeping curtsy)*
                        Monsieur . . .
                                A message for you:
                From our good cousin we desire to know
                When and where we may see him privately.

Cleopatra: queen of
ancient Egypt
Caesar: Cleopatra's
consort
Beatrice: the idealized
heroine in *The
Divine Comedy* by
Dante, an Italian
poet of the late thir-
teenth and early
fourteenth centuries

■ **Scene vi** ■■■■■■

CYRANO   *(Amazed)*
                          See me?

DUENNA   *(An elaborate reverence)*
                                    We have certain things to tell you.
                          *(*CYRANO *is so utterly taken aback as to be speechless. The*
                          DUENNA, *oblivious to his reaction, continues.)*
                          To-morrow, at the first flush of the dawn,   5
                          We hear Mass at Saint Roch. Then afterwards,
                          Where can we meet and talk a little?

CYRANO   *(Catching* LE BRET's *arm)*
                                                        Where?—
                          To-morrow?—Ah . . . the shop of Ragueneau . . .
                          The pastrycook at Rue St. Honoré . . .

DUENNA   We are agreed. Remember—seven o'clock.   10
                          (Reverence)
                          Until then—   ■ Scene vii ■

CYRANO   I'll be there.
                          (The DUENNA *goes out;* CYRANO *falls into the arms of* LE
                          BRET.*)*
                                    Me . . . to see me! . . .

LE BRET   You are not quite so gloomy.

CYRANO   After all,
                          She knows that I exist—no matter why!

LE BRET   So now, you are going to be happy.

CYRANO   Now! . . .
                          (Beside himself)
                          I—I am going to be a storm—a flame—   5
                          I need to fight whole armies all alone;
                          I have ten hearts, a hundred arms; I feel
                          Too strong to war with mortals—
                          (Shouts at the top of his voice)
                                              Bring me giants!

                          *(A moment since, the shadows of the comedians have
                          been visible moving and posturing upon the stage. The
                          violins have taken their places.)*

VOICE	*(From the stage)*	
	Hey—pst—less noise! We are rehearsing here!	

CYRANO   *(Laughs)*
We are going.

(He turns upstage. Through the street door enter CUIGY, BRISSAILLE, *a number of officers, and* LIGNIÈRE.*)*

CUIGY   Cyrano!

CYRANO   What is it?

CUIGY   Here—   10
Here's your stray lamb!

CYRANO   *(Recognizes* LIGNIÈRE*)*
                   Lignière—What's wrong with him?

CUIGY   He wants you.

BRISSAILLE   He's afraid to go home.

CYRANO   Why?

LIGNIÈRE   *(Showing a crumpled scrap of paper)*
This letter—hundred against one—that's me—
I'm the one—all because of little song—
Good song—Hundred men, waiting, understand?   15
Porte de Nesle—way home—Might be dangerous—
Would you permit me spend the night with you?

CYRANO   A hundred—is that all? You're going home!

LIGNIÈRE   *(Astonished)*
Why—

CYRANO   *(In a voice of thunder, indicating the lighted lantern which the* PORTER *holds up curiously as he regards the scene)*
       Take that lantern!
*(*LIGNIÈRE *precipitately seizes the lantern.)*
                     Forward march! I say
I'll be the man to-night that sees you home.   20

(To the officers)
You others follow—I want an audience!

CUIGY   A hundred against one—

CYRANO   Those are the odds!
March!
(To the officers)
          And you gentlemen, remember now,
No rescue—Let me fight alone.

(The comedians in their costumes are descending from the stage and joining the group.)

COMEDIENNE   *(To another)*
                                   But why
Against one poor poet, a hundred men?   25

(The VIOLINS join the procession which is forming. The lighted candles are snatched from the stage and distributed; it becomes a torchlight procession. The PORTER flings wide the great doors. We see in the dim moonlight a corner of old Paris, purple and picturesque.)

ALL   To the Porte de Nesle!

CYRANO   *(Taking his station as he speaks, erect upon the threshold)*
                    To the Porte de Nesle!
(He turns back for a moment to the COMEDIENNE.)
Did you not ask, my dear, why against one
Singer they send a hundred swords?
(Quietly, drawing his own sword)
                                   Because
They know this one man for a friend of mine!

(He goes out. The procession follows: LIGNIÈRE at its head, then the comediennes on the arms of the officers, then the comedians leaping and dancing as they go. It vanishes into the night to the music of the VIOLINS, illuminated by the flickering glimmer of the candles.)

(Curtain)

About the Play

1. How do the following characters describe De Guiche?
     Lignière (p. 359)
     First Marquis (p. 360)
2. How do the following characters describe Cyrano?
     Lignière (pp. 357-58)
     Ragueneau (pp. 356-58)
     Le Bret (pp. 356-58)
3. How do De Guiche and Cyrano differ?
4. Read Christian's speechs on page 355. Do you think that Christian is in love with Roxane's external or internal beauty?
5. Read Cyrano's speech on page 382. How does his love for Roxane differ from Christian's?

ACT II

The Bakery of the Poets

The shop of RAGUENEAU, *Baker and Pastrycook. The street, seen vaguely through the glass panes in the door at the back, is gray in the first light of dawn.*

Tables are covered with trays of cakes and rolls; others with chairs placed about them are set for guests.

One little table in a corner disappears under a heap of papers. As the curtain rises, RAGUENEAU *is seated there. He is writing poetry.*

RAGUENEAU	*(Raises his head; returns to mere earth)* Over the coppers of my kitchen flows The frosted-silver dawn. Silence awhile The god who sings within thee, Ragueneau! Lay down the lute—the oven calls for thee! *(Rises; goes to one of the cooks)* Here's a hiatus* in your sauce; fill up The measure.

■ Scene i ■

5   *hiatus:* interruption (in the process of making something)

Cook

How much?

Ragueneau

(Measures on his finger)
                        One more dactyl.

Cook

                                Huh?

Ragueneau

*(Moves to the fireplace and addresses the First
Pastrycook)*
Your rolls lack balance. Here's the proper form—
An equal hemistich* on either side,
And the caesura* in between.
(To another, pointing out an unfinished pie)
                        Your house
Of crust should have a roof upon it.
(To an APPRENTICE *holding a dish covered by a napkin)*
                        And you?   10

APPRENTICE

(Advances)
Master, I thought of you when I designed
This, hoping it might please you.

RAGUENEAU

                        Ah! A lyre—

APPRENTICE

In puff-paste—

RAGUENEAU

                And the jewels—candied fruit!

APPRENTICE

And sugar!

*(*LISE *enters;* RAGUENEAU *shows the lyre to* LISE, *with a
languid air.)*

RAGUENEAU

                Graceful—yes?

LISE

                        Ridiculous!

(She places on the counter a pile of paper bags.)

RAGUENEAU

Paper bags? Thank you. . . .
(He looks at them.)
                        No! My manuscripts!   15
The sacred verses of my poets—rent
Asunder, limb from limb—butchered to make
Base* packages of pastry! Ah, you are one

hemistich: a line of
verse shorter than
the normal line
caesura: pause

base: worthless

Of those insane Bacchantes* who destroyed
Orpheus!*

> Bacchantes: god-
> desses or priest-
> esses of Bacchus,
> wine, and revelry
> Orpheus: mythologi-
> cal singer whose
> music calmed
> beasts and even
> rocks and trees

LISE Your silly poets left them here   20
To pay for eating half our stock-in-trade:
We ought to make some profit out of them!

RAGUENEAU Ant! Would you blame the locust for his song?

LISE I blame the locust for his appetite!
There used to be a time—before you had 25
Your hungry friends—you never called me Ants—
No, nor Bacchantes!

RAGUENEAU What a way to use
Poetry!

LISE Well, what is the use of it?

RAGUENEAU But, my dear girl, what would you do with prose?
(Two children enter.)
Well, dears?

■ **Scene ii** ■

FIRST CHILD Three little patties.

RAGUENEAU *(Serves them)*
   There we are!
All hot and brown.

SECOND CHILD Would you mind wrapping them?

RAGUENEAU One of my paper bags! . . .
  Oh, certainly.
*(Reads from the bag, as he is about to wrap the patties
in it)*
"Ulysses,* when he left Penelope"*—
Not that one!
(Takes another bag; reads)
  "Phoebus,* golden-crowned"—
   Not that one. 5

> Ulysses: heroic king of
> Ithaca in Greek
> legend
> Penelope: Ulysses'
> faithful wife
> Phoebus: god of the
> sun

LISE Well? They are waiting!

RAGUENEAU	Very well, very well!—
	The Sonnet to Phyllis* . . .
	Yet—it does seem hard . . .

Phyllis: a country girl
addressed in Virgil's
Eclogues

LISE	Made up your mind—at last! Hmph!—Jack-o'-Dreams!
RAGUENEAU	*(As her back is turned, calls back the children, who are already at the door)*
	Pst!—Children—Give me back the bag. Instead
	Of three patties, you shall have six of them! 10
	(They make the exchange. The children go out. He reads from the bag, as he smoothes it out tenderly.)
	"Phyllis"—
	A spot of butter on her name!—
	"Phyllis"—

■ Scene iii ■

CYRANO	*(Enters hurriedly)*
	What is the time?

RAGUENEAU	Six o'clock.
CYRANO	One
	Hour more . . .
RAGUENEAU	Felicitations!*
CYRANO	And for what?
RAGUENEAU	Your victory! I saw it all—
CYRANO	Which one?
RAGUENEAU	At the Hôtel de Bourgogne.

felicitations: congratulations

CYRANO   *(Mechanically shaking hands with* LISE*)*
                          Oh—the duel!

RAGUENEAU   *(Fencing and thrusting with a spit, which he snatches up*
                 from the hearth)
                 The duel in Rime!

LISE   He talks of nothing else.   5
                 (Noticing CYRANO'S *hand)*
                 Your hand—what have you done?

CYRANO   Oh, my hand?—
                 Nothing.

RAGUENEAU   *(Suddenly stops his shadow-fencing)*
                 What danger now—

CYRANO   No danger.

LISE   I believe
                 He's lying.

CYRANO   Why? Was I looking down my nose?
                 That must have been a very cunning lie!
                 (Changing his tone; to RAGUENEAU*)*
                 I expect someone. Leave us here alone,   10
                 When the time comes.

RAGUENEAU
How can I? In a moment,
My poets will be here.

LISE
To break their . . . fast!

CYRANO
Take them away, then, when I give the sign.
—What time?

RAGUENEAU
Ten minutes after.

CYRANO
Have you a pen?

RAGUENEAU
(Offers him a pen)
An eagle's feather!

CYRANO
Ah—
(Takes up the pen; waves RAGUENEAU *away)*
Only to write—   15
To fold—To give it to her—and to go . . .
(Throws down the pen)
If I dare speak one word to her . . .
—One word
Of all the many thousand I have here!
Whereas in writing . . .
(Takes up the pen)
Come, I'll write to her
That letter I have written on my heart,   20
Torn up, and written over many times—
So many times . . . that all I have to do
Is to remember, and to write it down.

*(He writes. Through the glass of the door appear vague
and hesitating shadows. The* POETS *enter, clothed in rusty
black and spotted with mud.)*

■ Scene iv ■

LISE
(To RAGUENEAU*)*
Here come your scarecrows!

FIRST POET
Comrade!

SECOND POET
(Takes both RAGUENEAU's *hands)*
My dear brother!

THIRD POET	*(Sniffing)* Phoebus Apollo of the Silver Spoon!
FOURTH POET	Cupid of Cookery!
RAGUENEAU	*(Surrounded, embraced, beaten on the back)* These geniuses, They put one at one's ease!
FIRST POET	We were delayed By the crowd at the Porte de Nesle.
SECOND POET	Dead men 5 All scarred and gory, scattered on the stones, Villainous-looking scoundrels—eight of them.
CYRANO	*(Looks up an instant)* Eight? I thought only seven—
RAGUENEAU	Do you know The hero of this hecatomb?*
CYRANO	I? . . . No.
LISE	*(To RAGUENEAU)* Do you?
RAGUENEAU	Hmm—perhaps!
FIRST POET	They say one man alone 10 Put to flight all this crowd.
SECOND POET	Everywhere lay Swords, daggers, pikes,* bludgeons*—
CYRANO	*(Writing)* "Your eyes . . . Your lips . . ."
THIRD POET	Some savage monster might have done this thing!
CYRANO	"Looking upon you, I grow faint with fear . . ."
SECOND POET	What have you written lately, Ragueneau? 15

hecatomb: sacrifice or slaughter

pikes: spearheads
bludgeons: clubs

CYRANO   "Your Friend—Who loves you . . ."
                                          So. No signature;
                  I'll give it her myself.

RAGUENEAU   A Recipe
                  In Rime.

FIRST POET   Read us your rimes!

FOURTH POET   Here's a brioche*   *brioche:* soft roll
                  Cocking its hat at me.

                  (He bites off the top of it.)

FIRST POET   Look how those buns
                  Follow the hungry poet with their eyes!   20

RAGUENEAU   *(Coughs, adjusts his cap, strikes an attitude)*
                  A Recipe in Rime—

SECOND POET   *(Gives* the FOURTH POET *a dig with his elbow)*
                                      Your breakfast?

FOURTH POET   Dinner!

RAGUENEAU   *(Declaims)*
                  A Recipe for Making Almond Tarts

                  Beat your eggs, the yolk and white,
                      Very light;
                  Mingle with their creamy fluff   25
                    Drops of lime-juice, cool and green;
                      Then pour in
                  Milk of Almonds, just enough.

                  Dainty patty-pans, embraced
                      In puff-paste—   30
                  Have these ready within reach;
                    With your thumb and finger, pinch
                      Half an inch
                  Up around the edge of each—

> Into these, a score or more,   35
>   Slowly pour
> All your store of custard; so
>   Take them, bake them golden-brown—
>   Now sit down! . . .
> Almond tartlets, Ragueneau!   40

POETS   Delicious! Melting!

FOURTH POET   *(Chokes)*

Humph!

CYRANO   *(To* RAGUENEAU*)*

Do you not see
Those fellows fattening themselves?—

RAGUENEAU

I know.
I would not look—it might embarrass them—
You see, I love a friendly audience.
Besides—another vanity—I am pleased   45
When they enjoy my cooking.

*(*ROXANE *and the* DUENNA *appear outside the door.)*

CYRANO   *(Slaps him on the back)*

Be off with you!

RAGUENEAU   *(To the* POETS*)*
Come inside—we shall be more comfortable. . . .

(He leads the POETS *into an inner room. They go out.)*

CYRANO   If I can see the faintest spark of hope,
Then—
(Throws door open—bows)
   Welcome!
*(*ROXANE *enters masked, followed by the* DUENNA*, whom*
CYRANO *detains.)*
Pardon me—one word—

DUENNA

Take two.

CYRANO   Have you a good digestion?

■ **Scene v** ▬▬▬▬

DUENNA	Wonderful!
CYRANO	Good. Here are two sonnets, by Benserade*—

Benserade: seventeenth-century French poet

DUENNA	Huh?
CYRANO	Which I fill for you with éclairs.
DUENNA	Ooo! 5
CYRANO	—Do you love Nature?
DUENNA	Mad about it.
CYRANO	Then Go out and eat these in the street. Do not Return—
DUENNA	Oh, but—
CYRANO	Until you finish them. *(Down to* ROXANE*)* Blessed above all others be the hour When you remembered to remember me, And came to tell me . . . what?

■ **Scene vi** ■

ROXANE	*(Takes off her mask)* First let me thank you Because that man . . . that creature, whom your sword Made sport of yesterday—His patron, one— 5
CYRANO	De Guiche?—
ROXANE	—who thinks himself in love with me Would force himself upon me for—a husband—
CYRANO	I understand—so much the better then! I fought, not for my nose, but your bright eyes.
ROXANE	And then, to tell you—but before I can 10 Tell you—Are you, I wonder, still the same Big brother—almost—that you used to be When we were children, playing by the pond In the old garden down there—

CYRANO	I remember— Every summer you came to Bergerac! . . . 15
ROXANE	You used to make swords out of bulrushes—
CYRANO	Your dandelion-dolls with golden hair—
ROXANE	And those green plums—
CYRANO	And those black mulberries—
ROXANE	In those days, you did everything I wished!
CYRANO	Roxane, in short skirts, was called Madeleine. 20
ROXANE	Was I pretty?
CYRANO	Oh—not too plain!
ROXANE	Sometimes When you had hurt your hand you used to come Running to me—and I would be your mother, And say—Oh, in a very grown-up voice: *(She takes his hand.)* "Now, what have you been doing to yourself? 25 Let me see—" *(She sees the hand—starts.)* Oh!— Wait—I said, "Let me see!" Still—at your age! How did you do that?
CYRANO	Playing With the big boys, down by the Porte de Nesle.
ROXANE	*(Sits at a table and wets her handkerchief in a glass of water)* Come here to me.
CYRANO	—Such a wise little mother!
ROXANE	And tell me, while I wash this blood away, 30 How many you—played with?
CYRANO	Oh, about a hundred.

ROXANE   Tell me.

CYRANO   No. Let me go. Tell me what you
Were going to tell me—if you dared?

ROXANE   *(Still holding his hand)*
                                    I think
I do dare—now. It seems like long ago
When I could tell you things. Yes—I dare. . . . Listen: 35
I . . . love someone.

CYRANO   Ah! . . .

ROXANE   Someone who does not know.

CYRANO   Ah! . . .

ROXANE   At least—not yet.

CYRANO   Ah! . . .

ROXANE   But he will know
Some day.

CYRANO   Ah! . . .

ROXANE   A big boy who loves me too,
And is afraid of me, and keeps away,
And never says one word.

CYRANO   Ah! . . .

ROXANE   Let me have   40
Your hand a moment—why, how hot it is!—
I know. I see him trying . . .

CYRANO   Ah! . . .

ROXANE   There now!
Is that better?—
(She finishes bandaging the hand with her handkerchief.)
                    Besides—only to think—
(This is a secret.) He is a soldier too,
In your own regiment—

CYRANO   Ah! . . .

ROXANE   Yes, in the Guards,   45
            Your company too.

CYRANO   Ah! . . .

ROXANE   And such a man!—
            He is proud—noble—brave—beautiful—

CYRANO   *(Turns pale; rises)*
            Beautiful!—

ROXANE   What's the matter?

CYRANO   *(Smiling)*
                              Nothing—this—
            My sore hand!

ROXANE	Well, I love him. That is all.
	Oh—and I never saw him anywhere 50
	Except the *Comedie.*
CYRANO	You have never spoken?—
ROXANE	Only our eyes . . .
CYRANO	Why, then—How do you know?—
ROXANE	People talk about people; and I hear
	Things . . . and I know.
CYRANO	You say he's in the Guards:
	His name?
ROXANE	Baron Christian de Neuvillette. 55
CYRANO	He is not in the Guards.
ROXANE	Yes. Since this morning.
	Captain Carbon de Castel-Jaloux.
CYRANO	So soon! . . .
	So soon we lose our hearts!—
	But, my dear child,—
DUENNA	*(Opens the door)*
	I've eaten the cakes, Monsieur de Bergerac!
CYRANO	Good! Now go out and read the poetry! 60
	(The DUENNA *disappears.)*
	But, my dear child! You, who love only words,
	Wit, the grand manner—why for all you know,
	The man may be a savage, or a fool.
ROXANE	His curls are like a hero from D'Urfé.
CYRANO	His mind may be as curly as his hair. 65
ROXANE	Not with such eyes. I read his soul in them.

CYRANO	Yes, all our souls are written in our eyes! But—if he be a bungler?
ROXANE	Then I shall die— There!
CYRANO	*(After a pause)* And you brought me here to tell me this? I do not yet quite understand, Madame, 70 The reason for your confidence.
ROXANE	They say That in your company—It frightens me— You are all Gascons* . . .
CYRANO	And we pick a quarrel With any flat-foot who intrudes himself Whose blood is not pure Gascon like our own? 75 Is this what you have heard?
ROXANE	I'm so afraid For him!
CYRANO	*(Between his teeth)* Not without reason!—
ROXANE	And I thought You . . . You were so brave, so invincible Yesterday, against all those brutes!—If you, Whom they all fear—
CYRANO	Oh well—I will defend 80 Your little Baron.
ROXANE	Will you? Just for me? Because I've always been—your friend!
CYRANO	Of course . . .
ROXANE	Will you be *his* friend?
CYRANO	I will be his friend.
ROXANE	And never let him fight a duel?

Gascons: people of Gascony, reputed to be assertive and boastful

CYRANO	No—never.

ROXANE Oh, but you are a darling!—I must go—   85
You never told me about last night—Why,
You must have been a hero! Have him write
And tell me all about it—will you?

CYRANO   Of course . . .

ROXANE *(Kisses his hand)*
I always did love you!—A hundred men
Against one—Well . . . . Adieu. We are great friends,   90
Are we not?

CYRANO   Of course . . .

ROXANE   He *must* write to me—
A hundred—You shall tell me the whole story
Some day, when I have time. A hundred men—
What courage—

CYRANO *(Salutes as she goes out)*
                    Oh . . . I have done better since!

*(The door closes after her. CYRANO remains motionless,
his eyes on the ground. Pause. The other door opens;
RAGUENEAU puts in his head.)*

RAGUENEAU May I come in?

CYRANO *(Without moving)*
                    Yes. . . .
*(RAGUENEAU and his friends reenter. At the same time,
CARBON DE CASTEL-JALOUX appears at the street door in
uniform as Captain of the Guards; recognizes CYRANO
with a sweeping gesture.)*

CARBON   Here he is!—Our hero!

CYRANO *(Raises his head and salutes)*
Our Captain!

■ Scene vii ■

CARBON   We know! All our company
Are here—

CYRANO   *(Recoils)*
                    No—

CARBON   Come! They're waiting for you.

CYRANO   No!

CARBON   *(Tries to lead him out)*
Only across the street—Come!

CYRANO   Please—

CARBON   *(Goes to the door and shouts in a voice of thunder)*
                              Our champion
Refuses! He's not feeling well to-day!   5

*(Noise outside of swords and trampling feet approaching;
the* CADETS *noisily enter the shop.)*

RAGUENEAU   *(In astonishment)*
You are all Gascons?

CADETS   All!

FIRST CADET   *(To* CYRANO*)*
                    Bravo!

SECOND CADET *(Takes both of* CYRANO's *hands)*
                         Vivat!*   *Vivat:* Latin: "May you
                                                         live (long)!"

LE BRET   *(Enters; hurries to* CYRANO*)*
The whole town's looking for you! Raving mad—
A triumph! Those who saw the fight—

CYRANO   I hope
You have not told them where I—

LE BRET   *(Rubbing his hands)*
                         Certainly
I told them!

CITIZEN   *(Enters, followed by a group)*
                                      Listen! Shut the door!—Here comes   10
                  All Paris!

                  *(The street outside fills with a shouting crowd. Chairs and
                  carriages stop at the door.)*

LE BRET   *(Aside to CYRANO, smiling)*
                                      And Roxane?

CYRANO   *(Quickly)*
                                              Hush!

CROWD   *(Outside)*
                                              Cyrano!

                  *(A mob bursts into the shop. Shouts, acclamations,
                  general disturbance.)*

RAGUENEAU   *(Standing on a table)*
                  My shop invaded—They'll break everything—
                  Glorious!

SEVERAL MEN   *(Crowding about CYRANO)*
                                      My friend! . . . My friend! . . .

CYRANO   Why, yesterday
                  I did not have so many friends!

LE BRET   Success
                  At last!

FIRST MARQUIS   *(Runs to CYRANO, with outstretched hands)*
                                      My dear—really!—

CYRANO   *(Coldly)*
                                              So? And how long   15
                  Have I been dear to you?

SECOND MARQUIS   One moment—pray!
                  I have two ladies in my carriage here;
                  Let me present you—

CYRANO   Certainly! And first,
Who will present you, sir—to me?

LE BRET   *(Astounded)*
                                   Why, what
Do you mean?—

CYRANO   Hush!

EDITOR   *(With a portfolio)*
                   May I have the details? . . .   20

CYRANO   You may not.

LE BRET   *(Plucking* CYRANO's *sleeve)*
              Renaudot!—the editor
Of the *Gazette*—your reputation! . . .

CYRANO   No!

(The crowd arranges itself. DE GUICHE *appears, escorted
by* CUIGY, BRISSAILLE, *and the other officers who were
with* CYRANO *at the close of Act I.)*

CUIGY   *(Goes to* CYRANO*)*
Monsieur de Guiche!—
(Murmur; everyone moves.)
               A message from the Marshal
De Gassion—

DE GUICHE   *(Saluting* CYRANO*)*
             Who wishes to express
Through me his admiration. He has heard   25
Of your affair—

CROWD   Bravo!

CYRANO   *(Bowing)*
               The Marshal speaks
As an authority.

DE GUICHE   He said just now
The story would have been incredible

Were it not for the witness—

CUIGY

Of our eyes!

LE BRET

(Aside to CYRANO*)*
What is it?

CYRANO

Hush!—

LE BRET

Something is wrong with you;   30
Are you in pain?

CYRANO

(Recovering himself)
In pain? Before this crowd?
(His moustache bristles. He throws out his chest.)
I? In pain? You shall see!

DE GUICHE

(To whom CUIGY *has been whispering)*
Your name is known
Already as a soldier. You are one
Of those wild Gascons, are you not?

CYRANO

The Guards,
Yes. A Cadet.

CADETS

(In a voice of thunder)
One of ourselves!

DE GUICHE

Ah! So—   35
Then all these gentlemen with the haughty air,
These are the famous—

CARBON

Cyrano!

CYRANO

Captain?

CARBON

Our troop being all present, be so kind
As to present them to the Comte de Guiche!

CYRANO

(With a gesture, presenting the CADETS *to* DE GUICHE,
declaims:)
The Cadets of Gascoyne—the defenders   40
of Carbon de Castel-Jaloux:

Free fighters, free wooers, free spenders—
The Cadets of Gascoyne—the defenders
Of old homes, old names, and old splendors—
   A proud and a pestilent* crew!   45   *pestilent:* trouble-
The Cadets of Gascoyne, the defenders   making
   Of Carbon de Castel-Jaloux.

DE GUICHE   *(Languidly, sitting in a chair)*
                  Poets are fashionable nowadays
                  To have about one. Would you care to join
                  My following?

CYRANO   No, sir. I do not follow.   50

DE GUICHE   Your duel yesterday amused my uncle
                  The Cardinal. I might help you there.

LE BRET   Oh no!

DE GUICHE   I suppose you have written a tragedy—
                  They all have.

LE BRET   *(Aside to* CYRANO*)*
                              Now at last you'll have it played—
                  Your "Agrippine"!

DE GUICHE   Why not? Take it to him.   55

CYRANO   *(Tempted)*
                  Really—

DE GUICHE   He is himself a dramatist;
                  Let him rewrite a few lines here and there,
                  And he'll approve the rest.

CYRANO   *(His face falling again)*
                                Impossible.
                  My blood curdles to think of altering
                  One comma.

DE GUICHE   Ah, but when he likes a thing   60
                  He pays well.

CYRANO   Yes—but not so well as I—
              When I have made a line that sings itself
              So that I love the sound of it—I pay
              Myself a hundred times.

DE GUICHE   You're proud, my friend.

CYRANO   You have observed that?

CADET   (Enters with a drawn sword, along the whole blade of
              which is transfixed a collection of disreputable hats, their
              plumes dragged, their crowns cut and torn)
                              Cyrano! See here—   65
              Look what we found this morning in the street—
              The plumes dropped in their flight by those fine birds
              Who showed the white feather!

CARBON   Spoils of the hunt—
              Well mounted!

CROWD   Ha-ha-ha!

CUIGY   Whoever hired
              Those rascals, he must be an angry man   70
              To-day!

BRISSAILLE   Who was it? Do you know?

DE GUICHE   Myself!—
              (The laughter ceases.)
              I hired them to do the sort of work
              We do not soil our hands with—attacking
              An aging poet. . . .

              (Uncomfortable silence)

CADET   (To CYRANO)
                        What shall we do with them?
              They ought to be preserved before they spoil—   75

CYRANO   (Takes the sword, and in the gesture of saluting DE
              GUICHE with it, makes all the hats slide off at his feet)
              Sir, will you not return these to your friends?

DE GUICHE	My chair—my porters here—immediately!
	(To CYRANO *violently)*
	—As for you, sir!—
VOICE	*(In the street)*
	The chair of Monseigneur
	Le Comte de Guiche!—
DE GUICHE	*(Having recovered his self-control, smiling)*
	Have you read *Don Quixote?*
CYRANO	I have—and found myself the hero.
PORTER	*(Appears at the door)*
	Chair
	Ready!
DE GUICHE	Be so good as to read once more 80
	The chapter of the windmills.
CYRANO	*(Gravely)*
	Chapter Thirteen.
DE GUICHE	Windmills, remember, if you fight with them—
CYRANO	My enemies change, then, with every wind?
DE GUICHE	—May swing round their huge arms and cast you down
	Into the mire.
CYRANO	Or up—among the stars! 85

*(*DE GUICHE *goes out. We see him get into the chair. The officers follow murmuring among themselves.* LE BRET *goes up with them. The crowd goes out.)*

CYRANO	*(Saluting with burlesque politeness those who go out without daring to take leave of him)*
	Gentlemen . . . Gentlemen . . . .
LE BRET	*(As the door closes, comes down, shaking his clenched hands to heaven)*
	You have done it now—
	You've made your fortune!

■ Scene viii ■■■

CYRANO   There you go again,
                    Growling!—

LE BRET   At least this latest pose of yours—
                    Ruining every chance that comes your way—
                    Becomes exaggerated—

CYRANO   Very well,   5
                    Then I exaggerate!

LE BRET   *(Triumphantly)*
                              Oh, you do!

CYRANO   Yes;
                    On principle. There are things in this world
                    A man does well to carry to extremes.

LE BRET   Stop trying to be Three Musketeers in one!
                    Fortune and glory—

CYRANO   What would you have me do?   10
                    Seek for the patronage of some great man,
                    And like a creeping vine on a tall tree
                    Crawl upward, where I cannot stand alone?
                    No thank you! Dedicate, as others do,
                    Poems to pawnbrokers? No—no thank you!   15
                    Wear out my belly groveling* in the dust?   *groveling:* lying
                    No thank you! Scratch the back of any swine   prostrate
                    That roots up gold for me? Or use the fire
                    God gave me to burn incense all day long
                    Under the nose of wood and stone? No, sir,   20
                    I thank you! —But . . .

                                    To sing, to laugh, to dream,
                    To walk in my own way and be alone,
                    Free, with an eye to see things as they are,
                    To fight—or write. To travel any road
                    Under the sun, under the stars, nor doubt   25
                    If fame or fortune lie beyond the bourne*—   *bourne:* boundary
                    Never to make a line I have not heard
                    In my own heart; yet, with all modesty
                    To say: "My soul, be satisfied with flowers,
                    With fruit, with weeds even; but gather them   30

In the one garden you may call your own."
So, when I win some triumph, by some chance,
Render no share to Caesar*—in a word,
I am too proud to be a parasite,
And if my nature wants the germ* that grows   35
Towering to heaven like the mountain pine,
Or like the oak, sheltering multitudes—
I stand, not high it may be—but alone!

Render no share to Caesar: a reference to Matt. 22:21
wants the germ: lacks the seed

LE BRET   Alone, yes!—But why stand against the world?
This is but madness!

CYRANO   Method, let us say.   40
It is my pleasure to displease. I love
Hatred. Imagine how it feels to face
The volley* of a thousand angry eyes—
The bile* of envy and the froth of fear
Spattering little drops about me—You—   45
Good nature all around you, soft and warm—
You are like those Italians, in great cowls*
Comfortable and loose—Your chin sinks down
Into the folds, your shoulders droop. But I—
The Spanish ruff* I wear around my throat   50
Is like a ring of enemies; hard, proud,
Each point another pride, another thorn—
So that I hold myself erect perforce*
Wearing the hatred of the common herd
Haughtily, the harsh collar of Old Spain,   55
At once a fetter and—a halo!

volley: several shots fired at once
bile: bitterness

cowls: hoods

ruff: frilled collar

perforce: necessarily

LE BRET   Yes . . .
(After a silence, draws CYRANO's *arm through his own)*
Tell this to all the world—And then to me
Say very softly that . . . She loves you not.

CYRANO   *(Quickly)*
Hush!

(A moment since, CHRISTIAN *has entered and mingled with the* CADETS, *who do not offer to speak to him. Finally, he sits down alone at a small table, where he is served by* LISE.*)*

■ Scene ix ■■■■■■■

FIRST CADET   *(Rises from a table upstage, his glass in his hand)*
        Cyrano!—Your story!

CYRANO   Presently . . .

(He goes up, on the arm of LE BRET, *talking to him. The* CADET *comes downstage.)*

FIRST CADET   The story of the combat! An example
For—
(He stops by the table where CHRISTIAN *is sitting.)*
      —this young tadpole here.

CHRISTIAN   *(Looks up)*
                      Tadpole?

SECOND CADET   Yes, you!—
You narrow-gutted Northerner!

CHRISTIAN   Sir?

FIRST CADET   Hark,
Monsieur de Neuvillette: You are to know   5
There is a certain subject—I would say,
A certain object—never to be named
Among us: utterly unmentionable!

CHRISTIAN   And that is?

THIRD CADET   *(In an awful voice)*
              Look at me! . . .
(He strikes his nose three times with his finger, mysteriously.)
              You understand?

CHRISTIAN   Why, yes; the—

FOURTH CADET   Sh! . . . We never speak that word—   10
(Indicating CYRANO *by a gesture)*
To breathe it is to have to do with *him!*

FIFTH CADET   *(Speaks through his nose)*
He has exterminated several
Whose tone of voice suggested . . .

SIXTH CADET	*(In a hollow tone; rising from under the table on all fours)* Would you die Before your time? Just mention anything Convex* . . . or cartilaginous* . . .
SEVENTH CADET	*(His hand on* CHRISTIAN's *shoulder)* One word— 15 One syllable—one gesture—nay, one sneeze— Your handkerchief becomes your winding-sheet!* *(Silence. In a circle around* CHRISTIAN, *arms crossed, they regard him expectantly.)*
CHRISTIAN	*(Rises and goes to* CARBON, *who is conversing with an officer, and pretending not to see what is taking place)* Captain!
CARBON	*(Turns, and looks him over)* Sir?
CHRISTIAN	What is the proper thing to do When Gascons grow too boastful?
CARBON	Prove to them That one may be a Norman, and have courage. 20 *(Turns his back)*
CHRISTIAN	I thank you.
FIRST CADET	*(To* CYRANO*)* Come—the story!
ALL	The story!

CYRANO	*(Comes down)*
	                          Oh,
	My story? Well . . .
	(They all draw up their stools and group themselves around him, eagerly. CHRISTIAN *places himself astride of a chair, his arms on the back of it.)*
	                I marched on, all alone
	To meet those devils. Overhead, the moon
	Hung like a gold watch at the fob* of heaven,
	Till suddenly some Angel rubbed a cloud, 25

convex: curving outward
cartilaginous: made of cartilage

winding-sheet: cloth in which a corpse is wrapped

fob: watch chain

As it might be his handkerchief, across
The shining crystal, and—the night came down.
No lamps in those back streets—It was so dark—
Perilous! You could not see beyond—

CHRISTIAN   Your nose.

(Silence. Every man slowly rises to his feet. They look at
CYRANO *almost with terror. He has stopped short, utterly*
astonished. Pause.)

CYRANO   Who is that man there?

CADET   *(In a low voice)*
                              A recruit—arrived   30
              This morning.

CYRANO   *(Takes a step toward* CHRISTIAN*)*
                      A recruit—

CARBON   *(In a low voice)*
                              His name is Christian
              De Neuvil—

CYRANO   *(Suddenly motionless)*
                      Oh . . .
              (He turns pale, flushes, makes a movement as if to throw
              himself upon CHRISTIAN*.)*
                      I—
              (Controls himself, and goes on in a choking voice)
                      I see. Very well,
              As I was saying—
              (With a sudden burst of rage)
                      Perilous! . . .
              (He goes on in a natural tone.)
                              It grew dark,
              You could not see your hand before your eyes.
              I marched on, thinking how, all for the sake   35
              Of one poor poet
              (They slowly sit down, watching him.)
                              who wrote a rowdy song
              Whene'er he took—

CHRISTIAN   A noseful—

(Everyone rises. CHRISTIAN *balances himself on two legs of his chair.)*

CYRANO   *(Half strangled)*
                              —Took a notion.
Whene'er he took a notion—For his sake,
I might antagonize some dangerous man,
One powerful enough to make me pay—   40

CHRISTIAN   Through the nose—

CYRANO   *(Wipes the sweat from his forehead)*
                         Pay the Piper. After all,
I thought, why am I putting in my—

CHRISTIAN   Nose—

CYRANO   —My oar . . . Why am I putting in my oar?
The quarrel's none of mine. However—now
I am here, I may as well go through with it.   45
Come Gascon—do your duty!—Suddenly
A sword flashed in the dark. I caught it fair—

CHRISTIAN   On the nose—

CYRANO   On my blade. Before I knew it,
There I was—

CHRISTIAN   Rubbing noses—

CYRANO   *(Pale and smiling)*
                         Crossing swords
With half a score at once. I handed one—   50

CHRISTIAN   A nosegay—

CYRANO   *(Leaping at him)*
           GET OUT OF HERE! All of you!

(The Gascons tumble over each other to rush for the nearest exit. The lines following are heard brokenly in the confusion of getting through the door.)

FIRST CADET   The old lion wakes!

CYRANO   Leave me here alone with
That man!

SECOND CADET   He'll have the fellow chopped into
Sausage—

RAGUENEAU   Sausage?—

THIRD CADET   Mince-meat, then—

*(They are all gone: some through the street door, some by
the inner door to right and left. A few disappear up the
staircase. CYRANO arrives in front of CHRISTIAN, who has
not moved an inch. They stand face to face a moment and
look at each other.)*

CYRANO	To my arms!
CHRISTIAN	Sir? . . .
CYRANO	You have courage!
CHRISTIAN	Oh, that! . . .
CYRANO	You are brave— That pleases me.
CHRISTIAN	You mean? . . .
CYRANO	Do you not know I am her brother? Come!
CHRISTIAN	Whose?—
CYRANO	Hers—Roxane!
CHRISTIAN	Her . . . brother? You?
CYRANO	Her cousin. Much the same.
CHRISTIAN	And she has told you? . . .
CYRANO	Everything.
CHRISTIAN	She loves me?
CYRANO	Perhaps.
CHRISTIAN	*(Takes both his hands)* My dear sir—more than I can say, I am honored—
CYRANO	This is rather sudden.
CHRISTIAN	Please Forgive me—
CYRANO	*(Holds him at arm's length, looking at him)* Why, he is a handsome man, This fellow!

■ Scene x ▬▬▬

5

CHRISTIAN	On my honor—if you knew How much I have admired—
CYRANO	Yes, yes—and all 10 Those Noses which—
CHRISTIAN	Please! I apologize.
CYRANO	*(Change of tone)* Roxane expects a letter—
CHRISTIAN	Not from me?—
CYRANO	Yes. Why not?
CHRISTIAN	Once I write, that ruins all!
CYRANO	And why?
CHRISTIAN	Because . . . because I am a fool! Stupid enough to hang myself!
CYRANO	But no— 15 You are no fool; you call yourself a fool, There's proof enough in that. Besides, you did not Attack me like a fool.
CHRISTIAN	Bah! Any one Can pick a quarrel. Yes, I have a sort Of rough and ready soldier's tongue. I know 20 That. But with any woman—paralyzed, Speechless, dumb. If only I had words To say what I have here!
CYRANO	If I could be A handsome little Musketeer with eyes!—
CHRISTIAN	Besides—you know Roxane—how sensitive— 25 One rough word, and the sweet illusion—gone!
CYRANO	I wish you might be my interpreter.
CHRISTIAN	I wish I had your wit—

CYRANO	Borrow it, then!—

Your beautiful young manhood—lend me that,
And we two make one hero of romance!   30

CHRISTIAN   What?

CYRANO   Would you dare repeat to her the words
I gave you, day by day?

CHRISTIAN   You mean?

CYRANO   I mean
Roxane shall have no disillusionment!
Come, shall we win her both together? Take
The soul within this leathern jack* of mine,   35   *leathern jack:* padded
And breathe it into you?   leather garment
(Touches CHRISTIAN'S *heart)*
                              So—there's my heart
Under your velvet, now!

CHRISTIAN   But—Cyrano!—

CYRANO   But—Christian, why not?

CHRISTIAN   I'm afraid—

CYRANO   I know—
Afraid that when you have her all alone,
You lose all. Have no fear. It is yourself   40
She loves—give her yourself put into words—
My words, upon your lips!

CHRISTIAN   But does it mean
So much to you?

CYRANO   *(Beside himself)*
                    It means—
(Recovers, changes tone)
                              A Comedy,
A situation for a poet! Come.
Shall we collaborate? I'll be your cloak   45
Of darkness, your enchanted sword, your ring
To charm the fairy Princess!

CHRISTIAN   But the letter—
I cannot write—

CYRANO   Oh yes, the letter.
(He takes from his pocket the letter which he has written.)
                              Here.

CHRISTIAN   What is this?

CYRANO   All there; all but the address.

CHRISTIAN   I—

CYRANO   You may send it. It will serve.

CHRISTIAN   But why   50
Have you done this?

CYRANO   I have amused myself
As we all do, we poets—writing vows
To Chloris, Phyllis—any pretty name—
You might have had a pocketful of them!
Take it, and turn to facts my fantasies—   55
I loosed these loves like doves into the air;
Give them a habitation and a home.
Here, take it—You will find me all the more
Eloquent, being insincere! Come!

CHRISTIAN   First,
There must be a few changes here and there   60—
Written at random, can it fit Roxane?

CYRANO   Like her own glove.

CHRISTIAN   No, but—

CYRANO   My son, have faith—
Faith in the love of women for themselves—
Roxane will know this letter for her own!

CHRISTIAN   *(Throws himself into the arms of* CYRANO; *they stand
embraced)*
My friend!

(The door upstage opens a little. The First Cadet *steals in.)*

First Cadet   Nothing. A silence like the tomb . . .   65

I hardly dare look—
(He sees the two.)
                Wha-at?

(The other Cadets *crowd in behind him and see.)*

Cadets   No!—No!

Second Cadet   *(Slaps his knee)*
                                    Well, well!
Now we're allowed to talk about his nose?
(Calls, sniffing the air and grimacing)
That smell . . .
(He plants himself in front of Cyrano, *and looks at his nose in an impolite manner.)*
                You ought to know about such things;
What seems to have died around here?

Cyrano   *(Knocks him backward over a bench)*
                                Cabbage-heads!
(Joy. The Cadets *have found their old* Cyrano *again. General disturbance.)*

(Curtain)

About the Play

1. How does Cyrano react to the excessive praise and attention given to him by his fellow cadets when they hear of his victory over the hundred men? What does this tell us about Cyrano?
2. The central conflict of the drama is clearly revealed in Act II. (See especially pp. 400-403.) Would you describe the central conflict as man against a power greater than himself, man against man, or man against himself?
3. How does Christian describe himself to Cyrano (p. 420)?
4. Is Christian's description of himself consistent with what we have already learned about him in Act I?
5. What does Cyrano's willingness to help Christian win Roxane's love tell us about him?
6. Is Cyrano's action consistent with Le Bret's and Ragueneau's descriptions of him in Act I?

ACT III

Roxane's Kiss

A little square in the old Marais: old houses, and a glimpse of narrow streets. On the right, the house of ROXANE *and her garden wall, overhung with tall shrubbery. Over the door of the house, a balcony and a tall window; to one side of the door, a bench.*

At the curtain rise the DUENNA *is seated on the bench beside the door. The window is wide open on* ROXANE's *balcony; a light within suggests that it is early evening.*

DUENNA	*(Calls up to window)* Roxane! Are you ready? We will be late!	■ Scene i ■
ROXANE	*(Within)* I'm putting on my cape—	
DUENNA	Hurry, my dear— We'll miss The Tender Passion!*	

The Tender Passion: the topic of a forum held at a neighbor's house for entertainment and education

ROXANE   Coming!—

(Music of stringed instruments off-stage approaches; the
voice of CYRANO *can be heard accompanying.)*

DUENNA   What—?
A serenade?—How pleasant—

CYRANO   No, no, no!—
F natural, you natural born fool!   5
(Enters, followed by two PAGES, *carrying theorbos*)*

theorbos: musical
instruments; a type
of lute

FIRST PAGE   *(Ironically)*
No doubt your honor knows F natural
When he hears—

CYRANO   I am a musician, infant!—
A pupil of Gassendi.*

*(*CYRANO *snatches the instruments from the* FIRST PAGE
and continues the tune.)

Gassendi: French
seventeenth-century
mathematician,
musician, and
philosopher

ROXANE   *(Appears on the balcony)*
                                    Is that you,
Cyrano? Please—please don't go—I'll be down—
Wait—
(Goes in through the window)

DUENNA   *(Turning to* CYRANO*)*
                    Did you train these virtuosi?*

virtuosi: masters of
technique

CYRANO   No—   10
I won them on a bet from D'Assoucy.
We were debating a fine point of grammar
When, pointing out these two young nightingales
Dressed up like peacocks, with their instruments,
He cries: "No, but I KNOW! I'll wager you   15
A day of music." Well, of course he lost;
And so until to-morrow they are mine,
My private orchestra. Pleasant at first,
But they become a trifle—
(To the PAGES*)*
                    Here! Go play

A minuet to Montfleury—and tell him   20
I sent you!
(The PAGES *go up to the exit.* CYRANO *turns to the*
DUENNA.*)*
     I came here as usual
To inquire after our friend—
(To the PAGES*)*
        Play out of tune.
And keep on playing!
(The PAGES *go out. He turns to the* DUENNA.*)*
      Our friend with the great soul.

ROXANE   *(Enters in time to hear the last words)*
       He's beautiful and brilliant—and I love him!

CYRANO   Do you find Christian . . . intellectual?   25

ROXANE   More so than you, even.

CYRANO   I'm glad.

ROXANE   No man
       Ever so beautifully said those things—
       Those pretty nothings that are everything.
       Sometimes he falls into a reverie;
       His inspiration fails—then all at once,   30
       He will say something absolutely . . . Oh!

CYRANO   Really!

ROXANE   How like a man! You think a man
       Who has a handsome face must be a fool.

CYRANO   He talks well about . . . matters of the heart?

ROXANE   He does not *talk;* he rhapsodizes . . . dreams . . .   35

CYRANO   *(Twisting his moustache)*
       He . . . writes well?

ROXANE   Wonderfully. Listen now:
       (Reciting as from memory)
       "Take my heart; I shall have it all the more;

Plucking the flowers, we keep the plant in bloom—"
Well?

CYRANO   Pooh!

ROXANE   And this:
                              "Knowing you have in store
More heart to give than I to find heart-room—"   40

CYRANO   First he has too much, then too little; just
How much heart does he need?

ROXANE   *(Tapping her foot)*
                                        You're teasing me!
You're jealous!

CYRANO   *(Startled)*
                    Jealous?

ROXANE   Of his poetry—
You poets are like that . . . And these last lines . . .
Listen to this—

CYRANO   You know them all by heart?   45

ROXANE   Every one!

CYRANO   *(Twisting his moustache)*
                    I may call that flattering . . .

ROXANE   He is a master!

CYRANO   Oh—come!

ROXANE   Yes—a master!

CYRANO   *(Bowing)*
A master—if you will!

DUENNA   *(Comes downstage quickly)*
                              Monsieur de Guiche!—
(To CYRANO, *pushing him toward the house)*
Go inside—If he does not find you here,
It may be just as well. He may suspect—   50

ROXANE	—My secret! Yes; he is in love with me And he is powerful. Let him not know— One look would frost my roses before bloom.
CYRANO	*(Going into the house)* Very well, very well!
ROXANE	*(To* DE GUICHE, *as he enters)* We were just going—
DE GUICHE	I came only to say farewell.
ROXANE	You leave Paris?
DE GUICHE	Yes—for the front.
ROXANE	Ah!
DE GUICHE	And to-night!
ROXANE	Ah!
DE GUICHE	We have orders to besiege Arras.
ROXANE	Arras?
DE GUICHE	Yes. My departure leaves you . . . cold?
ROXANE	*(Politely)* Oh! Not that.
DE GUICHE	It has left me desolate— When shall I see you? Ever? Did you know I was made Colonel?
ROXANE	*(Indifferent)* Bravo.
DE GUICHE	Regiment Of the Guards.
ROXANE	*(Catching her breath)* Of the Guards?—

■ Scene ii ■

5

DE GUICHE

His regiment
Your cousin, the mighty man of words!—
(Grimly)

Down there
We may have an accounting!

ROXANE

(Suffocating)

Are you sure   10
The Guards are ordered?

DE GUICHE

Under my command!

ROXANE

(Sinks down, breathless, on the bench; aside)
Christian!—

DE GUICHE

What is it?

ROXANE

(Losing control of herself)
To the war—perhaps
Never again to—When a woman cares,
Is that nothing?

DE GUICHE

(Surprised and delighted)
You say this now—to me—
Now, at the very moment?—

ROXANE

(Recovers—changes her tone)
Tell me something: 15
My cousin—You say you mean to be revenged
On him. Do you mean that?

DE GUICHE

(Smiles)
Why? Would you care?

ROXANE

Not for him.

DE GUICHE

Do you see him?

ROXANE

Now and then.

DE GUICHE

He goes about everywhere nowadays
With one of the Cadets—de Neuve—Neuville—   20
Neuvillers—

ROXANE   *(Coolly)*
                                A tall man?—

DE GUICHE   Blond—

ROXANE   Rosy cheeks?—

DE GUICHE   Handsome!—

ROXANE   Pooh!—

DE GUICHE   And a fool.

ROXANE   *(Languidly)*
                                        So he appears . . .
                  (Animated)
                  But Cyrano? What will you do to him?
                  Order him into danger? He loves that!
                  I know what *I* should do.

DE GUICHE   What?

ROXANE   Leave him here   25
                  With his Cadets, while all the regiment
                  Goes on to glory! That would torture him—
                  To sit all through the war with folded arms—
                  I know his nature. If you hate that man,
                  Strike at his self-esteem.

DE GUICHE   Oh woman—woman!   30
                  Who but a woman would have thought of this?

ROXANE   He'll eat his heart out, while his Gascon friends
                  Bite their nails all day long in Paris here.
                  And you will be avenged!

DE GUICHE   You love me then,
                  A little? . . .
                  (She smiles.)
                          Making my enemies your own,   35
                  Hating them—I should like to see in that
                  A sign of love, Roxane.

ROXANE   Perhaps it is one . . .

DE GUICHE   *(Shows a number of folded despatches)*
Here are the orders—for each company—
Ready to send . . .
(Selects one)
        So—This is for the Guards—
I'll keep that. Aha, Cyrano!
(To ROXANE*)*
              You too,   40
You play your little games, do you?

ROXANE   *(Watching him)*
              Sometimes . . .

DE GUICHE   *(Close to her, speaking hurriedly)*
And you!—Oh, I am mad over you!—Listen—
In the Rue d'Orleans, the Capuchins*
Have their new convent. By their law, no layman
May pass inside those walls. I'll see to that—   45
Their sleeves are wide enough to cover me—
The servants of my Uncle-Cardinal
Will fear his nephew. So—I'll come to you
Masked, after everyone knows I have gone—
Oh, let me wait one day!—

Capuchins: those who wear hooded cloaks, i.e., priests

ROXANE   If this be known,   50
Your honor—

DE GUICHE   Bah!

ROXANE   The war—your duty—

DE GUICHE   *(Blows away an imaginary feather)*
              Phoo!—
Only say yes!

ROXANE   No!

DE GUICHE   Whisper . . .

ROXANE   *(Tenderly)*
           I ought not
To let you . . .

DE GUICHE   Ah! . . .

ROXANE | *(Pretends to break down)*
| Ah, go!
| *(Aside)*
| —Christian remains—
| *(Aloud—heroically)*
| I would have you a hero—Antoine . . .

DE GUICHE | Have me? . . .
| So you can love—

ROXANE | One for whose sake I fear.   55

DE GUICHE | *(Triumphant)*
| I go! Will that content you?
| *(Kisses her hand)*

ROXANE | Yes—my friend!

| *(He goes out.)*

DUENNA | *(As* DE GUICHE *disappears, making a deep curtsy behind his back, and imitating* ROXANE'S *intense tone)*
| Yes—my friend!

ROXANE | *(Quickly, close to her)*
| Not a word to Cyrano—
| He would never forgive me if he knew
| I stole his war!
| *(She calls toward the house.)*
| Cousin!
| *(*CYRANO *comes out of the house; she turns to him, indicating the house opposite.)*
| We are going over—
| Alcandre speaks to-night—and Lysimon.
| *(The two women cross the street;* ROXANE *motions to the* DUENNA *as the door opens.)*
| Enter . . .
| *(To* CYRANO*)*
| If Christian comes, tell him to wait.

■ Scene iii ■

CYRANO | Oh—
| *(*ROXANE *returns.)*
| When he comes, what will you talk about?
| You always know beforehand.

ROXANE	About . . .
CYRANO	Well?
ROXANE	You will not tell him, will you?
CYRANO	I am dumb. 5

ROXANE   About nothing! Or about everything—
I shall say: "Speak of love in your own words—
Improvise! Rhapsodize! Be eloquent!"

CYRANO   *(Smiling)*
Good!

ROXANE   Sh!—

CYRANO   Sh!—

ROXANE   Not a word!

(She goes in; the door closes.)

CYRANO   *(Bowing)*
Thank you so much—

ROXANE   *(Opens door and puts out her head)*
He must be unprepared—

CYRANO   Of course!

ROXANE   Sh!—
(Goes in again)

CYRANO   *(Calls)*
Christian!   10
(CHRISTIAN enters)
I have your theme—bring on your memory!—
Here is your chance now to surpass yourself,
No time to lose—Come! Look intelligent—
Come home and learn your lines.

■ Scene iv ■■■■

CHRISTIAN   No.

CYRANO

What?

CHRISTIAN

I'll wait
Here for Roxane.

CYRANO

What lunacy is this?   5
Come quickly!

CHRISTIAN

No, I say! I've had enough—
Taking my words, my letters, all from you—
Making our love a little comedy!
It was a game at first; but now—she cares . . .
Thanks to you. I am not afraid. I'll speak   10
For myself now.

CYRANO

Undoubtedly!

CHRISTIAN

I will!
Why not? I am no such fool—you shall see!
Besides—my dear friend—you have taught me much.
(ROXANE *appears in the doorway, opposite.*)
There she is now . . . Cyrano, wait! Stay here!

CYRANO

(Bows)
Speak for yourself, my friend!

*(He goes out. The door of the house across from
ROXANNE's opens; the guests begin to disperse.)*

■ **Scene v** ■

ROXANE

(Taking leave of the company)
Adieu . . . Adieu.

DUENNA

I told you so—We missed The Tender Passion!

(She goes into ROXANE's house.)

ROXANE

Adieu.
*(The guests disappear down the street; ROXANE turns to
CHRISTIAN.)*
Is that you, Christian? Let us stay
Here, in the twilight. They are gone. The air
Is fragrant. We shall be alone. Sit down   5
There—so . . .

(They sit on the bench.)
Now tell me things.

CHRISTIAN   *(After a silence)*

I love you.

ROXANE   *(Closes her eyes)*

Yes,
Speak to me about love . . .

CHRISTIAN   I love you.

ROXANE   Now
Be eloquent! . . .

CHRISTIAN   I love—

ROXANE   *(Opens her eyes)*

You have your theme—
Improvise! Rhapsodize!

CHRISTIAN   I love you so!

ROXANE   Of course. And then? . . .

CHRISTIAN   And then . . . Oh, I should be   10
So happy if you loved me too! Roxane,
Say that you love me too!

ROXANE   *(Making a face)*
                                   I ask for cream.
You give me milk and water. Tell me first
A little, how you love me.

CHRISTIAN   Very much.

ROXANE   Oh—tell me how you *feel!*

CHRISTIAN   *(Coming nearer, and devouring her with his eyes)*
                                   Your hand . . . If only   15
I might . . . kiss it—

ROXANE   Christian!

CHRISTIAN   I love you so!

ROXANE   *(Makes as if to rise)*
Again?

CHRISTIAN   *(Desperately, restraining her)*
                No, not again—I do not love you—

ROXANE   *(Settles back)*
That's better . . .

CHRISTIAN   I adore you!

ROXANE   Oh!—
(Rises and moves away)

CHRISTIAN   I know;
I grow absurd.

ROXANE   *(Coldly)*
                And that displeases me
As much as if you had grown ugly.

CHRISTIAN   I—   20

ROXANE   Gather your dreams together into words!

CHRISTIAN   I love—

ROXANE   I know; you love me. Adieu.

(She goes to her house.)

CHRISTIAN   No,
But wait—please—let me—I was going to say—

ROXANE   *(Pushes the door open)*
That you adore me. Yes; I know that too.
No! . . . Go away! . . .
(She goes in and shuts the door in his face.)

CHRISTIAN   I . . . I . . .

CYRANO   *(Enters)*
                         A great success!   25

CHRISTIAN   Help me!   ■ **Scene vi** ■

CYRANO   Not I.

CHRISTIAN   I cannot live unless
She loves me—now, this moment!

CYRANO   What makes you think
I can teach you right now—this moment?

CHRISTIAN   *(Catches him by the arm)*
                              —Wait!—
Look! Up there!—Quick—

(The light shows in ROXANE's window.)

CYRANO   Her window—

CHRISTIAN   *(Wailing)*
                         I shall die!—

CYRANO   Less noise!

CHRISTIAN Oh, I—

CYRANO It does seem fairly dark— 5

CHRISTIAN *(Excitedly)*
Well!—Well!—Well!—

CYRANO Let us try what can be done;
It's more than you deserve—stand over there,
Idiot—there!—before the balcony—
Let me stand underneath. I'll whisper you
What to say.

CHRISTIAN She may hear—she may—

CYRANO Less noise! 10

(The PAGES appear upstage.)

FIRST PAGE Hep!—

CYRANO *(Fingers to lips)*
Sh!—

FIRST PAGE *(Low voice)*
We serenaded Montfleury!—
What next?

CYRANO Down to the corner of the street—
One this way—and the other over there—
If anybody passes, play a tune!

PAGE What tune, O musical Philosopher? 15

CYRANO Sad for a man, or merry for a woman—
Now go!

(The PAGES disappear, one toward each corner of the street.)

CYRANO *(To CHRISTIAN)*
Call her!

CHRISTIAN Roxane!

CYRANO   Wait . . .
                (Gathers up a handful of pebbles)
                                         Gravel . . .
                (Throws it at the window)
                                              There!—

ROXANE   *(Opens the window)*
                Who's calling?

CHRISTIAN   I—

ROXANE   Who?

CHRISTIAN   Christian.

ROXANE   You again?

CHRISTIAN   I had to tell you—

CYRANO   *(Under the balcony)*
                        Good—Keep your voice down.

ROXANE   No. Go away. You tell me nothing.

CHRISTIAN   Please!—   20

ROXANE   You do not love me any more—

CHRISTIAN   *(To whom* CYRANO *whispers his words)*
                                No—no—
                Not any more—I love you . . . evermore . . .
                And ever . . . more and more!

ROXANE   *(About to close the window—pauses)*
                                A little better . . .

CHRISTIAN   *(Same business)*
                Love grows and struggles like . . . an angry child . . .
                Breaking my heart . . . his cradle . . .

ROXANE   *(Coming out on the balcony)*
                                Better still—   25
                But . . . such a babe is dangerous; why not
                Have smothered it new-born?

CHRISTIAN   *(Same business)*

                      And so I do . . .
And yet he lives . . . I found . . . as you shall find . . .
This new-born babe . . . an infant . . . Hercules!*

Hercules: mythical figure renowned for great feats of strength and endurance, including killing snakes in his cradle

ROXANE   *(Further forward)*
Good!—

CHRISTIAN   *(Same business)*

           Strong enough . . . at birth . . . to strangle those   30
Two serpents—Doubt and . . . Pride.

ROXANE   *(Leans over the balcony)*

                         Why, very well!
Tell me now why you speak so haltingly—
Has your imagination gone lame?

CYRANO   *(Thrusts* CHRISTIAN *under the balcony, and stands in his place)*

                     Here—
This grows too difficult!

ROXANE   Your words to-night
Hesitate. Why?

CYRANO   *(In a low tone, imitating* CHRISTIAN*)*
           Through the warm summer gloom   35
They grope in darkness toward the light of you.

ROXANE   My words, well aimed, find you more readily.

CYRANO   My heart is open wide and waits for them—
Too large a mark to miss! My words fly home,
Heavy with honey like returning bees,   40
To your small secret ear. Moreover—yours
Fall to me swiftly. Mine more slowly rise.

ROXANE   Yet not so slowly as they did at first.

CYRANO   They have learned the way, and you have welcomed them.

ROXANE   *(Softly)*
Am I so far above you now?

CYRANO   So far—   45
                       If you let fall upon me one hard word,
                       Out of that height—you crush me!

ROXANE   *(Turns)*
                                                I'll come down—

CYRANO   *(Quickly)*
               No!

ROXANE   *(Points out the bench under the balcony)*
                       Stand you on the bench. Come nearer!

CYRANO   *(Recoils into the shadow)*
                                                       No!—

ROXANE   And why—so great a *No?*

CYRANO   *(More and more overcome by emotion)*
                                       Let me enjoy
               The one moment I ever—my one chance   50
               To speak to you . . . unseen!

ROXANE   Unseen?—

CYRANO   Yes!—yes . . .
               Night, making all things dimly beautiful,
               One veil over us both—You only see
               The darkness of a long cloak in the gloom,
               And I the whiteness of a summer gown—   55
               You are all light—I am all shadow! . . . How
               Can you know what this moment means to me?
               If I was ever eloquent—

ROXANE   You were
               Eloquent—

CYRANO   —You have never heard till now
               My own heart speaking!

ROXANE   Why not?

CYRANO   Until now,   60
               I spoke through . . .

ROXANE   Yes?—

CYRANO   —through that sweet drunkenness
You pour into the world out of your eyes!
But to-night . . . but to-night, I indeed speak
For the first time!

ROXANE   For the first time—Your voice,
Even, is not the same.

CYRANO   *(Passionately; moves nearer)*
                                How should it be?   65
I have another voice—my own,
Myself, daring—
(He stops, confused; then tries to recover himself.)
                        Where was I? . . . I forget! . . .
Forgive me. This is all sweet like a dream . . .
Strange—like a dream . . .

ROXANE   How, strange?

CYRANO   Is it not so
To be myself to you, and have no fear   75
Of moving you to laughter?

ROXANE   Laughter—why?

CYRANO   *(Struggling for an explanation)*
Because . . . What am I . . . What is any man,
That he dare ask for you? Therefore my heart
Hides behind phrases. There's a modesty
In these things too—I come here to pluck down   75
Out of the sky the evening star—then smile,
And stoop to gather little flowers.

ROXANE   Are they
Not sweet, those little flowers?

CYRANO   Not enough sweet
For you and me, to-night!

ROXANE   *(Breathless)*
                        You never spoke
To me like this . . .

CYRANO   Little things, pretty things—   80
                    Arrows and hearts and torches—roses red,
                    And violets blue—are these all? Come away,
                    And breathe fresh air! Must we keep on and on
                    Sipping stale honey of tiny cups
                    Decorated with golden tracery,*   85   *tracery:* ornamental
                    Drop by drop, all day long? We are alive;   work
                    We thirst—Come away, plunge, and drink, and drown
                    In the great river flowing to the sea!

ROXANE   But . . . Poetry?

CYRANO   Love hates that game of words!
                    It is a crime to fence with life—I tell you,   90
                    There comes one moment, once—and God help those
                    Who pass that moment by!—when Beauty stands
                    Looking into the soul with grave, sweet eyes
                    That sicken at pretty words!

ROXANE   If that be true—
                    And when that moment comes to you and me—   95
                    What words will you? . . .

CYRANO   All those, all those, all those
                    That blossom in my heart, I'll fling to you—
                    Armfuls of loose bloom! Love, I love beyond
                    Breath, beyond reason, beyond love's own power
                    Of loving! Your name is like a golden bell   100
                    Hung in my heart; and when I think of you,
                    I tremble, and the bell swings and rings out:
                    "Roxane!" . . . along my veins, "Roxane!" . . . "Roxane!"

ROXANE   *(Very low)*
                    Yes . . . that is . . . Love—

CYRANO   Yes, that is Love—that wind
                    Of terrible and jealous beauty, blowing   105
                    Over me—that dark fire, that music . . .
                                                Yet
                    Love seeketh not his own!* Dear, you may take   *Love seeketh not his
                    My happiness to make you happier,   own:* an allusion to
                    Even though you never know I gave it you—   I Cor. 13:5
                    Only let me hear sometimes, all alone,   110

The distant laughter of your joy! . . .
$$\text{I never}$$
Look at you, but there's some new virtue born
In me, some new courage. Do you begin
To understand, a little? Can you feel
My soul, there in the darkness, breathe on you?   115
Oh, but to-night, now, I dare say these things
To you—

ROXANE   Yes, and I tremble . . . and I weep . . .
And I love you . . . and I am yours . . . and you
Have made me thus!

CYRANO   *(After a pause; quietly)*
$$\text{What is death like, I wonder?}$$
I know everything else now . . .
$$\text{I have done}$$ 120
This, to you—I, myself . . .
$$\text{Only let me}$$
Ask one thing more—

CHRISTIAN   *(Under the the balcony)*
$$\text{One kiss!}$$

ROXANE   *(Startled)*
$$\text{One?—}$$

CYRANO   *(To CHRISTIAN)*
$$\text{You! . . .}$$

ROXANE   You ask me
For—

CYRANO   I . . . Yes, but—I mean—
(To CHRISTIAN)
$$\text{You go too far!}$$

CHRISTIAN   She's willing!—Why not make the most of it?

CYRANO   *(To ROXANE)*
I did ask . . . but I know I ask too much . . .   125

ROXANE   Only one—Is that all?

CYRANO   All!—How much more
Than all!—I know—I frighten you—I ask . . .
I ask you to refuse—

CHRISTIAN   *(To* CYRANO*)*
                    But why?

CYRANO   Christian,
      Be quiet!

ROXANE   *(Leaning over)*
                What's that you say?

CYRANO   I'm angry with
Myself because I go too far, and so   130
I say to myself: "Christian, be quiet!"—

CHRISTIAN   Win me that kiss!

CYRANO   No.

CHRISTIAN   Sooner or later—

CYRANO   True . . .
That is true . . . Soon or late, it will be so
Because you are young and she is beautiful—
(To himself)
Since it must be, I'd rather be myself   135
The cause of . . . what must be.

ROXANE   Are you still there?
We were speaking of—

CYRANO   A kiss. What is a kiss?
A promise given under seal—a vow
Taken before the shrine of memory—
A sacrament* of blossoms, a new song
Sung by two hearts to an old simple tune—   5
The ring of one horizon around two souls
Together, all alone!

ROXANE   Hush! . . .

∇
■ **Scene vii** ■

sacrament: religious
rite

CYRANO	Why, what shame?— There was a Queen of France,* not long ago, And a great lord of England*—a queen's gift, A crown jewel!
ROXANE	Indeed!
CYRANO	Indeed, like him, 10 I have my sorrows and my silences; Like her, you are the queen I dare adore; Like him I'm faithful and forlorn—
ROXANE	Like him Beautiful—
CYRANO	*(Aside)* So I am—I forgot that!
ROXANE	Then—Come; . . . Gather your sacred blossom . . .
CYRANO	*(To* CHRISTIAN*)* Go! 15
ROXANE	Your crown jewel . . .
CYRANO	Go on!—
ROXANE	Your old new song . . .
CYRANO	Climb!—
CHRISTIAN	*(Hesitates)* No—Would you?—not yet—
CYRANO	*(Pushing him)* Climb up, animal!

(CHRISTIAN *springs on the bench and climbs by the pillars,*
the branches, the vines, until he bestrides the balcony
railing. They kiss.)

CYRANO	*(Very low)* Ah! . . . Roxane! . . .

a Queen of France:
Anne of Austria
a great lord of England:
George Villiers, duke
of Buckingham
(1592-1628), who,
while on a mission
to Paris, carried on a
flirtation with the
queen of France

I have won what I have won—
The feast of love—and I am Lazarus!
Yet . . . I have something here that is mine now   20
And was not mine before I spoke the words
That won her—not for me! . . . Kissing my words—
My words, upon your lips!
(The theorbos begin to play.)
                              A merry tune—
A sad tune. So! A Capuchin!
(The CAPUCHIN *enters upstage.* CYRANO *retreats out of sight, runs back on-stage, pretending as if he had arrived from a distance, and then calls up to the balcony.)*
                              Hola!

ROXANE   Who is it?

CYRANO   I. Is Christian there with you?   25

CHRISTIAN   *(Astonished)*
              Cyrano!

ROXANE   Good morrow, Cousin!

CYRANO   Cousin, . . . good morrow!

ROXANE   *(Sees the* CAPUCHIN *approaching)*
              I'm coming down.

              (She disappears into the house.)

CHRISTIAN   *(Aside, upon seeing the* CAPUCHIN*)*
                              Oh—not now . . .

CAPUCHIN   *(To* CYRANO *)*
                              She lives here,
              Madeleine Robin?

ROXANE   *(Appears on the threshold of the house with a lantern, followed by* CHRISTIAN*)*
                              What is it?

CAPUCHIN   A letter.

CHRISTIAN   Oh! . . .

■ Scene viii ■■■■

CAPUCHIN	*(To* ROXANE*)*
	Some matter profitable to the soul—
	A very noble lord gave it to me!

| ROXANE | *(To* CHRISTIAN*)* |
| | De Guiche! |

| CHRISTIAN | He dares?— |

ROXANE   It will not be for long;   5
When he learns that I love you . . .
(By the light of the lantern she reads the letter in a low
tone, as if to herself.)
                              "Mademoiselle:
The drums are beating, and the regiment
Arms for the march. Secretly I remain
Here, in Convent. I have disobeyed;
I shall be with you soon. I send this first   10
By an old monk, as simple as a sheep,
Who understands nothing of this. Your smile
Is more than I can bear, and seek no more.
Be alone to-night, waiting for one who dares
To hope you will forgive . . ." etcetera—   15
(To the CAPUCHIN*)*
Father, this letter concerns you . . .
(To CHRISTIAN*)*
                              —and you.
Listen:
(The others gather around her. She pretends to read from
the letter, aloud.)
        "Mademoiselle:
                    The Cardinal
Will have his way, although against your will;
That is why I am sending this to you
By a most holy man, intelligent,   20
Discreet. You will communicate to him
Our order to perform, here and at once
The rite of . . .
(Turns the page)
            —Holy Matrimony. You
And Christian will be married privately
In your house. I have sent him to you. I know   25
You hesitate. Be resigned, nevertheless,
To the Cardinal's command, who sends herewith

His blessing. Be assured also of my own
Respect and high consideration—*signed,*
Your very humble and—etcetera—" 30

CAPUCHIN A noble lord! I said so—never fear—
A worthy lord!—a very worthy lord!—

ROXANE *(To* CHRISTIAN*)*
Am I a good reader of letters?

CHRISTIAN *(Motions toward the* CAPUCHIN*)*
Careful!—

ROXANE *(In a tragic tone)*
Oh, this is terrible!

CAPUCHIN *(Turns the light of his lantern on* CYRANO*)*
You are to be—

CHRISTIAN *I* am the bridegroom!

CAPUCHIN *(Turns his lantern upon* CHRISTIAN; *then, as if some
suspicion crossed his mind, upon seeing the young man so
handsome)*
Oh—why, *you* . . .

ROXANE *(Quickly)*
Look here— 35
"Postscript: Give to the Convent in my name
One hundred and twenty pistoles"*—

CAPUCHIN Think of it!
A worthy lord—a *very* worthy lord! . . .
(To ROXANE, *solemnly)*
Daughter, resign yourself!

ROXANE *(With an air of martyrdom)*
I am resigned . . .
(While CHRISTIAN *opens the door for the* CAPUCHIN *and
invites him to enter, she turns to* CYRANO.*)*
De Guiche may come. Keep him out here with you. 40
Do not let him—

CYRANO I understand!

pistoles: European
gold coins

(To the CAPUCHIN*)*

How long
Will you be?

CAPUCHIN

Oh, a quarter of an hour.

CYRANO

(Hurrying them into the house)
Hurry—I'll wait here—

ROXANE

(To CHRISTIAN*)*

Come!

(They go into the house.)

CYRANO

Now then, to make
His Grace delay that quarter of an hour . . .
I have it!—up here—
(He steps on the bench, and climbs up the wall toward the balcony. The theorbos begin to play a mournful melody.)
Sad music—a man! . . .   45
(The music pauses on a sinister tremolo.)
Oh—very much a man!
(He sits astride of the railing and, drawing toward him a long branch of one of the trees which border the garden wall, he grasps it with both hands, ready to swing himself down.)
So—not too high—
(He peers down at the ground.)
I must float gently through the atmosphere—

DE GUICHE

(Enters, masked, groping in the dark toward the house)
Where is that cursed, bleating Capuchin?

■ Scene ix ■

CYRANO

What if he knows my voice?—Ah, no!—Tic-tac,
Bergerac—we unlock our Gascon tongue;
A good strong accent—

DE GUICHE

Here's the house—all dark—
Bothersome mask!—
(As he is about to enter the house, CYRANO *leaps from the balcony, still holding fast to the branch, which bends and swings him between* DE GUICHE *and the door; then he releases the branch and pretends to fall heavily as though from a height. He lands flatly on the ground, where he lies*

motionless, as if stunned. DE GUICHE *leaps back.)*
What's that?
(When he lifts his eyes, the branch has sprung back into place. He can see nothing but the sky; he does not understand.)
Why . . .
Where did this man   5
Fall from?

CYRANO

(Sits up, and speaks with a strong accent)
—The moon!

DE GUICHE

You—

CYRANO

From the moon, the moon!
I fell out of the moon!

DE GUICHE

The fellow's mad—

CYRANO

(Dreamily)
Where am I?

DE GUICHE

Why—

CYRANO

What time is it? What place
Is this? What day? What season?

DE GUICHE

You—

CYRANO

I'm stunned!

DE GUICHE

My dear sir—

CYRANO

Like a bomb—a bomb—I fell   10
From the moon!

DE GUICHE

Now see here—

CYRANO

(Rising to his feet, and speaking in a terrible voice)
I say, the moon!

DE GUICHE

(Recoils)
Very well—if you say so—

(Aside)

Raving mad!—

CYRANO

(Advancing upon him)
I am not speaking metaphorically!

DE GUICHE

Pardon.

CYRANO

A hundred years—an hour ago—
I really cannot say how long I fell—   15
I was in yonder shining sphere—

DE GUICHE

(Shrugs)

Quite so.
Please let me pass.

CYRANO

(Interposes himself)
Where am I? Tell the truth—
I can bear it. In what quarter of the globe
Have I descended like a meteorite?

DE GUICHE

Please move!

CYRANO

I could not choose my place to fall—   20
The earth spun round so fast—Was it the Earth,
I wonder?—Or is this another world?
Another moon? Whither have I been drawn
By the dead weight of my posterior?

DE GUICHE

Sir, I repeat—

CYRANO

(With a sudden cry, which causes DE GUICHE *to recoil
again)*
His face! What's this?—black!

DE GUICHE

(Carries his hand to his mask)
Oh!—   25

CYRANO

(Terrified)
Are you a native? Is this Africa?

DE GUICHE

—This mask!

CYRANO	*(Somewhat reassured)* Are we in Venice? Genoa?—
DE GUICHE	*(Tries to pass him)* A lady is waiting for me.
CYRANO	*(Quite happy again)* So this is Paris!
DE GUICHE	*(Smiling in spite of himself)* This fool becomes amusing.
CYRANO	Ah! You smile?
DE GUICHE	I do. Kindly permit me—

CYRANO   *(Delighted)*

Dear old Paris—   30

Well, well!—
(Wholly at his ease, smiles, bows, arranges his dress)
Excuse my appearance. I arrive
By the last thunderbolt—a trifle singed
As I came through the ether. These long journeys—
You know! There are so few conveniences!
My eyes are full of star-dust. On my spurs,   35
Some sort of fur . . . Planet's apparently . . .
(Plucks something from his sleeve)
Look—on my doublet—That's a Comet's hair!
(He blows something from the back of this hand.)
Phoo!

DE GUICHE   *(Grows angry)*

Monsieur—

CYRANO   *(As DE GUICHE is about to push past, thrusts his leg in the way)*

Here's a tooth, stuck in my boot,
From the Great Bear.* Trying to get away,
I tripped over the Scorpion* and came down   40
Slap, into one scale of the Balances*—
The pointer marks my weight this moment . . .
(Pointing upward)

See?

Great Bear: constellation Ursa Major
Scorpion: constellation Scorpio
Balances: constellation Libra

*(*DE GUICHE *makes a sudden movement.* CYRANO *catches his arm.)*
Be careful! If you struck me on the nose,
It would drip milk!

DE GUICHE   Milk?

CYRANO   From the Milky Way!

DE GUICHE   Heavens!

CYRANO   That's right—the heavens.
(Crossing his arms)
                                        Curious place—   45
Did you know Sirius* wore a nightcap? True!
(Confidentially)
The Little Bear* is still too young to bite.
(Laughing)
My foot caught in the Lyre* and broke a string.
(Proudly)
Well—when I write my book, and tell the tale
Of my adventures—all these little stars   50
That shake out of my cloak—I must save those
To use for asterisks!

DE GUICHE   That will do now—
I wish—

CYRANO   Yes, yes—I know—

DE GUICHE   Sir—

CYRANO   You desire
To learn from my own lips the character
Of the moon's surface—its inhabitants   55
If any—

DE GUICHE   *(Loses patience and shouts)*
                I desire no such thing! I—

CYRANO   *(Rapidly)*
You wish to know by what mysterious means
I reached the moon?—well—confidentially—
It was a new invention of my own.

Sirius: the brightest
    star

Little Bear: constella-
    tion Ursa Minor

Lyre: constellation
    Lyra

DE GUICHE	*(Discouraged)* Drunk too—as well as mad!	
CYRANO	I scorned the eagle Of Regiomontanus,* and the dove Of Archytas!*	60

Regiomontanus: a fifteenth-century German astronomer

Archytas: an ancient philosopher

DE GUICHE	A learned lunatic!—
CYRANO	I imitated no one. I myself Discovered not one scheme merely, but six—

(DE GUICHE has succeeded in passing him, and moves toward the door of ROXANE's house. CYRANO follows, ready to use violence if necessary.)

DE GUICHE	*(Looks around)* Six?	
CYRANO	*(With increasing volubility)* As for instance—Having stripped myself Bare as a wax candle, adorn my form With crystal vials filled with morning dew, And so be drawn aloft, as the sun rises Drinking the mist of dawn!	65
DE GUICHE	*(Takes a step toward CYRANO)* Yes—that makes one.	

CYRANO	*(Draws back to lead him away from the door; speaks faster and faster)* Or, sealing up the air in a cedar chest, Rarefy* it by means of mirrors, placed In an icosahedron.*	70

rarefy: purify

icosahedron: twenty-sided formation

DE GUICHE	*(Takes another step)* Two.	
CYRANO	*(Still retreating)* Again, I might construct a rocket, in the form Of a huge locust, driven by impulses Of villainous saltpetre* from the rear, Upward, by leaps and bounds.	75

saltpetre: the mineral potassium nitrate, so-called rock salt

DE GUICHE   *(Interested in spite of himself, and counting on his fingers)*
                                    Three.

CYRANO   *(Same business)*
                                            Or again,
                Smoke having the natural tendency to rise,
                Blow in a globe enough to raise me.

DE GUICHE   *(Same business, more and more astonished)*
                                            Four!

CYRANO   Or since Diana, as old fables tell,
                Draws forth to fill her crescent horn,* the marrow   80   *crescent horn: the*
                Of bulls and goats—to anoint myself therewith.   *shape of the moon*
                                                                                     in its first quarter

DE GUICHE   *(Hypnotized)*
                Five!—

CYRANO   *(Has by this time led him all the way across the street,*
                close to a bench)
                        Finally—seated on an iron plate,
                To hurl a magnet in the air—the iron
                Follows—I catch the magnet—throw again—
                And so proceed indefinitely.

DE GUICHE   Six!—   85
                All excellent—and which did you adopt?

CYRANO   *(Coolly)*
                Why, none of them. . . . A seventh.

DE GUICHE   Which was?—

CYRANO   Guess!

DE GUICHE   An interesting idiot, this!

CYRANO   *(Imitates the sound of waves with his voice, and their*
                movement by large, vague gestures)
                                Hoo! . . . Hoo! . . .

DE GUICHE   Well?

CYRANO   Have you guessed it yet?

DE GUICHE	Why, no.

CYRANO

(Grandiloquent)

The ocean!
What hour its rising tide seeks the full moon,   90
I laid me on the strand, fresh from the spray,
My head fronting the moonbeams, since the hair
Retains moisture—and so I slowly rose
As upon angels' wings, effortlessly,
Upward—then suddenly I felt a shock!—   95
And then . . .

DE GUICHE

(Overcome by curiosity, sits down on the bench)
And then?

CYRANO

And then—
(Changes abruptly to his natural voice)
The time is up!—
Fifteen minutes, your Grace!—You are now free;
And—they are bound—in wedlock.

DE GUICHE

(Leaping up)
Do *I* dream?
That voice . . .
(The door of ROXANE's *house opens; lackeys appear,
bearing lighted candles. Lights up.* CYRANO *removes his
hat.)*
And that nose!—Cyrano!

CYRANO

(Smiling)
Cyrano! . . .
This very moment, they have exchanged rings.   100

DE GUICHE

Who?   ■ Scene x ■■■■■■■
(He turns upstage. ROXANE *and* CHRISTIAN *appear, hand
in hand. The* CAPUCHIN *follows them, smiling and holding
aloft a torch. The* DUENNA *brings up the rear in a pleasant
flutter of emotion.)*
No!
(To ROXANE*)*
You?—
(Recognizes CHRISTIAN*)*
He?—
(Saluting ROXANE*)*
My sincere compliments!

(To CYRANO*)*
You also, my inventor of machines!
Your rigmarole* would have detained a saint   *rigmarole:* incoherent
Entering Paradise—decidedly   talk
You must not fail to write that book some day!   5

CYRANO   *(Bowing)*
                  Sir, I engage myself to do so.
                  (The CAPUCHIN *leads the bridal pair down to* DE GUICHE.*)*
                                    M'lord,
                  The handsome couple you—and God—have joined
                  Together!

DE GUICHE   *(Regarding him with a frosty eye)*
                                    Quite so.
                  (Turns to ROXANE*)*
                                    Madame, kindly bid
                  Your . . . husband farewell.

ROXANE   Oh!—

DE GUICHE   *(To* CHRISTIAN*)*
                                    Your regiment
                  Leaves to-night, sir. Report at once!

ROXANE   You mean   10
                  For the front? The war?

DE GUICHE   Certainly!

ROXANE   I thought
                  The Cadets were not going—

DE GUICHE   Oh yes, they are!
                  (Taking out the despatch from his pocket)
                  Here is the order—
                  (To CHRISTIAN*)*
                                    Baron! Deliver this.

ROXANE   *(Throws herself into* CHRISTIAN's *arms)*
                  Christian!

DE GUICHE   *(To* CYRANO, *sneering)*
                                    The bridal night is not so near!

CYRANO   *(Aside)*
                    Somehow that news fails to disquiet me.   15

CHRISTIAN   *(To* ROXANE*)*
                    Your lips again . . .

CYRANO   There . . . That will do now—Come!

CHRISTIAN   *(Still holding* ROXANE*)*
                    You do not know how hard it is—

CYRANO   *(Tries to drag him away)*
                                        I know!

                    (The beating of drums is heard in the distance.)

DE GUICHE   *(Upstage)*
                    The regiment—on the march!

ROXANE   *(As* CYRANO *tries to lead* CHRISTIAN *away, follows and
                    detains them)*
                                        Take care of him
                    For me—
                    (Appealingly)
                            Promise never to let him do
                    Anything dangerous!

CYRANO	I'll do my best— I cannot promise—	20

ROXANE   *(Same business)*
                      Make him be careful!

CYRANO   Yes—
          I'll try—

ROXANE   *(Same business)*
                  Be sure to keep him dry and warm!

CYRANO   Yes, yes—if possible—

ROXANE   *(Same business; confidentially, in his ear)*
                      See that he remains
          Faithful!—

CYRANO   Of course!—

ROXANE   *(Same business)*
                      And have him write to me
          Every single day!

CYRANO   *(Stops)*
                  That, I promise you!   25

Curtain

About the Play

1. List several lines from the play that reveal the character of De Guiche.
2. What adjectives might you use to describe De Guiche?
3. Why does Christian desire to "speak for himself"? What happens when he does so?
4. What does Roxane's response to Christian's "words of love" tell us about her?

5. Compare Roxane with Beauty from "Beauty and the Beast." What qualities do these two heroines have in common? How do they differ?
6. Reread Cyrano's speeches on pages 444-45. What do these speeches tell us about Cyrano's view of love? What does Cyrano's view of love tell us about him?

ACT IV

The Cadets of Gascoyne

The post occupied by the Company of CARBON DE CASTEL-JALOUX *at the siege of Arras.*

Tents; scattered weapons; drums, et cetera. It is near daybreak, and the east is yellow with approaching dawn. Sentries at intervals. Camp-fires.

The curtain rise discovers the CADETS *asleep, rolled in their cloaks.* CARBON DE CASTEL-JALOUX *and* LE BRET *keep watch. They are both very thin and pale.* CHRISTIAN *is asleep among the others, wrapped in his cloak, in the foreground, his face lighted by the flickering fire. Silence.*

LE BRET	Horrible!	■ Scene i ■■■■■

CARBON   Why, yes. All of that.

LE BRET   Frightful!

CARBON   *(Gesture toward the sleeping* CADETS*)*
Speak quietly—You might wake them.
(To the CADETS*)*
                              Go to sleep—

Hush!
(To LE BRET*)*
          Who sleeps dines.

LE BRET   I have insomnia.
This famine wastes us.
(Firing off-stage)

CARBON   Curse that musketry!

SENTRY   *(Off-stage)*
Halt! Who goes there?

CYRANO   Bergerac!

SENTRY   Halt! Who goes?—   5

CYRANO   *(Appears on the parapet*)*
Bergerac, idiot!

parapet: low wall
around the edge of a
roof or a bridge

LE BRET   *(Goes to meet him)*
                             You come again!

CYRANO   *(Signs to him not to wake anyone)*
                Hush!

LE BRET   Wounded?—

CYRANO   No—They always miss me—quite
                A habit by this time!

LE BRET   Yes—Go right on—
                Risk your life every morning before breakfast
                To send a letter!

CYRANO   *(Stops near* CHRISTIAN*)*
                             I promised he should write   10
                Every single day . . .
                (Looks down at him)
                             Hm—The boy looks pale
                When he is asleep—thin too—starving to death—
                If that poor child knew! Handsome, nonetheless . . .

LE BRET   Go and get some sleep!

CYRANO   *(Affectionately)*
                             Now, now—you old bear,
                No growling!—I am careful—you know I am—   15
                Every night, when I cross the Spanish lines
                I wait till they are all drunk.

LE BRET   You might bring
                Some food with you.

CYRANO   I have to travel light
                To pass through—By the way, there will be news
                For you to-day: the French will eat or die,   20
                If what I saw means anything.

LE BRET   Tell us!

CYRANO   No—
                I am not sure—we shall see!

CARBON
                                    What a war,
                When the besieger starves to death!

LE BRET
                                                Fine war—
                Fine situation! We besiege Arras—
                The Cardinal Prince of Spain besieges us—   25
                And—here we are!

CYRANO
                                Someone might besiege *him.*

CARBON   A hungry joke!

CYRANO   Ho, ho!

LE BRET
                                    Yes, you can laugh—
                Risking a life like yours to carry letters—
                Where are you going now?

CYRANO   *(At tent door)*
                                    To write another.

                (CYRANO goes into the tent. A little more daylight. The   ■ **Scene ii** ■■■■
                clouds redden. The town of Arras shows on the horizon.
                A cannon shot is heard, followed immediately by a roll of
                drums, far away to the left. Other drums beat a little
                nearer. The drums go on answering each other here and
                there, approach, beat loudly almost on the stage, and die
                away toward the right, across the camp. The camp
                awakes. Voices of officers in the distance.)

CARBON   *(Sighs)*
                Those drums!—another good nourishing sleep
                Gone forevermore.
                (The CADETS *rouse themselves.)*
                                    Now then!

FIRST CADET   *(Sits up, yawns)*
                                    How I hunger!

SECOND CADET   Starving!

ALL   *(Groan)*
                        Aoh!

CARBON   Up with you!

THIRD CADET   Not another step!

FOURTH CADET   Not another movement!

FIRST CADET   Look at my tongue—
I said this air was indigestible!   5

FIFTH CADET   My coronet for half a pound of cheese!

SIXTH CADET   I have no stomach for this war—I'll stay
In my tent—like *Achilles.* *

> *Achilles:* Greek hero in Homer's *Iliad* who removes himself from the war, shutting himself in his tent

CARBON   Cyrano!
Come out here!—You know how to talk to them.
Get them laughing—

CYRANO   *(Enters from tent and speaks to the* FIRST CADET, *who is
walking away, with his chin on his chest)*
                    You there, with the long face?   10

FIRST CADET   I have something on my mind that troubles me.

■ Scene iii ■

CYRANO   What's that?

FIRST CADET   My stomach.

CYRANO   So have I.

FIRST CADET   No doubt
You enjoy this!

CYRANO   *(Tightens his belt)*
                    It keeps me looking young.

SECOND CADET   My teeth are growing rusty.

CYRANO   Sharpen them!

THIRD CADET   My belly sounds as hollow as a drum.   5

CYRANO   Beat the long roll on it!

FOURTH CADET   My ears are ringing.

CYRANO   Liar! A hungry belly has no ears.

SIXTH CADET   I'll swallow anything!

CYRANO   *(Throws him the book which he has in his hand)*
                              Try the *Iliad.**

> *the Iliad:* Homer's epic poem about the Trojan War

SEVENTH CADET   The Cardinal, he has four meals a day—
What does he care!

CYRANO   Ask him; he really ought   10
To send you . . . a spring lamb out of his flock,
Roasted whole—

SIXTH CADET   And the salad—

CYRANO   Of course—Romaine!*

> *Romaine:* from Rome, seat of the Catholic church

FIFTH CADET   *(Shivering)*
I am as hungry as a wolf.

CYRANO   *(Tosses him a cloak)*
                              Put on
Your sheep's clothing.

FIRST CADET   *(With a shrug)*
                              Always the clever answer!

CYRANO   Always the answer—yes! Let me die so—   15
Under some rosy-golden sunset, saying
A good thing, for a good cause! By the sword,
The point of honor—by the hand of one
Worthy to be my foeman, let me fall—
Steel in my heart, and laughter on my lips!   20

VOICES   All very well—We are hungry!

CYRANO   Bah! You think
Of nothing but yourselves.
(His eye singles out the old fifer in the background.)
                              Here, Bertrandou,
You were a shepherd once—your pipe now! Come,

Breathe, blow—play to these belly-worshippers
The old airs of the South—
                        "Airs with a smile in them,   25
Airs with a sigh in them, airs with the breeze
And the blue of the sky in them—"
                              Small, demure* tunes   *demure: reserved,
Whose every note is like a little sister—   modest
Songs heard only in some long silent voice
Not quite forgotten—Mountain melodies   30
Like thin smoke rising from brown cottages
In the still noon, slowly—Quaint lullabies,
Whose very music has a Southern tongue—
(The old man sits down and begins to play.)
Listen, you Gascons! Now it is no more
The shrill fife—It's the flute, through woodlands far   35
Away, calling—no longer the hot battle-cry.
But the cool, quiet pipe our goatherds play!
Listen—the forest glens . . . the hills . . . the downs . . .
The green sweetness of night on the Dordogne . . .
Listen, you Gascons! It is all Gascoyne! . . .   40

*(Every head is bowed; every eye cast down. Here and
there a tear is furtively brushed away with the back of a
hand, the corner of a cloak.)*

CARBON   *(Softly to* CYRANO*)*
              You make them weep—

CYRANO   For homesickness—a hunger
              More noble than that hunger of the flesh;
              It is their hearts now that are starving.

CARBON   Yes,
              But you melt down their manhood.

CYRANO   *(Motions the drummer to approach)*
                                    You think so?
              Let them be. There is iron in their blood   45
              Not easily dissolved in tears. You need
              Only—

              (He makes a gesture; the drum beats.)

ALL   *(Spring up and rush toward their weapons)*
                    What's that? Where is it?—What?—

CYRANO   *(Smiles)*
                                                You see—
                    Let Mars snore in his sleep once—and farewell
                    Venus—sweet dreams—regrets—dear thoughts of home—
                    All the fife lulls to rest wakes at the drums!   50

THIRD CADET   *(Looks upstage)*
                    Aha—Monsieur de Guiche!

CADETS   *(Mutter among themselves)*
                                                Ugh!

CYRANO   *(Smiles)*
                                                Flattering
                    Murmur!

FIRST CADET   He makes me weary!

SECOND CADET   With his collar
                    Of lace over his corselet—

THIRD CADET   Like a ribbon
                    Tied round a sword!

SECOND CADET   A courtier always!

THIRD CADET   The Cardinal's nephew!

CARBON   Nonetheless—a Gascon.   55

FIRST CADET   A counterfeit! Never you trust that man—
                    Because we Gascons, look you, are all mad—
                    This fellow is reasonable—nothing more
                    Dangerous than a reasonable Gascon!

LE BRET   He looks pale.

FOURTH CADET   Oh, he can be hungry too,   60
                    Like any other poor devil—but he wears
                    So many jewels on that belt of his
                    That his cramps glitter in the sun!

CYRANO	*(Quickly)*

Is he

To see us looking miserable? Quick!—

(They all hurriedly begin to play games, on their stools, drums, or cloaks spread on the ground. CYRANO walks up and down, reading a small book which he takes from his pocket. DE GUICHE enters, looking pale and haggard. He goes to CARBON. They look at each other askance, each observing with satisfaction the condition of the other.)

■ **Scene iv** ■

DE GUICHE	Good morning! *(Aside)*

He looks yellow.

CARBON	*(Same business)*

He is all eyes.

DE GUICHE	*(Looks at the CADETS)*

What have we here? Black looks? Yes, gentlemen—
I am informed I am not popular;
The hill-nobility, barons of Béarn,
The pomp and pride of Perigord—I learn   5
They disapprove their colonel; call him courtier,
Politician—they take it ill that I
Cover my steel with lace of Genoa.*
It is a great offense to be a Gascon
And not to be a beggar!
(Silence. They play.)

Well—Shall I have   10

Your captain punish you? . . . No.

Genoa: a port city in northwestern Italy

CARBON	

As to that,

It would be impossible.

DE GUICHE	<div align="center">Oh?</div>

CARBON	

I am free;

I pay my company; it is my own;
I obey military orders.

DE GUICHE	<div align="center">Oh!</div>

That will be quite enough.

(To the CADETS*)*

          I can afford   15
Your little hates. My conduct under fire
Is well known. It was only yesterday
I drove the Count de Bucquoi from Bapaume,
Pouring my men down like an avalanche,
I myself led the charge—

CYRANO   *(Without looking up from his book)*

         And your white scarf?   20

DE GUICHE   *(Surprised and gratified)*

You heard that episode? Yes—rallying
My men for the third time, I found myself
Carried among a crowd of fugitives
Into the enemy's lines. I was in danger
Of being shot or captured; but I thought   25
Quickly—took off and flung away the scarf
That marked my military rank—and so
Being inconspicuous, escaped among
My own force, rallied them, returned again
And won the day! . . .
(The CADETS *do not appear to be listening, but here and
there those at the games remain motionless.)*

         What do you say to that?   30
Presence of mind—yes?

CYRANO

            Henry of Navarre*
Being outnumbered, never flung away
His white plume.
(Silent enjoyment among the CADETS *at this remark)*

> Henry of Navarre: the
> king of France
> (1589-1610)

DE GUICHE

         My device was a success,
However!
(Same attentive pause, interrupting the games)

CYRANO

        Possibly. . . . An officer
Does not lightly resign the privilege   35
Of being a target.
(Increasing satisfaction among the CADETS *as the games
resume)*

        Now, if I had been there—
Your courage and my own differ in this—
When your scarf fell, I should have put it on.

DE GUICHE	Boasting again!

CYRANO

          Boasting? Lend it to me
To-night; I'll lead the first charge, with your scarf   40
Over my shoulder!

DE GUICHE

          Gasconnade* once more!
You are safe making that offer, and you know it—
My scarf lies on the riverbank between
The lines, a spot swept by artillery
Impossible to reach alive!

Gasconnade: boastful talk

CYRANO

(Produces the scarf from his pocket)
          Yes. Here . . .   45

*(Silence. The CADETS stifle their laughter. DE GUICHE
turns to look at them. Immediately they resume their
gravity and their games. One of them whistles carelessly
the mountain air which the fifer was playing.)*

DE GUICHE

(Takes the scarf)
Thank you! That bit of white is what I need
To make a signal. I was hesitating—
You have decided me.

*(DE GUICHE goes up to the parapet, climbs upon it, and
waves the scarf at arm's length several times.)*

ALL

          What is he doing?—
What?—

SENTRY

(On the parapet)
          There's a man down there running away!

DE GUICHE

(Descending)
A Spaniard. Very useful as a spy   50
To both sides. He informs the enemy
As I instruct him. By this influence
I can arrange their dispositions.

CYRANO

          Traitor!

DE GUICHE

(Folding the scarf)
A traitor, yes; but useful . . .
          We were saying? . . .

Oh, yes—Here is a bit of news for you: 55
Last night we had hopes of reprovisioning
The army. Under cover of the dark,
The Marshal moved to Dourlens. Our supplies
Are there. He may reach them. But to return
Safely, he needs a large force—at least half   60
Our entire strength. At present, we have here
Merely a skeleton.

CARBON   Fortunately,
The Spaniards do not know that.

DE GUICHE   Oh, yes; they know
They will attack.

CARBON   Ah!

DE GUICHE   From that spy of mine
I learned of their intention. His report   65
Will determine the point of their advance.
The fellow asked me what to say! I told him:
"Go out between the line; watch for my signal;
Where you see that, let them attack there."

CARBON   *(To the* CADETS*)*
                                            Well,
Gentlemen!

*(All rise. Noise of sword belts and breastplates being
buckled on.)*

DE GUICHE   You may have perhaps an hour.   70

FIRST CADET   Oh—An hour!

(They all sit down and resume their games once more.)

DE GUICHE   *(To* CARBON*)*
                  The great thing is to gain time.
Any moment the Marshal may return.

CARBON   And to gain time?

DE GUICHE	You will all be so kind As to lay down your lives!
CYRANO	Ah! Your revenge?
DE GUICHE	I make no great pretense of loving you! 75 But—since you gentlemen esteem yourselves Invincible, the bravest of the brave, And all that—why need we be personal? I serve the king in choosing . . . as I choose!
CYRANO	*(Salutes)* Sir, permit me to offer—all our thanks. 80
DE GUICHE	*(Returns the salute)* You love to fight a hundred against one; Here is your opportunity! *(He goes upstage with* CARBON.*)*

CYRANO	*(To the* CADETS*)*
	        My friends,
	We shall add now to our old Gascon arms
	With their six chevrons,* blue and gold, a seventh—
	Blood-red!
	*(*DE GUICHE *talks in a low tone to* CARBON *upstage.
	Orders are given. The defense is arranged.* CYRANO *goes
	to* CHRISTIAN, *who has remained motionless with folded
	arms.)*
	        Christian?
	(Lays a hand on his shoulder)

CHRISTIAN	*(Shakes his head)* Roxane . . .
CYRANO	Yes.
CHRISTIAN	I should like 85 To say farewell to her, with my whole heart Written for her to keep.
CYRANO	I thought of that— *(Takes a letter from his doublet)* I have written your farewell.

chevrons: emblems of v-shaped stripes

CHRISTIAN   Show me!

CYRANO   You wish
To read it?

CHRISTIAN   Of course!
*(He takes the letter, begins to read, then looks up
suddenly.)*
                              What?—

CYRANO   What is it?

CHRISTIAN   Look—
This little circle—

CYRANO   *(Takes back the letter quickly, and looks innocent)*
                              Circle?—

CHRISTIAN   Yes—a tear!   90

CYRANO   So it is! . . . Well—a poet while he writes
Is like a lover in his lady's arms,
Believing his imagination—all
Seems true—you understand? There's half the charm
Of writing—Now, this letter as you see   95
I have made so pathetic that I wept
While I was writing it!

CHRISTIAN   You—wept?

CYRANO   Why, yes—
Because . . . it is a little thing to die,
But—not to see her . . . that is terrible!
And I shall never––
*(*CHRISTIAN *looks at him.)*
                     We shall never—
(Quickly)
                                        You   100
Will never—

CHRISTIAN   *(Snatches the letter)*
                     Give me that!
(Noise in the distance on the outskirts of the camp)

SENTRY	*(From the parapet)* Halt—who goes there? *(Shots, shouting, jingle of harness)*
CARBON	What is it?—
SENTRY	Why, a coach.
	(They rush to look.)
VOICES	What? In the Camp? A coach? Coming this way—It must have driven Through the Spanish lines—Why is it here?—Fire! No! The driver shouting—what does he say? 105 Wait—He said: "On the service of the King!"
	(They are all on the parapet looking over. The jingling comes nearer.)
DE GUICHE	Of the King?
	(They come down and fall into line.)
CARBON	Hats off, all!
DE GUICHE	*(Speaks off-stage)* The King! Fall in, Rascals!—
	(The coach enters at full trot. It is covered with mud and dust. The curtains are drawn. Two footmen are seated behind. It stops suddenly.)
CARBON	*(Shouts)* Beat the assembly— *(Roll of drums)*
DE GUICHE	Two of you, Lower the steps—open the door—
	(Two men rush to the coach. The door opens.)
ROXANE	*(Comes out of the coach)* Good morning!

(At the sound of a woman's voice, every head is raised. Sensation.)

■ Scene v ■■■■■■

DE GUICHE   On the King's service—You?

ROXANE   Yes—my own king—
Love!

CYRANO   *(Aside)*
God is merciful . . .

CHRISTIAN   *(Hastens to her)*
You! Why have you—

ROXANE   Your war lasted so long!

CHRISTIAN   But why?—

ROXANE   Not now—

CYRANO   *(Aside)*
I wonder if I dare to look at her . . .

DE GUICHE   You cannot remain here!

ROXANE   Why, certainly!   5
Roll that drum here, somebody . . .
(She sits on the drum, which is brought to her.)
                                    Thank you—There!
(She laughs.)
Would you believe—they fired upon us?
                                    —My coach
Looks like the pumpkin in the fairy tale,
Does it not? And my footmen—
(She throws a kiss to CHRISTIAN.*)*
                                    How do you do?
(She looks about.)
How serious you all are! Do you know,   10
It is a long drive here—from Arras?
(Sees CYRANO*)*
                                    Cousin,
I am glad to see you!

CYRANO   *(Advances)*
                                Oh—How did you come?

ROXANE   How did I find you? Very easily—
                  I followed where the country was laid waste
                  —Oh, but I saw such things! I had to see   15
                  To believe. Gentlemen, is that the service
                  Of your King? I prefer my own!

CYRANO   But how
                  Did you come through?

ROXANE   Why, through the Spanish lines
                  Of course!

FIRST CADET   They let you pass?—

DE GUICHE   What did you say?
                  How did you manage?

LE BRET   Yes, that must have been   20
                  Difficult!

ROXANE   No—I simply drove along.
                  Now and then some hidalgo* scowled at me   *hidalgo:* low-ranking
                  And I smiled back—my best smile; whereupon,   Spanish nobleman
                  The Spaniards being (without prejudice
                  To the French) the most polished gentlemen   25
                  In the world—I passed!

CARBON   Certainly that smile
                  Should be a passport!

DE GUICHE   *(To* ROXANE*)*
                                You must leave this place.

ROXANE   I?

LE BRET   Yes—immediately.

ROXANE   And why?

CHRISTIAN   *(Embarrassed)*
                                Because . . .

CYRANO   *(Same)*
                In half an hour . . .

DE GUICHE   *(Same)*
                                Or these quarters . . .

CARBON   *(Same)*
                                            Perhaps
                It might be better . . .

LE BRET   If you . . .

ROXANE   Oh—I see!   30
                You're going to fight. I remain here.

ALL   No—no!

ROXANE   He is my husband—
                (Throws herself in CHRISTIAN's *arms)*
                                I will die with you!

CHRISTIAN   Your eyes! . . . Why do you?—

ROXANE   You know why . . .

DE GUICHE   *(Desperate)*
                                            This post
                Is dangerous—

ROXANE   *(Turns)*
                            How—dangerous?

CYRANO   The proof
                Is, we are ordered—

ROXANE   *(To* DE GUICHE*)*
                            Oh—you wish to make   35
                A widow of me?

DE GUICHE   On my word of honor—

ROXANE   No matter. I am just a little mad—
                I will stay. It may be amusing.

CYRANO	What, A heroine—our intellectual?
ROXANE	Monsieur de Bergerac, I'm your cousin! 40
CADET	We'll fight now! Hurrah!

ROXANE	*(More and more excited)*
	                    I'm safe with you—my friends!
	Perhaps—
	(Looks at DE GUICHE*)*
	          The Count should leave us. Any moment
	Now, there may be danger.

DE GUICHE	This is too much! I must inspect my guns. I shall return— You may change your mind—There will yet be time— 45
ROXANE	Never!

*(*DE GUICHE *goes out.)*

■ Scene vi ■■■■

CHRISTIAN	*(Imploring)* Roxane! . . .
ROXANE	No!
ALL	We say she stays here!
CARBON	*(Advances ceremoniously, and addresses* ROXANE*)* Then please, Madame, would you open the hand That holds your handkerchief.
ROXANE	*(Opens her hand; the handkerchief falls.)* Why?

(The whole company makes a movement toward it.)

CARBON	*(Picks it up quickly)* My company Was in want of a banner. We have now The fairest in the army!

ROXANE   *(Smiling)*
                                        Rather small—   5

CARBON   *(Fastens the handkerchief to his lance)*
                Lace—and embroidered!

CADET   *(To the others)*
                                        With her smiling on me,
                I could die happy, if I only had
                Something in my—

CARBON   *(Turns upon him)*
                                        Shame on you! Feast your eyes
                And forget your—

ROXANE   *(Quickly)*
                                        It must be this fresh air—
                I'm starving! Let me see . . .
                                        Cold partridges,   10
                Pastry, something to drink too—that would do.
                Will someone bring that to me?

CADET   *(Aside)*
                                        Will someone!—

ANOTHER   Where on earth we are to find—

ROXANE   *(Overhears; sweetly)*
                                        Why, there—
                In my carriage.

ALL   Wha-at?

ROXANE   All you have to do
                Is to unpack, and carve, and serve things.
                                        Oh,   15
                Notice my coachman; you may recognize
                An old friend.

CADETS   *(Rush to the coach)*
                                Ragueneau!

ROXANE   *(Follows them with her eyes)*
                                        Poor fellows . . .

CADETS	*(Acclamations)* <div align="center">Ah!</div>Ah!
CYRANO	*(Kisses her hand)* Our good fairy!
RAGUENEAU	*(Standing on his box, like a mountebank* before a crowd)* <div align="center">Gentlemen!—</div>*(Enthusiasm)*
CADETS	<div align="center">Bravo!</div>Bravo!
RAGUENEAU	<div align="center">The Spaniards, basking in our smiles,</div>Smiled on our baskets! *(Applause)*
CYRANO	*(Aside, to* CHRISTIAN) <div align="center">Christian!—</div>
RAGUENEAU	<div align="center">They adored 20</div>The Fair, and missed— *(He takes from under the seat a dish, which he holds aloft.)* <div align="center">the Fowl!</div> *(Applause. The dish is passed from hand to hand.)*
CYRANO	*(As before, to* CHRISTIAN) <div align="center">Pst!—Let me speak—</div>
ROXANE	*(As the* CADETS *return with their arms full of provisions, calls)* Christian! Come here and make yourself useful. *(*CHRISTIAN *turns to her, at the moment when* CYRANO *was leading him aside. She arranges the food, with his aid and that of the two imperturbable footmen.)*
FIRST CADET	We are not going to die without a gorge— *(Sees* ROXANE; *corrects himself hastily)* Pardon—a banquet! *(Tumult; laughter)*

mountebank: one who sells quack medicines after drawing a crowd with jokes or tricks

ROXANE   *(Throws a tablecloth at the head of* CYRANO*)*
                                    Come out of your dreams!
              Unfold this cloth—

RAGUENEAU   *(Takes off one of the lanterns of the carriage, and*
              flourishes it)
                                    Our lamps are bonbonnières!*   25   *bonbonnières:* deco-
                                                                                    rated boxes of
                                                                                    candy

CYRANO   *(To* CHRISTIAN*)*
              I must see you before you speak with her—

RAGUENEAU   *(More and more lyrical)*
              My whip-handle is one long sausage!

ROXANE   *(Pouring drink; passing food)*
                                                We
              Being about to die, first let us dine!
              Never mind the others—all for Gascoyne!
              And if De Guiche comes, he is not invited!   30
              (Going from one to another)
              Plenty of time—you need not eat so fast—
              (Goes to CHRISTIAN*)*
              What would you like?

CHRISTIAN   Nothing.

ROXANE   Oh, but you must!—
              Some sausage and a biscuit?

CHRISTIAN   Tell me first
              Why you came—

ROXANE   By and by. I must take care
              Of these poor boys—

LE BRET   *(Who has gone upstage to pass up food to the* SENTRY *on*
              the parapet, on the end of a lance)
                                    De Guiche!—

CYRANO   Hide everything   35
              Quick!—Dishes, bottles, tablecloth—
                                          Now look
              Hungry again—

(To RAGUENEAU*)*
            You there! Up on your box—
—Everything out of sight?—

(In a twinkling, everything has been pushed inside the tents, hidden in their hats or under their cloaks. DE GUICHE *enters quickly, then stops, sniffing the air. Silence.)*

■ Scene vii ■

DE GUICHE   It smells good here.

CADET   *(Humming with an air of great unconcern)*
Sing ha-ha-ha and ho-ho-ho—

DE GUICHE   *(Stares at him; he grows embarrassed.)*
                              You there—
What are you blushing for?

CADET   Nothing—my blood
Stirs at the thought of battle.

ANOTHER   Pom . . . pom . . . pom!

DE GUICHE   *(Turns upon him)*
What's that?

CADET   Only a song—a little song—   5

DE GUICHE   You appear happy!

CADET   Oh yes—always happy
Before a fight—

DE GUICHE   *(Calls to* CARBON, *for the purpose of giving him an order)*
            Captain! I—
(Stops and looks at him)
                      First explain why
You're looking happy too!—

CARBON   *(Pulls a long face and hides a cup behind his back)*
                      No!

DE GUICHE   Here—I had
One gun remaining. I have had it placed

(He points off-stage.)
There—in that corner—for your men.

CADET   *(Simpering)*

                         So kind!—   10

DE GUICHE   *(Turns away with a shrug to* ROXANE*)*
Madame, have you decided?

ROXANE   I stay here.

DE GUICHE   You have time to escape—

ROXANE   No!

DE GUICHE   Very well—
Someone give me a musket!

CARBON   What?

DE GUICHE   *I* stay
Here also.

CYRANO   *(Formally)*
       Sir, you show courage!

FIRST CADET   A Gascon
In spite of all that lace!

ROXANE   Why—

DE GUICHE   Must I run   15
Away, and leave a woman?

SECOND CADET   *(To* FIRST CADET*)*
           He might want
Something to eat—what do you say?
(All the food re-appears, as if by magic.)

DE GUICHE   *(His face lighting up)*
          A feast!

THIRD CADET   Here a little, there a little—

DE GUICHE   *(Recovers his self-control; haughtily)*
                                        Do you think
                   I want your leavings?

CYRANO   *(Saluting)*
                                        Colonel—you improve!

DE GUICHE   I can fight as I am!

FIRST CADET   *(Delighted)*
                                        Listen to him—   20
                   He has an accent!

DE GUICHE   *(Laughs)*
                                        Have I?

FIRST CADET   A Gascon!—
                   A Gascon, after all!

                   (They all begin to dance.)

CARBON   *(Who has disappeared for a moment behind the parapet,
                   reappears on top of it)*
                                        I've placed my pikemen
                   Here.
                   (Indicates a row of pikes showing above the parapet)

DE GUICHE   *(Bows to* ROXANE*)*
                                   We'll review them; will you take my arm?

                   *(She takes his arm; they go up on the parapet. The rest
                   uncover, and follow them upstage.)*

CHRISTIAN   *(Goes hurriedly to* CYRANO*)*
                   Speak quickly!

                   (At the moment when ROXANE *appears on the parapet,
                   the pikes are lowered in salute, and a cheer is heard. She
                   bows.)*

PIKEMEN   *(Off-stage)*
                                        Hurrah!

CHRISTIAN   What is it?

■ Scene viii ■■

CYRANO   If Roxane . . .

CHRISTIAN   Well?

CYRANO   Speaks about your letters . . .

CHRISTIAN   Yes—I know!

CYRANO   Do not make the mistake of showing . . .

CHRISTIAN   What?

CYRANO   Showing surprise.

CHRISTIAN   Surprise—why?

CYRANO   I must tell you! . . .
It is quite simple—I had forgotten it   5
Until just now. You have . . .

CHRISTIAN   Speak quickly!—

CYRANO   You
Have written oftener than you think.

CHRISTIAN   Oh—have I!

CYRANO   I took upon me to interpret you;
              And wrote—sometimes . . . without . . .

CHRISTIAN   My knowing. Well?

CYRANO   Perfectly simple!

CHRISTIAN   Oh yes, perfectly!—   10
              For a month, we have been blockaded here!—
              How did you send all these letters?

CYRANO   Before
              Daylight, I managed—

CHRISTIAN   I see. That was also
              Perfectly simple!
                            —So I wrote to her,
              How many times a week? Twice? Three times? Four?   15

CYRANO   Oftener.

CHRISTIAN   Every day?

CYRANO   Yes—every day . . .
              Every single day . . .

CHRISTIAN   (Violently)
                            And that wrought you up
              Into such a flame that you faced death—

CYRANO   (Sees ROXANE returning)
                                        Hush—
              Not before her!

              (He goes quickly into the tent. ROXANE comes up to
              CHRISTIAN.)

ROXANE   Now—Christian!

CHRISTIAN   (Takes her hands)
                            Tell me now
              Why you came here—over these ruined roads—   20

Why you made your way among mosstroopers*
And ruffians*—you—to join me here?

ROXANE   Because—
Your letters . . .

CHRISTIAN   Meaning?

ROXANE   It was your own fault
If I ran into danger! I went mad—
Mad with you! Think what you have written me,   25
How many times, each one more wonderful
Than the last!

CHRISTIAN   All this for a few absurd
Love-letters—

ROXANE   Hush—absurd! How can you know?
I thought I loved you, ever since one night
When a voice that I never would have known   30
Under my window breathed your soul to me . . .
But—all this time, your letters—every one
Was like hearing your voice there in the dark,
All around me, like your arms around me . . .
(More lightly)
                                        At last,
I came. Anyone would! Do you suppose   35
The prim Penelope had stayed at home
Embroidering,—if Ulysses wrote like you?
She would have fallen like another Helen*—
Tucked up those linen petticoats of hers
And followed him to Troy!

CHRISTIAN   But you—

ROXANE   I read them   40
Over and over. I grew faint reading them.
I belonged to you. Every page of them
Was like a petal from your soul—
Like the light and the fire of a great love,
Sweet and strong and true—

CHRISTIAN   Sweet . . . and strong . . .
and true . . .   45

mosstroopers:
marauders who
infested the marshes
in Great Britain
ruffians: lawless, bru-
tal men

Helen: mythologi-
cal beauty over
whom the Trojan
War was fought

You felt that, Roxane?—

ROXANE

You know how I feel!

CHRISTIAN   So—you came . . .

ROXANE

So I came to say to you
"Forgive me"—(It is time to be forgiven
Now, when we may die presently)—forgive me
For being light and vain and loving you   50
Only because you were beautiful.

CHRISTIAN   *(Astonished)*

Roxane!

ROXANE   Afterwards I knew better. Afterwards
(I had to learn to use my wings) I loved you
For yourself too—knowing you more, and loving
More of you. And now—

CHRISTIAN

Now? . . .

ROXANE

It is yourself   55
I love now: your own self.

CHRISTIAN   *(Taken aback)*

Roxane!

ROXANE   *(Gravely)*

Be happy!—
You must have suffered; for you must have seen
How frivolous I was; and to be loved
For the mere costume, the poor casual body
You went about in—to a soul like yours,   60
That must have been torture! Therefore with words
You revealed your heart. Now that image of you
Which filled my eyes first—I see better now,
And I see it no more!

CHRISTIAN

Oh!—

ROXANE

You still doubt
Your victory?

CHRISTIAN   *(Miserably)*
                              Roxane!—

ROXANE   I understand: 65
                   You cannot perfectly believe in me—
                   A love like this—

CHRISTIAN   I want no love like this!
                   I want love only for—

ROXANE   Only for what
                   Every woman sees in you? I can do
                   Better than that!

CHRISTIAN   No—it was best before!   70

ROXANE   You do not altogether know me . . . Dear,
                   There is more of me than there was—with this,
                   I can love more of you—more of what makes
                   You your own self—Truly! . . . If you were less
                   Lovable—

CHRISTIAN   No!

ROXANE   —Less charming—ugly even—   75
                   I should love you still.

CHRISTIAN   You mean that?

ROXANE   I do
                   Mean that!

CHRISTIAN   Ugly? . . .

ROXANE   Yes. Even then!

CHRISTIAN   *(Agonized)*
                                   Oh . . . No!

ROXANE   Now are you happy?

CHRISTIAN   *(Choking)*
                              Yes . . .

ROXANE   What is it?

CHRISTIAN   *(Pushes her away gently)*
                                                        Only . . .
            Nothing . . . one moment . . .

ROXANE   But—

CHRISTIAN   *(Gestures toward the* CADETS*)*
                                        I am keeping you
            From those poor fellows—Go and smile at them;   80
            They are going to die!

ROXANE   *(Softly)*
                                    Dear Christian!

CHRISTIAN   Go—
            (She goes up among the Gascons who gather round her
            respectfully.)
            Cyrano!

CYRANO   *(Comes out of the tent, armed for the battle)*
                        What is wrong? You look—

CHRISTIAN   She does not
            Love me any more.

CYRANO   *(Smiles)*
                                    You think not?

CHRISTIAN   She loves
            You.

CYRANO   No!—

CHRISTIAN   *(Bitterly)*
                        She loves only my soul.

CYRANO   No!

CHRISTIAN   Yes—
            That means you. And you love her.

CYRANO   I?

CHRISTIAN   I see—
I know!

CYRANO   That is true . . .

CHRISTIAN   More than—

CYRANO   *(Quietly)*
                                  More than that.   5

CHRISTIAN   Tell her so!

CYRANO   No.

CHRISTIAN   Why not?

CYRANO   Why—look at me!

CHRISTIAN   She would love me if I were ugly.

CYRANO   *(Startled)*
                                  She—
Said that?

CHRISTIAN   Yes. Now then!

CYRANO   *(Half to himself)*
                              It was good of her   10
To tell you that . . .
(Change of tone)
                  Nonsense! Do you believe
Any such madness—
                  It was good of her
To tell you . . .
                  Do not take her at her word!
Go on—you never will be ugly—Go!
She would never forgive me.

CHRISTIAN   That is what
We shall see.

CYRANO   No, no—

CHRISTIAN   Let her choose between us!—

Tell her everything!

CYRANO   No—you torture me—   15

CHRISTIAN   Shall I ruin your happiness, because
I have a cursed pretty face? That seems
Too unfair!

CYRANO   And am I to ruin yours
Because I happen to be born with power
To say what you—perhaps—feel?

CHRISTIAN   Tell her!

CYRANO   Man—   20
Do not try me too far!

CHRISTIAN   I am tired of being
My own rival!

CYRANO   Christian!—

CHRISTIAN   Our secret marriage—
No witnesses—fraudulent—that can be
Annulled—

CYRANO   Do not try me—

CHRISTIAN   I want her love
For the poor fool I am—or not at all!   25
Oh, I am going through with this! I'll know,
One way or the other. Now I shall walk down
To the end of the post. Go tell her. Let her choose
One of us.

CYRANO   It will be you.

CHRISTIAN   Ah—I hope so!
(He turns and calls.)
Roxane!

CYRANO   No—no—

ROXANE   *(Hurries down to him)*
           Yes, Christian?

CHRISTIAN   Cyrano   30
Has news for you—important.

(She turns to CYRANO. CHRISTIAN *goes out.)*

ROXANE   *(Lightly)*
               Oh—important?

CYRANO   He is gone . . .
(To ROXANE*)*
        Nothing—only Christian thinks
You ought to know—

ROXANE   I do know. He still doubts
What I told him just now. I saw that.

CYRANO   *(Takes her hand)*
                Was it
True—what you told him just now?

ROXANE   It was true!
I said that I should love him even . . .

CYRANO   *(Smiling sadly)*
            The word   5
Comes hard—before me?

ROXANE   Even if he were . . .

CYRANO   Say it—
I shall not be hurt!—Ugly?

ROXANE   Even then
I should love him.
(A few shots, off-stage, are heard in the direction in which
CHRISTIAN *disappeared.)*
      Hark! The guns—

CYRANO   Hideous?

ROXANE   Hideous.

■ Scene x ■

CYRANO   Disfigured?

ROXANE   Or disfigured.

CYRANO   Even
Grotesque?

ROXANE   How could he ever be grotesque—   10
Ever—to me!

CYRANO   But you could love him so,
As much as?—

ROXANE   Yes—and more!

CYRANO   *(Aside excitedly)*
                                        It is true!—true!—
Perhaps—No! This is too much happiness . . .
(To ROXANE*)*
I—Roxane—listen—

LE BRET   *(Enters quickly; calls to* CYRANO *in a low tone)*
                    Cyrano—

CYRANO   *(Turns)*
                              Yes?

LE BRET   Hush! . . .

(He whispers a few words to him.)

CYRANO   *(Lets fall* ROXANE's *hand)*
Ah!

ROXANE   What is it?

CYRANO   *(Half stunned, and aside)*
                    All gone . . .

ROXANE   *(More shots)*
                              What is it? Oh,   15
They are fighting!—

(She goes up to look off-stage.)

CYRANO   All gone. I cannot ever
Tell her, now . . . ever . . .

ROXANE   *(Starts to rush away)*
                                        What has happened?

CYRANO   *(Restrains her)*
                                                        Nothing.

(Several CADETS *enter. They conceal something which
they are carrying, and form a group so as to prevent*
ROXANE *from seeing their burden.)*

ROXANE   These men—

CYRANO   Come away . . .

(He leads her away from the group.)

ROXANE   You were telling me
Something—

CYRANO   Oh, that? Nothing . . .
(Gravely)
                                        I swear to you
That the spirit of Christian—that his soul   20
Was—
(Corrects himself quickly)
            That his soul is no less great—

ROXANE   *(Catches at the word)*
                                        Was?
                (Crying out)
                                                Oh!—

(She rushes among the men, and scatters them.)

CYRANO   All gone . . .

ROXANE   *(Sees* CHRISTIAN *lying upon his cloak)*
                        Christian!

LE BRET   *(To* CYRANO*)*
                        At the first volley.

(ROXANE throws herself upon the body of CHRISTIAN.
Shots; at first scattered, then increasing.
Drums. Voices shouting.)

CARBON   *(Sword in hand)*

                                                    Here
They come!—Ready!—

(Followed by the CADETS, he climbs over the parapet and
disappears.)

ROXANE   Christian!

CARBON   *(Off-stage)*

                                        Come on, there, you!

ROXANE   Christian!

CARBON   Fall in!

ROXANE   Christian!

CARBON   Measure your fuse!

(RAGUENEAU hurries up, carrying a helmet full of water.)

CHRISTIAN   *(Faintly)*
Roxane! . . .

CYRANO   *(Low and quick, in CHRISTIAN's ear, while ROXANE is*
dipping into the water a strip of linen torn from her dress)
                    I have told her; she loves you.

(CHRISTIAN closes his eyes.)

ROXANE   *(Turns to CHRISTIAN)*

                                        Yes,   25
My darling?

CARBON   Draw your ramrods!

ROXANE   *(To CYRANO)*

                            He is not dead? . . .

CARBON	Open you charges!

ROXANE
                    I can feel his cheek
Growing cold against mine—

CARBON
                       Take aim!

ROXANE
                           A letter—
Over his heart—
(She opens it.)
          For me.

CYRANO
(Aside)
                 My letter . . .

CARBON
                    Fire!

(Musketry, cries and groans. Din* of battle.)   *din:* noise

CYRANO
(Trying to withdraw his hand, which ROXANE, *still upon her knees, is holding)*
But Roxane—they are fighting—

ROXANE
                    Wait a little . . .   30
He is dead. No one else knew him but you . . .
(She weeps quietly.)
Was he not a great wooer, a great man,
A hero?

CYRANO
(Standing, bareheaded)
         Yes, Roxane.

ROXANE
               A poet, unknown,
Adorable?

CYRANO
      Yes, Roxane.

ROXANE
                   A fine mind?

CYRANO
Yes, Roxane.

ROXANE
              A heart deeper than we knew—   35
A soul magnificently tender?

CYRANO   *(Firmly)*
                                                Yes,
                Roxane!

ROXANE   *(Sinks down upon the breast of* CHRISTIAN*)*
                                He is dead now . . .

CYRANO   *(Aside; draws his sword)*
                                        Why, so am I—
                For I am dead, and my love mourns for me
                And does not know . . .
                (Trumpets in distance)

DE GUICHE   *(Appears on the parapet, disheveled, wounded on the
                forehead, shouting)*
                                The signal—hark—the trumpets!
                The army has returned—Hold them now!—Hold them! 40
                The army!—

ROXANE   On his letter—blood . . . and tears.

VOICE   *(Off-stage)*
                Surrender!

CADETS   No!

RAGUENEAU   This place is dangerous!—

CYRANO   *(To* DE GUICHE*)*
                Take her away—I am going—

ROXANE   *(Kisses the letter; faintly)*
                                        His blood . . . his tears . . .

RAGUENEAU   *(Leaps down from the coach and runs to her)*
                She's fainted—

DE GUICHE   *(On the parapet; savagely, to the* CADETS*)*
                                Hold them!

VOICE   *(Off-stage)*
                                        Lay down your arms!

CADETS   No! No!

| CYRANO | *(To* DE GUICHE*)* |
| | Sir, you have proved yourself—Take care of her.   45 |

DE GUICHE	*(Hurries to* ROXANE *and takes her up in his arms)*
	As you will—we can win, if you hold on
	A little longer—

CYRANO	Good!
	(Calls out to ROXANE, *as she is carried away, fainting, by*
	DE GUICHE *and* RAGUENEAU*)*
	Adieu, Roxane!

(Tumult, outcries. Several CADETS *come back wounded and fall on the stage.* CYRANO, *rushing to the fight, is stopped on the crest of the parapet by* CARBON, *covered with blood.)*

| CARBON | We are breaking—I am twice wounded— |

CYRANO	*(Shouts to the Gascons)*
	Courage!
	Do not retreat, good men!
	(To CARBON, *holding him up)*
	So—never fear!
	I have two deaths to avenge now—Christian's 50
	And my own!
	(They come down. CYRANO *takes from him the lance with* ROXANE's *handkerchief still fastened to it. Then standing amid a hail of bullets, he declaims:)*
	Float, little banner, with her name!

(He rushes forward followed by a few survivors.)

(Curtain)

About the Play

1. How has Roxane changed since Act I?
2. What conflict emerges as a result of Roxane's growth?
3. Has Christian changed since Act I?
4. Why does Cyrano refuse to tell Roxane he loves her after Christian dies?
5. Is this action of Cyrano's consistent with what we know of him?

ACT V

Cyrano's Gazette

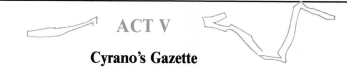

Fifteen years later, in 1655: the park of the convent occupied by the Ladies of the Cross, at Paris.

At the curtain rise the nuns are coming and going across the Park; several of them are seated on the bench around MOTHER MARGUÉRITE. *The leaves are falling.*

■ **Scene i** ■■■■

SISTER MARTHE   *(To* MOTHER MARGUÉRITE*)*
Sister Claire has been looking in the glass
At her new cap; twice!

MOTHER
MARGUÉRITE   *(To* SISTER CLAIRE*)*
                              It is very plain;
Very.

SISTER CLAIRE   And Sister Marthe stole a plum
Out of the tart this morning!

MOTHER
MARGUÉRITE   *(To* SISTER MARTHE*)*
                              That was wrong;
Very wrong.

SISTER CLAIRE   Oh, but such a little look!   5

SISTER MARTHE   Such a little plum!

MOTHER
MARGUÉRITE   *(Severely)*
                    I shall tell Monsieur
De Cyrano, this evening.

SISTER CLAIRE   No! Oh, no!—
He will make fun of us.

SISTER MARTHE   He will say nuns
Are so gay!

SISTER CLAIRE   And so greedy!

MOTHER MARGUÉRITE	*(Smiling)*

And so good . . .

SISTER CLAIRE	It must be ten years, Mother Marguérite, 10
	That he has come here every Saturday,
	Is it not?

MOTHER
MARGUÉRITE

More than ten years; ever since
His cousin came to live among us here—
Her worldly weeds among our linen veils.

SISTER MARTHE	None else can turn that happy sorrow of hers 15
	Into a smile.

ALL	He's such fun!—He makes us

Almost laugh!—And he teases everyone—
And pleases everyone—And we all love him—
And he likes our cakes, too—

MOTHER
MARGUÉRITE

He is so poor;
So very poor.

SISTER MARTHE	Who said?

MOTHER
MARGUÉRITE

Monsieur Le Bret. 20

SISTER MARTHE	Why does not someone help him?

MOTHER
MARGUÉRITE

He would be
Angry, very angry . . .
(Between the trees upstage, ROXANE *appears, all in black,
with a widow's cap and long veils.* DE GUICHE,
*magnificently grown old, walks beside her. They move
slowly.* MOTHER MARGUÉRITE *rises.)*
Let us go in—
Madame Madeleine has a visitor.

SISTER MARTHE	*(To* SISTER CLAIRE*)*
	The Duc de Grammont, is it not? The Marshal?

SISTER CLAIRE   *(Looks toward* DE GUICHE*)*
I think so—yes.—

SISTER MARTHE   He has not been to see her   25
For months—

NUNS   He's busy—the Court!—the Camp!—

SISTER CLAIRE   The world!

(They go out. DE GUICHE *and* ROXANE *come down in silence, and stop near the embroidery frame. Pause.)*

■ Scene ii ■

DE GUICHE   And you remain here, wasting all that gold—
For ever in mourning?

ROXANE   For ever.

DE GUICHE   And still faithful?

ROXANE   And still faithful . . .

DE GUICHE   *(After a pause)*
                        Have you forgiven me?

ROXANE   *(Simply, looking up at the cross of the convent)*
I am here.

DE GUICHE   Was Christian . . . all that?

ROXANE   If you knew him.

DE GUICHE   Ah? We were not precisely . . . intimate . . .   5
And his last letter—always at your heart?

ROXANE   It hangs here, like a holy reliquary.*

DE GUICHE   Dead—and you love him still!

ROXANE   Sometimes I think
He has not altogether died; our hearts
Meet, and his love flows all around me, living.   10

reliquary: relic used in religious ceremony, usually reputed to have belonged to some saint or martyr

DE GUICHE	*(After another pause)*
	You see Cyrano often?

ROXANE   Every week.
My old friend takes the place of my Gazette,
Brings me all the news. Every Saturday,
Under that tree where you are now, his chair
Stands, if the day be fine. I wait for him,   15
Embroidering; the hour strikes; then I hear,
(I need not turn to look!) at the last stroke,
His cane tapping the steps. He laughs at me
For my eternal needlework. He tells
The story of the past week—
(LE BRET appears on the steps.)
                                        There's Le Bret!—   20
(LE BRET approaches.)
How is it with our friend?

LE BRET   Badly.

DE GUICHE   Indeed?

ROXANE   *(To DE GUICHE)*
Oh, he exaggerates!

LE BRET   Just as I said—
Loneliness, misery—I told him so!—
His satires make a host of enemies—
He attacks the false nobles, the false saints,   25
The false heroes, the false artists—in short,
Everyone!

ROXANE   But they fear that sword of his—
No one dare touch him!

DE GUICHE   *(With a shrug)*
                                        H'm—that may be so.

LE BRET   It is not violence I fear for him,
But solitude—poverty—old gray December,   30
Stealing on wolf's feet, with a wolf's green eyes,
Into his darkening room. Those bravoes yet
May strike our Swordsman down! Every day now,
He draws his belt up one hole; his poor nose

| | Looks like old ivory; he has one coat   35 |
| | Left—his old black serge.* |

serge: woolen (one)

DE GUICHE   That is nothing strange
In this world! No, you need not pity him
Overmuch.

LE BRET   *(With a bitter smile)*
                         My lord Marshal! . . .

DE GUICHE   I say, do not
Pity him overmuch. He lives his life,
His own life, his own way—thought, word, and deed   40
Free!

LE BRET   *(As before)*
                         My lord Duke! . . .

DE GUICHE   *(Haughtily)*
                                    Yes, I know—I have all;
He has nothing. Nevertheless, to-day
I should be proud to shake his hand. . . .
(Saluting ROXANE*)*
                                             Adieu.

ROXANE   I will go with you.

                         *(*DE GUICHE *salutes* LE BRET, *and turns with* ROXANE
                         toward the steps.)

DE GUICHE   *(Pauses on the steps, as she climbs)*
                                    Yes—I envy him
Now and then. . . .
                                    Do you know, when a man wins   45
Everything in this world, when he succeeds
Too much—he feels, having done nothing wrong
Especially, heaven knows!—he feels somehow
A thousand small displeasures with himself,
Whose whole sum is not quite Remorse, but rather   50
A sort of vague disgust. . . . The ducal* robes
Mounting up, step by step, to pride and power,
Somewhere among their folds draw after them
A rustle of dry illusions, vain regrets,

ducal: belonging to a
duke

As your veil, up the stairs here, draws along   55
The whisper of dead leaves.

ROXANE   *(Ironically)*
                                        The sentiment
Does you honor.

DE GUICHE   Oh, yes . . .
(Pausing suddenly)
                          Monsieur Le Bret!—
(To ROXANE*)*
You pardon us?—
(He goes to LE BRET *and speaks in a low tone.)*
                    One moment—It is true
That no one dares attack your friend. Some people
Dislike him, nonetheless. The other day   60
At Court, such a one said to me: "This man
Cyrano may die—accidentally."

LE BRET   *(Coldly)*
Thank you.

DE GUICHE   You may thank me. Keep him at home
All you can. Tell him to be careful.

LE BRET   *(Shaking his hands to heaven)*
                                Careful!—
He is coming here. I'll warn him—yes, but! . . .

ROXANE   *(Still on the steps, to* SISTER CLAIRE *who approaches her)*
                                                Here   65
I am—what is it?

SISTER CLAIRE   Madame, Ragueneau
Wishes to see you.

ROXANE   Bring him here.
(To LE BRET *and* DE GUICHE*)*
                                He comes
For sympathy—having been first of all
A Poet, he became since then, in turn,
A Singer—

LE BRET   Bath-house keeper—

ROXANE   Sacristan*—   70   *Sacristan: church
                                                                                     officer in charge of
                                                                                     sacred vessels and
LE BRET   Actor—   vestments

ROXANE   Hairdresser—

LE BRET   Music-master—

ROXANE   Now,
               To-day—

RAGUENEAU   *(Enters hurriedly)*
                         Madame!—
               (He sees LE BRET.*)*
                         Monsieur!—

ROXANE   *(Smiling)*
                              First tell your troubles
               To Le Bret for a moment.

RAGUENEAU   But Madame—
               (She goes out, with DE GUICHE, *not hearing him.*
               RAGUENEAU *comes to* LE BRET.*)*
               After all, I had rather—You are here—
               She need not know so soon—I went to see him
               Just now—Our friend—As I came near his door,
               I saw him coming out. I hurried on
               To join him. At the corner of the street,   5
               As he passed—Could it be an accident?—
               I wonder!—At the window overhead,
               A lackey with a heavy log of wood
               Let it fall—

LE BRET   Cyrano!

RAGUENEAU   I ran to him—

LE BRET   No! The cowards!

RAGUENEAU   I found him lying there—   10
               A great hole in his head—

■ Scene iii ■■■■

LE BRET	Is he alive?

RAGUENEAU

> Alive—yes. But . . . I had to carry him
> Up to his room—Ah! Have you seen his room?—

LE BRET

> Is he suffering?

RAGUENEAU

> No; unconscious.

LE BRET

> Did you
> Call a doctor?

RAGUENEAU

> One came—for charity.   15

LE BRET

> Poor Cyrano!—We must not tell Roxane
> All at once . . . Did the doctor say?—

RAGUENEAU

> He said
> Fever, and lesions of the—I forget
> Those long names—Ah, if you had seen him there,
> His head all white bandages!—Let us go   20
> Quickly—there is no one to care for him—
> All alone—If he tries to raise his head,
> He may die!

LE BRET

> *(Draws him away to the right)*
> This way—It is shorter—through
> The Chapel—

ROXANE

> *(Appears on the stairway, and calls to* LE BRET *as he is
> going out by the colonnade which leads to the small door
> of the Chapel)*
> Monsieur Le Bret!—
> *(*LE BRET *and* RAGUENEAU *rush off without hearing.)*
> Running away
> When I call to him? Poor dear Ragueneau   25
> Must have been very tragic!
> *(She comes slowly down the stair, toward the tree.)*
> What a day! . . .
> Something in these bright autumn afternoons
> Happy and yet regretful—an old sorrow
> Smiling . . . as though poor little April dried
> Her tears long ago—and remembered . . .

■ Scene iv ■■■■■

(She sits down at her work. Two NUNS *come out of the house carrying a great chair and set it under the tree.)*
　　　　Ah—
The old chair, for my old friend!—

SISTER MARTHE
　　　　　　　　　　　　　　　The best one　　　5
In our best parlor!—

ROXANE
　　　　　　　　　　　Thank you, Sister—
(The NUNS *withdraw.)*
　　　　　　　　　　　　　There—
(She begins embroidering. The clock strikes.)
The hour!—He will be coming now—my silks—
All done striking? He never was this late.
(A dead leaf falls on her work; she brushes it away.)
What could keep him?—

NUN
(Appears on the steps)
　　　　　　　　Monsieur de Bergerac.

ROXANE
(Without turning)
What was I saying? . . . Hard, sometimes, to match
These faded colors! . . .
(While she goes on working, CYRANO *appears at the top of the steps, very pale, his hat drawn over his eyes. The Nun who has brought him in goes away. He begins to descend the steps leaning on his cane, and holding himself on his feet only by an evident effort.* ROXANE *turns to him, with a tone of friendly banter.)*
　　　　　　　　After fourteen years,
Late—for the first time!

CYRANO
(Reaches the chair, and sinks into it; his gay tone contrasting with his tortured face)
　　　　　　　　Yes, yes—maddening!
I was detained by—

ROXANE
　　　　　　　Well?

CYRANO
　　　　　　　　　A visitor,
Most unexpected.

ROXANE
(Carelessly, still sewing)
　　　　　　　　Was your visitor　　　5

■ Scene v ■■■■■

Tiresome?

CYRANO

    Why, hardly that—inopportune,
Let us say—an old friend of mine—at least
A very old acquaintance.

ROXANE

       Did you tell him
To go away?

CYRANO

    For the time being, yes.
I said: "Excuse me—this is Saturday—   10
I have a previous engagement, one
I cannot miss, even for you—Come back
An hour from now."

ROXANE

      Your friend will have to wait;
I shall not let you go till dark.

CYRANO

(Very gently)
       Perhaps
A little before dark, I must go . . .

*(He leans back in the chair, and closes his eyes. A breath
of wind causes a few leaves to fall.)*

ROXANE

(Smiling)
       Look—   15
(Looks away through the trees)
The leaves . . . Venetian red! Look at them fall.

CYRANO

Yes—they know how to die. A little way
From the branch to the earth, a little fear
Of mingling with the common dust—and yet
They go down gracefully—a fall that seems   20
Like flying!

ROXANE

    Melancholy—you?

CYRANO

       Why, no,
Roxane!

ROXANE

    Then let the leaves fall. Tell me now
The Court news—my gazette!

CYRANO   Let me see—

ROXANE   Ah!

CYRANO   *(More and more pale, struggling against pain)*
            Saturday, the nineteenth; the King fell ill,
            After eight helpings of grape marmalade.   25
            His malady was brought before the court,
            Found guilty of high treason; whereupon
            His Majesty revived. The royal pulse
            Is now normal. Sunday, the twentieth:
            The Queen gave a grand ball, at which they burned   30
            Seven hundred and sixty-three wax candles. Note:
            They say our troops have been victorious
            In Austria. Later: Three sorcerers
            Have been hung. Special post: The little dog
            Of Madame d'Athis was obliged to take   35
            Four pills before—

ROXANE   Monsieur de Bergerac,
            Will you kindly be quiet!

CYRANO   Monday . . . nothing.
            Lygdamire has a new suitor.

ROXANE   Oh!

CYRANO   *(His face more and more altered)*
                                  Tuesday,
            The Twenty-second: All the court has gone
            To Fontainebleau. Wednesday: The Comte de
                Fiesque   40
            Spoke to Madame de Montglat; she said No.
            Thursday: Mancini was the Queen of France
            Or—very nearly! Friday: La Montglat
            Said Yes. Saturday, twenty-sixth . . .
            (His eyes close; his head sinks back; silence.)

ROXANE   *(Surprised at not hearing any more, turns, looks at him,
            and rises, frightened)*
                              He has fainted—
            (She runs to him, crying out.)
            Cyrano!

CYRANO   *(Opens his eyes)*
                          What . . . What is it? . . .
                  (He sees ROXANE *leaning over him, and quickly pulls his*
                  hat down over his head and leans back away from her in
                  the chair.)
                                          No—oh no—   45
                  It is nothing—truly!

ROXANE   But—

CYRANO   My old wound—
                  At Arras—sometimes—you know. . . .

ROXANE   My poor friend!

CYRANO   Oh it is nothing; it will soon be gone. . . .
                  (Forcing a smile)
                  There! It is gone!

ROXANE   *(Standing close to him)*
                                  We all have our old wounds—
                  I have mine—here . . .
                  (Her hand at her breast)
                                          under this faded scrap   50
                  Of writing. . . . It is hard to read now—all
                  But the blood—and the tears. . . .

                  (Twilight begins to fall.)

CYRANO   His letter! . . . Did you
                  Not promise me that some day . . . that some day. . . .
                  You would let me read it?

ROXANE   His letter?—You . . .
                  You wish—

CYRANO   I do wish it—to-day.

ROXANE   *(Gives him the little silken bag from around her neck)*
                                          Here. . . .   55

CYRANO   May I . . . open it?

ROXANE   Open it, and read.

(She goes back to her work, folds it again, rearranges her silks.)

CYRANO
(Unfolds the letter; reads)
"Farewell Roxane, because today I die—"

ROXANE
(Looks up, surprised)
Aloud?

CYRANO
(Reads)
  "I know that it will be to-day,
My own dearly beloved—and my heart
Still so heavy with love I have not told,   60
And I die without telling you! No more
Shall my eyes drink the sight of you,
Never more, with a look that is a kiss,
Follow the sweet grace of you—"

ROXANE
         How you read it—
His letter!

CYRANO
(Continues)
    "I remember now the way   65
You have, of pushing back a lock of hair
With one hand, from your forehead—and my heart
Cries out—"

ROXANE
    His letter . . . and you read it so . . .

(The darkness increases imperceptibly.)

CYRANO
"Cries out and keeps crying: 'Farewell, my dear,
My dearest—' "

ROXANE
    In a voice. . . .

CYRANO
      "—My own heart's own,   70
My own treasure—"

ROXANE
(Dreamily)
    In such a voice. . . .

CYRANO
       —"My love—"

ROXANE	—As I remember hearing . . . *(She trembles.)* —long ago. . . . *(She comes near him, softly, without his seeing her; passes the chair, leans over silently, looking at the letter. The darkness increases.)*
CYRANO	"—I am never away from you. Even now, I shall not leave you. In another world, I shall be still that one who loves you, loves you 75 Beyond measure, beyond—"
ROXANE	*(Lays her hand on his shoulder)* How can you read Now? It is dark. . . . *(He starts, turns, and sees her there close to him. A little movement of surprise, almost of fear; then he bows his head. A long pause; then in the twilight now completely fallen, she says very softly, clasping her hands)* And all these fourteen years, He has been the old friend, who came to me To be amusing.
CYRANO	<div style="text-align:center">Roxane!—</div>
ROXANE	<div style="text-align:center">It was you.</div>
CYRANO	No, no, Roxane no!
ROXANE	And I might have known, 80 Every time that I heard you speak my name! . . .
CYRANO	No—It was not I—
ROXANE	<div style="text-align:center">It was . . . you!</div>
CYRANO	<div style="text-align:center">I swear—</div>
ROXANE	I understand everything now: The letters— That was you . . .
CYRANO	<div style="text-align:center">No!</div>

ROXANE   And the dear, foolish words—
That was you. . . .

CYRANO   No!

ROXANE   And the voice . . . in the dark . . .   85
That was . . . you!

CYRANO   On my honor—

ROXANE   And . . . the Soul!—
That was all you.

CYRANO   I never loved you—

ROXANE   Yes,
You loved me.

CYRANO   *(Desperately)*
                        No—He loved you—

ROXANE   Even now,
You love me!

CYRANO   *(His voice weakens.)*
                        No!

ROXANE   *(Smiling)*
                        And why . . . so great a "No"?

CYRANO   No, no, my own dear love, I love you not! . . .   90
(Pause)

ROXANE   How many things have died . . . and are newborn! . . .
Why were you silent for so many years,
All the while, every night and every day,
He gave me nothing—you knew that—You knew
Here, in this letter lying on my breast,   95
Your tears—You knew they were your tears—

CYRANO   *(Holds the letter out to her)*
                                      The blood
Was his.

ROXANE Why do you break that silence now,
Today?

CYRANO Why? Oh, because—

(LE BRET and RAGUENEAU enter, running.)

LE BRET What recklessness—
I knew it! He is here!

CYRANO *(Smiling, and trying to rise)*
Well? Here I am!

RAGUENEAU He has killed himself, Madame, coming here! 100

ROXANE He—You say . . . And that faintness . . . was that?—

CYRANO No,
Nothing! I did not finish my Gazette—
Saturday, twenty-sixth: An hour or so
Before dinner, Monsieur de Bergerac
Died, foully murdered.

(He uncovers his head, and shows it swathed in bandages.)

ROXANE Oh, what does he mean?— 105
Cyrano!—What have they done to you?—

CYRANO "Struck down
By the sword of a hero, let me fall—
Steel in my heart, and laughter on my lips!"
Yes, I said that once. How Fate loves a jest!—
Behold me ambushed—taken in the rear— 110
My battlefield a gutter—my noble foe
A lackey, with a log of wood! . . .
It seems
Too logical—I have missed everything,
Even my death!

RAGUENEAU *(Breaks down)*
Ah, monsieur!—

CYRANO Ragueneau,
Stop blubbering!

(Takes his hand)
                                    What are you writing now,   115
Old poet?

RAGUENEAU   *(Through his tears)*
                            I am not a poet now;
I snuff the—light the candles—for Molière!

CYRANO   Oh—Molière!

RAGUENEAU   Yes, but I am leaving him
Tomorrow. Yesterday they played "Scapin"—
He has stolen your scene—

LE BRET   The whole scene—word for
            word!   120

RAGUENEAU   Yes, yes: "What on earth was he doing there"
That one!

LE BRET   *(Furious)*
                    And Molière stole it all from you—
Bodily!—

CYRANO   Bah—He showed good taste. . . .
(To RAGUENEAU*)*
                                    The Scene
Went well? . . .

RAGUENEAU   Ah, monsieur, they laughed—and laughed—
How they did laugh!

CYRANO   Yes—that has been my life. . . .   125
Do you remember that night Christian spoke
Under your window? It was always so!
While I stood in the darkness underneath,
Others climbed up to win the applause—the kiss!—
Well—that seems only justice—I still say,   130
Even now, on the threshold of my tomb—
"Molière has genius—Christian had good looks—"
*(The chapel bell is ringing. Along the avenue of trees
above the stairway, the* NUNS *pass in procession to their
prayers.)*
They are going to pray now; there is the bell.

ROXANE   *(Raises herself and calls to them)*
Sister!—Sister!—

CYRANO   *(Holding on to her hand)*
         No,—do not go away—
I may not still be here when you return. . . .   135
(The NUNS *have gone into the chapel. The organ begins to
play.)*
A little harmony is all I need—
Listen. . . .

ROXANE   You shall not die! I love you!—

CYRANO   No—
That is not in the story! You remember
When Beauty said "I love you" to the Beast
That was a fairy prince, his ugliness   140
Changed and dissolved, like magic. . . . But you see
I am still the same.

ROXANE   And I—I have done
This to you! All my fault—mine!

CYRANO   You? Why no,
On the contrary! I had never known
Womanhood and its sweetness but for you.   145
My mother did not love to look at me—
I never had a sister—Later on,
I feared the mistress with a mockery
Behind her smile. But you—because of you
I have had one friend not quite all a friend—   150
Across my life, one whispering silken gown! . . .

LE BRET   *(Points to the rising moon which begins to shine down
between the trees)*
Your other friend is looking at you.

CYRANO   *(Smiling at the moon)*
           I see. . . .

ROXANE   I never loved but one man in my life,
And I have lost him—twice. . . .

CYRANO   Le Bret—I shall be up there presently   155
                In the moon—without having to invent
                Any flying machines!

ROXANE   What are you saying? . . .

CYRANO   The moon—yes, that would be the place for me—
                My kind of paradise! I shall find there
                Those other souls who should be friends of mine—   160
                Socrates—Galileo—

LE BRET   *(Revolting)*
                                    No!—No!—No!—
                It is too idiotic—too unfair—
                Such a friend—such a poet—such a man
                To die so—to die so!—

CYRANO   *(Affectionately)*
                                    There goes Le Bret,
                Growling!

LE BRET   *(Breaks down)*
                    My friend!—

CYRANO   *(Half raises himself, his eye wanders.)*
                           The Cadets of Gascoyne,   165
The Defenders. . . . The elementary mass—
Ah—there's the point! Now, then . . .

LE BRET   Delirious—
And all that learning—

CYRANO   On the other hand,
We have Copernicus—

ROXANE   Oh!

CYRANO   *(More and more delirious)*
                    "Very well,
But what on earth was he doing up there?—   170
What on earth was he doing there, up there?" . . .
(He declaims.)
    Philosopher and scientist,
    Poet, musician, duellist—
      He flew high, and fell back again!
    A pretty wit—whose like we lack—   175
    A wooer . . . not like other men. . . .
      Here lies Hercule-Savinien
    De Cyrano de Bergerac—
      Who was all things—and all in vain!
Well, I must go—pardon—I cannot stay!   180
My moonbeam comes to carry me away. . . .
(He falls back into the chair, half fainting. The sobbing of
ROXANE *recalls him to reality. Gradually his mind comes*
back to him. He looks at her, stroking the veil that hides
her hair.)
I would not have you mourn any the less
That good, brave, noble Christian; but perhaps—
I ask you only this—when the great cold
Gathers around my bones, that you may give   185
A double meaning to your widow's weeds
And the tears you let fall for him may be
For a little—my tears. . . .

ROXANE   *(Sobbing)*
                 Oh, my love! . . .

| CYRANO | *(Suddenly shaken as with a fever fit, raises himself erect and pushes her away)* |

         —Not here!—

Not lying down! . . .
(They spring forward to help him; he motions them back.)
      Let no one help me—no one!—
Only the tree. . . .
(He sets his back against the trunk. Pause.)
      It is coming . . . I feel   190
Already shod with marble . . . gloved with lead . . .
(Joyously)
Let the old fellow come now! He shall find me
On my feet—sword in hand—
(Draws his sword)

| LE BRET | Cyrano!— |

| ROXANE | *(Half fainting)* |

            Oh,
Cyrano!

| CYRANO | I can see him there—he grins— |

He is looking at my nose—that skeleton   195
—What's that you say? Hopeless?—Why, very well!—
But a man does not fight merely to win!
No—no—better to know one fights in vain! . . .
You there—Who are you? A hundred against one—
I know them now, my ancient enemies—   200
(He lunges at the empty air.)
Falsehood! . . . There! There! Prejudice—Compromise—
Cowardice—
(Thrusting)
    What's that? No! Surrender? No!
Never—never! . . .
    Ah, you too, Vanity!
I knew you would overthrow me in the end—
No! I fight on! I fight on! I fight on!   205
*(He swings the blade in great circles, then pauses, gasping.
When he speaks again, it is in another tone.)*
Yes, all my laurels you have riven away*   *riven away:* torn apart
And all my roses; yet in spite of you,
There is one crown I bear away with me,
And to-night, when I enter before God,
My salute shall sweep all the stars away   210

From the blue threshold! One thing without stain,
Unspotted from the world, in spite of doom
Mine own!—
(He springs forward, his sword aloft.)
                    And that is . . .

*(The sword escapes from his hand; he totters, and falls
into the arms of* LE BRET *and* RAGUENEAU.*)*

ROXANE   *(Bends over him and kisses him on the forehead)*
                              —That is . . .

CYRANO   *(Opens his eyes and smiles up at her)*
                                    My white plume. . . .

                    (Curtain)

About the Play

1. Read Le Bret's speech on page 507, lines 29-33. What does Le Bret fear for Cyrano? Why?
2. How has De Guiche changed?
3. Read Haggai 1:6. How could this verse apply to De Guiche?
4. How has De Guiche's attitude toward Cyrano changed?
5. On page 522, lines 138-42 Cyrano makes reference to the fairy tale "Beauty and the Beast." You have already made some comparisons between Roxane and Beauty. List several other similarities between the fairy tale and the play.

About the Author

Edmond Rostand (1868-1918) wrote French verse drama in the Romantic style for an audience that craved plays full of heroism, wit, and poetic language. *Cyrano de Bergerac,* Rostand's best-known work and the one which established his reputation, more than satisfied the desires of his audience.

The son of a poet, Rostand studied the liberal arts in Paris and enjoyed composing plays for a form of puppet theater called "marionette theater." He wrote his first play at age twenty; more and better plays, as well as poems and essays, followed.

Cyrano de Bergerac was written in 1897 when Rostand was thirty-one. Another play followed in 1900, and by 1901 Rostand's reputation as a French playwright was secure. After his election in 1901 to the prestigious French Academy, a sickly Rostand retired and went to live in the country. In 1910 he wrote another play in the form of a fable. Featuring the well-known French character Chanticleer the Rooster, this play was not a success. Rostand, however, continued to write poetry and drama well into World War I. At his death in 1918, Rostand was considered the unofficial poet laureate of France.

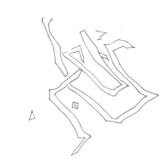

Index

Photo Credits

Cover: (from left to right) Unusual Films, Suzanne R. Altizer, Unusual Films, Brad Carper, George R. Collins, Unusual Films

Altizer, Suzanne R.: 222-23 (large)

Carper, Brad: 305 (small)

Collins, George R.: 155 (small), 223 (small)

Ramsey, Wade K.: 304-5 (large)

U. S. Air Force: 65 (small)

Unusual Films: viii-1 (both), 3, 64-65 (large), 68, 154-55 (large), 157, 344-45 (both), 347, 349, 357, 363, 373, 384, 392, 401, 418, 435, 441, 456, 461, 473, 488, 502, 514, 523